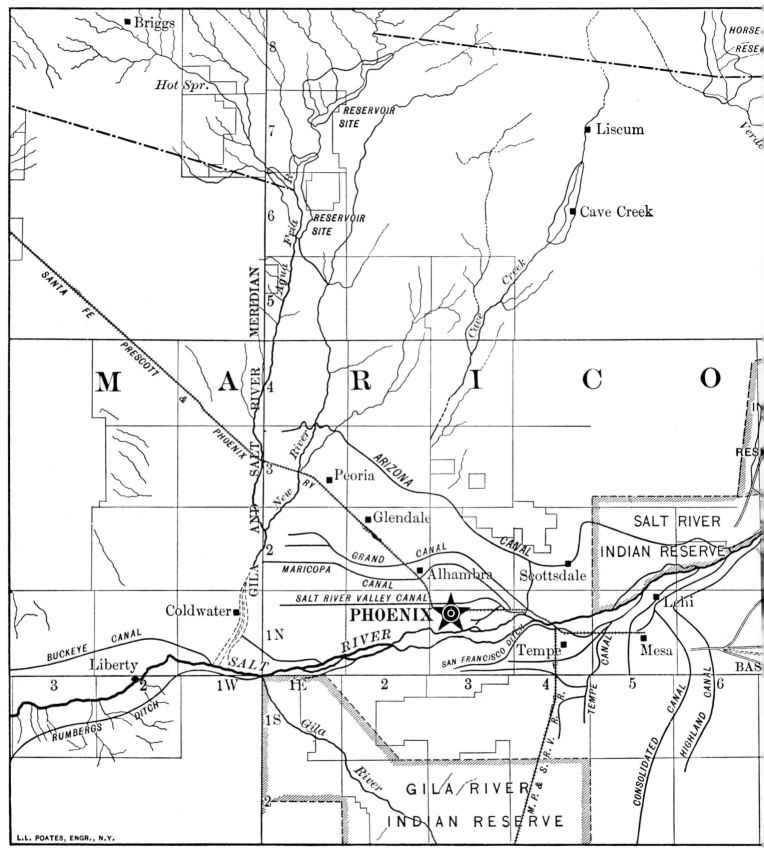

L.L. POATES, ENGR., N.Y.

MAP OF SALT

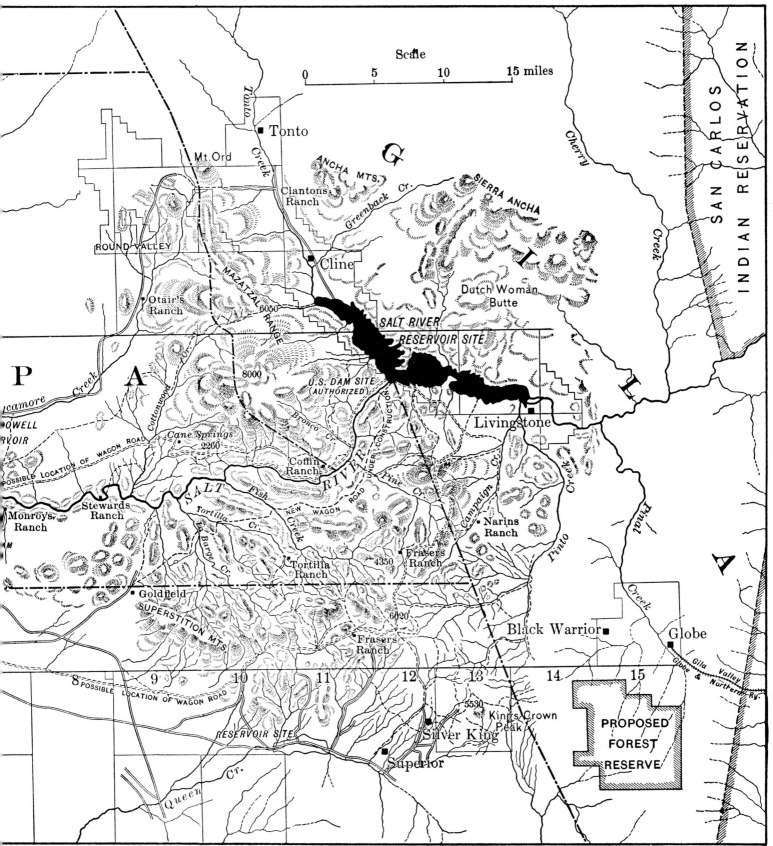

VALLEY, ARIZONA.

ROOSEVELT DAM:

A History to 1911

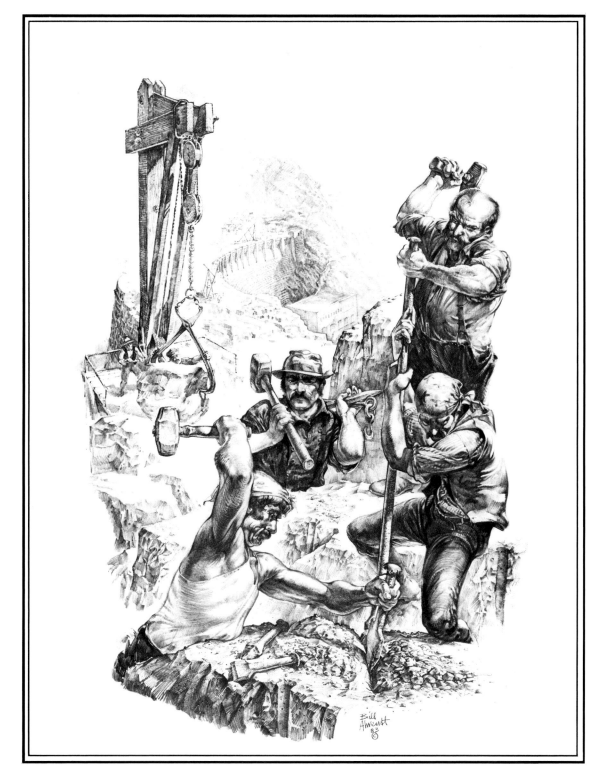

Earl A. Zarbin

ROOSEVELT DAM:
A History to 1911
Earl A. Zarbin

Typography by Dorothy Martin
Cover Art by Bill Ahrendt
Editing by Virginia Brew and Richard Stahl
Layout by Mark Woodruff
Printing by COL Press, Inc., Phoenix
Binding by Roswell Bookbinding, Phoenix
Photos Courtesy of Salt River Project

Design and Production by
Michael McCabe, Wordcrafters, Phoenix

Supported by
The Central Arizona Museum
and
The Arizona Republic, Phoenix

Published by
Salt River Project, Phoenix

To my wife, Dorothy,
who provided the most encouragement.

Foreword

Roosevelt Dam's importance to the growth of the Salt River Valley cannot be overemphasized. While it is certain a dam would have been built at the dam site someday, its contruction came at a time propitious for capturing the progressive mood of the nation.

After seventy-five years, the dam and its associated works have justified their initial $10.5 million cost many times over. They remain the backbone against which further development took place.

Roosevelt Dam originally was conceived for water storage, but, with passage of the National Reclamation Act of 1902 and federal instead of local or private financing, electric generating capacity beyond the power necessary to build the dam was added. From this dual development of stored water and hydroelectric generation emerged the Salt River Project as it is today.

When I began the research that led to writing this book, my intent was to gather material to rewrite an historical novel. The novel dealt with events in the Salt River Valley, but incompletely. Before revising it, I wanted a better understanding of how the Valley developed.

It took no special insight to understand that water was central to the Valley's progress. However, no history was available to tell how it all came about—and this work does not fulfill that ideal. Bits and pieces of the history are scattered here and there, leaving many questions unanswered.

If I truly wanted answers, I decided there was one place where I might begin to get them—from early newspapers. I thought about this for some months because I perceived it would be a lot of work to go through the newspapers. Finally, I told myself that if I really were serious about getting answers, I had to make the time to look through the old papers. The one convenient time, without having to come to work early or leave late, was my lunch hour.

Fortunately, my employer, **Phoenix Newspapers, Inc.,** in its library had copies of old Phoenix newspapers on microfilm. Marcella Bagley, head librarian, showed me how to use the microfilm reader. For the next five years and more I spent not only my lunch hour in the microfilm room, I began going to the office an hour or two early several days each week. On weekends, days off, and vacations, I spent as much time as I could reading microfilm at the newspaper and the Hayden Library at Arizona State University.

As the years passed, the novel got sidetracked. I had begun to find some answers. I also realized there were stories to be told if I could figure out how to tell them. The most dramatic and meaningful of these stories revealed the struggle to build a water storage dam on the Salt River at the Tonto Basin, the eventual site of Theodore Roosevelt Dam.

Eventually, it occurred to me to write the Roosevelt Dam story as I learned of it—by reading the early newspapers. This accounts for the chronologic approach in the text. In some cases, I have been able to enlarge upon and clarify certain incidents, thanks to documents made available principally by the Salt River Project Archives. But for the most part, newspaper reports were the source for the manuscript.

Last, I thank the people who have aided me in one way or another in the preparation of this manuscript. So much time has elapsed in this respect I do not know the names of all of them, mainly because when I began the research I had no prescience there would be a manuscript, and because I did not record them. Nonetheless, some names remain prominent because the individuals helped in educating and encouraging me. Of those, with the exceptions of Susie Sato of the Arizona Historical Foundation and Julian DeVries and Ben Cole, coworkers, all are employees at the Salt River Project, chief among them Larry Doerschlag, Paul Weimann, Joe Gacioch and Dick Lynch.

Earl Zarbin, August 1983

Table of Contents

page

Foreward 10

April 15, 1915 13

EPOCH I

1878 - 1898 19

November 30, 1898 - June 1902 29

EPOCH II

July - November 1902 43

December 1902 - March 1903 51

April - July 1903 61

EPOCH III

August 1903 - March 1904 75

March 1904 - February 1905 87

March - August 1905 101

September 1905 - February 1906 113

March - August 1906 127

September 1906 - February 1907 139

March - August 1907 151

September 1907 - February 1908 163

March - August 1908 171

September 1908 - February 1909 185

March - August 1909 197

September 1909 - February 1910 211

March - August 1910 219

September 1910 - February 1911 235

March 1-18, 1911 241

Index 247

April 15, 1915

To the several thousand persons gathered about the speakers' stand at the south end of Roosevelt Dam on April 15, 1915, there could well have seemed something divine about the moment. When the event they were there to celebrate was proposed, it was to mark the first time a million acre-feet of water had accumulated in the reservoir behind the dam. But the celebration had been delayed, and in the interval Roosevelt Lake had filled. The evening before the celebration, water began running over the dam's spillways for the first time, and now the thousands were gathered on the dam to give their thanks and to witness the spectacle.

The *Arizona Gazette,* published in Phoenix in the heart of the valley receiving the benefits of the stored water, described the scene and the feelings of the people on the dam:

With bared heads and reverent hearts, 3,000 people yesterday celebrated the first filling and overflowing of the great Tonto reservoir . . .

For two days the roads were filled with cars headed for the dam, and there were gathered for the occasion representatives of every walk of life. There were several of the men whose foresight and perseverance in the face of insurmountable difficulties had made the great project possible, and there too were the men whose children and grandchildren would reap the fruits of the labors of the undaunted pioneers. [1]

At a meeting of the directors of the Phoenix Chamber of Commerce, in early February 1915, the chamber proposed the celebration at Roosevelt Dam. C. H. Fitch, the U.S. Reclamation Service engineer in charge of the dam and its associated works in the Salt River Valley, said on February 12 that he was almost certain a million acre-feet of water would be in the reservoir within a month. The gauge in the lake at the dam was at elevation 182.15, which meant the water in storage totaled 739,463 acre-feet. This was an immense quantity of water, standing in stark contrast to the low stage of a year earlier. In Phoenix, there was a great sense of optimism among the businessmen. Snow was on the watershed, and the weather was cool. [2]

On February 20, members of the chamber lunched at the Arizona Club with their counterparts from other Valley communities to discuss the "High Water at Roosevelt Dam Celebration." Fitch and John P. Orme, president of the Salt River Valley Water Users' Association, whose members were entitled to receive the water stored in the reservoir, predicted there would be a million acre-feet of water in storage by March 18, the fourth anniversary of the formal dedication of the dam by former President Theodore Roosevelt. Fitch thought that would be an ideal time for the dedication because the nights were not so cold, "the days are splendid, and the rains will have brought out the most brilliant flower displays all over the mountains." He said the Reclamation Service would develop regulations for traveling on Roosevelt Road (today's Apache Trail, officially Arizona 88) between Mesa and Roosevelt, and would provide accommodations at Fish Creek Station and at Roosevelt. [3]

Orme said that the Water Users' Association's Board of Governors and Council had passed a joint resolution endorsing the celebration. "We believe it will be a fine thing to make the people realize the value of having a reservoir full of water," Orme said. [4]

Romaine Fielding, whose Lubin Motion Picture Co. was headquartered in Phoenix, said he would make a full reel of film for the Chamber of Commerce, and representatives of Mesa, Tempe, and Chandler promised their cooperation. [5]

Another planning session was held February 24, at which March 18 was settled upon as the official date for the celebration. However, it was pointed out the next day that the Southern Arizona Fair was scheduled in Tucson March 17-19. As a courtesy to the fair, the date of the high water celebration was changed to April 15. [6]

Meantime, the level of Roosevelt Lake continued to climb toward one million acre-feet, reaching 991,108 acre-feet at 6 p.m. March 8. The Reclamation Service received a letter from Eph Penrod of the White Mountains, part of which provide runoff for the Salt River watershed. Penrod wrote:

I have been in these parts 25 years, and there never has been so much snow. You better warn the people in the lowlands that if the snow goes out with a warm rain there is liable to be terrible floods. [7]

At 6 p.m. March 10, the water in storage behind Roosevelt Dam reached 996,833 acre-feet and the water level 201.25 feet. Twenty-four hours later, the water in storage totaled 1,004,009 acre feet. [8]

The high water celebration arrangements committee met in Mesa March 12 and appointed a committee to call on Governor George W. P. Hunt to declare April 15 a holiday. Invitations to attend the celebration were sent to mayors of cities, chambers of commerce, and railroad officials. Barbecue tickets were distributed around the Valley, including Higley and Gilbert. [9]

On March 13, the Reclamation Service issued an official statement concerning the snow conditions on the Salt River watershed and the potential for water runoff:

With the existing conditions in the snow fields of the upper watershed of the Salt River, it is difficult to conceive that the spring melting can occur under weather conditions so unfavorable as to possibly affect the realization of the confidently expected capacity storage in the Roosevelt reservoir this spring, and under normal conditions it seems probable that considerable excess water will necessarily run to waste. [10]

When the arrangements committee met March 24, it decided it would be too much trouble to serve a barbecue, so it abandoned that in favor of basket lunches and hot coffee. To pay for the celebration, the cost of which was estimated at $275, the committee approved a $1 charge for every car going over the road. Sheriff Jeff Adams of Maricopa County agreed to provide a motorcycle patrol, while signs were to be posted at all points of danger. Mechanics to aid motorists needing repairs were to be stationed at several locations. Driving rules were to be printed. Mesa people agreed to supply trucks to carry food, gas, oil, repair parts, and cheese.

Glendale was to provide sugar, Tempe, milk, and Phoenix, bread and coffee. [11]

Word came March 29 that the battleship *Arizona* would be launched in June at the U.S. Navy yard in Brooklyn, New York, and it was expected that Hunt would name an Arizona delegation to attend the launching, which would include a young lady to dedicate the dreadnought by breaking a bottle of water over the ship's bow. It was first projected the water for the dedication would come from the Hassayampa River, but later it was decided it should be from the first water over the spillways at Roosevelt Dam. [12]

At 6 a.m. April 6, the water in storage at Roosevelt Dam reached 1,253,329 acre-feet and the depth of the lake at the dam, 218.10 feet, or 6.90 feet below the top of the spillways. It was considered virtually certain the reservoir would fill and water would be over the spillways by the day of the celebration. [13]

Hunt issued a proclamation April 12 making April 15 a holiday in Maricopa and Gila counties to celebrate the filling of Roosevelt Lake. [14]

The morning of April 14, the Reclamation Service issued a statement:

Water is pouring in at the rate of hundreds of thousands of miners' inches over the Salt River intake weir. The Tonto (Creek) is contributing three thousand miners' inches. Twelve thousand acre-feet was the gain in the twenty-four hours at six o'clock this morning. [15]

Publisher Dwight B. Heard of the *Arizona Republican,* acting for the arrangements committee, planned to be at the dam when the first water went over the spillways, to capture some of it in a demijohn for later use at the dedication of the battleship *Arizona.* Heard was delayed, however, so he arranged by telephone to have the *Republican* reporter at the celebration, Robert Paul Holliday, get the water. [16]

Throughout the day April 14, cars carrying celebrators streamed out of Phoenix toward Tempe, Mesa, and the Roosevelt Road to the dam. Said the *Republican:*

traffic assumed an almost metropolitan appearance along Van Buren street. Autos, rigs, motorcycles, saddle horses and camp outfits were seen wending their ways toward the Superstitions.

The newspaper described the procession of autos as a "motorcade," and by evening crowds of visitors were camped along Roosevelt Lake, at the nearby U.S. Reclamation Service headquarters, and at Roosevelt (also called Newtown) one and a half miles above the dam on the south side of the reservoir. Thousands of electric lights had been placed on the dam and strung on poles along the road to Roosevelt. Fireworks were touched off from a barge toward the center of the lake and from shore, at Roosevelt, where there also was dance music. [17]

At 8:30 p.m. April 14, Fitch and other Reclamation Service engineers decided the water going over the spillways had become a stream and set that as the official time for the reservoir coming full. Several parties made claim to getting the first water, but the honor undoubtedly went to a Reclamation Service engineer named Dorman. Fitch put some of that water into a quart bottle, which later was set in a copper-bound flask. The top of the flask was fitted with a handle so Esther Ross, 17, of Prescott, named by Hunt to christen the *Arizona,* could swing it against the battleship's bow. The launching occurred June 19, but the bottle swung by Miss Ross was overly protected by the flask and failed to break. [18]

Early the morning of April 15, the dam visitors rushed to see the water flowing over the spillways dash against the rocks 225 feet below. The water was two inches over the spillways in the morning, but increased gradually through the day to almost six and a half inches by 6 p.m. At noon, the 3,000 persons at the south end of the dam were quieted by Charles H. Akers of the *Gazette,* chairman of the committee on speakers. Behind him, Roosevelt Lake filled the Tonto Basin and spread out in a wing shape, reaching far up the Salt River and Tonto Creek. Roosevelt Lake contained 1,378,180 acre-feet of water. [19]

Akers introduced Fielding, who offered the invocation, and then the speakers, beginning with Joseph H. Kibbey, chief author of the articles of incorporation of the Water Users' Association. Kibbey gave a brief history of the dam and added:

This dam is the regional reserve bank of Arizona, upon which the whole state may draw. The history of this work includes four epochs, of which this occasion marks the beginning of the last—successful, everlasting, proven true and able—it will stand here for ages to supply our lands with irrigation water.

Prosperity is assured the Salt River Valley and through the Valley to the entire state.

Blighted fields in Salt River Valley are forever saved. There will be no more parched acres where we live. [20]

George H. Maxwell, called "the father of the (national)

Joseph H. Kibbey

reclamation act," spoke next. Maxwell, executive director of the National Irrigation Association, had assisted Kibbey in the drawing of the articles of incorporation. He said he could not name every man who aided in the irrigation movement, but his mention of Benjamin A. Fowler, first president of the Water Users' Association, brought a burst of appreciative applause. Fowler, although a latecomer to the Salt River Valley in 1899, played a leading role in the water storage movement. Illness had kept him from the celebration. [21]

Maxwell said no "section of the West extended more loyal cooperation to the national irrigation movement than the Salt River Valley," both before and after the passage of the National Reclamation Act. He said Roosevelt Dam was,

but a stepping stone to something so much bigger that the mind can hardly grasp it.

That great future toward which we are now struggling with even greater faith than in the old days is the time when every drop of water that now runs to waste in the west will be saved and stored and used to bring forth the fruits of the earth for humanity's use and benefit. [22]

Louis C. Hill, who had been the U.S. Reclamation Service's chief engineer in charge of the overall construction of Roosevelt Dam and its associated works, told the crowd the water in the reservoir represented "A bank account on which you can draw at need for four years at least with a certainty that your checks will be honored. . . ." If the dam had been finished in 1905, he said, there would have been no shortage of water in all the years since. He continued:

Conserve your water as the careful man does his bank account accumulated by years of self-denial. Add to it by utilizing your underground water, not by wasting it, and no shortage can harm you. . .

In ten years the assessed valuation of Maricopa County has jumped to nearly $70,000,000. The population has nearly doubled. The country and the towns have taken on new life. Energy and hope have replaced listlessness and despair. The man who believed the Roosevelt Dam never would be built or if built would never fill, or if filled would never stand, is replaced by the man who knows it is built, is filled and is here. The optimist is crowding out the pessimist. [23]

State Senators John Bacon of Gila County and O. S. Stapley of Maricopa County were the next speakers, followed by William J. Murphy, the original contractor for construction of the Arizona Canal in the Salt River Valley, and one of the men involved in uniting the north side canals into a single water delivery system. Murphy said the people had come to the dam "in some sense like pilgrims to a sacred shrine." He recalled plans for a dam were made many times and companies organized:

But the job was too big for us, too big for any capital to which we had access. Yet while hope was long deferred, we did not altogether lose faith that somehow, sometime, the great consummation should be realized. . .

The project has been expanded beyond our wildest dreams. We did not think much about water power in the early days. We certainly had no conception of the importance of this unique feature of the project; we had no sense of its value; we had no vision of this power canal and its concrete dam twenty miles above us, of this 200-foot waterfall carrying energy down to the great power plant below us, or of the other power plants that have been built and of still others yet to be built, giving us a grand total of 28,000

horsepower. This power will all be ultimately utilized and produce a very large net revenue.

He predicted that Phoenix, like Babylon, would have a population of 3 million. [24]

R. M. Turner, with the Bank of Chandler, spoke from the point of view of a newcomer, explaining how Roosevelt Dam's construction had caused him and thousands of others to come to the state to live. [25]

Congressman Carl Hayden spoke next. Hayden, like many land owners with early water rights, had opposed the articles of incorporation of the Water Users' Association. On this occasion, he reminded the visitors that unlike other government works, the government was to be repaid the costs of construction, but that the time period for payment had been extended from 10 to 20 years, with no payment in any year to exceed 6 percent of the total cost. "In practical effect," he said, "the water user pays nothing on the principal of his debt to the government but cancels his obligations by paying simple interest for twenty years." Hayden, with a rose in hand, said it was,

despair that the people on the Salt River Valley are this day burying forever. With this rose, which I pluck from the pall of despair, I dedicate these impounded waters that they may flow for all time down the canyons of the river to bless the lands that lie below. [26]

The last speaker was U.S. Senator Henry Fountain Ashurst of Arizona. Ashurst said the U.S. government was "a very conservative institution," and it would not have built the Roosevelt Dam and other projects if it had not received "satisfactory assurances that these projects are practicable and wise." He said that while the water users might have "differed as to detail they are all agreed as to the beneficence of the object attempted to be achieved by the construction of this project." In conclusion, he said:

Irrigation of the west is a project so big and yet so simple that it appeals to the millions. It works its magic spell on the patriotic imagination of the masses and kindles fires of unselfish sentiment, for it is poetical yet practical. It is practical because it requires a good judgment and sound common sense to succeed. It is poetical because all the rich imagery of the Bible comes from the familiarity with the desert, and we in the mind's eye can see that the mighty prophet was thinking of irrigation and God's goodness to man when he said, "He turneth the wilderness into a standing water, and dry ground into water springs." [27]

1. *Arizona Gazette* (Phoenix), April 16, 1915.
2. *Arizona Republican* (Phoenix), February 13, 1915.
3. *Ibid.,* February 21, 28, 1915.
4. *Ibid.*
5. *Ibid.*
6. *Ibid.,* February 25, 26, 1915.
7. *Ibid.,* March 9, 1915.
8. *Ibid.,* March 10, 11, 1915.
9. *Gazette,* March 13, 1915.
10. *Ibid.*
11. *Republican,* March 25, 27, 1915.
12. *Ibid.,* March 30, April 15, 1915.
13. *Gazette,* April 6, 1915.
14. *Republican,* April 13, 1915.
15. *Ibid.,* April 15, 1915.
16. *Ibid.*
17. *Ibid.; Gazette,* April 15, 1915.
18. *Republican,* April 15, 17, June 20, 26, 1915.
19. *Ibid.,* April 16, 1915; *Gazette,* April 15, 1915.

20. *Ibid.*
21. *Gazette,* April 15, 19, 1915; *Republican,* April 16, 1915.
22. *Gazette,* April 19, 1915.
23. *Ibid.,* April 16, 1915.

24. *Ibid.*
25. *Ibid.*
26. *Ibid.,* April 16, 23, 1915; *Republican,* April 16, 1915.
27. *Gazette,* April 16, 1915.

EPOCH I

1878 - 1898

Lincoln Fowler, who may have been the first settler in the Tonto Basin country in 1876, later moved to the Salt River Valley and became a Republican candidate for the Assembly of the Legislature of the Arizona Territory in 1884. The Republicans held a rally at the plaza in Phoenix the evening of Saturday, October 25, 1884. Fowler was the last speaker and by the time he was introduced, the hour was late. For this reason, according to a report in the *Arizona Gazette,* Fowler said,

he would make no speech, and yet in a few minutes' talk he made by far the most practical observations of the evening. On the water question, he took up a proposition new and feasible—namely, the survey by the general government of our streams, with a view of improving the same for irrigating purposes; ascertaining where water diverts by subterranean channels from the main course; practical points for establishing reservoirs and like details. The idea is a good one and will sooner or later be adopted. [1]

A few days later, the **Phoenix Daily Herald** published an article signed by Fowler providing a fuller explanation of what he had in mind. He called for a "thorough hydrographic survey of the Gila and Salt rivers and other streams of the Territory and their valleys" by the federal government. He said the streams should be mapped and possible reservoir sites identified. Fowler noted that all of the streams in Arizona, with the exception of the Colorado River, were unnavigable. His proposal should not be regarded as a novelty, he said, because Congress for a long time had appropriated money for the improvement of navigable streams within the United States, and by an act of March 3, 1873, had created a three-member commission to conduct topographical and other examinations of the San Joaquin, Tulare, and Sacramento valleys in California. The commission's major conclusions, in Fowler's words, were,

That experience of other countries shows that irrigation works can be most effectually carried on by the government. State and national governments should at once combine their efforts to inaugurate this enterprise by an instrumental survey to ascertain what lands are irrigable and at what expense of construction, the amounts of water that can be furnished each tract of land, the best methods of delivery, probable cost, etc. All accessible information from foreign irrigation systems should be collected and disseminated. A system of uniform law and regulations should be established. Land and water should be inseparably united. [2]

Fowler urged the territorial Legislature to adopt a memorial to Congress asking for government aid in conducting such surveys. He proposed that the territory's delegate to Congress pursue the matter and that the people petition Congress directly. Fowler said that since the time of the Pharaohs, government had been involved in irrigation works. He cited the work of the British government in India, and pointed out that the storage of water was receiving attention in neighboring California. In Arizona, he said,

there are many places upon the Salt river, Verde, Tonto creek and Gila river that could be utilized for the purpose of storage of the flood waters of winter for irrigation during the summer months. [3]

The movement for involving the federal government in constructing canals and water storage reservoirs can be traced to 1873 or earlier. In July 1873, the **Arizona Citizen** of Tucson published an article saying that "The subject of irrigating the vast plains of the United States is annually becoming one of deeper interest." The newspaper reported that a convention on the subject was planned, and delegates met in Denver, Colorado, in October 1873. They formed a National Central Committee of Irrigation composed of the governors of nine western states and territories, including Governor Anson P. K. Safford of Arizona. The committee, which apparently had no future role in the irrigation movement, sent a memorial to Congress proposing enactment of a law to aid development of the arid region between the 99th meridian and the Pacific Ocean. The memorial argued that the irrigation needs of the West were "too extensive and costly for either individuals, private corporations, territorial, or state governments." It said agriculture, and settlement of the public domain, would remain "confined to the immediate valleys of the watercourses" until the national government provided assistance through the construction of reservoirs, which would be used to provide water for stamp mills at gold and silver mines before the flow was used to "enrich and fertilize the arid plains." The memorialists said the federal government had established precedents for providing aid by donating land to various states to aid in the construction of canals for navigation and for building railways. They asked Congress to grant the states and territories one-half of all non-mineral arid lands, the sale of which would be used to construct irrigating canals and reservoirs to reclaim the "arid waste lands." They asked that the states and territories be given exclusive control of the construction and maintenance of the canals and reservoirs, that they be permitted to issue bonds to raise funds for the construction, that the laws for settlement of the public domain be made more strict, and "that no title shall issue until the claimant shall be a bona fide, actual settler upon the land claimed." [4]

"The water question" alluded to by the **Gazette,** not enough water in the Salt River to irrigate all the land that could be cultivated, except in periods of flood, apparently became a matter of serious concern with the construction of the Grand Canal in 1878. At that time the Salt River Valley had, not including small, independent ditches or those dug by Indians, 11 recognized canal companies. [5]

American settlement of the Salt River Valley began in 1867, and the claims to Salt River water by 1878 exceeded 6,600,000 acre-feet of water per year, [6] or 5.5 times the average yearly normal inflow (as measured in later years). [7] Most of the claims to water were not exercised. In the early years of agricultural development, the main cares of the settlers, aside from breaking the land and getting their crops in, were digging, extending, and maintaining the irrigation ditches, and building and replacing their rock and brush dams, which were carried away by rises in the river. Their cultivation of hay, grain, and vegetables "was confined to that period of the year when the water in the river was very abundant," [8] which was usually in the late fall, winter, and early spring. Even in those months, however, the flow in the river could be erratic, varying widely year to year. Winter runoff sometimes made the Salt River "unfordable for weeks, while during the hot, dry weather or summer, it is sometimes reduced to a mere brook." [9]

Articles of incorporation of the Grand Canal Co. were filed with the secretary of the territory June 20, 1878. The canal, with its head on the north side of the Salt River, about one and one-half miles east of Tempe, was intended to supply water to 10,000 acres of ground north of the earliest north side canals, the Salt River Valley and the Maricopa. It was "the opinion of well informed persons that in supplying this ditch (Grand Canal), together with the several others that receive from the same source, the balance of water remaining will not amount to much." [10] Reacting to the threat of an inadequate water supply,

a mob tore out the dam of the Grand Canal just after its construction under the impression that there was not water enough to irrigate the land it would cover with the half-dozen sections then under cultivation under older canals. . . [11]

In the spring of 1879, the water in the Salt River was "at as low a stage as ever known by white inhabitants of this valley," and some of the farmers under the canals serving the lower valley were likely to lose their crops. The writer of those words observed that while the water flow immediately below the Maricopa Canal Company's dam was 700 or 800 miners' inches (40 miners' inches equaling one cubic foot, hence, seventeen and one-half to 20 cubic feet per second, or about 35 to 40 acre-feet in 24 hours), a short distance downstream in the ditch of the Salt River Valley Canal Co. there were more than 5,000 miners' inches. This meant, he said, that most of the water was passing through the sand under the dams at the heads of the respective ditches. To remedy this, "the business of irrigation (must be) thoroughly systematized" by the construction across the river of an impervious dam built down to bedrock to raise the water and divert it into a single head to supply the entire north side of the river. This meant the dam had to be built at the head of the Valley (at that time, the upper Valley was considered to be today's Papago Park, north of Tempe). The alternative, the writer said, would be lawyer-enriching litigation aimed at determining "the priority of right in ditch franchises." [12]

Other proposals to resolve the water question were to grow crops that required less water than wheat and barley (sugar cane, broom corn, cotton, and flax were suggested) and to bore artesian wells. According to the *Herald*, "The formation of this valley is well calculated for wells of this character," but none was successfully drilled. [13]

In May 1879, the crops of the farmers under the Griffin and Farmers' canals on the north side of the river southwest of Phoenix were suffering terribly from a lack of water. The farmers had been told that the "Mormons (who began settling on the south side of the Salt River, about six miles east of Tempe, in 1877) had taken at least one-half of the water out of the river, and that they flooded the desert with the greater portion of it." A group of stockholders from the Griffin and Farmers' canals decided to visit the Mormons to learn the truth of the story, and to divert the water back into the river—by force, if necessary. Saturday morning, May 17, fourteen farmers, armed and mounted, rode up the river, crossed at Hayden's Ferry (Tempe), and continued on to Mesa City. There, the farmers "were well treated and entertained, which surprised us somewhat, as we had held the belief that the people were a set of ill-bred ruffians." The Mormons said they were themselves short of water, which the visitors could readily see by looking into the Mesa Canal. "Being convinced that the Mormons were not the vicious, meddlesome, and selfish people they had been represented to be," the farmers rode several miles northeast to Jonesville (later Lehi), the first of the Mormon settlements. There they were met by Daniel Webster Jones, leader of the settlement, who insisted that the visitors camp the night. The next morning, they inspected the Mormons' farms and the Utah Canal. Jones told them he believed the oldest ditches should be protected in their water rights and should not be deprived of the water by the larger ditches, such as the Grand Canal. Satisfied the Mormons were not responsible for the short supply of water, the farmers returned home. [14]

While the visit to the Mormons ended peacefully, the shortage of water led to a shooting the morning of June 14, 1879, three miles west of Phoenix. Early that day, Michael Huff turned water from a ditch onto a parcel of land. Later, farmer John Ellis diverted the water to his own ground. Ellis went for breakfast. While he was gone, Huff returned the water to the land he had been irrigating. Ellis, seeing what had happened, came out with a shotgun and when about 50 yards away fired at Huff, a part of the load striking him in the head and neck. Huff survived, and Ellis was given a 21-month sentence in the territorial prison at Yuma after being found guilty of assult with a deadly weapon. [15]

At a meeting of the stockholders of the Grand Canal Co., on August 30, 1879, a resolution was adopted directing the president to appoint a committee of five "to confer with the directors and owners of all the canals in the valley below Hayden's Ferry, in regard to the feasibility of consolidating all the canals in the valley having their head below the Grand Canal, and taking the water from the river at one place; and also as to the advisability of inviting capital from abroad to take out the same." [16]

But this was not to be. The Farmers' Canal Co., Griffin Ditch Co., and Monterey Ditch Co. joined in a suit asking for an injunction to stop the Grand Canal Co., the Tempe Canal Co., and the Mesa Canal Co. from taking water from the river ahead of the plaintiffs. For an unexplained reason, the Utah Canal, started in 1877, was omitted from the suit. The Salt River Valley Canal Co. and the Maricopa Canal Co. presumably were not named because their claims to water preceded the others, both canals tracing their origins to the Swilling Irrigating and Canal Co. in 1867. Before the case was tried, the Tempe Canal Co. was dropped as a defendant. The plaintiffs asked that the court affirm them in the quantity of water taken from the river, i.e., 3,500 miners' inches for the Farmers', 1,800 inches for the Griffin, and 1,500 for the Monterey, and permanently restrain the defendants from interfering with their water supplies. In answer, the Grand and Mesa companies maintained that between the diversion points of their ditches and those of the plaintiffs, the river divided into three channels to a width of one mile, and that in the dry season the water disappeared in the sands of the river only "to rise again below the mouths of plaintiffs said ditches." For these reasons, the Grand and Mesa canals argued "that if all the water appropriated by them were left free to flow past their respective points of appropriations, the same, together with a considerable amount more, would disappear by the same means, and never flow into the mouths of plaintiffs' said ditches." Judge DeForest Porter acknowledged the priority of right of the Farmers', Griffin and Monterey ditches, but ruled against a permanent injunction, saying, in effect, that the amount of water taken by the defendants would make no material difference to the plaintiffs if it had been allowed to flow past the defendants' canals. [17]

By then, there was more water in the river than the farmers could use, but agitation for doing something about the water question continued into and throughout 1880. In an editorial April 30, the *Territorial Expositor,* published in Phoenix, had some suggestions, among them making the water "a part of the land," which would give the land "a permanent valuation," and construction of one main canal on the north side. The newspaper said, "Congressional aid would be very acceptable, but there is little or no hope in that direction." It said private enterprise would have to do the work, and invited comment from readers. Attorney Alexander D. Lemon responded, calling for construction of a cement dam "at a point high enough up the river from which a main trunk canal can be taken out that would cover all the land available for irrigation in the valley." Lemon said the dam should be near the present dam of the Grand Canal where the bedrock came close to the surface. He proposed one management, with water users receiving water for fixed periods of time. He agreed that water should be tied to the land, and that the corporation should be required to sell water to landowners. However, the amount of cultivated land should not exceed the water supply, and, in years of shortage, the water should be divided pro rata. Moreover, the priority to the water should depend upon continued occupation of the land. Meetings were called and held to consider the question, but no resolution was reached, and in December 1880, the *Gazette* called for a legislative solution. Assemblyman-elect Peter J. Bolan and Councilmen-elect Rube S. Thomas and Albert C. Baker, all of Maricopa County, called for unity in developing an act for introduction when the territorial Legislature met in January 1881. The views of the county's two other Assembly members, Nathaniel Sharp of Hayden's Ferry, and J. R. McCormack of Globe, were not disclosed. [18]

Late in February 1881, Bolan introduced in the Assembly a bill to establish for each of the canals the priority of its right to the use of Salt River water and the amount. The canals, in order of priority, and the quantity of water to which each was entitled as established in Bolan's bill, were as follows: Salt River Valley, 3,500 miners' inches; Griffin, 1,000 inches; Wilson, 200 inches; Tempe, 2,300 inches; Prescott, 300 inches; Farmers', 1,200 inches; Monterey, 800 inches; San Francisco, 1,300 inches; Maricopa, 2,500 inches; Utah, 800 inches; Mesa, 1,200 inches, and Grand, 3,500 inches. [19]

The measure, while reportedly meeting with general favor in Phoenix, was opposed by Tempe Canal water users, who insisted they were entitled to 8,000 miners' inches. Among the Tempe people in Prescott working against Bolan's bill was Charles Trumbull Hayden, proprietor of Hayden's Ferry and owner of the flour mill at the site. When the bill came up for debate in March, Bolan challenged the right of Sharp to vote because he was one of the Tempe Canal water users. Sharp retorted that "self-preservation is the first law of nature," and the bill was overwhelmingly defeated. [20]

In July 1881, the Salt River Valley Canal Co. notified the operators of the Grand, Utah, and Mesa canals that legal proceedings would begin if the three companies failed to allow sufficient water into the river to meet the needs of the Salt River Valley Canal. Almost immediately after, summer rains eased the water shortage, but a letter writer told the *Herald* that turning the water into the river from the three threatened canals would not have helped the Salt River Valley Canal. The writer alluded to an experiment two years earlier in which the water to the Utah and Mesa canals was cut off, but, before the water reached the Phoenix area, it sank into the river's sandy bottom. [21]

On May 19, 1882, the *Gazette* reported the prospect of a canal being "taken out on the north side of the Salt River, about a mile below the mouth of the Verde." This was the future Arizona Canal for which the water right had been located in March 1882. The head of the canal was to be about 25 miles east of Phoenix, putting it farther upstream than any of the others. The promoters intended to open for settlement about 100,000 acres of land north and northeast of the Grand Canal. Articles of incorporation for the Arizona Canal Co. were filed with the Maricopa County recorder on December 20, 1882, and construction began in May 1883. It was announced that the canal would carry 40,000 miners' inches of water, and along its course there would be a drop where waterpower could be developed. The dam that was to divert water into the Arizona Canal was to have a masonry foundation "laid with hydraulic cement and the upper portion crib-work filled in with concrete or rock and earth." The exact length of the dam was undetermined, but it was estimated it would be at least 300- to 500-feet at a minimum. These plans gave the farmers under the lower canals cause to worry about whether any water would be left for them. Others saw the canal, with its 16-foot waterfall (the Arizona Falls at today's 56th Street and Indian School Road), as an opportunity to bring electricity to Phoenix to light buildings, run streetcars, pump water, and operate factories. The Arizona Canal promoters, however, gave their immediate attention to allaying fears that the Arizona Canal would take all the water. They said repeatedly there was enough water for everyone. [22]

The possibility of building a reservoir on the Hassayampa River at Walnut Grove west of Crown King in Yavapai County for mining purposes was raised in the early 1880s. In June 1884, a report said that English capitalists were considering building an 80-foot high dam at Walnut Grove to store water and to convey it by canal to the Weaver Mining District. A later report said the dam would be 100-feet high. [23]

In September 1884, the Arizona Canal Co. reported it expected to open an office the following month to begin selling water rights. The *Herald* said the company had worked "so quietly that our people seem to fail to realize the magnitude of the great work." By then, the newspaper said, "the great work. . .is now nearly completed," meaning a canal 40 miles in length. Actually, the company's dam and head works were still to be finished and a formal offer to sell water rights was some months ahead. Meantime, the directors of the other canals in the Valley monitored the activities of the Arizona Canal Co. They were not going to permit the canal company to take water from the river without a fight. [24]

Judge Porter, elected to the territorial Assembly in November 1884, had his own ideas about how to solve the water question in Maricopa County, and when the Legislature met in January 1885, he gave notice he intended to introduce a bill consolidating the canals on both sides of the Salt River and adjusting water distribution. In an editorial January 24, the *Herald* said consolidating the canals on each side of the river "is just the thing needed in the valley," but the *Gazette* opined, three days later, that, while the theory was good,

the vital objection to its practical adoption is the almost assured certainty that an oppressive and damaging monopoly will arise therefrom. In irrigating countries, the control of water for purely speculative purposes is all wrong,. . . The Gazette *and the people of Maricopa County will certainly oppose all schemes in this direction, in the spirit of self-defense.* [25]

Ten days later, the *Gazette* reported that a petition containing 325 names opposed to resolving the water question through legislation was sent to the Legislature in Prescott. The newspaper said the signatures included those of every director of the canal companies on the north side of the river. It said a similar protest was expected to be fashioned on the south side of the river. On March 12, the *Gazette* said:

We objected to the passage of any act disturbing present water rights, and laws radically changing our system of irrigation, and nothing further than a "notice" of a bill to this effect was heard of in the halls of our legislature. [26]

Runoff in the Salt and Verde rivers was high in March 1885 and a wing of the Arizona Canal dam washed away. The Arizona Canal Co. decided to make major improvements to the dam. Nevertheless, an advertisement in the *Gazette* of June 1, 1885, announced the completion of the Arizona Canal and the company's readiness "to furnish water for irrigating purposes." Virtually all of the land under the canal had been entered under the Desert Land Act of 1877, which permitted an individual to acquire up to 640 acres for reclamation "by conducting water upon the same, within the period of three years" after the date of filing with the federal government. Upon making proof of compliance at the end of three years, the land cost the buyer $1.25 per acre. Compliance could be made by having water on the ground or by owning a perpetual water right from a chartered irrigating company. The Arizona Water Co. offered perpetual water rights, meaning the water could not be severed from the land. This was different from the custom then prevailing in the Valley. The perpetual rights were sold by the company for $500 for each 80 acres. [27]

The *Gazette* of June 3 carried a report of a party of men exploring the Salt River Canyon to determine whether it was practical to float logs in the river from the Sierra Anchas, east of the Tonto Basin, to Phoenix. The adventurers launched a boat about four miles above where Tonto Creek empties into the Salt River and continued down the river to the head of the dam of the Grand Canal. The explorers reported that, in the box canyon of the river, the walls sometimes towered 1,000 feet above them, and the newspaper said,

In years to come the Box canon (sic) of the Salt River will be utilized as a reservoir. . .[28]

Later that summer when the water in the river was down, complaints were made about the Arizona Canal. The complaints prompted a letter to the *Herald* from an "Old-Timer," who suggested water for all the north side canals be taken through the Arizona Canal. He suggested the water be divided for the other canals after it passed below the Arizona Falls, which was the plan adopted in 1889 after the Arizona Improvement Co., successor to the Arizona Canal Co., bought controlling interest in the Salt River Valley, Maricopa, and Grand canals. [29]

Old-Timer's letter drew a response in the *Gazette*, which said the Arizona Canal had a right to water only when the older canals did not need it. The newspaper said: that for the Arizona Canal "a wise plan (is) to go up in the Box canon (sic) or elsewhere and build reservoirs; then they will always have water whether it rains in this immediate section or not. This will ultimately be done we think. . ." [30]

On March 25, 1886, the *Gazette* published a long article saying chances were good the Hassayampa River reservoir at Walnut Grove would be built. The story said Wells H. Bates, who conceived the idea of constructing the reservoir, visited the Weaver Mining District in company of Professor W. P. Blake of Yale, a mineralogist, and that building the dam depended upon his report to a syndicate of capitalists. Bates said he thought Blake would make a flattering report. The dam would be 80-feet high and of sufficient length to reach solid ground on each side. The project would cost at least $250,000 and would include an iron water main running 14 miles to the gold-bearing gravel beds. In addition, three-inch pipes would convey water to various points on the plateau west of the Hassayampa, to make it feasible to graze cattle. [31]

In April 1886, the *Gazette* said in an editorial reservoirs would be constructed "when the value of our lands are thoroughly appreciated and the efficacy of irrigation in the production of all crops understood." The newspaper said reservoirs should come as public works "free from the monopoly which private capital would exercise in the distribution of water and the absolute control of the lands." The editorial scorned the idea of using Colorado River water to irrigate the desert and called for construction of reservoirs on the Gila, Salt, and Verde rivers, using labor from the territorial prison at Yuma to build them. [32]

Delegate to Congress C. C. Bean of Arizona, in May 1886, presented to the U.S. House of Representatives a bill to provide for the reclamation of desert lands. The measure, authored by Lincoln Fowler, provided for turning over the desert lands to the Western states and territories. Proceeds from the sale of the land at $1.25 per acre were to be used exclusively for the reclaiming of the land through construction of canals, reservoirs, and artesian wells. The bill also called for "a complete topographical and hydrographical survey of the Territories." [33]

In Prescott in late June, the Walnut Grove Water Storage Co. completed the purchase of four ranches at a cost of $45,500, including the Abner Wade ranch where the Walnut Grove Dam was to rise. The cost of the reservoir and 60 miles of pipeline was put at not less than $500,000. The company was said to have paid up capital of $1 million in addition to the money already expended. Work was to begin in September and, when it was finished, not less than 100,000 head of cattle were to be placed on the range. The *Hoof and Horn,* published in Prescott, said the purchase of the ranches was important because,

it is the first time in the history of Arizona, or for that matter in the entire southwest, that the oft discussed proposition of storing the surplus of winter water for use during the dry season will be practically and scientifically tested by a company with sufficient capital to guarantee its not being hampered in its operations by any lack of funds. If success crown this effort the importance of Arizona as a permanent stock growing country is increased a hundred fold. [34]

Arizona Democrats, meeting in convention in September, made construction of reservoirs a part of their party platform, while the *Gazette* the following month said the territory was financially unable to do the necessary hydrographic work on the streams. The newspaper continued,

therefore, congress will have to be invoked to do the work in the public interest the same as the government improves harbors and rivers for the general good. That portion of the public domain dependent upon irrigation is as much entitled to the improvement of its streams and catchments as are the states bordering the sea coast or the Great Lakes to have their rivers made navigable at government expense. [35]

The Arizona Canal Company's reconstructed dam in the Salt River was completed in December 1886. It was described as being 900-feet long and "built at an acute angle across the river running upstream from the mouth of the canal to a rocky point on the opposite side of the river and to which it is firmly united as it is to the rocks at the mouth." The dam had a base 40-feet wide built in sections that were hinged together. Cribs made of heavy timbers were built atop the upstream half of the base and were filled with rocks. The lower half formed an apron. For 50 feet on the upstream side, the river had been filled with rock and brush. The top of the dam was 22-feet wide and was planked. [36]

By January 1887, construction of the Walnut Grove Dam was well underway, and it was announced its size would be increased from a planned 40-feet thick and 85-feet high to 124-feet thick and 110-feet high. An electric light plant had been ordered so the work could progress night and day. The contractors, Nagle & Leonard of San Francisco, advertised for 200 workers, including quarrymen, blacksmiths, stonemasons, carpenters, and laborers. [37]

The morning of February 4, 1887, Commissioner J. W. Crenshaw of the U.S. District Court in Phoenix granted a temporary order restraining the Arizona Canal Co. from diverting water into its canal. The order had been sought by the Salt River Valley, Maricopa, Grand, Mesa, Utah, Tempe, and San Francisco Canal companies, which, on February 7, filed suit against the Arizona Canal Co. They asked in the suit that the Arizona Canal Co. be stopped from interfering with the flow of the river and be ordered to remove its dam. By the time the suit came to trial in March 1890, it had been amended five times, and the plaintiffs were Michael Wormser, owner of the San Francisco Canal, and the owners of the Tempe Canal, and the defendants were the Salt River Valley, Maricopa, Grand, Mesa, Utah, Highland, and Arizona canals. The Arizona Canal was then under the control of the Arizona Improvement Co., which at the time its articles of incorporation were recorded in May 1887, had acquired or was soon to acquire, the majority of the stock in the Salt River Valley, Maricopa, and Grand Canal companies and planned to supply all the north side canals with water through the Arizona Canal. The Arizona Improvement Co. withdrew the Salt River Valley, Maricopa, and Grand Canal companies as plaintiffs from the lawsuit, while the south side companies, except for Wormser and the Tempe Canal owners, removed themselves. The south side companies withdrew because an agreement was worked out with the Arizona Improvement Co. about how the water of the river should be divided. This contract, which was signed in 1890, in the period between the taking of testimony in the lawsuit and the decision by Judge Joseph H. Kibbey, gave the Mesa and Utah canals one-third of the water and the north side canals two-thirds, after deducting the amounts to which the San Francisco and Tempe canals were entitled. [38]

In June 1887, the *Gazette* printed a letter written by Jerome B. Barton, who said:

Now is the time to move in the matter of storing water for summer use and shortages in dry seasons. Let the citizens and farmers unite on both sides of the river in an association for the purpose of storing water, and issue stock to raise means to prosecute the work, and secure the most eligible sites now, for the time is not far distant when the most available places will be secured by parties whose object will be to open up new lands, and the old locators and settlers will have to take other and more expensive sites or be at the mercy of the first water storage companies.

Barton said that in part of 1876-77 he had been employed to look for a railroad pass from Phoenix to the forests of the mountains to the east and northeast, and there were "Boxed canons (sic) with small but permanent streams, with large watersheds that will give us a large supply of water with a small outlay compared with the benefits received." He said the idea was not new, and it was one of King S. Woolsey's "pet schemes." Woolsey, who died in 1879, was a rancher, Indian fighter, irrigator, legislator, and businessman. [39]

By the last half of 1887, the Salt River Valley had a touch of reservoir fever, and the *Herald* said there were large syndicates operating on both sides of the river preparing to unite "to build vast reservoirs on the Verde and upper Salt River that will secure enough water to irrigate every foot of this valley where water can be got onto it." The newspaper said the water storage company would be the largest in the United States, but the company never materialized. The Walnut Grove Dam, meantime, was described as "a huge success. . .and demonstrates beyond a doubt the practicability of constructing and operating great storage reservoirs in our mountains." Completed, the Walnut Grove Dam was 135-feet thick at bedrock, tapering to 10 feet at its 110-foot height. It was 175-feet wide across the stream and 400-feet long on top. The dam was built with masonry walls with the interior filled with rocks. The cost was $400,000. In December, the *Herald* reported "A gentleman who has visited the locality of the junction of Tonto Creek with the Salt River says a basin or lake can be made there, by building a dam across the Salt below Tonto, which will afford an abundance of water to irrigate Salt River Valley throughout the year." The gentleman thought this could be done for $1 million. In January 1888, the newspaper said the company that built the Walnut Grove Dam was looking for another location to build a dam and suggested the Tonto Basin site. [40]

Valley residents continued to talk about water storage, but nothing was decided. William A. Hancock, attorney, farmer, surveyor, land promoter, and canal projector, including the Arizona Canal, wrote in September 1888, that it was becoming well understood for two or three months in the summer the natural flow of the Salt River would not cover all the irrigable lands, and a system of storage reservoirs along the Salt and Verde rivers was necessary. Hancock noted while no actual surveys had been made of the reservoir sites, the cost of building the reservoirs was estimated at between $1 million and $1,500,000. The real question confronting the Valley was devising "some means by which money can be secured by the best and most practical means." Hancock suggested the issuance of bonds "secured by a lien upon the property of the county to be benefited by the outlay." He proposed placing the matter in the hands of a board of commissioners appointed for the purpose, or giving authority to the county board of supervisors. Hancock said the time to begin developing water storage was "at once. . .(because) if we delay too long, serious difficulty and possible loss to the farmers and horticultural interests of the valley may be encountered." [41]

Congress, on October 2, 1888, appropriated $100,000 for the United States Geological Survey under direction of the secretary of the interior to survey the arid region of the West to determine to what extent the lands could be reclaimed by irrigation and to select sites for reservoirs for water storage and flood prevention. The law withdrew from public settlement both the reservoir sites and the lands susceptible to irrigation from the water stored in them. [42]

On February 14, 1889, the U.S. Senate created a Select Committee on Irrigation and Reclamation of Arid Lands. The evening of April 7, 1889, the Phoenix Chamber of Commerce adopted resolutions inviting the committee to visit Phoenix. Henry K. Kemp, chamber president, sent a letter to Senator William M. Stewart of Nevada, chairman of the select committee, asking the committee to come. Stewart replied the committee expected to arrive in Arizona in September. [43]

Richard J. Hinton, irrigating engineer for the U.S. Geological Survey and author of a book about Arizona, sent letters in May to the City of Phoenix and Governor Lewis Wolfley asking that factual data concerning irrigation be gathered for presentation to the senate select committee. Phoenix referred the letter to the chamber of commerce, while Wolfley sent copies of the letter to boards of supervisors in the counties. [44]

The coming of the senate committee renewed interest among Valley canal men in developing a water storage plan, and a preliminary meeting was held in Phoenix on June 29, which resulted in a general invitation for all canal interests to attend a meeting July 6. At the meeting, County Supervisor C. R. Hakes suggested the county appropriate some money so a survey could be conducted to locate the best reservoir sites, their capacities, and costs. On July 12, the supervisors appropriated $500 for the survey over the protests of Hakes, who wanted a larger expenditure so the survey could be complete and a report made (the survey party's expenses came to $599.67). County Surveyor William Breckenridge was directed to make the survey assisted by John R. Norton, foreman of the Arizona Improvement Co., and one other person. The third member of the survey team was James H. McClintock, a newspaperman and a director of the Tempe Normal School. They departed, accompanied by a factotum, the morning of July 18. [45]

Thomas E. Farish, territorial immigration commissioner, prepared a report for the U.S. Geological Survey in which he said the 13 canals in the Salt River Valley (he did not include Indian canals) had a length of 175 miles and covered 250,000 acres of land, of which 187,500 had been reclaimed and 125,000 were annually cultivated. Farish added:

All the water in the Salt River has been appropriated and nothing further can be done in the way of land reclamation under this stream without the construction of storage reservoirs. [46]

Breckenridge, Norton, McClintock, and their packer/cook returned to Phoenix the morning of August 10. Breckenridge, in a report to the county supervisors, and McClintock, in an article published in the *Herald,* said the most available dam site was on the Salt River, about 400 yards below its junction with Tonto Creek. The river at that point was about 200-feet wide, and the canyon walls were nearly vertical for about 100 feet before sloping back about one foot for each one foot of rise. The canyon walls were approximately 800-feet high, and a 200-foot-high dam would create a V-shaped lake, backing the water up the Salt River for 16 miles and up Tonto Creek for 10 miles. Bedrock was thought to be not more than a dozen feet below the river bed. There was an abundance of limestone and sandstone, with timber available in the Sierra Ancha Mountains, about 20 miles distant. Breckenridge estimated the cost of the dam and reservoir at not more than $1,500,000, "and it would supply water enough to irrigate all the land in the valley from the Arizona Canal dam to Yuma." The lake would be the largest artificial reservoir in the world. McClintock offered these further comments:

Surely the general government can find at no other place a more eligible site for water storage than this presents, and it should now be made the aim of our representative citizens to see that Congress is properly informed and to push matters so that, either by governmental aid or assisted private enterprise, the necessary one-half million dollars shall be forthcoming for the construction of the dam, and that the prosperity of Central Arizona shall be established as firmly as the eternal rocks.

A watertight bedrock dam just below the junction of the Salt and Verde, from which would be supplied all the canals of the valley, is a necessary concomitant to this enterprise, and would needs be effected before the full benefits of the summer storage flow could be enjoyed. This would be a costly undertaking to be entirely borne by the people of the valley, and yet would be the most economical move that could be made in canal circles. Besides the saving of the never ending expense of repairs to our brush dams, there would be saved from the underground flow fully 7,000 miners' inches. [47]

Two members of the Senate Select Committee on Irrigation, Stewart and John H. Reagan of Texas, arrived in the Valley on September 4. Hinton and John Wesley Powell, director of the U.S. Geological Survey, were with them. Among the Valley residents who gave testimony were Farish, Breckenridge, Fowler, and William J. Murphy, president of the Arizona Improvement Co. and the contractor who built the Arizona Canal. At 8 p.m. September 4, about 500 persons gathered at the city plaza and heard Stewart speak about irrigation and silver coinage. Stewart predicted that when 65 million people realized what could be done with irrigation in the West, they would eagerly unite for its development. He also advised the people never permit the separation of water from the land. He said water and land, like the union of states, must be inseparable forever. The senators departed for Tucson the following morning. [48]

In November 1889, construction of a lower Walnut Grove Dam on the Hassayampa River was in progress, about 17 miles downstream from the big dam. The lower dam was intended to be 57-feet high and about 200-feet long on top. It was to measure 60-feet wide at the base and taper to 10 feet at the top. Its form of construction was to be the same as the big dam, with masonry walls and an interior filled with rocks. Work also was planned on a central dam between the first two. The central dam was intended to provide electrical power for use in some of the mining sections. [49]

On February 21, 1890, about 9 p.m., the Salt River began a sudden rise that in three hours made it 15-feet deep. Thereafter, it rose more slowly, reaching a peak of 17 feet at 1 p.m. February 22 and washing out 200 feet of the railroad bridge connecting Phoenix and Tempe. [50]

Heavy rain—a solid sheet—also fell February 21 over the watershed of the Hassayampa River. By 8 p.m., the Walnut Grove Dam's 750-acre reservoir was full and water began running over the top. Early the morning of February 22, water was as much as 13 or 15 feet over the dam. At 2:20 a.m., the structure gave way. The water from the reservoir formed a huge wall as it raced through the canyon. It swept away the lower dam and caught entire families sleeping in the main construction camp, a couple of miles below. An estimated 45 to 70 persons lost their lives. Some persons considered the dam's failure to be a serious setback for water storage. But the *Herald* demurred:

Already preliminaries are being arranged for the reconstruction of the Walnut Grove dam and for the building of yet another large reservoir dam in that region. The bursting of that dam so far as water storage in Arizona is concerned was simply a benefit to capital that will invest in like structures in the future. That dam was most carelessly constructed and much money was wasted on it, but good dams can be constructed in this country easier than almost anywhere else; the thing that was to be learned was the demands that would be made on such structures. We have just had one terrible lesson as to that. [51]

The Walnut Grove Dam was not rebuilt.

In July 1890, Dexter M. Ferry, head of D. M. Ferry & Co. of Detroit, Michigan, a seed firm, and his partner, C. C. Bowen, visited the Salt River Valley at the invitation of Dr. Alexander J. Chandler, territorial veterinarian. Chandler, who had worked for Ferry and Bowen before coming to Arizona in 1887, wanted them to invest in a scheme for consolidating the canals south of the Salt River and acquiring land. One of the ideas they considered was construction of a masonry dam 460-feet long and 34-feet high upstream of the Arizona Dam and below the confluence of the Salt and Verde rivers. While this scheme fell through, in January 1891, with Chandler as the front man, they took over the management of the Mesa Canal and enlarged it to a point about one mile northeast of Mesa. From there, the flow was divided to travel in three directions. The western branch fed the Utah Extension Canal and Tempe Canal, the southern branch, the Mesa Canal, and the eastern branch, the Consolidated Canal, which turned south for 19 miles to the border of the Gila River Indian Reservation. The Consolidated Canal was owned by the Consolidated Canal Co., incorporated in March 1892, by Chandler, Ferry, and Bowen. The western branch was only two-miles long and, before passing water to the Tempe Canal, had a drop of 35 feet. It was at the drop that Chandler constructed a 500-horsepower electric generating plant, which in 1897 was used to pump well water and later to provide power for Mesa and Tempe. [52]

Congress on August 30, 1890, repealed the part of the law of October 2, 1888, withdrawing public lands from entry except for reservoir sites. [53]

The first National Irrigation Congress was held September 15-17 in Salt Lake City, Utah. Among the Arizona delegates were Lincoln Fowler, who was credited with developing the idea of ceding desert lands to the states and territories so they could be sold with the proceeds going toward reclamation projects, and William J. Murphy. The aim of the convention was to induce the federal government to cede the arid lands, and such a resolution was adopted. [54]

Articles of incorporation for the Rio Verde Canal Co. were filed in Phoenix on December 18, 1891. Subsequently, the company made claims to construct dams and reservoirs on New River and the Verde River. One of the locations on the Verde River was at the Horseshoe site. Though the company, in connection with the Horseshoe reservoir, bored a 700 foot tunnel through a mountain, excavated about 20 miles of canals in Paradise Valley northeast of Phoenix, and sold water rights, it never delivered a drop of water. [55]

Judge Kibbey's decision in the lawsuit started against the Arizona Canal Co. in 1887 was made March 31, 1892. By then, the suit was known as *M. Wormser, et al. v. The Salt River Valley Canal Co., et al.* In it Kibbey ruled that water appropriated for the reclamation of desert land cannot subsequently be segregated from the land. He acknowledged, however, once an appropriation of water was made, it might be abandoned. He said a person who abandoned water "exhibits a want of good faith toward the government by whose bounty he obtained title" to lands. Kibbey said agreements for prorating of water among the canal companies were illegal, but his ruling was ignored. He said irrigators with diversion points along the river below those of canal companies with diverting points above should be required to take water from the latter, provided it was delivered at no greater cost. Kibbey said that would result in a saving of water. He said canal companies were common carriers subject to competition; if a canal company had no customers, it could not divert water. Kibbey, by means of a chart, listed the number of quarter sections (each quarter section consisting of 160 acres) of land for which each canal could divert water, beginning with the year 1869 and continuing through 1889. The chart showed 946 quarter sections, or 151,360 acres of land, of which 105,760 acres were on the north side of the river and 45,600 acres on the south side. The decree established that the San Francisco and Tempe canals were entitled to divert water for virtually all quarter sections under them before the Arizona Canal could take any water. Kibbey did not attempt to establish the water rights of individual irrigators. [56]

In May 1892, the *Herald* said "construction of the dam on the Salt River in the box canyon will probably begin within a year." It said "the process of securing the funds is going on more favorably now than for the past year or two," but no details of these efforts were offered and nothing came of them. In December 1892, the *Herald* said prophetically:

When the necessity for water for irrigation purposes squeezes the people of the Salt and Gila valleys hard enough, then the important matter of water storage will assume some importance. At present, though everybody knows that the time will come in the near future, yet no move is being made to meet the necessity. The loss of a few years crops will commence, however, and then there will be plenty of water. [57]

Articles of incorporation for the Hudson Reservoir and Canal Co. were filed February 18, 1893, by C. D. Baker and D. A. Abrams, both of Phoenix, but it was not until April that the extent of the company's plans, including a dam 225-feet high in the box canyon of the Salt River below Tonto Creek, were disclosed. Attorney Wells Hendershott, who had arrived in Phoenix the previous October reportedly on behalf of New York capitalists interested in investing in Arizona, said the scheme involved construction of two additional dams on the Salt River, the first a diversion dam about 10 miles above the confluence of the Salt and Verde rivers, and the second six miles above the mouth of Cottonwood Creek. Papers were being prepared to gain title to the reservoir sites as required by territorial and federal laws. The *Arizona Republican* said,

This is the active beginning of that irrigation scheme, which has been the dream of capitalists for years, making a lake of Tonto basin. The profits from its accomplishment have always been apparent, but the stupendous prospective cost until now has stood in the way of the fulfillment of the dream. [58]

Despite the newspaper's prognostication and considerable expenditure of money by the Hudson company, the dam went unbuilt.

Another attempt by Valley farmers to organize for construction of water storage reservoirs began with a meeting of Mesa Canal stockholders June 4, 1893. The stockholders approved a resolution offered by Ethelbert W. Wilbur, company secretary, calling for a meeting of canal company directors and other interested citizens in Tempe on June 15. That meeting was attended by representatives of the Arizona, Grand, Mesa, Utah, Tempe, and Highland canals (this latter canal was organized on the south side of the river in 1887 to water land east of Mesa; it was not a successful enterprise) and the proposed Rio Verde Canal. The participants agreed that the only feasible way to increase the water supply was to build reservoirs, but they could not agree on how funds should be raised. In addition, farmers from the north side did not want anyone connected with the management of canals involved, but this was unacceptable to the south siders because they owned their canals themselves. Finally, it was decided that a five-member committee representative of all the men interested in irrigation and development of reservoirs be named to plan what to do next. Their answer was to call for another committee, composed of 12 members, to arrange for a general meeting. The 12-member committee met June 20 and scheduled a general meeting July 15. This meeting convened in Patton's 720-seat opera house at 20 S. Center St., Phoenix. Alex Trippel of the Mesa Canal, an engineer and the first speaker, said an ordinary association of farmers could not accomplish the work of water storage, and it was necessary to raise funds either through legislation or by bonding. He said there could be no objection to a private corporation if the landowners could be guaranteed proper water service. Trippel said an objection to a large storage dam was it would be filled with sediment and silt; hence, many small reservoirs would be better, but William Hancock said the silt problem was exaggerated, and he argued for a well-financed company to build a reservoir. Jerry Millay, the meeting chairman, said farmers with the earliest existing water rights should be admitted to a cooperative reservoir project at a lower cost than later appropriators, but the water should be distributed pro rata. He suggested a mortgage of 10, 20, or 30 years upon the land to be benefited, with trustees selected by the farmers to oversee the construction of the reservoirs. He proposed a convention with elected representatives in numbers based upon the acreage under each canal. Wilbur said the real question was whether the reservoir would be owned by private capital or the people, while W. C. Collier wanted t know how it was to be paid for, suggesting it be underwritten by federal lands ceded to the territory when it became a state and sold for that purpose. E. F. Kellner, a merchant and landowner, called for an election of a committee by the people to form a plan of action, but Wilbur proposed Millay appoint a committee. One man objected, saying he was unwilling to have his interests passed upon by men selected in that manner. Millay responded it was this spirit of jealousy that had cursed the country. J. H. Broomell moved the chair appoint two men from the south side and two from the north side, who would select a committee of 10 equally divided between the two sides to develop a reservoir plan, which would later be submitted to the people. The committee was appointed, but it apparently was unable to develop a satisfactory plan because it was not heard from again. [59]

The *Herald* commented:

The great scheme of water storage for the Salt and Gila valleys continues to be pushed publicly and privately. There is one certain method of securing it and one certain method of receiving all the benefits that may be derived from water storage, and that is for the property owners of this valley in the form of a great corporation in which each shall hold nontransferable stock except with the transfer of his property, to take hold of the matter, the prior rights of earlier locations of water being carefully provided for. [60]

In the months that followed, little, if anything, was done by farmers in the Valley toward construction of reservoirs, provoking the *Herald* of February 23, 1895, to say, "It is now doubtful whether the old idea of great reservoirs on the rivers will ever materialize." [61]

James A. Fleming and James H. McClintock, both of Phoenix, and A. J. Doran of Florence, all appointed as delegates to the fourth National Irrigation Congress in Albuquerque, New Mexico, scheduled for September 16-19, met in Phoenix July 19 and agreed to issue a letter asking the municipalities, irrigation districts, and convention representatives to join in trying to bring the 1896 congress to Phoenix. Their efforts were successful. [62]

Representatives of seven canal companies met in Phoenix on July 20, 1895, to discuss what was to be done to preserve the water rights of the canals. They maintained that for several years less water had been available and blamed this on diversions by new settlers upstream. John W. Woolf and H. F. Robinson were assigned to tour the Verde River to learn the extent of upstream diversions. They reported September 1 that, from the mouth of the lower Verde River southward, they found nine ditches, nearly all within the former Fort McDowell Military Reservation, with an estimated 800 to 900 miners' inches being diverted from the river by three ditches. The blame for less water was simply that less rain had fallen over the watershed, although in the full year 1895 the total runoff was 1,621,000 acre-feet. The problem was 592,000 acre-feet came down the river in January and only 18,000 acre-feet in July. [63]

Arthur Powell Davis, hydrographer for the U.S. Geological Survey, arrived in Florence in December 1895 with a party of men to investigate ways to secure water for the Pima and other Indians on the Gila River Indian Reservation. As part of the investigation, Davis surveyed the Buttes dam site, about 14 miles east of Florence on the Gila River, and a dam site on Queen Creek, north of the reservation. He also considered pumping water from the ground, and possible "purchase of water from companies contemplating storage on Salt River." Davis reported late in 1896 the Hudson Reservoir and Canal Company's contemplated dam at the Tonto Basin would store more than 800,000 acre-feet of water. "Judging from the topography of the reservoir site and the character of rock at the dam site," Davis wrote, "it is entirely probable that a safe reservoir could be built capable of impounding an enormous quantity of water, somewhere in the neighborhood of the astonishing figures (800,000 acre-feet) given above." However, he said, the water could not be carried by a gravity canal to the eastern end of the reservation, where much of the farming had been done in the past. But, the water could be taken to Sacaton and the central part of the reservation. Davis was unable to obtain a figure at which the Hudson company was willing to supply water. He also thought it was "undesirable to enter into contracts with private companies," and recommended against buying water as a solution to supplying the Pimas. Davis' supervisor, Frederick H. Newell, in transmitting Davis' report to Charles D. Walcott, director of the Geological Survey, noted that while promoters and capitalists had embarked upon a number of Salt River water storage projects, none had been completed, "and their achievement depends, to a certain extent, upon the share that the Government may take in the construction" by granting a large body of land. Newell said, as Davis had shown,

it would be preferable as a business proposition for the Government to do all the work and dispose of the benefited land, keeping the increased value to repay the cost of the project. The Government, not having exclusive control of the reservoir, would not be sure of the successful completion or of proper maintenance. [64]

Newell attended the National Irrigation Congress meeting in Phoenix December 15-17, 1896. Another of the delegates was George H. Maxwell of California, who introduced a resolution, which was approved, calling for "construction of storage reservoirs by the federal government where necessary, to furnish water for the reclamation and actual settlement of public lands." The convention, adopting another resolution proposed by Maxwell, severely restricted its support for ceding the public lands to the states and territories so they could sell them to underwrite the costs of reclamation. The resolution favored cession of the public lands "only upon conditions so strict that they shall absolutely insure the settlement of such lands by actual settlers in small tracts and absolutely prevent their monopoly in large bodies under private ownership." [65]

In 1897, Davis visited the Tonto Basin dam site and wrote a tract titled, *Irrigation Near Phoenix, Arizona.* In this paper, Davis put the number of principal water reservoir sites surveyed by individuals, corporations, and the government at eight, including Tonto Basin. Of the latter, he said:

It would probably be impossible to find anywhere in the arid region a storage project in which all conditions are as favorable as for this one. The capacity of the reservoir, in proportion to the dimensions of the dam, is enormous. The lands to be watered are of remarkable fertility, in a climate of which may be classed as almost semitropic, and are vastly greater in area than the water can supply. To a considerable extent they are already settled upon, and the water is in lively demand. The character of rock at the dam site is said to be excellent for the construction and foundation of the dam. . . .There can be no doubt. . .that in this reservoir site lies one of the most important possibilities for the future of the agriculture of southern Arizona. [66]

The "lively demand" for water alluded to by Davis became more acute as 1897 passed into 1898 because Arizona and the Valley were entering a period of severe drought. In April 1898, A. Redewill, a piano salesman who traveled the state from his Phoenix headquarters, reported there were no signs of snow visible on the mountains from which the rills and streams that fed the Salt River got their water. Unless there was a snow storm in the mountains, there would be a lack of water, Redewill said. He said the remedy was for Maricopa County to sell two million dollars' worth of bonds, refundable in 50 years at 5 percent interest, and dam the Salt River. [67]

1. *Arizona Republican* (Phoenix), March 19, 1911; *Arizona Gazette* (Phoenix), October 27, 1884.

2. *Phoenix Daily Herald* (hereafter Herald), October 30, 1884.

3. *Ibid.*

4. *Arizona Citizen* (Tucson), July 12, November 15, 1873.

5. *Salt River Herald* (Phoenix), August 17, 1878; *Territorial Expositor* (Phoenix), February 25, 1881.

6. *Salt River Herald,* May 4, 1878.

7. Interview with Howard Alexander, Salt River Project, August 21, 1981.

8. *M. Wormser, et al, v. The Salt River Valley Canal Co., et al,* No. 708, Second Judicial District, Territory of Arizona, Maricopa County, Decision, Joseph H. Kibbey, March 31, 1892, p. 5, Salt River Project Archives (hereaftr SRPA).

9. Alfred J. McClatchie, *Utilizing Our Water Supply,* University of Arizona Bulletin No. 43, Tucson, Arizona, July 28, 1902, pp. 62-65.

10. *Salt River Herald,* July 6, August 17, 1878.

11. *Herald,* January 15, 1892, April 11, 1888.

12. *Expositor,* May 9, 1879; *Herald,* August 20, 1879.

13. *Herald,* July 12, 1879.

14. *Expositor,* May 23, 1879; *Mesa Tribune,* July 12, 1969; Frank T. Pomeroy, *The Genealogical and Historical Magazine of the Arizona Temple District* (October, 1925), Vol. II, No. 4, p. 38.

15. *Herald,* June 14, October 17, 31, 1879.

16. *Ibid.,* September 3, 1879.

17. *Ibid.,* September 10, December 15, 1879; *Expositor,* September 12, October 31, November 7, 1879, August 20, 1880.

18. *Herald,* December 29, 30, 1879, January 20, July 21, August 4, 6, 1880; *Expositor,* April 30, May 7, July 23, 30, 1880; *Gazette,* December 8, 11, 1880.

19. *Expositor,* February 25, 1881.

20. *Ibid.,* March 4, 11, 1881; *Gazette,* March 7, 1881.

21. *Herald,* July 25, 1881.

22. *Gazette,* May 19, December 20, 1882, May 8, November 20, 1883; *Herald,* May 7, July 9, 11, September 19, December 24, 29, 1883, September 22, 1884.

23. *Herald,* June 4, 30, 1884.

24. *Ibid.,* September 22, 24, 1884; *Gazette,* July 19, September 29, October 4, November 14, 1884.

25. *Herald,* January 23, 24, 1885.

26. *Gazette,* February 6, March 12, 1885.

27. *Gazette,* April 2, 4, June 1, 3, 1885, April 27, 1886; *Citizen,* March 31, 1877; *Herald,* September 28, 1886.

28. *Gazette,* June 3, 5, 6, 9, 1885.

29. *Herald,* October 1, 1885; McClatchie, *op. cit.,* pp. 81-82.

30. *Gazette,* October 1, 1885.

31. *Ibid.,* March 25, 1886; *Herald,* July 1, 1886, quoting *Hoof and Horn* (Prescott).

32. *Gazette,* April 20, 1886.

33. *Herald,* May 27, 1886.

34. *Gazette,* April 20, 1886; *Herald,* July 1, 1886, quoting *Hoof and Horn.*

35. *Gazette,* September 10, October 4, 1886.

36. *Herald,* December 24, 1886; *Gazette,* October 9, 1886.

37. H. A. Bigelow, *Journal-Miner* (Prescott), reprinted in the *Gazette,* January 22, 28, 1887; *Herald,* October 8, 1888.

38. *Herald,* February 4, 1887; *Gazette,* May 24, 1887; Kibbey, *Wormser v. Salt River Valley Canal;* McClatchie, *op. cit.,* p. 88.

39. *Gazette,* June 24, 1887; *Herald,* July 2, 1879.

40. *Herald,* July 9, August 4, October 7, December 15, 1887; *Phoenix Weekly Herald,* October 6, 1888, January 9, February 27, 1890.

41. W. A. Hancock, *Herald,* September 8, 1888.

42. F. H. Newell, *The History of the Irrigation Movement, First Annual Report of the U.S. Reclamation Service* (Washington: Government Printing Office, 1903), pp. 20-21.

43. Newell, *op. cit.,* pp. 4-5; *Herald,* April 9, 16, 1889.

44. *Herald,* June 4, 6, 1889.

45. *Ibid.,* July 2, 6, 13, 19, August 15, 20, 1889.

46. *Ibid.,* July 16, 1889.

47. *Ibid.,* August 14, 15, 1889.

48. *Ibid.,* September 4, 5, 1889.

49. *Ibid.,* November 12, 1889; *Phoenix Weekly Herald,* February 27, 1890.

50. *Herald,* February 22, 1890.

51. *Ibid.,* February 24, March 4, March 5, 1890; *Phoenix Weekly Herald,* February 27, 1890.

52. *Herald,* July 18, 1890, January 12, 1891, January 25, 1897; *Gazette,* reprinted *Tempe Daily News,* July 30, 1892.

53. *Herald,* September 2, 1890; Newell, *op. cit.,* p. 3.

54. *Herald,* July 29, December 28, 1891; Newell, *op. cit.,* p. 6.

55. *Herald,* December 18, 21, 1891; *Gazette,* April 28, 1893, March 5, April 16, 1896.

56. Kibbey, *op. cit.,* pp. 48, 56, 61, 72; *Gazette,* April 3, 1892.

57. *Herald,* May 16, December 20, 1892.

58. *Gazette,* February 19, 1893; *Republican,* April 20, 26, 1893.

59. *Republican,* June 10, 16, 21, July 16, 1893; *Herald,* December 13, 1887, September 8, 1888; *Gazette,* June 4, 16, 1893; *Arizona Weekly Gazette* (Phoenix), July 20, 1893.

60. *Herald,* July 26, 1893.

61. *Ibid.,* February 23, 1895.

62. *Ibid.,* June 20, July 19, September 18, 1895.

63. H. F. Robinson and J. W. Woolf, *Report on Use of Water From Verde River,* September 1, 1895, SRPA; McClatchie, *op. cit.,* p. 69.

64. *Florence Tribune,* reprinted *Gazette,* December 16, 1895; Arthur P. Davis, *Report on the Irrigation Investigation of the Pima and Other Indians on the Gila River Reservation, Arizona* (Washington: Government Printing Office, 1897), SRPA; F. H. Newell to C. D. Walcott, November 11, 1896, included in Davis' report.

65. *Herald,* December 16, 18, 1896; Newell, *op. cit.,* p. 7.

66. Arthur P. Davis, *Irrigation Near Phoenix, Arizona,* U.S. Geological Survey, Water Supply & Irrigation Paper, No. 2 (Washington: Government Printing Office, 1897), reprinted by SRPA, pp. 39-40.

67. McClatchie, *op. cit.,* p. 69; *Gazette,* April 16, 1898.

November 30, 1898 - June, 1902

Fulfilling my promise to call a meeting after election, of water consumers and other parties interested, to formulate, with their assistance, a feasible plan to secure water storage for Maricopa County, I hereby call a public meeting at the city hall, Phoenix, December 12, 1898, at 1:30 p.m. to which all persons interested are invited. Aaron Goldberg. [1]

In November 1898, Goldberg was elected to the Council of the Arizona Legislature. Like many other persons, he shared the view that because private capital had failed to build water storage reservoirs, the matter was now up to the Legislature. The December 12 meeting began at 2 p.m. and ended almost three hours later with the appointment of a Water Storage Committee of 10 members to consider the feasibility of a water storage project. Among the members were Governor Nathan Oakes Murphy, a fervent advocate of the cession of arid lands to the states and territories for reclamation purposes; Lincoln Fowler, credited with developing the idea of cession; Winfield Scott, orange grower and founder of Scottsdale; Alexander J. Chandler, who united the canals south of the Salt River into a single water delivery system and developed the Valley's first hydroelectric plant; John W. Woolf, a prominent land owner under the Tempe Canal; and Goldberg, a Phoenix merchant. [2]

If the Legislature agreed, Goldberg said, a committee should be sent to Washington to either secure direct aid from the federal government for construction of a reservoir, or to get concessions of public land that would accompany statehood. Another important factor to him was the safety of any dam that was built. Chandler doubted the government would build a reservoir, adding, "We want to adopt the most feasible plan that we can carry out, not what we think ought to be done." J. K. Doolittle of the Rio Verde Canal, W. W. Miller of the Arizona Canal, and Henry H. Mann of the Hudson Reservoir and Canal Co. doubted Congress would provide money for a reservoir and advocated relief from taxation to induce private capital to build dams. [3]

On December 20, the Water Storage Committee elected Goldberg permanent chairman (replacing Murphy, originally selected but unable to serve) and R. E. Daggs, secretary. The meeting ended with Goldberg appointing subcommittees to consider construction by a corporation, by securing government aid, and by individual ownership. [4]

On December 28, a committee of farmers, calling themselves "prior appropriators," met in the Good Templars hall over the Dorris Brothers' Furniture Store in Phoenix to form the Maricopa County Farmers' Cooperative and Protective Association. These men, who worked in harmony with Goldberg's committee, either owned or rented land to which water had been applied in 1880 or earlier. Some of them thought the prior appropriators were entitled to the present water in the river and should not be asked to contribute to construction of a reservoir. [5]

Goldberg's Water Storage Committee met January 3, 1899, to hear reports from the corporation and individual ownership subcommittees. The first subcommittee proposed legislation providing for the creation of irrigation districts with power to tax land to raise funds for reservoir construction.

In explanation of this proposition, F. A. Gulley said the tax would "force unoccupied land, held for speculation, to help pay for general improvement of the country and enhancement of all land values." The individual ownership subcommittee proposed formation of a district or a company of 750,000 acres or 750,000 shares, respectively, with stock and nontransferable water rights in the company limited to landowners on the basis of one share per acre. A committee was appointed to work with a legislative committee named by the prior appropriators. [6]

Dwight B. Heard, who, with his father-in-law, Chicago wholesale hardwareman Augustus C. Bartlett, was to establish the 7,000-acre Bartlett-Heard Land and Cattle Co., wrote to Goldberg about water storage. Heard thought if the U.S. government could "be induced to construct the needed storage works and operate the same on a strictly civil service basis the results would undoubtedly be satisfactory," but he said it was improbable that it would happen for many years. He believed the idea that people of the Valley should "bond their lands and construct a reservoir themselves would be found impracticable," which meant they must look toward private capital. In any event, Heard argued that owners of ground irrigated only when the river flooded "should expect to pay more for storage water than those located under the old canals" because the stored water would give their land productive value. Similarly, Heard wrote, "land under newer canals should bear the principal costs of the water storage" since they would "reap the greatest benefit." He said the water rights for such land were presently of indefinite value, while, with water storage, they "would become decidedly valuable." [7]

Murphy's message to the Legislature in January 1899 included a request for legislation dealing with water storage. He said:

I deem it of the greatest importance that some plan be devised to expedite and insure water storage and that legislation be had to aid and encourage the construction of reservoirs and for the purpose of controlling and regulating the distribution of water. [8]

In response, the Legislature approved a bill exempting from taxation for 15 years reservoirs and canals constructed for water storage, but it failed to accept a measure to form an irrigation commission to work on behalf of water storage. The failure to approve the commission drew a note of regret from Frederick H. Newell, hydrographer for the U.S. Geological Survey:

I have long appreciated the necessity of water storage in Arizona and am doing whatever is possible to forward it. We now have a field party operating along the Gila River under a clause in the Indian appropriations bill. Their work is narrowly restricted by law, so that we cannot take up the question of larger public importance. If this could be done I have no doubt but that the results would be beneficial. Until the people of Arizona express themselves clearly and emphatically on the subject it of course is improbable that congress will take action. [9]

In ensuing months, Murphy pushed the idea of ceding the arid lands to the states and territories, even making an appearance in June before the Trans-Mississippi Congress at Wichita, Kansas. The congress rejected a resolution calling for cession of arid lands and approved one asking for government aid for irrigation. [10]

Among the men at the congress were many who regularly attended the National Irrigation Congress. These men had decided the work of the irrigation congress needed to be continued throughout the year to bring public sentiment to the cause of federal help for reclamation. As a result, while in Wichita they organized the National Irrigation Association with George H. Maxwell of California picked to head the executive committee. [11]

When the National Irrigation Congress met at Missoula, Montana, September 25-27, it too rejected the ceding of arid lands by a vote of more than 10 to 1. The vote against cession followed a speech in opposition by Myron H. McCord, former governor of Arizona. The congress unanimously adopted a resolution calling for federal aid in construction of reservoirs. [12]

Despite the overwhelming rejection of cession by the National Irrigation Congress, Murphy continued to support cession throughout the remainder of his career as governor. McCord, in a speech October 20 before the Arizona Agricultural Association in Phoenix, gave a number of reasons for opposing ceding of arid lands, the most important being that "the easiest, quickest, and best way to reclaim the arid lands and permit their settlement and cultivation is to have the government build the great dams. . ." He said if the arid lands were ceded they would be "gobbled up by land-grabbing syndicates" and speculators as were swamplands given to the states between 1850 and 1860. McCord said the advocates of national irrigation aimed to have the federal government build reservoirs only "in places beyond the point where private capital can be reasonably expected to go. . .". [13]

At the end of October, John F. Wilson, Arizona's delegate to Congress, returned from a visit to the proposed site of the San Carlos dam on the Gila River below the San Carlos Indian Reservation. Wilson said he would ask for an appropriation to build the San Carlos dam, which would furnish water for the Gila River Indian Reservation and would permit the opening of other lands for non-Indians. The U.S. Geological Survey reported a masonry dam at San Carlos forming a reservoir containing 241,396 acre-feet of water would cost $1,038,926. Frederick Newell proposed "That the San Carlos dam should be built as the first step to be taken for the storage of water upon the Gila," and Wilson in December introduced a bill for the construction of the dam. The *Phoenix Daily Enterprise* said that,

Should this become a law the entrance wedge will have been started towards establishing government reservoirs. . . .Every citizen in the territory should assist our delegate in his efforts to secure the passage of this measure. With the establishment of one reservoir, the feasibility of the scheme will be apparent to all. [14]

A few days later, farmers and businessmen gathered in Phoenix at the Dorris Theater to hear an address by Maxwell. In addition to attacking cession, he charged that apathy and lack of unity in the West retarded the program of national irrigation. Maxwell said the best plan to get reservoirs was to support construction of the San Carlos dam. In response, McCord offered resolutions, which were unanimously approved, endorsing construction of the San Carlos reservoir, supporting federal construction of water storage dams, and opposing cession. [15]

In March 1900, former Senator Warner Miller of New York arrived in the Valley to investigate the plan of the Hudson Reservoir and Canal Co. to build a dam at the Tonto Basin, 60 miles northeast of Phoenix. In an interview, Miller said he thought the plan was feasible and if properly carried out would settle the water question and would prove a financial success. He added:

The water power at the dam would prove a great source of revenue. It could be utilized to supply the mines and people of Globe with light and power at reasonable prices and Phoenix would also harness all of its moving appliances to this great industrial giant. This of itself would be a great revenue getter. The horsepower to be secured from the construction of this dam is beyond man's power to compute. But one thing is certain, and that is, it would be ample to move all the machinery and supply all the light needed in Gila and Maricopa counties, and have an abundance left for other uses. [16]

The evening of April 17, the Phoenix and Maricopa County Board of Trade, successor to the Phoenix Chamber of Commerce, appointed a five-member Committee on Water Storage to agitate the question of selling bonds in the name of the county to build water storage reservoirs. S. M. McCowan, superintendent of the Phoenix Indian School, was named chairman of the committee. Other members were Benjamin A. Fowler, J. Ernest Walker, Vernon L. Clark and B. Heyman. They met the night of April 19 to discuss the issue and to talk with Sims Ely, secretary of the Hudson company. The committee concluded that if private efforts to build the Tonto Basin reservoir were unsuccessful, it would be necessary for the public to step in, and the best way to do that was to bond the county. Before that could be done, however, congressional approval would be necessary, and it was agreed the committee would prepare legislation for approval of the Board of Trade before having it presented to Congress. Ely said it would take about a year for the bonding bill to get through Congress and if, at the end of that time, the Hudson company was unable to get the financing to build, it would find some agreement fair to the company and the people so they could build and the company step aside. Meantime, Ely said, the company was pursuing private investment and construction of the reservoir. Measures in that direction, he said, had been passage of the law exempting the reservoir from taxation, the completion of important engineering work, and the signing of contracts with the canal companies, which assured the reservoir company of a profitable income ($300,000 per year). The committee decided it would be necessary from then on to carry out a careful campaign in favor of water storage, and when Eastern capitalists learned the people were ready to bond themselves for the reservoir, it would convince the men with money the Tonto Basin dam was a good investment.

The committee believed a vote to bond the county would carry because no one could deny it would double the value of every acre in the Valley before the dam was finished, and it would make Phoenix a city of 50,000 people. [17]

McCowan made a report on behalf of the Water Storage Committee at a meeting of the Board of Trade the evening of May 1. The committee said there were two ways to increase the existing water supply: by protecting forest reserves so they would not be denuded of trees and vegetation, and by constructing underground dams to bring to the surface waters wasted in the sands of the rivers. The best way to preserve surplus waters so they could be made available in dry periods was through construction of reservoirs. The committee noted proposals had been made for diverting water stored in a reservoir at the Tonto Basin far enough up the canyon of the Salt River to reach large tracts of land south of the river not under any existing canals and on the Gila River Indian Reservation. The committee said large tracts of uncultivated land already existed under the Arizona, Consolidated and Highland canals. [18]

The report examined four possible ways to raise money for reservoirs: federal appropriations, federal government cession of lands to states and territories, private enterprise, and voting bonds to be sold by Maricopa County. The committee thought direct government aid "not worth considering." Similarly, the committee believed if it waited for government initiative in the ceding of land "we may, perhaps, in the course of a generation or two, look down from above on the beginning of the undertaking." If the Hudson company built the reservoir, the committee pointed out, it would be the people and not the companies who paid the $300,000 yearly guarantee made in the contracts between Hudson and the canal companies. This would be accomplished by the canal companies increasing the price of water from $1.25 to $2.25 per acre. This left the fourth proposition, voting bonds, which, the committee said, "has many points in its favor over any of the others." Principally, ownership and control of the reservoir would be in the hands of the people. The committee said ownership by the public should extend to the canal companies, but the lowest estimate of their cost was $4 million. Added to an estimated $2,500,000 for building the Tonto Basin dam, the committee doubted that $6,500,000 in bonds could be sold in a county with an assessed valuation of $10 million. The committee believed that for between $2 million and $3 million the reservoir site could be acquired from the Hudson company and the dam built. The committee recommended the preparation of a bill for introduction in Congress and a program "to educate and enlighten the people on the importance, extent, and designs of the irrigation movement by the distribution of literature, mass meetings, etc." [19]

In July, Charles C. Randolph, editor and owner of the *Arizona Republican,* returned from a trip to the East where he had met with some capitalists and talked with them about water storage. Randolph said he was told the drawback to the Hudson company's reservoir was the immense sum of money it required, but if the people of Maricopa County showed their faith in the project by issuing $500,000 in

bonds, it might help in raising the funds. As a result, July 19 the *Republican* printed an editorial proposing the county issue $500,000 in bonds, the money being made available to the Hudson Reservoir and Canal Co. contingent upon its raising $2 million to $2,500,000 for the dam construction. For the $500,000, the newspaper proposed the county receive preferred stock in the company. Once the company began paying dividends, the paper said, the county could market the stock or retain it. The newspaper invited comments from readers about the proposal. [20]

The *Arizona Gazette* reacted by calling it a plan by grafters to divide $500,000. The newspaper identified the plotters as Governor Murphy, his brother, Frank, a prominent Arizona railroad man, and Russell A. Alger of Detroit, a wealthy lumberman with holdings in Michigan and Minnesota. Alger and several other capitalists had visited the Valley in June and had spoken favorably of the Hudson company's proposition. Alger, like former Senator Miller of New York, was prominent in Republican Party politics, and it is possible their interest in the Tonto Basin dam was stirred by Detroit seed company owners Dexter M. Ferry and C. C. Bowen, partners with Chandler in the Consolidated Canal Co. [21]

The *Gazette* said the people would never vote bonds for a reservoir unless it included ownership of the dam and the canal companies. The *Enterprise* said before the county became a small shareholder in the reservoir company the question of who owns the water should be settled. The paper said the water and land should be inseparable, but an Arizona court had said ownership of water was vested in the canal companies. "If the water belonged to the people, then it was proper they should contribute to increase the water supply," the *Enterprise* said. "Under other circumstances they should not." [22]

On August 12, the *Gazette* printed a letter from William Christy, banker, rancher, and cohort of William J. Murphy in north side canal operations, calling for a mass convention of Valley water users to form a plan for a water storage reservoir. He proposed a committee of 25 composed of two members from each canal, two members from Phoenix, and one each from Mesa, Glendale and Tempe. He suggested the formation of a corporation, the Salt River Valley Water Storage and Reservoir Co., with each landowner paying $1 per acre per year for 10 years. With 250,000 acres in the corporation, $2,500,000 would be raised. By paying the $1 in advance, which was the method for paying for water, at the end of three years $1 million would be in hand; the corporation could then bond itself for $1 million. Christy proposed city lots pay $2 per year. He calculated the bonds would be paid off with the last four yearly payments. He proposed water rights cover the number of acres of land owned by the certificate holder and that the certificate (water right) be permanently fixed to the land. He said each certificate of stock should be entitled to vote the number of acres represented by the stock in the election of directors or managers. [23]

Other schemes for getting water storage were printed in the newspapers, and on August 15, the *Gazette* suggested the

Board of Trade call a meeting of citizens to take up the water storage question. The *Gazette* said it proposed the Board of Trade "because it is the only organized commercial body in existence in this county, and has for its membership some of the best and most progressive men in this county." The following day, the newspaper reported farmers were circulating a petition calling for a meeting, and on August 23, the *Republican* printed a notice for a meeting "at Dorris' Theater at 10:00 a.m. Friday, August 31."[24]

McCowan was elected chairman of the August 31 meeting. He believed the county should own and control the water storage works; without ownership there was no control. McCowan said he agreed with all others that the federal government should build the reservoir, "but in our time. . .[it] is extremely improbable."[25]

The meeting heard a variety of plans, finally approving a Christy proposal to appoint a committee of 25 made up of two members each from the north side canals, two each from the Consolidated, Tempe, Mesa and Utah canals, one each from the San Franicsco, Highland, and Buckeye canals, three from the city of Phoenix and one each from Tempe, Glendale and Mesa. McCord opposed a motion by John C. Adams, owner of the Adams Hotel in Phoenix, to include the Water Storage Committee of the Board of Trade. McCord said the meeting had been called in the interest of the farmers, but it had been almost taken out of their hands. Adams replied that there was no antagonism between the businessmen and the farmers, that town and country had a community of interest, and Adams' motion was approved. The meeting adjourned so the 25 members could be selected. After their names were reported, the new committee met with the Board of Trade committee and elected Benjamin Fowler permanent chairman of the Salt River Valley Water Storage Committee. Frank H. Parker was named secretary. Subcommittees were appointed to investigate the importation of water from the Colorado River, the quantity of storable water, silt in reservoirs and reservoir sites.[26]

Fowler, besides presiding at the general meetings of the committee in the following months, became a candidate for the Territorial Assembly. He was successful at the November 6 general election, and a week later he was selected by the Water Storage Committee to represent the water users at the ninth National Irrigation Congress, which met in Chicago November 21 through 24. Fowler, meantime, met with Secretary of the Interior Ethan A. Hitchcock in Washington and gave him a letter in which the Water Storage Committee offered to provide $1,500 to match an equal amount from funds of the U.S. Geological Survey for use in investigating "all of the physical conditions of topography, water flow, depth of bedrock, amount of sediment carried by the water, and other facts. . .preliminary to the construction of systems of water storage." Fowler noted Geological Survey officials were agreeable to the proposition.[27]

In making the proposal to Hitchcock, Fowler may have been following the advice of Maxwell, whom Fowler had consulted about how to proceed toward water storage. Maxwell had suggested that Fowler "get" the Geological

Survey to begin work immediately on the McDowell reservoir on the Verde River and on the Tonto Basin site as soon as the latter "can be secured for the benefit of the people." Maxwell proposed that a Landowners Cooperative Water Co. build the McDowell reservoir and the federal government build at Tonto Basin. He suggested elimination of the system of floating water rights, which permitted water to be shifted from one piece of land to another. He said water and land should be tied together and the distinction between natural flow of water in the river and stored water be extinguished so the only thing to be determined in distributing the water would be priority of right. He proposed capital stock of 300,000 acres, one share for each acre with subscriptions for shares limited to landowners, and the canal companies to be bought with the proceeds from 20-year, low-interest bonds.[28]

Fowler also sought the advice of attorney George W. Kretzinger of Chicago, who suggested,

that you take immediate steps for the incorporation of a new company stating in detail and with clearness its objects and purposes, which shall include (a) the construction of reservoirs and dams; (b) the acquirement of the entire present canal and irrigating system in the Salt River Valley; (c) the enlargement and extension of said canals; (d) the acquirement of all other facilities and all franchises for water in your valley; (e) also the purpose to construct, operate and maintain an electric power system.

Kretzinger said once the company was formed, it should enter into a contract by which Maricopa County would issue bonds to aid in the construction, the bonds being dependent upon approval by Congress and a vote of a majority of legal voters in Maricopa County. He said the company's bonds should be used to buy the canals and for security to the county if required.[29]

At a meeting of the Water Storage Committee on December 11, attended by Fowler, the committee outlined the steps it should take. In addition to drafting a bonding bill for introduction in Congress, a work already in progress, the first thing to be done was the survey and engineering work at the reservoir sites, including plans, specifications, and estimated costs. This would be followed by working out an agreement with the canal companies for the delivery of water, then incorporation. The company would have a capital stock of $3 million divided into 300,000 shares to be sold at $8 per share in the first year and at $10 per share thereafter. Each share would represent one acre of land and the right to water in the reservoir, which would be non-transferable except in the sale of the land. The corporation would issue $1,500,000 in bonds for 10 and 20 years, with the bonds secured by all of its property and franchise. The intent was to make the landowners the permanent owners of the reservoir.[30]

Meantime, Charles Walcott, director of the Geological Survey, authorized hydrographer Authur P. Davis to begin the examination of possible reservoir sites on the Verde River. Davis was invited to speak to the Water Storage Committee on December 31. At the meeting, Heard proposed, and the committee agreed, the Geological Survey should be asked to extend Davis' work to the Salt River, and the committee should raise money for that purpose.[31]

The committee worked the rest of the day on the bonding bill, which, when completed was to be sent to Fowler, who had gone to Washington to help prepare the way for it. The bill was put in final form January 1, 1901. Its key provisions were: upon petition by at least 50 taxpayers, authorize the Maricopa County Board of Supervisors to call an election asking for permission to issue up to $2 million worth of municipal bonds for "acquirement" of property necessary for the operation of reservoirs, including control of water stored, "which property shall be forever exempt from taxation;" to require at least two-thirds approval of votes cast; at the same time as the bond election, to elect five property owners to a Maricopa County Board of Water Storage Commissioners, who would issue the bonds, and would appoint a president from their own number, and a secretary and treasurer who need not be commission members; to order the director of the U.S. Geological Survey to appoint an engineer to prepare plans for the reservoir; to create an advisory board whose members would be a representative of the Geological Survey, the irrigation expert of the U.S. Department of Agriculture, and an engineer named by the U.S. secretary of war, the board to have charge of all matters relating to the construction of the water storage works; to have the U.S. government guarantee the interest on the bonds, in exchange for which an additional 700,000 gallons of water would be delivered daily for irrigation on the Salt River Indian Reservation. [32]

At the committee's meeting January 8, the possible purchase of the Hudson company's dam site was discussed. The price was said to be $200,000, but the committee thought it was too much. Christy favored buying it for $50,000, while John R. Norton believed the company had lost its right to the site because it had failed to use it. Chandler thought the site could be bought for less than $50,000, and McCowan said the company unquestionably was entitled to something. [33]

On January 14, Randolph sent a story from Washington reporting that the bonding bill was unacceptable to Arizona's delegate, John Wilson. Wilson said the measure was too complicated because it would have to be referred to too many departments. He said the bill should be constructed so that it required as little time as possible before Congress. Fowler was told that the Army would not work under civilian officials. [34]

A few days later, another dispatch from Randolph gave more details about the unacceptable features of the bonding bill. If nothing else, Randolph wrote, the bill would never be approved because of the provision calling for the U.S. government to guarantee the interest on the bonds. If everything else were correct, that one provision would kill it, he said. Among other defects, the bill did not set a time for an election, which meant the Board of Supervisors might put it off indefinitely; it did not specify whether the water storage commissioners were to be owners of "real" or "personal" property; it did not provide for the commissioners to adopt bylaws, which meant changes would have to be approved by Congress; the duties of the secretary and treasurer outlined in the bill belonged in the bylaws; the bill would give the

advisory board, composed entirely of outsiders, power over expenditures without any recourse of the people to protest; it was unclear as to whether the commissioners or the advisory board would have the authority to award contracts and to employ labor. While there was no possibility the bill would be introduced as it arrived in Washington, Randolph said it might be possible to win approval of a stripped-down measure. He suggested that it be a simple enabling act prepared by someone in Washington. [35]

The Water Storage Committee discussed the situation January 17. One proposal was to let Wilson introduce a bill that reflected his views, but this met objections because it might lead Congress to believe that Maricopa County did not know what it really wanted. Governor Murphy told the committee he doubted county bonds could be sold unless they were guaranteed by the national government or were convertible into territorial bonds. While he said he favored cession of arid lands, he was open to any better idea. Murphy suggested a pared-down bond bill be written and passed through the Legislature. He said that could be done in 10 days, and all Congress would have to do is ratify it with an act of as few words as possible. He said Congress as a whole would not listen to ideas of federal aid. Hence, the problem before the committee and people was difficult of solution. Norton proposed the appointment of a committee to draft a bonding bill. A committee of five was named. [36]

In Murphy's message to the Legislature January 22, he proposed passage of a bill sanctioning:

the bond issue in some form, either in the amount suggested, with a plan for municipal construction and ownership, or for a lesser amount to aid private enterprise based upon an exchange of securities—and subsequently secure congressional approval of the legislative act. The procedure would not call for extended investigation by Congress nor the taking of the time of that body in the consideration of a lengthy bill. [37]

Fowler, at a meeting of the Water Storage Committee on February 6, suggested that Maxwell and Elwood Mead, irrigation engineer for the U.S. Department of Agriculture, be invited to Phoenix to advise the committee during the legislative session, and that was done. Mead, however, could not come. [38]

A week later, the committee discussed raising $1,500 for the Geological Survey as pledged in the letter Fowler delivered to Hitchock the previous November. The committee thought the sum should be provided by the board of supervisors, but the supervisors maintained they did not have authority under the law to make the appropriation. A committee was appointed to discuss the matter with the supervisors and to prepare legislation that would permit them to allot money for that purpose. [39]

On February 16, Fowler introduced a memorial, subsequently approved, calling upon the national government to build reservoirs. Fowler said the memorial, which noted the platforms of both the Republican and Democratic parties contained planks favoring national aid for irrigation, was word for word from a resolution adopted at the National Irrigation Congress in November. He said the movement for national irrigation had been extended throughout the Eastern part of the country and had the support of businessmen who had come to see reclamation as an opportunity for broad, new markets. [40]

At a meeting February 24, the Water Storage Committee decided a bill for bonding the county should be drafted for introduction in the Arizona Legislature. The *Republican,* in reporting the committee would consider the bonding bill at a meeting March 9, complained that "Months have been squandered in worthless quibbling" and that nothing had been accomplished since the Legislature convened. It continued:

The life of the present legislature is short. If anything is to be done it must be done quickly. If we expect to resurrect the territorial funding bill so we may avail ourselves of its guarantee, and thus make our county bonds saleable, it is high time some strenuous work be inaugurated and pushed through. It is worse than senseless to sit idly by waiting for government aid. It is folly— it is criminal folly. The government will not help us now. And why should we wait? If storage is a good business proposition, why not provide the funds and control the matter ourselves. [41]

The committee approved the form of the bill, and it was introduced by Fowler on March 11, the same day Maxwell arrived in Phoenix. [42]

A few days later, Fowler introduced a substitute measure for the bonding bill. The substitute, which had been prompted by the Water Storage Committee's desire to get the county supervisors to contribute $1,500 to the Geological Survey, provided for the appointment of a five-member Board of Water Storage Commissioners by the judge of the U.S. District Court. The bill would apply in any county with an assessed valuation of $8 million or more, which meant Maricopa County, and directed that the board of supervisors, upon the request of 50 registered voters, ask the judge to make the appointments. The bill directed that the commissioners serve one-year terms and be allowed to make a one-time tax levy of three mills per $1 on all taxable property, which would raise about $15,000. The measure empowered the commissioners to take all steps necessary for construction of reservoirs, including buying sites and contracting with canal companies for water delivery. [43]

Legislators were slow to act on Fowler's substitute, and with adjournment only a few days away, the *Republican,* the morning of March 20, condemned the inactivity because it believed the farmers would get no help from the federal government. The newspaper said that in the U.S. House of Representatives the only reservoir bill that had any chance of passage was offered by Representative Frank C. Newlands of Nevada, and it had been shamefully handled and defeated. The paper continued:

And is the Newlands bill what we want? Let us see.

It provides that the secretary of the interior may select sites. That means that sites will be selected in states having a political pull. . . It provides that reservoirs may be constructed in localities where there is sufficient desirable PUBLIC LANDS. That means that the government may confiscate the McDowell or Tonto Basin sites, dam them, store therein the flood waters and carry this water right by our homes and farms and reclaim the PUBLIC LANDS below Peoria.

And what will the poor valley do then? The lands we are living on; where our homes are; where our capital is invested are not public lands. Consequently we will have no right to the use of the stored water. Originally, the Newlands bill contained a clause

giving the secretary the right to conduct water to public lands or lands that had already been redeemed, but that clause was striken out, and such discretionary power killed.

Again, the bill does not provide for a gift of a reservoir to any locality by the government. The building of a dam constitutes a loan and users of water must reimburse the government for all expenditures. Then what do we gain by federal aid? Do we want it? Do we want the government to complete the Tonto scheme, store all the water that our ditches cannot carry, and reclaim more public lands? How will we be benefited by such action? [44]

That same day, both the House and Council approved Fowler's Board of Water Storage Commissioners' bill, including an amendment allowing the commissioners to levy the three mill tax for two years. Governor Murphy signed the bill the same day. [45]

The substitution of the measure to create the Board of Water Storage Commissioners, in preference to the bill to bond the county, undoubtedly was influenced by Maxwell, who did not believe Congress would approve enabling legislation that would put the burden of taxation for irrigation bonds upon the entire county. Maxwell, of course, was committed to the idea of national irrigation, and he told Fowler, legislators, and others at a March 19 meeting at the Dorris Theater that if the people of Arizona would work in harmony, a federal reservoir would be under construction inside the territory within two years. Maxwell was certain something would be accomplished in the next session of Congress. He said the Senate was friendly to irrigation, and he cited a couple of bills for which senators boosted appropriations. The House had never before discussed the subject, he said, but in the session just closed two committees had reported favorably on bills creating a construction fund through the sale of public lands. He said the bills had been reported too late for consideration. [46]

Maxwell said government aid "will come with a rush" as soon as the country's business interests demanded it. He had a plan for accomplishing this. He said nearly every man in the Valley from the East Coast knew a congressman, or knew someone who knew a congressman, and it was necessary for all to appeal directly to them by letter. In addition, every businessman should ask his wholesale contacts in the East to write to their congressmen in favor of national irrigation. If this were done by every town in the West, the influence upon the congressmen would become irresistible, Maxwell said. For the plan to be effective, he said, it was necessary to have a local organization, and he met with a group of businessmen March 26 for that purpose. The businessmen selected a five-member committee to direct the work. Among them were Fowler and Clark. [47]

Davis in mid-April informed the Water Storage Committee that the funds available for Geological Survey work in Arizona were exhausted, and it would be impossible to do any work at the Tonto Basin unless local funds were contributed. Davis said it would be unwise to undertake the work with less than $3,000, but $4,000 would be a better guarantee of success, should there be unexpected difficulties. He said for another $1,000 an accurate contour map of the area could be made. [48]

Fowler, Davis, and Frank P. Trott, the water

Arthur P. Davis

commissioner under the Kibbey Decree, accompanied by 30 members of the Water Storage Committee, appeared before the board of supervisors on April 15 to ask it to request Judge Webster Street to appoint the Board of Water Storage Commissioners. The supervisors said they would take the issue up the following morning, which they did, adopting an appropriate resolution. Street was advised of the action. He said he would look at the law and act upon it after being formally notified of the supervisors' request. The supervisors sent their request later that day, and Street, on April 18, appointed as commissioners Heard, Charles Goldman, and W. D. Fulwiler, all of Phoenix, J. T. Priest of Tempe, and Joseph G. Peterson of Mesa. The same day, Davis' crew departed for Globe and the Tonto reservoir site. On April 30, the commissioners organized and elected Priest as chairman and Fulwiler as secretary. They then appropriated $5,000 to support Davis' work. [49]

The Water Storage Committee also met April 30 and decided to continue its work until there was nothing left to do. [50]

President William McKinley and the interior secretary, Hitchcock, visited Phoenix on May 7. In a speech to the people at the capitol, McKinley was interrupted by sustained applause when he said,

You need a few more people, and to my mind there is nothing that will facilitate immigration like irrigation. [51]

At the end of June, the *Republican* printed an editorial in favor of government construction of reservoirs (which it did not expect would ever happen), and in opposition to the county subsidizing any private scheme (a subject about which the newspaper was ambivalent). The newspaper again analyzed the Newlands bill, showing that as it was written it would not help the Valley. The paper believed the

government would build the San Carlos dam to aid the Gila River Indian Reservation, and once that was done, it would foreclose construction of another reservoir—at Tonto Basin—in Arizona. The *Republican* concluded that the Valley's only salvation was construction of the Tonto Basin dam by private capital. This was a theme it was to repeat many times in the months ahead along with its belief that the national government would not provide the Valley with a reservoir, and the national irrigation movement meant little to the Valley because its program was aimed at reclaiming arid public lands to benefit homeseekers from the crowded East. [52]

Davis' boring crew completed its work at the Tonto Basin in early July, but Davis would not make the results of his work public. He reported his findings to the Board of Water Storage Commissioners, but they declined to give the results for business reasons. Davis did say that four lines of prospecting holes for bedrock were drilled across the canyon from one bank to the other, and the results were said to be satisfactory. It also was reported the water storage capacity of the reservoir was larger than expected, but, again, no details were provided. Davis met with the commissioners July 7, and they agreed to provide up to $2,000 to match a similar amount from the Geological Survey for a hydrographic survey of the Salt River and its tributaries. [53]

President McKinley was shot September 6, in Buffalo, New York, and died September 14. He was succeeded by Vice President Theodore Roosevelt, who, in his first message to Congress on December 3, endorsed the national irrigation movement with these words:

Great storage works are necessary to equalize the flow of streams and to save the flood waters. Their construction has been conclusively shown to be an undertaking too vast for private effort. Nor can it best be accomplished by the individual states acting alone. Far-reaching interstate problems are involved; and the resources of single states would often be inadequate. It is properly a national function, at least in some of its features. It is as right for the national government to make the streams and rivers of the arid region useful by engineerng works for water storage as to make useful the rivers and harbors of the humid region by engineering works of another kind. The storing of the floods in reservoirs at the headwaters of our rivers is but an enlargement of our present policy of river control, under which levees are built on the lower reaches of the same streams.

The government should construct and maintain these reservoirs as it does other public works. Where their purpose is to regulate the flow of streams, the water should be turned freely into the channels in the dry season to take the same course under the same laws as the natural flow.

The reclamation of the unsettled arid public lands presents a different problem. Here it is not enough to regulate the flow of streams. The object of the government is to dispose of the land to settlers who will build homes upon it. To accomplish this object water must be brought within their reach.

The pioneer settlers in the arid public domain chose their homes along streams from which they could themselves divert the water to reclaim their holdings.

Such opportunities are practically gone. There remain, however, vast areas of public land which can be made available for homestead settlement, but only by reservoirs and mainline canals impracticable for private enterprise. These irrigation works should be built by the national government. The lands reclaimed by them should be reserved by the government for actual settlers, and the cost of construction should so far as possible be repaid by the land reclaimed. The distribution of the water, the division of the streams among irrigators, should be left to the settlers themselves in conformity with state laws and without interference with those laws or with vested rights. . .

The reclamation and settlement of the arid lands will enrich every portion of the country, just as the settlement of the Ohio and Mississippi valleys brought prosperity to the Atlantic states. The increased demand for manufactured articles will stimulate industrial production, while wider home markets and the trade of Asia will consume the larger food supplies and effectually prevent western competition with eastern agriculture. Indeed, the products of irrigation will be consumed chiefly in upbuilding local centers of mining and other industries, which would otherwise not come into existence at all. Our people as a whole will profit, for successful home-making is but another name for the upbuilding of the nation. [54]

Roosevelt said the initial work would "of necessity be partly experimental in character" because it would be necessary to find out what "can and cannot be safely attempted." He said "whatever the nation does for the extension of irrigation should harmonize with, and tend to improve, the condition of those now living on irrigated land," [55] which suggests that the question of federal aid for lands in private ownership had not been ruled out.

The **Republican** observed that if Roosevelt's words were carried out, Arizona would likely be among the first to benefit because an appropriation of $1,040,000 for the San Carlos reservoir had been "strongly recommended" by Hitchcock. The **Gazette** said that "if the strongest friend of a

Theodore Roosevelt

national system of irrigation had written that part of the message, he could not have made it much stronger or better." [56] Indeed, Roosevelt's words may have come from the pen of Maxwell.

A week later, a conference of senators and representatives from the West agreed to make the bill originally proposed by Newlands and Senator Henry Hansbrough of North Dakota the basis for a national reclamation act. [57]

Meanwhile, the Board of Water Storage Commissioners, based upon the survey and maps prepared under Davis, filed an application with the federal land office for a dam site on the Salt River a quarter of a mile downstream from the Hudson Reservoir company's location. The commissioners asked the canal companies to supply information concerning the number of acres actually under cultivation and susceptible of irrigation; the companies failed to respond, however, so the commissioners in late November employed men to obtain the data. The commissioners attempted to develop contracts with the canal companies for the delivery of water from a water storage reservoir. Developing a scale of prices was the biggest problem because the old companies objected to paying the same price as new companies, which were not entitled to water until after the old ones. [58]

The commissioners at a December 19 meeting discussed a new county bond enabling act for submission to Congress. They thought a county tax of $1 per year per acre on the 275,000 acres that could be irrigated would be most equitable, but rejected it because it would not benefit all persons directly. If the reservoir cost $2 million, the interest would be $125,000 annually, and $150,000 would remain for the sinking fund to pay off the principal. The dam's cost could be reduced if cement were made at the site, and the commissioners reported that was being investigated. [59]

The **Gazette** and the **Enterprise** joined in expressing doubts about the value to the Valley of the proposed national irrigation law. The **Gazette** worried that if the government got control of the Tonto Basin site and built a storage reservoir,

would not the water thus conserved be forever taken away from the lands now owned and cultivated here in this valley? This is a serious matter, and one that the people living here should thoroughly investigate before it is too late. The people of Phoenix and the county of Maricopa can much better afford to contribute liberally of their means than to have anything so serious happen, as would be the result of the government taking the water that now comes to land under cultivation and use it upon lands not now under cultivation, but belonging to the government. Let us look into this matter and see where our duty lies, before it is too late. [60]

The **Enterprise** said if the proposed national plan was in effect, the government would build the Tonto Basin reservoir, provide the existing canals with their appropriated water, and use the balance to develop new lands. The paper said:

at present the most feasible plan for this valley seems to be the one adopted by the county water storage commission, which is to ask congress to allow Maricopa County to issue bonds and construct the reservoir. This might increase our taxes some, but in the long run [will be compensated by] the enhancement in the value of property and the general improvement of the country. [61]

Fowler left for Washington, D.C., the morning of January 15, 1902, to represent the Board of Trade in testifying on behalf of statehood for Arizona and for national irrigation. He said he favored the government building the Tonto Basin dam provided the water was for the lands under the present canals, but if it meant opening up thousands of new acres, the county would be better off issuing $2 million worth of bonds and building the reservoir itself. The *Republican* said Fowler could not "get rid of the idea that Congress and the administration can be brought to abandon the proposed San Carlos reservoir and appropriate the necessary money for a dam on Salt River."[62]

On February 4, the Board of Water Storage Commissioners issued a report on its work. It said if the dam was 200 feet above the river bed, it would store 981,125 acre-feet of water and would cover 14,617 acres. The exact cost of the dam was uncertain, but it would be approximately $2,500,000. However, the manufacture of cement at the site, and the installation of a hydroelectric plant to develop power for use in the dam construction, would reduce the cost to about $1,800,000. The report said plans, specifications, and estimates would be presented to the commissioners in the near future.[63]

Soon after, a letter from Fowler arrived. He said he expected some kind of reclamation bill "under inspiration of the president's powerful personality," but Governor Murphy returned from Washington and said the confusion over an irrigation bill was so great he doubted anything would be done except for a possible appropriation to begin work on the San Carlos dam. He was wrong. A few days later, the House rejected a $50,000 appropriation for the San Carlos project under charges it was intended as an entering wedge for national irrigation. The House also defeated all other proposals for appropriations for reservoir construction. The *Republican* supposed—incorrectly, it was soon to learn—the House's action was,

sufficient to convince the most visionary of the local hopefuls that it is moonstruck folly to expect an appropriation for the benefit of the Salt River Valley.[64]

The Senate on March 1 approved the Hansbrough-Newlands bill for national irrigation, with one vote against it. It was sent to the House, where it was expected to be amended.[65]

On March 6, the contents of the Maricopa County Enabling Act, drafted by the Board of Water Storage Commissioners for submission to Congress, were revealed along with a statement that the act had been sent to John F. Dillon of New York, who was described as "the most eminent authority in the country on legislation relating to bond issues." After Dillon approved it, it was to be sent to Marcus A. Smith, Arizona's delegate to Congress, for introduction. The bill asked Maricopa County be authorized to issue up to $2,250,000 in bonds for reservoir work, including "developing and delivering water power," upon approval by a majority vote of property taxpayers. It directed the governor of Arizona, the district court judge of Maricopa County, and the chairman of the board of supervisors appoint a five-member board of water

commissioners, who thereafter would be elected. The bonds were to be issued for 50 years at a rate of interest not exceeding 5 percent. If the revenues from water storage and power works were insufficient to pay the interest and principal due on the bonds, the commissioners were authorized to impose a tax on property within the reservoir district to raise the money.[66]

The *Republican* criticized the bill because it limited the issuance of bonds for the reservoir to county ownership. The newspaper said the voters should have an opportunity to approve alternatives if they rejected county ownership. Alternatives might be "a moderate subsidy to a private corporation, or. . .bonds to guarantee the interest on bonds of a corporation, or. . .a limited amount of bonds to be exchanged for bonds of a reservoir company." The newspaper said the commissioners apparently were unable to agree upon alternatives, which was "short-sighted" of them. The paper said the bill would meet opposition in Washington, including from "the extreme, one-idea people who can think of nothing but 'national irrigation'."[67]

The following day, the commissioners approved a second proposed bill, which was to be supplemental to the first. Prepared by Heard, who represented the National Irrigation Association in Phoenix, it called for a $1 million appropriation from Congress for construction of the Salt River dam, provided the taxpayers of Maricopa County first approved the issuance of bonds to build the reservoir. Heard's bill provided for the reservoir plans to be approved by the U.S. Geological Survey and for the survey to cooperate in the supervision of the construction. This bill, as the enabling act of a year earlier, provided for the delivery of an additional 700,000 gallons of water daily to the Salt River Indian Reservation for irrigation.[68]

The House Irrigation Committee reported favorably on the Hansbrough-Newlands bill, but a minority report denounced it as an "unfair, unwise, and improvident scheme, so vast and expensive that the ordinary mind is staggered at its mere contemplation." The report also charged: "the land grant railways are behind this scheme and are the real beneficiaries." The accusation was partially correct. Western railroads contributed liberally to the National Irrigation Association.[69]

On March 12, the 30-member Water Storage Committee, which had been created by the citizens August 31, 1900, voted 17 to 2 that the bonding bill be changed to elect the water storage commissioners at the time of the bond election. They also agreed the bonds, to win approval, should be supported by a two-thirds vote rather than a simple majority.[70]

Dillon returned the enabling act along with his amendments at the end of March. Opposition to some of Dillon's changes, especially one to allow 20 percent of the bondholders to begin foreclosure proceedings if interest on the bonds was not paid for six months, raised a storm of protest. The opposition was so great, the Board of Water Storage Commissioners sent a wire to Smith in Washington asking him to not introduce the bill until further advised. The commissioners met with Phoenix businessmen and water users from both sides of the river to work out their differences over the changes. The commissioners agreed to extend the default period on the bonds to one year (some persons thought there was no likelihood of defaulting on either interest or principal because funds could be raised by tax revenue, if no other way). They also finally assented to a two-thirds vote for passage of the bonds, to the election of three commissioners from north of the river and two from south, and to the publication before the election of the terms of the contracts with at least 8 of 12 canal companies named in the bill, the general plan for the control and distribution of water and electricity, and a brief general description of the reservoir plans. The reworked enabling act was mailed to Dillon on April 8 accompanied by a letter introducing Heard, who was going to New York and Washington to represent the commissioners in an effort to get the measure through Congress.[71]

Davis arrived in Phoenix on April 17 and submitted the report of his investigation of the Tonto Basin reservoir site to the Water Storage Commissioners. It put the cost of a dam 217 feet above the river bed at $1,909,387, including an estimated $91,000 for a cement plant, $300,000 for the manufacture of 150,000 barrels of Portland cement, $800,970 for the dam, $188,360 for a power house, equipment, and canal, $50,000 for excavation of the foundation and river diversion, $31,450 for outlet tunnels and lining, $11,600 for tunnel gates and machinery, $26,000 for viaducts across spillways, $15,000 for roads and telephones, $9,000 for outlet towers, shafts and houses, $243,507 for engineering and contingencies of 15 percent, and $42,500 for damage to private lands. Of the dam, Davis wrote,

The proposed structure is to be built on a circular curve, convex upstream, the back having a radius of 400 feet, and the face a shorter radius from the same center. The dam is to be of uncoursed rubble masonry, and to have a section on modern conservative ideas as a simple gravity structure, and the added stability due to its curved form will greatly increase its factor of safety. The rock of which the dam will be constructed will be excavated from the spillway and is a tough, close-grained sandstone.

If 1,000 acre-feet were taken as the average annual inflow of sediment, Davis estimated it would take 500 years for the reservoir to fill. He said it probably would take 100 years before the loss of storage capacity would be serious. Once the dam was built, it was expected the electric power developed could be used at neighboring mines or in the Valley for pumping water.[72]

On April 19, the Maricopa County Enabling Act was introduced in the House by Smith, but few persons in the Valley expected it would be passed in that session of Congress. Smith had written earlier in April that 15,000 bills already had been introduced, and action would be taken on no more than 1,000.[73]

Little was printed about the Hansbrough-Newlands Act or the bonding bill until after mid-May. The *Republican* published a dispatch saying Roosevelt was "showing lively interest in (the reclamation act's) status." The newspaper reported there was opposition to the bonding bill because the county bonds could be converted to territorial bonds.

The *Prescott Journal-Miner* called to the attention of Yavapai County residents a clause in the bill it said threatened the water rights of Verde River farmers, but the *Republican* pointed out existing rights were protected.[74]

On the night of May 27, about 300 businessmen and citizens from both sides of the river met with Frank Murphy at the Adams Hotel. He was asked to comment about the enabling act. He said he did not know its status, but he would use his influence with the Santa Fe and Southern Pacific railroads to have them lobby for it. Woolf said the bill had been reported favorably by a House committee. Murphy, informed there was no alternative should the people reject issuing $2,250,000 in bonds, suggested the bill be amended to allow the people to vote on bonds not to exceed $1 million to aid a private corporation in construction of the reservoir. The businessmen voted to ask the Water Storage Commissioners to immediately seek such an amendment, and the commissioners met the next day. They voted to send telegrams to Heard, Smith, Fowler and Governor Murphy asking them to amend the enabling act to include the $1 million provision, to remove the Verde River provision found objectionable by Yavapai County, and to eliminate the requirement contracts had to be made with at least two-thirds of the canal companies before an election could be held. The commissioners also voted to send Trott to Washington. This turn of events elated the businessmen, commissioners and others, but a letter from Ethelbert W. Wilbur of Mesa, who was in Washington, warned of opposition to the bill from the secretary of the interior and others.[75]

The *Republican* reported June 5 the advice from Washington was that the outlook for the bonding bill was not favorable, while a June 8 dispatch said the fate of the Hansbrough-Newlands bill was uncertain. The next day, Trott telegraphed that Congress would not consider the enabling act unless Heard and Wilbur changed their opposition to eliminating the clause requiring contracts with two-thirds of the canals. The *Republican* pointed out Heard personally represented the San Francisco Canal (the Bartlett-Heard Land and Cattle Co. acquired the canal when it bought the estate of Michael Wormser in 1900). Heard, Wilbur, Trott and Fowler replied to the Water Storage Commissioners by wire June 10:

Nothing but united action can save the enabling act. We have agreed to change the canal contract clause to six, making no other changes. Let all friends of the valley unite on that basis.[76]

On June 11, the *Republican* printed an editorial reporting Maxwell and "the 'national irrigation' crowd" had boasted within the last week that if the Hansbrough-Newlands Act became law, as expected,

the Tonto Basin site will be taken over by the government for "home-making on the public lands." How would the people of the Salt River Valley like to see the flood waters of the Salt River diverted from their lands for all time, and used on the public lands for new settlers beyond Mesa? And yet this is what many misguided citizens of the valley, such as Dwight B. Heard, B. A. Fowler, Judge Stilwell and a few others, have unwittingly been working for when they talked "national irrigation" as the solution of the storage problem for this community.[77]

The Water Storage Commissioners met June 12 and

voted to reject the proposal from Heard, Wilbur, Trott and Fowler. The commissioners telegraphed insisting their resolution of May 28 be followed, but south side water users expressed opposition to the amendments and support for Heard and Wilbur in resisting the changes. [78]

Newell on June 12 sent Davis' report concerning water storage on the Salt and Verde rivers to Walcott. Included was this statement:

The Salt (River) and Tonto (Creek) both occupy comparatively open valleys above (the) gorge and have a moderate fall. The combined effect is one of the most capacious reservoir sites in the West. The dam might be built to a height of 300 feet or more, if such a height were justified by the water supply. [79]

The Hansbrough-Newlands bill was approved by the House on June 13, and the *Republican* said,

There is every reason to expect that Arizona will be the first beneficiary of the new law. It is known that the president and the secretary of the interior are very anxious to have the San Carlos reservoir constructed... The urgent needs of the Pima and Maricopa Indians, so frequently pointed out by the governor of the territory and other officials, leave no room for question as to where the initial reclamation by the government will begin.

We take great pleasure in congratulating our neighbors of the Gila valley and the people of Florence upon the bright prospects before them. [80]

Governor Murphy sent a message June 13 saying the enabling act, with or without amendments, had no chance of passage. [81]

Davis wired to the Water Storage Commissioners on June 13 for authority to begin the survey for the power canal proposed for construction in connection with the Tonto Basin dam. [82]

The Senate concurred in the House amendments to the Hansbrough-Newlands bill and Roosevelt signed the measure into law on June 17. This news did not reach readers of Phoenix newspapers until June 19 when the *Republican* printed a 15-word story on the front page below a one line, one column headline, "IRRIGATION BILL SIGNED." The story, in its entirety, said:

Washington, June 18—The president today notified the senate that he had approved the Hansbrough-Newlands irrigation bill. [83]

The impact of the bill upon the Salt River Valley was unknown. There were no celebrations or expressions of gratitude. Newspaper readers had been told repeatedly the

law would be of no value to them. The *Republican* on June 18 said "the possibilities of relief through the national irrigation act are well worth considering," but did not describe "the possibilities." Indeed, it continued to print stories about the wrangling between Heard and the other Water Storage Commissioners. [85]

Heard had sent a letter saying unless the commissioners receded from their May 28 resolution, the enabling act would fall. However, if agreement could be reached upon the bill as introduced or upon the compromise suggested by himself, Trott and Fowler, the measure could succeed, Heard said. The commissioners discussed the situation June 18, and while they continued to favor an amendment of the enabling act, they wired Heard and Smith they were willing to abandon their position in the interest of passing the bill. [86]

The commissioners also approved Davis' request to begin the power canal survey, the *Republican* saying, June 19,

Unless the water storage bill is passed and the bonds are voted, there can be no water power canal, but sometime there will be a reservoir built, either by the county or by private capital, and the information obtained by the survey will not be wasted. [87]

Governor Murphy returned to Phoenix on June 25 and said he regarded the reclamation bill as the entering wedge of the national reclamation movement. Murphy said the aim of the leaders of the national irrigation movement was to make new homes, not improve old ones, and they did not contemplate storing water to benefit lands whose titles were in private ownership. It was expected Hitchcock would order the building of the San Carlos dam. Murphy said at no time did the county bonding bill have a chance of passage. [88]

About the enabling act, the *Republican* said:

If anything has been gained by the agitation which has been going on at Washington, it has been the getting of the bill before the congress and the giving of the people of the valley five months (when Congress would reconvene) in which to get together upon some plan. Unless they do, Mr. Trott says that there is nothing to be hoped for in the way of legislation. [89]

Because the bonding bill was dead and because the Water Storage Commissioners believed all the preliminary work for the construction of the Salt River reservoir was done, they sent their resignations to Judge Edward Kent of the U.S. District Court in Phoenix. Kent refused to accept them because of conditions in the Valley but said he would reconsider in September. [90]

1. *Phoenix Daily Enterprise,* November 30, 1898; *Arizona Gazette* (Phoenix), December 1, 1898.
2. *Gazette,* December 1, 13, 14, 1898.
3. *Ibid.,* December 13, 1898; *Enterprise,* December 13, 1898.
4. *Gazette,* December 16, 21, 1898.
5. *Arizona Weekly Gazette* (Phoenix), December 31, 1898.
6. *Ibid.,* January 7, 1899.
7. Dwight B. Heard to Aaron Goldberg, December 30, 1898, reprinted *Weekly Gazette,* January 14, 1899.
8. *Gazette,* January 18, 1899.
9. *Ibid.,* February 28, March 4, April 5, 1899; F. H. Newell to Thomas Boyle, March 28, 1899, reprinted *Gazette,* April 5, 1899.
10. *Gazette,* June 1, 7, 1899.
11. *Ibid.,* June 4, 1899; F. H. Newell, *The History of the Irrigation Movement,* First Annual Report of the U.S. Reclamation Service

(Washington: Government Printing Office, 1903), p. 8, Salt River Project Archives (hereafter SRPA).
12. *Gazette,* September 29, 1899; *Enterprise,* September 28, 1899.
13. *Gazette,* October 21, 1899.
14. *Enterprise,* October 31, December 27, 1899; F. H. Newell to C. D. Walcott, December 1, 1899, contained in *Water Supply and Irrigation Papers of the United States Geological Survey,* No. 33 (Washington: Government Printing Office, 1900), p. 1, partially reprinted by SRPA.
15. *Gazette,* December 31, 1899.
16. *Ibid.,* March 16, 1900.
17. *Ibid.* April 18, 20, 1900; *Arizona Republican* (Phoenix), April 20, 1900; *A Report to the Phoenix and Maricopa County Board of Trade,* April, 1900, SRPA.
18. *Republican,* May 2, 1900; *Gazette,* May 2, 1900; *A Report to*

the...Board of Trade.

19. *A report to the...Board of Trade.*
20. *Republican,* July 19, August 3, 1900.
21. *Gazette,* June 12, 22, August 1, 1900.
22. *Ibid.,* July 22, 1900; *Enterprise,* July 21, 1900.
23. William Christy, *Gazette,* August 12, 1900.
24. *Gazette,* August 15, 16, 28, 1900; *Enterprise,* August 9, 15, 1900; *Republican,* August 16, 23, 1900.
25. *Gazette,* August 31, 1900.
26. *Ibid.,* August 31, September 12, 1900, May 1, 1901; *Enterprise,* September 1, 1900.
27. *Republican,* November 4, 1900; *Enterprise,* November 15, 1900; B. A. Fowler to E. A. Hitchcock, November 20, 1900, SRPA.
28. George H. Maxwell to B.A. Fowler, *Memorandum of Suggestions for Salt River Valley Water Storage Committee,* circa October or November 1900, SRPA.
29. G. W. Kretzinger to B. A. Fowler, December 6, 1900, SRPA.
30. *Gazette,* November 30, December 5, 11, 1900.
31. Charles Walcott to E. A. Hitchcock, January 14, 1901, SRPA; *Republican,* January 1, 1901.
32. *Republican,* January 1, 4, 1901.
33. *Ibid.,* January 9, 1901.
34. *Ibid.,* January 15, 1901.
35. *Ibid.,* January 18, 1901.
36. *Ibid.*
37. *Ibid.,* January 23, 1901.
38. *Ibid.,* February 6, 1901.
39. *Ibid.,* February 13, 1901.
40. *Ibid.,* February 17, 19, 1901.
41. *Ibid.,* February 24, March 8, 1901.
42. *Ibid.,* March 10, 12, 1901.
43. *Enterprise,* March 15, 1901.
44. *Republican,* March 20, 1901.
45. *Ibid.,* March 21, 1901; *Enterprise,* March 27, 1901.
46. *Republican,* March 12, 19, 1901.
47. *Ibid.,* March 19, 28, 1901; *Enterprise,* March 27, 1901.
48. *Republican,* April 16, 17, 1901.
49. *Ibid.,* April 16, 17, 19, 22, May 1, 1901; *Enterprise,* April 27, 1901.
50. *Republican,* May 1, 1901.
51. *Ibid.,* May 8, 1901; *Enterprise,* May 8, 1901.
52. *Republican,* June 28, September 22, October 6, November 3, 22, 1901, January 11, 19, 29, 1902.
53. *Ibid.,* July 6, 7, 8, 1901.
54. *Ibid.,* September 7, 14, December 4, 1901.
55. *Ibid.,* December 4, 1901.
56. *Ibid.,* November 25, December 4, 1901; *Gazette,* November 29, December 4, 1901.
57. *Republican,* December 11, 1901.
58. *Ibid.,* December 20, 1901, February 4, 1902.
59. *Ibid.,* December 20, 1901.
60. *Gazette,* December 7, 1901.
61. *Enterprise,* December 19, 1901.
62. *Gazette,* January 16, 1902; *Republican,* January 16, 1902.
63. *Republican,* February 4, 1902.
64. *Ibid.,* February 16, 21, 23, 1902.
65. *Ibid.,* March 2, 1902.
66. *Ibid.,* March 6, 1902.
67. *Ibid.*
68. *Ibid.,* March 8, 1902; *Gazette,* February 5, March 8, 1902.
69. *Republican,* March 8, 11, 1902, April 24, 1904; *Gazette,* April 21, 1904.
70. *Republican,* March 13, 1902; *Gazette,* March 13, 1902.
71. *Enterprise,* March 31, April 7, 1902; *Republican,* April 4, 5, 8, 9, 1902.
72. *Republican,* April 27, 1902.
73. *Ibid.,* April 8, 20, 1902.
74. *Ibid.,* May 18, 20, 1902.
75. *Ibid.,* May 28, 29, 1902; *Gazette,* May 28, 1902.
76. *Ibid.,* June 5, 9, 10, 11, 1900.
77. *Ibid.,* June 11, 1902.
78. *Ibid.,* June 13, 1902
79. Arthur P. Davis, *Water Storage on Salt River, Arizona,* U.S. Geological Survey, Irrigation Paper No. 73 (Washington: Government Printing Office, 1903), p. 23.
80. *Republican,* June 14, 1902.
81. *Ibid.*
82. *Ibid.*
83. *Ibid.,* June 19, 1902.
84. *Ibid.,* June 18, 1902.
85. *Ibid.,* June 19, 20, 1902.
86. *Ibid.,* June 19, 1902; *Gazette,* June 19, 1902.
87. *Republican,* June 19, 1902; *Gazette,* June 19, 1902.
88. *Republican,* June 26, 1902.
89. *Ibid.,* June 28, 1902.
90. *Ibid.,* July 4, 1902.

Epoch II

July - November 1902

Salt River Valley farmers and businessmen were slow to learn how the Hansbrough-Newlands Act might affect their efforts to get the Tonto Basin reservoir. Not until July 15, four weeks after the law was signed, did J. T. Priest, vice president of the Salt River Valley Water Storage Committee and chairman of the Board of Water Storage Commissioners, and Frank H. Parker, secretary of the committee, issue a call for,

A mass meeting of the water users and citizens of the Salt River Valley. . .at the court house in Phoenix at 10 a.m. Saturday, July 19, 1902, for the purpose of considering a plan to secure, if possible, the construction by the United States government of the Tonto Basin reservoir under authority of the Hansbrough-Newlands irrigation act passed by Congress at its last session. [1]

The *Arizona Gazette* said the call for the meeting was prompted by an announcement that Frederick H. Newell, chief hydrographer for the U.S. Geological Survey, had left Washington, D.C., to visit the states and territories included in the irrigation law. In the same article, the newspaper quoted Newell at length about how the Geological Survey, a branch of the U.S. Department of the Interior, intended to proceed. Among his remarks were these:

The impression has gone out that we are to enter upon the construction of the Gila River (San Carlos dam), Truckee River and St. Mary's River projects before perfecting other surveys. This is erroneous. These three projects are perhaps further along than others, and were cited as typical ones when the plan was under consideration of having the government build one or two experimental systems. But the act is much broader than then proposed. It authorizes the secretary to build where he pleases. It is our idea, therefore, to make surveys in all sixteen states and territories interested before deciding upon any particular project. We may find new projects where, for certain reasons, such as demand for lands, abundance of water, etc., it may be desirable to enter upon construction soon. [2]

The *Arizona Republican* thought the meeting would be good because there was nothing to be done about the Maricopa County Enabling Act until Congress met again. The newspaper said "there would certainly be nothing lost by an effort meantime to have the Secretary of the Interior adopt the Tonto site for one of the first reservoirs," but it did not believe that would be done without making some sort of provision to provide water to the Gila River Indian Reservation. The paper said the reservation could be provided with sufficient water from the Tonto Basin reservoir to irrigate 15,000 acres—"as large an area as the Indians could cultivate"—by extending the Consolidated or the Highland canals, both of which "run to the borders of the reservation." [3]

The *Los Angeles Times* reacted to this proposal in an editorial, "Salt River Schemers," saying the statement "that the Indians might be supplied with water from (the Tonto) reservoir—may be taken with a grain of salt." The *Times* expressed concern the San Carlos project would be neglected if the government took up the Tonto Basin dam. The newspaper said the people of the Salt River Valley "were not particularly well affected toward the national irrigation

movement," and the persons attempting to use it were "a few speculators." [4]

The meeting called by the Water Storage Committee was not very productive. Issues that had divided the ranchers and canal men for many years were raised, among them the priority of their rights to water. There was even an objection to government's building the reservoir for fear the people would lose control of the water. [5] The meeting ended with the adoption of a resolution expressing the willingness of the people to repay the government the cost of construction of a dam "upon satisfactory terms and conditions being made," and a direction to the meeting chairman, Dr. J. M. Ford, to appoint three persons to go to Washington to inform Hitchcock of the merits of the Tonto Basin reservoir. [6] A few days later, Ford named Benjamin Fowler, William Christy, and John W. Woolf. [7]

By then, Fowler was on his way back to the Valley from Washington. He sent a telegram to his wife in which he reportedly said he was bringing a definite proposition from the government for building the dam. [8]

Dwight B. Heard, one of the Water Storage Commissioners, also had been in Washington. He had gone to lobby on behalf of the enabling act, returning to Phoenix July 21. He told newspapermen he thought there was a good chance for the reservoir to be built if the people worked together, [9] and he invited a group of men from around the Valley to meet with him the night of July 24 at the Adams Hotel to explain what he thought had to be done to get it built. He told them some form of association or organization would have to be formed to secure title to the dam site from the Hudson Reservoir and Canal Co. and turn it over to the government. The normal flow of the river and the order in which the land was to receive water had to be determined and settled by judicial decree. Lastly, Secretary of the Interior Ethan A. Hitchcock was a friend of the Indians and any plan would have to include an arrangement to furnish them water.

Heard said Fowler would explain more fully when he returned, and at the end of the meeting the men present signed a call for a meeting August 2 at the courthouse. [10]

On July 27, the *Gazette* printed a story announcing,

All the public lands in Maricopa County which would probably be irrigated from the Tonto Basin reservoir have been withdrawn from settlement by Milton R. Moore, registrar of the land office at Tucson, who is acting under instructions from the Department of the Interior. . . It is presumed that this land is withdrawn from settlement on account of the probable selection of the Tonto Basin as a site for the reservoir, and that as soon as the selection is made the lands will then be reopened to settlement under the new law. [11]

The Interior Department's withdrawing the public land from entry was the first in a number of signals the Valley would get in the months following that indicated the readiness of the government to build the dam and reservoir.

Two days after the land withdrawal, Fowler was back and he was interviewed by the *Gazette* and the *Republican*.

Benjamin A. Fowler

Fowler said the report that he had a definite proposition from the government was wrong, but a plan had been outlined that could lead to construction of the dam. He confirmed what Heard had said about the need for an organization and the settling of water rights issues, and added the water rights would have to be made inseparable from the land. Once the dam was built, the people would have to repay the government the cost of construction within 10 years but no interest would have to be paid on the money. Moreover, before the Interior Department made a decision about which reservoirs would be built, surveys would have to be conducted and cost estimates made. All of this would take time, which meant it would take from 12 to 15 months before construction would start on any reservoir, Fowler said. [12]

He said there were many reasons why the government wanted to make the Tonto Basin reservoir one of the early projects. The first was the conditions were more favorable there than anywhere else. Another was the success of the project would give a strong impetus to the national irrigation movement. [13]

Fowler said if the government should build the San Carlos reservoir, it would not mean the end of the Tonto. But he said he knew of no reason why both should not be built, and he thought it probable both sites would be selected. [14]

What needed to be done, he said, was for the people of the Valley to adjust their differences, to dispose of them one at a time until all the government's requirements had been met. [15]

At the meeting August 2, Fowler reiterated what he had said in the interview, adding the government did not want to be involved in litigation. He said the canals would have to become the property of the landowners and each share of stock in the organization would represent one acre of land. [16]

Fowler put a deadline on when he thought the Valley water users ought to have their problems resolved. This was January 1, 1903, "for, by that time, the government will be ready to begin on the first reservoir, and if we are not our chance is gone," he said. [17]

Fowler extolled George H. Maxwell, executive director of the National Irrigation Association, saying "it was through him the President called the conference which changed the (reclamation) bill so as to admit of the construction of reservoirs for land under private ownership." [18]

Maxwell had agreed to come to the Valley to address the people if they wanted him, Fowler said. [19]

He also said the government had no special desire to come to the Valley, "but there are certain officials who want to build the first reservoir at Tonto, simply because it will in the future serve as a model for others." [20]

Heard spoke next. He listed a number of government officials who approved of the general features of the plan outlined by Fowler, or who otherwise gave encouragement. The list included the most important persons in the Interior Department, starting with Secretary Hitchcock. Others were Charles D. Walcott, director of the U.S. Geological Survey; Gifford Pinchott, head of the Bureau of Forestry; Arthur P. Davis of the Geological Survey, and Newell. In addition, support was given by Secretary of Agriculture James Wilson and Elwood Mead, who headed the Agriculture Department's irrigation investigations. [21]

"After the adjournment of Congress," Heard said, "I had a special conference with President Roosevelt on the needs of this community. The President is an enthusiastic friend of the West, but nothing but the cleanest, fairest measures can hope to secure his support. He showed much interest in the presentation of the needs of the Salt River Valley, but stated that the selection of the government projects would be entirely in the hands of the Secretary of the Interior, Mr. Hitchcock, acting upon the advice of Mr. Walcott, director of the Geological Survey, and Mr. F. H. Newell, of the Survey. The President expressed the utmost confidence in the business ability, judgment, and experience of these gentlemen, and stated frankly that the projects selected would be chosen entirely on their merits and on no other grounds. . . He indicated that if the Salt River reservoir project had the special merits claimed for it, and was approved by the Secretary of the Interior, he knew of nothing to interfere with the construction." [22]

Heard dispelled any concern the reservoir would not be built because most of the land was in private ownership, whereas the reclamation act before being amended to include areas such as the valley was intended to open public lands for settlement. He said Interior Department officials had assured him there was no problem. [23]

Finally, he said there would be no government interference with the vested rights of landowners to the use of water, and he believed the Mann family of New York was ready to negotiate the sale of the reservoir site. The Manns owned the site through the Hudson Reservoir and Canal Co. [24]

At the conclusion of his talk, Heard was loudly cheered. His remarks had set the stage for Parker to propose a resolution calling for the formation of a Water Storage Conference Committee "to make such adjustments and secure such agreements as may be required by the Department of the Interior prior to the consideration of the construction of the Tonto Basin reservoir." [25] The committee was to have 26 members, with the management of 10 canals each appointing one member. The canals were the Arizona, Grand, Maricopa, and Salt River Valley on the river's north side, and the San Francisco, Tempe, Utah, Mesa, Consolidated, and Highland on the south side. Water users under seven canals—Arizona, Grand, Maricopa, Salt River Valley, Tempe, Utah, and Mesa—were to appoint two members each, and the Maricopa County Board of Trade was to name two from the city of Phoenix.

The Conference Committee members were to be named within five days and were to meet August 9 to organize and begin their work. [26]

Two other motions were made and adopted. The first was to invite Maxwell to the Valley to address the farmers and businessmen; the second was for the meeting chairman, Dr. Ford, to appoint a committee of three to work with the Water Storage Commissioners to acquire the Tonto Basin dam site. In that connection, Christy said the commission had the power to negotiate for the site and it would have $20,000 available to help buy it. [27]

Fowler left the night of August 2 for Los Angeles, where he met Newell and traveled with him to San Francisco to meet Maxwell. [28] Five days later, Fowler sent a telegram from Los Angeles to Christy saying Fowler and Maxwell would arrive in Phoenix the next day. Fowler suggested Maxwell meet with the Conference Committee Saturday morning, August 9, and with the public in the afternoon. [29]

Christy, president of the Valley Bank, also received a letter from Newell in response to an inquiry from Christy asking the best course to pursue in getting the reservoir. Newell said neither he,

nor my assistants can properly advise you, yet it may be allowable to call attention to the fact that the interpretation of the reclamation law, and its application to particular, circumstances, may properly be entrusted to its principal advocate and exponent, Mr. George H. Maxwell. Further than this, my acquaintance with Mr. B. A. Fowler of your valley, and the favorable impression he had made through his efficient yet conservative action, leads me to the belief that whatever he may recommend to you will be based upon a complete knowledge of proper methods and feasible ends. [30]

If there had been any doubt Maxwell and Fowler were the right men to guide the Valley, Newell's endorsement should have set it permanently aside.

Meantime, the Water Storage Commissioners met and voted to make its records available to the Conference Committee, to allocate $12,000 for the purchase of the reservoir site on the condition the rest of the cost be contributed from other sources, and to buy a replica of the completed dam and ancillary works created by the Geological Survey. Heard had informed the commission he had seen the replica while in Washington. [31]

Saturday morning, with 24 of the 26 members present, the

George H. Maxwell

Water Storage Conference Committee met at the Board of Trade. Fowler was elected permanent chairman, Parker, secretary, and Ward Hughes, assistant secretary. [32]

This was followed by comments from Maxwell, who said his role in developing a proposition for the reservoir would be to advise whether he thought it would be acceptable to the nation. This did not mean, he said, there would be approval of all he suggested, but the way to find out was to talk it out. The spirit of the discussions was up to them, he said.

"If you can rise to the proper height," Maxwell said, "if you can realize the fact as a whole community that the building of this reservoir by the government will practically wipe out all trouble that confronts you today, and the moment that the secretary of the interior puts his signature to the order for that reservoir it doubles the value of every piece of property in the city of Phoenix and in this valley, you can well afford to sink absolutely out of sight every local personal difference of every kind and unite together to bring about the completion of a common plan which will unite this whole community as one man to make the fight—because it will be a fight, there is no question about that—to get the government to come in here and build these works."

Maxwell, contrary to views expressed by Heard and Fowler, said he did not see any need to be concerned about the normal flow of the river. He said there was no such thing as normal flow. To him, the flow in the river was varying and irregular, so establishment of a normal flow meant creation of a theoretical abnormal flow. When there was water enough for everyone, the question of normal flow would be of no interest, he said.

As to the priority of the right to use water, he did not believe this would either be interferred with or surrendered.

". . .it seems to me that when you build this reservoir," Maxwell said, "you create beyond question such an increased supply that if you do not undertake to spread it over too much land, you will absolutely eliminate all causes of conflict over priority of rights. . . No man will spend his substance in litigation over priority rights."

The public meeting in the afternoon attracted more than a thousand persons to hear Maxwell and was held in the courthouse yard.

Maxwell began by saying he had heard a remark on the street that morning that the people could not get together. He said the difficulty of doing that could not be one-hundredth of the problem of having to unite the people of the East, West and South to get the National Reclamation Act through Congress.

He said if the people of the Valley could get together, he believed a contract for the reservoir could be let in under six months. He said a couple of conditions had to be met to accomplish this. The first was no one but the farmers of the Valley were to benefit, i.e., the reservoir was not to be built for the benefit of the canal companies, which meant the distribution of water had to be under the control of the landowners. He said the canals might be obtained through the sale of bonds, which would mean debt, but when paid off, the farmers who were the landowners and water users would own them.

The second condition was whatever the plan, it had to be economically sound. The advantage of government construction of the reservoir was that the money for it would be loaned interest free and not a cent would have to be repaid until after it was completed. Thus, there would be a savings of water as well as interest, Maxwell said.

If you expect the irrigation association to help you in this matter," Maxwell said, "we must be able to go before the Eastern people and assure them that the government has absolutely a cinch on the payments, and we must be able to see that the government gets its full share every year. The government will take no chance of a controversy or a failure to pay any part of what is due. In other words, when you have brought together in a line the lands and the interests in the valley who are willing to assume the burden of paying the government for that reservoir, you must so unite them that they act together in everything that is done and that the government will have nothing whatever to do except to open the gate of the reservoir and let the water out as you need it any year upon the condition that the fixed annual sum, which is to be paid to the government as a whole before the right to the water vests for the year."

Maxwell thought landowners without priority rights might pay more for the reservoir than those with water rights. He urged that, when a plan was drawn up, it be sent to Washington with Fowler, who had the confidence of the Eastern people. Maxwell said there would be no controversy between the Tonto and San Carlos propositions. Last, he said he had been asked to return to help in the plan, and he would do so if invited, which he was. [33]

The Conference Committee had enlisted attorney Joseph H. Kibbey to draw up a plan on how to proceed. [34] Kibbey, as judge of the U.S. District Court of the 2nd judicial district, Arizona Territory, in 1892 authored the decision in the case of *Michael Wormser, et al, v. the Salt River Valley Canal Co., et al,* and had remained in the Valley as one of its foremost water and legal authorities. [35]

While Kibbey labored over his plan, public discussion on the north side of the river centered around how to assure the water would be delivered from the reservoir. One idea was to perpetually lease the canals from the companies; another was to make a contract providing for perpetual delivery of water at a fixed rate; a third was to buy the canals, but the farmers objected to mortgaging their land to do that. Many of the farmers under the Grand, Maricopa, and Salt River Valley canals expressed willingness to buy their own waterways, but not the Arizona Canal. [36]

One suggestion for acquiring the canals was to ask Congress to pass a law creating an irrigation district taking in lands served by the north side canals, including those in Phoenix, with authority to issue bonds. It was suggested the same law could contain an appropriation of money to construct the reservoir, which the farmers would repay at the rate of $1.50 per acre per year for 10 years. The farmers favored this approach because they did not think it involved mortgaging their ground or giving up any rights. [37]

The *Republican* printed a letter from S. M. McCowan, former part-owner and editor of the newspaper and the superintendent of the Phoenix Indian School, saying the Geological Survey office in Washington had the plans for constructing the Tonto dam "all completed today down to the smallest detail." He wrote that was "where the government would like to initiate the work of dam construction for irrigation purposes."

"Aside from the government's scientific interest," McCowan said, "it don't give a tinker's dam for the material welfare of any citizen in the valley. It wants to demonstrate success, and knowing that all the elements of success cluster around Tonto, it would be glad to commence there."

All the people had to do, he said, was to accept whatever conditions the government desired. He advised the Conference Committee against concocting "a pretty little scheme of its own."

McCowan added, "The welfare of the Pima Indians need not be considered in this connection." [38]

Kibbey's plan was presented at a meeting of the Water Storage Conference Committee on September 4. In the document, Kibbey gave his interpretation of the congressional intent in passing the reclamation act and what he thought was implied in the legislation. Kibbey's views were unquestionably influenced by the earlier expressions of Maxwell, Fowler, and Heard. Key among these were those dealing with the settlement of water priority issues and control of the distribution of water.

Kibbey divided the water question into two classes, the water users and the water carriers, or canal companies. As to the first, they had to resolve "the question of time and extent of appropriation of water." There were two methods for accomplishing this: first, with the agreement of all the water users, submit the matter to arbitration, with the determination to be made a decree of the court from which there would be no appeal; second, make all the water users plaintiffs or defendants in a suit instituted in U.S. District Court. As to the canal companies, assuming they maintained their autonomy, "questions of their relative rights to divert and carry water" would have to be settled.[39]

"All these questions," Kibbey said, "are preliminary to and are independent of any consideration of the administration of stored water and are questions in the determination of which the government probably cannot, and certainly will not, engage. They must be settled before we can go to the government at all." [40]

About the distribution of water, Kibbey said, "It is extremely desirable that the means. . .shall be under the immediate and exclusive management and control of the water users." He described various ways in which that could be accomplished. First, if the canal companies retained their independent status, the water users' association, to be organized by the farmers, could either perpetually lease them or the companies could deliver the water at an agreed upon reasonable cost, but, in either case, the association would have the right of purchase. Second, the canals could be purchased outright, their maximum value being the cost of constructing a new system of canals. Third, the canals could be acquired through the power of eminent domain, which was considered the simplest plan. Fourth, the association could construct its own canals and distribution system, which would make the old canals valueless. [41]

Other Kibbey proposals were: the water users form and incorporate an association with membership limited to landowners or homesteaders who had, or would have, rights to the use of the stored water; the number of shares in the corporation be equal to the number of acres to receive stored or other water and the value of the capital stock be equal in sum to the cost of the reservoir; the acceptance of shares signify agreement to pledge the land as collateral for payment of all assessments and to submit water rights questions to settlement; the power for operating the association be invested in a council with general legislative powers and a board of directors for immediate management; the division of the country into districts conforming as nearly as possible to the lands supplied by the individual canal systems, so that the cost of acquiring a canal or of constructing a new one could be assessed against the shareholders of the area benefited; the stockholders be allowed one vote each at all corporate elections regardless of the number of shares owned; the individual shareholder deal directly with the secretary of the interior "in initiating or perfecting any individual right" (Maxwell, in his speech to the people August 9, said the government probably would prefer to deal with the association); the estimate of the amount of land to be served by the reservoir be low because it would be easier to expand than to contract the acreage to be served; the water from the reservoir be apportioned "in the order of the existing appropriations and if there be a surplus then to new lands acquired by homesteading." [42]

In consideration of the Indians on the Gila River Reservation, Kibbey said they could be furnished with electricity produced at the dam to pump water. This, he said, "would afford them a greater, more certain, more constant, and a more reliable supply of water than they ever had." The source of the pumped water was constantly being renewed, he said.

Kibbey said the power would be produced at one-fourth the present cost and in quantities to "produce a handsome income" from the cities and towns in the Valley. The amount used by the Indians "would hardly make an appreciable diminution of the whole amount developed." [43]

He said an important duty of the association would be to stop the diversions of water upstream on the Salt and Verde rivers, which across the past 15 years had caused a constant reduction in the water flowing through the Valley. This had been going on so long, he said, there was little hope efforts would be made to stop it without unity among the farmers. Whether the government built the Tonto reservoir or not, there had to be unification of interest if they were to avoid a disastrous end. [44]

Summing up, Kibbey told the Conference Committee the reservoir proposition was "almost dazzling" when viewed from the position of the "extremest pessimist."

"Take the cost of the reservoir and of the system of distribution at the highest it can be expected," he said. "Reduce the amount of land to be irrigated to the least extent, within the certain knowledge of the most incredulous. Make liberal allowance for faults, improvidence, carelessness, mistakes, and unskillful management and administration. Take into consideration disaster by flood. Ignore possible income from other sources other than from the stockholders themselves, and yet the result is of such magnificent proportions as to be alluring." [45]

Before adjourning, the Conference Committee selected an executive committee of 11 members to make it easier to transact immediate business. The committee, and the interests they represented, were: Fowler, Arizona Canal; Christy, Grand Canal; Lin R. Orme, Maricopa Canal; Parker, Salt River Valley Canal; John W. Woolf, Tempe Canal; Hezekiah Simkins, Utah Canal; Ward Hughes, San Francisco Canal; Dr. Ethelbert W. Wilbur, Mesa Canal; Dr. Alexander J. Chandler, Consolidated Canal; W. H. Wallace, Highland Canal, and Frank T. Alkire, city of Phoenix. [46]

The Conference Committee next met September 26. That morning, Maxwell arrived back in Phoenix and informed the committee he would remain until October 4, when he had to leave for Colorado Springs, Colorado, site of the 10th National Irrigation Congress, October 6-9. Vice presidents of the congress included Fowler, Heard, and William J. Murphy.

Maxwell gave general endorsement to the Kibbey plan, after which M. E. Messinger of the Arizona Canal water users proposed that the committee consider the organization of a water users' association. However, Wilbur proposed there be two associations, one for the north side of the river and the other for the south side. He gave as the reason for this the different administration of the canals on the two sides of the river, the north side being controlled by corporations and the south side more generally by the water users. Wilbur said once the two associations were formed, they could organize a joint company to deal with the government. The idea was supported by Chandler and James F. Johnson of the Utah Canal, but it was argued by others that all of the benefits of two associations could be accomplished by a parent corporation embracing the entire valley and by the formation of district or subordinate associations, which conformed to the Kibbey plan.

Christy said he too favored the idea of north side and south side organizations, but said the first thing to do was to form the parent company. He said the water users' association should be incorporated with a capital stock of 250,000 shares valued at $10 each. He agreed each share should represent one acre of land but proposed each landowner should have as many shares as acres.

This raised the question of the provision of the reclamation law that limited delivery of water to a maximum of 160 acres owned by one person. It was thought that this limitation applied in virgin country where the government was contracting with individuals but not in a settled district where the government would deliver the water to an association, which would distribute it. The matter was laid aside, and discussion returned to a motion by Christy that a committee of five be named to draw up articles of incorporation. Wilbur suggested the Executive Committee be given the task, and the motion was passed unanimously. The committee was instructed to report on its work the following Monday. [47] It apparently was sometime after the approval of this motion that Heard replaced Hughes on the Executive Committee. [48]

The Executive Committee's real work, at that point, was to reach agreement as to what was to go into the articles rather than to provide the language. [49] The committee worked each day, but it was unable to finish its task by Monday. [50] From its meeting place at the Adams Hotel, Maxwell issued a statement: "Throughout the long session there was a steady discussion of the details of the general plan with every promise of ability to satisfactorily adjust all of the various questions arising." [51]

Little was said about areas of disagreement, but one sticky point was how many acres should be included in the reservoir area. It was the old problem of more irrigable acres under the canals than could be supplied adequately with water. [52]

By Tuesday afternoon, Maxwell announced all the important matters had been agreed upon, and the plan would be presented to the Water Storage Conference Committee Thursday morning. Last minute changes delayed the meeting until one o'clock in the afternoon. The plan was a statement of reclamation law interpretation, Valley conditions, and principles for unifying the water users. The plan restated many of the ideas presented in the Kibbey plan, but, significantly, the Executive Committee reported it saw no need for determining water priority and rights issues before government approval of the reservoir.

While concurring on the need for early adjudication of these questions, the committee said, "It is not necessary, however, in our judgment that this should be done as a condition precedent to the construction of the reservoir or before its construction should be authorized and begun by the government." [53]

The committee also took a firm stand on the provision of the reclamation law limiting water deliveries to 160 acres to any one landowner. The committee declared no landowner be able to acquire a reservoir right unless, before the completion of the dam, he bring himself into compliance with the law. In addition, it said the first opportunity to obtain reservoir rights should be for lands already under cultivation. [54]

The committee took no position about how the canals should be acquired, but agreed the water users' association should take control of the water from the government at the reservoir and should apportion it among the canals, which should be united into a single company. At the same time, the committee said it must be recognized "that no plan could now be devised or carried into effect under which the government would assume control or acquire the ownership of the distributing canal systems in the Salt River Valley." [55] Each canal was to be "under the control and management of its local board selected by the landowners under each system separately." [56]

The committee said the association should be formed with 250,000 shares, the shares to have a par value of $12.50 each payable to the government at the rate of $1.25 per acre for 10 years, beginning at a time to be set by the secretary of the interior. Although providing for 250,000 shares, the committee said it would be unwise to irrigate more than 200,000 acres with the entire water supply including the natural flow of the Salt and Verde rivers, the flood waters to be stored, and the water to be developed from beneath the ground with the power to be generated at the dam. It was estimated no more than 20,000 acres could be supplied with pumped water. [57]

The committee recommended the construction of a reservoir with a water storage capacity of 1,478,750 acre-feet. It estimated the cost of the reservoir at $2,549,231. [58]

The association was to include all landowners wishing to obtain reservoir rights. It was to collect from the landowners all money due the government. It was to be governed by a board through which all business of common interest was to be conducted, such as development of pumping plants, protection of the water supply, and purchase of the reservoir site. [59]

Last, the committee proposed the preparation of a subscription book which was to be signed by landowners indicating approval of the plan and pledging to "subscribe for the number of shares and acreage set opposite their respective names, subject to their approval of the articles of incorporation and by-laws of the merger association to be hereinafter prepared." [60]

The Conference Committee agreed to employ Kibbey to prepare the articles of incorporation with instructions to have them ready by October 15. The committee also called a mass meeting at 3 o'clock the afternoon of October 2 to hear a talk by Maxwell before he departed for the National Irrigation Congress. [61]

At the meeting, Maxwell explained that signing the subscription book obligated no one to anything but would be an indication of progress to the interior secretary. Maxwell said the farmers had to "transform the canal companies into landowners' companies" so that the government would know it was dealing with the people, and the water would be distributed properly. He said the farmers could not expect the government to invest $2,500,000 and collect this money back in small amounts from the water users; there had to be a common channel—an association—through which business could be transacted.

Maxwell was loudly applauded when he said syndicates owning more than 160 acres would have to subdivide their holdings into tracts of that size. He said this would prevent Eastern corporations from coming to the Valley and getting more than that amount. The water also had to go to bona fide residents of the section.

He foresaw great possibilities for the electric power to be developed, suggesting there would be enough to light every farm house in addition to pumping water. [62]

Kibbey begain writing the articles of incorporation, and Conference Committee members began soliciting signatures for the subscription book. By October 15, the day Kibbey was to have completed the articles, signatures representing about 25,000 acres had been obtained, but the articles were not done, and they were not to be for several months. The Conference Committee instructed the Executive Committee to meet with Kibbey to assist him in preparing the articles. [63] Simultaneously, the committee members canvassed the ranches and farms for signatures. By early December, the committee had received signatures for 140,000 acres, and there was hope 40,000 acres more would be represented. [64]

At the end of October, the Conference Committee received a letter from Maxwell, who emphasized the need for securing "as many subscriptions as possible to the approval of the plan for the formation of the water users' association." In addition, he urged that a list of landowners under each canal system be developed to include a description of the land, the nature of the water right, and the number of canal company shares. His idea was to prepare a draft of the articles of incorporation and take them up separately with each canal company with the aim of consolidating the companies. [65]

Maxwell said he planned to be back in the Valley by November 7, but he did not return until November 30. [66] His journeys included a trip to Washington, where he met with President Roosevelt. [67]

Davis arrived in Phoenix November 5. He told newspaper reporters he had come for two purposes: first, to investigate the Valley's underground water supply, and, second, to make preparations for a survey of the power canal, which was to provide the water for generating electricity at the dam site. The canal was to be at least 15-miles long and the water was to have a fall of 180 feet, which would develop 1,200 horsepower. [68]

A reporter for the *Phoenix Enterprise* asked Davis if he thought the Tonto Basin reservoir would be built.

Davis answered: "Of course I cannot speak for the government. . .but I see no reason why the government should not build the dam. It has spent quite a sum of money getting the facts in the case, and if the people pursue the proper policy, I think they should succeed."

Did Davis think the people had adopted a proper plan? "I do," Davis said, then explained his and the government's position.

"While I am not the deciding factor in the location of a dam," he said, "I do not think the government would construct a project that I would not recommend, and I would not recommend any project where the water is turned over to a corporation to carry to the farmers. The law is positive and direct on this point, and as long as the canals are owned by private corporations I would not feel disposed to recommend that the dam be built. But I see that your committee has recommended that the farmers organize and buy the canals. If this is done, the matter will be simplified. Of course the government could construct canals, and this will be done where new irrigation systems are established, but your system is already in the hands of private owners and until it is gotten into a shape where the government can control it, or have the people control it, I would not consider the project feasible under present law." [69]

A few days later in a speech to the Oasis Club at Coffee Al's, Davis said the Tonto dam site was so nearly ideal that if the land in the Valley were public, the government would no doubt begin construction at once. He made it clear the people were not waiting for the government but the government for the people. [70]

In mid-November, a model of the Tonto dam and reservoir ordered by the Water Storage Commission in August went on exhibit at the Board of Trade. However, instead of being a duplicate of the one seen by Heard, it was the original made for the Geological Survey.

"The geological commission in its desire to help along the preliminary work here, kindly forwarded the original model. . .and will itself take the duplicate as soon as it is completed," the *Republican* stated.[71] The article continued:

The dam is to be 210-feet high and the cost of the entire enterprise is estimated at approximately $2,000,000 and is to impound 840,000 acre-feet of water. The water storage commission and the engineers are now figuring on plans for building the dam forty feet higher than this model calls for, thereby nearly doubling its capacity and impounding 1,400,000 acre-feet of water. . .

But the unique feature of the whole enterprise and a feature but few have learned the details of is the scheme of development of electric power. A canal will be dug, heading at the upper end of the reservoir site, capable of carrying the minimum flow of the river whether there is impounded water at hand or not. This canal will skirt the reservoir basin along the water level when the basin is full, finally passing round one end of the dam in a channel cut in the rock waste way, some feet down through a hole in the rock then out and over the precipice to the powerhouse. The construction of this canal will be the first work in carrying out the big project and a corps of engineers will begin its survey in a few days. . .[72]

1. *Arizona Gazette* (Phoenix), July 16, 1902.
2. *Ibid.*
3. *Arizona Republican* (Phoenix), July 15, 1902.
4. *Los Angeles Times,* quoted in *Republican,* July 22, 1902.
5. *Republican,* July 2, 1902.
6. *Ibid.*
7. *Ibid.,* July 24, 1902.
8. *Ibid.,* July 22, 1902.
9. *Ibid.*
10. *Ibid.,* July 25, 1902; *Phoenix Daily Enterprise,* July 30, 1902.
11. *Gazette,* July 27, 1902.
12. *Ibid.,* July 30, 1902; *Republican,* July 30, 1902.
13. *Ibid.*
14. *Ibid.*
15. *Ibid.*
16. *Ibid.,* August 3, 1902.
17. *Gazette,* August 3, 1902.
18. *Ibid.*
19. *Ibid.*
20. *Ibid.*
21. *Enterprise,* August 4, 1902.
22. *Ibid.*
23. *Ibid.*
24. *Ibid.*
25. *Ibid., Gazette,* August 3, 1902; *Republican,* August 3, 1902.
26. *Ibid.*
27. *Gazette,* August 3, 1902; *Enterprise,* August 4, 1902.
28. *Enterprise,* August 3, 1902.
29. *Republican,* August 8, 1902.
30. *Ibid.*
31. *Republican,* August 5, 1902.
32. *Republican,* August 10, 1902; *Gazette,* August 10, 1902.
33. *Ibid.*
34. *Republican,* Sept. 5, August 17, 1902.
35. Joseph H. Kibbey, decision in *Wormser v. Salt River Valley Canal Co.,* March 31, 1892.
36. *Republican,* August 17, 1902.
37. *Enterprise,* August 19, 1902.
38. *Republican,* August 16, 1902.
39. Joseph H. Kibbey, address to Water Storage Conference Committee, September 4, 1902, in *Proceedings of First Conference of Engineers of the Reclamation Service* (Washington: Government Printing Office, 1904), pp. 132-140; *Republican,* September 7, 1902.
40. *Ibid.*
41. *Ibid.*
42. *Ibid.*
43. *Ibid.*
44. *Ibid.*
45. *Ibid.*
46. *Republican,* September 5, 1902.
47. *Ibid.,* September 25, 1902.
48. *Ibid.,* January 22, 1903.
49. *Enterprise,* September 29, 1902.
50. *Republican,* September 29, 1902.
51. *Enterprise,* September 29, 1902.
52. *Ibid.*
53. Report of the Executive Committee of the Water Storage Conference Committee of the Salt River Valley, October 2, 1903, in *Proceedings of Reclamation Service,* pp. 143-147; *Republican,* October 3, 1902.
54. *Ibid.*
55. *Ibid.*
56. *Ibid.*
57. *Ibid.*
58. *Ibid.*
59. *Ibid.*
60. *Ibid.*
61. *Ibid.*
62. *Ibid.*
63. *Republican,* October 16, 1902.
64. *Ibid.,* December 2, 1902.
65. *Ibid.,* November 1, 1902.
66. *Ibid.*
67. *Gazette,* November 25, 1902.
68. *Republican,* November 6, 15, 1902; *Gazette,* November 6, 1902; *Enterprise,* November 8, 1902.
69. *Enterprise,* November 8, 1902.
70. *Republican,* November 11, 1902.
71. *Republican,* November 15, 1902.
72. *Ibid.*

December 1902 - March 1903

By December 1902, having received positive indications from the federal government of its willingness to build the Tonto Basin dam and reservoir, the people of the Salt River Valley found themselves in the throes of forming an organization to deal with the government.

If there was any doubt about the government's readiness to build, it should have been dispelled by the words of George H. Maxwell, the executive director of the National Irrigation Association, and the chief figure in persuading Congress to adopt a national irrigation law. Maxwell had volunteered to assist the Salt River Valley water users in the development of an organization to work with the government in seeking approval for the reservoir and planned to remain in the Valley until it was built.

In November, Maxwell had been to Washington, D.C., to meet with President Theodore Roosevelt and Secretary of the Interior Ethan A. Hitchcock. On Maxwell's return to Phoenix, a reporter for the **Phoenix Enterprise** asked him, "Do you think the Secretary of the Interior will recommend the building of the Tonto Dam?"

"Most assuredly I think he will," Maxwell answered. "Everything is all right in Washington, and it only remains for the people of this valley to perfect their organization and get it in proper shape. As soon as your people do this, the order for the building of the Tonto Basin reservoir will be given by Mr. Hitchcock." [1]

Maxwell told the **Arizona Republican** that no more work had to be done in Washington to get the reservoir. Everybody there was in favor of it. [2]

What remained to be done involved completing the articles of incorporation for an organization and signing enough acres into it to assure the government it would be repaid the money it advanced for building the dam. That would be followed by making some sort of arrangement with the canal companies for the delivery of water or for acquiring them. Members of the Water Storage Conference Committee, which was leading the organizing efforts, reported nothing discouraging in dealing with the canal companies. [3]

Little information filtered out about the work of preparing the articles of incorporation. On December 10, Joseph H. Kibbey, who was employed to prepare the articles, and Maxwell told the Conference Committee's Executive Committee that the two of them could get the work done much faster if they were left alone to do it themselves. The Executive Committee voted to leave the preparation of the articles to them. [4]

In the interim, the **Arizona Blade,** published in Florence by Thomas Weedin, launched an attack on Maxwell, saying, the words he had spoken on his return to Phoenix had "struck terror to the hearts of the people of Casa Grande Valley." [5] The **Arizona Gazette** responded,

There was and is no necessity for the people of Pinal County to go into hysteria because the San Carlos dam will not be built first...

Neither Mr. Maxwell nor any other man in the (Salt River) valley is fighting the San Carlos scheme. In fact, all agree that the dam should be built; but the people here contend, and rightly, that they are entitled to the first dam because the conditions are most favorable for its construction. More work has been done and it is nearer the construction stage than any proposition in the west. . . Mr. Maxwell is not trying to "blow the San Carlos dam out and the Tonto dam in," as stated in the Blade, but he is assisting the people of the Salt River Valley in settling up a few of their differences which have grown out of the water question, or rather the lack of water to irrigate the lands under cultivation. When Mr. Maxwell expressed his opinion that the Tonto dam would be built and that work would begin within a few months, he was merely stating what he believed to be facts, and without the least prejudice against the San Carlos dam. In fact, Mr. Maxwell has spoken in the kindliest terms of that scheme, and as soon as he has completed the work mapped out here he will willingly assist the people of the Casa Grande valley, if his services are needed. [6]

In the months to come, this was the course the citizens of the Salt River Valley were to take in respect to the San Carlos dam: the construction of the Tonto reservoir did not mean the San Carlos dam should not be built and as soon as the Tonto was assured and underway, attention would be turned to helping the people of Pinal County—and the Indians on the Gila River Reservation—get the San Carlos reservoir.

Reclamation Service engineer Arthur P. Davis gave a series of lectures about the Tonto dam in Phoenix, Tempe and Mesa. At one of them, Davis said the greatest drawback to the construction of most reservoirs was the cost of cement. He said it once had been feared this would be the situation at the Tonto site, but a search revealed the finest quality of lime 1,900 feet from the dam and the finest clay only a little more than two miles distant. He put the total cost of building a cement plant and manufacturing 200,000 barrels of cement at not more than $500,000. This compared to $1,800,000 if the cement had to be bought elsewhere and shipped in. [7]

On December 24, Kibbey and Maxwell presented the articles to the Executive Committee. [8] From then through January 2, the committee met in four all-day sessions, [9] but what the committee talked about was not disclosed. The **Republican** of January 3, 1903, explained,

None of the deliberations of the committee have been made public, not because it was desired that a close veil of secrecy should be thrown about the proceedings but it was surmised that many changes would be made. It was thought better to wait until the articles have been made complete and then when they are given to the public there will be no erroneous impressions of them to be removed. All members of the executive committee are pleased with the result of their long labors and they see no serious obstacles in the rest of the way. [10]

The harmony inferred by the **Republican's** statement was not true, but the people were not informed of it. Some serious differences existed, but Frederick H. Newell, chief of the Reclamation Service, was due in Phoenix in a couple of days and Maxwell, Kibbey and the committee majority undoubtedly hoped he could help overcome the problems.

Newell, accompanied by Davis, had toured the Colorado

River valley from Needles to south of Yuma,[11] and they arrived in Phoenix the afternoon of January 5. Almost at once, Newell went into a long conference with a delegation from Florence, which was there to push for construction of the San Carlos dam. Subsequently, it was announced Maxwell would leave for Florence on June 8 to assist the Pinal County water users in their work to get a reservoir.[12]

Davis left for Globe the night of January 5, while Newell had long conferences with Arizona Governor Alexander O. Brodie, Benjamin A. Fowler, Maxwell, Kibbey and others.[13] Newell, afterward, said he was "very favorably impressed with the work and progress that has been made by the Water Storage Conference Committee."[14] He said any report submitted by Fowler "will have great influence with Secretary Hitchcock."[15]

Newell also said there were three survey parties in the field in connection with the construction of the Tonto Basin dam. One was gathering information about the Valley's underground water; the second was for surveying the power canal; the third was surveying the Salt River from the Tonto Basin dam site to the head of the Arizona Canal.[16]

The following afternoon, Newell addressed the Water Storage Conference Committee and other interested citizens. Officially, he said he was not supposed to talk and he asked the people to forget it if he should say something he should not.[17]

Newell said there was nothing unique or preeminent about Arizona's claim for assistance. "Each locality feels

Frederick H. Newell

that they have the only place to begin the construction of reservoirs, a place where they must have water," he said. "It is the same story from them all and it is hard for one at a distance to judge of the merits, so it remains for the sections to present their propositions to the government and the one that gets there first with a business proposition will be the one to receive the benefits."[18]

However, Newell said the Valley people had been "hard at work upon a proposition. . .and the results should attract attention all over the world, although I do not know just what you have accomplished. I would not discuss it, if I did, further than to say that I believe you will be considered most favorably as the site for a reservoir, as an ideal one. I hope to be able before long to come here and not leave until the dam and reservoir have been completed."[19]

Newell's statement that he did not "know just what you have accomplished" seems improbable because when the differences over the articles of incorporation became public, Maxwell, Kibbey and others argued the views of the minority were contrary to Interior Department instructions.[20] Once the articles were near completion, Newell and Davis were the only Interior Department representatives to visit Phoenix and they could have seen them before they were revealed to the full Water Storage Conference Committee, January 17. Newell and Davis, and more likely Newell, had the final word on disputes with the minority about the meaning of the reclamation law and what the Interior Department required in the articles. Indeed, Maxwell said the articles, after being approved by the majority of the Conference Commitee and before being taken to Washington, already had the unofficial endorsement of Newell.[21]

Newell, in remarks to the Conference Committee January 6, left no question as to his own importance in the decision process. He explained that because Secretary Hitchcock had so many departments to oversee and was so busy, "The spending of the money for the reservoirs he has practically placed in the hands of the Geological Survey."[22] Newell said the head of the Geological Survey, Charles D. Walcott, also had many things to look after, so the reclamation work had been assigned "to a board of engineers of which I have the honor to be the head."[23]

When Newell concluded, Ethelbert W. Wilbur of the Mesa Canal asked how soon Hitchcock would make a decision about the construction. Newell said he did not believe it would occur until after Congress adjourned March 4. Even then, he said, it would take time for contracts to be let and the length of time it would take to build depended upon the conditions. In this connection, Newell said, it would help if there was a railroad, or even a wagon road, from the Valley to the Tonto Basin county.[24]

Maxwell, as announced, went to Pinal County where he told the people the first thing to be done was to do what had been done in the Salt River Valley, which was the harmonizing of the various interests so the government could build the reservoir if it wanted to. If conditions were right, there was no reason why the government should not build both reservoirs, he said.[25]

The harmonizing of interests to which Maxwell alluded was, of course, an illusion. The Executive Committee completed work January 14 and Fowler and Parker announced a meeting of the general committee would be held at the Board of Trade at 9 a.m. January 17 "to pass upon the articles of incorporation of the Salt River Valley Water Users' Association. . ." [26] Immediately, rumors began circulating about a split in the Executive Commitee and the possibility of two reports instead of one. [27] The rumors were correct.

Fowler began the meeting, explaining the articles were intended to open the way for future business with the government. He said the articles had been recommended for adoption. It took about an hour to read them aloud. When this was done, Wilbur arose and announced a minority report had been prepared and it would be read by Dwight B. Heard. The third member of the minority was John W. Woolf, [28] a landowner under the Tempe Canal and a member of the Territorial Assembly.

The minority report charged that the articles differed "so radically in a number of vital principles" adopted by the Water Storage Conference Committee that many water users might not join the association, thereby "endangering the success of the whole proposition." [29]

If the government built the reservoir and too few acres were subscribed for reservoir rights, "the cost per acre to those who did subscribe would be so great, or the water so thinly distributed, as to make the success of the proposition prohibitive from a business standpoint," the report said. [30]

Specifically, the minority charged the articles failed to adequately protect existing water rights, as provided in the reclamation law and the Conference Committee's general plan, and "the principle of autonomy of the several canal divisions and local control. . .are practically eliminated." [31]

The minority objected to making all assessments "a lien on the lands of the shareholders as well as upon the shares of stock appurtenant to said lands and all rights and interests represented by such shares." [32] They thought assessments "should be proportioned. . .according to the benefits derived" from the construction of the dam, and each canal district should pay for its own operation. [33]

Heard, Woolf and Wilbur had these further suggestions: that should a landowner, through no fault of his own, fail to meet his obligations, he "not forfeit his present vested rights to the use of water for the irrigation of his lands;" that a provision be made that the articles not be binding "until a reasonable number of shares have been subscribed," so that landowners could make an approximate estimate of what reservoir rights would cost; and that the articles be amended to eliminate the danger of pooling "all existing water rights on all lands subscribed." [34]

The *Republican* reported the minority report "caused a sensation in the meeting and not a little indignation." [35] The newspaper writer revealed his own indignation by continuing:

The minority report presented no alternatives to the articles as drawn and dealt with nothing which the whole committee could pass upon intelligently, wherefore the proceeding could have no

effect except that of meeting the ends of a small element which heretofore has fallen heir to much caustic criticism from the public. [36]

Maxwell, in remarks recorded by a stenographer, said until the reading of the minority report he had,

felt that there was no very serious danger in the way of the construction of this reservoir. I confess that this so-called minority report came to me as something in the nature of a shock. Now, I think it is perfectly fair and just to all to say that the points at difference between the minority of the committee and the majority of the committee have been well understood for quite a number of days. If the minority committee had submitted somthing which the minority suggested should be adopted in place of what the majority suggested, no harm could have been done. This document does not do that, but does make certain general statements which, if disseminated through this community between now and the time when you will meet again will, in my judgment, create a widespread misconception which it will take days and weeks to remove. [37]

Maxwell said "as one of the counsel for the committee who prepared those articles. . .they conform absolutely in every particular and do not depart in the slightest degree, in any way, vitally or otherwise, from the plan adopted by the general Conference Committee. Judge Kibbey and I sat down with that plan before us and drew those articles with the determination that there should be no departure from that plan and I believe that we succeeded." [38]

He warned if the community got the idea the articles contained the defects stated in the minority report, there was "grave danger of a delay in working out this proposition, which ought to be avoided if possible." [39]

The Conference Committee rejected the minority report. The committee decided to read and adopt the articles [40] section by section and then as a whole. Before the discussion ended several hours later, Heard proposed that section 1 of article 4 be amended so landowners would not be forced to take pumped water. Kibbey said that detail should be taken up after the association's organization and did not belong in the articles. Maxwell agreed no one should be forced to take pumped water. The committee adjourned until 9 a.m. Tuesday, January 20. [41]

The Phoenix newspapers failed except in a general way to report the contents of the minority report. The newspapers left unclear what the split was about, but before the Tuesday meeting the *Gazette* and the *Republican* commented editorially. The former said if the people reserved any conclusions until the articles were presented to them, "they will be fully satisfied," [42] while the latter raised an old fear that should they fail, "the government in the near future will itself arrange for acquiring the (dam) site and will proceed to store the flood waters of the Salt River for the benefit of public lands available." [43]

The *Gazette* added:

If there are any interests like those of Mr. Heard which cannot adapt themselves to the conditions of the national irrigation act, they should not stand in the way of a plan which will be for the benefit of the great mass of the people of the valley. [44]

When the Conference Committee reconvened, the articles were changed without dissent to prevent water from being used for manufacturing purposes. [45]

The minority, heeding Maxwell's criticism, came ready

with proposed amendments [46] to the articles, and Wilbur offered the first one when section 3 of article 5 came up. [47] Section 3 provided for the forfeiture of all rights if the shareholder failed to comply with the rules and regulations of the Interior Department. The minority interpreted section 3 to mean existing entitlements to water could be lost. The amendment would have specifically excluded from forfeiture vested rights in the Salt and Verde rivers held by the landowner at the time he became a shareholder in the association. The majority said the amendment was unnecessary because article 14 protected "the present vested rights of any person to the prior use, or delivery, of the natural appropriated flow of the waters" of the two rivers. Heard said the amendment was intended to prevent any ambiguity or contradiction in the articles. [48]

Kibbey demurred, arguing the amendment would allow present owners of water rights to withdraw from the association, after contracts for construction of the dam were signed, for failing to pay assessments. He said the secretary of the interior would never agree to such a situation.

"We have got to show the Secretary. . .we are willing to put our present irrigated land in as a part of the capital of this association, and in this way make up the 200,000 acres to be served by the basin," Kibbey said. [49]

The amendment was defeated by a vote of 13 to 8. [50]

Section 8 of article 5 was strongly disputed. It made all rights to water appurtenant to the land. The minority proposed an amendment that would have limited appurtenance to water stored in the reservoir or otherwise developed by the government. This would have left intact for vested water rights the system of floating rights by which water was shifted from one piece of land to another. The water right was considered property and was rented, leased, bought, sold, transferred, mortgaged and used as collateral.

Wilbur was a forceful proponent of keeping water rights separate from the land. He also believed if section 8 was not amended, it would compel the owners of vested rights to pool them with those who had no rights except from the reservoir. [51]

To the minority, there was a contradiction in the National Reclamation Act because, on the one hand, it required water be appurtenant to the land but, on the other, it forbade interference with existing rights. Nevertheless, Kibbey said the secretary of the interior would never consent to the amendment and its acceptance would destroy any chance for the reservoir. [52]

Kibbey also said there would be no pooling of water rights, explaining, "Every person who has rights shall still retain them. If A was the first man to take out water and Z the last, A will be served with water first and Z last. When there is enough water to go around all will have plenty, and when there should be a shortage, A will be served first, B next and so on. But no man shall be furnished any more water than he can advantageously use." [53]

The amendment was defeated as was a persistent proposal by Heard for a "regulation right" in the reservoir. [54] According to Fowler, Heard contended "that if the flood water which belonged to him could be held back in the

government reservoir and the flow 'regulated,' he would have all the water needed for his 7,000 acres." [55]

"To have conceded this point," Fowler said, "would have been equivalent to a complete evasion of the provisions of the reclamation act, limiting the acreage on which a water right could be issued to 160 acres." [56]

Maxwell said the substitute the minority proposed for article 9 would have given the landowners entire local control over the various canal systems. He said this was unacceptable because it would deny the government any recourse should a canal division decide to withdraw from the association after the ranchers subscribed to the stock. [57]

Under the minority's amendments, the expenses of each canal system would have been met by the landowners within the division and the power for levying assessments would have been given to a locally elected three-member board of water commissioners. The majority favored assessments apportioned equally against each share of stock. The articles also provided for the appointment of the board of water commissioners by the Board of Governors of the Water Users' Association, which was to have responsibiilty for the daily management of the organization.

Maxwell said local assessments would give the local boards control over the Board of Governors, an action which would postpone the reservoir. He said the minority was going directly opposite to government recommendations. [58]

The substitute was defeated, so by the time the meeting adjourned nine of the 20 articles had been accepted, and the remainder were expected to be adopted before the next day passed. [59] Only one major question remained, [60] and this concerned article 13, which also dealt with assessments and placing government liens on the land. [61]

The fight over assessments was partly a restatement of the minority's position about how the cost of the individual canal operations should be met. The minority pointed out the expense of running some canals was high, but Kibbey said this was "due to mismanagement and under cooperative management the costs would be reduced to a minimum and equalized." [62] The minority concurred assessments should be divided equally among all shareholders when common benefits were to be derived.

The minority preferred "a lien on the right to the use of water" instead of "a lien on the lands of the shareholders," which led Maxwell to remark, "The effort of the minority seems to be to perpetuate the conflicting insecure conditions which have been the curse of this valley." [63]

Maxwell also said the reservoir system, if it became a reality, should be thought of as a single system, not a series of individual systems, and should be operated on an equal basis. He said the quarreling that had resulted from the conflicting systems the past 20 years should have been a lesson for them. [64]

Heard, in presenting the amendments, said the minority's views had been misunderstood by some, and misinterpreted by others. He said the amendments were offered in the belief they would be best for the reservoir movement. [65]

Woolf said the minority was handicapped in explaining

its position because things would be said that should not be said in public. He attacked the articles as being arbitrary and said they would change conditions in the Valley. It should be kept in mind, he said, that conditions in part of the Valley, his own, were nearly as outlined in the reclamation law in that the people owned the canals, while in the other part of the Valley this was not so. Given these circumstances, he thought it unjust to require equal assessments among the canals. Nonetheless, the amendments were defeated, and the articles in their entirety were adopted with pledges of support from the south side minority. [66]

Fowler later summarized opposition to the articles:

The opposition of the minority was due, first, to a reluctance to abandon old and adopt new methods; second, to an unwillingness to accept the principle, laid down in the National Irrigation Act itself, that water should be appurtenant to the land; third, to a fear of jeopardizing capital invested in so-called "floating water rights," which, it was feared, would become valueless if water was attached to the land; fourth, to unwillingness on the part of owners of large holdings to subdivide, as required by said act, who yet wanted to become beneficiaries under it; fifth, to a fear of a merger of the canal systems into one association, and consequent loss of local control; sixth, to ignorance of the plan proposed and the benefits expected; seventh, to pure selfishness and personal interest. [67]

Immediately after the articles were adopted, there followed what the *Enterprise* described as a "love feast" [68] and the Water Storage Conference Committee named Fowler as the first president of the Water Users' Association and Wilbur as the vice president. The Conference Committee named them and the other members of the Executive Committee to serve as the Board of Governors until the first annual election, April 5, 1904. [69] The Conference Committee then wrote into the articles the names of 30 men to serve as the first Council, which was the association's legislative branch, with responsibility for writing its bylaws. [70]

Also written into the articles were the names of the incorporators. They were identified, the *Republican* said, so "the reader may understand. . .the unanimity of action in the adoption of the articles of incorporation. . .it will be noted that includes the representatives of every hitherto conflicting interest in the valley." [71] Forty-one men were named. [72]

However, the "love feast" did not last long and by the time the articles were filed with the Maricopa County recorder, two of the original governors had withdrawn as well as 14 members of the Council. Of the 49 men who became incorporators, the names of 23 were not among the original list.

Before the Conference Committee adjourned just before noon January 22, 1903, it decided not to dissolve itself so it would be available should its counsel be needed. It passed a resolution thanking the newspapers for having withheld publication of the articles previous to their adoption and it called a mass meeting of citizens for 10 a.m. Saturday at the Dorris Opera House so the articles could be explained and the landowners encouraged to subscribe to them. Fowler, Heard and Christy were appointed to make arrangements for the meeting. [73]

The capital stock of the Water Users' Association was divided into 250,000 shares with a par value of $15 for a total of $3,750,000. For each acre of land, owners could obtain one share up to a maximum of 160. In elections, each share represented one vote. Each share carried with it a right to water for irrigating the land it represented in an amount proportionate to all stored and developed water, but "the whole amount of water actually delivered from all sources [could] not exceed the amount necessary for the proper cultivation of said lands." [74]

The articles did not follow completely the recommendations approved by the Water Storage Conference Committee on October 2, 1902, but the plan contained a statement which permitted changes.

"It must be understood," the plan said, "that *all the recommendations contained in this report and embodied in the plan proposed are subject to any modification which should be advised by the Secretary of the Interior. . ."* [Emphasis added.] [75]

"It was a comparatively simple proposition to reach a general outline agreement in October," Fowler said, "but quite another to blaze a new trail—to formulate, without precedent or guide, articles of incorporation which should be broad in scope, clear in statement, carefully worded and legally phrased, just to all interests and adapted to existing conditions." [76]

The articles became the model for water users' associations in other areas, [77] including Pinal and Yuma counties in Arizona.

The day after the articles were adopted, it was decided to hold two meetings at the opera house at 10 a.m. and 2 p.m. To encourage the attendance of farmers and ranchers from the eastern part of the Valley, round trip railroad tickets from Tempe were sold for 35 cents and from Mesa for 50 cents. [78]

However, the morning session "was not largely attended as had been expected but the theater was well filled in the afternoon." [79] The reason the building was not packed, according to the *Republican,* "was because a large part of the water users are already so well satisfied with the situation they did not care to waste any more time till there was an opportunity to get up the (subscription) books and sign something." [80] The accuracy of that statement remained to be demonstrated.

Kibbey, the main speaker in the morning, took a conciliatory approach toward the minority.

"There have been differences in the committee," he said, "but they arose from honest motives and were the result of men looking at the proposition from different viewpoints. Any subject that causes thought is sure to cause difference of opinion, and any matter that can be unanimously settled by a body of men either requires but little thought or is hardly worth the disposition." [81]

Kibbey reviewed the articles, praising especially the provision in the reclamation law that made water appurtenant to the land.

"The contrary system of floating water rights has been the cause of more pernicious litigation than any other phase in irrigation problems, and the new law will eliminate all this," he said. [82]

Maxwell gave the principal address in the afternoon, explaining the articles and remarking that if the dam had been built ten years before, the annual increase in farm production would have been $2,500,000, enough to have paid for the reservoir each year. He said he had asked Christy, president of the Valley Bank, to calculate the weight of that much gold, and it came to 10,325 pounds.

"Just think, now, if we had that 10,325 pounds of ten and twenty dollar gold pieces here on the platform, representing the prosperity of the country, don't you suppose it would arouse your interest," Maxwell said. "And suppose that we had an annual harvest festival and that sum was to be distributed, don't you suppose that the festival would be well attended?" [83]

Maxwell said the Tonto reservoir would be built but never by private capital. If a landowner did not want to join the Water Users' Association, that did not bother Maxwell.

"No man need come into this association unless he wants to," he said. "If he has speculative water rights and thinks they are more valuable to him than this grand scheme or plan, let him hold onto them and carry them to the grave with him if he wants to." [84]

In addition to Maxwell and Kibbey, other lawyers spoke at the morning and afternoon meetings. While some of them expressed reservations, all endorsed the articles as being fair and urged the farmers and ranchers to join the association. However, no one could subscribe for shares because the Water Users' Association was not yet a legal entity. It would not come into lawful existence until the articles were filed with the county recorder. Because of this, Fowler announced another mass meeting at the opera house for the next Saturday, [85] but this was delayed until February 9. [86]

Kibbey and Maxwell spoke at a meeting of Tempe Canal owners January 31. Kibbey told them that by joining the association, they would not lose their right and title to the Tempe Canal nor would they have to buy and pay for the Arizona Canal or any other. Maxwell, who spoke for more than two hours, said he was not there to plead for them to join the association. He said the dam would be built, and if they did not join, their children and grandchildren would have occasion to curse them for a terrible error. [87]

On February 3, Maxwell spoke to farmers under the Utah and Mesa canals, saying should the reservoir not be built, they had lost nothing, but there was everything to gain, which had been the purpose of writing the articles. For those who had floating water rights, he said they would have until the reservoir was completed, and until certificates of ownership in the Salt River Valley Water Users' Association were issued, to attach the rights to land. Maxwell said it would take at least three years to build the dam. [88]

Meantime, the Conference Committee sent letters January 31 to those who had been selected as incorporators, asking them to come to Room 8 in the Nicholson Building in Phoenix to sign the articles before February 6, the day it was hoped they would be ready for filing with the county recorder. [89]

There was hope opposition to the articles was fading, but it did not turn out that way. The Conference Committee received a letter from Woolf saying he could not in good conscience sign the articles, and Heard said he would not sign because his views were different. [90] The minority's third prominent member, Wilbur, said he did not agree with the articles, but thought it was better if everyone signed them. He was ill so the committee on February 5 sent the engrossed copy of the articles in care of W. H. Wallace to Mesa to get Wilbur's signature. [91]

The Conference Committee also announced the subscription books would be ready for signing Monday morning, [92] and it agreed to recommend to the Board of Governors an assessment of 10 cents per share be levied to pay association expenses until 1904. The committee estimated that 160,000 acres would sign so $16,000 would be raised. The committee also named subscription committees for all but the Tempe and San Francisco canals [93] and issued a formal call for a mass meeting Monday afternoon, saying in part:

Prompt action is imperative to the immediate success of this great movement. If you delay, you delay your own progress and that of the entire valley.

Mr. Maxwell will leave Phoenix on Tuesday morning, to be gone about a month. He will go to Washington and it should be made evident before then that the landowners of this valley want the Salt River reservoir built immediately. The only way to demonstrate this is to subscribe to the articles of incorporation. [94]

The articles were filed with the county recorder at 4:15 p.m. Saturday, February 7. [95] Replacing Woolf and Heard on the Board of Governors were M. A. Stanford and Sam F. Webb. Both men originally had been named to serve on the Council. [96]

On the same day the articles were filed, the majority of the Tempe Canal water users, among them Woolf and Heard, voted to keep their canal out of the association and adopted the following resolution:

That the shareholders of the Tempe Canal. . .approve of the amendments to the articles of incorporation; and that our representatives are hereby authorized to use every means in their power to have these amendments adopted, either through the secretary of the interior or otherwise. [97]

The Tempe Canal shareholders, at this or another meeting, voted to send Carl Hayden to Washington to explain the minority position. The shareholders also appointed a five-member committee to investigate and make estimates of the cost of building a groundwater pumping system for use in the summer months. The committee included Woolf, Heard and Hayden. [98] After Arizona statehood, Hayden served as its first congressman in the U.S. House of Representatives and later as U.S. senator.

The action of the Tempe Canal in going after pumped water prompted the *Gazette* to observe:

One of the first objections raised by the minority members of the Water Storage Conference Committee to the articles adopted recently was that the shareholders were not guaranteed that subterranean water would not be forced on them, and one of the first things done by the minority members after withdrawing from the organization was to put on foot a plan whereby the Tempe Canal could be furnished with the same kind of water. [99]

About the Tempe Canal's decision to stay out of the association, the *Gazette* said, "it improves the chances for securing the reservoir. The action can have no effect other than to remove all objections to the articles. . ." [100] The *Republican* made the same assessment adding, "It can now be shown to the government that the lands for which a reservoir is sought are lands which will provide a large proportion of new homes for settlers. . ." [101]

On February 8, the *Gazette* printed a small item from Washington saying the interior secretary in a few days would make a decision on the first sites for reservoir construction. Newell recommended three sites, but they were not named. [102]

Before the mass meeting the next day, Vernon L. Clark was elected temporary chairman of the Council. W. M. Messinger, A. J. Peters, W. A. Wilson, William MacDonald and J. Wilfred Broomell were named to serve on the committee on bylaws. [103]

At the mass meeting, Maxwell explained why the minority amendments if adopted would ruin any chance of ever getting the reservoir. He was confident the articles would be approved by the interior secretary inasmuch as they already had the unofficial endorsement of Newell. [104] Maxwell said the Water Users' Association was open to all people in the Valley, but if the south siders elected to stay out, they could never say their rights had been denied. [105]

Maxwell left for Washington the next day, undoubtedly with a copy of the articles, and the *Republican* reported 5,000 acres has been signed into the association. [106] Despite the mass meetings and favorable newspaper stories, progress in getting signatures was slow. Meetings were held in Mesa and Lehi, the latter an area served by the Utah Canal, to explain the articles and to hear objections to them. [107] Subscription committee members said they found opposition in two sections of the Valley. [108] The sections were Tempe and Lehi, but many north side farmers with old water rights did not come in at once, either. One thing said to have influenced some of the south siders to sign up was a report government engineers were running a line for a new canal east of Mesa to bring in 50,000 acres of desert land. [109]

Meanwhile, the people of Florence and surrounding country adopted their own articles of incorporation and signed in acreage as they continued their pursuit of the San Carlos dam. Kibbey advised them in the preparation of the articles. [110]

On March 12, Secretary Hitchcock, on recommendation of the Geological Survey, gave provisional approval to the articles of the Salt River Valley Water Users' Association and to the construction of the Tonto Basin dam and four other projects. This meant for the Valley, pending the adoption of the articles by the water users, the Reclamation Service could proceed with such preliminary work as construction of roads, purchase of land and preparation of contracts. [111]

By then, too, Hayden was in Washington where he met with Hitchcock and Charles D. Walcott, director of the Geological Survey. After apparently conferring with them, Hayden on March 13 sent a letter to Hitchcock in which he asked "whether the government can deal with any form of organization in receiving payments from reservoirs." If the government could, Hayden asked the Interior Department to "determine upon some general form of organization to be taken as a basis in organizing every reservoir district" with a provision that where local conditions required it, changes be permitted with the interior secretary's approval. [112]

Hayden also asked Hitchcock to determine "as soon as practicable" the particular form of organization to be used in the Salt River Valley and "whether it is possible. . .for the government to enter into contracts with the owners of vested rights to the natural appropriated flow of streams upon which reservoirs are to be constructed to deliver them a regulated flow from the reservoirs in lieu of such vested rights." [113]

News of Hitchcock's provisional approval of the articles and construction of the Tonto Basin project was published in Phoenix March 13. The *Republican's* story, filed by Charles C. Randolph, included his observation,

At the end of the line it would appear that it is up to the people of the Salt River Valley. If they comply with the government requirements the reservoir undoubtedly will be constructed. I have it on good authority that there will be no delay on the part of the government once the way is made clear for beginning the work. [114]

Coincidental with this news, Maxwell returned from Washington and said, "The Interior Department is ready to issue the order for the construction of the dam just as soon as the people of the Valley are ready and the sooner the conditions are complied with, the sooner will that reservoir be constructed. There is nothing to be done in Washington toward securing the reservoir. What remains to be done must be done right here in the Valley." [115]

Maxwell cautioned the longer the delay in construction the more opportunity for some other place to get ahead of the Tonto Basin dam. [116]

He also thought it was wrong that committees should be traveling about the Valley canvassing for subscriptions for shares. "The landowners should go at once—everyone of them—to the office of the association and see that they are enrolled as subscribers in the association," he said. [117]

Maxwell's wife, son and daughter had accompanied him to Phoenix. He recalled he had promised the people the previous August that he would remain in the Valley until the dam was built and he intended to make good his word. From the train station, the family went directly to the Broomell ranch, which took water from the Maricopa Canal. Maxwell soon bought the ranch for $8,000. [118]

The *Republican* now used the fact that government engineers were running canal lines outside the irrigated area to warn farmers to get into line and to attack the minority, which continued to raise questions about the articles. The newspaper said,

A crisis impossible of exaggeration has been reached in the history of this valley. It is impossible to conceive of a greater calamity than the diversion of the flood waters of the river for all time to lands not embraced under our own canals. . .

The Hammer club comprises a very limited membership, but it has had sufficient influence so far to cause the movement for storage to proceed haltingly and slowly. Do the knockers propose

to continue their tactics? And will the businessmen of Phoenix and the ranchers of this valley have so little firmness as to permit these tactics to continue? [119]

The *Gazette* made the same points, reporting that it was "said that the government would order an investigation of the normal flow of the Salt River, together with the exact amount of water used for irrigation purposes, with the idea of constructing the reservoir to impound the flood waters for the use of the new lands." [120]

Fowler sent letters to nonresident landowners informing them of the association and its plans, telling them,

Finally, we wish to impress upon you the fact heretofore suggested that this is the only plan proposed, the only one suggested, and the only one that can have any hope of success. [121]

At a meeting of the Board of Governors March 16, it was revealed that 40,000 acres had been subscribed. Maxwell and others expressed surprise that there should be any hesitancy to sign up. [122] Fowler read a letter from a Washington official, probably Newell, that said,

From certain newspaper clippings I observe there is a disposition to hold back among some of the people. I do not understand the basis of this opposition unless it be from the large landowners because it affords them no chance for personal gain. A careful reading of the law shows that it was constructed for the benefit of all landowners and will prevent speculation in land and water rights. I understand that the Secretary of the Interior will most rigidly enforce the law with regard to the small landowner and protect that interest. He will also require for the government complete security for the investment. Before the government starts to work on the reservoir a full plan must be worked out by the people and complete security given that the expenditure will be returned to the government. Anything that looks like speculation will be opposed and the water shall be the basis of such rights. I am positive that the Secretary of the Interior will not discuss the matter until the full plan has been presented to him. [123]

The people were chided by the *Gazette* for having shown not "the slightest enthusiasm" when the news came that the Tonto dam had received tentative approval. The *Gazette* contrasted the reaction with Montrose, Colorado, when it was learned there that Washington had selected the Gunnison tunnel as one of the first projects. "...excitement and enthusiasm were at fever heat," the newspaper said, then quoted a dispatch:

The telephone lines were in continuous use with country towns and farms. Men were congratulating each other on the streets and general rejoicing was heard everywhere. Enemies of years joined hands in congratulations.

The *Gazette* added, editorially:

In view of this, is it any wonder why people say that it is time for Arizona to wake up? When the announcement was made yesterday that the Board of Governors had received subscriptions to but 40,000 acres of land the effect was startling. There should have been not less than 150,000 during that time. [124]

Augustus C. Bartlett, president of the Bartlett-Heard Land and Cattle Co., who was visiting from Chicago, undertook in a letter to Walcott on March 16 to explain the position of large landowners, denying they had any "desire to secure advantages in the use of stored water over their neighbors owning small bodies." Bartlett said his company would not benefit "except it may be through the possible willingness of the Secretary of the Interior to grant us regulated flow in exchange for a larger quantity of intermittent water." [125]

Bartlett denied accusations that his company wanted "to postpone water storage." Rather, he said, the water users would "follow any suggestions that come directly from the Secretary of the Interior. They only want to know what is necessary to secure water." [126]

He said he had learned,

from a number of water users, who are among the most substantial and reliable in the valley, that an Association has been formed containing some features that appear to them as unfair, inconsistent and speculative, and that the farmers are being coerced into joining, through persistently reiterated statements that "this is the only plan which the Secretary of the Interior will consider; and the consequent fear that the reservoir will not be built; or if built, they will receive no benefit, unless they acquiesce in this initiative movement."

...notwithstanding all the pressure which has been brought to bear by this (Water Users') Association through a large number of solicitors who have been in the field for nearly two months, I am informed that they have secured about the same acreage as was "signed up" in a few days under the original plan adopted October 2, 1902. [127]

Hitchcock, on March 21, replied to Hayden's March 13 letter saying that the interior secretary could "deal with an organization in receiving payments from the individuals who have contracted for water rights," and it was not "necessary nor advisable at the present time to determine upon a general form of organization to be taken as a basis in organizing every reservoir district." [128]

Further, "The particular form of organization for the Salt River Valley may be modified in the future as necessities may require, but for the present the form already adopted is considered sufficient." [129]

As to "a regulated flow from the reservoirs," Hitchcock said, "It is probably possible in completing the details of distribution to make arrangements whereby the owners of vested water rights may be benefited," but it was not essential to make that determination then and could "safely be left for the initiation by the local organization of water-users. Their united opinion upon the matter should have weight in the final determination." [130]

Hitchcock also addressed the situation in the Salt River Valley,

where there are several thousand owners of small tracts who desire to be supplied with water under the terms of the law, and in other similar cases, it is clearly essential to insure unity of purpose and to secure the best results, that such owners unite in an organization which will act as the agent for the individuals. It is also essential that such organization as a whole guarantee that the payments be made and that the strongest possible security be given the government for the faithful performance of contracts which may be made.

In the case now presented, it appears that such an organization has been made and after many weeks of conference and debate, articles have been adopted and signatures are being obtained to these articles. There is, however, a minority consisting mainly of large landowners who are in opposition and it is this minority which is appealing from the action of the majority. [131]

Hayden reacted to Hitchcock's comments about the minority by sending another letter, saying they were not "speculators in desert lands," and that the lands under the

Tempe Canal were "subdivided into as small, if not smaller, average individual holdings as any other sections of the valley." [132] Hayden added:

There are also a large number of farmers under the other old canals who agree with us in objecting to the present form of these articles. The members of the Geological Survey were sadly misinformed when they gave you this information. [133]

He told Hitchcock, "The articles were adopted upon the plea of Mr. George H. Maxwell that if they were not accepted in the form he desired, in his opinion, the Secretary of the Interior would not order the construction of the reservoir." [134]

Hayden said that the Department of the Interior had vital concerns, "such as the nature of the security offered for the faithful performance of contracts with the government," while the people living under the reservoir had concerns which were theirs alone, not the government's, "such as the payment of assessments for maintenance of canals, etc." [135]

If the Interior Department would point out in what way the minority's amendment conflicted with the reclamation law or department policy and would draw up "the form of those articles wherein the Department is concerned. . .the same will be accepted without dissent," Hayden said. He enclosed with his letter a copy of the letter sent by Bartlett to Walcott. [136]

By March 23, the Water Users' Association reported the acres subscribed exceeded 50,000. While subscriptions were not coming in as fast as Fowler and the soliciting committees desired, they said they believed their approach of not pressing the farmers and giving them every opportunity to understand what they were signing was the right one. [137]

It also was revealed that Walcott would arrive in Phoenix in two days. The *Republican* expected his presence would "be of great benefit to the storage movement and is surely a strong indication that the government is in earnest in respect of the Tonto enterprise," [138] while the *Gazette* thought it "should convince those who have held back for fear there might be some hitch and the valley would fail to secure this reservoir." [139]

Walcott's visit to Arizona was prompted by his desire to see some of the five projects that had received preliminary approval from Hitchcock. Walcott said he has been authorized "to make estimates and plans of the Tonto

reservoir," as well as to look into aspects of the proposition. The Salt River Valley and the Tonto Basin were the first on his list of places to visit. [140]

Casa Grande Valley water users took advantage of Walcott's arrival to argue in behalf of the San Carlos reservoir. On March 28, Walcott met with Dr. G. M. Brockway, Charles D. Reppy and W. Y. Price of Florence. The Pinal County men contended construction of the Tonto reservoir could not be accomplished except through a perversion of the national irrigation law. In addition, they argued, under the law the amount of money Arizona could expect was insufficient to build more than one reservoir and the reasons to build the San Carlos dam were more compelling that those to build the Tonto Basin dam. [141]

Walcott's presence also may have inspired Woolf to write a long essay, published March 30, 1903, by the *Enterprise,* expanding upon his opposition to the articles. Woolf questioned whether it was necessary for landowners who owned their own canals to join an association, or corporation, in order to receive the benefits of the National Reclamation Act. He contended the law contemplated the formation of some form of organization only after the government had turned the irrigation works over to the landowners, and that was not to happen until "the payments required. . .are made for the major portion of the lands irrigated. . ." [142]

Woolf argued the law did not mean that the organization whatever its form should "become the agent of the government to keep its accounts, assess, collect and pay to the government the money due to it from the individual members of the organization." He pointed out that section 5 of the reclamation law provided "annual installments shall be paid to the receiver of the local land office." He concluded from this that the government would "in all cases deal directly with the individual landowners or entryman as the case may be, through the general land office, just as it has always heretofore dealt with the public lands." [143]

The same day Woolf's letter was published, Walcott left on a trip during which he viewed the Salt River Valley, the Arizona Dam on the Salt River, the Tonto Basin and dam site, and the proposed location for a dam on the San Pedro River at the abandoned town of Charleston, 30 miles above Benson. [144]

1. *Phoenix Enterprise,* December 1, 1902.
2. *Arizona Republican* (Phoenix), December 2, 1902.
3. *Ibid.*
4. *Arizona Gazette* (Phoenix), December 11, 1902.
5. *Gazette,* December 9, 1902.
6. *Ibid.*
7. *Republican,* December 17, 1902.
8. *Ibid.,* December 25, 1902; *Gazette,* December 23, 1902.
9. *Republican,* December 28, 1902, January 2, 3, 1903; *Gazette,* December 31, 1902.
10. *Republican,* January 3, 1903.
11. *Ibid.,* January 5, 1903.
12. *Ibid.,* January 7, 1903.
13. *Gazette,* January 6, 1903.
14. *Ibid.*
15. *Ibid.*
16. *Ibid.*
17. *Republican,* January 7, 1903; *Gazette,* January 7, 1903.
18. *Ibid.*
19. *Ibid.*
20. *Gazette,* January 21, 1903.
21. *Ibid.,* February 10, 1903.
22. *Ibid.,* January 7, 1903.
23. *Ibid.*
24. *Ibid.*
25. *Republican,* January 12, 1903.
26. *Gazette,* January 16, 1903.
27. *Enterprise,* January 17, 1903.
28. *Republican,* January 18, 1903; *Gazette,* January 18, 1903.
29. Minority Report, Salt River Valley Water Storage Conference Committee, January 17, 1903. National Archives, Record Group 48, Lands & Railroad Division, Salt River Project Archives (hereafter SRPA).
30. *Ibid.*

31. *Ibid.*
32. *Ibid.*
33. *Ibid.*
34. *Ibid.*
35. *Ibid.*
36. *Ibid.*
37. *Ibid.; Gazette,* January 18, 1903.
38. *Ibid.*
39. *Ibid.*
40. See Articles of Incorporation, Salt River Valley Water Users' Association, SRPA.
41. *Gazette,* January 18, 1903.
42. *Ibid.*
43. *Republican,* January 19, 1903.
44. *Gazette,* January 18, 1903.
45. *Enterprise,* January 20, 1903; *Gazette,* January 21, 1903.
46. See proposed amendments of the minority to the Articles of Incorporation, Salt River Valley Water Users' Association, SRPA.
47. *Enterprise,* January 20, 1903.
48. *Ibid.*
49. *Ibid.*
50. *Ibid.*
51. *Gazette,* January 21, 1903.
52. *Ibid.*
53. *Gazette,* January 25, 1903.
54. *Republican,* January 21, 1903.
55. *Proceedings of First Conference of Engineers of the Reclamation Service* (Washington: Government Printing Office, 1904), p. 142.
56. *Ibid.*
57. *Gazette,* January 21, 1903.
58. *Ibid.*
59. *Ibid.*
60. *Republican,* January 21, 1903.
61. *Enterprise,* January 21, 1903.
62. *Gazette,* January 25, 1903.
63. *Enterprise,* January 21, 1903.
64. *Ibid.*
65. *Ibid.; Gazette,* January 21, 1903.
66. *Gazette,* January 22, 1903.
67. *Proceedings of. . .Reclamation Service,* pp. 141-142.
68. *Enterprise,* January 21, 1903.
69. *Gazette,* January 22, 1903; *Republican,* January 22, 1903.
70. *Ibid.,* J. C. Adams, N. M. Broadway, J. Wilfred Broomell, W. W. Dobson, B. A. Fickas, Frank Fowler, S. S. Green, James Johnson, Cyrus G. Jones, Will Kay, W. J. Kingsbury, M. W. Messinger, John P. Orme, Charles Peterson, J. T. Priest, L. J. Rice, M. A. Stanford, C. S. Stewart, I. V. Stewart, Joseph Stuart, Fred Tait, H. J. Underhill, H. G. Van Fossen, A. P. Walbridge, Henry E. Ware, Sam F. Webb, Henry Wilkie, William Wilson, T. W. Pemberton, Neils Peterson.
71. *Republican,* January 22, 1903.
72. *Ibid., Gazette,* January 22, 1903. Adams, Alkire, Broadway, Broomell, Chandler, Christy, Dobson, Fickas, F. A. Fowler, Frank Fowler, Green, Heard, Johnson, ·Jones, Kay, Kingsbury, Messinger, John Orme, Lin Orme, Parker, Pemberton, Charles Peterson, Neils Peterson, Priest, Rice, Simkins, Stanford, Stewart, Stewart, Stuart, Tait, Underhill, Van Fossen, Walbridge, Wallace, Wilson, Woolf, Ware, Webb, Wilbur, Wilkie.
73. *Gazette,* January 22, 1903.
74. *Salt River Project, Final History to 1916,* unpublished manuscript, Vol. I, p. 27, SRPA.
75. *Proceedings of. . .Reclamation Service,* pp. 143-147; *Republican,* October 3, 1903.
76. *Ibid.,* p. 142.
77. *Final History to 1916,* Vol. I, p. 18.
78. *Republican,* January 23, 1903.
79. *Ibid.,* January 25, 1903.
80. *Ibid.*

81. *Gazette,* January 25, 1903.
82. *Ibid.*
83. *Ibid.*
84. *Ibid.*
85. *Ibid.; Republican,* January 25, 1903.
86. *Republican,* February 3, 1903.
87. *Ibid.,* February 1, 1903.
88. *Ibid.,* February 4, 1903.
89. *Ibid.,* February 1, 1903.
90. *Gazette,* February 6, 1903.
91. *Ibid.; Republican,* February 6, 1903.
92. *Republican,* February 6, 1903.
93. *Gazette,* February 6, 1903.
94. *Republican,* February 6, 1903.
95. *Book 13, Articles of Incorporation, Maricopa County Recorder's Office,* pp. 603-630, Phoenix, Arizona; *Arizona Republic* (Phoenix), June 17, 1977.
96. *Final History to 1916,* Vol. I, p. 38, Council members, Vol. I, p. 35, incorporators, Vol. I, p. 19.
97. *Gazette,* February 10, 1903.
98. *Ibid.*
99. *Gazette,* February 11, 1903.
100. *Ibid,* February 10, 1903.
101. *Republican,* February 10, 1903.
102. *Gazette,* February 8, 1903.
103. *Ibid.,* February 10, 1903.
104. *Ibid.*
105. *Republican,* February 10, 1903.
106. *Ibid.,* February 11, 1903.
107. *Republican,* February 13, 21, 26, 1903; *Enterprise,* February 16, 1903.
108. *Republican,* March 11, 1903; *Enterprise,* March 9, 1903.
109. *Republican,* March 9,1903.
110. *Enterprise,* February 10, 1903; *Republican,* February 26, 1903.
111. *Final History to 1916,* pp. 18, 57-58; *Republican,* March 14, 1903; *Gazette,* March 14, 1903.
112. Carl Hayden to E. A. Hitchcock, March 13, 1903, SRPA.
113. *Ibid.*
114. *Republican,* March 14, 1903.
115. *Gazette,* March 14, 1903.
116. *Ibid.*
117. *Republican,* March 14, 1903.
118. *Gazette,* May 13, 1903.
119. *Republican,* March 15, 1903.
120. *Gazette,* March 15, 1903.
121. *Ibid.*
122. *Republican,* March 17, 1903; *Gazette,* March 17, 1903.
123. *Gazette,* March 17, 1903.
124. *Ibid.*
125. A. C. Bartlett to Charles D. Walcott, March 16, 1903, SRPA.
126. *Ibid.*
127. *Ibid.*
128. E. A. Hitchcock to Carl Hayden, March 21, 1903, SRPA.
129. *Ibid.*
130. *Ibid.*
131. *Ibid.*
132. Carl Hayden to E. A. Hitchcock, March 25, 1903, SRPA.
133. *Ibid.*
134. *Ibid.*
135. *Ibid.*
136. *Ibid.*
137. *Republican,* March 24, 1903.
138. *Ibid.*
139. *Gazette,* March 26, 1903.
140. *Republican,* March 26, April 19, 1903; *Gazette,* March 26, 1903.
141. *Republican,* March 29, 1903.
142. J. W. Woolf, *Enterprise,* March 30, 1903.
143. *Ibid.*
144. *Enterprise,* April 20, 1903.

April - July 1903

A heavy flow of water came down the Salt River in the first days of April 1903. Water five-feet deep poured over the Arizona Dam. [1] At Tempe, the river ran six feet below the "famous flood of 1891 when the bridge of the Maricopa & Phoenix (rail)road was lifted from its piers and carried away." [2] In some places, the river ran a mile wide, and the telegraph wires came down. The rushing water damaged the Utah and Tempe canals, and the steel cable used to guide the ferry across the river at the Tempe Crossing broke. [3]

Frank P. Trott estimated "a discharge equaling the maximum stage of water on the second of the month would fill the reservoir in less than ten days." [4]

On April 10, while at the camp of the U.S. Geological Survey in the Tonto Basin about 15 miles above the dam site, Charles D. Walcott wrote a report about his "investigation of the conditions affecting irrigation in the Salt River Valley of Arizona accompanied by certain recommendations in relation to the Department [of the Interior] dealing with the problem of building a storage reservoir in the Tonto Basin for supplying water to the lands in public and private ownership in the Salt River Valley." [5]

In the report, which Walcott sent to his boss, Secretary of the Interior Ethan A. Hitchcock, Walcott said the ideal irrigation system in the Valley should include provision for "a permanent diversion dam in the Salt River just below the mouth of the Rio Verde with one large main canal on the north side and one on the south side." He said the cost of maintaining the present canals and delivering water varied from 50 cents to $1.50 per acre. [6]

Walcott said the Salt River Valley Water Users' Association's articles of incorporation were sufficient to carry out repayment to the government of construction of the dam and to take care of water delivery, but, "The modifications proposed by the minority would, if adopted, weaken the security of the Government through the Association and would make the administration of the distributing system complex and impracticable." He also said the minority modifications would "seriously limit the power of the Government to enforce its rules and regulations through the Association." [7]

Walcott recommended to Hitchcock that the citizens of the Valley be informed Walcott had been granted authority to acquire the "necessary property, rights of way, etc., preliminary to the construction of irrigation work on the Salt River," and "construction remains subject to the feasibility of obtaining the necessary rights, and the adjustment of private claims. . ." The property and private claims included the dam site belonging to the Hudson Reservoir and Canal Co. and the ranches of Tonto Basin settlers whose land would be flooded when the reservoir filled. [8]

Walcott also proposed Hitchcock inform the people,

That the Department has considered the appeal of the minority of the Salt River Valley Water Storage Conference Committee and decided that any interposition on the part of the Department would *appear to be unnecessary and tend rather to delay and complicate affairs and would not result to advantage in the execution of the law.* [9]

On April 17, Walcott was in Phoenix when he received a telegram from Hitchcock approving the April 10 report and proposals. Hitchcock said Walcott could make known to the Water Users' Association the contents of the telegram. Walcott immediately informed Benjamin A. Fowler, president of the association, he would like to meet with the Board of Governors, the leaders of the minority, and representatives of the press at 9:30 a.m. the next day. [10]

At the gathering, Walcott recounted his visit to the Tonto Basin. With him, he said, had been civil, consulting, and electrical engineers, as well as an expert in the manufacture of cement." [11] Walcott continued:

We found everything of the most favorable character. The bedrock, at 24 feet, is most satisfactory. The foundations are solid, and the abutting walls are as good as any engineer could ask for. We also found that the maps were correct in relation to the area that could be covered by water, and that a dam built to a height of 230 feet above the level of the stream bed would store all the water that would be apt to be available in any one year. The power proposition was pronounced by the engineer to be entirely feasible, and if this reservoir is constructed I think that this will be one of the first things undertaken, to facilitate construction of the dam, the operations of the cement works, etc. We found abundant supply of lime and an abundance of clay, and all the things necessary for the manufacture of hydraulic cement at this site. This will be a great economy, of course, as it will save the hauling of cement to the dam. [12]

He said he had informed Hitchcock of these findings, and the interior secretary had officially authorized him to inform the people of Hitchcock's approval, which, for the most part, was a restatement of Walcott's recommendations. However, the final sentence of Hitchcock's statement was new. It said,

As a whole the articles of incorporation of the association are approved. [13]

This statement drew applause. [14]

Walcott said he wished to add some personal observations, one being, "if in the early fall satisfactory proof has been given to the Interior secretary that security will be given for the money expended, work will undoubtedly be begun at an early day." [15]

"As you know," he said, "you have conditions here which are found nowhere else. . .And there is no other project that I know of. . .where the decisions [sic] remains with the people whether the work shall be done or not." [16]

At the meeting's end, Dwight B. Heard, John T. Woolf, and Ethelbert W. Wilbur asked Walcott to meet with them in the afternoon so they could present a compromise. Walcott consented, and at 3 o'clock they, along with members of the majority and the press, gathered. Wilbur spoke at length on the need for harmony and compromise, and Woolf said "that he and his associates would willingly give security to the government for the money expended by the government, but they were not inclined to sign articles which made the security run to the association." [17]

Woolf said the association might make unfair assessments for maintenance. The landowners under the older canals worried they might have to pay more than their share of maintenance costs, [18] but the fears of some of the ranchers went much deeper. For example, one farmer argued that a private individual who asked a rancher "to put a mortgage on his land in order to build him a reservoir. . . would make himself ridiculous. Then why should the government ask such a thing?" [19] This farmer expressed concern about the government buying the canals at exorbitant prices with the burden for paying falling on the landowners. [20] Some of the farmers, among them John P. Orme, who in later years would become the second president of the Water Users' Association, were willing to pay the costs of buying their own canal, but they wanted assurance they would not be taxed to pay for others. [21]

Heard presented Walcott with five proposed amendments and a new section to the articles. [22] The *Arizona Republican* characterized the amendments as nothing new, [23] while the new section dealt with a regulation right in the reservoir, to wit:

That the distribution of said natural appropriated flow of water to which our present vested rights entitle us shall be regulated through the use of the reservoir, thus greatly increasing the duty of and the beneficial use of such reservoir. [24]

Little was said about the merits of the minority proposals. Most of the discussion was about whether they should be considered. When the speeches were over, Walcott said it would be useless to submit any modifications of the articles to Hitchcock unless they were sent by the Water Users' Association. That ended the meeting, but the Board of Governors decided to take up the minority ideas the next Tuesday. [25]

While Walcott was in Arizona, there was no effort to gather subscriptions for shares in the association, [26] but by Tuesday morning another 3,000 acres had been signed. Still, this was not as good as hoped for. [27]

The governors met, deciding not to consider making changes in the articles but enlarging the committee to obtain subscriptions. [28]

In an editorial, the *Phoenix Enterprise* said it would take three years to build the reservoir, which would give the people time to fight out their differences. "Right now the thing to do is to get the reservoir," the *Enterprise* said. [29]

This produced an immediate letter to the editor from Maxwell, who concurred with the editorial, and admonished:

Delays are dangerous to such a degree that if the people of this valley realized how delay might jeopardize construction of this reservoir there is not a man in the valley who would not have his name enrolled as a shareholder in the association for all his land within twenty-four hours. . .

To DELAY now while differing ideas as to various points in the articles are exploited and argued back and forth between the many landowners who entertain all sorts of different views, would be to run a risk of losing the reservoir altogether—a risk which is simply appalling when we consider the consequences of the loss to the people of this valley. . .

The majority of the shareholders in the association can make any modifications they choose in the articles at any time, provided the

change be approved by the secretary of the Interior. The secretary of the Interior has not said by any means that the articles cannot be changed. On the contrary, he says: "The particular form of organization for the Salt River Valley may be modified in the future as necessities may require."

What more could any one ask for? To waste precious time and run the risk of losing the reservoir by wrangling for weeks and months over questions that we will have three years to thresh out while the reservoir is being built, is a policy so utterly suicidal that it is very hard to believe that the people of this valley will be led into such a fatal blunder. [30]

On April 25, the soliciting committees met to lay plans for getting subscriptions to the articles as quickly as possible. The committee members decided to make individual visits to the farmers. In addition, it was decided to call meetings of landowners under the various canals, the first being a meeting of Maricopa Canal owners Saturday, May 2. [31]

Most of the men who appeared for that meeting, which was attended by Maxwell, had not signed for shares. Maxwell had bought a ranch under the canal and his presence gave the farmers a chance to ask questions. Primarily, they were interested in knowing how a rancher, after signing for shares, could withdraw from the association. They were under the impression the moment they signed, their land was irredeemably mortgaged to the Water Users' Association. Maxwell said by remaining in the association, a rancher would be eligible for a reservoir right when the dam was completed. If a man did not take that right, he would be no worse off than he was before, and the water he might have taken would go to new lands. Those who believed in water storage were willing to bet that when the reservoir was completed no one would want to drop out. [32]

The farmers also wanted to make certain before signing the articles the association would own the canal through which they received water, and they would be assessed in buying the canals only for the one delivering water to them. They were told it was expected these matters would be attended to through a bylaw to be approved by the Water Users' Council, and through a resolution of the governors urging the water users under each canal to organize separate organizations to work independently or together in arranging to acquire the canals.

A committee of five was appointed to work with the water users of the other north side canals—the Grand, Salt River Valley, and Arizona—in developing a purchase plan. John Orme, who presided at the meeting, was selected chairman of the committee, and Maxwell was asked to serve as an adviser. [33]

Fowler read a letter at the meeting from Reclamation Service engineer Arthur P. Davis. Davis wrote the only thing holding up the purchase of machinery for the preliminary construction was the signing of sufficient land into the association. Davis said Walcott had given him instructions to wait until that happened.

Orme told a newspaperman as soon as the canal questions were resolved, he would sign the articles, and he believed the others who had held out would, too. [34]

However, when the Council met May 4, Kibbey advised

there was no need for a bylaw until the landowners or their committees determined the terms and conditions for buying the canals from the Arizona Water Co. and they petitioned the association to take action. Not until then would there be something for the Council to consider. [35]

The governors, in approving the resolution urging the landowners to organize to buy their canals, suggested they adjust among themselves their respective rights to the water carried. The governors wanted this done before the canals came under association management. Under the Maricopa Canal, some landowners held shares of stock in the canal, some owned water rights, some owned both shares and water rights, and some possessed neither. [36]

The resolution created some confusion, raising the impression the landowners under each canal would acquire their canals without regard to the association or to other canals. Maxwell later explained no canal could be acquired without approval of landowners under all the canals. He said the Arizona Canal Co. would not dispose of the canals piecemeal but all at the same time. Once this happened, the landowners under one system would stand the expense of paying only for theirs and not the others. If the Arizona Canal Co. set too high a price, the government could condemn the property, or it could build parallel canals, which would make the company's useless. For this reason, it could be expected the price would not be exorbitant. [37]

On May 5, a group of Valley residents left by train for the Grand Canyon where they were to meet President Theodore Roosevelt. [38] Arizona Governor Alexander O. Brodie met the president's train in Albuquerque, New Mexico, the same day. [39] At the Grand Canyon, Roosevelt gave a speech in which he said,

Arizona is one of the regions from which I expect most development through the wise action of the national congress in passing the irrigation act. The first and biggest experiment now in view under that act is the one that we are trying in Arizona. I look forward to the effects of irrigation, partly as applied by and through the government, still more as applied by individuals, and especially by associations of individuals, profiting by the example of government, possibly by help from it—I look forward to the effects of irrigation as being of greater consequence to all this region of country in the next fifty years than any other movement whatsoever. [40]

Years later, in April 1912, Thomas F. Weedin of Florence, Arizona, a newspaper editor and enemy of the construction of the Tonto reservoir ahead of the San Carlos dam, told a subcommittee of the U.S. House of Representatives it was Brodie who induced Roosevelt to order the building of the Tonto Basin dam. Weedin said when he learned Roosevelt was to visit the Grand Canyon, he arranged for a friend in Albuquerque to deliver to the president an article about the controversy over which dam should be built first. Weedin said this was so Roosevelt,

would have an opportunity to read it between Albuquerque and Grand Canyon, because I knew a committee was going up from here [Phoenix] to the Grand Canyon to interview him in this reservoir proposition, and when he got to the Grand Canyon and this committee waited on him and presented their case to him, he pulled out the paper and he says, "Here are a lot of facts and figures that I desire you to answer before I can take any stand on this

proposition," and some of them said that was a little paper published in Florence of not much consequence, and Mr. Roosevelt says, "He seems to be quoting facts and figures you do not seem to be able to answer, and I would like an answer before I consent to this change [of building the Tonto before the San Carlos]."

Well, the committee returned, and after Mr. Roosevelt had gone back to Washington, Gov. Brodie immediately went back, and Gov. Brodie, as I am informed from friends in Washington, went to President Roosevelt and made a personal effort on behalf of this [Tonto] reservoir site, and I am informed. . .that President Roosevelt called Secretary Hitchcock in and said, "Mr. Hitchcock, I want you to do in this reservoir matter whatever my friend, Gov. Brodie, wants done." As a result of that the reservoir site was adopted and was built and was named the Roosevelt Reservoir. [41]

While Weedin's account ignores Brodie's presence at the Grand Canyon and the previous approval of the Tonto's construction pending the signing of sufficient acreage into the Water Users' Association, there apparently was some truth to the story of Brodie's interceding with Roosevelt on behalf of the Tonto dam. Confirmation for this came from Joseph L. B. Alexander. Alexander and Brodie were both Arizonans and both enlisted in Roosevelt's Rough Riders and served in Cuba with the future president during the Spanish-American War in 1898. They were brother officers, Alexander entering service as a lieutenant and Brodie, a West Point graduate, as a major. Roosevelt, as president, named Brodie governor of the Arizona Territory and Alexander U.S. attorney.

Alexander said he delayed writing his account of Brodie's intercession until all of the participants to whom "publicity might cause embarrassment" had died. [42] He said he was told the story by Brodie upon the latter's return from a trip to Washington. According to Alexander, Brodie's account was that while construction of the Tonto reservoir was pending, Hitchcock had,

some doubt. . .as to his power and authority. . .to expend money in the construction of projects for the irrigation of lands held in private ownership. It was to remove that doubt and obtain from Mr. Hitchcock a favorable decision for the construction of the Roosevelt dam that Colonel Brodie visited Washington. However, after a short talk with the Secretary he found Mr. Hitchcock still inclined to believe that he had no authority under the reclamation law to construct the reservoir. [43]

Brodie informed Roosevelt of the situation,

Whereupon Colonel Brodie stated, Colonel Roosevelt said, "While the execution of the reclamation law is delegated to the Secretary of the Interior, and ordinarily, I would not interfere with the exercise of his discretion as to what lands should have reservoirs constructed for their irrigation, yet inasmuch as Arizona has no Senators to urge the rights and claims of its people, I feel that I should speak for them, and from what you tell me, I am convinced that the farmers of Salt River Valley should have the reservoir built for them. I will ask Mr. Hitchcock to come to the White House this evening and I want you to meet him here at 8 o'clock and we will consider the matter."

Colonel Brodie said that on that same evening, he met Secretary Hitchcock at the White House and that Colonel Roosevelt said to Mr. Hitchcock, "Mr. Secretary, Colonel Brodie is my friend, and whatever he tells you, you can depend upon. I am deeply concerned with the welfare of the people of Arizona and believe that the reservoir which Colonel Brodie wants constructed under the reclamation law for the people of Salt River Valley ought to be built, and I hope you may find it possible under the law to build it. I shall feel greatly gratified if it can be done."

Colonel Brodie said that after that statement, Colonel Roosevelt left him and Mr. Hitchcock alone to talk the matter over and from thence on he found the Secretary more favorable toward the construction of the Roosevelt dam than he had been theretofore, and that before he left Washington, Mr. Hitchcock assured him that the reservoir would be built because the President wished it. [44]

Weedin and Charles D. Reppy of Florence may have been the two most persistent opponents of the Tonto construction. Reppy, like Weedin, was a newspaper editor, but he also was a mining engineer and rancher. Reppy clipped newspaper and other articles unfavorable to the Tonto site and sent them to Hitchcock and Roosevelt. In the eyes of Weedin, Reppy and other Casa Grande Valley water users, the enemies were Maxwell, Walcott, Fowler and Frederick H. Newell, chief engineer of the Reclamation Service, who allegedly conspired to dump the San Carlos dam in favor of the Tonto.

The main arguments by Weedin, Reppy, et al; were these:

Construction of the San Carlos reservoir was the wedge used in winning passage of the national reclamation law. Besides serving as the "great exemplar of the noble National Irrigation policy of reclaiming arid public lands in order that home-seekers might find homes; it was also to succor something like 7,000 Pima Indians. . .who are starving because they are deprived of their water by white settlers." [45]. Immediately upon passage of the irrigation act, "there was a sudden cessation of aching for the starved Pimas" in favor of "the Salt River Valley, with its 20,000 live Americans and the fertile irrigated farms of Phoenix and vicinity." [46] Further, "though no man knoweth how it hath come about. . .the Government is to spend $2,500,000, not to reclaim public lands, but to improve the present property of private citizens of the Salt River Valley." [47] Because "there are in the Salt River Valley 50,000 acres more land now under private ownership than the whole reservoir can serve when built. . .it means. . .that not an acre of public land will be made available for the homesteader." [48] ". . .the object of the National Irrigation Act was not exactly to double the value of property already held by a community as prosperous as that of the Salt River Valley. . ." [49] Rather, the reclamation law was sought and approved "to make available for new home-seekers the now unproductive millions of arid acres in the West." [50]

During his Arizona visit, Walcott was questioned about construction of San Carlos reservoir. Walcott said the depth to bedrock was 65 feet, which made construction of the dam almost impracticable. In addition, he said construction was remote because the site was on an Indian reservation and an act of Congress would be required to make the location available. [51]

The clincher, however, for not undertaking the San Carlos project [aside from the desire of the Reclamation Service engineers to build at the Tonto Basin, so they could demonstrate quick success] was the Indians could not mortgage or put a lien on their land in order to assure the federal government it would be repaid for building the dam, reservoir, and associated works. [52]

Weedin and Reppy may not have been able to counter the last argument, but they brushed away the alleged impediments caused by depth to bedrock and the Indian reservation location of the San Carlos site.

Weedin pointed out the Geological Survey, i.e., Newell and Walcott, had recommended the San Carlos reservoir as feasible and "as an ideal storage proposition," [53] and Hitchcock in 1901 had urged Congress to appropriate $1,040,000 for its construction. [54] At that time the maximum depth of bedrock was estimated to be 74 feet, while Walcott in April 1903 was saying it was 65 feet. Weedin said the discovery that bedrock was not as deep as thought "will call for a reduction of nearly one-fifth in the estimates of the cost of the dam and bring the total considerably below one million, or two-thirds less than the estimated cost of the Tonto dam." [55]

Reppy said all that was necessary to segregate the San Carlos site from the Indian reservation was for the president to issue an executive order. The reservation had been created by such an order, and a presidential proclamation had been issued "a few weeks previous in order to cut off mines [from the reservation] owned by Geo. B. Chittenden and others, of Washington, D.C. If it could be done for a private purpose it certainly could be for a great public good." [56]

Reppy, Weedin, and the other Florence area farmers must have known theirs was a lost cause, but they continued to fight. The Casa Grande Valley Water Users' Association authorized a pamphlet, "Shall the National Irrigation Law Be Used As a Great Graft?" and Reppy raised the specter of "acts of bribery and corruption" and "an 'irrigation ring' whose members are preparing to feather their nests and to bring scandal upon a great and beneficient law that will probably cause its repeal." [57]

On May 9, Weedin's *Arizona Blade* printed a long article, "MAXWELL'S BUNCO GAME On the National Irrigation Association," in which Maxwell and "his cohorts" were accused of "obtaining a wrong administration" of the reclamation law. It was noted Maxwell was reported by the Phoenix newspapers to have invested $12,000 in a Valley ranch, "But whether or not he had bought it with his 'hard earned dollars' or just accidentally fallen heir to it, we did not ascertain." [58]

The *Blade* argued the Tonto reservoir, contrary to what Maxwell was telling members of the National Irrigation Association, could not store enough water to demonstrate "the benefits of National Irrigation to the entire country," so that if built, it would allow Maxwell and "the large landowners and land syndicates to unload their holdings on unsuspecting 'outsiders' at an advance of about five hundred per cent. . .And this they will do before the final completion of the dam and before the inadequacy of the water supply becomes generally known." [59]

The *Republican* reported May 10 that 70,000 acres had been subscribed for, and "It is only a matter of time, but it is taking more time than it ought to." [60] The newspaper lashed out at an argument that water users should not subscribe for shares because they would be members of a corporation, [61] and charged, without naming them, "A little coterie of men who do not want the reservoir at all, unless their pet interests are given an advantage, have not hesitated to impose upon ranchers by inventing one fake after another." [62]

The two weeks that began on Sunday, May 24, were fateful and eventful in the effort to sign the farmers and ranchers into the Water Users' Association. It began on Monday, May 25, with a decision by Judge Edward Kent in the case of *H. G. Van Fossen v. the Salt River Valley Canal Co.* Kent's ruling established the right of Van Fossen, though neither a shareholder in the canal nor the owner of a water right, to receive water for his land through the canal company. [63] While various interpretations were made as to the effect of the decision, it was seen by some as an assist to the association by decreasing the value of floating water rights and by putting all farmers on an equal footing in their right to have water delivered whether or not they had a contractual relationship with a canal company. [64] The decision allowed a canal company to charge for the delivery of water, but it did not deal with the priority of Van Fossen's right to water relative to that of other water appropriators. [65]

The next day, the *Arizona Gazette* published a letter from Dr. L.C. Toney, who had subscribed for 160 shares in the association, stating the number of acres signed was "nearly a hundred thousand," and prophetically warning there would "'come a time,' and not very far away either, when an ultimatum will be given to the water users" to join the association or forget the reservoir. [66]

Both the *Republican* and the *Enterprise* chose that day to editorially warn the people of Florence that attacking Maxwell and Fowler, and fighting the inevitability of the Tonto Basin reservoir would not get the San Carlos dam for them. [67] The *Enterprise* deplored efforts by some Arizonans to have the General Assembly of the Presbyterian Church of the United States, meeting in Los Angeles, approve a resolution calling for the appropriation of irrigation funds for the San Carlos reservoir. These men, the *Enterprise* said,

are putting up the argument that the Florence project is for the Pima Indians, and that by building the Tonto dam the government is taking bread out of the mouths of the Pimas and starving them to death. Who ever saw a starving Pima? White men have starved, Yuma Indians have grown thin, but the Pima Indian is and always has been as round as a barrel and as fat as a dry-goods box. [68]

The newspaper said the people at Florence became concerned about the Pimas only after the settlers in the Upper Gila Valley began to appropriate the water previously stolen from the Indians through the Florence canal. [69]

The *Republican* also reported, "The strength of the opposition [to the articles] began to peter rapidly as soon as the ranchers tumbled that technical arguments against the plan of organization really meant opposition to the reservoir." [70] The next day, the paper said Maxwell, M. A. Stanford, and others had begun personal visits to all the landowners who had not signed in the expectation "that in this way a large additional acreage will be secured." [71] The *Enterprise* noted May 28 that Maxwell and Stanford said "that they are succeeding beyond their expectations." [72]

That newspaper also reported the government contemplated abandoning the portion of the Arizona Canal east of the Crosscut Canal that linked the Arizona with the Grand Canal, at today's 48th Street in Phoenix. The paper said the government would build a new canal, but first it was going to replace the Arizona dam with a masonry dam. From there, a new canal would be built to reclaim 50,000 acres of desert land east of Camelback Mountain in Paradise Valley and then drop south to connect with the Crosscut Canal. [73] The Arizona Canal was to be re-routed to create a water fall for the generation of 16,000 horsepower of electricity, which would be worth $800,000 per year. [74]

The *Arizona Democrat* published an editorial May 29 with the title, "A PUBLIC ENEMY," in which it said it had been,

informed that D. B. Heard has succeeded in getting up an "agreement" for the Tempe farmers to sign which he claims will secure these men all of the rights under the reservoir, and at the same time permit, what he is pleased to call, "local control." The facts in the case are that Heard is deceiving the farmers of this valley and doing it, we believe, for selfish and unworthy purposes. . .

The farmer who believes that he cannot sign the articles. . .with justice to himself has an absolute right and it is his duty to refuse to sign, but the man or coterie of men who scheme and plot to destroy and delay the construction of the Tonto reservoir is an enemy of this valley and ought to be treated as such. D. B. Heard, in our opinion, is one of this class of men, and we warn him now that should he by his machinations cloud this proposition and retard its construction, that the valley of the Salt River will be far too circumscribed to hold his kind of people. The men of this valley have for years hoped and toiled in the interest of this storage dam, and they will not tolerate the meddlesome inexcusable interference of men who were sent into Arizona by rich fathers-in-law in a palace car. The Democrat *entertains no ill feeling towards Mr. Heard, but we do say that he has done more by innuendo and misleading assertions to injure the valley than has any other man who ever infested the territory, and it is about time that he was calling a halt.* [75]

Dwight B. Heard

The *Republican* printed a dispatch from its Washington correspondent, Charles C. Randolph, in which he said its purpose was to warn, "That there is grave danger to the valley in delay." [76]

Randolph wrote that Hitchcock would like to begin construction by November 1, but because of the time required to advertise for contracts and dispose of bids and to allow contractors to prepare for the work, the interior secretary had to know the decision of the landowners as early as possible. Should construction not begin by the close of the year, there would "be grave danger of an indefinite postponement," Randolph said. [77]

He repeated what had been said time and again, that work would not begin "until the required amount of land has been subscribed," [78] adding:

In the course of the conversation with the secretary of the Interior this afternoon he spoke of the advantages of a reservoir to the valley and declared that under no circumstances would he authorize one to be built there unless the people agreed to the conditions as set forth. It is believed at the department that the rights of the landowners are thoroughly safeguarded in the articles of the Water Users' Association and surprise is expressed that the government's attitude has been misrepresented by opponents of the reservoir.

In view of the conditions as they appear at this end of the line, the friends of the reservoir in Phoenix would do well to exert themselves during the next thirty days. The old saw about looking a gift horse in the mouth is regarded here as applicable to existing conditions in the valley. In the case of this particular horse, there are plenty of communities in the arid regions that would be willing to accept it and pledge themselves not to hunt for defects. [79]

The *Enterprise* reprinted Randolph's article that afternoon, plus the news that "a high official in Washington who speaks authoritively for the secretary" had sent a communication "which is in the nature of an ultimatum to the people of the Salt River Valley." [80] According to the *Enterprise,*

The communication states the fact that the department is in receipt of a letter from Mr. D. B. Heard, asking if the secretary of the Interior would consider the changes in the articles. . .proposed by the minority, if presented by an organization, and says that a letter would be written to Mr. Heard informing him that the department was opposed to the proposed changes; that the Tonto Basin reservoir would be built on the plan proposed by the Water Users' Association, or not at all; and that the secretary regarded the proposed amendments as contrary to good public policy.

. . .the communication stated unreservedly that the people of this valley must go before the secretary immediately if they wanted this reservoir, as the irrigation moneys would be appropriated to other projects if there was much longer delay. [81]

A reporter interviewed Frank H. Parker, secretary of the association, and learned that about 90,000 acres were signed, but Parker said it was expected there would be 100,000 acres before another week passed. Parker said he was uncertain how many acres the government would require. [82]

Meanwhile, Fowler, learning of a meeting planned by the Tempe Canal owners the next day, sent a telegram to Walcott:

Heard claims inside information concerning government policy in reservoir construction that government will not insist on lien, will consent to local and divided control, will approve minority amendments. Can we deny? [83]

Saturday morning, May 30, the *Republican* printed another "DANGER!" story, this time warning that communities in Colorado, Utah, and Idaho wanted the Salt River reservoir postponed and their projects started. Interior Department officials pointed out the curious circumstance that the model organization adopted by these communities was based upon the plan adopted and approved for the Salt River Valley, but the only place from where objections came was Phoenix. The chief objector was identified as Heard, who had been informed "that prolonged delay will lead to failure and the indefinite postponement of the Tonto Basin reservoir." [84]

The article quoted an Interior Department official who was not named as saying that the decision of the Tempe Canal owners to remain out of the Water Users' Association was "gratifying news."

"While the valid arguments in favor of beginning work on the Salt River are many," he said, "a serious objection raised has been the contention that the reservoir would directly benefit so many districts that are already prosperous. It greatly strengthens the enterprise, from the viewpoint of the government, to have a substantial area of desert land included. The withdrawal of the Tempe landowners materially simplifies the situation."

The official also said that neither the Tempe nor other dissenting landowners would later be allowed to join the association. [85]

The *Gazette* printed an editorial, "SAVE THE RESERVOIR," calling upon the directors of the Board of Trade, when they met the next Tuesday, "to investigate and see just who it is that is jeopardizing the valley's future." But the *Gazette* let on that it already knew who to blame, saying, "The methods that have been adopted by D. B. Heard. . .who is now being looked upon as an enemy to the future welfare of what promised to be a modern paradise, should be condemned in the severest terms." [86]

The *Enterprise* came to Heard's defense, labeling, "this war that is being made on Dwight B. Heard. . .purely a bit of slimy spite work." Heard had a right to fight for changes in the articles "without being slandered and abused." The way to get the reservoir was "to get the farmers to sign up, and abusing Mr. Heard is not going to make them sign up." [87]

The *Republican* also carried the news the General Assembly of the Presbyterian Church had passed resolutions that,

urgently requests the honorable secretary of the Interior to take steps without delay for the erection of a reservoir at San Carlos on the Gila River, as recommended by himself in a report to Congress prior to the passage of the irrigation law, June 17, 1902, and under which he has power to act. [88]

Reppy saw to it Hitchcock and Roosevelt were furnished with copies of the resolution. [89] Earlier resolutions calling for building the San Carlos dam had been approved by the Presbyterian Synod of New Mexico, Pima and Papago pupils of the Tucson Indian Industrial School, and the Tucson Chamber of Commerce. [90]

The stockholders of the Tempe Canal assembled at one o'clock Saturday afternoon, May 30, in the Odd Fellows'

Hall in Tempe. Also present were at least five north siders, including Maxwell. They and other non-stockholders were excluded from the meeting until the canal owners completed their business, which was approving a petition to Hitchcock averring their desire for the reservoir and their willingness to regard the document as a binding contract. It was approved with a single dissenting vote. [91]

The petition for the most part was a restatement of the minority positions, including the request for modifying the articles to provide for a reservoir regulating right. The most significant concession of the minority was agreeing to a lien on the land to assure the payment of all assessments. The minority also wanted the articles modified to limit to 200,000 acres the amount of land to be irrigated within the reservoir district. [92]

When the meeting was opened to the public, the chairman, J. Webster Johnson, said the petition would be read, and all persons agreeing with it were invited to unite with the Tempe Canal owners. Woolf read the petition, then Heard explained its origin, saying he and others who held similar views believed some definite plan should be submitted to Hitchcock. Heard said they thought the secretary had been provided partial information "from prejudiced sources." He said he knew Hitchcock had approved the "Maxwell" plan but still believed the articles could be changed if a clear and strong showing were made. Heard also attempted to refute the idea he and the others were "kickers," because they were as anxious for the reservoir as anybody. [93]

Maxwell was asked to comment. He began by saying he thought it was useless to address Tempe Canal stockholders, but he would give his opinion of the petition. He said from a legal standpoint, Hitchcock could not approve it, and it had as much chance as a petition calling for government construction of a pipeline to the head of the Tempe Canal should it be discovered the moon was a monstrous sphere containing an everlasting supply of water. [94]

In an editorial, the **Republican** questioned, "What any sane man could expect to gain by again taking the subject to the secretary," then provided its own answer:

It looks very much, indeed, as if, finding it impossible to carry through their pet projects, they have determined to defeat the reservoir altogether. [95]

The newspaper expressed concern Hitchcock would form an unfavorable opinion of the people and "their business sagacity," and warned another month's delay "may mean the loss of the reservoir." [96]

On Monday, Fowler received an answer to his wire of May 29. Walcott telegraphed:

. . .minority amendments were not approved and will not be taken up. The department will insist on central unified control of canal systems and best security on water and land. No one has a right to claim inside information as to intentions of the department. [97]

That same day, many of the men engaged in pump irrigation in the Valley met at the Water Users' Association offices to talk about their relationship to the organization. One thing they discussed was the quality of the groundwater,

and Dr. Alexander J. Chandler, at that time perhaps the most successful pump irrigator in the Valley, said the only problem he had with underground water was getting enough of it. That was a statement all of them agreed with. Maxwell told them no member of the association could be compelled to take pumped water, but he saw no reason why a member should not be able to get electric power without paying any more for it than he would for his share of reservoir water. [98] Those among the pumpers who had not subscribed for shares indicated they probably would join the association. [99]

Before the day ended, 5,511 acres of land were signed into the association, some of it by persons "who have been slow to accept salvation." [100] To celebrate the signing of 100,000 acres, the Board of Trade called a mass meeting for 2 p.m. Saturday, June 6. [101]

Tuesday, June 3, the **Enterprise** published a long letter from Heard presenting his side of the reservoir question. He said he would "treat with dignified contempt. . .the slanderous personal attacks," and would get to the "vital question. . .in which the holders of all speculative idle lands are ranged on one side. . .supporting the present articles. . .and a large number of conservative, practical and responsible farmers. . .who are not so much interested in the ability of the speculators to unload" on the other. [102]

"The people of this valley should decide whether they wish a speculative, unloading proposition or a clean-cut business proposition which will make for the permanent prosperity of this community" with construction of the reservoir, Heard wrote. [103]

He said, "under the present articles legitimate farmers, with well-developed places and valuable water rights, are asked to put up the bulk of the security and apparently will receive the least benefit, while the speculative holders of idle lands. . .put up the least security and receive the greatest benefit."

Then Heard got to the central point of his argument:

It is well known in this community that under the excitement of a boom, which the construction of the reservoir is bound to create, these homeseekers and colonists to whom they sell will find, if the present plans are carried out, that the water supply is not sufficient to enable them to farm properly. . .

The fact that under the most favorable conditions of distribution and economical use, we cannot expect to irrigate with the reservoir (in view of our known water supply) more than 200,000 acres, and the fact that we already have under canals, within the reservoir district, 254,000 acres of patented land is what really causes the present friction over the articles. [104]

Saturday morning, committees from the Salt River Valley, Maricopa, and Grand canals met and passed a resolution calling for the immediate signing of all land under them "in order that the proposition of this valley may be presented to the secretary of the Interior. . .within ten days. Every delay from this time on endangers our project." [105]

The reasons for specifying 10 days in the resolution were that private correspondence from Washington said great political pressure was being brought upon Hitchcock to postpone the Tonto project; that Hitchcock had never been strongly inclined toward the Tonto Basin and had been talked into it by members of the Geological Survey; that

Hitchcock was becoming exasperated by the controversy over the articles and he was thinking of turning down the project if the wrangling didn't stop; that he would not consider again the minority amendments; that he was leaving for his summer vacation June 18, and he would not issue the order to make contracts for construction of the reservoir unless sufficient acreage had been signed by that date. [106]

At the mass meeting Saturday afternoon, Fowler read the resolution approved by the canal committees and the telegram he had received from Walcott. Fowler announced that 105,000 acres had been signed, and said the government was ready to spend $3 million for the reservoir and charge no interest. In addition, he said other improvements contemplated by the government for the Valley would almost equal in cost the building of the dam. [107]

Among the speakers introduced by chairman of the day J. A. Marshall were several who had withheld their lands from the association but who had now signed. They included John R. Norton and John Orme. Norton told the crowd of men, women, and children,

It's now time to bury the hatchet. The government can build a reservoir for us all. Every man can and will get his rights. The older ranchers who have stood back are not apologizing for their honest convictions, but they want a reservoir and want it bad.

Orme said he had "been one of those honestly opposed to the articles of incorporation; one of those who have sometimes been maligned by the papers, and I still differ honestly, but in order to get the reservoir, I have signed the articles and advise every man to sign and leave all details to an honest secretary of the Interior." Orme said he would continue his fight, but he would work to protect his rights under the reservoir. [108]

Marshall introduced Maxwell as "The daddy of them all," to which Maxwell said:

To be called the daddy of them all is rather an overpowering introduction. I think that if I had been the daddy of you all, I would have disciplined you better so that you could have been brought into line more easily and with greater promptness. [109]

Maxwell said it was inexplicable to him there should ever have been any doubts, "but as I look upon the keen faces before me I think the sand storm has passed." He repudiated the idea there was a speculative class of lands and predicted the Tempe Canal Co. would come to curse the day it followed bad advice. [110]

When the last speech was over, Heard was invited to the platform. He asked Maxwell a series of prepared questions. [111] The *Republican* said the confrontation between the two men was "a rewinnowing of the chaff from which the grain had long ago been extracted," but it "gave the great body of water users an opportunity to express in public their approval of Mr. Maxwell's stand and alternatively their disapproval of Mr. Heard's efforts that have resulted in delaying the movement already nervously near to the danger line." [112]

In an editorial the next day, the *Republican* hailed Maxwell as "the great Emancipator of the arid West," and said Heard "should not flatter himself that his motives are misunderstood." The newspaper charged that should Heard succeed in getting the benefits of stored water for his 7,000 acre ranch without having to cut it into 160-acre tracts, "it would mean a gain to him and his associates of at least $250,000." [113]

In the week that followed, 30,000 acres were subscribed into the association, bringing the total to 135,000. [114] Heard departed for Chicago and Washington, [115] where he intended to make another attempt to have Hitchcock accept the minority view. On June 10, Fowler wrote to Newell in Los Angeles to inform him that 120,000 acres had been signed. Newell replied June 13, saying, "it would be well to proceed somewhat cautiously in receiving more subscriptions and endeavor to consolidate as much as possible." His advice was that signatures not be accepted indiscriminately, but that future members should be limited "to localities where best economy can be secured in future administration." [116]

At the same time Newell was writing these words, the *Republican's* Washington correspondent was sending a dispatch saying at least 150,000 and possibly 180,000 acres would be demanded by the Interior Department. Randolph said while the news from the Valley "caused much satisfaction in the Interior Department," he reminded readers,

If it were not that the Tonto Basin site presents ideal conditions for a reservoir the flouting of the government's offer by a portion of the valley's population unquestionably would have been sufficient provocation to turn the government's attention in another direction. . .

. . .but for the enthusiasm displayed at the mass meeting in Phoenix last week and the assurances conveyed in recent dispatches to the secretary of the Interior and the director of the Geological Survey that the required acreage would be subscribed, the outlook for building of the reservoir would not be nearly as bright as it is at this writing. [117]

In the midst of this, C. R. Olberg, a Geological Survey engineer, said the government intended to begin immediately the construction of a wagon road from the Valley to the Tonto Basin. [118] Olberg and H. A. Storrs, an electrical engineer, had just arrived in Phoenix from the dam site, having traveled the 30-mile length of the box canyon of the Salt River, which begins near the junction with Tonto Creek. Storrs was working out the details of the proposed cement plant to be built just above the dam site. [119]

Friday night, June 19, Fowler sent the following wire to Walcott:

Total acreage signed tonight one hundred fifty thousand. Will make it twenty thousand more next week without Tempe. The small landowners are all coming in. [120]

The *Republican* printed that news the morning of June 20 along with a dispatch from Randolph that said Heard had met with Hitchcock. The report said Heard had failed to sway Hitchcock or Walcott but had created the impression he would accept the situation and would advise others to do the same. [121]

Heard had met with Hitchcock on June 17, the first anniversary of the signing of the reclamation act by Roosevelt. Hitchcock, besides refusing to alter the Water Users' articles, declined commemorating the anniversary of the irrigation law by signing an order that day for construction of the Tonto Basin reservoir, as urged by Heard. Hitchcock could not issue such an order because the work of the Reclamation Service was not far enough along. [122]

The first word from Heard on his Washington meetings came in a telegram to Norton:

Satisfactory conference with Secretary Hitchcock. Am confident the reservoir is assured. Will return next Saturday with definite plans to stop friction and ill-will. [123]

The Tempe Canal stockholders met and discussed Heard's wire, but no one was certain exactly what he meant. Some south siders interpreted it to mean some new plan had been devised that was "satisfactory" to Hitchcock. [124]

On June 22, the governors adopted a resolution that no lands from outside the reservoir district described in the articles should be signed into the association. The resolution was adopted in response to applications for shares made by landowners outside the district. [125] On returning from the East Coast, Brodie told reporters he had talked with Hitchcock and the reservoir was a certainty. [126]

The *Los Angeles Times* published an editorial June 26 saying, while the Pima and Maricopa Indians on the Gila River were "fully deserving of relief. . .as a measure of justice," that should not "blind us to the fact that the unfortunate white settlers of the Salt River valley also have some claim upon the consideration of the country." The *Times* said, too, it should not be ignored that the Gila Valley people protesting construction of the Tonto reservoir "are the same who, by the construction and operation of the Florence canal, first deprived those Indians of their vested irrigation rights." [127]

The *Republican* praised the *Times,* saying the California paper "for a time had cobwebs in its eyes," but now had "made a careful canvas of the situation, and sets forth its findings in. . .a plain, fair and fearless statement." [128] As might be expected, the *Times* editorial produced some outrage at Florence. [129]

Heard returned Saturday, June 27, and said Walcott and Hitchcock now realized that no matter the differences over the articles, there was united opinion on the need for the reservoir. Heard said while he believed the articles would have to be modified, he would sign lands under the Maricopa, Grand, and Mesa canals after conferring with the stockholders of the Tempe and Utah canals. He said he had told Walcott that as the articles presently stood, he could not recommend to the owners of land with vested water rights that they sign into the association. However, he said he would urge each water user to act upon his own judgment. [130]

Heard said Hitchcock and Walcott also had decided to limit the land to be served to 200,000 acres, as recommended by the Water Storage Conference Committee in its unanimous resolution in October 1902. [131]

On Monday, Heard conferred with several of the large landowners under the Tempe Canal, and it was reported they were still determined to remain out of the association. [132] To get supplemental water, they planned to begin a pumping enterprise, and three of the stockholders, Hayden, C. G. Jones, and I. V. Stewart, gave notice in the Maricopa County recorder's office they had located a site for a diversion dam on the Salt River, at which they intended to divert 375 cubic feet of water per second into a canal for the generation of electric power. The canal was to follow a generally westerly course for a distance of 10.4 miles, where the water was to drop 60 feet to produce the power before being returned to the river. It was estimated enough power could be generated to pump 125 cubic feet of water per second, or almost 250 acre-feet per 24 hours. The cost of the project was estimated at $300,000. [133]

Not all of the Tempe Canal landowners were in agreement, and one of them signed into the association for 160 acres and predicted some of his neighbors would subscribe, too. [134]

The Governors met and ordered the books for subscription to the capital stock of the association be closed at the end of the business day July 13. [135] A couple of days later, Fowler received a letter in which Newell suggested the books be closed July 15 or 31. Thereafter, it was to be up to Hitchcock to decide whether the subscription of land was large enough to insure repayment or whether public lands were to be included. [136]

Heard wrote to Walcott July 3 informing him of the Tempe Canal's plans for a diversion dam and pumping plant. Heard wanted to know if the proposal would interfere with Reclamation Service plans. [137] That same day, Heard signed about 615 acres into the association, which was all the land he owned individually, none of it part of the Bartlett-Heard Land & Cattle Co. [138]

Arthur P. Davis, the Reclamation Service engineer in charge of the preliminary work for the Tonto reservoir, returned to Phoenix July 4. He praised the work of the Water Users' Association and said the dam would be built just as soon as Hitchcock issued the order. [139] Davis said the power canal would cost somewhat more to construct in certain places than had been expected, so he had ordered a re-survey in those locations. Concerning the routes for proposed roads, Davis quipped he had found some excellent lines for airships. [140]

Davis and Kibbey, at Heard's invitation, met with him, Hayden, Woolf and Jones at Heard's office July 10 to discuss the Tempe Canal situation. In particular, they were talking about the proposed pumping plant as an alternative for the Tempe Canal, should it remain outside the reservoir project, when a messenger arrived with two telegrams, one for Davis from Newell and the other for Heard from Walcott. Newell told Davis,

Heard wrote July 3rd regarding proposed Tempe power plant. Walcott wires him that public lands were withdrawn to prevent such interference with our plans. Notify all concerned.

Walcott's telegram said:

Proposed Tempe plant will interfere with government plan. Lands were withdrawn to prevent such further interference.

As a result of the conference Davis agreed to meet at 10 o'clock the following morning with the Tempe Canal stockholders in the Odd Fellows' Hall in Tempe. [141]

The meeting opened with the stockholders hearing a report comparing the costs to them of the Tonto reservoir with the price of building either a hydropower or a steam plant to generate electricity to operate pumping plants. During this discussion, Heard and others pointed out the figures concerning the Tonto project were not accurate. Davis confirmed this, saying the costs presented were based upon the calculations he had made for the original dam. Since then, he said, the height of the dam had been raised, but no new estimates of costs had been announced. Davis provided new figures and a new comparison was made, but it involved only the dam and a steam-generated power plant because the telegrams from Newell and Walcott had rendered the hydroelectric proposal moot. The comparison showed an initial cost to the canal company of $454,500 for the Tonto dam and $191,395 for the steam plant. However, after 10 years, the annual cost for each acre under the Tonto was projected at $1.11 and with the steam plant $2.12. The canal stockholders took no action on the pumping plant.

The most important thing Davis said, in answering questions about the reservoir, was that with the present water supply he did not think more than 180,000 acres would be accepted for irrigation and the area might be smaller.

Heard spoke next, recapitulating the four things for which he said he had fought: "That the acreage be adjusted to the water supply; that the priorities be protected; that water users have control of canals, and that there be 'equitable assessment' in the raising of money." Heard said he believed the first two were fully satisfied by what Davis had said. The other two were less essential, but, if the Tempe Canal landowners would join the association, they could fight for them, and eventually the interior secretary would approve them, he said. He then urged each man to join of his own decision and not because he advised it. However, as a company, the Tempe Canal owners made no decision about what they would do. [142]

The governors met Monday. Acting on Davis' recommendation, they delayed closing the books until 6 p.m. Friday, July 17 to give the Tempe Canal landowners an opportunity to join the association. At the end of the day, it was announced 190,000 acres had been subscribed, 3,000 of them from under the Tempe Canal. [143] The governors followed up the next day by opening an office in Tempe where Tempe Canal owners could sign. [144]

At the close of business Friday, the association reported 195,000 acres had been subscribed, approximately 6,000 in the Tempe district. About 140,000 acres had been signed on the north side of the river, and 55,000, on the south side. [145]

On July 21, the governors authorized Fowler to go to Washington to present a report on the association's progress. [146] Fowler left for Denver July 24, where he was to meet Newell and Davis before continuing to Washington. [147] Commenting upon Fowler's mission, the **Republican** said:

> *There was a time when it did not seem within the bounds of possibility for this valley to share in any of the benefits of a national irrigation law.*
>
> *The propaganda. . .was for water storage for public lands. The lands here had already passed into private ownership. Apparently, there was not a shadow whereon to found a hope that the government could do anything for us. But Maxwell and Fowler, with that faith which moves mountains and with a perseverance and diplomacy that made their campaign one of the most notable ever witnessed in Washington, stemmed an adverse current for months and organized a glorious victory. When the national reclamation law was at last enacted it was seen that Maxwell and Fowler had succeeded in so amending the bill that it permitted the Salt River valley to be covered by the provisions of the law. The clauses in the law which enable the secretary of the Interior to accept the plan of the Water Users' Association are clauses which were placed in the statutes because of the persistent work of George H. Maxwell and B. A. Fowler. For all time, the dam on the Salt River will be a monument that will honor these men. [148]*

1. *Phoenix Daily Enterprise,* April 2, 1903.
2. *Arizona Republican* (Phoenix), April 3, 1903.
3. *Arizona Gazette* (Phoenix), April 7, 1903.
4. *Republican,* April 5, 1903.
5. Charles D. Walcott, letter and Report on Irrigation in the Salt River Valley, Arizona, April 10, 1903, Salt River Project Archives (Hereafter SRPA).
6. *Ibid.*
7. *Ibid.*
8. *Ibid.*
9. *Ibid.*
10. *Republican,* April 18, 1903; *Gazette,* April 18, 1903.
11. *Republican,* April 19, 1903.
12. *Ibid.*
13. *Ibid.*
14. *Ibid.*
15. *Ibid.*
16. *Ibid.*
17. *Republican,* April 19, 26, 1903.
18. *Ibid.,* April 26, 1903.
19. *Enterprise,* April 17, 1903.
20. *Ibid.*
21. *Ibid.,* May 3, 1903.
22. *Ibid.,* April 19, 1903.
23. *Ibid.*
24. *Ibid.,* June 3, 1903.
25. *Ibid.,* April 19, 1903.
26. *Ibid.*
27. *Ibid.,* April 21, 1903.
28. *Ibid.,* April 22, 1903.
29. *Ibid.*
30. *Ibid.,* April 23, 1903.
31. *Gazette,* April 26, 1903.
32. *Republican,* May 3, 1903.
33. *Ibid.,* May 3 and 5, 1903.
34. *Ibid.,* May 3, 1903.
35. *Ibid.,* May 5, 1903.
36. *Ibid.*
37. *Gazette,* May 20, 1903.
38. *Ibid.,* May 5, 1903.
39. *Republican,* May 6, 1903.
40. *Ibid.,* May 7, 1903.
41. *Report in the Matter of the Investigation, of the Salt ad Gila Rivers—Reservations and Reclamation Service* (Washington: Government Printing Office, 1913) pp. 54-55 (hereafter *Report in the Matter of Investigation*). The article Weedin presented to the House subcommittee of the Committee on Expenditures in the Interior Department and reprinted in the *Report in the Matter of Investigation,* pp. 55-66, could not have been the one seen by Roosevelt. Roosevelt was at the Grand Canyon May 6, 1903, while

the reprint at pp. 55-66, includes on p. 56 quotations from a letter from Dwight D. Heard to the *Phoenix Enterprise,* June 3, 1903, and on p. 60 an article from the *Globe-Times,* May 27, 1903. The article at pp. 55-66 was undoubtedly published in July, 1903, a copy of which was sent by Charles D. Reppy to E. A. Hitchcock, July 28, 1903, National Archives, Record Group 48, Lands and Railroads, Reclamation, "Miscellaneous Projects" records, 1807-1903, SRPA.

42. Story of How Roosevelt Dam Came to Attention of T. Roosevelt, Phoenix History Project, Alexander Collection, Box No. 1, undated, Phoenix Historical Society, Phoenix, Arizona.

43. *Ibid.*

44. *Ibid.*

45. Charles F. Lummis, "Lost in the Shuffle," *Out West,* June, 1903, quoted in letter from Charles D. Reppy to E. A. Hitchcock, June 6, 1903, National Archives, Record Group 48, Lands and Railroads, Reclamation, SRPA. In the July, 1903, edition of *Out West,* quoted in the *Enterprise,* July 10, 1903, Lummis wrote that after talking over the Tonto Basin and San Carlos propositions with men from the Geological Survey, he was "convinced that there is no Senegambian in the woodpile. The point is simply that, as experts in a new experiment, they believe the Tonto reservoir is a better 'opener' than the San Carlos. They stand for the San Carlos later, and for relief of the parched Pimas at once,—by pumping."

46. Lummis, Reppy to Hitchcock, June 6, 1903.

47. *Ibid.*

48. *Ibid.*

49. *Ibid.*

50. *Ibid.*

51. *Republican,* April 13, 1903; reprinted from the *Arizona Silver Belt* (Globe), *Republican,* June 29, 1903; editorial reprinted from the *Los Angeles Times,* June 26, 1903.

52. *Republican,* June 29, 1903, editorial reprinted from *Los Angeles Times,* June 26, 1903; *Enterprise,* June 4, 1903. It was apparently for this reason that the portion of the Salt River Indian Reservation lying within the reservoir district of the Salt River Valley Water Users' Association, approximately 14,000 acres south of the Arizona Canal, was not included in the association.

53. *Report in the Matter of the Investigation,* pp. 55-130.

54. *Republican,* November 25, 1901; *Gazette,* November 29, 1901; Charles D. Reppy to E. A. Hitchcock, June 6, 1903, National Archives, Record Group 48, Lands & Railroads, Reclamation, SRPA.

55. *Report in the Matter of the Investigation,* p. 55.

56. Reppy to Hitchcock, June 6, 1903.

57. *Ibid.*

58. *Arizona Blade* (Florence), May 9, 1903, Arizona State Archives.

59. *Ibid.*

60. *Republican,* May 10, 1903.

61. *Ibid.,* May 12, 1903.

62. *Ibid.,* May 21, 1903.

63. *Ibid.,* May 26, 1903.

64. *Ibid.; Enterprise,* May 26, 1903.

65. *Republican,* May 26, 1903.

66. *Gazette,* May 26, 1903.

67. *Republican,* May 26, 1903; *Enterprise,* May 26, 1903.

68. *Enterprise,* May 26, 1903.

69. *Ibid.*

70. *Republican,* May 26, 1903.

71. *Ibid.,* May 27, 1903.

72. *Enterprise,* May 28, 1903.

73. *Ibid.; Gazette,* May 27, 1903.

74. *Enterprise,* May 28, 1903.

75. *Arizona Democrat* (Phoenix), May 29, 1903.

76. *Republican,* May 29, 1903.

77. *Ibid.*

78. *Ibid.*

79. *Ibid.*

80. *Enterprise,* May 29, 1903.

81. *Ibid.*

82. *Ibid.*

83. *Republican,* June 7, 1903.

84. *Ibid.* May 30, 1903.

85. *Ibid.*

86. *Gazette,* May 30, 1903.

87. *Enterprise,* May 30, 1903.

88. *Republican,* May 30, 1903; Resolutions Adopted by the General Assembly of the Presbyterian Church of the United States in Los Angeles, California, May 29, 1903, National Archives, Record Group 48, SRPA.

89. Reppy to Hitchcock, June 6, 1903.

90. *Blade,* November 29, 1902, March 21, 1903, Arizona State Archives; National Archives, Record Group 115, San Carlos, 429A, March 1903; National Archives, Records of the Bureau of Reclamation, Record Group 115, Project File 1902-1919; San Carlos 429-429A, Box 531, National Archives, Record Group 48, Lands and Railroads, Reclamation, SRPA.

91. *Republican,* May 31, 1903.

92. *Ibid.*

93. *Ibid.*

94. *Ibid.*

95. *Ibid.*

96. *Ibid.*

97. *Republican,* June 7, 1903.

98. *Gazette,* June 2, 1903.

99. *Republican,* June 2, 1903.

100. *Ibid.*

101. *Republican,* June 3, 1903.

102. *Enterprise,* June 3, 1903.

103. *Ibid.*

104. *Ibid.;* Heard told the subcommittee of the House Committee on Expenditures in the Interior Department, which conducted hearings in Phoenix, Arizona, April 23-May 2, 1912, that in payment for the Salt River reservoir and dam he "was very favorable to what is known as a graduated plan. . .I was in favor of a graduated plan under which those lands that had old and well-established water rights would have to pay less money than the lands which had no water rights." Quoted in *Report in the Matter of the Investigation,* p. 366.

105. *Republican,* June 7, 1903; *Gazette,* June 7, 1903.

106. *Enterprise,* June 6, 1903; *Gazette,* June 7, 1903; *Republican,* June 7, 1903.

107. *Republican,* June 7, 1903; *Gazette,* June 7, 1903.

108. *Republican,* June 7, 1903.

109. *Republican,* June 7, 1903; *Gazette,* June 7, 1903.

110. *Ibid.*

111. *Gazette,* June 7, 1903.

112. *Republican,* June 7, 1903.

113. *Ibid.*

114. *Republican,* June 14, 1903.

115. *Ibid.,* June 12, 1903.

116. *Ibid.,* June 16, 1903.

117. *Ibid.,* June 14, 1903.

118. *Gazette,* June 9, 1903.

119. *Republican,* June 9, 1903.

120. *Ibid.,* June 20, 1903.

121. *Ibid.*

122. *Enterprise,* June 27, 1903; *Republican,* June 28, 1903.

123. *Ibid.,* June 20, 1903; *Republican,* June 21, 1903.

124. *Republican,* June 23, 1903.

125. *Ibid.*

126. *Enterprise,* June 23, 1903; *Gazette,* June 23, 1903.

127. *Republican,* June 29, 1903.

128. *Ibid.*

129. Reppy to Hitchcock, July 28, 1903; *Blade,* August 22, 1903.

130. *Republican,* June 28, 1903.

131. *Gazette,* June 28, 1903.

132. *Republican,* June 30, 1903; *Gazette,* June 30, 1903; *Enterprise,* June 29, 1903.

133. *Gazette,* June 30, 1903; *Enterprise,* June 29, 1903.

134. *Republican,* June 30, 1903.

135. *Ibid.*

136. *Ibid.,* July 2, 1903.

137. *Ibid.,* July 11, 1903.

138. *Ibid.,* July 3, 1903; *Report in the Matter of the Investigation,* p. 366.

139. *Gazette,* July 5, 1903; *Republican,* July 5, 1903.

140. *Republican,* July 7, 1903.

141. *Ibid.,* July 11, 1903.

142. *Ibid.,* July 12, 1903.

143. *Ibid.,* July 14, 1903; *Enterprise,* July 14, 1903.

144. *Gazette,* July 15, 1903.

145. *Republican,* July 18, 1903.

146. *Enterprise,* July 22, 1903.

147. *Republican,* July 24, 1903.

148. *Ibid.,* July 26, 1903.

EPOCH III

August 1903 - March 1904

On August 3, 1903, the Board of Governors of the Salt River Valley Water Users' Association got some good but not unexpected news: The U.S. Geological Survey had approved the association's application for construction of a dam and reservoir at the Tonto Basin site on the Salt River. The governors received the news in a letter from Benjamin A. Fowler, association president, who had gone to Denver, Colorado, to meet with Frederick H. Newell, chief of the Reclamation Service, and Arthur Davis, engineer in charge of the preliminary work for the Tonto reservoir. Fowler wrote the application was being forwarded to Secretary of the Interior Ethan A. Hitchcock for his approval. In addition, Fowler said, orders were being issued by the Reclamation Service, which meant moving ahead with the project. [1]

Soon after, there was tangible evidence the Reclamation Service was doing something more than making surveys. Charles P. Mullen, in charge of keeping the engineers in supplies, came to Phoenix and purchased eight mules, two wagons, six scrapers, shovels, a stove, and groceries. [2] The *Arizona Republican* reported the supplies were for use in construction of a 23-mile-long road from Livingston to timberland in the Sierra Anchas, a line of mountains to the north and northeast where the Reclamation Service intended to operate a portable sawmill to supply lumber for building the cement mill and other structures at the reservoir site. [3] The sawmill was to have several locations, [4] the first of them near the falls of Wild Rose Creek, about 35 miles from the dam site. [5]

Mullen said the entire route for a road between the dam and Phoenix had not been selected, [6] while the *Arizona Silver Belt,* in Globe, reported,

The proposed wagon road to Phoenix is not seriously talked of for the reason that it is impracticable. It would cost probably $150,000, an amount out of all proportion to the benefit that would be derived from it, and the farmers would have to pay for it. Besides, a wagon road from the mouth of Tonto to Phoenix available for freighting is impossible. Globe will handle all the freight. [7]

The *Silver Belt* had reported earlier the Gila Valley, Globe and Northern Railway, which served Globe, already had received inquiries concerning the movement of large quantities of cement, fuel oil, and steel. [8]

Mullen also had the job of buying the land of settlers in the Tonto Basin, [9] at up to $30 an acre. [10] Some believed that once it became known the government intended to go ahead with the reservoir, owners of land in the basin to be flooded would ask exorbitant prices for their acreage. Because of this, it was decided in advance to have private parties take options on as much ground as they could get. In this way, some of the property was "secured at nominal prices," [11] but publication of what was happening caused problems, and some owners refused to sell. [12] A few of the owners and the govenment could not agree on price, so the U.S. Department of Justice took them to court. At least one of these cases did not end until 1918 when the governors agreed to pay $5,000

to Marion Braddock for the submerging of his ground; in addition, he retained title to the land. [13] Some of the options were paid for with property tax funds collected for use by the Maricopa County Board of Water Storage Commissioners. [14] In 1916, the value of the submerged land, including the price paid for the dam site, was put at $152,415.79. [15]

On August 19, the *Arizona Gazette* printed a story from Denver saying the government had advertised for bids for construction of the cement mill near the site of the proposed reservoir and for erection of a telephone line. [16] The advertisement said the steel and timber cement mill building would be built "on the Salt River, opposite the mouth of Tonto Creek, requiring about eight tons of structural steel and iron." [17] The telephone line was to run from Phoenix to Livingston via Mesa, Goldfield, and Fish Creek. [18]

The advertisement for bids had been made without Secretary Hitchcock's formal approval for construction of the reservoir. Davis was questioned about this by a Phoenix newspaperman, and the engineer explained this was the same way the Reclamation Service had begun work on its first project, the Truckee River diversion dam in Nevada. Davis said:

The official act of the government in its decision to build the Nevada project consisted of the request for bids to construct the dam, made by myself, and the acceptance of the lowest bid by authority of the secretary. Work began on that project at once, and I presume the same will be true in the case of the Tonto Basin project. [19]

Davis said the bids, which would be received until September 21, included machinery for the manufacture of cement and for a temporary power plant to provide electricity for use in the construction work. [20]

Before August ended, Louis C. Hill, a former professor of physics and electrical engineering who had joined the Reclamation Service, arrived in Phoenix, [21] and on August 24, 1903, he took charge of all field operations in connection with the Tonto reservoir. [22] In addition, letters from Fowler warned political pressures were still being brought on Hitchcock to reverse himself on the Tonto dam. [23] Fowler said there were persistent rumors an effort would be made at the National Irrigation Congress at Ogden, Utah, September 15-18, to pass a resolution condemning the Tonto Basin project as a speculative scheme for the benefit of lands in private ownership. He expressed concern over the effect this might have on Hitchcock. [24] This prompted Vernon Clark, Phoenix businessman and irrigator, and several others to announce they would attend the congress to assist Fowler and George H. Maxwell, executive director of the National Irrigation Association. [25]

On September 1, Davis appeared before the Maricopa County Board of Trade to bring the members up-to-date on what was happening. He discussed the cement mill, saying it would be nearly a year before cement could be manufactured. He said all the contracts to be let would be awarded before Christmas. Davis spent most of the time discussing the desirability and the cost of a wagon road between Mesa and the dam site. He said the road from Globe would be shorter than from Mesa,

but to offset the differences, the advantages are with Mesa, as we would be forced to come here for our forage and labor, which would be a great deal cheaper than at Globe, which is only a mining camp and sparsely settled. Another possible advantage would be railroad rates, which may be a very important factor, but there must be a large difference in the Globe railroad rates and the rates here to make up for the difference in wagon rates. . .

All things considered, we would prefer that the freight came this way. If we could have a road whereby we could make the distance in one day with a buggy and two days with a wagon, it would be a great improvement over the inconveniences we have to endure by going by way of Globe. [26]

Davis said, however, that because the road from Globe was shorter and better, the Reclamation Service had about concluded the road to Mesa would be too expensive to undertake under the irrigation act. For $5,000 or $6,000, he said, the road from Globe could be shortened from 43 miles to about 38 or 39 miles, while the road from Mesa might cost between $150,000 and $200,000. He said it was over this route the power transmission line as well as the telephone line would have to be constructed. Eleven miles of the route through the Salt River Canyon was in very rough country known as Fish Creek Hill, but should the people of the Valley agree to pay for that portion of the road at a cost of about $100,000, Davis said he believed the government "would be justified in building the balance out of the reclamation fund." [27] He also had heard the rumor a trolley line was going to be built from Mesa to the Tonto Basin: if true, he said, "the matter of freight would be settled, for wagons could not compete with electricity." [28] The rumor proved untrue.

Davis said two roads were then under construction, the lumber road, and a three-mile road from the site of the cement works to the clay hills. Davis said about 12,000 tons of clay would be needed. [29] The clay deposits were about one- and one-half miles north of the river while the cement works were to be constructed south of the river.

During excavation for the power canal, clay was found south of the river and closer to the mill building, so the clay road north of the Salt was little used. The one- and one-half miles of the road south of the river formed part of the regular freight road to Globe until water backed up by the reservoir flooded it. [30]

Some work had been done on a road from the dam site toward the head of the power canal, and work was to begin on the telephone road, Davis said. [31] The latter road was to become the freight road between the dam and Mesa.

After hearing Davis, Board of Trade members discussed raising money for the Fish Creek Hill portion of the road. Some suggested bonding the county, while others thought Phoenix, Tempe, and Mesa should supply the funds. [32]

The Board of Trade also named Davis as one of its representatives to the National Irrigation Congress, [33] but Davis later said he would have been there anyway under orders from Newell. Davis said he spent most of his time at the congress discussing engineering problems confronting the Reclamation Service in the various projects. [34]

At the congress, Charles C. Reppy of Florence, Pinal County, Arizona, wanted a resolution adopted demanding Congress enact a law prohibiting the spending of any reclamation fund money where any land was owned by private persons. Maricopa County Supervisor John P. Orme, returning to Phoenix from the Utah meeting, said Davis killed the Reppy proposal by saying there was not a single feasible irrigation project in the nation that did not involve some privately owned land; that the Tonto Basin project was the most feasible in the West, and that the San Carlos dam was not recommended because the depth to bedrock made it impractical and because it would have benefited no one but the Indians, something not contemplated by the reclamation act. [35]

Orme said Reppy "printed and circulated the bare-faced statement that Newell, Davis and Maxwell had been bribed, and he showed a picture of Mr. Maxwell's residence east of town, probably with a view of making it appear that this house was the bribe that was given to Mr. Maxwell. All of his accusations fell flat and were unheeded." [36]

Bids for the Reclamation Service work in the Tonto Basin were opened September 23 in Denver but the bidders and the amounts were not disclosed. [37]

The governors met October 5 and passed a resolution authorizing Fowler to appoint a committee of three,

Louis C. Hill

including himself, to discuss the advisability of building a road from the Valley to the dam site. The resolution invited the Board of Trade and the Phoenix, Tempe, and Mesa councils to appoint similar committees. [38]

In the days that followed, each of the towns and the Board of Trade complied, with Davis telling the Phoenix council the government could construct a trail sufficient for erecting the transmission line for $25,000. If the Valley residents were willing to raise $100,000, he was sure the government would increase its spending by another $50,000 to provide a good freight road. [39]

Davis also made arrangements for office space in the rooms of the Water Users' Association, Nicholson Building, 34 North Center Street, thereby making Phoenix his headquarters. [40]

On October 14, [41] Hitchock issued an order to Charles D. Walcott, director of the U. S. Geological Survey, to make contracts for the preliminary work on the Tonto reservoir. [42] In addition, the Reclamation Service was authorized to exercise the options it had taken on land in the Tonto Basin. Those were due to expire October 20. [43]

In reporting these matters, Charles C. Randolph, Washington correspondent of the **Republican,** wrote,

A source of annoyance to the [Interior] department is the attitude of several holders of land in the reservoir site who appear determined to hold up the government for excessive sums for their holdings. It is the policy of the department to avoid litigation and it will be liberal with land owners but it will not submit to extortions of the kind mentioned. . . There is no doubt that contracts would have been let some time ago but for obstacles created by land owners. [44]

Accounts of Hitchcock's actions were published the morning of October 15. Former Phoenix Mayor Walter Talbot and Clark, along with many others, viewed the announcement about the contracts as the culmination of the long struggle to get a reservoir. Talbot and Clark decided the time had come to celebrate. They took up a collection and then got some posters out announcing a meeting at 3 p.m. at the Board of Trade. They arranged for the Pioneer Band to play that night, and they bought all the fireworks they could find in the city. [45]

At the meeting, it was quickly agreed "a jollification meeting" [46] was in order that night, the details to be looked after by a committee of five that included Talbot and Clark. Another committee of three was assigned to send telegrams of appreciation to President Theodore Roosevelt, Hitchcock, Walcott, Newell, Davis, and Maxwell. [47] A vote of thanks was given to Fowler and a request he speak. Fowler thanked the group for its vote. He said that much remained to be done, but he was certain with cooperation, loyal support of each other, and patience, success was assured. [48]

Shortly after 7 p.m., the Pioneer Band marched up and down Washington Street, First Avenue, and Adams Street, with the crowd stopping in front of the Adams Hotel at Center and Adams. All the while, cannon crackers, little torpedoes, and other fireworks were set off so that "the Fourth of July was as nothing in comparison." [49]

The men chosen to speak at the jollification were on the balcony of the Adams Hotel. The four stories of the hotel were a blaze of electric lights. Among the speakers were Governor Alexander O. Brodie, attorney Joseph L. B. Alexander, hotelman John C. Adams, and Fowler. Various of the speakers made mention of Fowler and Maxwell. Credit also was given to Joseph H. Kibbey, legal counsel. [50]

Alexander recalled there was a time when he, as many others, had been in doubt as to whether the reservoir would be built. But those doubts had been allayed after Brodie had returned from Washington and told Alexander the president had expressed a desire the dam be built. Alexander closed by saying the people should support the construction of the Tonto Basin road. [51]

When the speeches were over, the Pioneer Band marched to the newspaper offices and gave serenades, the merrymaking continuing until late. [52]

Davis returned to Phoenix October 18. In an interview, he said preparatory work for construction of the power canal would go on while the cement works were being built. He said some cement would be required for the power canal. [53]

Another visitor was Edward T. Duryea of Colton, California, a government specialist in the manufacture of Portland cement. Duryea explained how the cement would be produced. He said the plant would be as small as any made but still would cost $100,000. Its capacity would be 300 barrels a day. The plant would be within 2,000 feet of the dam site. Just behind the plant location was a hill from which limestone would be taken. The limestone overlaid the mountain, so it would be necessary to quarry. The clay with which the limestone would be mixed was three miles distant. The heat for the kilns through which the mixture would pass would be furnished by burning oil. It would take 11 gallons of oil for each barrel of cement. The oil, purchased in California, would cost one cent a gallon. Delivered to Phoenix, it would cost two cents a gallon, or to Globe, three cents. It would take another five cents to deliver to the cement plant. Adding the cost of labor and electric power, the expense of producing 200,000 barrels was put at $2 a barrel. Duryea estimated that if the cement was bought in the marketplace, by the time it was delivered to the dam site it would cost $8 per barrel. [54]

Duryea also said the conditions for the manufacture of cement were as favorable at the site of the San Carlos dam as they were at the Tonto Basin. [55]

On October 22, the committee to build the road to Tonto Basin, under the chairmanship of Kibbey, issued a report in the form of a proposed federal law that would allow Phoenix, Tempe, and Mesa to sell bonds to raise money for construction of the road. [56] Congressional approval was needed because of an 1886 law known as the Harrison Act. The act limited territories and their political subdivisions from issuing bonds without first receiving permission from Congress.

In late October, about 200 men were working on the various works at the Tonto Basin. One-half of them were Apache Indians from the San Carlos Reservation. They were paid $1.50 per day plus board. The white men received $2 per day, rations, and lodging. [57]

Hitchcock announced on October 31 bids for building the power canal would be received by the Interior Department until December 8. The bids would be,

for the construction of about eighteen miles of canal, pressure pipes and tunnels, together with headworks, spill-ways and gates, for the diversion and conduction of about 200 cubic feet of water per second, from Salt River, about 25 miles north of Globe, Arizona, for power purposes. Proposals must be submitted in three bids, one for tunnels, one for pressure pipes, and one for other structures. [58]

Fowler and Kibbey presented the governors the results of the road committee's work on November 3, 1903. The governors authorized Fowler to go to Washington to work for passage of the proposed law to allow the cities of Phoenix, Tempe, and Mesa to bond themselves for building the Tonto Basin road. The governors also authorized Fowler and Kibbey to negotiate a lease for office space on the second floor of the new post office building, on the southeast corner of Monroe and Center. [59]

The next week, Louis Hill, Henry A. Storrs, a government electrical engineer, and two others arrived in Phoenix from the Tonto Basin over the route of the proposed wagon and telephone road. [60] Hill said excavation for the cement mill foundation was progressing and preparations for making brick necessary for erection of the building almost was finished. [61] Soon after, it was announced the Interior Department was asking bids for a thousand barrels of cement for use in the cement mill foundation, the temporary powerhouse, and other structures. [62]

Davis also had worked up the specifications for bids on driving a 500-foot tunnel through a solid rock formation on the north side of the river, at the dam site. The tunnel was to be used to divert the river around the dam site while the dam foundation was built. It was thought that diversion, plus water diverted into the power canal, would leave the dam site comparatively dry. After the dam was built, irrigation water would flow through the tunnel, which would have two headgates, one at the upper end for use only if there was some need to repair the one which would be farther down. The material for the headgates had not been selected, but both steel and bronze were being considered. [63]

Storrs said the telephone line would be about 75-miles long, but only about 50 miles would have to be constructed because the government contemplated acquiring the poles of the Arizona Water Co. between Phoenix and the Arizona Dam. He said most of the poles would be iron, but about 25 miles would be wood. Delivering the poles to where they would be raised would be difficult because of their weight and the terrain. [64] The contractor for the telephone line, James R. Thorpe of Denver, had gone to San Francisco, California, to purchase poles. [65]

Meantime, the Gila Valley and Globe Telephone Co. arranged to extend its line 24 miles from Globe to Livingston, receiving a contribution of $800 from Globe merchants for construction. The money was to be repaid by free use of the line until the debt was paid and by reduced tolls thereafter. [66]

Globe businessmen, as well as some in the Salt River Valley, talked about opening small stores and other commercial enterprises at the government town site on a high bluff three-quarters of a mile upstream of the dam. [67] The government welcomed all enterprise without limitation, except that the sale of liquor would be prohibited there and at construction camps. [68]

The new town lacked a name. The Globe people discussed it, coming up with the name Olberg after Charles R. Olberg, a Geological Survey engineer involved in much of the preliminary work. [69] Olberg, however, protested the town being named after him, [70] and it wasn't long before the place was called Roosevelt. [71]

Norman H. Livingston, who operated a store at Livingston about 11 miles upstream at the mouth of Pinto Creek, may have been the first shopkeeper at Roosevelt. He also planned to operate a restaurant and a hay and grain business. E. F. Kellner & Co. of Globe planned to open a store within a few weeks. [72]

In late November, a letter from Fowler arrived. He said the bonding bill could not be passed in the "present extra session" of Congress, but it would be introduced early in December and no opposition was expected. [73]

Fowler also found himself in the midst of a controversy involving the cement industry. A couple of the cement manufacturers, one of them George Stone of San Francisco, president of the Pacific Portland Cement Co., visited Hitchcock and told him that the government had no business making cement, and it would be illegal for it to do so. [74]

According to a dispatch from Randolph, the *Republican's* correspondent, Stone informed Hitchcock that permitting the Geological Survey to make the cement at the Tonto Basin would be detrimental to the Republican Party. Stone argued the product the government intended to make would be inferior. However, should it be manufactured successfully, this might encourage other persons to enter the business and cheapen the cost, thereby destroying the industry. Stone threatened to try to get a bill through Congress to prevent the government from making cement. He also intimated cement could be delivered to the reservoir site for under $5 per barrel. Randolph said this compared with the $2.50 per barrel it would cost if made at the dam site and the $9.50 per barrel being asked by the "cement trust." [75]

Stone denied there was a cement trust, but acknowledged there was an association of Portland cement manufacturers. He said he could supply the government with cement at $1.75 per barrel f.o.b. Adding the cost of railroad shipping, the cement could be delivered in Phoenix at $3.25 per barrel, or Globe at $3.55, provided he got the contract for the entire estimated 200,000 barrels. Added to the price would be the wagon haul to the dam from Globe, which would mean another $1.90 for a total of $5.45 per barrel. [76]

As soon as Fowler learned about the cement makers' insistence on supplying the cement, he began lining up support from senators and representatives to protect the Water Users' Association's interests. [77]

In Phoenix, Davis said that, even if the cement price came

down to $5.50 per barrel, that would still be more than double what it would cost to produce at the site. [78]

Davis also said that contracts for the cement machinery and buildings already had been received as well as proposals for hauling the materials to the Tonto Basin. Based on these expenses, he said the cement plant would cost less to build than estimated. If a reduction in the cost of transporting the oil could be secured, the price per barrel of cement would be even lower. [79]

"The cost would not be more than $2 per barrel after the mill has been completed," Davis said. [80] He suggested the government invite bids from manufacturers to produce cement at the dam site, which would eliminate the cost of freight. It also would force the successful bidder to do the work as decided by the Reclamation Service, but this was a matter for Hitchcock to decide, Davis said. [81]

The cement makers met with Interior Department officials November 25. After the meeting, department officials announced they would ask for bids on 200,000 barrels of cement, letting it also be known the government had given up, at least temporarily, the idea of making its own cement. The bids were expected to take one of two forms: the government to furnish at the site a 250-barrel per day mill and power to operate it, or the cement to be manufactured elsewhere, shipped to Globe or Phoenix by rail, and hauled to the Tonto Basin. The manufacturers and Interior Department agreed to ask the railroads for reduced rates; if the railroads agreed, the lowest bids would be sought from the makers and the government's plant abandoned. [82]

Davis said that, if the cement mill at the Tonto site was given up, it was certain the dam and reservoir "can never be built for the original estimate." [83]

The *Republican* suggested a cement company be organized in the Valley should there be a call for bids. [84] The *Gazette* proposed the ranchers of the Water Users' Association take control of the cement plant, [85] while the *Enterprise* said protests to the Interior Department's decision should be sent through Fowler. [86]

On December 2, work was shut down on the Tonto road above Goldfield about 22 miles northeast of Mesa. [87] Although newspapers described the halt in work as temporary, [88] apparently to allow for a more complete survey of the road, [89] "rumors respecting it had grown from a mole hill into a mountain." [90] One rumor was work had been suspended at the Tonto Basin, and another was Davis had been replaced. [91] Davis had left for the reservoir site soon after the road work had stopped. [92] When he returned December 23, Davis said the rumors were wrong. Everything was proceeding nicely, and there was nothing to worry about, he said. [93] This included demonstrating for prospective bidders the character of the work connected with the power canal and preparing the cement mill foundation. Material for the telephone line was being distributed, [94] and the road to the sawmill site was completed. [95] In addition, J. E. Sturgeon of Tempe signed an agreement to farm the land in the Tonto Basin acquired by the government from settlers. [96]

On December 18, the road bonding bill was approved by the U.S. House of Representatives, [97] and on December 19 Newell testified about the cement question at a special joint meeting of the Senate and House Committees on Irrigation. Newell said the government would manufacture cement at the dam site if that was the cheapest way to get it. He said it was doubtful the cement makers could deliver it cheaper. If there was any possibility that could happen, it would be because of the high price of shipping oil from California to the Tonto Basin. But even then, Newell said he did not think the private cement makers could produce it for less. [98]

First supplies to Roosevelt were freighted from Globe. A typical teamster, February 6, 1904.

Davis had been criticized for not calling for bids, but Newell said Davis had obtained figures "from California manufacturers nearest to the dam site, showing the lowest price of cement, delivered at the site, would be $9 per barrel." Newell said if bids had been solicited, it would have spared him criticism too, but he thought Davis was justified in considering the $9 per barrel figure was made in good faith. Newell said Davis had not considered the quotation to be a starting point for future negotiations. He said Davis was a frank person, and he expected the cement makers would be the same. Davis should not be censured because he overlooked the finagling that went on in negotiating prices. [99]

Bids were opened December 23 at the Interior Department for construction of the 500-foot tunnel on the north side of the river. [100] On January 6, 1904, bids were opened for the power canal, [101] and two days later the department received bids for the delivery of 1,000 barrels of cement at Globe, the low bid being $4.80 per barrel. The same news dispatch reporting the cement bid said the government engineers, in calculating the cost of cement delivered at the dam, learned a mining company at Globe was paying $6.80 per barrel. Adding the cost of carrying the cement 40 miles over the mountain trail, they had come up with the $9 per barrel estimate. [102]

Cement at $9 per barrel would have made the building of a masonary dam prohibitive. This had led to the search for materials to determine whether cement could be produced there. Eight rock and clay samples were sent to the cement works at Colton for analysis. Test results showed a good quality material could be made. [103]

The same day the bids for the cement were opened, the Senate passed the bonding bill. It was expected it would reach the president for his signature on January 12. [104] However, Roosevelt did not sign it until January 21. [105] Fowler wrote the delay in signing "was caused by the fact of it being a bill affecting the territory and hence necessitating several references and no little red tape." [106]

Meantime, the consulting and construction engineers involved with building the various Reclamation Service projects were called to Washington to discuss the cement situation. The principle involved in manufacturing cement for the Tonto Basin project was identical to that which would apply to the other projects. The cement manufacturers maintained the government had no,

duty to enter into the manufacture of any class of commodities. If the government can erect cement plants to avoid the cost of railroad transportation, middlemen's profits and manufacturer's profits, it is its duty to erect mills for the manufacture of blankets, clothing, shoes, etc., worn by its soldiers and sailors, to manufacture iron for its building construction, to operate mines for its gold and silver currency, etc. . . in no case should the government enter into any competition with the general public. [107]

The cement industry argued if the dam should be built and collapse because of poor quality cement made by the Reclamation Service, millions of dollars invested by the government and private land holders would be lost. The government would be without any security, which the private makers would provide if given the contract to make the cement, and the only punishment to the government men might be the firing of an incompetent superintendent. The manufacturers said they would be willing to produce cement at the dam site provided the material found there met the qualities of Portland cement of known character, but they wanted the option of supplying it from their own mills. If the cement was produced at the site, the government would own the mill, but it would provide the bidder electrical power free for its operation. In outlining these conditions in a letter to Hitchcock, the Portland cement industry said,

We, however, do not recognize that the government in the construction of a dam, should, without requesting bids from cement manufacturers for the cement to be supplied, proceed to construct and operate a cement works as part of the construction of the dam—such cement works and operations of the same being no part of that which would be called for in bids for the construction of the dam, or materials entering therein. [108]

The letter added it was a source of gratification to the industry to find "that the high price at which it was claimed cement would cost at this time, arose from the excessive cost of transportation, and not from excessive factory price of the material." [109]

A government engineer associated with the Tonto Basin project, probably Davis, had told the **Enterprise** it "would not be very comfortable to have outside contractors there." He said the contractors probably would not be satisfied with the mill, nor would they want to work for six months and stop for six months, if that were necessary. [110] Another problem was government laborers were restricted to working eight hours per day, which was two hours less than private companies. This was a 20 percent advantage in favor of the cement makers. [111]

Another time, Davis said he did not want to be handicapped by the presence of a private cement maker, and he expressed confidence that would not happen. [112]

Nonetheless, in accordance with its November commitment, the Interior Department called for bids on January 25. It specified the quantity at between 150,000 and 250,000 barrels. [113] Correspondent Randolph of the **Republican** said this amounted "to a practical abandonment of the project for a cement factory at the site," but he said the Geological Survey had received assurances the bid would be about $4 per barrel, delivered at the site. He said the Globe, Gila Valley and Northern Railroad had made material concessions. The bids were to be opened February 29. [114]

While this was going on, progress continued on all phases of the work, including road building—except for the section above Goldfield. Engineer W. A. Farish of the Reclamation Service reported that much of the work was in rock, [115] which was one reason why the **Silver Belt** had written if "some of the Phoenix enthusiasts would visit the box canyon and see the character of the work being done to make it possible to construct the transmission line, we think their hearts would fail them on the wagon road proposition. The excavating is nearly all in solid rock and very slow and expensive." [116] Despite this, by mid-January eight miles of the road from the dam site west toward Fish Creek Hill had been constructed. [117] In addition, work on a high line road to shorten the distance to Globe was progressing. [118]

Five miles of telephone poles had been put up from the

Arizona Dam in the direction of the Tonto Basin. [119] The men putting up the telephone line expected to reach Mormon Flat by February 1. [120] In all, about 400 men were employed, including 30 on the telephone line and 75 on the cement plant. Hill, the engineer supervising the work, said the mill foundation was in and the building was going up. Fifteen men were cutting trees and sawing lumber in the mountains, furnishing 5,000 to 6,000 feet of lumber a day. Thirty were at a cadastral survey camp south of Mesa. Ten were surveying. The remainder were building roads and freighting supplies from Globe. [121]

The power canal contracts had been let for the excavation of about 600,000 yards of material, the drilling of 7,000 feet of tunnel in connection with building the power canal and the manufacture of pressure pipe. [122]

The tiny community of Roosevelt had a barber shop, a drugstore, a meat market, a shoe shop, a livery stable, two restaurants, two lodging houses, and three general stores. Two doctors were present. One of them was in private practice, and the other worked for the government. A private party had put up a town hall where dances were held on Saturday night. [123] A 40,000-gallon water reservoir was built above the cement mill site. Plans were made to pipe water in three miles from Cottonwood Canyon through one- and one-half and 2-inch pipes, eliminating the camp's dependence on river water. [124]

In mid-January, Kibbey was summoned to Washington to confer with Reclamation Service officials about legal matters in connection with the water storage project. [125] While the nature of the legal matters was not disclosed, one of them involved writing a contract between the Water Users' Association and the Interior Department, providing for repayment of the money advanced for building the reservoir and associated works. As it turned out, Kibbey also was involved in government negotiations to acquire the rights of the Hudson Reservoir and Canal Co. at the Tonto Basin.

The day before leaving for Washington, Kibbey met with land owners under the Salt River Valley, Maricopa, and Grand canals to discuss formation of canal districts in accordance with article 9 of the Water Users' Association articles of incorporation. The landowners approved the form of a petition to be submitted to the Council calling for the creation of the districts. The owners under each canal then met separately to sign the petition for their canal. The petition was the work of a 21-member committee of landowners from the three canals headed by John R. Norton. [126] The landowners also discussed how their relative rights to water would be determined. If there always was enough water, this would not be a problem. But should there be a miscalculation in the number of acres that could be served or should drought occur, the priority of rights had to be known, and the Reclamation Service insisted this question be settled in the beginning. Just how this would be done was not decided, but the filing of a friendly lawsuit or finding another means were discussed. [127]

Rumors had circulated in the Valley the Hudson Reservoir and Canal Co. was demanding $100,000 for its claims in the Tonto Basin. According to the February 11 *Gazette,* the demand had been put to the Interior Department by former Governor Nathan O. Murphy and Sims Ely, who was secretary of the Hudson company as well as editor of the *Republican.* ". . . owing to the demands for $100,000, the construction work on the Tonto reservoir has been delayed," the *Gazette* said. It said local attorneys and those in Washington denied the Hudson company had any claim to the reservoir site, and, if it did, its claims were not worth a third of the price demanded. The newspaper gave two reasons why there had been no public discussion: first, those with knowledge of the situation did not want "to create any unnecessary agitation in the valley," and, second, there was confidence that Fowler and Kibbey would take care of the people's interest. If claims of the Hudson company were established, the Water Users' Association would pay a just sum, the paper said. [128]

The following day, the *Gazette* reported the Mann family of New York, owners of the Hudson company, claimed their right to the Tonto dam site did not expire until October 1905, "and if they hold out, operations on the government reservoir cannot begin until then, and probably not until after the case has been carried to the court. This might delay the dam for several years." [129]

On February 13, the *Enterprise* reported a compromise price of $40,000 was to be paid to the Hudson Reservoir and Canal Co. The newspaper commented:

This means that the farmers of Salt River Valley will have to pay forty thousand dollars for something which neither by them nor by the government, prior to the institution of the Murphy and Ely claim, was ever taken into consideration. . . If nothing else arises. . . active work will be begun at Tonto in a short time. But for the institution of this claim work might have been under way nearly if not quite three months ago. [130]

The next morning, Sunday, February 14, the *Gazette* editorially accused Ely, Murphy and the *Republican* of trying to hold-up their neighbors. The *Gazette* said when the Water Users' Association was formed, the people,

did not for a moment believe that any citizen, resident or property owner, who would be benefited by the construction of the Tonto reservoir, would ever be guilty of attempting a hold-up and virtually rob his friends and neighbors of $100,000, every dollar of which is equal to a drop of blood. . .

Had the graft been attempted in the open and by outsiders, the people would have known how to meet them on the field but to have those who owe their present and future to the people, turn traitor and strike in the dark, is more than the limit. . . [131]

The *Republican* chose the same Sunday morning to comment, asserting that accusations against it and charges that the work on the reservoir might be delayed were inspired by the newspaper's desire for an uninstructed delegation to the Republican National Convention of 1904. The *Republican* maintained if it could be shown it "is connected with any object in opposition to the welfare of the people of the valley," its influence in the delegation matter would be weakened. It said, "the newspapers. . . being served by the Washington grapevine service" were urging an instructed delegation to the GOP convention. [132]

The *Republican* said it was uncertain about the claims of the Hudson company. The newspaper said a member of the

Water Users' Association reported he had been informed by the Interior Department the Hudson company's right was valid. The paper said it also had learned the agreement to pay $40,000 had been reached with the consent of Fowler and Kibbey. Regarding the charge the dam had been threatened, the *Republican* said:

There has been at no time a cessation of operations at the dam, as the grapevine papers well know. There was last fall a discontinuance of work on the cement mill in consequences of the appeal made to the Interior Department by a representative of the cement manufacturers. Even that work is now resumed in part. All the time a small army of men has been employed in the various operations possible before the actual work of dam building is commenced. . .

The Republican *seldom wastes so many words on misrepresentation so utterly silly as this is. We are not sure now that we have not been recklessly extravagant.* [133]

The *Republican's* words fueled the flames of journalistic self-righteousness. For readers not privy to the behind-the-scenes maneuvering, it helped produce only a bit more understanding of what allegedly happened.

The *Enterprise* said it was a Democratic newspaper and it was indifferent to what Republicans did. It charged the so-called legality of the Hudson Reservoir and Canal Co. claim had been fixed "not by exhaustive investigation before an unbiased tribunal," but by Murphy's "intimate acquaintance with Secretary Hitchcock" and by Murphy's representations as a lobbyist for the Santa Fe Railroad. The newspaper said the Hudson company people had "performed no work since 1891, except to relocate the site and amend their plans from time to time." It said by the time Kibbey and Fowler became involved, they confronted "a condition, and not a theory," and their fight was "for as small a hold-up as possible." As to the *Republican,* the *Enterprise* said:

Certain it is that the negotiations have been carried on in the dark, consummated in the dark, and much uneasiness is being caused the Republican *by the present expose.* [134]

The *Gazette's* response was to accuse the *Republican* of knowing "nothing of honest motives" and of never advocating "any cause except when its managers saw a chance for a rake-off. Honest men consider a denunciation by the *Republican* as a high compliment. . . " The *Gazette* reached a crescendo in vituperativeness:

The history of the Republican *is a continued story of graft, grab, pilfer and steal, and it has become so thoroughly saturated with evil designs that the common ordinary foot pad, outlaw and moral degenerate are angels in comparison.* [135]

Meanwhile, the owner of the *Republican,* George W. Vickers, sent a telegram to Kibbey recounting the statements appearing in the *Enterprise* and *Gazette.* He asked Kibbey to respond. Kibbey sent a wire, which was published in the *Republican* the morning of February 16:

Work was not held up on the Tonto dam site by threats of litigation by the Hudson Reservoir company. There is no conclusive action yet by the Interior Department, but the situation is satisfactory to Mr. Fowler and myself. Governor Murphy had nothing to do with the matter that I know of. Mr. Ely, secretary of the company, was present at the hearing, but not as principal in presenting it. Mr. Ely's connection with the matter has been entirely fair. [136]

The hearing to which Kibbey referrred apparently was

one conducted by an advisory board of five engineers appointed in January by the Geological Survey. Kibbey and Fowler represented the Water Users' Association at the hearing, while Henry R. Mann, president, and Ely appeared for the Hudson Reservoir and Canal Co. The advisory board decided $40,000 should be paid to the company, an action the *Gazette* said was taken February 16. The *Gazette* correspondent in Washington reported Kibbey had told him:

If the company had held out in the demand for $100,000, it might have caused delay in the work on the Tonto dam indefinitely, by litigation, especially, as it was contended that the franchise was self-forfeiting by the mere lapse of time, but might require a judicial declaration of forfeiture. [137]

Concerning the Kibbey telegram printed in the *Republican,* the *Gazette* said:

The alleged telegram from Judge Kibbey might have been secured through misrepresentation. . . [138]

Ely returned to Phoenix February 19. Upon learning about what he said were "a lot of falsehoods concerning the settlement between the government and the Hudson Reservoir and Canal," Ely wrote an article to set the record straight. He said it was lies that the company either delayed or threatened to delay the Tonto reservoir, that there had been graft, that the negotiations were secret, that political influence was involved, and that Murphy was involved in any manner. [139]

Ely said he several times had stated in public before water committees of Valley citizens the company would ask at least $100,000 and probably $200,000 for its claims. He said the owners could have delayed construction indefinitely and might have recovered as much as $200,000, but, "They did not wish to be obstructionists on the eve of success—although it was a success in which everybody but themselves would share." [140]

That ended the controversy over purchase of the dam site. The last step in the transaction was the filing by the government of a deed to the property with the county recorder on July 25, 1904. [141]

Three members of the Board of Governors, Alexander J. Chandler, Frank Alkire, and Ethelbert W. Wilbur, met with Hill February 19. Hill informed them the wagon road to the reservoir site had been named the Phoenix-Roosevelt road, with the length between Mesa and Roosevelt about 60 miles. He also presented a list of the estimated construction costs of the road between certain points, the most expensive being two miles at Fish Creek Hill at $6,000 per mile. Hill's estimate was $78,100. He also said the grade at no place would exceed six percent. Based on Hill's figures, the three governors decided to recommend a bond issue of $80,000 for the three cities. [142]

At a meeting March 1, the joint road committee met with Hill and Davis. After an extended discussion, it was decided the cities should provide $75,000 for construction of the freight road. The committee adopted a resolution asking the cities to hold bond elections in the following amounts: Phoenix $67,500, Tempe $4,000, and Mesa $3,500. [143]

Even as the committee acted, work on the road continued.

U.S. Reclamation Service engineers, laborers and Roosevelt townspeople, February 2, 1904.

Thorpe said it was a road worth seeing and was being constructed regardless of expense. He said it was 10 miles from Roosevelt to the mouth of Fish Creek, and the road was being blasted out of solid rock by blowing off the ends of the mountains which run down the canyon. Thorpe said the terrain reminded him of European highways, but the primal virginity of the Tonto country had been destroyed by the vigorous road building. [144]

Hill and Duryea came in over the road, reporting travel was not now so serious an undertaking. From their camp, they traveled by wagon to the end of the road, then 27 miles by horseback, then by carriage to Mesa, and then by rail to Phoenix. [145]

The telephone poles had been set to the top of Fish Creek Hill and wire men were not far behind. [146] The telephone from the dam site to Globe was finished and the first message was spoken February 12. [147] A temporary electric plant was operating at Roosevelt, furnishing power for lights. [148]

In late February, some of the government officials moved their operations to the north side of the river opposite Roosevelt. A suspension bridge was to be constructed over the river. A number of men were laid off pending the start of work on the power canal. [149]

On February 27, the Council divided the land signed into the Water Users' Association into 10 districts from which one governor and three council members would be elected April 5. [150]

Davis and Kibbey returned to the Valley, and Davis said the cement bids would be opened February 29, and it was unlikely there would be any bids to manufacture the cement at the dam site. He said if the low bid was near estimates made by government engineers, a contract would be awarded. [151]

Kibbey reported he expected the government had by now signed the contract with the association, and he expected a copy at any time. He said it had to be ratified by members of the association. He also said Davis had informed him that by March 1, the government would have spent or would have under contract $1 million on the Tonto Basin project. [152]

Kibbey said the government would build the cement works regardless of the bids. The cement mill would be built as a precautionary measure. The reason was that the government was not going to award the entire cement contract at once. And on subsequent bids, if too high for the dam's construction, the government could produce the cement itself. Kibbey said he expected the low bid to be less than $2.75 per barrel. This would earn the manufacturer no money, but he said the makers figured they would make money by keeping the government out of the business. [153]

On March 1, Kibbey received a telegram from Fowler saying he had the approved contract, and he would have it with him when he arrived in Phoenix on Saturday, March 5. [154] A community reception was planned to honor Fowler and Kibbey for securing the contract. [155]

News of the cement bids was received March 2 in a telegram to Davis from Newell. There were three bids for delivery of cement at the dam site: $4,89, $5.40 and $5.70. [156] There also was an informal bid to deliver cement at $3 per barrel to Globe. Davis wired Newell to reject all bids. Davis said the government could make the cement at $3 per barrel. He said this was an uncontroverted fact. He said no manufacturer had investigated producing the cement at the dam site. A reporter for the **Republican** asked if the government would call for new bids or proceed to make the cement. Davis said he could not answer that question, [157] but the Interior Department the next day announced all cement bids had been rejected. [158] On March 4, the department said the government would make its own cement. [159]

The reception for Fowler was postponed until Monday, March 7, because he did not arrive in Phoenix until Saturday night. [160] Sunday night, with Davis present, Fowler gave a long interview on his affairs in Washington. He said Kibbey and Davis arrived as the contract negotiations began and their services were indispensable in explaining conditions to clerks in the Interior Department who knew nothing about the Valley and its conditions. Fowler said he did not believe anyone could have taken the place of Kibbey in this work. Fowler said what actually was signed was a memorandum of agreement between the government and the Water Users' Association. Once it was ratified by the association and the shareholders, it would be returned to Washington and serve as the contract. [161]

In the meantime, there would be no delay in the actual work, Fowler said. He added the work would go on because of the government's strong faith in the honest purpose of the people. He said Davis would have stopped the work six months ago were it not for that faith. Davis concurred, saying, "The government felt justified in keeping on, by the great interest of the valley in the enterprise." Davis said a delay of a year would have been of incalculable damage to the farmers, perhaps by as much as $2 million. [162]

Fowler said the work in the Valley was being watched with great interest. He said the government's approval of what had been done was so high the articles of incorporation and other documents prepared for the Water Users' Association had been copied by other associations. Davis said there was something about which Fowler would not speak, and this was the offer of a position in the Reclamation Service to assist in organizing other water users' associations. Davis said the salary offered was almost twice the amount Fowler received from the association, but he turned down the job because his services were needed in the Valley. [163] Fowler was paid $2,000 per year. [164]

The reception for Fowler and Kibbey outside the courthouse began at 2:30 p.m. with music by the Pioneer and Indian School bands. The **Republican** said the turnout of people was greater than the one 18 months earlier when George Maxwell pointed the way to get the reservoir, and the previous June when the gathering of enough acres signed into the association was celebrated. [165]

Fowler and Kibbey were compared to returning war heros. County attorney Albert C. Baker said the Rough Riders had not done as much for the country as had Kibbey and Fowler. Davis said they had accomplished more than people realized because they had induced the government to commit itself to a definite plan, when the most that could reasonably have been expected was a tentative and conditional agreement. But in this instance, the government was proceeding on the faith of the people represented by them, Davis said. [166]

Kibbey and Fowler spoke, Kibbey reviewing events leading to the proposed contract, and Fowler stressing the responsibility placed on the people and the confidence expressed in them by the government in the memorandum of agreement.

"This agreement with the government means that we will get the dam, and get the water," Kibbey said. "It will not, after the dam is built, be a question of whether or not to plant crops, or whether or not the season may be dry, for the water will be here, and we will know just what we have to depend upon." [167]

Fowler urged the passage of the road bonding bill and read a letter from Newell recommending the road as a matter of convenience and economy. Fowler also read a letter from Hitchcock, which had accompanied the memorandum. Hitchcock said the proposed agreement,

will secure the most economical distribution of the water upon the lands that can profitably be benefited thereby, will avoid conflicts that might otherwise arise in the distribution of the water, will be most effective in preventing any interference with vested rights that have heretofore been acquired, will equitably distribute the cost of construction, maintenance, and operation of the works, and will assure the government reimbursement of all money expended in and upon the project. [168]

Fowler also said the contract for the power canal had been let at a price of about $500,000, and within 90 days 1,000 men would be at work in the Tonto Basin. [169]

At the conclusion of his remarks, the assembly adopted a resolution giving the "warmest kind of thanks and gratitude of the people" to Fowler, Kibbey, Davis, and Maxwell. [170]

1. *Arizona Republican* (Phoenix), August 4, 1903.
2. *Arizona Gazette* (Phoenix), August 14, 1903.
3. *Republican*, August 15, 22, 1904; *Salt River Project, Final History to 1916*, Vol. I. p. 67, 72, unpublished manuscript, Salt River Project Archives (herafter SRPA).
4. *Final History to 1916.* Vol. I, P. 67.
5. *Gazette*, August 16, 1903.
6. *Ibid.*, August 14, 1903.
7. *Arizona Silver Belt* (Globe), August 22, 1903, reprinted in the *Gazette*, August 25, 1903.
8. *Silver Belt*, reprinted in the *Gazette*, August 11, 1903.
9. *Gazette*, August 19, 1903.
10. *Ibid.*, September 2, 1903.
11. *Ibid*, September 2, 1903.
12. *Ibid.*
13. *Republican*, January 8, 1918.
14. *Ibid*, September 2, 1903; *Gazette*, September 2, 1903.

15. *Final History to 1916,* Vol. I, p. 120.
16. *Gazette*, August 19, 1903.
17. *Ibid.; Republican*, August 23, 1903.
18. *Gazette*, August 21, 1903.
19. *Enterprise*, September 1, 1903.
20. *Republican*, September 2, 1903.
21. *Ibid.*, August 27, 1903.
22. Arthur P. Davis, *Second Annual Report of the Reclamation Service, 1902-1903* (Washington: Government Printing Office, 1904) p. 72.
23. *Enterprise*, August 28, 1903.
24. *Ibid.*, August 31, 1903.
25. *Ibid.*, August 28, 1903.
26. *Gazette*, September 2, 1903.
27. *Ibid.; Republican*, September 2, 1903.
28. *Republican*, September 2, 1903; *Gazette*, September 4, 1903.
29. *Ibid.*

30. *Final History to 1916,* Vol I., p. 73.
31. *Republican,* September 2, 1903.
32. *Gazette,* September 2, 1903.
33. *Republican,* September 2, 1903.
34. *Ibid.,* October 1, 1903.
35. *Enterprise,* September 25, 1903.
36. *Ibid.*
37. *Republican,* September 24, 1903.
38. *Ibid.,* October 6, 1903.
39. *Ibid.*
40. *Ibid.,* October 8, 1903.
41. Davis, *Second Annual Report of the Reclamation Service,* p. 72, said Secretary Hitchcock on October 12, 1903, approved the award of contracts for various work associated with the Tonto Basin project.
42. *Ibid.* The contractors and the work they were to do: Wilcox & Rose, Riverside, Calif., erect building for manufacture of cement; Hendrie & Bolthoff, Denver, Colo., electric motors for cement mill; Babcock Electric Manufacturing Co., generators for temporary power plant; Stillwell-Bierce and Smith-Vaile Co., water wheels for temporary power plant; Allis-Chalmers Co., machinery for manufacturing cement: James R. Thorpe, telephone line from Arizona Dam to Livingston; *Republican,* October 15, 1903.
43. *Republican,* October 15, 1903.
44. *Ibid.*
45. *Republican,* October 16, 1903; *Gazette,* October 16, 1903.
46. *Republican,* October 16, 1903.
47. *Ibid.; Gazette,* October 16, 1903.
48. *Republican,* October 16, 1903.
49. *Gazette,* October 16, 1903.
50. *Ibid.; Republican,* October 16, 1903.
51. *Ibid.*
52. *Ibid.*
53. *Republican,* October 19, 1903.
54. *Ibid.,* October 22, 1903.
55. *Ibid.*
56. *Ibid.*
57. *Gazette,* October 20, 1903; *Enterprise,* October 28, 1903.
58. *Republican,* November 6, 1903.
59. *Ibid.,* November 3, 1903.
60. *Ibid.,* November 11, 1903; *Gazette,* November 10, 1903.
61. *Republican,* November 11, 1903.
62. *Ibid.,* November 18, 1903.
63. *Ibid.,* November 14, 1903; *Gazette,* November 19, December 24, 1903; Louis C. Hill, *Third Annual Report of the Reclamation Service, 1903-1904,* (Washington: Government Printing Office, 1905) p. 146.
64. *Gazette,* November 10, 1093; *Final History to 1916,* Vol. 1, p. 62.
65. *Republican,* November 8, 1903.
66. *Ibid.,* November 30, 1903.
67. *Ibid.,* November 11, 1903; *Final History to 1916,* Vol. I., p. 60.
68. *Republican,* November 11, 1903.
69. *Silver Belt,* undated, reprinted *Enterprise,* November 17, 1903.
70. *Enterprise,* November 25, 1903.
71. *Republican,* January 31, 1904; Omar A. Turney, who was with the U. S. Geological Survey in the Tonto Basin and later was an engineer in the Salt River Valley, took credit for giving the name Roosevelt to the town; *Republican,* October 11, 1914; another story about how the name Roosevelt came in to use was told in the *Republican,* April 13, 1908, crediting unnamed censors in Washington who decided the name Tonto, which "in the Apache language means 'fool,'" was inappropriate for the dam. They thereupon decided to name the dam after President Theodore Roosevelt.
72. *Silver Belt,* undated, reprinted *Enterprise,* November 17, 1903.
73. *Republican,* November 22, 1903.
74. *Ibid.*
75. *Ibid.,* The cement manufacturers interpreted the Republican Party platform of 1900, which promised protection of home industries, to include the cement business. Instead of doing that, the administation proposed going into competition with it, they argued. Moreover, the industry had contributed liberally to the campaign of William McKinley and his running mate, Theodore Roosevelt, *Republican,* March 7, 1904.
76. *Republican,* November 24, 1903.
77. *Gazette,* November 22, 1903.
78. *Ibid.,* November 24, 1903.
79. *Republican,* November 24, 1903.
80. *Gazette,* November 24, 1903.
81. *Ibid.*
82. *Ibid.,* November 26, 1903.
83. *Enterprise,* November 26, 1903.
84. *Republican,* November 28, 1903.
85. *Gazette,* November 29, 1903.
86. *Enterprise,* November 26, 1903.
87. *Republican,* December 4, 1903.
88. *Ibid.; Gazette,* December 3, 1903.
89. *Republican,* December 16, 1903.
90. *Ibid.,* December 4, 1903.
91. *Ibid.,* December 15, 24, 1903.
92. *Ibid.,* December 15, 1903.
93. *Ibid.,* December 24, 1903.
94. *Ibid.,* December 23, 1903.
95. *Enterprise,* November 30, 1903.
96. *Republican,* December 16, 17, 1903.
97. *Ibid.,* December 19, 1903.
98. *Ibid.,* December 22, 1903.
99. *Ibid.*
100. *Gazette,* December 24, 1903.
101. *Republican,* January 8, 1904.
102. *Enterprise,* January 8, 1904.
103. *Final History to 1916,* Vol. I. p. 80.
104. *Republican,* January 9, 1904.
105. *Gazette,* January 22, 1904.
106. *Republican,* February 2, 1904.
107. *Gazette,* January 2, 1904.
108. *Ibid.*
109. *Ibid.*
110. *Enterprise,* November 26, 1903.
111. *Republican,* December 22, 1903.
112. *Enterprise,* December 18, 1903.
113. *Republican,* January 26, 1904, March 4, 1904.
114. *Ibid.,* January 27, 1904.
115. *Gazette,* January 8, 1904.
116. *Silver Belt,* undated, reprinted *Enterprise,* November 25, 1903.
117. *Gazette,* January 13, 1904.
118. *Ibid.*
119. *Ibid.*
120. *Republican,* January 26, 1904.
121. *Ibid.; Enterprise,* February 1, 1904.
122. *Republican,* February 2, 29, 1904.
123. *Ibid.*
124. *Enterprise,* February 1, 1904; *Republican,* February 13, 1904.
125. *Republican,* January 16, 1904.
126. *Ibid.,* January 17, 1904.
127. *Ibid.*
128. *Gazette,* February 11, 1904.
129. *Ibid.,* February 12, 1904.
130. *Enterprise,* February 13, 1904.
131. *Gazette,* February 14, 1904.
132. *Republican,* February 14, 1904.
133. *Ibid.*
134. *Enterprise,* February 15, 1904.
135. *Gazette,* February 16, 1904.
136. *Republican,* February 16, 1904.
137. *Gazette,* February 17, 1904.
138. *Ibid.*
139. *Republican,* February 20, 1904.

140. *Ibid.*
141. *Ibid.,* July 6, 1904.
142. *Ibid.,* February 20, 1904.
143. *Ibid.,* March 2, 1904.
144. *Ibid.,* February 11, 1904.
145. *Ibid.,* February 19, 1904.
146. *Ibid.,* February 14, 1904.
147. *Ibid.,* February 18, 1904.
148. *Ibid.,* February 14, 1904.
149. *Gazette,* March 1, 1904.
150. *Republican,* February 28, 1904.
151. *Ibid.,* February 29, 1904.
152. *Ibid.,* March 1, 1904.
153. *Ibid.*
154. *Ibid.,* March 2, 1904.
155. *Ibid.,* March 4, 5, 6, 8, 1904.
156. *Republican,* March 3, 1904, gives the low bid at $4.81 per barrel, but *Final History to 1916,* Vol. I, p. 82, puts the price at $4.89 per barrel delivered at Roosevelt. "This was probably based upon cash f.o.b. factory of but little more than $1 per barrel and nearly $3.89 for freight by rail and wagon."
157. *Republican,* March 3, 1904; *Gazette,* March 3, 1904.

158. *Republican,* March 4, 1904.
159. *Ibid.,* March 5, 1904.
160. *Ibid.,* March 6, 1904.
161. *Ibid.,* March 7, 1904.
162. *Ibid.*

163. *Ibid.* According to the *Republican,* June 10, 1903, Fowler was hired by the U. S. Geological Survey in 1902 to do "a cadastral survey" of the Valley, but quit when he was made president of the Water Users' Association. The *Enterprise,* June 9, 1903, said Fowler's salary from the Geological Survey was more than what the association paid him.

164. *The Taming of the Salt* (Salt River Project: Phoenix, 1970), p. 76.

165. *Republican,* March 8, 1904; *Gazette,* March 8, 1904.
166. *Republican,* March 8, 1904.
167. *Gazette,* March 8, 1904.

168. E. A. Hitchcock to C. D. Walcott, February 25, 1904, reprinted in *Republican,* March 8, 1904, and *Gazette,* March 8, 1904.

169. *Gazette,* March 8, 1904.
170. *Ibid.; Republican,* March 8, 1904.

March 1904 - February 1905

The evening of March 9, 1904, the Phoenix City Council met and voted to call a bond election April 11 to provide money to help the Reclamation Service build the Roosevelt road between Mesa and the Tonto Basin. Mayor Walter Bennett, in answer to a question about who would own the road when it was finished, said it would be a public thoroughfare under control of and maintained by the federal government. This would continue until the time for the farmers to take control of the reservoir and pay for it. [1]

At a meeting March 15 with the Maricopa County Board of Trade, Benjamin A. Fowler said the government would maintain the road until the Water Users' Association had finished paying for the dam. Fowler, president of the association, said that would be about 15 years from then. He said the question of ultimate ownership had not been decided, nor had the possibility of the sale of a franchise for use of the road by a railroad or electric trolley. Deciding those matters right then was less important than getting the road, he said. [2]

Louis C. Hill, Reclamation Service engineer in charge of the work at the Tonto Basin, said March 21 the government would keep the road in good repair as long as it retained possession of the dam. If building the road cost more than the $75,000 to be put up by Phoenix, Tempe, and Mesa, the government would pay the deficiency, he said. [3]

Opposition to the road seemed minimal. In answer to one argument there was no hurry in completing the road, so there was no real hurry in voting on the bonds, Arthur P. Davis said there was the greatest urgency. Davis, in overall charge of operations on the Tonto Basin project for the government, said that if the bonds were approved, the road would be built in four months but in three months machinery needed at the dam site would be carried over it. In addition, there would be a savings to the farmers in the cost of transportation. [4] It was acknowledged that because the road from Mesa would be longer than from Globe, the wagon haul would cost more, but this was partly offset by the higher railroad rates to Globe. [5] More than that, getting to Globe was inconvenient. [6]

Frederick H. Newell, chief engineer of the Reclamation Service, had written to Fowler concerning the road the previous December. Newell said,

It is essential in order to secure supplies and labor at reasonable cost to have quick communication with the center of population and of business in the Salt River Valley, and avoid the long round-about railroad route and wagon transportation. . .

It is for the advantage of the people of Salt River valley to have this wagon road built as speedily as possible as it will reduce the ultimate cost of the works, which they must pay for and will facilitate every step of the proceedings. . . Trade and commerce between the cities of the valley and the construction and mining camps in the mountains will be vastly increased. [7]

Another plus, Newell said, was it would help reduce the cost of building the power transmission line. [8]

Another point of opposition in Phoenix was the road would provide greater benefits to Mesa and Tempe, which were closer to the Tonto Basin. To this, the *Arizona Republican* said in an editorial: "A more narrow, shortsighted view could not be entertained, and, happily, such a view is not held by many." [9]

The Water Users' Association issued a pamphlet, "Facts to Be Considered by the Voters of Phoenix, Tempe and Mesa Concerning the Tonto Road, and Voting Bonds for Aiding in its Construction." [10] The pamphlet, written by Joseph H. Kibbey, [11] the association's counsel, explained the economic advantages to the Valley:

For the next four years the money expended at Tonto for labor and food supplies, both of which can be obtained in the Salt River valley, if not barred by the difficulty and cost of transportation, will exceed $1,500 per day for every business day in the year; $1,000 for labor and $500 for food supply. In other words, if the food supply is obtained from this valley there will be expended here, on that account alone, more than $500 per day; and by locating the employment office here there will be a continual stream of laborers, numbering well up into the thousands, going and coming through the city for several years, each one of whom would leave here more or less cash, and to whom the total wages would exceed $1000 per day. The greater part of wages paid to men engaged in any work is expended where paid or at the city nearest and most convenient to the place of payment. Can we afford to lose this additional capital which would inevitably be put in circulation here. [12]

Another argument was the Valley demand for cement for irrigation ditches, sidewalks, and construction could be supplied at one-half the present market cost by the government plant at the Tonto Basin. The pamphlet said the cement could be hauled very cheaply by teamsters who otherwise would return to the Valley with empty wagons. [13]

Finally, the pamphlet said that, if the people failed to support the bonds, the government would "hereafter deal at arms' length and take nothing of the good faith and promise of co-operation for granted." [14]

On March 21, the governors of the Water Users' Association approved the form of contract between the association and the Interior Department for building the Tonto dam. [15] The document was sent to the Council, which gave its approval, and, on March 28, the governors set May 10 as the date the association shareholders would vote on it. [16]

The governors also adopted a resolution instructing that the names of settlers upon school lands not be included among those eligible to vote. This was done because although the lands had been signed into the association, the settlers did not hold title. [17] The school lands consisted of sections 16 and 36 of each township and were reserved by the national government for use by the Arizona Territory to benefit the public schools. The persons farming those sections obtained leases from the territory with the proceeds from the leases placed in a trust fund to benefit the schools.

There were a number of other persons signed into the association who were ineligible to vote. These included farmers who leased lands but did not hold clear title (the holders of title could vote). Others who could not vote were corporations, estate administrators, executors, trustees, guardians, minors and residents of town sites, such as Phoenix, unless they owned land subscribed into the reservoir district which was outside the municipal boundaries. [18]

Nonresidents of Arizona could vote if they owned land and they happened to be in the Valley when the election was held. But they could not vote by proxy. Women holding title to land were eligible to vote. [19]

The governors' decision to deny the vote to school land farmers applied to the election of association officers April 5 as well as to the contract election. The decision drew a protest from T. P. Coughlin, who wrote:

Settlers upon (school) land are either entitled to all the rights and privileges of any other member of the association or they are not members of the association at all. If said settlers have no voice in the affairs of the association, every acre of school land is illegally subscribed upon the books of the association and every dollar paid by the aforesaid settlers to the association should be returned. If, upon the other hand, should it be decided by the secretary of the Interior that these settlers have rights in the association then the coming election will be illegal. These settlers were asked to subscribe their land and done so in good faith. They were only asked for their lease upon the land and the 10 cents per acre. Their rights of franchise as American citizens was not questioned. And the mere fact that they lease land from the territory should not in itself be such a heinous crime that they should lose their right of suffrage. [20]

The school lands problem was not resolved until 1915 when the Arizona Legislature passed a law allowing lands in sections 16 and 36 to be sold. In 1917, the governors agreed to include on the association voting list occupants of school lands who had secured purchase contracts from the State of Arizona and had recorded them with the county recorder. [21]

A mass rally to discuss the Roosevelt road bonds was held the evening of March 29 at the Dorris theater. Carl Hayden, a member of the Tempe City Council, said he was against the bonds at first because he did not see how they could help Tempe. He changed his mind, he said, because the road would be built sometime, and there was no other time when it could be built so cheaply. In addition, the road would have the benefit of government engineering skills and government construction, which meant there would be no graft.

"We would not be sure of that if we were building the road ourselves," Hayden said. [22]

Hill answered questions and described the road, saying in two places the up grade would be six percent, and, in one place, Fish Creek Hill, 10 percent, but the latter would not be in the direction of the dam. He said other routes had been examined and found unsuitable. [23]

By the end of March, 140 men were working on the Roosevelt road between Fish Creek Hill and the dam. [24] Construction also continued on the High Line road, [25] which branched off the road from Globe to Livingston about six miles above the latter place. The High Line road ran for 20 miles to the dam site. Originally, it crossed south of the power canal line about a mile above Roosevelt, then continued into the town. This lower road would later be flooded by the reservoir. The High Line road also went to the cement mill and eventually was to link with the Roosevelt road. Like the Roosevelt road, the grade of the High Line

road toward the dam did not exceed six percent, while 10 percent was the steepest grade toward Globe. [26]

The telephone line was completed from the Arizona Dam to Fish Creek Hill and from Roosevelt east to the point on the Salt River where the cement diversion dam was to be constructed to divert water into the power canal. [27] The survey for the power canal line was completed, and two contracts were signed for its construction, one for excavation and the other for tunnel work. [28] Davis went to Los Angeles to be present at some tests of steel-reinforced concrete pipe, which would be used to convey the power canal water across canyons and washes. There was a possibility the pipe would be used in the canal penstock, but a decision on the material had not been made. Wood stave and iron were among other materials suggested. [29]

A 300-foot-long suspension bridge, suspended from two wire cables attached to the canyon walls, was in place over the river. [30] One hundred men worked at quarrying and installing slabs of limestone for the foundation at the cement mill, which was half completed. [31] Contracts were signed for the cement mill machinery and for the mill building. [32]

At Roosevelt, about 60 tents provided living quarters for many of the men. The town had a dozen frame buildings. There were now four general merchandise stores, four restaurants, and a post office. Roosevelt was described as "a live, up-to-date little town with electric lights and paved streets." [33]

On April 2, by a vote of 68 to 2, property owners in Mesa approved selling $3,500 in bonds for building the Roosevelt road. [34] Three days later, Fowler was reelected president of the Water Users' Association in the organization's first election for which 986 persons were eligible to vote. [35] Neither Fowler nor Dr. Ethelbert W. Wilbur, vice president, was opposed in the election. [36]

At the same time, an unsigned circular was distributed through Phoenix urging property taxpayers to vote against the wagon road bonds. The circular said Phoenix should do nothing to build up Mesa and Tempe. It argued the cost of hauling oil from Mesa would be 20 cents per hundredweight higher than from Globe, and all freight "will go that way." [37]

The circular went into italics over a statement by Fowler in Washington, D.C., that the road was not "vitally" necessary. [38] The evening of April 9, at the final meeting on behalf of the bonds, Fowler charged the circular misrepresented his views. He acknowledged telling a congressional committee that while the road did not have to be built, it was very important and a proper business move, and the people strongly supported it. He said he was sure the people would demonstrate this at the election. [39]

Other speakers, including Kibbey and hotelman John C. Adams, said building the road was a business proposition, which would increase prosperity. Davis also spoke, repeating some of the business arguments for the road, adding the dam's electric power plant and transmission line would be a constantly growing enterprise whose initial cost would be less with the road. He said the dam would attract tourists and the lake behind it would provide fishing, boating, and other vacation opportunities. He said the road would be a good one, permanent in nature, and would be built for the money asked. [40]

On April 11, while Phoenix voters were approving the bonds 686 to 38, [41] Davis met with the governors and told them the extended drought in the country was an unlooked for condition and if it continued could affect the number of acres for which association shares could be issued. He said the policy of limiting the number of shares within the number of acres that could be safely irrigated would be adhered to rigidly. The Interior Department now estimated 200,000 acres could be irrigated, 160,000 acres from the natural flow of the river and impounded water, and 35,000 to 40,000 acres from the underground supply. The estimated cost of the project was $3,600,000, or a cost of $18 per acre if 200,000 acres were included in the reservoir district. If the drought continued and the estimated acreage was reduced to 180,000, the cost would be $20 per acre, and if, 150,000, it would be $24 per acre. [42]

Davis said, however, it was doubtful any such reduction would be necessary. "It is only mentioned to show the most extreme conditions possible," he said. [43]

The governors ordered a letter to be sent to shareholders urging them to vote in the election to ratify the contract with the government. The governors said a large vote would "show the government our appreciation of what they are doing for us." Shareholders were warned they could not vote if they had failed to pay the previously levied assessment of 10 cents per acre. [44]

In addition, a pamphlet containing a draft of the proposed contract and a copy of Hitchcock's letter of February 25, 1904, to the director of the U.S. Geological Survey, was distributed to shareholders. [45]

On April 30, property tax payers in Tempe approved their portion of the Roosevelt road bonds 54 to 10, [46] but it also was learned the government would be unable to continue building the road until the bonds were sold and the money became available. Hill and Davis at first had said approval of the bonds would be sufficient to continue building, but they now said they needed the money. Fearing the red tape involved in selling the bonds could take up to two months, delaying construction of the road by that much, the *Phoenix*

Enterprise said "some method must be devised to raise some money prior to that time." [47]

Hill, discussing the work in the Tonto Basin, said it had been decided to construct the dam's sluicing tunnel on the south side instead of the north side of the river, and the work of excavating the tunnel's approaches was in progress. He said there would be 8,700 feet of tunnels along the route of the power canal, and this work was in progress, too. [48]

The telephone line, constructed on high ground so it would not be flooded when the reservoir filled, was completed from the site of the power canal diversion dam about six miles upstream from Livingston, to the Arizona Dam where it connected to Phoenix over the line of the Arizona Water Co. Hill spoke over the line from Livingston to Phoenix April 17. [49]

However, the telephone service was unsatisfactory for two reasons. First, the end of the line in Phoenix was in the office of the Arizona Water Co., [50] and second, the line between the Arizona Dam and the water company office ran along the ground. [51] As a result, the Reclamation Service in late December 1904, began construction of its own line from the Arizona Dam. This line, with poles set 35 to the mile, was 27 miles long and connected with the Reclamation Service office and the Consolidated Telephone, Telegraph and Electric Co. in Phoenix. Wooden poles were used inside the city and iron poles outside. The Arizona Water Co. was allowed to place its own new line on the poles. The government line was completed in February 1905. Later that year, a branch line was run to Mesa off the Phoenix-Arizona Dam connection. [52]

In the last week of April, a measles epidemic broke out in Livingston. [53] At Roosevelt, construction of new buildings continued, [54] while at the cement mill the building began going up. Contractors for the power canal also got underway with the excavation and tunneling. [55] Also, construction was soon to begin on a second and larger temporary steam power plant, which was to be a few hundred feet from the site. [56]

The High Line road to Globe was completed, [57] and W. B. Lewis, operator of the stagecoach line from Globe to Roosevelt, increased service from three times a week to daily. [58]

Two views of government sawmill in the Sierra Ancha Mountains.

Meantime, government employees began traveling over the route of the uncompleted Roosevelt road to reach the dam site. The Bowen & Grover stage line carried the first government passengers in wagons from Mesa to Mormon Flat, where the travelers switched to mules for the remainder of the journey. [59] Other men seeking employment walked or rode horseback to the Tonto Basin. [60]

Bowen & Grover began construction of a road house at Mormon Flat. [61] Other stage stations were being established along the road at Goldfield, at Weekes Ranch a mile east of Goldfield, [62] and at Fish Creek. [63]

Freighting outfits also began departing from Phoenix for the dam site. [64]

On May 6, Fowler left for Denver where he met with Davis and Hill to ask if there was some way the government could advance the money for the Roosevelt road. They told him no. Before Fowler began the return trip, he sent a telegram to Vernon L. Clark, putting in motion a previously agreed upon alternative plan to raise between $20,000 and $25,000, the amount Davis and Hill indicated would be needed to keep the road work going until the bonds were sold. The local banks agreed to put up the money by accepting the personal notes of financially solid men, up to a maximum of $300 apiece. Mayor Bennett of Phoenix assured the banks the City Council would repay the funds as soon as the cash for the bonds was received. A meeting was called the night of May 17 at the Board of Trade [65] where the plan was explained. Dr. Alexander J. Chandler of Mesa said the same proposal had worked in his city. Chandler said 10 men were asked to sign notes but 20 responded. The Board of Trade agreed to the plan, assigning Fowler, Frank Alkire, and Walter Talbot to carry it out. By the time the meeting ended, they had 52 names. [66] Five days later, the committee had 148 notes. [67]

The night of May 23, the Phoenix city council sold its bonds to a Denver company for a total of $69,750. [68] A week later, Hill was notified $20,000 secured by notes was in the bank at Phoenix, and checks drawn against the city of Phoenix for the road construction would be approved. Hill reported 150 men were at work at the Roosevelt end of the road and 150 would be put to work at Fish Creek Canyon. [69] By mid-June, almost 400 men were at work on the road. [70]

On May 10, shareholders in the Water Users' Association gave their approval of the contract for the dam. The vote was 24,602 to 240. It was said the 240 votes were cast by two men in the lower end of the Valley who may not have fully understood how to mark the ballot. Based on the vote, the governors adopted a resolution authorizing the association president and secretary to enter into a contract with the government. [71]

On May 28, the Council acted upon the petitions from the landowners under the Salt River Valley, Maricopa, and Grand canals and approved the formation of three canal districts. [72]

The Water Users' Association office was moved to the post office building on May 31. [73]

Frederick Newell arrived at Globe June 4. He met Fowler there, and they traveled together to the Reclamation Service headquarters camp at Livingston. With Hill, they spent the next few days visiting the sawmill in the Sierra Anchas and touring the other work. On Wednesday afternoon, June 8, they started for Phoenix, camping at Fish Creek overnight. They arrived in Mesa Thursday night. They reached Phoenix about noon June 10, and that afternoon Newell met with the Maricopa County Board of Supervisors to encourage it to put the road between Mesa and Goldfield into good shape for heavy hauling. [74] The supervisors had been warned that if the road was not readied for heavy hauling, machinery might have to be sent via Globe. Davis had suggested $5,000 for the work, but the supervisors said they did not have the money. [75] They later agreed to fix the eight miles between Mesa and the point where the road entered Pinal County. They said they had no jurisdiction beyond that point. [76]

The greatest obstacle to all of the road work at that time was the drought. The problem was getting water to the workers. Hill said the white men could not work far distances from water. He said Indians would work in those locales. He said the Indians, who also worked for cheaper wages, would walk four miles for water. He said it would require about 12 barrels of water each day at the camps, which was too costly and would wear out the horses needed to pack it in. [77]

At the Tonto Basin, a force of men drilled holes in the riverbed searching for bedrock on the line of the dam. When finished there, they intended to drill for bedrock in the Salt River upstream at the site of the power canal diversion dam. [78]

In Roosevelt, two large boilers and the engine for the new steam power plant were in place and a brick building to house them was going up. This was the first brick building, and it was made with bricks produced at Roosevelt. [79] Construction also was in progress for an ice plant and for an office building for the Reclamation Service. [80]

Dust was held down on the streets of Roosevelt by means of a large sprinkling wagon. [81] Druggist Warren Barnett served ice cream sodas from his soda fountain for 25 cents, [82] and Saturday night dances were held at a new dance hall erected by restaurant owner Richard Baker. [83] The tents in which the workers lived were moved higher up the hill. [84]

Signs of oil were found in the Tonto Basin, and the smell of it was detected in the sluicing tunnel. Hill said the indications of oil were not sufficient to justify the expense of bringing in a heavy drilling rig to explore for it. [85]

Construction of the sluicing tunnel was progressing from both ends, and by the end of June, 230 feet had been tunneled. About 4,000 feet of tunnel work on the power canal was completed and ready for concrete lining, but excavation work was hampered by a shortage of men. [86]

Hot springs near Roosevelt were being used by some persons to bathe, and some used the warm water to do their laundry. [87]

On June 19, the governors, acting upon the recommendation of landowners under the three canal divisions that had been created, named three commissioners for each. Maricopa Canal landowners split on who they

Indian teamsters making fill on the High Line road, circa March 1904.

wanted for commissioners, and petitions nominating two groups were offered. The governors selected the men with the greatest number of signatures, Dwight B. Heard, C. C. Hurley, and Henry Ware. [88]

The governors also granted a month's leave of absence to Fowler, who had been asked by Newell to join him in inspecting irrigation projects in Colorado and Idaho. Fowler was instructed to deliver the signed contract to Newell. Fowler also was authorized to go to Washington if necessary to explain details and make an early plea for signing by the government. [89]

Late in June, commissioners from the three canal divisions urged water users under the Arizona Canal to create another division and to select commissioners. One purpose in asking the Arizona Canal landowners to do this was so water users under the four canals could unite their efforts to acquire the canals from the Arizona Water Co. [90]

On July 5, the governors passed a resolution authorizing Kibbey to file the lawsuit that would determine the priority of water rights in the Valley. The governors did this in the following language:

That the attorney of the association, Judge Kibbey, be authorized and instructed to institute a comprehensive suit to determine the relative rights of all persons using or diverting water from the flow of the Salt and Verde rivers for the purposes of irrigation, mining and manufacturing, to use and to divert water for the purposes aforesaid, at such time and in such manner as to him may seem wise and expedient, and to that end to take any and all steps which may to him seem expedient or necessary to speedily settle and determine the present vested rights to the use of water for said purposes, from the flow of the Salt and Verde rivers and their tributaries. [91]

The *Arizona Gazette* reported Kibbey would select one of the water users with the oldest claims to become the plaintiff in the suit, and all others would be defendants. These defendants were to include users upstream on the Verde and Salt rivers who diverted water claimed by Valley farmers. [92]

A few days later, the U.S. Department of Justice filed suit to close a saloon operated by Charles W. Williams near the mouth of Pinto Creek and the Salt River. The suit alleged the saloon was greatly interfering with construction operations. [93] Hill said that while the saloon and gambling house were three or four miles from the nearest contractor's camp and a dozen miles from the dam site, teamsters and others from the camps patronized the business. He said the camps were usually quiet, except when the men returned drunk from the saloon. A man had been sent to ask Williams to close, but he refused, saying he had been there before the land was withdrawn for the Tonto Basin reservoir. [94] But the saloon was on government land and an injunction closing it was granted. [95]

Rain, the first in nine months, fell in the Valley and over some of the watershed July 21. At midday, 750 cubic feet per second was measured at the Arizona Dam, which was 10 times more than the water flowing in the river the day before. However, the flow fell to 500 cubic feet per second by evening. [96]

The night of July 22, heavy showers fell over parts of the Tonto Basin, and the government camp at Livingston was flooded by two feet of water coming from Pinto Creek. The creek itself ran five-feet deep and a quarter-mile wide. [97]

The morning of July 23, water ran two-feet deep over the Arizona Dam. The Arizona Canal was supposed to carry a maximum of 750 cubic feet per second diverted by the dam. This left about 7,000 cubic feet per second going over the dam. Before dark, the water made the Salt River unfordable at Tempe. [98]

However, very little of the water reached the parched land, and the north side farmers met July 26 to talk about it. Before the meeting, County Supervisor John P. Orme and others went to the office of the Arizona Water Co. to ask about what happened to the water. The conversation between Orme and William B. Cleary, general manager of the company, became heated, and Cleary punched Orme in the face. The *Republican* reported,

The blow was not a heavy one and was not intended to do any bodily damage, but it did no moral good. It aroused a great deal of inflammation and was the principal topic of conversation on the street during the forenoon. Later in the day a party of water users again visited the canal office and the subject was further talked over. Mr. Cleary expressed regret at the occurrence and offered to apologize to Mr. Orme for his hasty and violent action. The apology was readily accepted and the gentlemen shook hands. [99]

The farmers met again July 27. This time they drew up petitions that were presented to Cleary. The petitions, which were signed by the commissioners appointed for the Maricopa, Grand, and Salt River Valley canals and by a committee appointed for the Arizona Canal, said the canals were "largely filled with sand, silt, debris, weeds and brush" and could not carry the water for which the farmers had paid. The petition concerning the Grand Canal pointed out that it was "without any head or diversion dam." The farmers demanded the conditions,

be remedied at once and that you inform us immediately whether you will comply with this demand. [100]

Cleary accepted the petitions and said they would be referred to the directors of each canal company. He said he would let the farmers know as expeditiously as possible what would be done. [101]

That morning, water again began going over the Arizona Dam. It reached a depth of two and one-half feet before dropping to two feet and continued at that depth until late afternoon. This put a good head of water in the canals. [102]

Word came from Livingston that Charles R. Olberg, one of the government engineers, and Dr. Ralph F. Palmer, the government physician, had come down with typhoid. [103]

Palmer, in an autobiography, *Doctor on Horseback,* said Dr. Richard D. Kennedy of the Old Dominion Mine Hospital at Globe was called to the camp and gave Palmer the same treatment the latter had devised for other patients:

This was to put the patient in a canvas tarp with several inches of water in it and a cake of ice at the head and foot. Then four to six men would hold the sides and ends up and swish the cold water around by rolling the patient in the canvas. It was a very effective treatment from a fever standpoint but as my 105 degree temperature began to respond I sure wanted to beg off. Anyway, there is an end to all things and all the typhoid cases recovered. [104]

Another heavy rain fell in the Tonto Basin July 26. Pinto Creek rose three feet while a rise of eight and one-half feet was measured that night at the Tonto dam site. The high water swamped part of the road between there and Fish Creek Hill and swept away supplies at one of the road camps. [105]

Hill reported the specifications for the dam were nearing completion, but it would take some time yet for the detailed drawings to be finished. [106] He said drawings and specifications for the regulating gates in the sluicing tunnel were almost ready. [107]

A daily mail service was started August 1 between Globe, Livingston, and Roosevelt. [108]

In Phoenix, the farmers representing the various north side canals met. Besides talking about canal conditions, they named Heard as chairman. Heard, in turn, appointed Orme to act in his place while Heard spent a month vacationing in California. [109]

Another result of the farmers' meetings was the incorporation, August 6, of the Appropriators' Canal Co. The purpose of the incorporators, Orme, Patrick T. Hurley, Thomas Armstrong Jr., W. H. Wilkey, and Lincoln Fowler, was to reestablish the head of the Grand Canal to capture the water that came over the Arizona Dam and to use it to irrigate lands under the Grand, Maricopa, and Salt River Valley canals. Part of the contention was that the Arizona Canal was big enough only to keep itself and one other of the canals filled at the same time. Reopening the head of the Grand Canal was expected to make it possible to keep all four north side canals full. Men and horses were sent to begin the work. [110]

The Grand Canal at that time received its water through the Crosscut Canal that dropped south from the Arizona Canal along the line of today's 48th Street in Phoenix. The farmers said the Grand Canal could carry more water than was being delivered through the Crosscut. Cleary, when questioned about what was happening, said so far as he knew there was no objection to the Appropriators' Canal. [111]

The capital stock of the company was $50,000, and landowners under the three canals the Appropriators' intended to serve were asked to buy stock. Each share of stock represented an acre of ground and a proportionate amount of the additional water that was to be brought through the canal. [112]

At 8 p.m. Sunday, August 7, Munc Price of Reedsville, North Carolina, a rodman on one of the Reclamation Service survey crews, died of typhoid fever in the hospital at Roosevelt. [113] Price's death was the first among the men associated with the Tonto Basin project.

The same day Price died, the Salt River at Roosevelt rose about two feet higher than it had from the storms two weeks earlier. The high water was caused by rains that fell in the Sierra Anchas. The water carried a couple of inches of mud into the sluicing tunnel. [114]

By then, the larger steam power plant was operating day and night supplying electricity for a steam hoist at the cement mill and for other machinery plus the ice plant, the machine shop, and carpenter shop. [115] The ice plant was soon producing two tons of ice each day. [116]

On August 11, Secretary of the Interior Ethan A. Hitchcock signed the contract with the Water Users' Association for construction of the dam. [117]

A few days later, lawsuits were brought against the Grand, Maricopa, and the Salt River Valley canal companies by about 50 farmers. The suits complained the companies had failed to perform their duties as common carriers with the result the plaintiffs' "trees and vines are already destroyed and their fields of alfalfa reduced in extent and productiveness." The suits asked that if the companies failed to make adequate repairs or did not stop allowing other companies from appropriating water that was rightfully theirs, that the companies be placed in receivership. One of the attorneys for the farmers was Thomas Armstrong Jr., one of the incorporators of the Appropriators' canal. [118]

Rains fell all night in the Tonto Basin August 15 filling the intake tunnel for the power canal with five feet of water and mud. Water got into several of the other tunnels, but they were drained and damage was light. [119]

By the end of August, six camps had been established for men working on the Roosevelt road. [120]

The digging of the sluicing tunnel was completed. The tunnel excavations from both ends were within a quarter-inch of the engineers' lines when they met. [121] The tunnel was 13-feet wide, 11-feet high, and 480-feet long. Besides sluicing the reservoir, the tunnel was intended to divert the river around the dam while it was being built. When the reservoir was full, it was expected that 10,000 cubic feet of water per second could be discharged through the tunnel. [122]

Construction of the sluicing tunnel,

presented many great difficulties; a rise in the river of two feet would flood both portals, together with their long approaches, with mud and river debris, which could only be removed by men tramming it out in practically water tight cars. This occurred not less than three times during the progress of the work. Another bad feature was the intense heat. Several hot springs were encountered and the temperature rose to 130 degrees Fahrenheit. This water emitted a steam-like vapor which was almost suffocating. The men worked stripped to the waist, coming out at short intervals for a breath of air.

Machine drills driven by compressed air were used in the construction. . . On account of the isolated situation of the work, it was difficult to get experienced drillers. The common laborers were largely Mexicans and Apache Indians. [123]

Excavation of the power canal tunnels was nearly done, and the work of lining them with concrete continued. [124] The Reclamation Service employed a new contractor to operate the sawmill, and about 8,000 feet of lumber were cut daily. About 5,000 feet of lumber were used in the power canal tunnels, and the remainder were used in the work at Roosevelt and at the dam site. [125]

Hill passed through Phoenix on September 16 on his way to Denver for the opening of the bids for the sluicing tunnel gates. He reported the cement mill building was completed, and the foundations were in for the manufacturing machinery. By October 1, he expected it would be possible to drive a team of horses from one end of the Roosevelt road to the other. The road was almost finished except to the top of Fish Creek Hill and bridges over Lewis and Pranty, Fish, and Ash creeks. [126] The Fish Creek Hill work was some of the most difficult and expensive to be done.

The road climbs the hill going towards Mesa on a 10 percent grade, for the most part along the foot of a vertical cliff several hundred feet high, the cliff being so steep as to necessitate rock fills 75 feet in height in order to get the required width of roadway. In other places, rock cuts 60 to 70 feet in depth were necessary. Some short sections of this road were very expensive to construct, the cost probably reaching $25,000 or more per mile. [127]

On September 17, Republicans held their territorial convention in Prescott, and Fowler was selected as the party's nominee for delegate to Congress. Fowler's name was placed in nomination by Kibbey, who also introduced a successful resolution pledging the support of Fowler and the GOP to the construction of the San Carlos dam and other favorable irrigation projects. [128] The Democrats, two days earlier, approved a plank urging the building of the San Carlos dam. They nominated Marcus A. Smith for delegate. [129]

The Post Office Department advertised for bids for a mail route between Mesa and Roosevelt, [130] and Sheldon S. Baker, a chemist for the Geological Survey, reported that 90 percent of the salt found in the Salt River was caused by the flow of water over large salt deposits in Carrizo Creek. Cibecue Creek contributed about 5 percent of the salt found in the river. [131]

A court hearing was held September 28 by Judge Edward Kent on the request that the Salt River Valley, Maricopa, and Grand canal companies be placed in receivership. Kent indicated the farmers were asking for too much, but he said he would consider their plea that the companies be required to repair and improve the canals, dam, and headgates. [132]

October opened with Kent's denying all of the farmers' pleas by dismissing the cases. [133]

George H. Maxwell, executive director of the National Irrigation Association, came to Phoenix to campaign on behalf of Fowler's candidacy. Before a filled Dorris theater the night of October 14, Maxwell extolled Fowler and defended the national irrigation movement's financial backing by the railroads. He also denied he had gained financially. Before becoming involved in the irrigation movement, his income as a lawyer had ranged between $10,000 and $26,000 per year, he said. Moreover, he had contributed $10,000 to the movement, getting the money by mortgaging property. Maxwell said he had repaid $1,000 of that and was paying 8 percent interest on the balance. [134] While in Phoenix, he arranged the sale of his ranch for $15,000. [135]

About 11 a.m. Tuesday, October 18, Robert Schell was fatally injured while doing some blasting on the Roosevelt road about 15 miles from the dam site. He put in a dynamite charge and either made the fuse too short or miscalculated the time needed to get away. Schell caught the full effect of the blast. His right arm was almost entirely blown away, and the concussion threw him at least 30 feet. He landed on his back on a rock. Schell, described as "rather an old man," died about 9 o'clock that night before a doctor summoned from Mesa could reach him. [136]

The general election was held November 8, and Fowler lost to Smith by 872 votes—9,522 to 10,394. [137]

On November 14, the contract for three pair of gates to be installed in the sluicing tunnel was let to the Llewellyn Iron Works of Los Angeles for $102,000. [138] The government took over operation of the sawmill, while work had fallen a little behind on the power canal because of the inability to get enough workers during the hot weather. The power canal contractors were urged to hire additional men so there would be no delay in its completion. [139]

In Washington, the Interior Department on November 23 announced bids would be received at the Reclamation Service office in Phoenix until 9 a.m. February 8, 1905, *for the construction of a masonry dam and two bridges on Salt River, about 70 miles east of Phoenix, Ariz. The dam will contain about 300,000 cubic yards of masonry. Specifications, form of proposal, and plans may be inspected at the office of the chief engineer of the Reclamation Service, Washington, D.C., or at the office of the district engineer of the Reclamation Service, Roosevelt, Ariz. . . Proposals must be marked: "Proposal for the construction of the Roosevelt dam, Salt River, Arizona."* [140]

The last of the machinery for use in the cement mill was delivered in November. The machinery had been expected earlier, but delays occurred because the contractors were slow in making shipment and because freighters to haul it from Globe to Roosevelt were scarce. [141]

By the end of November, the Roosevelt road was in good enough shape to warrant the beginning of a movement in Mesa for its use as a bicycle trail. The Mesa people were especially concerned with the condition of the road from Mesa to Goldfield. This was the old road. It was soft and they were afraid it would soon be cut up by heavy traffic. They wanted the road made smooth so that each time a wheel passed over the road it would be packed down and hardened. [142]

John Holdren, who won the contract to deliver mail between Mesa and Roosevelt, bought a couple of heavy carriages to carry the mail. [143] The mail service began December 5. [144]

It was announced from Livingston that the Reclamation Service would soon open bids for delivering 50,000 barrels of oil from Mesa to the cement mill at Roosevelt. Tanks with capacities of 1,000 barrels were to be built at Mesa for handling the oil. [145] A tank with a 2,000 barrel capacity was built near the cement mill. [146] The government hoped to begin the manufacture of cement by February 1, 1905. [147]

In early December, only the bridge across Ash Creek was not in place on the Roosevelt road. Hill reported people were managing to get around the creek, but it would take a couple of weeks to take care of some of the rough spots along the road. Thereafter, he said, a crew would be kept busy repairing the road where it settled and where rocks fell on it. The stage carrying the mail and passengers made the trip from Mesa to Roosevelt in one day with three changes of horses. [148]

The governors met December 5 and adopted a resolution that the contracts of landowners who applied for stock in the association and failed to pay the preliminary assessment of 10 cents per acre by January 15, 1905, be returned to such persons as having been rejected. The resolution did "not apply to school lands or lands on the waiting list" hoping to get into the association. Frank H. Parker, association secretary, said payment had been made on 150,000 acres and about 45,000 acres were delinquent. The association needed the money to operate. [149]

Early the morning of December 9, two Indian children burned to death at an Indian camp near the work on the power canal. The children made a fire of dried brush and fell asleep nearby. Somehow, their clothing caught fire. The children were about 7 years old. [150]

Orville H. Ensign, electrical engineer for the Reclamation Service, was aboard the stage Friday, December 16, when it made the trip from Roosevelt to Mesa in eleven and one-half hours. Ensign said the only break in the ride was at Ash Creek, which the passengers had to walk over. He said the bridge was expected to be completed by the next Tuesday. The worst part of the road was from Goldfield to Mesa, but workmen had started to change some of the grades and to harden it. Ensign said the horses trotted most of the way, upgrade as well as downhill. [151]

Christmas was celebrated at Roosevelt with a Christmas tree and Christmas eve dancing plus a children's program held in the school house. [152]

Because a portion of the Roosevelt road ran along the river past the dam site and was subject to flooding, construction started in January 1905 on a new road at a higher elevation from the cement mill to pass over a hill and connect with the Roosevelt road. [153] The part of the road immediately downstream from the dam was built high on the mountain to avoid the south side spillway. There, and farther down the canyon, rock cuts of from 20 feet to 60 feet were made. To protect the workers, life lines were used in many instances. [154]

Workmen also began blasting away the mountain to prepare a shelf for the temporary and permanent power plants. Originally, the engineers had planned to put the temporary hydroelectric power plant inside the reservoir at a point 80 feet above the low flow of the river. Various objections to this led to a new plan to locate the temporary plant on the site of the permanent powerhouse, immediately below the dam. Hence, much of the work for the temporary plant was later used in the permanent powerhouse. [155]

The shelf on which the permanent powerhouse was to rise was 25 feet above the river channel, but the temporary plant went into a recess 10 feet higher up, hollowed out of the mountainside. This was done to protect the temporary installation from possible flooding and from damage by falling rocks during future blasting. [156]

The temporary power plant was to be connected with the power canal by means of a tunnel 500-feet long. The tunnel was to be lined with a 7-foot diameter steel pipe set in concrete. [157]

Another work in progress was the excavation inside the sluicing tunnel of the chamber in which two sets of three identical gates were to be installed, the first set of service gates to control the release of water and the other set to serve as emergency gates should repairs be necessary. The excavation was about 120 feet inside the tunnel from the upstream portal. The service gates would be set in the downstream end of the chamber and the emergency gates 10 feet farther upstream. [158]

On Thursday, January 5, 1905, the Reclamation Service opened bids in Phoenix for the purchase and delivery of 50,000 barrels of oil to Roosevelt and for the hauling of freight. The oil bids took into consideration the railroad freight rates from the California oil fields to Mesa and Globe and the hauling of oil from those two points to Roosevelt. Three bids were entered that included the cost of the oil and its delivery, the lowest being $3.48 per barrel by C. R. Eager & Co. of Los Angeles, and the highest $4.49. Seven bids were made for hauling freight, the lowest being $13.60 per ton by Wolf Sachs of Tempe, and the highest $18.50. [159] The contracts were later awarded to Eager Co. [160] and Sachs. [161]

The *Gazette* reported January 6 the Reclamation Service had "under consideration the designing of an ideal distributing canal system for the entire Salt River valley" based upon the cadastral survey of the Valley made by government engineers. The newspaper called this,

a piece of good news to the people of the valley. For while we have always been looking forward to the big dam as something that would put new life and vigor into our section, yet we had not considered anything with reference to the method which would be used by the government in distributing the water from the dam... This ideal canal system is something that few had thought of before. [162]

Apparently it was unknown to the *Gazette* editors that Charles D. Walcott, director of the U.S. Geological Survey, had described the "ideal irrigation system for the Salt River valley" in a report April 10, 1903, to the Interior secretary. This system called for a permanent diversion dam and one large main canal on each side of the river by which to convey water to laterals for distribution to the land. This system contemplated the selection of a water commissioner by the settlers for each canal, subject to approval by the government engineer in charge. Once the majority of payments had been made to the government for the cost of building the reservoir, the water users were expected to take control of the distribution system, subject to rules and regulations established by the Interior secretary. [163]

The *Republican,* on January 7, echoed the *Gazette* report of the previous day, the *Republican* adding "an ideal distributing canal system. . .is a part of the work of reclamation in the valley which was not generally contemplated in the beginning." [164]

In later years, the things "not generally contemplated in the beginning" became a sore point with many of the shareholders in the Water Users' Association because they had to pay for the work. As the cost of the project rose from the initial projection of about $15 per acre toward $50, $55 and $60 per acre, some of the farmers became bitter and resentful.

Heavy rains and snow began falling over the watershed of the Salt and Verde rivers the night of January 7. Within a few days, the area of the Tonto Basin, from the power canal diversion dam to the Roosevelt dam site, was covered with water. The washes and creeks ran with torrents, and most of the roads became impassable. The river at Roosevelt rose 16 feet above its usual level. Before the storm passed, almost 6 inches of rain fell, and the Sierra Anchas were covered with snow. [165]

Rain started falling over the Salt River Valley the morning of January 9. [166] The morning of January 10, a report came in from the Arizona Dam that two feet of water was flowing over. By that night it was three feet, and the water continued to rise so that by the night of January 11 it was more than four-feet deep. [167]

The high water in the river gave the operators of the Appropriators' Canal a chance to try out the newly installed headgates. A flow estimated at more than 125 cubic feet of water per second ran into the canal for a distance of six or seven miles before being diverted back into the river through a waste way. [168]

At a session of the Arizona Supreme Court January 13, it was announced the U.S. Supreme Court had upheld the lower courts in the case of *Henry E. Slosser v. the Salt River Canal Co.* brought in 1895. The lower courts held that Slosser had a right to water for his land even though he was not a shareholder in the canal company and had not rented a water right from a stockholder. [169]

A reporter for the *Republican* wrote an account of a trip over the Roosevelt road, saying "It is the wagon road of America" with nothing like it elsewhere in the U.S. He reported it had been opened for freight a few days earlier, and the teamsters were disturbed by rumors automobiles were going to use it. The freighters said there were hundreds of sharp curves from which a driver could not see 30 feet ahead, and, if automobiles were met at such points, the horses would scare and plunge over the bluffs. Their own lives would be endangered, and they predicted problems if automobiles tried to use the road. [170]

The writer said the roadbed, beyond Goldfield, was made of disintegrated granite and tuff, a volcanic rock. The wooden bridges, constructed from lumber cut in the Sierra Anchas, were substantial, and there were few heavy grades. He said "the road is as smooth as Washington street" and would be ideal for bicycles except for the grades. However, the road needed widening at the curves so freight teams could pass. [171]

Teams were encounted on every mile, and stations for tourists had been established and were being improved. The scenery was "indescribably beautiful and grand," with the "stupendous canyon of Fish Creek. . .a repetition of the Grand Canyon on a minor scale." For miles, the road followed a "shelf in the cliffs, from which a stone can be tossed hundreds of feet below. It skirts palisades which are more magnificient than the famed palisades of the Hudson." [172]

On January 16, Kibbey filed in the U.S. District Court the lawsuit of *Patrick T. Hurley v. Charles F. Abbott and others.* This was the suit to determine the order in which land in the Valley was to receive water from the river. In reporting the filing of the suit, the *Republican* said in the "complaint there are sixty folios of names containing altogether more than 5,000." All the water users in the Valley and along the upper Verde River were made defendants. [173]

The complaint said Hurley owned the southeast quarter of section 14, township 1 north, range 2 east (Lower Buckeye road to Durango, between 27th and 31st avenues), and his right to appropriate 120 miners' inches of water annually to irrigate the 160 acres dated from as early as 1870. The water claim of 120 inches was for more than 2,100 acre-feet per year. Hurley asked his water appropriation be secured to him against encroachments from all other water users. [174]

Among the new arrivals at Roosevelt was Chester W. Smith of Connecticut, who was to take charge of the dam construction when it started. A dance was held in the new government dining room, [175] which was located on the mountainside above the High Line road near a group of permanent houses for Reclamation Service officials. These houses were occupied by, among others, Hill, Palmer, Duryea, and their families. [176] Storekeepers in Roosevelt were pleased by business, and the town with its "good many restaurants and lodging houses. . .springing up. . .is taking on quite a metropolitan air." [177] The town lots were leased "for business purposes at no rental but under restriction as to conduct, especially in regard to liquor, which was prohibited within a three-mile limit over the entire project." [178]

The new building at Roosevelt to house the Reclamation Service offices was nearing completion, with part of the government staff there and the rest at Livingston. [179] About 20 families were camped at Livingston or nearby. [180] Tents were pitched on three sides of the ranch house, which once was headquarters for the H. Z. ranch. The building was whitewashed, as were all the trees and fence poles. The entire office force assisted in the raising of a 50-foot flagpole, brought in from the Sierra Anchas January 31. A flag was run up and lowered at sunset, with Frank Nash, a one-time government scout in the Apache wars, sounding retreat. [181]

A number of water users under the Grand, Maricopa, and Salt River Valley canals met and decided to have a single law firm represent them in *Hurley v. Abbott,* in order to reduce the expense of answering and being represented. They drafted a letter to be sent to others similarly situated, inviting them to join. [182]

Water users served by the Arizona Canal met under the auspices of the Arizona Canal Water Users' Protective Association. Kibbey explained the purpose of the *Hurley* suit. While the water users agreed with the object of the suit, many of them thought there might be a simpler and less expensive way to achieve the same thing. Some suggested a cooperative agreement using the Kibbey Decree of 1892 as the basis for a settlement. The association appointed a committee of 10 men to study the effect of the lawsuit. [183]

Heavy rain fell again in early February, and by Saturday, February 4, the country was awash in water. The floodplain of Cave Creek, which entered the Valley northwest of Phoenix, was filled with water, and the *Republican* reported:

There had never been so much water within the limits of Phoenix since the flood of 1891. All of the city west of the east line of the capitol grounds was submerged or surrounded. Nothing could be seen of the grounds but the trees and shrubbery, and the water at its highest point was beginning to creep under the doors of the capitol building. . . A great section of the Maricopa canal went out and the water poured through without obstruction. [184]

The Salt River at Tempe reached a point higher than at any time since 1891, which meant water was pouring over the Arizona Dam. [185] On February 6, the water coming over the dam ranged between six- and seven-feet deep. [186]

Hill arrived in Phoenix from the dam site on Tuesday, February 7. He said the worst problem at Roosevelt was the road at the dam site, which had been covered by water 15-feet deep but was at a depth of six or eight feet when he had left. [187] He had come to Phoenix for the opening of the bids for the dam, but this was postponed until February 23 because the arrival of some of the Reclamation Service

consulting engineers had been delayed by the weather. [188] The bidders, about 20 in number, met with Hill at the appointed hour. They handed over their bids, then he read to them the official notice of postponement, and returned the bids unopened. The contractors protested the length of the delay and sent a telegram to Secretary Hitchcock contending that the engineers would arrive in two or three days. They asked for an earlier date for the bid opening. They wanted to avoid the expense of remaining in Phoenix or of going home and returning, [189] but Hitchcock, the next day, replied the new day having been announced, it would be impracticable to order an earlier opening. [190]

Hill, on February 8, did open bids for the delivery of wood to the dam site. The wood was to be burned at the cement mill. J. E. Sturgeon of Tempe offered the lower of two bids, $4.35 per cord for 100 cords of cottonwood and $5.60 per cord for 500 cords of mesquite wood. Sturgeon already was furnishing the government camps with a large part of their meat supply, and he had other interests in the Tonto Basin. [191]

On February 10, President Theodore Roosevelt sent the name of Joseph H. Kibbey, attorney general of Arizona, to the U.S. Senate to succeed Alexander O. Brodie as governor. [192] Roosevelt earlier had named Brodie assistant chief of the Records and Pension Bureau of the U.S. Army, an appointment that had been confirmed in January by the U.S. Senate. [193]

Arizona Canal water users met February 11 to consider the findings of the committee appointed to recommend how to react to *Hurley v. Abbott.* The committee majority advised joining with the water users under the other canals in encouraging the suit and making an early answer to it, but a motion to adopt the recommendation failed by a 3 to 1 margin. Among those opposed to the majority was William J. Murphy, the owner of more land under the canal than probably anyone else. The majority of the water users favored taking no action except to urge the withdrawal of the suit and to accept whatever summons was made upon them. [194]

Thomas Armstrong Jr. filed an answer to *Hurley* on February 13. He asked that Hurley be required to prove his claim. Armstrong also said he was the owner of two tracts of land the water appropriations for which were made in 1869. He said he was entitled to a constant flow of 33/80 of an inch or one-half inch of water for each acre. He asked the court to establish his right to that volume of water and to restrain Hurley or anyone else from taking it. [195]

Long-time residents of the Tonto Basin said it had been many years since they had seen so much water in the Salt River. Stages and freight were delayed, and teams could not get across the river to bring in lumber from the Sierra Anchas. An effort to start a ferry at Griffin's Ford, over which all the wood was carried, failed because the cable used was too weak. [196] Stronger cable was procured, and in another week a ferry was running to carry provisions across the river for the men at the sawmill. [197]

Teamsters continued to have difficulty getting freight from Globe to Roosevelt and Livingston. In some places, the road was described as having no bottom. The Roosevelt road continued to be covered by water in the vicinity of the dam. [198]

Hill came in from the Tonto Basin for the opening of the dam bids. He reported everything was going smoothly except for the freighting. He said the final touches were being put on the upper 10 miles of the power canal and the lower part, about nine miles long, would require another four months of work. The uncompleted sections required the heaviest work. [199]

The penstock for the power canal was under construction. Hill said the power canal would develop 5,000 horsepower, and another 2,500 horsepower would be developed through penstocks placed in the dam. He said seven miles downstream there was a place to develop another 2,500 horsepower and just above the mouth of the Verde River, 4,500 horsepower. [200]

Hill said the cement plant was ready to begin grinding raw materials, with the only thing holding up the grinding the inability to bring in oil over the road from Globe. Four carloads of an order of 1,500 barrels were in Globe awaiting delivery. [201]

Twenty-two bids were opened February 23 for construction of the dam. The low bid of $1,147,600 was made by John M. O'Rourke & Co. of Galveston, Texas.

O'Rourke proposed to build the dam in 24 months, while the second lowest bidder, Roderick & Wood of St. Louis, proposed to take 17 months at a cost of $1,187,200. The high bid was $2,685,900 and called for a 30-month construction period. [202] The height of the dam above the low water mark was to be 230 feet, and the reservoir when full was to contain 1,100,000 acre-feet of water. [203]

The following day, the *Republican* said, "The people generally are feeling quite jubilant over the figures presented. . . The cost is materially less than had been predicted by many who were disposed to take a pessimistic view of things." [204]

The newspaper also pointed out the government specifications called for the dam to come into use when 150 feet above the level of the riverbed. By that time four-fifths of the masonry work would be completed, but the reservoir would hold only about a third of its capacity compared to when it was completed. The newspaper said,

The reasons are obvious why the last one-fifth of the work will be the fifth that will provide for the holding of two-thirds of the water when the basin is full. [205]

Kibbey was confirmed as governor by the U.S. Senate on February 27. [206] He took office the afternoon of Tuesday, March 7, 1905. [207]

1. *Arizona Republican* (Phoenix), March 9, 1904.
2. *Ibid.,* March 16, 1904.
3. *Ibid.,* March 22, 1904.
4. *Ibid.,* March 16, 1904.
5. *Ibid.,* April 7, 1904.
6. F. H. Newell to B. A. Fowler, December 18, 1903, Salt River Project Archives (hereafter SRPA).
7. *Ibid.*
8. *Ibid.*
9. *Republican,* March 13, 1904.
10. *Ibid.,* March 23, 1904.
11. *Ibid.,* March 16, 1904.
12. *Ibid.,* March 23, 1904.
13. *Ibid.*
14. *Ibid.*
15. *Ibid.,* March 22, 1904.
16. *Ibid.,* March 29, 1904.
17. *Ibid.,* March 29 and 30, 1904.
18. *Ibid.,* March 30, 1904.
19. *Ibid.*
20. *Ibid.,* April 1, 1904.
21. *Ibid.,* February 7, 1917.
22. *Ibid.,* March 30, 1904.
23. *Ibid.*
24. *Phoenix Enterprise,* March 31, 1904.
25. *Ibid.*
26. *Salt River Project, Final History to 1916,* unpublished manuscript, Vol. I, p. 73, SRPA.
27. *Enterprise,* March 31, 1904; *Republican,* March 17, 1904.
28. *Republican,* March 17, 1904; *Final History to 1916,* Vol. I, p. 157. Robert Sherer & Co. received the contract for power canal excavation. John Tuttle won the contract for tunnel construction for the power canal.
29. *Republican,* March 12, 1904.
30. *Ibid.,* March 25, 1904.
31. *Enterprise,* March 31, 1904.
32. *Ibid.,* March 16, 1904.

33. *Ibid.,* March 31, 1904.
34. *Republican,* April 2, 1904.
35. *Ibid.,* April 2, 6 and 7, 1904.
36. *Ibid.,* April 6 and 7, 1904.
37. *Ibid.,* April 7, 1904.
38. *Ibid.*
39. *Ibid.,* April 10, 1904.
40. *Ibid.*
41. *Ibid.,* April 12, 1904.
42. *Ibid.*
43. *Ibid.*
44. *Arizona Gazette* (Phoenix), April 13, 1904.
45. Morris Bien to B.A. Fowler, February 24, 1905, reprinted *Republican,* November 19, 1905.
46. *Republican,* May 1, 1904; *Enterprise,* May 3, 1904, reported the vote was 56 to 10.
47. *Enterprise,* April 30, 1904.
48. *Republican,* April 21, 1904; *Final History to 1916,* Vol. I, p. 157.
49. *Republican,* April 16 and 21, 1904.
50. *Ibid.,* May 13, 1904.
51. *Final History to 1916,* Vol. I., p. 64.
52. *Ibid.; Republican,* Dec. 1, 1904.
53. *Republican,* May 1, 1904.
54. *Ibid.,* April 16, 1904.
55. *Ibid.,* May 1, 1904.
56. *Ibid.,* April 21 and 23, 1904.
57. *Ibid.,* May 1, 1904.
58. *Ibid.,* April 25, 1904.
59. *Ibid.,* April 14, 1904.
60. *Ibid.,* April 21, 1904.
61. *Ibid.,* April 16, 1904.
62. *Ibid.,* April 28, 1904.
63. *Ibid.,* April 18 and 21, May 1, 1904.
64. *Ibid.,* May 4, 1904.
65. *Ibid.,* May 17, 1904.
66. *Ibid.,* May 18, 1904.
67. *Ibid.,* May 23, 1904.

68. *Ibid.,* May 24, 1904.
69. *Ibid.,* May 31, 1904.
70. *Final History to 1916,* Vol. I, pps. 76-77.
71. *Republican,* March 17, 1904.
72. *Ibid.,* May 29, 1904.
73. *Ibid.,* June 1, 1904.
74. *Ibid.,* June 11, 1904.
75. *Ibid.,* May 24, 1904.
76. *Ibid.,* June 11, 1904.
77. *Ibid.,* June 12, 1904; *Gazette,* June 14, 1904.
78. *Republican,* June 8, 1904.
79. *Ibid.,* June 8, July 10, August 24, 1904.
80. *Ibid.,* June 19, 1904.
81. *Ibid.,* June 26, 1904.
82. *Ibid.,* April 26, June 26, 1904.
83. *Ibid.,* April 10, June 26, 1904.
84. *Ibid.,* June 26, 1904.
85. *Ibid.,* June 28, July 10, 1904.
86. *Ibid.,* July 10, 1904.
87. *Ibid.,* June 28, 1904.
88. *Arizona Republican Weekly* (Phoenix), June 9, 1904; *Republican,* June 19, 1904.
89. *Republican,* June 19, 1904.
90. *Ibid.,* June 9, and 26, 1904.
91. *Ibid.,* July 6, 1904.
92. *Gazette,* July 6, 1904.
93. *Ibid.,* July 9, 1904; *Republican,* July 9, 1904.
94. *Gazette,* July 10, 1904; *Republican,* July 10, 1904.
95. *Republican,* August 13, 1904.
96. *Ibid.,* July 22, 1904.
97. *Ibid.,* July 26 and 28, 1904.
98. *Ibid.,* July 24, 1904.
99. *Ibid.,* July 27, 1904.
100. *Ibid.,* July 28, 1904; *Gazette,* July 28, 1904.
101. *Ibid.*
102. *Republican,* July 28, 1904.
103. *Ibid.*
104. Ralph F. Palmer, *Doctor on Horseback,* (Mesa: Mesa Historical and Archaeological Society, 1979) p. 106.
105. *Republican,* July 30, 1904.
106. *Ibid.*
107. *Gazette,* July 30, 1904.
108. *Republican,* August 5, 1904.
109. *Ibid.,* August 1, 1904.
110. *Ibid.,* August 7, 1904; *Gazette,* August 7, 1904.
111. *Republican,* August 7, 1904.
112. *Ibid.*
113. *Ibid.,* August 12, 1904.
114. *Ibid.*
115. *Ibid.*
116. *Ibid.,* August 24, 1904.
117. *Ibid.,* August 12, 1904.
118. *Ibid.,* August 17, 1904.
119. *Ibid.,* August 24, 1904.
120. *Ibid.*
121. *Ibid.,* September 2, 1904.
122. *Final History to 1916,* Vol. I., p. 93; Louis C. Hill, *Fourth Annual Report of the Reclamation Service, 1904-05.,* (Washington: Government Printing Office, 1906), p. 74.
123. *Final History to 1916,* Vol. I., pp. 93-94.
124. *Republican,* September 2, 1904.
125. *Ibid.,* August 24, 1904.
126. *Ibid.,* September 17 and November 3, 1904.
127. *Final History to 1916,* Vol. I., pp. 75-76.
128. *Republican,* September 18, 1904.
129. *Ibid.,* September 16, 1904.
130. *Ibid.,* September 20, 1904.
131. *Ibid.,* September 27, 1904.
132. *Ibid.,* September 29, 1904.

133. *Ibid.,* October 2, 1904.
134. *Ibid.,* October 15, 1904.
135. *Ibid.,* November 12, 1904.
136. *Ibid.,* October 19, 1904.
137. *Ibid.,* November 10, 1904.
138. *Final History to 1916,* Vol. I, p. 105.
139. *Republican,* December 17, 1904.
140. *Ibid.,* December 6, 1904.
141. *Final History to 1916,* Vol. I, p. 83.
142. *Republican,* November 29, 1904.
143. *Ibid.,* December 3, 1904.
144. *Ibid.,* December 9 and 27, 1904.
145. *Ibid.,* December 6, 1904.
146. *Final History to 1916,* Vol. I, p. 83.
147. *Republican,* December 6, 1904.
148. *Ibid.*
149. *Ibid.*
150. *Ibid.,* December 14, 1904.
151. *Ibid.,* December 17, 1904.
152. *Ibid.,* December 27, 1904.
153. *Ibid.,* January 4 and February 8, 1904.
154. *Final History to 1916,* Vol. I, p. 75.
155. *Ibid.,* p. 113.
156. *Ibid.,* p. 114; *Republican,* January 4, 1905.
157. *Final History to 1916,* Vol. I, p. 113.
158. *Ibid.,* pp. 104-105; *Republican,* January 4, 1905.
159. *Republican,* January 6, 1905.
160. *Final History to 1916,* Vol. I, pp. 84-85.
161. *Republican,* February 3, 1905.
162. *Gazette,* January 6, 1905.
163. C. D. Walcott to E. A. Hitchcock, April 10, 1903, Report on Irrigation in the Salt River Valley, National Archives, Record Group 48, Lands & Railroad, Reclamation, SRPA.
164. *Republican,* January 7, 1905.
165. *Ibid.,* January 21, 1905.
166. *Ibid.,* January 10, 1905.
167. *Ibid.,* January 12, 1905.
168. *Ibid.,* January 13, 1905; *Gazette,* January 12, 1905.
169. *Gazette,* February 12, 1899, and January 13, 1905; *Republican,* January 14, 1905.
170. *Republican,* January 10, 1905.
171. *Ibid.*
172. *Ibid.*
173. *Ibid.,* January 17, 1905.
174. *Ibid.*
175. *Ibid.,* January 21, 1905.
176. *Ibid.,* December 6, 1904.
177. *Ibid.,* January 21, 1905.
178. Palmer, *op.cit.,* p. 86.
179. *Republican,* January 23, 1904.
180. *Ibid.,* January 11, 1905.
181. *Ibid.,* February 16, 1905.
182. *Ibid.,* January 24, 1905.
183. *Ibid.,* January 29, 1905.
184. *Ibid.,* February 5, 1905.
185. *Ibid.*
186. *Ibid.,* February 7, 1905.
187. *Ibid.,* February 8, 1905.
188. *Ibid.*
189. *Ibid.,* February 9, 1905.
190. *Ibid.,* February 10, 1905.
191. *Ibid.,* February 9, 1905.
192. *Ibid.,* February 11, 1905.
193. *Ibid.,* January 27, 1905.
194. *Ibid.,* February 12, 1905.
195. *Ibid.,* February 14, 1905.
196. *Ibid.,* February 22, 1905.
197. *Ibid.,* February 27, 1905.
198. *Ibid.,* February 28, 1905.
199. *Ibid.,* February 23, 1905.

200. *Ibid.*
201. *Ibid.*
202. *Ibid.,* February 24, 1905.
203. *Gazette,* February 15, 1905.

204. *Republican,* February 24, 1905.
205. *Ibid.,* February 25, 1905.
206. *Ibid.,* February 28, 1905.
207. *Ibid.,* March 8, 1905.

March - August 1905

Two men died in the first two days of March 1905, at the Tonto Basin. The first was Alex McGalvey, one of the men working on the extension of the Roosevelt road above the dam site. McGalvey fell from a 300-foot-high cliff to the rocks below. Though several men were working near him, no one saw him fall. One of his companions missed him. They looked over the edge of the cliff and saw him on the rocks. This happened March 1. [1]

The next day, Mills Van Wagenen, 20, of Globe, was with three other men on the suspension bridge over the Salt River watching Osborne Richins take flow measurements. A heavy rock broke free from the side of the mountain and crushed one of the cables holding the bridge between the canyon walls. The bridge tipped as it dropped about 20 feet to the water, spilling all of the men but Richins into the swift-running river. Richins, stream gauger for the Reclamation Service, grabbed one of the wires along the side of the bridge. Van Wagenen, an inexperienced swimmer, was swept away. [2] His body was found 16 days later caught in some branches at the head of the Utah Canal, about eight miles below the junction of the Salt and Verde rivers. [3] He had been employed by the government. [4]

Two of the men who had been on the bridge, Will Galpin and Ellis Palmer, swam to safety, while the fourth man, an unidentified stranger, was pulled to safety by Richins. [5]

Ah Soo, a Chinese employed as a cook at the Reclamation Service's headquarters camp, almost drowned when he attempted to swim the river following a hunt for game. He was saved by several Indians camped on the north side of the river. [6]

A different kind of event, a wedding, the first at Roosevelt, took place at 4:30 p.m., March 5. John D. Houston, a Roosevelt businessman, married Rose E. Velasco. The bride had been born at old Fort McDowell and had been reared in Phoenix. [7]

The Tonto Basin had several days of clear weather, then rain fell again. The deluges of water, besides bringing freighting to a virtual standstill, washed out the railroad in the vicinity of Globe. The Salt River Valley too had a few days of respite from the rain, but it began falling again, and the flow in the river continued high. Water poured over the Arizona Dam. [8]

By March 16, 10.42 inches of rain had fallen in Phoenix, which was nearly twice the 5.57 inches that fell in all of 1904. [9] One old-timer, Henry Morgan, said he had not seen a rainy season equal to this one except in the spring of 1864 or 1865. Twice in March, the water flow at the Roosevelt dam site reached between 50,000 and 60,000 cubic feet per second. [10]

On March 17, seven feet of water was measured coming over the Arizona Dam at 4 o'clock in the afternoon. [11] Two spans of the Phoenix & Eastern Railroad bridge dropped into the Salt River at Tempe, but a second railroad bridge, the Maricopa & Phoenix, withstood the burrowing water.

The river carved acreage away from bordering farms, and at the Center Street crossing south of Phoenix, it was said to be the highest in 14 years. [12]

Despite the miserable conditions and the boggy road between Mesa and Goldfield, [13] Wolf Sachs on March 21 sent out his first freight wagon on the Roosevelt road. [14] The *Arizona Republican* reported,

Wednesday two more of Wolf Sachs' six-mule teams came up to Mesa and loaded with grain and hay and supplies for the Tonto Dam. This makes five outfits on the road... Mesa, with the starting of the oil teams and the teams for handling the merchandise and supplies, takes on the air of a hustling mining camp in the early days, less the drunkenness and noise. [15]

There was no way to get the supplies directly to Roosevelt because the over-the-hill road had not been completed, and the road along the river past the dam site remained under water. [16] There were two ways to get the supplies to the camp: one choice was to send it via pack trains and the other was to haul the goods upriver in a boat. Neither method was appealing, but until the river went down or the Roosevelt road was completed, those were the options. [17]

Word came from Washington, D.C., that the contract for construction of the Roosevelt Dam had been awarded to John M. O'Rourke & Co. of Galveston, Texas. [18]

Benjamin A. Fowler, president of the Water Users' Association, called the governors and attorneys in the city into conference March 27 to discuss the water priority lawsuit of *Hurley v. Abbott*. [19] Fowler, who had returned from Washington the previous week, revealed to them letters written to him February 23, 1905, by Arthur P. Davis, assistant chief engineer of the Reclamation Service, and February 24, 1905, by Morris Bien, supervising engineer, expressing concern over opposition to the lawsuit. Davis wrote,

It was distinctly understood from the first that such an adjudication would be made at the earliest possible date, and it is a great surprise and disappointment that this policy does not meet with universal favor. . . . It is (a) necessary preliminary to any intelligent determination on the part of the association or on the part of the government as to how much water will be available for distribution to the lands that have been pledged for the payment of the cost of the reservoir.

A large proportion of the lands that have been thus pledged are in tracts greater than 160 acres, and under the terms of the reclamation act, must be sold to persons who are eligible to perfect a water right under that act. No intelligent purchase or sale of such lands can be made until it is known whether or not they will be irrigated by the proposed project, and this uncertainty attaches to a very large proportion of the lands in the reclamation district. Their sale depends upon their status with regard to water rights, which cannot be settled until after a judicial decree and a determination as to whether they will be included in the area served by the reservoir. . . .

If this adjudication is not made as soon as practicable, it will be necessary for the government to determine in some other way the lands to be served by the reservoir which will lead to dissatisfaction and litigation, and will necessitate an eventual adjudication such as is now proposed with the delay and loss that such a delay will occasion. [20]

Bien said opposition to *Hurley* came as a surprise to him,

because one of the fundamental ideas urged upon the consideration of the secretary of the interior in February 1904, for immediate action on the draft of contract then submitted was that this was a necessary preliminary to adjudication of these claims to the use of water. [21]

Bien reminded Fowler the secretary had stated this in his letter of February 25, 1904, to the director of the U.S. Geological Survey, and the letter had been printed as part of the draft of the contract circulated in a pamphlet to shareholders in the Water Users' Association before the association's election ratifying the contract. The secretary had said,

Unless some agreement or understanding as to the distribution of all the waters made available by means of the reservoir can be arrived at, so that its use can be made uniform by one system, a conflict between the users of the increased supply and the owners of the vested rights in the natural flow of the stream would seem to be inevitable. [22]

Bien said failure to carry out the adjudication would be regarded by the secretary as a "direct violation of [the terms of the contract], leaving him free of any obligation specified in it." He warned if the adjudication was not accomplished "there is grave doubt whether any storage would be possible by the Reclamation Service for the benefit of the members of the association." He concluded:

Unless adjudication of these individual water rights is carried through by the association, the main purpose of its existence is not realized. It is doubtful, therefore, whether the department would undertake to operate the storage system in the face of the serious conflicts of rights that must necessarily arise if no adjudication of these rights has been made. [23]

There was no apparent disagreement among either the governors or the attorneys as to the need for the adjudication, but no definite action was taken. [24]

The Council of the Water Users' Association met April 1 at the Board of Trade to discuss the situation. About 100 persons were present, including Governor Joseph H. Kibbey, association attorney, who argued the lawsuit was absolutely necessary. He said he had heard talk of a settlement by agreement, but nothing had come of it. He said the suit would go on, and the expense would be much greater if the water users waited to receive summons before replying. [25]

William J. Murphy, though not a Council member, was allowed to speak. He expressed strong opposition to *Hurley,* contending the suit would continue for years and would be expensive to every landowner. Murphy said he believed the letters from Davis and Bien had been solicited. [26]

Fowler followed Murphy, and said he had asked for the letters while he was in Washington. Fowler said the opposition to the suit was discussed with Reclamation officials, and all of them said it was necessary. He said he did not want to return to Arizona as the bearer of messages but thought it would be better if letters were addressed to him. Fowler said he doubted an agreement could be reached to which all water users would subscribe. He said he had been informed by the court that, unless an agreement was unanimous, it was worthless. The suit was the only option. [27]

Again, nothing definite was done. [28]

The election of association governors took place April 4. A week later, Fowler wrote to Davis, telling him, "in several of the districts the election turned on 'suit or no suit' to establish prior rights." Fowler said Dr. Alexander J. Chandler had engineered the election of W. J. Kingsbury, who, like Chandler, opposed *Hurley.* Fowler said that, as the board then stood, it was split for and against the lawsuit, with Fowler providing the necessary sixth vote in favor. Among the farmers elected to the Board of Governors was Maricopa County Supervisor John P. Orme. [29]

Fowler reported that there had been,

so many determined threats of vigorous litigation and determination to carry the suit on demurrer and other technicalities to the United States Supreme Court, and thus delay action, that it has seemed to me best to find some other way, if it is possible, by which these rights can be adjudicated. [30]

If some other way could not be found, Fowler said the suit would have to be pushed, even if it took years to settle, which "causes apprehension throughout the business community." In addition to such large landholders as Chandler and Murphy, the real estate men opposed the suit. [31] The suit was a threat to land sales under the larger canals [Chandler's Consolidated, Murphy's Arizona] where the appropriations of water were the youngest. Although Chandler and Murphy were shareholders in the Water Users' Association and they knew the government insisted upon determining the priority of rights before distribution of water from the reservoir began, they apparently preferred maintaining the status quo for as long as they could. They were comfortable with the situation as it was, and they could not know, as no one could, what the court might do.

The weather improved in the Tonto Basin so freighting between there and Globe began to return to normal. The Reclamation Service office in Phoenix reported oil was beginning to arrive in Roosevelt from Globe, and the cement mill would soon start up. [32]

The Council met April 8 to discuss *Hurley.* At length, the Council adopted two resolutions. The first, appointed the Council chairman, C. T. Hirst, and a councilman from each district to prepare a report for the Council outlining "the best means of promptly adjusting the rights to the use of irrigating water." The second, invited any person having a plan to adjust the rights to present it in writing and to explain it in person at a meeting scheduled April 22. [33]

Heavy rains again descended on the Tonto Basin country April 8, [34] and word came April 12 from Roosevelt that the water in the river was higher than at any other time that year. The water was reported to be 25-feet deep. [35]

At 4 o'clock on the afternoon of April 12, the water coming over the Arizona Dam was 7.7-feet deep. [36] In the forenoon the following day, with nearly eight feet of water topping the dam, timbers began to slough away.

By 3 p.m., it was estimated the hole in the dam was 200-feet wide. [37] The *Republican* said,

The importance of this misfortune is not alone in the property loss to the canal company. . .it very seriously affects nearly all the north side ranchers, for the reason that it may mean an entire lack of irrigation water for their crops later on, when the dry season comes and the rain stops. And it could not occur at a more critical time, for the crops now are all growing, and if there is a shortage it will be during the season when they are maturing. [38]

The dam was 1,100-feet long and about ten feet high, with aprons slanting into the river bed on both the upstream and downstream sides. Six inches to seven feet of water had come over the dam since January 10. [39] The last time the dam had broken was in 1891 when almost 18 feet of water topped it. [40]

A general meeting of water users April 13 resulted in the unanimous adoption of a resolution urging the governors and Council of the Water Users' Association to do everything possible to expedite *Hurley v. Abbott* and for all shareholders to file their answers. The resolution also urged all water users agree that the evidence adduced in *M. Wormser, et al, v. the Salt River Valley Canal Co., et al,* which resulted in the Kibbey Decree,

as to the cultivation and right to the use of water on particular lands under the several canals, be admitted as competent evidence in the suit of Hurley v. Abbott, et al, and be considered determinative of the rights to the use of water upon said several tracts of lands therein tabulated as of date of the decision. . . .[41]

The Kibbey Decree set forth the number of quarter sections of land entitled to water under the canals between the years 1868 and 1889. A table included with the decision showed 946 quarter sections irrigated under eight canals. The decree did not deal with the rights of individual lands receiving water through the canals. [42]

On April 14, the break in the Arizona Dam was said to be about 300 feet. [43] A report from Tempe said the greater part of the timbers had lodged in the river between there and Mesa, and in one place a man could almost cross on them without getting wet. [44] William B. Cleary, general manager of the Arizona Water Co., which operated the dam, said April 15 the management already was planning to begin repairs when the water went down. The break in the dam was said to have grown larger, [45] and by April 17, it was estimated to be 400-feet wide. [46]

The break in the dam also caused two hydroelectric power plants, which depended upon the Arizona Canal for water, to cease operations. The Evergreen power station was on a crosscut canal on the Salt River Indian Reservation, and the Arizona Falls plant was at today's 56th Street and Indian School Road in Phoenix. The two stations supplied electricity to the Phoenix Light & Fuel Co. for distribution in Phoenix. The company maintained a steam power plant for backup. [47]

The cement mill at Roosevelt began operating April 17, [48] but it was not to run at full capacity until 1906. There were two reasons. First, the electric generating capacity of the temporary steam power plant was insufficient. It was not until April 2, 1906, that the cement mill received electricity from the temporary hydroelectric power plant so it could run at capacity. Second, the grinding of the cement was slower than anticipated. This problem was resolved by the purchase of a second tube mill for grinding cement. It was installed in November 1905, increasing the capacity of the cement mill by about 50 percent. [49]

Once the mill was operating at capacity, it took two months to fill the storage space set aside for cement. The mill was closed from June through September 1906. Until August 1909, when all the cement required had been manufactured, the mill shut down three more times, May and November 1907, and August 1909. The capacity of the mill was about 10,000 barrels per month, but its highest single month's production was 14,000 barrels. The total output was 338,452 barrels. The cost of manufacturing, including depreciation of the plant, was $1,063,542.36, or $3.14 per barrel, which was $1.75 per barrel less than the low bid of $4.89 for delivering the product at Roosevelt. The Reclamation Service figured the savings to the farmers was $591,487. [50]

The dam contractor, John M. O'Rourke, and his business partner, George N. Steinmetz, after visiting the dam site, came to Phoenix April 21 and met with local businessmen and Reclamation Service officials. O'Rourke told a newspaper reporter it would take about four months before active work would begin. He said the temporary power plant had to be in operation and machinery purchased. In the interim, quarries would be opened and cables, trams, derricks and other equipment readied. O'Rourke said one advantage was the quarries would be on the hills overlooking the dam site, which eliminated the need for building railroads. He estimated 300 to 500 men would be employed, depending upon the stage of the work. The part of the work on which he hoped to employ the most men was the laying of the foundation. He said the work would be pushed as fast as possible, regardless of the season. The first work would be the excavation of the dam site. If water came along and filled the hole, it would be taken out at the earliest opportunity and the work continued until the dam was built. [51]

Stockholders of the Appropriators' Canal Co. met April 22. Because of the damage to the Arizona Dam, they now envisioned the role of the Appropriators' as supplying water at all times for land under the Grand Canal. The Appropriators' stockholders voted to raise and spend $7,500 for construction, including building three bridges, and to meet with directors of the Grand Canal to ask permission to connect the Appropriators' Canal to the Grand Canal. [52]

The Council also met April 22 and discussed two plans proposed to the subcommittee appointed April 8 for facilitating settlement of the priority suit. Both plans involved dividing the land into classes according to the priority of appropriation and establishing 40 miners' inches as the amount of water to which each quarter section of land should be entitled. A plan offered by C. B. Wood proposed continuing the distribution of water to the Tempe and San Francisco canals as provided by the Kibbey Decree. The plan proposed designating lands irrigated between 1868 and 1875, as described in the Kibbey Decree, as Class A. Other classes proposed were land irrigated between 1875 and 1880 Class B, 1880 to 1885 Class C, and 1885 to 1890 Class D. Lands no longer irrigated were to be excluded. Since the plan "would protect every *legitimate right*" of the lands to be irrigated, estimated at between 100,000 and 110,000 acres, Wood believed "the suit to all intents and purposes would be settled." Kibbey condemned Wood's plan as impracticable, [53] undoubtedly because it contained no provision for determining the priority rights of individual lands. It also smacked of Dwight B. Heard's rejected proposal for a reservoir regulating right by which the reservoir would provide water for already existing rights.

Frank H. Parker, the association secretary, offered the second plan. Parker's plan proposed using tables prepared by the Maricopa County Board of Water Storage Commissioners, showing 120,000 acres (750 quarter sections) in actual cultivation in 1901. Until the priorities of the landowners were determined, Parker wanted them to agree the 750 quarter sections had the first right to water and the water would be divided equally. He also thought it would be an advantage if the number of quarter sections with first rights to the flow of the Salt and Verde rivers was reduced to 700 quarter sections. These were to be designated Class A lands. Lands with occasional irrigation, estimated to include 300 to 400 quarter sections, were to be Class B. Parker proposed the Kibbey Decree be used to locate the 700 quarter sections in Class A. [54]

Neither plan was acceptable to the Council, which adopted a resolution calling for a Committee of Sixteen to make a concerted effort,

to unite the owners of cultivated lands both within and without the association, on some form of an agreement as to the use of the natural appropriated flow of the Salt and Verde rivers. Said agreement to be used as a stipulation in the suit of Hurley vs. Abbott, et al., *and to be binding upon all parties signing such agreement.* [55]

After it was pointed out the resolution seemed to favor cultivated lands over uncultivated lands, an amendment to the resolution was added:

Said committee shall be empowered to work out a compromise plan for the lands within the association, if in their study of the situation they find such a plan feasible. [56]

A resolution named to the Committee of Sixteen the president of the association, Fowler; vice president, Dr. Ethelbert W. Wilbur; the secretary, Parker; and the chairman of the council, Hirst. Hirst and Fowler were authorized to name seven members of the Council, three governors, and one representative each from lands under the Tempe and San Francisco canals not in the association. [57] The appointments were made April 24. Heard was named to represent the San Francisco Canal. [58]

The Roosevelt road opened for traffic April 24, and the first stage went over it that night. [59] The cost of building the 63 miles of the road was $350,644. [60] Opening the road did not mean an end to road construction. There were more roads to be built in addition to maintenance, repairs, and improvements.

Fowler left for Washington April 25. He considered the breaking of the Arizona Dam as an opportunity for the Water Users' Association to acquire the north side canal system from the Arizona Water Co. and to press the Interior Department for construction of a permanent solid masonry diversion dam. [61]

On April 26, the management of the Grand Canal announced it was willing to meet with representatives of the Appropriators' Canal to work out an agreement under which Grand Canal water users could get water while the Arizona Dam was being repaired. Lloyd B. Christy, president of the Grand Canal, and Cleary, secretary, offered to lease to the Appropriators' the portion of the Grand Canal from its headgates opposite Tempe westerly to its intersection with the Crosscut Canal, provided the Appropriators' repaired it. Christy and Cleary also said they were willing to pay for water delivery to the Crosscut until the Arizona Dam was diverting water and the Arizona Canal was supplying water into the Crosscut. [62]

The proposition proferred by Christy and Cleary was immediately rejected by Appropriators' Canal officials because it would have defeated and undone everything they had accomplished. The Appropriators' came up with a counter proposition consisting of two plans: first, the Appropriators' would complete its canal from the river to the intersection of the Grand Canal within four weeks and would supply water for six months without cost to the Grand Canal. This would be done provided the Grand Canal would obtain permission from its associated corporation, the Arizona Water Co., for the Appropriators' to extend its canal across a quarter section of land owned by the Arizona Water Co. lying between the western end of the Appropriators' and the Grand Canal. The Appropriators' offered to pay reasonable damages for permission to cross the quarter section.

Second, the Appropriators' would allow the Grand Canal to complete the Appropriators' Canal within four weeks and the Appropriators' would pay the construction costs. The Appropriators' would give the Grand Canal a lien on the Appropriators', and would allow the Grand Canal to remain in possession of it, rent free, until the cost was repaid with interest. In exchange, the Grand Canal would supply water to the landowners until such time as the Grand Canal again obtained water through the Arizona Canal. [63]

The two sides met April 29, but could not agree to a compromise. The Appropriators' officials decided to go ahead with the construction of their canal, paralleling the Grand Canal, and prepare to go to court over their digging across the quarter section owned by the Arizona Water Co. [64]

The Reclamation Service announced it would accept bids for construction of a sand crushing plant at Roosevelt until 2 p.m. May 15. The sand would be used in the cement and concrete work at the dam. [65]

Hill reported the high water in the river had filled the sluicing tunnel with sand. He said the sand could easily be flushed out with water when the tunnel was needed. He also said preliminary work for the gates was continuing. The chamber above the tunnel was completed, and workmen were about 40 feet away from having drilled through from the top downward. [66]

Hill said about 5,000 yards of rock had been removed from the south wall of the canyon to accommodate the temporary power plant. The rock had been dumped into the riverbed, and nearly all of it had been carried away by the floods. Hill said that was the only good turn the river had done for them. [67]

About 120 feet of the power canal penstock had been excavated as an uprise, and Hill said another force would begin working downward in a few days. As soon as wood could be supplied for fuel, compressed air drills would be used in the excavation, he said. [68]

The rainy weather had seriously delayed progress, Hill said, but about 500 government employees were at work. [69] The main headquarters was now at Roosevelt, with the engineers and office workers occupying the Reclamation Service's new building at Roosevelt. [70]

On May 1, the governors adopted a resolution giving delinquent stockholders until June 1 to pay the preliminary assessment of ten cents per share without penalty. The Council adopted a bylaw imposing a penalty of two cents per share for the first 30 days of delinquency after June 1 and one cent per share for each succeeding 30-day period. The Council adopted another bylaw permitting landowners qualified to become shareholders to apply for stock. Upon payment of the ten cents per share, the land would be placed upon the "waiting list" for later decision by the secretary of the interior as to which land in the reservoir district would get water. The bylaws could not become effective until approved by the interior secretary, an action that took place October 25, 1905. The period for paying the ten cents per share was extended until June 1, 1906. [71]

A traction engine to haul oil in 34 barrel tanks on specially built wagons between Mesa and Government Well passed through Tempe en route to Mesa on May 1, 1905, on the Maricopa & Phoenix Railroad. Government Well was about two and one-half miles northeast of Goldfield on the Roosevelt road and was the point at which the road began its passage through the mountains.

The traction engine, owned by C. R. Eager & Co., weighed 23 tons and stood on three wheels, two at the rear and the third centered at the front. The wheels were 57-inches high with tires 42-inches wide and required a road 14-feet wide. To accommodate the engine, which was equipped with a gasoline fueled marine corrugated boiler, the Reclamation Service laid out a new road from Mesa to Government Well and built extra strength bridges. Pulling a full load of four wagons with filled tanks, totaling 58,432 pounds, the traction engine chugged along at about three miles per hour. At Government Well the wagons were hitched to six-horse teams for the haul to Roosevelt. A second traction engine was put in service in September. [72]

The Committee of Sixteen met May 6 to consider the Kibbey Decree and other data, including tables showing river water flows, water distribution, cultivated acreage, and contracts between the various canals. In addition, Parker announced that printed copies of the complaint in *Hurley v. Abbott* and printed forms to make formal answer to the suit were available at the Water Users' Association offices. Kibbey had drawn up the form to make formal answer; the water user had only to fill in appropriate blanks. [73]

On May 6, Fowler delivered a letter in Washington, D.C., to Frederick H. Newell, chief engineer of the Reclamation Service, in which Fowler said the Arizona Water Co. "would gladly unload" the injured Arizona Dam and the company's canal interests, and the Water Users' Association "would gladly purchase," provided the Interior Department would appoint a commission or board to determine the price and terms. Fowler also asked the government to replace the Arizona Dam with a,

permanent masonry diversion dam for the benefit of the whole valley, with head gates, at either end to supply main distributing canals, on both the north and south sides of the river, which, in the early future, will be consolidated under the administration of the Salt River Valley Water Users' Association. [74]

Before writing the letter, Fowler had been in New York City getting the agreement of Hiram R. Steele, vice president of the Arizona Water Co., and his associates for the sale of the company to the Water Users' Association. None of this was known to the water users until after Fowler returned to the Valley in June.

Newell replied to Fowler's letter at once—on May 6. Newell said the government already had spent and would spend more money on the Salt River project than authorized by the reclamation act [section 9 of the act provided funds derived from the sale of public lands be spent on projects within the state or territory where the lands were sold]. For that reason, he said, "it has therefore become necessary to scrutinize with great care all propositions for additional expenditures." [75]

After reminding Fowler that, "All the dealings of the Reclamation Service with the people of the valley. . .have been based upon. . .a proper adjustment of [vested water] rights before any new expenditures are undertaken in the valley or any stored water is furnished for irrigation," Newell said the question of building the diversion dam would be investigated. He closed the letter by asking Fowler to urge upon the Water Users' Association the immediate "adjustment of the existing water rights, in order that the government may proceed without delay or uncertainty." [76]

Newell did not comment upon Fowler's request for the appointment of a board to determine the value of the Arizona Water Co. holdings, but they undoubtedly discussed this. Fowler commuted back and forth between Washington and New York, trying to bring together a satisfactory arrangement for the purchase of the water company.

The Committee of Sixteen, on May 9, appointed a three-member subcommittee, Heard, Parker, and Wilbur, to consider the substitution of a regulated flow for the fluctuating flow of water. The committee had determined the regulated flow coming from the reservoir would be less than the average amount of water actually delivered. [77] Heard unquestionably was the chief exponent of the regulated flow, which would have provided the regulation right in the reservoir for which he had fought unsuccessfully when the association's articles of incorporation were written.

The subcommittee issued its report May 13, including a recommendation that a daily regulated flow be adopted. However, the daily regulated flow was abandoned after ensuing meetings of the full committee indicated it would be impossible to get agreement on it among all water users. [78]

Meanwhile, work on the Appropriators' Canal progressed, with a new head at the level of the river bottom built a mile and a half farther upstream. [79] Cleary reported the repair work at the Arizona Dam and the Arizona Canal would proceed faster if more animals could be obtained. The canal was filled with sand for a distance of two miles. The break in the dam measured 190 feet, and some of the cribbing still stood in the breach. [80]

Bids for the sand crushing plant were opened May 15, and the lowest of four, $5,531.86, came from the Mine and Smelter Supply Co. of El Paso, Texas, which received the contract. [81] The same day, the first two tanks of oil were sent out from Mesa by freight train. The traction engine was ready for work, but the road was not in good enough shape. Oil was arriving at Roosevelt from Globe for use at the cement mill, and some of the cement was used to line the power canal. Hill reported more than 200 feet of the power canal penstock had been excavated. [82]

The Orange Growers' Association, made up of 20 orchardists, met May 18 and decided to order four pumps from a San Francisco company for use in drawing water from the river at the head of the Arizona Canal. Since the Arizona Water Co. was not supplying the water for which they had paid, the ranchers did not see how anyone could object to their plan. The aggregate capacity of the pumps was 1,850 miners' inches (91.5 acre-feet in 24 hours). [83]

Secretary of the Interior Ethan A. Hitchcock, on May 18, agreed to appoint three "disinterested engineers or experts" to calculate the value of the Arizona Water Co., as proposed by Fowler and Steele. Charles D. Walcott, director of the U.S. Geological Survey, informed Fowler of the decision by letter May 22. Walcott said that agreement to appoint the board was done "upon the distinct understanding that the United States does not at this time assume the obligation to pay the amount appraised nor to purchase the property at any price or in any event, this question to be left for future decision when the value of the property, as determined by the Commission, shall become known." [84]

Fowler sent a letter May 23 to the Interior Department in which he enclosed a form of contract for the sale of the Arizona Water Co. to the Water Users' Association. He asked Hitchcock to approve the contract form. [85]

On May 24, 3,000 acres of the Salt River Indian Reservation on the north side of the Salt River and 900 acres on the south side were signed for stock in the Water Users' Association. The land was signed in upon the recommendation of William H. Code, irrigation engineer for the U.S. Bureau of Indian Affairs. Authority for Joseph B. Alexander, superintendent of the Indian reservation, to enroll the Indian land was given by Hitchcock on May 18. Alexander was told to,

take such steps as may be necessary to carry out the recommendations of Inspector Code with respect to signing up on the waiting list of the Water Users' Association for reservoir rights for the Indians. . . [86]

The Indians on the Salt River Reservation were never issued reservoir rights, their land being omitted when the interior secretary designated which acreage within the reservoir district would receive stored water. One reason for this was the land would have been subject to a lien for the payment of all assessments of the association. [87]

The pumps ordered by the Orange Growers' Association arrived by train May 24. They were immediately loaded on four-horse wagons for movement to the head of the Arizona Canal. Foundations for the pumps and two engines to run them, one gasoline and the other steam, already were in place. [88] Two of the pumps were in operation by May 28, but more power was needed to start the others. The two working pumps produced about 1,500 inches of water, but the water was not going far because the Arizona Canal still had not been cleaned. The pumps were started in the hope the water would wash some of the sand downstream and help open the canal. [89]

Meanwhile, some of the orange growers hauled water in to irrigate trees and installed pumps for that purpose. [90] The pumps at the head of the Arizona Canal failed to get sufficient water down the canal to do any good, so the Orange Growers' Association closed them down June 15. [91] In addition, the Arizona Water Co. expected to have water in the Arizona Canal a few days thereafter. Repairs involving the Arizona Dam included the construction of a gravel dike that circled the breach to keep water from passing through. The dike, intended as a temporary work while new cribbing was built in the river to fill in the break, ran to the head of the canal. Water was turned down the canal June 18. [92]

Hitchcock, on June 1, wrote to Fowler, saying,

I have concluded that the interests of the government will be best subserved and the situation much simplified by the purchase of the property of the Arizona Water company directly by the United States, provided that such property can be acquired, including all outstanding interests controlled by the company, for a satisfactory consideration. [93]

Despite this explicit statement, Hitchcock added "that this proposed action has no significance or effect beyond the ascertainment of the value of the property controlled by the Arizona Water company. . ." [94]

That same day, Concord stagecoaches arrived at Mesa. They were ordered from a San Francisco firm by William A. Kimball for a stage line between Mesa and Roosevelt. One seated eight passengers and the other ten. It was announced the stages would go into operation at once, making stops at Goldfield, Morman Flat, and Fish Creek to change horses. The stage office in Roosevelt was at Warren Barnett's drug store, and in Mesa, in the former post office building. The competition no doubt prompted J. Holdren & Sons, the existing stage line, to report a 14-passenger automobile had been ordered for use between Mesa and Government Well. It was promised the auto, which would have a speed of 20 miles an hour, would make a daily round trip between the two points. [95]

Fowler and Steele, on June 7, sent a letter to Hitchcock in which they described the property of the Arizona Canal Co. to be appraised. The property included the Arizona Canal and Dam; all contracts, including one allowing the Phoenix Light & Fuel Co. to develop hydroelectric power with water flowing in the Arizona Canal; controlling interest in the Grand, Salt River Valley, Maricopa, and Water Power (Crosscut) canals, and all water rights and property owned under the canals. They said the "appraisement shall be governed by the rules that would apply if the property was being taken by condemnation proceedings." They concluded,

that this appraisement is to be made with a view of said property being taken over by the United States government as an integral part of the irrigation system for said valley if the government shall hereafter elect to do so but that the government is in no way obligated to make said purchase. [96]

In Phoenix on June 7, Cleary, on behalf of the Arizona Water Co., warned the Appropriators' Canal company to cease its operations. [97] The Appropriators' had built a flume under the Crosscut Canal, and men and teams were excavating a canal paralleling the Grand Canal. The flume was 20-feet wide and three-feet deep. The Arizona Water Co. claimed the land on which the Appropriators' Canal was being extended. [98] The Arizona Water Co. filed suit June 9, and a temporary injunction was issued to halt the canal digging. [99]

Water users under the Grand, Maricopa, and Salt River Valley canals met June 10. Landowners under the latter two adopted a resolution calling upon the Arizona Water Co. to repair the Joint Head Dam (a short distance east of today's 48th Street on the north side of the Salt River in Phoenix) and to clean the sand out of the Salt River Valley Canal so it could carry an adequate amount of water. The situation between the Arizona Water Co. and the Appropriators' Canal was discussed, and Lincoln Fowler said he had tendered the water company $250 in gold for the strip of land near the Crosscut through which the Appropriators' had run. The strip of land was 60-feet wide and a mile long. An answer to the Arizona Water Company's lawsuit had been made by the Appropriators', including the filing of a condemnation proceeding for the strip of land. [100]

Hitchcock wrote to Benjamin Fowler June 10, telling him a commission would be appointed to appraise the Arizona Water Co. Hitchcock also advised him that, while this was being done with the understanding the government was under no obligation to buy, "It must be. . .understood that if any purchase shall be made by the government it must be to the property as an entirety." [101]

On Monday, June 12, a flow of 6,000 inches of water ran through the Appropriators' Canal into the Grand Canal west of the Crosscut Canal. The farmers also decided to improve the Joint Head Dam themselves. [102]

When the case of the Arizona Water Co. against the Appropriators' Canal Co. came up in court, attorney Thomas Armstrong Jr. said the Appropriators' had ignored the temporary injunction because the farmers needed the water. Cleary asked for 30 days in which to prepare evidence, but Judge Edward Kent denied the request and set a hearing for the following day. Cleary also sent men and teams to work on the Joint Head Dam. [103]

After hearing arguments June 13, Kent took under advisement whether to dissolve the injunction. He also set June 14 to hear the Appropriators' condemnation suit. Meantime, under the direction of Heard, work continued on the Appropriators' Canal, and it was expected that within a few days water would be turned into the Salt River Valley and Maricopa canals as well as the Grand Canal. [104]

Hitchcock, on June 14, approved the appointments of George Y. Wisner, W. H. Sanders, and A. E. Chandler to serve as a commission to appraise the property of the Arizona Water Co. [105] The same day, Hitchcock wrote to Fowler and Steele telling them of the action. [106]

Also on that day, Kent ruled the Appropriators' could have the strip of land owned by the Arizona Water Co. The only testimony concerned the value of the land, put by the Appropriators' at $10 to $15 per acre for the approximately eight acres involved. The ground had never been cultivated and was covered with virgin brush. Cleary put the value of the land between $40 and $50 per acre. He testified the bush was a valuable crop cultivated by the Arizona Water Co. for use in the construction and repair of the Joint Head Dam. Kent ordered the Appropriators' to execcute a bond of $300 until the value of the land was determined. [107]

The *Republican,* in an editorial, pointed out the significance of Kent's ruling in the Appropriators' condemnation case:

If the Appropriators' canal can invade the territory of the Arizona Water company. . .what is to prevent it. . .from constructing a system of canals which will parallel the old system?

And if this privilege exists, what becomes of the value of the property and rights heretofore enjoyed by the Arizona Water company? That such value has been greatly lessened is the natural conclusion.

. . .the new state of affairs would seem to give the ranchers a decided advantage in negotiating with the Arizona Water company for the acquirement of its holdings. To put it bluntly, the way seems clear for the ranchers to construct a new system of canals in the event that they cannot reach satisfactory terms with the owners of the old canal system. [108]

Benjamin Fowler returned to Phoenix on June 17. He said he would report on what had been accomplished at a meeting of the governors on Monday. He added the trip east had been made advisable by the breaking of the Arizona Dam and the discussions had involved the system of water distribution. [109]

The Grand, Maricopa, and Salt River Valley canals' water users met and adopted resolutions calling for completion of the Appropriators' Canal, delivery of water from it to the Maricopa and Salt River Valley canals, purchase of stock in the Appropriators' by water users under the three older canals, and construction of a permanent dam at the Joint Head. [110]

Soon after, extension of the Appropriators' Canal began. By the end of October 1905, the canal's length was said to be 30 miles plus 20 miles of laterals. It was estimated the canal could provide water for 38,000 acres, about 15,000 acres of which could get water from no other canal. [111]

At the governors' meeting June 19, Fowler revealed the exchange of correspondence with Hitchcock. Fowler said he had told the officers and directors of the Arizona Water Co. it seemed almost providential the Arizona Dam had been injured, though he did not expect them to see it that way because the company eventually had to sell or lose its property through depreciation should another water delivery system be provided. He said while there was nothing to bind the government in buying the Arizona Water Co. holdings, he was sure that, if all was satisfactory, including acceptance by the people, it would be done. [112]

Fowler said the masonry diversion dam project would begin at once, which suggests Fowler convinced Newell (if Newell needed convincing) there would be "a proper adjustment of (vested water) rights" in the Valley, but this could not be accomplished "before any new expenditures were undertaken" [the quotes are from Newell's May 6 letter to Fowler]. Fowler said the project would include a few miles of canal construction on the south side of the river and probably some on the north side because the Arizona Canal should be enlarged. [113] The governors passed a resolution endorsing Fowler's actions. On June 26, a letter was sent to Hitchcock notifying him of the "hearty approval" of Fowler's actions by the governors. The governors noted,

both the Articles and the Contract (with the government) were adopted and ratified without taking the acquisition of the distributing system by the Government into consideration; that matter at that time at least, was left to be accomplished under the other provisions of the Articles.

. . .the proposition that the Government should acquire the distributing system on the North side is so incomparably better from every point of view than any other method suggested, that it meets with almost instant approval. [114]

Hill revealed on June 20 that for the past month a crew had been making measurements of the Arizona and other north side canals preparatory to making computations for use by the Appraisal Commission. He could not say, however, when the commission would meet. [115]

The Committee of Sixteen met June 24 and adopted a resolution "to use every possible effort to secure prompt judicial determination of the existing rights to the use of water in the Salt River Valley." The resolution was in response to Newell's May 6 letter to Fowler. [116]

A similar resolution was passed by the Council June 27. [117]

At Roosevelt, the afternoon of June 26, fire swept through a row of five tents occupied by Reclamation Service personnel. The tents were located on three terraces on an elevation above the town. The tents had board sides and floors and double roofs. A strong west wind jumped the fire from tent to tent. [118]

Reclamation officials issued another warning against liquor, which was being smuggled in in small quantities. Saloons were located at Mormon Flat and Fish Creek, along the Roosevelt road, and another was near the summit of the High Line road to Globe. Would-be operators of tent saloons made applications to open within the reservoir district but were rejected. A territorial law prohibited the establishment of a saloon within six miles of a government camp. [119]

The lower end of the power canal was nearing completion. On the upper end, six miles below the intake,

workmen began the installation of formed-in-place steel reinforced concrete pipe across Pinto Creek with a machine known as the "concrete alligator." The alligator, designed by Fred Teishman of the Reclamation Service, poured a jointless concrete pipe. The seven-inch-thick pipe, with an internal diameter of five feet three inches, was sunk ten feet below the creek bed. The Pinto Creek crossing was 2,400 feet, the longest of three waterways transversed with pipe. The others were Cottonwood Creek, three miles above the powerhouse, and School House Wash, about six miles east of the Roosevelt dam site. The Cottonwood Creek crossing was 540 feet and School House Wash 93 feet. Over other narrower waterways small wood flumes or concrete structures were used. [120]

The original plan for installing the pipe was to lay twin lines across Pinto Creek. The first few hundred feet of pipe were made with cement shipped from Colorado. One hundred and twenty feet were fashioned in 24 hours. Thereafter, the pipe was made by cement manufactured at Roosevelt. Demands of other portions of the construction for the cement and several floods delayed completion of the first Pinto Creek line until November 1905. In addition, the cement made at Roosevelt was slower setting. That and mechanical problems caused the builders to abandon the continuous round-the-clock installation of the pipe. [121]

Once the first line was finished at Pinto Creek, operations were switched to Cottonwood Creek. This was because all the water that would be needed to provide power at the dam could be carried in one line, and Hill wanted the electricty as soon as possible. The Cottonwood pipes were constructed through the winter, the pipe being made at the rate of 24 feet per day. The second Pinto line, started in March 1906 and completed about August 1, was built at the rate of 40 feet per day. [122]

The "concrete alligator" had a tendency to travel off line or grade, a problem that was partially solved with a steering apparatus. However, it was necessary about every eight or ten days to halt work in order to level and straighten the machine. [123]

Construction also began on a new road up Tonto Creek to replace the lower road, which would be flooded when the reservoir filled. [124]

On July 3, the governors instructed Kibbey to make certain by August 1 that all defendants in *Hurley v. Abbott* either had answered or had been served notice to answer, and to prosecute the case as promptly as possible to its conclusion. The governors also levied a seven cent annual assessment on each acre in the association. [125]

Davis, in a July 3 letter to Fowler, said bedrock borings for the diversion dam would be done in the fall "after the summer torrents of July and August have passed." Another letter from Davis said the Appraisal Commission would arrive about October 1. [126]

Residents of the Tonto Basin were shocked by the murders of rancher Sam Plunkett, 40, and one of this workers, Ed A. Kennedy, about 65, at Plunkett's ranch about a mile east of the mouth of Pinto Creek. Plunkett was supposed to meet July 14 with Reclamation Service officials.

When he failed to keep the appointment, messengers were sent to the ranch and the bodies were found inside the ranch house. Both men had been stabbed and their bodies mutilated with a butcher knife. Their skulls had been crushed with an iron from a wagon tongue. From the decomposition of the bodies, authorities estimated the men had been dead 48 hours before the crime was discovered. Robbery appeared to be the motive, and two Mexicans who had worked for Plunkett were suspected. Hill detailed Al Sieber, who had served 20 years as chief of Army scouts at San Carlos, to go after the killers. But the Indian trackers put to work by Sieber were on a cold trail. They were able to trace the movements of the suspects in the area, but the murderers had fled. [127]

The slayings prompted Hill to say Roosevelt was known as a decent and orderly camp, and it was going to remain that way. If robbery or other heinous crimes were committed, the offenders would be hunted and brought to justice regardless of expense. [128]

Hill reported the excavation of the penstock tunnel was completed. The incline of the tunnel was at a 40 percent grade with an overall length of 610 feet. It was expected the volume of water coming down the penstock tunnel would produce 5,000 horsepower of electricity. The excavation was difficult work; the combination of extreme heat and poor ventilation caused the men much discomfort. Compared to that, the installation of the steel lining would be easy, Hill said. [129]

A new tent hospital was opened at Roosevelt by Dr. Ralph Palmer, who also was in charge of sanitation. Strict rules governed the disposal of garbage and refuse, and Palmer developed a septic tank to handle sewage from the houses on the hill occupied by Reclamation officials. [130]

O'Rourke, the dam contractor, was busy putting in a camp on the opposite side of the river from Roosevelt and making other preparations. The camp was on a plateau about 1,000 feet above the dam site. [131]

George A. Mauk bought Joe Schell's stage station along the Roosevelt road, about three miles above Fish Creek. Improvements were underway at the Mormon Flat station operated by Fred Nelson. The Goldfield station was taken over by the Weekes brothers on a lease from C. A. Hall & Co. [132]

Stockholders in the Mesa Canal Co. met July 27 to consider their response to *Hurley.* After hearing their attorney, Webster Street, they instructed him not to answer until a summons was served. When he did answer, Street was to argue that the contract of 1890 between the Arizona Water Co. and the other canals, with the exception of the Tempe and San Francisco canals, had settled the water question among the canals as well as between Hurley and the Mesa Canal. Street said he thought the aim of *Hurley v. Abbott* was to break the 1890 contract. He said he thought the Water Users' Association was going to adopt a means other than a suit to resolve priority questions. He said he did not see how the suit could settle the rights of anyone but Hurley, a view, he said, that was shared by most other attorneys. Street contended that few persons had ever complained about the 1890 agreement. (The statement ignored the years of litigation the agreement had brought on between the Arizona Water Co. and the minority shareholders under the north side canals.) [133]

The 1890 contract provided that from the water remaining after the Tempe and San Francisco canals received theirs, the Mesa and Utah canals got one-third and the Arizona and the other north side canal companies were to get the remainder. [134]

Attorney Alexander Buck, in a letter to the *Republican,* took issue with statements *Hurley* could not settle the priority question among all water users. Buck said,

The title to the water to which each land owner is entitled and the order in which he should receive the same can be settled by a proper appearance in the suit. . . By filing a cross bill, each water user separately makes each and every other water user a defendant to all intents and purposes and the court will then act as justice and equity requires.

I know very well that certain of the canal companies are going to contend that the title of the water for each land owner in the valley cannot and ought not to be settled through the medium of a suit for that purpose. But that is not to be wondered at as they have, by making certain rules and regulations, violated every natural and constitutional right that the land owners have to the appropriation and use of water and forced them to sign illegal contracts arbitrarily. [135]

By the time the clerk of the U.S. District Court closed for business August 2, answers to *Hurley* numbered 489. It was estimated that under 1,000 answers would ultimately be filed. Though residents of Phoenix, Tempe, and Mesa were named individually in the suit, it was expected that the cities would make answer for all of them. Attorney Buck printed a notice in the *Republican* offering to handle answers through to the end of the suit for ten cents per acre. Buck said that by answering by August 15 the landowners could save the cost of service of summons, which he estimated would be from $4 to $6. [136]

On August 3, the *Phoenix Gazette* reported the Interior Department was considering raising the height of Roosevelt Dam and building a power plant on Fish Creek [137] (the Horse Mesa Dam was built by the Water User's Association on the Salt River just above Fish Creek between 1924 and 1927). Fowler was asked about raising the dam's height when he returned August 5 from a trip to Roosevelt. Fowler said because of the flow in the river in the spring and summer, the governors, among them himself, Wilbur, and Chandler, began agitating for raising the dam. Hill had agreed, and the matter was being considered in Washington. Fowler said he favored it because the storage capacity of the reservoir would be increased by about one-third at a cost probably not to exceed $200,000. He said the governors were to consider the matter Monday, August 7. [138]

Fowler also said when the dam was first seriously considered, four sets of plans were drawn. The No. 4 plan, which called for the highest dam, was favored, but the water in the river had been low for so long that, when bids were solicited, the dam height was reduced 20 feet. [139] The original plan of the Reclamation Service was for a dam to store water at a maximum depth of 190 feet, which would flood 13,459 acres and have a capacity of 840,775 acre-feet of water. As the time approached for bids, the Reclamation Service put the height at 210 feet above low water. This would flood 15,000 acres and store 1,125,160 acre-feet. The height of the spillway finally settled on was 220 feet above low water. The reservoir was to cover 16,329 acres and store 1,284,205 acre-feet. The dam proper was to be 20 feet higher than the spillway crest. A four-foot parapet was to put the total height of the dam, from the lowest foundation to the top of the parapet, at 284 feet. [140]

The governors on August 7 adopted a resolution in favor of adding 20 feet to the dam's height. [141] An identical resolution was approved by the Council on September 9. [142]

The first summonses in **Hurley v. Abbott** were issued August 7 and were directed at the defendant canal companies. Issuance to individual defendants was to start the following week. [143]

About 2:30 p.m. August 16, a severe summer thunderstorm struck the Tonto Basin. A small funnel-shaped cloud was seen northwest of Roosevelt, and winds blew at the rate of 80 to 90 miles an hour. Tents were wrecked. The building with the heaviest damage was the Monarch bowling alleys where the entire roof was blown off. Roofs also were stripped from some adobe buildings. [144]

The Knox automobile bought by the J. Holdren & Sons stage line arrived in Mesa August 22 and made its first run to Government Well August 25. Dubbed the "Red Terror," the auto weighed about 3,500 pounds and cost $3,000. The auto was intended to reduce by at least three hours the 12-hour trip from Mesa to Roosevelt. Holdren stages departed at 6 a.m. and arrived at 6 p.m. The auto was expected to reach Government Well at 8:30 a.m. where passengers would transfer to the regular horse-drawn stage. The auto would wait at Government Well for the in-coming stage, which arrived about 2 p.m. About 90 minutes was taken off the time from Roosevelt to Mesa. [145]

Two carloads of machinery and one carload of mules for J. M. O'Rourke & Co. arrived in Mesa. The equipment included cable and cars for the tramway over the Roosevelt dam site. [146]

---

1. *Arizona Republican* (Phoenix), March 4 and 8, 1905.
2. *Ibid.,* March 4, 5 and 8, 1905; *Arizona Silver Belt* (Globe), undated, reprinted *Arizona Gazette* (Phoenix), March 9, 1905.
3. *Republican,* March 19, 1905.
4. *Ibid.,* March 8, 1905.
5. *Ibid.,* March 4 and 8, 1905.
6. *Ibid.,* March 4, 1905.
7. *Ibid.,* March 9, 1905
8. *Ibid.,* March 8, 13 and 21, 1905.
9. *Ibid.,* March 17, 1905.
10. *Ibid.,* March 14, 1905; *Salt River Project, Final History to 1916,* unpublished manuscript, Vol. I., p. 114, Salt River Project Archives (hereafter SRPA).
11. *Republican,* March 18, 1905.
12. *Ibid.,* March 20, 1905.
13. *Ibid.*
14. *Ibid.,* March 24, 1905.
15. *Ibid.,* March 25, 1905.
16. *Ibid.,* March 24, 1905.
17. *Ibid.,* April 30, 1905.
18. *Ibid.,* March 17, 1905.
19. *Ibid.,* March 26 and 28, 1905.
20. A. P. Davis to B. A. Fowler, February 23, 1905, reprinted in *Republican,* March 28 and November 19, 1905; Report of the Committee of Sixteen, Phoenix, Arizona, November 1905, SRPA.
21. M. Bien to B. A. Fowler, February 23, 1905, reprinted in *Republican,* March 28 and November 19, 1905; Report of the Committee of Sixteen.
22. *Ibid.*
23. *Ibid.*
24. *Ibid.*
25. *Gazette,* April 1, 1905.
26. *Ibid.*
27. *Ibid.*
28. *Ibid.*
29. B. A. Fowler to A. P. Davis, April 11, 1905, National Archives, Record Group 115, 261 Salt River, 1902-1919, SRPA.
30. *Ibid.*
31. *Ibid.*
32. *Republican,* April 8, 1905.
33. *Ibid.,* April 9, 1905.
34. Fowler to Davis, April 11, 1905.
35. *Republican,* April 13 and 21, 1905.
36. *Ibid.*
37. *Ibid.,* April 14, 1905; *Gazette,* April 13, 1905.
38. *Republican,* April 14, 1905; *Gazette,* April 14, 1905.
39. *Ibid.*
40. *Gazette,* April 13, 1905.
41. Gerard H. Matthes to L. C. Hill, April 20, 1905, Salt River Project Vault, Kent #119, SRPA.
42. *M. Wormser, et al., plaintiffs, v. The Salt River Valley Canal Co., et al., defendants,* No. 708, Joseph H. Kibbey, decision, March 31, 1982, Second Judicial District, District Court, Territory of Arizona.
43. *Gazette,* April 15, 1905; *Republican,* April 15, 1905.
44. *Republican,* April 15, 1905.
45. *Ibid.,* April 16, 1905.
46. *Gazette,* April 18, 1905.
47. *Republican,* April 18, 1905.
48. *Ibid.,* April 21 and 27, 1905.
49. *Final History to 1916,* Vol. I, pp. 87-88.
50. *Ibid.,* pp. 89-90.
51. *Republican,* April 22, 1905.
52. *Ibid.,* April 23, 1905.
53. Matthes to Hill, April 20, 1905; *Republican,* April 23, 1905.
54. *Ibid.*
55. *Ibid.*
56. *Ibid.*
57. *Ibid.*
58. *Republican,* April 25, 1905.
59. *Ibid.,* April 27, 1905.
60. *Final History to 1916,* Vol. I, p. 74.
61. *Republican,* June 18 and 20, 1905.
62. *Ibid.,* April 27, 1905.
63. *Ibid.*
64. *Ibid.,* April 30, 1905.
65. *Ibid.,* April 25 and May 16, 1905.
66. *Ibid.,* April 27, 1905.
67. *Ibid.*
68. *Ibid.*
69. *Gazette,* April 26, 1905.
70. *Republican,* April 30, 1905.
71. *Ibid.,* May 2, 1905, May 6, 1905.
72. *Ibid.,* May 2, 7, 13, 16 and 24, August 16 and September 14, 1905.
73. *Ibid.,* May 6, 1905.

74. B. A. Fowler to F. H. Newell, May 6, 1905, SRPA.
75. Newell to Fowler, May 6, 1903, reprinted *Republican,* June 20, 1905.
76. *Ibid.*
77. Report of the Committee of Sixteen.
78. *Ibid.*
79. *Republican,* May 15, 1905.
80. *Ibid.,* May 18, 1905.
81. *Ibid.,* May 16, 1905; *Final History to 1916,* Vol. I, p. 115.
82. *Republican,* May 16, 1905; *Gazette,* May 16, 1905.
83. *Republican,* May 19, 1905.
84. C. D. Walcott to B. A. Fowler, May 22, 1905, SRPA.
85. *Republican,* June 20, 1905.
86. John F. Truesdell, Memorandum as to certain questions concerning the water rights of the Salt River Indian Reservation in Arizona, December 18, 1914, SRPA.
87. *Ibid.*
88. *Republican,* May 25, 1905.
89. *Ibid.,* May 29, 1905.
90. *Ibid.,* May 29 and June 3, 1905.
91. *Ibid.,* June 16, 1905.
92. *Ibid.,* June 20 and September 8, 1905.
93. E. A. Hitchcock to B. A. Fowler, June 1, 1905, reprinted *Republican,* June 20, 1905.
94. *Ibid.*
95. *Republican,* April 18, June 2, 4 and 14, 1905.
96. B. A. Fowler and Hiram S. Steele to E. A. Hitchcock, June 7, 1905, reprinted *Republican,* June 20, 1905.
97. *Republican,* June 8, 1905.
98. *Ibid.,* June 9, 1905.
99. *Ibid.,* June 10 and 11, 1905.
100. *Ibid.,* June 11, 13, 14 and 15, 1905.
101. E. A. Hitchcock to B. A. Fowler, June 10, 1905, reprinted *Republican,* June 20, 1905.
102. *Republican,* June 12, 1905.
103. *Ibid.,* June 13, 1905.
104. *Ibid.,* June 14, 1905.
105. E. A. Hitchcock to C. D. Walcott, June 14, 1905, SRPA.
106. *Ibid.*
107. *Republican,* June 15, 1905.
108. *Ibid.,* June 18, 1905.
109. *Ibid.*
110. *Ibid.*
111. *Ibid.,* July 3 and 5, August 17, September 8, 13 and 18, October 19 and November 1, 1905.
112. *Ibid.,* June 19, 1905.
113. *Ibid.,* June 19 and July 30, 1905.
114. J. H. Kibbey to E. A. Hitchcock, June 26, 1905, SRPA; *Republican,* June 27, 1905; *Final History to 1916,* Vol. II, p. 220.
115. *Republican,* June 21, 1905.
116. *Ibid.,* June 25, 1905.
117. *Ibid.,* June 28, 1905.
118. *Ibid.,* June 28 and August 31, 1905.
119. *Ibid.,* May 25 and June 29, 1905; Ralph F. Palmer, *Doctor on Horseback* (Mesa: Mesa Historical and Archaeological Society, 1979), p. 119.
120. *Gazette,* June 30, 1905; *Final History to 1916,* Vol. I, pp. 158-161.
121. *Final History to 1916,* Vol. I, p. 178.
122. *Ibid.*
123. *Ibid.,* p. 180.
124. *Gazette,* June 30, 1905.
125. *Republican,* July 4, 1905.
126. A. P. Davis to B. A. Fowler, July 3, 1905; mentioned in *Republican,* July 9 and 12, 1905.
127. *Republican,* July 15, 19 and 25, 1905; *Gazette,* August 1, 1905.
128. *Republican,* July 19, 1905.
129. *Gazette,* July 14, 1905; *Republican,* July 19, 1905.
130. *Gazette,* July 14, 1905; Palmer, *op. cit.,* p. 109.
131. *Gazette,* July 18, 1905.
132. *Republican,* July 26 and 28, August 3, 1905.
133. *Ibid.,* July 28, 1905; Alfred J. McClatchie, *Utilizing Our Water Supply* (University of Arizona, Tucson, July 28, 1902), Bulletin No. 43, Agriculture Experiment Station. p. 89.
134. McClatchie, *op. cit.,* p. 88.
135. *Republican,* July 30, 1905.
136. *Ibid.,* August 3, 1905.
137. *Gazette,* August 3, 1905.
138. *Republican,* August 6, 1905.
139. *Ibid.*
140. *Final History to 1916,* Vol. I, pp. 124-125; *Sixth Annual Report of the Reclamation Service, 1906-1907,* (Washington: Government Printing Office, 1908) p. 63.
141. *Republican,* August 8, 1905.
142. *Ibid.,* September 10, 1905.
143. *Ibid.,* August 8, 1905.
144. *Ibid.,* August 20, 1905.
145. *Ibid.,* August 23 and 26, 1905.
146. *Ibid.,* August 29, 1905.

September 1905 - February 1906

In early September, the flow of water in the Salt River was unusually high. On September 6, the *Arizona Republican* reported "some disquieting news": the gravel dyke, put across the river to divert water into the Arizona Canal and to protect the Arizona Dam, was washing away. The news came from Dan McDermott, canal superintendent, who did not think the dam would be injured. However, he had instructed the zanjeros, the men who operated the gates in the canal, to alert the farmers so they could fill their water tanks. [1]

The following day, it was learned the dyke had washed away for a few hundred feet. Since only about a third of the dam had been repaired, this meant the water was flowing through, and the river crossing below Phoenix was unfordable. McDermott estimated it would take 20 days to repair the dyke once the water receded. [2]

Coincidentally, Hiram R. Steele, an attorney and vice president of the Arizona Water Co., and his son, Porter, a New York City lawyer, arrived in town. Steele said he was sorry to learn about the damage to the dyke, and work would continue on the dam until it was repaired. [3]

Steele came to Phoenix to confer with the governors of the Water Users' Association. He met first with Governor Joseph H. Kibbey, association attorney. Kibbey told him the farmers did not like the way the water company operated, and the association intended to have control of the north side canals. Steele's meeting with the governors September 13 was private, but it was learned he gave a detailed description of the company's financial difficulties. At the meeting's end, it was announced the water company was willing to sell provided fair terms could be reached. Steele indicated he would like to have from the association an idea of what it was willing to pay. He was told the governors were not in a position to make an offer and whatever was done would require ratification by the shareholders. However, the governors were willing to entertain a proposition from him. It was to be understood, of course, that whatever was done would not interfere with the work of the commission appointed by Secretary of the Interior Ethan A. Hitchcock to appraise the Arizona Water Company's property. Nor would any deal be consummated without the interior secretary's approval and the government's advancing the money. [4]

On September 15, Judge George Holt of the U.S. District Court in New York City appointed Hiram Steele as the receiver for the Arizona Water Co. The receivership had been applied for by the New York Trust Co., which was trustee for $300,000 worth of bonds issued by the water company in 1899. The trust company alleged a default in the payment of interest on the bonds. The *Republican* reported that while Steele was in Phoenix he had intimated that a receivership might be the solution to the company's problems. [5]

William B. Cleary, local manager of the Arizona Water Co., said he understood the receivership was made as a means of raising money quickly for repair of the dam. The *Republican* thought the receivership would be an advantage for the Valley because it would mean the immediate repair of the dam. The newspaper explained certificates issued by the receiver would have a direct lien on the company's property ahead of the mortgage securing the bonds. The paper also thought the receivership would make easier the acquisition of the company by the Water Users' Association. The *Republican* foresaw quick negotiations between the association and the bondholders, with the federal government doing little beyond approving the price. [6]

However, the *Arizona Gazette* reported September 20 the Arizona Water Co. owners wanted $1,500,000, while the farmers were willing to pay from $300,000 to $350,000. It also said the minority stockholders in the older canal companies, the Salt River Valley, Maricopa, and Grand, expected to receive a part of the proceeds. The farmers under those canals were willing to pay for their own waterways, less the 49 percent interest they held, but they did not want to pay for the Arizona Canal. They believed that should be paid for by the landowners under it. [7]

Two employees of the Phoenix post office, Ernest W. Reid and B. W. Hoover, together made a $20 wager they could ride their bicycles to Roosevelt and back in 39 hours. The wager was accepted by four of their friends, who contended the road between Mesa and Government Well was so bad Reid and Hoover could not do it. The friends were wrong. The bicyclists departed from the post office at 4 a.m. September 24 and made it back 38 hours and 12 minutes later. [8]

About the time Reid and Hoover started their bicycle trip, high water in the Salt River began washing away another section of the dyke at the Arizona Dam. A portion of the dyke that had sloughed away earlier and had been replaced remained intact. [9]

U.S. District Court Judge Edward Kent in Phoenix, on September 26, named Steele to act as ancillary receiver of the Arizona Water Company's property in the Valley. The ancillary bill of complaint filed with the court by the New York Trust Co. provided the financial history of the water company. On January 1, 1899, the company gave a deed of trust for its property to the New York Security & Trust Co., predecessor of the New York Trust Co., to secure bonds not to exceed $300,000. The Arizona Water Co. was indebted in the sum of $256,000 and interest thereon but had defaulted on the latter. In addition, joint notes of the Maricopa, Grand, and Salt River Valley Canal companies, of which the Arizona Water Co. held a majority of stock, had been given for money advanced to repair the Arizona Dam. [10]

Louis C. Hill, the Reclamation Service engineer in charge of the Salt River project, reported there was being hauled over the Roosevelt road approximately 1,500,000 pounds of freight per month, including five tons of oil daily. When the amount of oil rose to between 18 and 20 tons daily, as required in the contract of C. R. Eager & Co., the monthly total of freight would be about 2,500,000 pounds. [11] In connection with that, the oil delivery contract was sold by Eager & Co. to Shattuck and Desmond, also of Los Angeles, on September 23 at Mesa. [12]

Hill said the sawmill in the Sierra Anchas had been closed and moved to Roosevelt, but a half-million feet of lumber remained to be hauled. This undoubtedly included poles that J. M. O'Rourke & Co., the dam contractor, intended to use in the construction of cofferdams in the riverbed above and below the dam site before starting excavation for the dam foundation. O'Rourke planned to build a large flume between the cofferdams to carry the normal flow of the river over the dam site. Hill said if the flow of the river was too much for the flume, part of the water might be diverted through the sluicing tunnel. He said O'Rourke had been delayed in getting started because one piece of machinery was not shipped until four months after it was ordered. The machinery was en route then, he said. [13]

The condition of the Roosevelt road from Mesa to Government Well continued to concern Hill and the Good Roads Association of Mesa. The heavy wagons had pulverized the soil to a bed of dust four inches thick. Hill said he would see the road was graveled if the association could persuade the Maricopa County Board of Supervisors to grade the 12 miles to the county line. It was estimated grading the road would cost $1,200. However, the only bid was $5,500, and the supervisors rejected it. The supervisors asked for new bids, and Shattuck and Desmond offered to do the grading for $1,500, which was accepted. By the end of January 1906, the grading was completed and only the graveling remained to be done. [14]

Letters from Steele and the Water Users' Association president, Benjamin A. Fowler, who had gone to the East Coast, were received by Kibbey. The letters, which concerned the sale of the Arizona Water Company's property, were read by Kibbey to the governors when they met October 2. Steele thought the water company should get $700,000, but he wanted the governors to set a price and to permit Fowler to act for the association. Fowler said he was willing to do it but not without instructions. He also intimated that, while he did not think it was right the governors should say what the association would pay, if a figure was sent to him he would be better able to act. It also appeared from the letters Hill had suggested to Steele and Fowler that, if the government were assured the association would take over the water company's property, the Reclamation Service might at once build the cement diversion dam, and the expense of repairing the Arizona Dam would be saved. Fowler said he did not think the government would build the diversion dam until it had some estimate of the price of the water company's holdings. [15]

Kibbey told the governors the water company should initiate the negotiating. He believed the company was more anxious to sell than the association was to buy. The governors did not want to offer more than might be necessary to buy. They also thought it was customary for the seller to put a price on his goods before the haggling started. At the governors' instructions, Kibbey sent telegrams to Steele and Fowler:

To Steele, New York City:

The board of governors met today and directed me to say that it adheres to its position that negotiations must be initiated by a proposition from a representative of the water company interests.

To Fowler, Washington, D.C.:

The board has considered the matter. It directs me to say that it can undertake no negotiations without a proposition from the water company as a basis. Every circumstance suggesting desirability of prompt action has been considered by the board and it is deemed by it that expedition is more advantageous to the water company than to the association. If negotiations fail, it will be because the water company has not initiated them by making a proposition. It remains with the water company to expedite matters. The board thinks this should be the place of negotiations. [16]

By September 1905, teamsters hauled 1,500,000 pounds of freight per month to Roosevelt.

without a proposition from the water company as a basis. Every circumstance suggesting desirability of prompt action has been considered by the board and it is deemed by it that expedition is more advantageous to the water company than to the association. If negotiations fail, it will be because the water company has not initiated them by making a proposition. It remains with the water company to expedite matters. The board thinks this should be the place of negotiations. [16]

Judge Kent, on October 3, issued an order confirming an order of the U.S. District Court in New York authorizing Steele to issue a receiver's certificate for $100,000 to be sold at not less than par with interest not to exceed 6 percent per annum. The money was to be used as follows: $38,134 to pay previous expenses incurred in repairing the Arizona Dam; an estimated $45,000 to repair the dam, and $15,000 for other debts. The request for the receiver's certificate showed that the New York Trust Co. was the trustee for $256,000 in first mortgage bonds and $646,499 in second mortgage bonds. There also was $55,000 in unsecured bonds. Among the bondholders were the Aetna Insurance Co. of Hartford, Connecticut, and the Middletown National Bank of Middletown, Connecticut. [17]

Kibbey received a telegram from Steele October 4 regretting the governors' position. Steele said it would be impractical for him to set a price without authority of the court. He said he thought the bondholders would agree to asking the court to give permission, but he expressed the fear that because of the governors' attitude he might not be able to raise money for repair of the Arizona Dam. He asked for suggestions on how the company and association could work together. [18]

The following day, the Arizona Canal Protective Association met at the Glendale school house for the purpose of trying to aid the Water Users' Association in acquiring the Arizona Canal. William J. Murphy said the meeting should deal solely with the Arizona Canal because the men assembled could not speak for water users under the other canals. The association adopted a resolution urging the Water Users' Association to "acquire" the canal (the word "purchase" was rejected so as not to limit the governors as to the kind of arrangement). Committees were appointed to ask Steele to have the canal cleaned and the dam repaired at once, and to enlist other water users into the Protective Association. Without water for the next season's crops, association members were worried they would not be able to grow sugar beets for a proposed sugar beet factory at Glendale. [19]

The first of the Protective Association committees met October 6 with Charles J. Hall, Steele's representative in Phoenix. Hall said there were no funds available to clean the canal. Dr. E. P. Palmer, committee chairman, suggested the water users be allowed to clean the canal themselves and to take their pay in water when the receiver could deliver it. Hall promised to send a wire to Steele seeking his permission. Meantime, the water company expected to turn water into the Arizona Canal by October 9, which it did. [20]

Chester W. Smith, Reclamation Service engineer in charge of building Roosevelt Dam, reported the O'Rourke company had driven the first piles into the riverbed for construction of the first cofferdam. [21] Visitors to Roosevelt estimated the population at more than 2,000 and the traveling time from the Valley to the Tonto Basin as nine hours or less. [22] The *Republican* was delivered there the afternoon of publication. [23] The turbine wheels for generating electricity from the power canal were being installed. [24] The Reverend J. P. Hutchison of Ellsworth, Ohio, arrived to minister to the community. [25]

The nearest point for liquor was now seven miles, partly because the project boundaries had been extended from one to three miles south of the river. [26] That did not halt the smuggling of liquor, legal and otherwise. Fitting into the legal category were patent medicines sold at the drugstore until an article in the *Ladies' Home Journal* revealed their high content of alcohol. Hill halted their sale. [27] Another time, Hill stopped one of Kimball's stages after it had entered the reservation and demanded the manifest, which disclosed four bottles of wine and 29 bottles of whiskey. The bottles were broken. [28] Dr. Ralph E. Palmer, in his autobiography, *Doctor on Horseback,* written in 1951, told of a similar incident. Palmer said he and two other government workers accompanied Hill, who carried a 30-30 rifle when he ordered stage driver Joe Phelps to stop just inside the three-mile limit. In the boot was found a case of whiskey. Hill ordered all but two bottles destroyed, allowing Dr. E. G. Lind, the disbursing officer, to take two into camp. [29] To enforce the liquor ban, Hill employed Jim Holmes, a former Texas Ranger, who carried two .38 Colt automatics. Palmer said Holmes could keep an ordinary tomato can "in the air shooting alternately from right and left hips until there was nothing left of the can or both guns were empty." [30]

Shareholders in the Appropriators' Canal Co. met October 7 and reelected Lincoln Fowler as president and John P. Orme, Patrick T. Hurley and Charles Goldman to the board of directors. The members turned down a motion to not deliver water to any water user who at the same time was getting water through another system. [31]

It was learned October 10 that Steele had no objection to the farmers cleaning the Arizona Canal, but he first wanted a report on its condition from superintendent McDermott. Some days later, the Arizona Water Co. began cleaning all the north side canals and repairing the dyke above the Arizona Dam. [32] Kibbey received a letter from Steele reiterating the request the Water Users' Association initiate action for purchase of the water company. [33]

Stockholders of the Maricopa, Grand, and Salt River Valley canals met October 18 to elect directors. Also adopted by the first two companies was a resolution introduced by Lincoln Fowler calling for committees of five stockholders and five water rights owners from each canal to develop a plan for selling and transferring their interests to the government. Salt River Valley Canal shareholders had adjourned before the resolution was approved. [34]

At Roosevelt, O'Rourke's men blasted out rock to prepare for erecting stations from which cable would be strung to carry tram cars across the canyon. Rock and other materials were to be lowered from the cars to the dam. The quarters for the men at Camp O'Rourke were about complete, and an ice and cold storage plant was under construction. A telephone was installed in the O'Rourke company office. Some of O'Rourke's workers, under the direction of his partner, John Steinmetz, installed hydraulic machinery to be used in the foundation excavation. Others stripped loose rock from the face of the north side of the canyon. Piles for the upper cofferdam had been driven. [35]

About 100 children were enrolled in the school, and Sunday church services were held regularly in Baker's hall and at the Reclamation Service building. The Reverend Thomas C. Moffatt, territorial missionary of the Presbyterian Church, arrived to aid in starting a church, and a movement was begun to build a tent church. [36]

A new bakery opened, and Dr. Ralph Palmer bought the drugstore. The telephone depot was moved from the Sultan-Newman Co. store to the Roosevelt Mercantile Co. A new piano was to be installed in Baker's hall, and a stage was constructed there in anticipation of the coming of theatrical groups. [37]

Kibbey received a letter from Fowler, who said he believed the Arizona Water Co. would sell for $350,000. Fowler wrote he was not authorized to speak on behalf of the company, but that was the price he had deduced. Fowler thought it must have been a shock to the owners to learn a property they had valued in the spring at more than a million dollars had fallen in worth to $200,000. The governors met October 28 and instructed Kibbey to wire Fowler that $350,000 was too much. There was talk the government had calculated the company's holding to be worth $250,000, but there was no confirmation for this. [38]

The evening of October 31, Ranger Holmes killed a Mexican, "L. Arbiso," after Arbiso was arrested for selling liquor to Indians. While trying to escape, he shot a deputy in the arm. Holmes and the deputy, a government teamster named Bagley, had arrested Arbiso at an Indian camp along Tonto Creek below Camp O'Rourke. In searching Arbiso, two bottles of whiskey were found, but no weapon. Holmes and Bagley, accompanied by the prisoner, spent several hours searching unsuccessfully for more liquor along Tonto Creek. Arbiso had not given them any trouble. As they walked toward the suspension bridge to cross the river to return to Roosevelt, Holmes was in the lead followed by Bagley and Arbiso. Suddenly, as they passed a clump of cottonwoods, Arbiso crouched behind a stump, produced a .44 caliber revolver, and fired a shot. The bullet struck Bagley in the arm. Before Arbiso could shoot a second time, Holmes killed him. Bullets hit Arbiso in the head, near the heart, and in each thigh. Bagley was treated by Dr. Palmer, who said the slug "entered the back of the right elbow and ranged down to the wrist severing nerves and tendons. He recovered from the wound but was left with a crippled right arm." [39]

Directors of the Board of Trade met November 4 to discuss the situation between the Water Users' Association and the Arizona Water Co. The directors thought there was too little time for the two parties to engage in the diplomacy of negotiating a price. They believed it would be better to pay the company more than its property was worth, if necessary, in order to assure the government would begin work at the head of the Arizona Canal. They thought that the loss to the Valley of next year's crop, especially if the sugar beet factory could not be given a thorough testing, might be greater than the depreciation of the water company's property. The water company was doing nothing about the permanent repair of the dam. The directors appointed a committee to discuss the situation with the governors. [40]

The **Republican** reported neither the association nor the water company had made a proposition, but there was a rumor Kibbey had offered $200,000. Another rumor was the company would make a proposal November 6. [41]

The latter rumor proved correct. When the governors met the morning of November 6, a letter of that date signed by Hall had been handed to Frank H. Parker, association secretary:

A telegram from H. R. Steele, receiver of the Arizona Water company, states that the bondholders will accept $350,000 for their canal interests, provided the government will take charge now and maintain works, etc. [42]

Present at the meeting besides the governors were committees from the Board of Trade and the Arizona Canal Protective Association. Dwight B. Heard was there representing the minority interests of stockholders in the Grand, Maricopa, and Salt River Valley canals. Lincoln Fowler also was there on behalf of the Appropriators' Canal Co., and as a member of a committee appointed by the Maricopa Canal Co. [43]

The governors thought $350,000 was too high. They said even if the offer were accepted, the water company was unable to give the government clear title, and they believed that would be necessary before the Reclamation Service could do anything. Engineer Hill was called into the meeting, and he agreed with the governors' assessment of what the government would do. However, he thought the Reclamation Service would take charge at the Arizona

Cement mill (top), powerhouse and footbridge over Salt River, November 11, 1905.

Canal head just as soon as an agreement was made. Asked when the appraisers appointed by the interior secretary would arrive to place a value on the Arizona Water Company's holdings, Hill said they were expected November 25, and he did not believe they could arrive much earlier. The governors decided to inform Steele, through Benjamin Fowler, they preferred to wait until the appraisers had acted before responding to Steele. The men at the meeting unanimously endorsed the governors' decision. [44]

Lincoln Fowler told the governors that, whenever the government desired to incorporate the Appropriators' Canal into the water distribution system, the company would willingly sell for its cost of about $40,000. Heard asked that, in considering the value of the Arizona Water Co., a price be placed on the minority interests. [45]

Kibbey, in a letter to Benjamin Fowler, said no one would take the Arizona Canal as a gift if he had to operate and maintain it. Kibbey did not think the holdings of the Arizona Water Co. worth $250,000. Fowler expected the company to await the report of the Appraisal Commission, which also was to consider building the Roosevelt Dam higher. [46]

Judge Kent approved an order on November 10 from the New York court allowing the receiver to sell land and water rights owned by the water company. The property was listed in two series, the first embracing 16 tracts of land under the Arizona Canal valued at $50,075 for purposes of the mortgage, and water rights under the canals as follows: Arizona $380,350; Grand $7,925; Maricopa $4,400, and Salt River Valley $3,000. The value of Arizona Canal water rights was put at $800 each and for the other canals at $400. The second series offered 12 tracts of land for $58,275 and these water rights: Grand $19,200; Maricopa $16,204; Salt River Valley $17,600, and Arizona $2,000. In this series, all water rights were valued at $400 each. [47]

The Committee of Sixteen finished its work November 19 and presented a report to the Council, which adopted it. The committee determined there were 127,512 acres of cultivated land in the Valley receiving water from the canals as follows: Grand, Maricopa, and Salt River Valley, 50,505 acres; Arizona, 23,440; Tempe, 21,000; Mesa, 14,122; Utah, 10,927; San Francisco, 4,328; Highland, 2,870; Broadway, 320. The committee was unable to arrive at any agreement as to the use of the natural flow of the Salt and Verde rivers above 60,000 miners' inches (2,970 acre-feet per day). It made a number of recommendations, including the water users under each canal adjust among themselves their individual rights; the water users under the canals and parties to *Hurley v. Abbott* agree among themselves how the water should be divided after apportioning at all times 500 miners' inches to Indian lands served by the Arizona Canal and 100 miners' inches to the Broadway Canal through the San Francisco Canal in periods when the river flow was above 6,000 miners' inches; the San Francisco and Tempe canals receive 64 miners' inches per quarter section of land less 200 miners' inches when the flow was between 6,000 and 52,000 miners' inches, but the 200 miners' inches be restored proportionately from the other canals whenever water passed the Utah Dam, or when a permanent diversion dam

should be built for the south side of the river in which the two canals owned an interest; after deducting the miners' inches for the San Fransisco and Tempe canals, the Arizona Canal receive "an arbitrary quantity" of 1,001 to 8,848 miners' inches when 6,000 to 58,000 miners' inches were in the river; the Grand, Maricopa, and Salt River Valley canals divide 2,746 to 26,729 miners' inches under the same conditions; the Mesa Canal 755 to 7,347 miners' inches and the Utah Canal 580 to 5,640 miners' inches under those conditions; the Highland Canal receive the flow of the rivers between 58,000 and 60,000 miners' inches; the agreement be binding when the owners of three-quarters of the cultivated and irrigated acreage had signed, including at least three-quarters of those under the San Francisco, Tempe, Maricopa, Grand, Salt River Valley, Mesa, and Utah canals; and the agreement not affect rights to the flood waters exceeding 60,000 miners' inches. [48]

Minority members of the Salt River Valley, Grand, and Maricopa canals met behind closed doors November 21 to discuss the value of their holdings, to place a price on them, and to do what they could to get the most for them. The value placed on each canal ranged from $30,000 to $50,000. If the highest value was placed on them and $200,000 was paid for the Arizona Canal, that would put the price at $350,000, [49] the amount proposed by Steele. The **Republican** pointed out,

It is a somewhat peculiar situation for the owners of these (minority) interests are, for the most part, men who are as much interested as anybody can be in the success of the projects of both the Appropriators' Canal company and the Water Users' association, for the latter of which it has been proposed that these old canal interests shall be bought by the government. Though these men will in a way be dealing with themselves they naturally desire to get as much as possible from the wreck of their former holdings. [50]

The meeting ended with the appointment of a committee of six, including a stockholder and a water right owner from each canal, to meet with the government Appraisal Commission, which was expected to arrive in a few days. [51]

On November 22, articles of incorporation for the Mesa-Roosevelt Stage Co. were filed by William A. Kimball, owner of the Kimball Stage line. The new company, which included E. S. Shattuck and D. L. Desmond of the Shattuck & Desmond Co., took over both the Kimball and J. Holdren & Sons lines. [52] That same evening, one of two stages carrying a theatrical company to Roosevelt overturned near Mormon Flat, causing a severe cut on the forehead to actress Florence Stanley. [53] This was one of a series of accidents. In another accident stage driver Frank Nash suffered a fractured leg when he jumped from the stage as it raced out of control down the hill into Roosevelt. [54] The theatrical group performed **Miss Hursey From Jersey** the night of November 23, at Baker's hall in Roosevelt. Attendance was so good the show was repeated the following night. [55]

Snow fell the morning and the night of November 22 at the Tonto Basin. ". . .the snow line was remarkably low for this time of the year," the **Republican** was informed by Frank G. Hough from Roosevelt. [56]

The Appraisal Commission and Arthur P. Davis,

assistant chief engineer of the Reclamation Service, arrived in Phoenix on November 25. [57] They were ready to begin work, but rain the next day kept them from going out. The river began to rise very rapidly. Valley residents knew the flood was bad because at 5 a.m. Monday, November 27, a large section of the old Maricopa & Phoenix railroad bridge across the Salt River at Tempe dropped away. With it went the Western Union and telephone lines. By 7 a.m., the water going over the Arizona Dam was nine-feet deep. [58] The *Republican* reported:

The Arizona Dam is no longer useful as a basis of calculation. At noon yesterday the gauge at that point showed ten feet over the point where the crest of the dam ought to be and a little later it rose to eleven feet. Still later it was 11 1/2 feet. [59]

The only thing the citizens had to compare with the flow of water was the flood of February 1891, the greatest in the Valley since the settlement by white men. In that year, the water was 17 or 18 feet over the Arizona Dam. The flow in the river rose to 276,000 cubic feet of water per second, then dropped before rising a few days later to 291,000 cubic feet per second. In that flood, the river broke into the Maricopa and Salt River Valley canals and carried the water into Phoenix. Following that flood, a levee to protect the city was built from the Joint Head of the Maricopa and Salt River Valley canals, east of today's 48th Street, along the north side of the river. The night of November 27, 1905, the water rose to within a few inches of the top of the levee. Two men walked the levee that night with instructions to telephone the sheriff from a nearby farmhouse in the event of a break. Meanwhile, officers alerted Phoenix residents to the danger. The crest of the flood passed about 11 p.m., and the river dropped 14 inches in the next hour. [60] It was later estimated the peak flow in this flood was 200,000 cubic feet per second. [61]

"Phoenix is greatly depressed by the present state of affairs," the *Republican* said the morning of November 28. The full extent of damage was unknown because the river was still high, but it was learned damage to the Appropriators' Canal along the river was extensive. The water had eaten away large sections of the canal's south bank. That night, the river broke into the joint canal of the Maricopa and Salt River Valley canals, but Phoenix escaped flooding because the river was dropping. The river also carried away a portion of the north approach of the Maricopa & Phoenix railroad's steel bridge at Tempe, putting out of business the last of the three railroad structures at that point. The water earlier had washed away piling and wooden structural work on the Phoenix & Eastern railroad bridge, part of which had been lost in the flood the previous spring. However, the Maricopa & Phoenix expected to quickly make repairs and to return its steel bridge to service. Arrangements were made for the Phoenix & Eastern to use the bridge. [62]

Valley residents knew what brought the flood. "It was generally believed the flood of yesterday was due in the main to rains melting the snow on the Verde watershed and another big flood was reported to be coming down Salt River," the *Republican* said. [63] From Roosevelt, the newspaper's correspondent wrote:

The highest water since the flood of 1891 was in the Salt river on Monday, Nov. 27. During last week a great deal of snow fell in the mountains north and east of here. The warm rain which fell all day Sunday melted the snow, bringing the water down in torrents. [64]

The water in the river at Roosevelt began rising very rapidly at 5 p.m. November 26. The suspension bridge, still the only means of crossing the river without a boat, went out at 5:30 a.m. November 27. The water continued to rise until reaching its peak at 11:30 a.m., 35 feet 10 inches, which was "12 feet above last year's highest mark." [65] The discharge of the river had risen from a little more than 2,000 cubic feet per second to almost 130,000 cubic feet per second, [66] racing through the canyon at about 12 miles an hour. [67] Tonto Creek furnished almost as much water as the Salt and covered the flats up Tonto Creek, the water reaching the hills. The Indian tents and shacks along the creek were washed away, and a few tents and houses occupied by whites were carried off or flooded. The sluicing tunnel was filled with sediment, and a sandbar covered its outlet. All of the work on the cofferdam and flume performed by O'Rourke was swept away along with a pile driver, logs, timber, a blacksmith shop, and assorted equipment. One person drowned. He was not identified. A mule and horse tied to a wagon near the sluicing tunnel were carried down the river, but the mule broke loose and swam to shore. Much of the excavation for the Pinto Creek pipeline was filled in, and the pipe already installed was partly filled with sediment. At the intake of the power canal, the river washed away hundreds of feet of soil and came up to the bank of the canal. The telephone line between Roosevelt and Phoenix went out, as did the road, which was not reopened for traffic until December 9. The telephone line was restored December 12. A new suspension bridge was completed December 1. [68]

The Appraisal Commission went into the field November 27, [69] and two days later the minority stockholders of the Maricopa, Grand, and Salt River Valley canals met to better define their position. After rejecting a resolution offered by Heard to accept for their stock interests "our proper legal proportionate part of the purchase prices," they adopted a proposal to accept for their "interests such proportionate amount as the board of appraisement. . .may fix upon said canals." They also asked, "That payment for each interest be made to the party interested personally." [70]

On December 1, Davis and Hill returned from a trip to Roosevelt via the Arizona Dam. They crossed the river above the Arizona Dam by boat without any difficulty. They reported the dam badly damaged; although several hundred feet of it was intact, it was ruined and the river plunged downstream without obstruction. The bank of the Arizona Canal for one and one-half miles was broken in a number of places. [71]

Appropriators' Canal Co. members met December 2 to consider repairs. They were uncertain whether to make the repairs temporary or permanent, but agreed they should coordinate their efforts with the desires of the Reclamation Service. However, Hill and George Y. Wisner, a member of the Appraisal Commission, told the Appropriators' they did not believe it was within their authority to advise what should be done. The Appropriators' called upon Hall to ask if the Arizona Water Co. would be interested in having the Grand Canal's water carried through the Appropriators' Canal. Hall said he doubted the water company would make such an arrangement. [72]

The Appraisal Commission visited Kibbey at the capitol building and called a closed meeting for Monday, December 4, to hear from representatives of the Arizona Water Co., the minority stockholders, the Appropriators' Canal Co., and the Water Users' Association. [73]

Attorney C. F. Ainsworth appeared before the commission on behalf of the Arizona Water Co. He put the value of the company's property at $608,176.03, not including water rights nor the balance due on contracts for the sale of water rights "for the reason that we understand the commission is not to consider the water appropriations or water rights. We also have omitted from this statement the headgates and that portion of the Arizona Dam remaining at the head of the Arizona Canal." [74]

The water company's itemized statement placed the original construction of the Arizona Canal at $381,514.86, then deducted $34,312.60 for the cost of removing silt, reducing its value to $347,202.26. Other items included the contract with the Phoenix Light & Fuel Co., $100,000; cost of laterals, $31,551.09; zanjero houses, $1,000; tools and implements, $18,200; one-third interest in Crosscut and Power canals, $9,658.81; interest in Salt River Valley Canal, $25,373; interest in Maricopa Canal, $32,800; interest in Grand Canal, $30,450; interest in Crosscut and Power canals through majority holdings in the Grand Canal, a part-owner of the Crosscut and Power canals, $5,553.81; interest in the Crosscut and Power canals through the Salt River Valley Canal, $6,384.46. [75]

The value of the contract with the Phoenix Light & Fuel Co. was derived in the following manner: the contract was made for 25 years and had 20 years to run. In the five years in which it had been in force, Phoenix Light & Fuel had paid about $6,000 per year to the Arizona Water Co., or 6 percent interest on $100,000, so it was estimated to be an asset worth $100,000. [76]

Heard and attorney Louis H. Chalmers presented statements on behalf of the minority interests in the Salt River Valley, Maricopa, and Grand canals. Heard spoke for the minority shareholders, and asked the Appraisal Commission to include the right of landowners to have water carried in the canals as part of the appraisement, but he objected to including the right to use water in establishing the value of the canals. Chalmers, appearing for water rights owners, argued the water rights represented easements in the canals with "a larger and more tangible interest in those canals" than those held by the shareholders. As such, he contended, the water rights should be appraised and their value paid to the owners of water rights and not to the companies claiming ownership of the canals. [77]

Lincoln Fowler read a brief giving the history and a description of the Appropriators' Canal. He said its ditch and intake head were superior to others. His comments were viewed as an invitation for the government to buy the canal any time it was needed. [78]

Following lunch, Kibbey spoke and said the Arizona Water Company's holdings should be worth no more than it would cost to construct a replacement system. He said the contract with the Phoenix Light & Fuel Co. had no value because the Arizona Water Co. was without a dam to deliver water to operate the hydroelectric plants. Kibbey said it would cost several hundred thousand dollars to build a new dam to collect $100,000 from Phoenix Light & Fuel across the next 20 years. He termed the contract a liability. [79]

Kibbey said the commission should not consider the value of either shares or water rights. He said the manner in which distribution of the proceeds of the sale of the water company's holdings was of no concern to either the government or the Water Users' Association. Therefore, the minority interests had no standing before the commission, he said. [80]

Ainsworth summed up the water company's position, saying Kibbey was wrong about the Phoenix Light & Fuel Co. contract because whoever bought the water company would have to fulfill the agreement. [81]

Several days later, Benjamin Fowler was asked by the Interior Department to come to Washington to aid in negotiations with the Arizona Water Co., should the interior secretary approve the work of the Appraisal Commission and agree to buy the company. The sooner this happens, the *Republican* said, "the sooner work will be started on the new diversion dam and the sooner can the government engineers determine what is feasible in respect of getting a temporary water supply for the valley next spring." [82]

The Interior Department on December 8 awarded a $43,750 contract to the General Electric Co. of Schenectady, New York, for electrical equipment to be used in the Roosevelt Dam powerhouse. [83] In this connection, Hill said the idea of a temporary electric plant had been abandoned. Instead, the water wheel, generator, and auxiliary machinery installed for use with the power canal and its penstock were to be the initial unit of the permanent power plant. He said it was thought the power generated from this first unit would be sufficient for the dam construction. When it was determined more power would be needed, the government decided to ask for bids on three additional water wheels and generators and options on two others. One unit was to be supplied within a year and the other two within two years. It was on these units the Interior Department had let the contract, Hill said. Once the dam was finished, the power would become available for pumping water in the Valley. [84]

It also was learned December 8 the Appraisal Commission had completed its report and set a price on the Arizona Water Co. holdings, but the report's contents were not revealed. [85]

The estimated cost of repairing the Appropriators' Canal was put at $3,600, the construction to include 3,000 feet of new ditch along the river. [86] The price of doing the minimal amount of work to get water in the Arizona Canal was estimated at $1,850 by H. F. Robinson. Hall had no objection to the Arizona Canal Protective Association's undertaking this work, but he advised against a second plan of extending the head of the Arizona Canal 4,000 feet upstream, at a cost of $10,000 to $15,000, until the government took some action in respect to buying the water company. [87]

The Protective Association met December 21 and voted to ask the farmers under the Arizona Canal to contribute 20 cents per acre toward canal repair. The work was to begin only after $2,000 had been collected, and any water would be divided among those who had contributed. The members also agreed that, if the government showed no inclination within a reasonable time of extending the canal, the association would do it. [88]

The Water Users' Association received a letter from Benjamin Fowler December 22 in which he said a favorable recommendation on the Appraisal Commission's work would be sent to Secretary Hitchcock. Fowler said details on the valuation of the water company would be made public by Hitchcock's office. [89]

On December 28, Parker received the following telegram from Fowler:

Appraisal of entire canal property is $304,161. Minority interest totals about $36,000. Have written full details. [90]

The *Republican's* Washington correspondent, Charles C. Randolph, provided a breakdown of the Appraisal Commissions' valuations: Arizona Canal, $191,086; power canal (for the Evergreen generating station on the Salt River Indian Reservation), $2,553; laterals and sublaterals, $25,029; Arizona Crosscut, $15,730; Maricopa and Salt River Valley canals Joint Head, $12,612; Maricopa Canal, $19,960; Salt River Valley Canal, $10,203; Grand Canal, $20,488; zanjero stations (houses), $1,000; telephone line, $500, and dredge and tools, $5,000. After the minority interest was deducted, $268,161 was left for the Arizona Water Co. [91]

The Appraisal Commission's estimates of the value of the canals were based upon the cost of constructing them by the excavation of various materials. The commission said the Arizona Water Co. and the Reclamation Service engineers were in close agreement about the quantity of materials but not upon their classification. The materials were rock, cemented gravel, cemented earth, and earth. The classification was referred back to the engineers, who came to an understanding and joined in a report to the commission. [92]

The commission concluded the contract between the Arizona Water Co. and the Phoenix Light & Fuel Co. was a liability because "it precludes the development of power by the United States or the Salt River Valley Water Users' Association. . . For this reason the Commission has appraised the value of the power canal and contract at the cost to construct the canal." [93]

Because the doctrine of prior appropriation of water applied in Arizona, and water would be delivered only to lands with rights by appropriation, the commission ruled there were no water rights to be purchased. The commission also said the Arizona Water Co. made no mention of rights-of-way, and the commission fixed no value on them because "little, if anything, would have to be paid for right-of-way

privileges" if the canals had to be constructed at the present time. Such construction would be over public lands and lands belonging to members of the Water Users' Association. [94]

Word came from Roosevelt that O'Rourke would not resume work in the riverbed until the cable and trams had been erected across the canyon. Once this was done, it was expected that, should another flood occur, whatever machinery was in the riverbed could be quickly removed. O'Rourke planned two cables over the river, each about 100 feet above the top of the dam, when completed. Two cable towers, each about 50-feet high, were to be built on each side of the river. The cables, three inches in diameter, would each be about 1,000-feet long. One cable was to be located just over the upstream face of the dam and the other, a little farther downstream, so any part of the dam could be reached during construction. [95]

O'Rourke's men also built a 16-room house for occupation by his chief aides and their families, blasted away canyon walls to form spillways, and prepared for the dam building. The spillways were to be 20 feet lower than the road on top of the dam and were to be 200-feet wide. The rock exploded from the mountainsides was hard red sandstone. It was to be used in the construction of the dam. This rubble was to be set in cement within the dam, while the exterior was to be huge blocks weighing up to 10 tons, laid with overlapping joints. [96]

Efforts to attend to both the spiritual and physical needs of the people at Roosevelt continued. Reverend Moffatt apparently got the people to abandon the idea of a tent church and began getting pledges of money and materials for construction of a building. The Reverend J. C. Mergeler was to take charge of the church. Arrangements were made for two dentists to visit the camp. [97]

The Arizona Canal Protective Association held its annual meeting January 6. Besides electing officers, members agreed to begin the minimum work to repair the Arizona Canal. [98]

Fowler, on January 13, wired Parker that the,

Secretary has formally offered to purchase. Now waiting Water Company's answer. [99]

Fowler also had written there was opposition to the government purchase of the Arizona Water Co. and construction of the diversion dam, all of which would cost about $700,000. Fowler said some groups believed Arizona was getting too large a part of the money available to the Reclamation Service. He thought if the government bought the water company and built the diversion dam that would be about the last large expenditure the Salt River project could expect. Including the $700,000, the total allotment to the project would be approximately $4,500,000. [100]

The Grand Canal Co. directors on January 15 offered to let the Appropriator's Canal Co. use the Grand Canal without charge provided it be returned to the owners in good condition upon the completion of negotiations between the Arizona Water Co. and the government. The Appropriators' the next day rejected the offer, principally because some Grand Canal water users were not Appropriators'

U.S. Reclamation Service headquarters camp at Roosevelt, January 26, 1906.

subscribers, but if there was water in the canal they would expect delivery under their Grand Canal water rights. [101]

Frederick H. Newell, chief engineer of the Reclamation Service, passed through Phoenix January 17 on his way to Roosevelt. Hill met him in Mesa. [102]

The *Gazette* reported January 22 the Arizona Water Co. would accept the Appraisal Commission's price of $304,161 for its property provided the government would take care of the minority stockholders. The *Gazette* thought this was a complication that would not block the negotiations for any length of time. [103]

Newell returned to Phoenix the next day and reported the water in the river at Roosevelt was coming in at too great a volume to permit O'Rourke to excavate for the foundation of the dam. About the proposed diversion dam for the Valley, he said the borings were disappointing because the depth to bedrock was greater than expected. He said it was impossible at the moment to say where the dam would be located. What would be done with the head of the Arizona Canal would depend upon the negotiations with the water company. Meantime, good progress was being made on repairing and cleaning the canal below the old head. [104]

The *Gazette* on the afternoon of January 24, reported that, "unless the water company accepts the Interior Secretary's offer within a reasonable length of time, the government will take steps to put in a parallel system that will render the Arizona Water Company's system absolutely valueless." The *Gazette* called its report "semi-official," because neither Newell nor Hill were the sort of men who would give out such information. The newspaper said the delaying tactics of the Arizona Water Co. had made the Granite Ripples the "ideal spot" at which to build the cement diversion dam, though Newell was said to have expressed the opinion bedrock there was very deep. In paralleling the Arizona Canal, a little land above Scottsdale would have to be omitted. The *Gazette* said the Appropriators' Canal could be purchased for $40,000 and with some enlargement could replace both the Grand and Maricopa canals and even furnish water to some lands under the Salt River Valley Canal. In any event, the newspaper said the Granite Ripples

site was a strong candidate for the diversion dam. Granite Ripples, also known as Granite Reef, was about three miles downstream from where the government engineers had been boring. [105]

A telegram from Fowler to Kibbey January 25 said the negotiations with the water company were going well. This set off a rumor that agreement had been reached. Hall immediately wired Steele, who replied there had been no agreement. [106]

The Arizona Canal Protective Association met January 26. It was disclosed more sand was in the canal than expected, and the cost of cleaning was higher than anticipated. The canal head was then two-feet higher than the water level in the river, which meant a rise in the river of that or more would put water in the canal without diversion works. A committee visited Hill, who assured its members the government was prepared to act at once to get water into the canal, as soon as word came from Washington the negotiations had been successfully concluded. He did not outline what work was planned, but he estimated it would take 40 to 60 days to carry through. [107]

On January 27, Hall received the following telegram from W. W. Miller, general counsel for the Arizona Water Co. and the bondholders:

If you have any copies of the first deed to the New York Surety and Trust company, send them to me immediately. We need them in our foreclosure proceeding. [108]

Tuesday afternoon, January 30, Steele sent a telegram saying the first bondholders intended to foreclose. This was interpreted to mean the government's offer would soon be accepted and was a step in clearing title to the property so it could be turned over to the government. [109]

News came from Roosevelt the health record of the camp had been broken with the death of a laborer for O'Rourke in late January: Mike Mojeskowitz had died from acute pneumonia after an illness of four days. A bucket brigade saved the store of E. F. Kellner & Co. from destruction when fire broke out, apparently from a candle left burning. On a more positive note, the camp was entertained by the Roosevelt Peerless Orchestra and the Mormon Trio, and Spud Shepherd had opened a dancing school. [110]

In early February, repairs were completed to the Appropriators' Canal. Water enough for all users was in it. The canal was said to be in condition for anything less than a rise of 15 feet in the river. There was no water in the Grand Canal, but farmers could get it through the Appropriators' if they bought stock. Both the Maricopa and Salt River Valley canals were getting water through the Joint Head. The Arizona Canal repairs were completed, and the farmers hoped for the river to rise to put in water. [111]

There were further reports on the river borings at Granite Reef, with the *Gazette* saying the dam might be built there even if there was a fissure. "...if the site is selected the cement work may be carried only a portion of the way into the fissure—far enough to make the dam stable, but not to prevent some underflow," the newspaper said. [112] Engineer Wisner said the Granite Reef site seemed the best yet found. [113]

Almost nothing was heard about the negotiations for the sale of the Arizona Water Co., but on February 5 the governors reviewed letters from Fowler concerning the negotiations. The governors did not think the public should be informed about what Fowler wrote. The governors also discussed the latest rumors, including one the water company had announced its refusal of the government offer and another it had decided to rebuild the Arizona Dam. [114]

The morning of February 9, the *Republican* printed a pessimistic account of the negotiations,

> The Republican *is prepared to state definitely that there is no possibility within a reasonable time, if ever, of an agreement between the government and the Arizona Water company... That matters have reached a point beyond which they can go no further has been known in Phoenix for several days, though there has been a lingering hope against hope.* [115]

The *Republican* regarded the Arizona Water Company's position "as blackmail," and said the farmers under the Arizona Canal were faced with two choices because of the immediate need for water. These were to assess themselves to raise $36,000 to buy the minority interests, or to raise and spend $20,000 for the temporary extension of the head of the Arizona Canal. Buying the minority holdings offered the best choice, according to the *Republican*, because it meant the government could immediately take over. Other alternatives were too much to expect, such as the minority stockholders sacrificing their interests "for a nominal sum. . .for the good of the cause," or too time consuming, such as building a parallel canal, condemning the Arizona Water Co. property, or asking Congress to allow Phoenix taxpayers to help through the issuance of bonds. [116]

Later that day, Hall sent a telegram to Steele pointing out the extreme need of the farmers for water. Hall asked that permission be granted to them to extend the canal to a new head. [117]

The next day, the *Gazette* printed a telegram it had sent to Secretary Hitchcock asking if it was true negotiations had been broken off:

> *Being represented here that negotiations between government and the Arizona Water company are broken off. Farmers being urged to raise thirty-six thousand dollars to purchase minority interests—the three hundred and four thousand to go to Arizona Water company. Meeting to be held this afternoon. Please wire us immediately our expense whether or not negotiations broken off.* [118]

The reply was sent by W. Scott Smith, Hitchcock's private secretary:

> *Telegram received. Negotiations not broken off, but still going on. The government desires to protect all interests. The offer to the Arizona Water company for canals was three hundred and four thousand dollars to include the thirty-six thousand dollars minority interests. This offer has not yet been accepted.* [119]

In addition, the *Gazette* printed a reply from Fowler to a telegram sent to him:

> *Replying to your telegram, negotiations have not been broken off, but are still continuing with prospect of settlement.* [120]

The *Gazette* also printed statements from Kibbey, Hall, and Parker that they knew nothing about the *Republican's* report that the negotiations had broken down. The *Gazette*

accused the *Republican* of taking part in a scheme "to literally blackmail the citizens of the valley, particularly those farmers on land lying under the Arizona Canal" into paying $36,000 to the Arizona Water Co. The *Gazette* charged the water company with deliberately letting the negotiations drag along "until such time as it thought the valley would be forced to accept a counter offer." The *Gazette* demanded the *Republican* name the persons who said there was "no possibility within a reasonable time, if ever, of an agreement." [121]

The *Gazette* offered its own solution for meeting the needs of the Arizona Canal water users. This was for the Arizona Canal Protective Association to show Judge Kent "that an intolerable condition exists, that neither the water company nor its receiver is making a reasonable effort to furnish water and ask for the appointment of a receiver in their interest." [122]

The newspaper also printed a telegram from Fowler in answer to a wire from Kibbey asking if work by the farmers on the Arizona Canal would in any way interfere with the negotiations. Fowler said:

> *Ranchers work on canal, providing company consents, need not interfere with pending negotiations.* [123]

The executive committee of the Arizona Canal Protective Association met the afternoon of February 10 and passed resolutions to not approve the *Republican's* proposal to buy the minority interests and to investigate the possibility of asking Kent to appoint a receiver to act independently of Steele or to force Steele to sell a certificate to get funds to build the extension. [124]

The *Republican* on Sunday morning, February 11, reported Steele had replied favorably to Hall's telegram asking the farmers be allowed to extend the Arizona Canal. Steele said the bondholders committee overseeing the receivership had no objection, but permission had to be granted by the court, which was in charge of the water company's property. [125]

The *Republican* defended its proposal that the Arizona Canal water users raise $36,000 to buy the minority interests by saying the idea had been revived by members of the Arizona Canal Protective Association, but none of them attended the executive committee meeting. The proposal, however, had led to a flurry of telegrams to Washington, D.C., seeking advice toward raising the money. Randolph sent a dispatch advising,

> *the people of the valley possess their souls in patience a while longer, with the comforting assurance that their interests are being properly safeguarded.*
>
> *There are many things I cannot speak of at this time without breaking faith, but when the history of this negotiation is written up I am confident that not only the water users' association but the community as a whole will be impressed and satisfied with the wise, conservative policy persistently and deligently followed by President B. A. Fowler in this whole matter. It would seem as if the negotiations ought to be brought to a close before the month ends.* [126]

In an article February 13, the *Republican* examined the plight of the Arizona Canal farmers, ranchers, and orchardists. "Should it prove a dry season it is not unlikely

Dam contractor John M. O'Rourke & Co.'s camp (center),
February 21, 1906.

that most of their trees would perish, while lack of water
would eliminate them from consideration in the matter of
pasture and stock raising," the newspaper said, adding, the
failure to get water would mean the inability to grow a good
sugar beet crop for the initial season of the new sugar beet
factory. However, the article said the sugar beet seed could
be sown as late as the latter part of March—something that
would not be done at all unless the farmers could be assured
at least a partial water supply. [127]

The Arizona Canal Protective Association convened
February 14 to hear from its attorneys about seeking
appointment of a local receiver or compelling Steele to issue
a receiver's certificate. Attorneys Julius M. Jamison and
Walter Bennett advised against either action because they
would involve litigation, which meant delay. Further,
should Steele be compelled to issue a receiver's certificate, no
one would want to buy it, which meant the Arizona Canal
farmers would have to put up the money. While they would
get their money back once the government bought the
Arizona Water Co., the company would, in the meantime,
own the canal extension, and the farmers would have to pay
the company for the delivery of water. But if the farmers
built the extension themselves, they would own it. Since they
had Steele's assurance they could use the canal, they would
not have to pay for the water. Winfield Scott, a member of
the executive committee and an orange grower, reported
Reclamation Service W. A. Farish estimated it would take
$16,000 to build the extension with a bottom width of 12
feet, capable of carrying 160 cubic feet of water per second.
The expense of paying zanjeros to tend the canal would cost
about $7,000 for the summer. Those costs were less than the
$25,000 farmers had paid the water company the previous
season to irrigate 17,000 acres at a price of $1.50 per inch of
water. [128]

Ralph Murphy, association secretary, said he had been in
telephone communication with Hill at Roosevelt and Hill

had asked construction of the extension not begin until he
had received a reply to a telegram sent to Hitchcock advising
him of the situation. The association voted to construct the
extension but adjourned until Saturday, February 17, to
give Hitchcock an opportunity to answer Hill. The members
also talked about how money would be raised. They
expected Phoenix merchants to contribute, as they had to
the earlier canal repair. [129]

On February 16, Cleon M. Etter and George L. Hewitt
posted a notice of appropriation of 50,000 miners' inches of
water from the Salt River on behalf of the Arizona Canal
Protective Association. They said the canal head would be
"about 3,700 to 4,000 feet above the present partially washed
out dam of the Arizona Water Company." [130]

The morning of February 17, the **Republican** printed a
dispatch from Randolph saying an all-day meeting February
16 between representatives of the water company,
government, and Fowler had ended without an agreement,

*But it may be said that the outlook is favorable and there is a
strong probability that a definite conclusion will be arrived at
tomorrow.* [131]

The newspaper also reported Hitchcock had withdrawn
from public entry sections 13, 14, 23, and 24 of township 2
north, range 6 east, which included the Granite Reef
Diversion Dam site. The area also took in the projected new
head for the Arizona Canal. [132]

Saturday afternoon the members of the Arizona Canal
Protective Association approved recommendations from its
executive committee that Indians on the Salt River
Reservation be offered water in exchange for labor in
building the canal extension, that Hall seek a court order
giving the farmers free use of the canal until the government
could furnish water, that a committee to solicit donations
among the Phoenix business houses be named, that there be
a solicitor for each lateral to take subscriptions for the
construction work, and that the assessment be $1.50 per acre
with previous subscriptions of 20 cents per acre to be
deducted from the $1.50. [133]

The membership had just approved a motion of Dr. John
V. Foss that the association incorporate when a dispatch to
the **Phoenix Enterprise,** reporting the successful conclusion
of negotiations, was brought to the meeting. [134] The story,
sent by Myron H. McCord, said:

*WASHINGTON, Feb. 17—Special—Receiver Steele and C. F.
Ainsworth, attorney for him, closed the contract with the
government today for the sale of the Arizona company's canals, W.
J. Murphy putting up the difference to make the deal go.*

*The government will take immediate possession of the Arizona
canal.*

*The government will proceed to construct a dam at the head of
the canal. Great credit is due to W. J. Murphy and Ainsworth for
this result.* [135]

After votes of thanks to Murphy and Fowler, the
Protective Association named the men to seek subscriptions
from farmers along the laterals and accepted subscriptions
for 3,361 acres from the members present. The executive
committee was instructed to be ready to turn the work over
to the government should the details of the settlement of the
negotiations be as reported. [136]

The *Gazette* that afternoon also contained reports that agreement with the Arizona Water Co. had been reached. It printed telegrams from Ainsworth and Fowler. Ainsworth wired Hall:

The government purchased canal today and takes immediate possession of the Arizona. [137]

Fowler's telegram was sent to Parker:

Agreement reached for sale of canal system subject to the approval of the secretary of the interior. Pending such approval, publication of details and terms denied. [138]

Sunday morning, the *Republican* provided further but incomplete information about the purchase, including an admonition from Fowler that Arizona Canal "farmers should energetically push plans for supplying irrigation water for the summer." This was because the government had decided not to take control of the Arizona Water Co. properties until title had been perfected. However, this was not immediately disclosed. [139]

Randolph reported there was a difference of $40,000 between what the water company demanded and the government would pay, and Murphy provided that "by contracting to take enough water rights [from the company] to meet the differences in the figures." Murphy arrived in Washington February 16 with the hope of effecting a settlement with Steele, and according to Randolph, they had labored "until far into this morning." [140]

Fowler, writing to the Board of Governors on February 19, said the government had been unaware of the Murphy-Steele deal "until agreement was reached with the Water Company." The Murphy-Steele agreement was a paper transaction in which Murphy agreed to provide 200 acres of land, valued at $200 per acre, in exchange for the water company's unissued water rights, which the Appraisal Commission had determined were valueless. [141]

The *Republican* on February 19 printed a telegram from Ainsworth in which he reported, "the government added $10,000 to the award for the Arizona canal." [142] That same day, Smith, Hitchcock's private secretary, wired the *Gazette* the $10,000 was "added to the engineers' estimate of the value of the canals for right-of-way." [143] This brought the total the government would pay for the water company's holdings to $314,161, including the minority's interest. Ainsworth said Hitchcock would sign his approval February 20, but he was wrong. The agreement was sent to the U.S. Department of Justice. The Interior Department was concerned about the effect of the acquisition upon the contract between the Arizona Water Co. and the Phoenix Light & Fuel Co. [144]

Hill sent word the morning of February 19 to the Arizona Canal Protective Association to proceed with its plans for building the canal extension. The association executive committee immediately began the mobilizing of a camp outfit and buying supplies, including 1,000 pounds of dynamite for rock work. McDermott was employed to hire men and teams and to take charge of the work. The men were to begin going to the work site the following morning. The work on the extension began the day after that. [145]

The night of February 19, Ranger Holmes killed an Indian, Matze, also known as "T. A. Twenty-five," at Cottonwood Canyon about two miles east of Roosevelt. Officers had been called to an Indian camp because some of the Apaches living there had gone on a drinking spree and some women were assaulted. As Holmes and a couple of other officers approached, Matze, who was standing beside a wagon, started raising a rifle to his shoulder and Holmes shot him. Dr. Palmer went to the scene the following morning and examined the body, which "was lying on the ground beside the wagon. There was no need to do more than determine the direction the five bullets had taken in passing through the body. They were to the fraction of an inch in the same location as the five holes in the Mexican bootlegger, so there was no question as to the author." [146]

At Roosevelt, the largest explosion to have occurred up to this point in construction of the dam took place the morning of February 22, to clear away rock. About 1,000 pounds of powder was set off simultaneously by an electric battery, and more than 2,000 cubic yards of rock shook free from the canyon wall and slid into the river. An observer said the mass was "the whole end of a mountain." The first of O'Rourke's steel cables over the river was put in place February 23, and the second one was expected to be finished the following week. O'Rourke's men were paid $2.50 per day and up. They lived in tents with cement floors, stoves, and spring beds. [147]

Construction of a jail in Roosevelt was completed. It was a ferro-concrete structure with walls, roof, and floor more than a foot thick. "The fact that the thing will be as hot as an oven during the summer months will, we believe, have such an effect upon the minds of would-be offenders of the law that they will think twice before committing a crime," the *Republican's* correspondent wrote. [148]

The Roosevelt office of the Mesa-Roosevelt Stage company was removed from the Roosevelt drugstore and placed in a building erected by Shattuck and Desmond. Business was so good the company added three extra express stages each week. [149]

The Reclamation Service employed a photographer, J. Morgan Miller, who succeeded Walter Lubkin. On the last day of February, the body of Jim Austin, also known as Coal Oil Jim, was found on a sandbar about a half-mile below the Roosevelt dam site. An autopsy conducted by Dr. Palmer showed Austin was beaten to death with a blunt instrument. [150]

1. *Arizona Republican* (Phoenix), September 7, 1905.
2. *Ibid.,* September 8, 1905.
3. *Ibid.*
4. *Ibid.,* September 14, 1905.
5. *Ibid.,* September 16 and 17, 1905.
6. *Ibid.,* September 17, 1905.
7. *Arizona Gazette* (Phoenix), September 20, 1905.
8. *Republican,* September 24 and 27, 1905.
9. *Ibid.,* September 26, 1905.
10. *Ibid.,* September 27, 1905.
11. *Ibid.,* September 28, 1905.
12. *Ibid.,* September 24, 1905.
13. *Ibid.,* September 28 and 29, November 7, 1905; *Gazette,* September 28 and October 30, 1905.
14. *Republican,* September 24, 28 and 28, October 21 and 24, 1905;

Gazette, September 29 and December 5, 1905, January 30, 1906.

15. *Gazette,* October 2, 1905; *Republican,* October 3, 1905.
16. *Ibid.*
17. *Republican,* October 4, 1905.
18. *Ibid.,* October 5, 1905.
19. *Ibid.,* October 6, 1905.
20. *Ibid.,* October 7 and 10, 1905.
21. *Ibid.*
22. *Ibid.*
23. *Ibid.,* October 12, 1905.
24. *Ibid.,* October 17, 1905.
25. *Ibid.,* October 14, 1905.
26. Richard E. Sloan, Land and Water Rights, Salt River Project, cities order of Commissioner W.A. Richards, General Land Office, U.S. Department of the Interior, July 21, 1905, Salt River Project Archives (hereafter SRPA).
27. *Republican,* October 13, 1905.
28. *Ibid.*
29. Ralph E. Palmer, ***Doctor on Horseback,*** (Mesa: Mesa Historical and Archaeological Society, 1979), pp. 117-118.
30. *Ibid.,* p. 112.
31. *Republican,* October 8, 1905.
32. *Ibid.,* October 11, 22 and 24, 1905.
33. *Ibid.,* October 12, 1905.
34. *Ibid.,* October 19, 1905.
35. *Ibid.,* October 14 and 27, November 5, 1905; *Gazette,* October 30, 1905.
36. *Republican,* October 27 and November 8, 1905.
37. *Ibid.,* October 27, November 4, 5, 12 and 27, 1905.
38. *Ibid.,* October 29, 1905.
39. *Ibid.,* November 2 and 5, 1905; *Gazette,* November 1, 1905; Palmer, *op. cit.,* pp. 112-113.
40. *Republican,* November 5, 1905.
41. *Ibid.*
42. *Ibid.,* November 7, 1905.
43. *Ibid.*
44. *Ibid.*
45. *Ibid.*
46. *Ibid.,* November 10, 1905; *Gazette,* November 10, 1905.
47. *Republican,* November 11, 1905.
48. Report of the Committee of Sixteen to the Salt River Valley Water Users' Association, November, 1905, SRPA; *Republican,* November 19, 1905.
49. *Republican,* November 22, 1905; *Gazette,* November 22, 1905.
50. *Republican,* November 22, 1905.
51. *Ibid.*
52. *Gazette,* November 23, 1905.
53. *Republican,* November 23, 1905.
54. *Ibid.,* November 14 and 18, 1905.
55. *Ibid.,* November 27, 1905.
56. *Ibid.*
57. *Salt River Project, Final History to 1916,* Vol. II, p. 216, unpublished manuscript, SRPA.
58. *Gazette,* November 27, 1905; *Republican,* November 28, 1905.
59. *Republican,* November 28, 1905.
60. *Ibid.,* November 28 and 29, 1905; *Gazette,* November 28, 1905.
61. U.S. Geological Survey, Phoenix, conversation with Earl Zarbin, December, 1979.
62. *Republican,* November 28, 1905; *Gazette,* November 28 and 29, 1905.
63. *Republican,* November 28, 1905.
64. *Ibid.,* December 3, 1905.
65. *Ibid.*
66. *Final History to 1916,* Vol. I, p. 134.
67. *Republican,* December 3, 1905.
68. *Ibid.,* December 3, 5, 13 and 16, 1905; *Final History to 1916,* Vol. I, p. 167.

69. *Republican,* November 28, 1905.
70. *Ibid.,* November 30, 1905.
71. *Ibid.,* December 2, 1905.
72. *Ibid.,* December 3, 1905.
73. *Ibid.,* December 4, 1905.
74. *Ibid.,* December 5, 1905.
75. *Ibid.*
76. *Ibid.*
77. *Ibid.; Final History to 1916,* Vol. II, pp. 232-236.
78. *Republican,* December 5, 1905.
79. *Ibid.*
80. *Ibid.*
81. *Ibid.*
82. *Ibid.,* December 7, 1905.
83. *Ibid.,* December 9, 1905.
84. *Ibid.,* December 19, 1905.
85. *Ibid.,* December 9, 1905.
86. *Ibid.,* December 13, 1905.
87. *Ibid.,* December 20, 1905; *Gazette,* December 22, 1905.
88. *Republican,* December 22, 1905; *Gazette,* December 22, 1905.
89. *Final History to 1916,* Vol. II, p. 216.
90. *Republican,* December 29, 1905.
91. *Ibid.; Final History to 1916,* Vol. II, p. 230.
92. *Final History to 1916,* Vol. II, pp. 225, 227 and 228.
93. *Ibid.,* p. 227.
94. *Ibid.,* pp. 229-230.
95. *Republican,* December 19, 1905, February 10, 1906.
96. *Gazette,* January 1 and 24, 1906; *Republican,* March 16, 1906.
97. *Republican,* January 3, 8 and 14, 1906.
98. *Ibid.,* January 7, 1906.
99. *Ibid.,* January 14, 1906.
100. *Ibid.*
101. *Ibid.,* January 16 and 17, 1906.
102. *Ibid.,* January 18, 1906.
103. *Gazette,* January 22, 1906.
104. *Republican,* January 24, 1906.
105. *Gazette,* January 24, 1906; *Republican,* January 25, 1906.
106. *Republican,* January 26, 1906.
107. *Ibid.,* January 27, 1906.
108. *Ibid.,* February 1, 1906.
109. *Gazette,* January 31, 1906.
110. *Republican,* January 20 and February 1, 1906.
111. *Gazette,* February 7, 1906.
112. *Ibid.,* February 3, 1906.
113. *Republican,* February 5, 1906.
114. *Ibid.,* February 6, 1906.
115. *Ibid.,* February 9, 1906.
116. *Ibid.*
117. *Ibid.,* February 11, 1906.
118. *Gazette,* February 10, 1906.
119. *Ibid.*
120. *Ibid.*
121. *Ibid.*
122. *Ibid.*
123. *Ibid.*
124. *Ibid.; Republican,* February 15, 1906.
125. *Republican,* February 11, 1906.
126. *Ibid.*
127. *Ibid.,* February 13, 1906.
128. *Gazette,* February 14, 1906; *Republican,* February 15, 1906.
129. *Ibid.*
130. *Gazette,* February 17, 1906.
131. *Republican,* February 17, 1906.
132. *Ibid.*
133. *Ibid.,* February 18, 1906.
134. *Ibid.*
135. *Phoenix Enterprise,* February 17, 1906.
136. *Republican,* February 18, 1906.
137. *Gazette,* February 17, 1906.

138. *Ibid.*

139. *Republican,* February 18, 1906; B.A. Fowler to Board of Governors, Salt River Valley Water Users' Association, February 19 and 28, 1906, SRPA.

140. *Republican,* February 18, 1906.

141. Fowler to Board of Governors, February 19, 1906.

142. *Republican,* February 19, 1906.

143. *Gazette,* February 20, 1906.

144. *Republican,* February 19, 1906; Fowler to Board of Governors, February 28, 1906.

145. *Republican,* February 20, 1906.

146. *Enterprise,* February 20, 1906; *Republican,* February 23, 1906; Palmer, *op. cit.,* pp. 113-114.

147. *Republican,* February 26 and 28, 1906; *Gazette,* February 14, 1906.

148. *Republican,* February 26, 1906.

149. *Ibid.,* February 14 and 28, 1906.

150. *Gazette,* February 28, 1906; *Republican,* March 25, 1904, April 23, 1904, March 4, 1906; Palmer, *op. cit.,* p. 114.

March - August 1906

The evening of March 1, 1906, the church at Roosevelt was dedicated, and a subscription was started to erase an $85 debt remaining on the building and a new organ. Those attending the dedication contributed $110. [1]

Soon after, three Indian policemen from San Carlos arrived to round up all the Indians to return them to the reservation; but those employed by the government resisted. The matter was settled by allowing the employed Indians and their dependents to stay, but the idle and those perceived as troublemakers were ordered to go. [2]

The executive committee of the Arizona Canal Protective Association met March 3 and decided that 10 acres would be the minimum acreage for which subscriptions for water delivery would be accepted. This was the same minimum imposed by the Arizona Water Co. [3]

One note of discouragement for the committee was the farmers were signing fewer acres to pay for construction of the canal extension than had been anticipated. In addition, some of the farmers thought they could deduct from the $1.50 per acre assessment for the extension all of what they earlier had contributed for canal repairs. For example, farmer A, who paid $20 at the rate of 20 cents per acre for 100 acres for repairs, signed up 20 acres for the extension at the rate of $1.50 per acre, or $30, and attempted to deduct the $20 from the $30. The committee said this was not what was intended by allowing a 20 cent per acre credit for the earlier contribution for repairs. The deduction was meant to be a straight credit of 20 cents off $1.50 per acre, so that farmer A signing up 20 acres for the extension owed $30, minus $4, for an obligation of $26. The association appealed to the farmers to sign up as much land as they could as quickly as possible, in order to avoid a shortage of funds. [4]

About 125 men and 35 teams were employed on the extension. There was some disappointment because some of the ground the extension was to go through was rock instead of loose gravel. This was offset, however, because it was found the canal would not have to be as deep as thought—five and one-half instead of eight and one-half feet. The farmers also planned to build a brush dam. [5]

On March 6, Judge Edward Kent approved an ancillary decree of foreclosure against the Arizona Water Co. The decree, sought by the New York Trust Co., New York City, had been entered there earlier by Judge George Holt. Special masters for carrying out the decree were named, Charles J. Hall in Phoenix and Payson Merrill in New York City. The following day, a "notice of foreclosure sale" was published in the *Arizona Republican.* [6]

In Washington, Secretary of the Interior Ethan Allan Hitchcock on March 7 approved the contract for purchasing the Arizona Water Co. Benjamin A. Fowler, president of the Salt River Valley Water Users' Association, sent telegrams to Frank H. Parker, association secretary, and Frank T. Alkire of the Arizona Canal Protective Association. Fowler also asked Alkire to wire back information concerning the "progress and prospects for successful (canal) extension." Alkire's reply said:

Just returned from Arizona head. Work one-third completed. Temporary relief only. Arizona ranchers in bad shape. Funds coming in slowly. Congratulations. [7]

Late the afternoon of March 8, J. E. Boone of Phoenix

Camp Roosevelt as seen from north side of Salt River, March 6, 1906.

was seriously injured in an accident on the road descending into Roosevelt. Boone, accompanied by his wife and their child, was hauling a load of supplies from Mesa for his brother-in-law, Roosevelt grocer William N. Curtis. When the wagon came to the top of the hill, Mrs. Boone told her husband she did not like the looks of the steep road. She and the child alighted from the wagon and were walking behind it when Boone urged the two horses pulling the wagon to move forward. As he started down, the heavily loaded wagon crowded upon the horses. The animals, unable to hold the load, and the brake on the wagon apparently giving away, tore down the hill. Boone tried unsuccessfully to turn the team into the bank of the road. Finally, he jumped. Some witnesses said he fell under the wheels of the wagon, while others thought he was trampled by the horses. Both of Boone's legs were badly crushed above the knees, and Dr. Ralph Palmer, the government's physician, contemplated amputating them. One of the horses escaped injury when the harness tore free, but the other was badly hurt, and the wagon was demolished. Sugar, rice, flour, and canned goods were scattered in every direction. [8]

Cleon M. Etter, directing the building of the Arizona Canal extension, reported March 9 that he and Dan McDermott, canal superintendent, expected to complete the extension by April 1 and to turn water into it that day. Etter said more than a thousand pounds of powder were being exploded each day to blast away rock. [9]

The *Republican,* on March 9, also published a letter from Charles C. Randolph, Washington correspondent, lauding Fowler in the negotiations leading to the agreement by the Interior Department to buy the Arizona Water Co. [10]

Rain began falling over the watersheds March 12 and by that night, the river began to rise at Roosevelt. The rain continued through the night, and between 9 and 10 a.m. Tuesday, March 13, the river reached its maximum height of 21.8 feet, which was about 15 feet more than the gauge normally recorded. [11]

A large head of water passed the Arizona Dam Tuesday morning, and about 400 cubic feet of water per second entered the Arizona Canal. The farmers were alerted to be ready to take water. The water ran four-feet deep over the ends of the portion of the Arizona Dam that remained, but it was impossible to know what had happened where the Arizona Canal extension was being excavated—the water was a solid sheet from one side of the river to the other. By Tuesday night, the water in the Arizona Canal had caused a break in the bank between the Arizona Falls (at today's 56th Street) and the Crosscut Canal (at 48th Street). [12]

Water was in the Arizona Canal for a rather short time because, very late Tuesday night or early Wednesday, March 14, the canal bank gave way near the head in the same spot as the previous November. The break was judged to be about 160 feet, or about half the size of the one repaired by the farmers. There were several other breaks, but it was impossible to determine the conditions because a surge of water from the Verde River made the depth of the Salt River a little deeper than the day before. The Protective Association executive committee met and decided at the earliest possible moment repairs would be made to the canal bank. [13]

J. E. Sturgeon of Tempe reported several freighters lost their wagons and loads when the water came up suddenly on the Roosevelt road. A telephone report from Roosevelt indicated it would take a week to fully repair the wagon road. The O'Rourke company benefited from the high river because it washed away from the foundation site some of the waste rock dumped there from the quarries. [14]

Etter telephoned from the Arizona head the afternoon of March 15, reporting the breaks in the canal did not appear to be as serious as first thought. A hole in the headgate had been patched so no more water was in the canal, about 900 feet of which had been filled with sand three-feet deep. Etter asked that additional men and supplies be sent, and they were started on their way. It was estimated the peak flow in

Sections of canal built to develop electricity with falling water, March 6, 1906.

the river March 14 had been 50,000 cubic feet per second. By March 15, it had dropped to 10,000 cubic feet per second. [15]

The head of the Appropriators' Canal was wrecked. The directors of the company blamed the problem on a dyke built by the county and the railroads to protect the Pacific & Eastern bridge. The Appropriators' directors said the dyke had thrown the current of the river to the north, which led to the damage to the canal head. The directors estimated repairs would cost $2,000. They talked about bringing suit against the county and the railroads. [16]

Boone, the teamster hurt March 8, died the night of March 15. His right leg had been amputated the night of March 14. Because the road to Phoenix was impassable, he was buried at Roosevelt. Other news from Roosevelt: preparations were started for the construction of the cement diversion dam at the head of the power canal; a newspaper, the *Roosevelt Tattler,* was published; the Roosevelt Tennis Club was preparing for an April tournament, and boxing contests, a favorite amusement, were resumed. [17]

President Fowler of the Water Users' Association arrived back in Phoenix Saturday morning, March 17. He declined to talk about the details of the negotiations for the purchase of the Arizona Water Co., but said there were many times when it seemed agreement had been accomplished. Saturday afternoon, Fowler attended a meeting at which members of the Arizona Canal Protective Association approved articles of incorporation for the Arizona Canal Water Users' Association. Fowler told the meeting that unless the federal government set some new precedent, work on the Granite Reef Diversion Dam could not be expected to begin until the summer of 1907. He said the water users had to help themselves because the government would not aid them until it had acquired title to the Arizona Water Co. property, which would take several months at the earliest. He said he would sign his own acreage into the new association and urged others to do the same, it having been brought out earlier that only about half the land for which water had been bought from the water company had been subscribed for building the extension. The association members adopted a resolution that land subscribed at $1.50 per acre for the extension would share in the distribution of water, while land for which 20 cents per acre had been paid for canal repairs would get flood water. [18]

On March 22, the *Republican* began a campaign to reelect Fowler president of the Water Users' Association by publishing an editorial in his favor and a statement of endorsement from Arizona Governor Joseph H. Kibbey, association counsel. The editorial said, "in all probability" Fowler would be unopposed, but that afternoon the *Phoenix Enterprise* reported,

there are one or two men who are trying to array the farmers against Mr. Fowler, but we also remember that the leader in this contest is the selfsame individual who resorted to everything in sight to defeat the government proposition entirely. . .(it was) ill becoming (of) this man at this day, when everything he opposed is in perfect working order, to come in again, and seek to inject his spleen into this campaign. We give him fair warning to keep out. We know his motives, and his purposes, and neither will bear the scrutiny of the public.

That "selfsame individual" was Dwight B. Heard, who was supporting Dr. Ethelbert W. Wilbur of Mesa for president. Wilbur, the association vice president, ran on a Farmer's Ticket that included candidates for the Board of Governors in five of the ten association districts. Among Wilbur's supporters were C. T. Hirst and John P. Orme. [19]

In endorsing Fowler, Kibbey said Reclamation Service officials might view Fowler's defeat "as a slap at the service." Kibbey also made available for publication a letter he had received March 13 from Frederick H. Newell, chief engineer of the Reclamation Service, in which Newell praised Fowler, saying he had "never met a man of more persistent effort and tireless energy, combined with patience and tact." [20]

At Roosevelt on March 22, the Reclamation Service ran water through the entire length of the power canal and down the penstock through which electric power was developed. The operation of the power canal meant eliminating the $150 per day expense of supplying fuel to generate electricity for operating the cement mill. However, the Reclamation Service decided that three additional tunnels and 2,500 feet of new power canal had to be dug because of the March floods. As originally constructed, the line of the power canal, about two miles below the intake, was a half-mile from the river. The land in between had been covered by a heavy growth of cottonwood trees, which ranged in size from two to three feet in diameter, and a thick forest of mesquite trees. In the flood of November 1905, the Salt River had taken a sharp turn to the south and had washed away a large part of the land. The March floods washed away even more, so that the distance between the river and the canal had been reduced in places to from 20 to 25 feet. The Reclamation Service engineers considered this too close and ran a new line for the canal. Construction on what was known as the Wehrili cutoff, the name derived from the family that formerly owned the land, began in April and was completed in August. While this work progressed, the original line of the canal was used to generate electricity. [21]

The articles of incorporation of the Arizona Canal Water Users' Association were filed with the county recorder March 23. The directors until the first annual election were E. E. Jack, president; Etter, vice president; John W. Foss, secretary; Winfield Scott and F. A. Woolsey. [22]

The same day, the shareholders of the Grand, Maricopa, and Salt River Valley canals met separately and approved resolutions authorizing the sale of the companies at the price established by the government Appraisal Commission. [23]

High water again came down the Verde and Salt rivers on March 25, but the breaks in the Arizona Canal had been repaired, and men and teams at the site continued working on the extension. The next day, the water got into the canal, and the only fear was that it would rise too high and wash out the banks. That happened on March 27. There were three breaks, all in locations where the canal bank had been carried away before. [24]

At Roosevelt, George S. Steinmetz, a partner in John M. O'Rourke & Co., the dam contractor, was saved from drowning in the Salt River by a workman, Tom Carlton. Steinmetz was crossing the river on a horse when the animal lost its footing and Steinmetz was plunged into the river. [25]

The *Enterprise* on March 26 attacked Wilbur's candidacy for president of the Water Users' Association, charging that Wilbur had been,

violently opposed to the entire reservoir plan as represented by the Water Users' Association. He and Dwight B. Heard led a bitter, relentless warfare against the proposition. . .Mr. Wilbur is a good man, but elect him, and that arch enemy of the north side canal system, D. B. Heard, will control the policy of the association. [26]

The following morning, the *Republican* said,

In the campaign which is being directed against President Fowler an effort is being made to renew the animosity of the south side against the north side and to stir up the ancient quarrel which existed between the settlers under the old canals and those under the Arizona canal. [27]

The *Republican* said in all the discussion it had heard concerning the April 3 election, "we have heard no reason for trading horses while crossing the stream." [28]

There also was talk on the street of putting the Appropriators' Canal Co. into the hands of a receiver. The company had debts of about $35,000, and several suggestions had been made for avoiding receivership. These were to charge $3 per acre for delivery of water, which was considered unlikely, or to issue bonds. [29]

On March 30, the *Republican* said in a news article the effort to defeat Fowler was being made, "by means of reports so villainously false that there is positively no foundation of fact for them to rest upon." The newspaper charged Wilbur had tried "to trap the officials of the Reclamation Service into some statement that may be construed into a depreciation of the services of Mr. Fowler" by sending a message to Newell in which he asked, in substance, "Will the interests of the Water Users' Association be endangered or jeopardized by the defeat of Mr. Fowler?"

According to the newspaper, Newell did not reply, but George Y. Wisner, who had been a member of the Appraisal Commission, sent a wire that said, "The government has great confidence in the Water Users' Association and its president." [30]

In an editorial, the *Republican* said, "the campaign conducted by the friends of Dr. Wilbur is to be deprecated." The paper said the aim of Fowler's friends was "to solidify all the interests of the valley," while Wilbur's supporters "are doing their utmost to disintegrate the valley and create conflicting interests." [31]

The accusations against Fowler included the following: he received a $10,000 commission in the sale of the Arizona Water Company's property to the government; he approved the government's paying $1 million or $1,250,000 for the Arizona Water Co.; he had an interest in several sections of new lands and expected to profit through their sale; and he favored the interests of the owners of new lands over those who had prior rights to water. [32]

The *Gazette,* on March 30, printed a story reviewing Fowler's record in the effort to get water storage for the Valley, saying "it must be remembered that in the time covered from 1900 to the present practically his entire time has been given over to the cause of irrigation and his every

effort has been crowned with success." [33]

The *Republican,* the same day, published a statement from Fowler summarizing his activities on behalf of the Water Users' Association. Fowler explained the decision to award $10,000 additional to the Arizona Water Co. for the Arizona canal right-of-way was made at a conference attended by Charles D. Walcott, director of the U.S. Geological Survey; Arthur P. Davis, assistant chief engineer of the Reclamation Service, and Morris Bien, supervising engineer and legal counsel. Fowler said representatives of the water company, during the negotiations, had brought up that the right-of-way had not been considered. Fowler said he had assented to a schedule of properties to be bought from the water company, but he had agreed to no price. He said he had informed Hiram Steele, vice president of the water company, the people "would not, under any circumstances, give even half of the bonded indebtedness, which was roughly estimated at $900,000." [34]

The afternoon of March 31, Fowler and Kibbey spoke at a meeting at the Dorris theater. Fowler repeated the origins of the $10,000 additional that went to the Arizona Water Co. and that it was not a commission to him. He denied being involved in the speculation of land, saying he had no ground beyond the 40 acres which he had held for years. He argued on behalf of the adjudication of prior rights, which was a defense of the rights of the older landowners, and said he was running for reelection on his record of the past six years. [35]

Kibbey repudiated each of the charges made against Fowler. Kibbey said the pitting of new lands versus old lands was a false issue. He said he did not care what Fowler's views were on that matter because the protection of the prior rights was provided by the articles of the association and the lawsuit of *Hurley v. Abbott.* Kibbey said a repudiation of Fowler would be a repudiation of the Reclamation Service. [36]

Heard published a pamphlet April 2 addressed to members of the Water Users' Association. He charged that statements saying he opposed construction of Roosevelt Dam were being "circulated solely for the purpose of hurting Dr. Wilbur, who it is well known I am supporting for the office of president of the Water Users' Association." Heard said Fowler had "done much excellent work. . .in the promotion period of our reservoir project," but there were now local problems that needed solving, and "Dr. Wilbur's practical experience makes him the better man for the position of president of our association." Heard said Fowler's supporters were attempting "to change the conservative character of the Board of Governors,' and to dictate to the farmers of the valley. . ." [37]

Election day, April 3, the *Republican* said in an editorial that the defeat of Fowler would mean the "derangement" of future plans because the Reclamation Service would not "engage in any foolish discussion with those who wanted things done differently." To support this, the newspaper published a letter on the front page that Kibbey received April 2 from Newell. Newell wrote:

Your letter of March 20 has been received. I have also a number of telegrams from persons in the Salt River valley asking for my

Wilbur and the Farmer's Ticket were defeated. Fowler received 32,500 votes and Wilbur 20,041. Heard called upon all water users to support Fowler for the best interests of the Valley. Some of the farmers had gone to the polls in automobiles, reportedly making it the first election in Arizona in which that form of transportation was used. [39]

The Reclamation Service consolidated its office and engineering forces in its building at Roosevelt-on-the-hill. An Indian died from drinking wood alcohol. Dr. Palmer was called to the Indian camp near the power canal intake. There he found the Indian sitting on the ground against a log. The body was viewed by a coroner's jury before being taken to the hospital at Roosevelt, where Palmer performed an autopsy. The stomach contents revealed the presence of wood alcohol. Palmer said engineer Hill, informed that the Indian had been at a road house about four miles outside camp on the Globe road, was able to have the place closed down. [40]

The *Gazette* said April 6 that work on the Granite Reef Diversion Dam would begin soon. The newspaper said the government was going to build a new road from Desert Wells, eight miles east of Mesa, to the diversion dam site. The paper said supplies would be carried on this road and that cement for the dam would be hauled in from Roosevelt. [41]

Hill reported the electricity generated through the power canal at Roosevelt was being used intermittently. Hill said O'Rourke was ready to renew work in the river when the water was at low stage. Meantime, both of O'Rourke's large tramway cables were in place across the canyon and Reclamation Service engineers were preparing for the installation of a second unit for the power plant. O'Rourke also began construction of a cableway from the cement mill to the dam site. [42]

On April 7, all the property of the Arizona Water Co. was sold to Porter Steele, the son of the receiver, Hiram Steele. [43]

Hill was asked April 9 by the executive committee of the Arizona Canal Water Users' Association to take control of the canal's water distribution. He declined, saying, until the government had full title he did not want to inject it in local affairs to that extent. However, he was willing to attend meetings and give advice. The executive committee, which wanted water distribution under the direction of an impartial party, then conceived the idea of asking the court to take over water distribution. Judge Kent said he could not say what he would do until the matter should come before him. [44]

Hill, Fowler, H. J. McClung, and F. H. Ensign made a trip April 10 by Cadillac automobile to the Evergreen power plant on the Salt River Indian Reservation and to the head of the Arizona Canal. McClung and Ensign were stockholders in the Pacific Gas & Electric Co., which was to take over the property of the Phoenix Light & Fuel Co. in

mid-May. Ensign was the Pacific Gas & Electric manager. Although the newspapers failed to report it, the men discussed running a line from the power plant to Granite Reef to supply the government with electricity for construction of the diversion dam. The men working on the Arizona Canal were unable to say just when water would be turned into the canal, which was the source of water for operation of the Evergreen power plant. [45]

In Roosevelt, Mrs. Pearl Hunter, 21, of Glazier, Texas, was killed the evening of April 13 when a small revolver fell from a coat pocket as she started up the stairs of the hotel. The revolver discharged when it struck the step. The bullet entered Mrs. Hunter's nose and lodged in her brain. She died in four or five minutes. She and her 4-year-old daughter had just arrived by stage and were entering the hotel to rent a room, Mrs. Hunter carrying the coat on her arm. An aunt came from Rye, about 35 miles north of Roosevelt, to arrange for burial in the local cemetery. [46]

E. E. Bacon, the owner of the Roosevelt hot springs, for the third time put up a building for the accommodation of customers. The first building had been carried away by the floods in November 1905, and the second, in the March flood. [47]

Members of the Appropriators' Canal Co., at a stormy meeting April 14, amended the articles of incorporation to increase the allowable indebtedness from $25,000 to $33,000, the sum the company then owed. Much of the criticism at the meeting was directed at Lincoln Fowler, company president, but others spoke in his defense. A committee was named to study the books and report at another meeting. [48]

Heard and his wife, accompanied by her parents, the A. C. Bartletts, visited the Roosevelt dam site and on their return reported O'Rourke had begun construction of the cofferdam above the upper face of the dam. [49]

Wolf Sachs of Mesa sold his government freighting contract to Shattuck & Desmond. [50]

On April 26, the Arizona Canal Water User's Association met and adopted a resolution providing that the price of

U.S. Reclamation Service mess house at Roosevelt.

stock would be $1.50 and only holders of shares, when fully paid, would be eligible for water. Each share of stock represented one acre. It was decided McDermott would be in charge of distributing water, which was expected to be turned into the canal the following week. McDermott was instructed not to hire any zanjero who was a landowner. [51]

The same day in Washington, Davis, acting chief engineer of the Reclamation Service, addressed a letter to Hill advising him he had authority to construct the Granite Reef Diversion Dam. Davis said:

You will therefore please report to this office at once what part of the work it is desirable to construct at this time by force account, and the details of the estimated cost, in order that authority may be secured from the Department. [52]

Water began flowing in the Arizona Canal April 29, but it only came in a foot deep, which could do little more than wet the canal. A group of men who intended to take over management of the Arizona Canal Water Users' Association proposed the construction of a rock dam to raise the water level. [53]

The change in management was accomplished May 4 with the voluntary resignations of the officers. The new officers elected were Alkire, president; Benjamin Fowler, vice president; J. W. Dorris, secretary, and Alex Silva, treasurer. These men, along with W. M. Ward, were elected to serve as members of an executive committee to operate the association. [54]

The *Republican* explained the switch in management this way:

Certain gentlemen who were not interested in the directorate. . .have been advancing money and credit to the association, but their favors had been so large that they did not deem it wise business judgment to further finance it, at least, to the amount necessary, unless they were given complete control of its management. . .they thought that if they were expected to furnish the credit for the completion of the enterprise and the performance of any new work that may be necessary, they should have charge. [55]

The old board, before resigning, employed R. H. Collins to supervise the dam work. The new board promised a "square deal" to all the farmers and ranchers in the distribution of water. Water in the canal had reached lateral 15, north of Alhambra (Grand Avenue and Thomas Road) but none was as yet going to the farmers. By May 7, water was near the west end of the canal, and it was hoped all the farmers would at least get water for stock. [56]

Meantime, construction began on the rock dam with the dumping of rock into the Salt River at the water's edge. The rock was taken from quarries on the north side of the river. To convey the rock, a railroad was built from the quarries to the dam, continuing atop the dam as it was extended across the river. Timbers for the railroad came from river drift, and the rails were loaned by the Southern Pacific. The plan was to make the dam 20-feet wide at the base and at least seven-feet high. The rock was hauled in two mule-pulled cars that measured six-feet wide and 10-feet long. The middle and lower sides of the dam were first built up. The largest rock was deposited on the upper and lower sides to weigh down the lighter material in the middle. It was thought the dam

would withstand any ordinary flood. Although the dam was not completed until the last days of June, by the fourth week in May 5,000 inches of water were flowing in the Arizona Canal. Another 1,000 inches were added by chinking and puddling the dam, and on May 22 the Arizona Canal Water Users' Association authorized Collins to add one and one-half feet to the height of the dam in the hope it would add another couple of thousand inches to the run. By then, water had been distributed to farmers with cattle and hogs, and the orchardists were the next to irrigate. Water for all other farming purposes became available May 25. By month's end, the canal was carrying more than 9,000 inches of water and some farmers who had not joined the association were doing so. Others were paying to increase the number of acres for which they could get water. [57]

On the afternoon of May 17 at Roosevelt, W. J. Evans of Globe died in the large swimming pool at the Roosevelt hot springs. Evans had been in town three days seeking employment with the Reclamation Service as an accountant and bookkeeper. He went to the hot springs and rented a bathing suit. He made one headfirst dive into the water and did not come up. A post mortem by Dr. Palmer showed Evans had an enlarged heart. The doctor thought the shock of the dive into the water had caused the heart to stop. [58]

Hill reported the cofferdam had been completed on the upstream side of the Roosevelt dam site and that sheet piling was being driven into the river bed for the lower cofferdam, which was 250 feet downstream. To give the sheet piling a secure anchorage, rock was dumped behind the wooden structure so it could withstand the ordinary flow of the river or any small flood. The piling of the upper cofferdam was 13 feet above the ordinary water line except for 80 feet in the center, which was two feet above the water. When the time came to divert the water through the sluicing tunnel, the plan was to raise the 80 feet if necessary. The foundation of the dam, which was to be 165-feet wide at bedrock, was located between the two dams. The excavation of the material for the foundation was to be accomplished with hydraulic machinery. For rocks and boulders too large to be removed in this fashion, five large derricks were erected. Electricity for the operation of the derricks was furnished through the power canal penstock and power plant. Hill said it was hoped the hydraulic machinery could be started about the first of July. [59]

Hill said the sluicing tunnel was being lined with concrete, and grillwork was being erected at the intake to keep out driftwood, large rocks, and other debris that might clog the tunnel. He said the grillwork would have been put in sooner, but the upper end of the tunnel had been blocked off by blasting of rock from the mountainside. He said the tunnel gates would not be installed until the dam was well underway. [60]

Once the excavation was finished, a small triangular section of the big dam would be built up from bedrock across the channel. The base of this first section was to be 40-feet wide. The 30-foot-high face was to form the face of the big dam. The hypotenuse of the triangle would be from the normal water level to the lower side of the base. The lower face of the small dam was to be rough and uneven, against which the rest of the foundation would rise. Once the small triangular dam was in, there would be no need for the upper cofferdam. If floods came, the worst that could happen would be the filling of the hole between the lower side of the small dam and the downstream cofferdam. Hill said it would be the work of but a day or two to pump out the water and clear away any debris. [61]

On June 1, the Salt River Valley Water Users' Association opened its books for registration of all land within the reservoir district not signed into the association and for the re-signing of those acres for which their owners had failed to pay the earlier assessments. The landowners who had not paid the assessments had the option of paying them and not re-signing. Shareholders who failed to pay their assessments within 30 days faced a penalty of two cents per acre and an additional one cent per acre for every 30 days delay thereafter. [62]

Judge Kent, on June 1, signed an ancillary decree confirming the sale of the Arizona Water Co. A decree confirming the sale already had been signed in New York City by Judge Holt. [63]

Phoenix property owners who had not done so were urged to deed their water rights to the mayor in trust so that a single answer could be made for all residents in the suit of **Hurley v. Abbott.** The mayor already held in trust the water rights for the original city limits, Seventh Street to Seventh Avenue, between Van Buren and Harrison, and for all or parts of five additions to the city. The **Republican** said the city was,

vitally interested in the case, not alone because of its indirect interests in the welfare of the whole valley but because eventually it is possible power from the Roosevelt dam may be obtained to be used in connection with the municipal water works system. [64]

The Salt River Valley Canal and Maricopa Canal companies on June 6 asked the U.S. District Court to issue injunctions against the Appropriators' Canal Co., the Grand Canal Co., and the Arizona Canal Water Users' Association to stop them from appropriating any flow of the Salt River that interfered with the plaintiffs' diverting 10,000 inches of water. The suit was aimed particularly at the Appropriators' Canal Co., which, since a lower level in the river, had been taking most of the water that had come downstream. When Frank Trott, water commissioner under the Kibbey Decree, attempted to regulate the amount of water the Appropriators' Canal was taking, company officials turned him away, saying he had no authority over the canal. The aim of the injunction suit was to bring the Appropriators' Canal under the jurisdiction of the court and the commissioner. [65]

At a hearing June 8, Judge Kent indicated he would give the Appropriators' Canal the old water delivery schedule of the Grand Canal, which had no head in the river through which to get water. Kent took that action the following day. He also ordered that the Arizona Canal Water Users' Association receive the water formerly taken by the Arizona Water Co., and the water available for distribution to the four north side canals be diverted in equal shares of one-

Baggage belonging to Italian rockmen loaded for transportation to Roosevelt, June 12, 1906.

quarter each. It had been brought out at the hearing that about 10,500 acres of land were being irrigated from each of the canals. [66]

On June 13, the *Gazette* reported work on the Roosevelt Dam would begin in a few days—the work was the start of the excavation of the dam site to bedrock. That day, the Reclamation Service began the diversion of the river through the sluicing tunnel. The water, when at the height of the lowest level of the upper cofferdam, flowed through the tunnel at the rate of 1,300 cubic feet per second. [67]

The site of the excavation was 2,500 feet below the junction of the Salt River and Tonto Creek. In locating the site, the government drilled three lines of holes across the stream in search of bedrock. The Reclamation Service reported the first line of holes drilled was about 1,600 feet below a line of six holes drilled by the Hudson Reservoir & Canal Co., which showed the bedrock consisted of sandstone and broken quartz and varied in depth between 23 and 64.5 feet. The first line of nine holes made by the government found bedrock in the red sandstone at depths of between 20 and 38 feet. The second line, 100 feet below the first, also contained nine holes, and the sandstone bedrock was from 21 to 24.6-feet deep. The third line, 100 feet below the middle line, had seven holes, and the bedrock, black slate, ranged in depth from 21.9 to 31 feet. The Reclamation Service said,

The final location of the dam was made so that the upper [first] and middle [second] lines came practically in the foundation. The bedrock is described as being a hard, tough, fine-grained sandstone, in well defined strata, dipping upstream at an angle of 29 degrees from the horizontal, approximately at right angles to the dam. The canyon, at the level of the river, was but little more than 200 feet wide. [68]

The plan was to excavate the foundation site using two hydraulic pumps; it was thought the work would be started in a few days. [69]

O'Rourke found it difficult to get all the labor he wanted for the job. The spring and summer heat was one reason; other reasons were the remoteness of the site, the difficulty of the work, and the long hours. As a result, O'Rourke worked the men day and night to accomplish as much as he could while the water in the river was low. On June 12 and 13, 80 Italians, who were expert rockmen, arrived from Pittsburgh, Pennsylvania, by special train. Already on hand were several hundred Italian laborers. Late in June, O'Rourke's partner, Steinmetz, left for Galveston, Texas, where he expected to employ 120 Negro laborers for work at the dam. They, along with the Italians and Mexicans, did the heavier labor. [70]

The afternoon of June 13, a meeting of attorneys opposed to **Hurley v. Abbott** was held in the office of attorney E. J. Bennitt. They discussed seeking an injunction to stop the Salt River Valley Water Users' Association from spending money on the suit and to seek recovery of the funds already expended. It was pointed out the suit was started at the insistence of the Interior Department, not the association. The next day, some of the ranchers who favored the suit said an injunction proceeding would only delay the inevitable and raise the costs. The governors decided to invite Reclamation Service officials from Washington to discuss the situation. [71]

By June 21, the road from Desert Wells to Granite Reef was almost completed. Another indication the diversion dam would soon be under construction came the next day when it was disclosed the Interior Department and the Pacific Gas & Electric Co. had concluded a contract by which the government would use power from the Evergreen station for that purpose. The government agreed to pay three and one-half cents per kilowatt hour for electricity. The *Gazette* recalled the power station had been abandoned because the Interior Department had refused to include the contract between the Arizona Water Co. and the Phoenix Light & Fuel Co. in the deal for the water company's property. A telephone wire which tapped the Roosevelt-Phoenix line was extended to the south side of the river a few days later. [72]

At the end of June, a rumor circulated that John Orme was going to oppose Lincoln Fowler for the presidency of the Appropriators' Canal Co., and for that reason Orme was considering not seeking reelection to the Maricopa County Board of Supervisors. [73]

The morning of June 30, Benjamin F. Lofgreen took the place of Joe Phelps as the stage driver, carrying the mail between Mesa and Roosevelt. Phelps took charge of Government Well for Shattuck & Desmond. [74]

On July 2, the *Republican* reported plans for the Granite Reef Diversion Dam had arrived in Phoenix. They were drawn by A. L. Harris, an assistant engineer in the Reclamation Service office at Roosevelt. The newspaper said all that was lacking was an official announcement the dam would be built, but this would come "contingent only upon the Arizona Water Co. transferring a good title" to the government. A description of the dam was furnished, including the following:

The upper face of the dam will be almost perpendicular, though there will be a batter or slant of one foot in ten. As the dam will rise but fifteen feet above the natural mud channel of the river this slant will scarcely be noticed.

At the bottom of the excavation the base will be 31-1/2 feet wide. At the top the dam will be 7-1/2 feet wide, rounded with what the engineers call an "O Gee" curve on the down stream face, merging into a slope of 4 on 7 and that in turn into the apron, which is further lengthened by over twenty feet of solid concrete slabs, laid on a foundation of rock filling several feet in thickness. . . .

Taking the upper face of the dam, the solid masonry will be 26

Looking upstream at site of Roosevelt Dam on the Salt River, April 16, 1906.

feet high, 15 feet of which will be above the natural riverbed and eleven feet below. This masonry structure, 31-1/2 feet wide at the bottom, will rest on a steel reinforced foundation. The steel plate will rest on piling, driven if possible, to bedrock. [75]

The main dam was to be 1,100-feet long, with the Arizona Canal heading into the river at the north end. The Arizona Canal headgates were designed to permit a flow of 2,000 cubic feet per second and the headgates for the South Canal at the south end 1,500 cubic feet per second. The dam was designed for a flood flow of 165,000 cubic feet per second, which was expected to rise about 12 feet over the crest. [76]

The hydraulic pumps began removing water from between the cofferdams at the Roosevelt dam site on July 6. Hill said the removal of the material between the dams had not begun because the upper cofferdam leaked. He said it would not start until the dam had been tightened up by silt. There was not much of that because the water was too clear. [77]

A deed from Porter Steele, conveying the property of the Arizona Water Co. to the U.S. government, was filed in the Maricopa county recorder's office July 9. [78]

Hill reported July 13 that the lower cofferdam had been made stronger and hardly leaked at all, while large quantities of brush were piled against the upstream side of the upper cofferdam to try to stem the leaks there. Water and debris were being removed from the excavation site, and enough water was out so that the men could wade in the middle of the stream. Hill said the points of many big rocks were sticking up through the water. Large arc lights were placed over the space between the cofferdams so the men could work night and day. [79]

A spate of accidents occurred, one of the more serious involving a black laborer named Thomas Reed on July 17. Reed and several other workers were filling skips with dirt and stone at the north side of the dam site when, about 150 feet above, where another gang was stripping rock and preparing a foundation for a derrick, a rock weighing about 12 pounds fell down the mountainside. Warning calls came from above and below, and Reed's companions started to get out of the way. Reed evidently thought the alert concerned an empty skip being lowered near him and remained immobile. Some of the men who were with Reed turned back to try and push him aside, but it was too late. The falling stone hit a projecting rock, bounded into the air, and came down on Reed's head. Fellow workers rushed to him. Blood oozed from his mouth and ears, and his skull was fractured in two places, one fracture extending from the back of the head to the bridge of his nose. The laborers thought he was dead, but he suddenly opened his eyes and groaned. He was taken to the hospital, and surgery was performed that night. He was given little chance to survive, but a week later he was doing well, and the doctors expected him to fully recover. [80]

Deeds transferring to the federal government the Grand Canal Co., the Salt River Valley Canal Co., the Maricopa Canal Co., and the Water Power Canal Co. were recorded July 18. The **Republican** said this meant the Interior Department soon would announce officially the location of

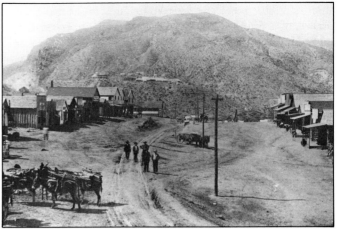

Roosevelt street scene 1906. Camp O'Rourke in background.

the proposed diversion dam. The same day, government crews were reported to have completed borings at Granite Reef. [81]

To assist in pumping out the water from between the cofferdams at Roosevelt, O'Rourke, the afternoon of July 19, telephoned to Phoenix to rent the centrifugal pumps ordered by the Arizona Orange Growers' Association after the Arizona Dam had gone out in 1905. [82]

Heavy rains in the mountains upstream from Roosevelt produced a runoff that washed large quantities of dirt and rubbish into the Salt River. The heavy sediment helped stop the leaks in the upper cofferdam, which allowed all the water to be pumped out from between the cofferdams. [83]

Secretary Hitchcock on July 24 authorized the construction of the Granite Reef Diversion Dam "by force account," which meant the Reclamation Service would do the work without putting it out to bid by private contractors. [84]

The contract between the Salt River Valley Water Users' Association and the Department of the Interior for construction of Roosevelt Dam was filed in the county recorder's office July 25. The **Republican** said the contract was "an imposing typewritten document, bound in leather, the title in gold letters." [85]

The afternoon of July 25, stage driver Lofgreen was waiting for a team of horses to be changed at Tortilla Flat when he suddenly collapsed. He was carried into the stage station, where he died about an hour later. The cause of death was sunstroke. [86]

Davis arrived in Roosevelt July 26. He spent the next couple of days conferring with Hill and inspecting the construction. While Davis was there, more hard rain fell. The river rose. While it did not pass over the upper cofferdam, the flood percolated through, and the pumps, including those brought in from the Valley, were kept busy. [87]

Davis, Hill, Bien, and W. H. Sanders of the Reclamation Service met July 31 with the governors and attorneys and others opposed to **Hurley v. Abbott.** Kibbey presented the Water Users' Association view of the suit, while attorneys W. H. Stillwell, Julius M. Jamison, Charles C. Woolf, Ralph Murphy, C. S. Steward, and Charles Peterson argued against it. But none of the opponents of the suit offered a plan as to how water rights could otherwise be settled. Some thought adoption of the Committee of Sixteen's report would be sufficient, but, it was pointed out, it dealt with placing 60,000 miners' inches of water and there were times when there was much more than that. In addition, a million inches or more had been appropriated, so the court would still have to be involved. Davis and Bien, in the absence of some other solution, said they favored the court suit. [88]

Hill was asked how long it would take to build the diversion dam. He said it would take a year if there were not too many floods. A load of lumber was at Mesa ready for hauling, to begin the preliminary work. He said the freighting might begin that day. [89]

Concerning the diversion dam construction, Hill said two-thirds of the dam would be on solid rock and the rest on a foundation of sheet piling to a great depth. [90]

The night of July 31 brought some bad news to the farmers under the Arizona Canal. Rains over the watershed of the Verde River brought a six-foot rise during the night, causing an estimated $4,000 damage to the Arizona Canal, headgates, and dam. Water ran over the dam, but the railroad track on top remained in place. However, the dam settled a foot or two in the river. Other rains north of the Valley caused flooding along Cave Creek, which washed through the banks of the Arizona Canal in four or five places. About 60 feet of canal were washed away at Evergreen. [91]

Davis, Bien, and Hill met privately the morning of August 1 with opponents of *Hurley v. Abbott.* These were men who had asked for a closed meeting and had not attended the meeting the day before. Davis said later nothing came out of the conference that could not have been stated publicly. In the afternoon, the engineers, Fowler, and Kibbey discussed the means by which owners of land in excess of 160 acres could dispose of their land before stored water became available for delivery. [92]

The governors met August 6 and by a vote of four to two decided to serve notice of *Hurley v. Abbott* upon the ranchers of the upper Verde River valley. Ralph Murphy strongly opposed the action, but Kibbey favored it. [93]

Repair work on the Arizona Canal was expected to be finished by Saturday, August 11, which also was the first day of operation of the sugar factory in Glendale. [94]

From attorney C. F. Ainsworth, who had been in Washington, it was learned the Interior Department was still examining the abstract giving the government title to the Arizona Water Co. property. Ainsworth paid off the costs of some judgments that had been pending against the north side canal companies. [95]

Bert Royce closed the Roosevelt bowling alley at Roosevelt because he could not afford to pay the $30 monthly license fee imposed by the Gila County Board of Supervisors. The Negro string band from O'Rourke's camp entertained the people of Roosevelt-on-the-Hill. About 30 Negro women, the wives of some of the laborers, arrived at Camp O'Rourke. O'Rourke & Co. provoked an ice price war when it limited its sale of the product to a single buyer, the

operator of a soda fountain, who sold the ice for two and one-half cents per pound. Ice was soon being brought by wagon from Globe by a half-dozen men, which pushed the price down to one-half cent per pound. This was below the cost of buying it and transporting it to Roosevelt. The men shortly got together and reduced the ice wagons to one, but ice continued to be made available at several stores. The price, however, went back to two and one-half cents per pound. [96]

Contractor Collins on August 18 began putting a two-foot high brush and stone crest atop the rock dam near the head of the Arizona Canal extension. However, heavy rains fell over the watersheds and two days later water again topped the dam. Collins telephoned August 20 that the flow in the river was 300,000 inches compared to the average flow that summer of between 20,000 and 40,000 inches. The following day, the river fell. Damage appeared slight, except for a small break in the Arizona Canal, where it crossed Paradise Valley. [97]

The situation at Roosevelt appeared more perilous. The river had risen on Monday, August 20. On Tuesday, it rose even more and sent water over the low point along the upper cofferdam. Many were afraid the flood would undermine and sweep away the sheet piling, which would have caused another long delay in the excavation. Just before midnight August 21, the river began falling rapidly. The cofferdam held, but Steinmetz said the water had washed out a channel six-feet deep and 40-feet wide in front of the cofferdam. That would have to be repaired, and the water would have to be pumped out of the excavation. Hill estimated that it would take four or five days at most. [98]

O'Rourke said the excavation in one area was then within six feet of bedrock. Once bedrock was reached, he said a trench a few feet in depth, running the length of the dam, would have to be blasted out of the bedrock. He said this was necessary to tie the foundation to the bedrock. Once done, as large a force of men as could possibly be employed would work at erecting the dam. He said should a flood of large proportions seem imminent, the cables from the overhead trams would be used to remove the machinery from the river bed. [99]

On August 27, the first load of cement for construction of the Granite Reef Diversion Dam was started by freighter from Roosevelt. The extension of a power line from Evergreen to the diversion dam site was started. The work of repairing the upper cofferdam in the river at Roosevelt was nearly completed, and all the water in the river was diverted through the sluicing tunnel. [100]

---

1. *Arizona Republican* (Phoenix), March 8, 1906.
2. *Ibid.,* March 10 and 14, 1906.
3. *Ibid.,* March 4, 1906.
4. *Ibid.*
5. *Ibid.,* March 4, 6 and 12, 1906.
6. *Ibid.,* March 7 and 8, 1906.
7. *Ibid.,* March 8, 1908.
8. *Ibid.,* March 14 and 21, 1906; *Phoenix Enterprise,* March 10 and 13, 1906, said the woman was Curtis' wife and the child, 3 years old, was theirs. The *Enterprise* gave his initials as J.D.

9. *Republican,* March 10, 1906.
10. *Ibid.,* March 9, 1906.
11. *Ibid.,* March 15, 1906.
12. *Ibid.,* March 14, 1906.
13. *Ibid.,* March 15, 1906.
14. *Ibid.,* March 16, 1906.
15. *Ibid.*
16. *Arizona Gazette* (Phoenix), March 17, 1906.
17. *Republican,* February 19, March 8, 10, 21 and 22, 1906.
18. *Ibid.,* March 18, 1906.
19. *Ibid.,* March 22 and April 4, 1906; *Gazette,* June 30, 1906; *Enterprise,* March 22 and 30, 1906; Dwight B. Heard, pamphlet, "To the Members of the Salt River Valley Water Users' Association." April 2, 1906, Salt River Project Archives (hereafter SRPA).
20. *Republican,* March 22, 1906.
21. *Ibid.,* March 30 and April 8, 1906; *Salt River Project, Final History to 1916,* unpublished manuscript, Volume I, p. 167, SRPA.
22. *Republican,* March 24, 1906.
23. *Ibid.*
24. *Ibid.,* March 26, 27 and 28, 1906.
25. *Ibid.,* March 30, 1906.
26. *Enterprise,* March 26, 1905.
27. *Republican,* March 28, 1906.
28. *Ibid.*
29. *Gazette,* March 28, 1906.
30. *Republican,* March 30, 1906.
31. *Ibid.*
32. *Ibid.,* April 1, 1906.
33. *Gazette,* March 30, 1906.
34. B.A. Fowler, *Republican,* March 31, 1906.
35. *Republican,* April 1, 1906.
36. *Ibid.*
37. Heard, pamphlet, April 2, 1906.
38. *Republican,* April 3, 1906.
39. *Ibid.,* April 4 and 10, 1906.
40. *Ibid.,* April 8, 1906; Ralph F. Palmer, *Doctor on Horseback,* (Mesa: Mesa Historical and Archaeological Society, 1979), pp. 114-115.
41. *Gazette,* April 6, 1906.
42. *Republican,* April 8, 10 and 12 and May 5, 1906.
43. *Ibid.,* April 8, 1906.
44. *Ibid.,* April 14, 1906.
45. *Ibid.,* April 11, 1906.
46. *Ibid.,* April 14 and 19, 1906.
47. *Ibid.,* April 14, 1906.
48. *Ibid.,* April 15, 1906; *Gazette,* April 14, 1906.
49. *Republican,* April 19, 1906.
50. *Gazette,* April 17, 1906.
51. *Republican,* April 26, 27 and 29, 1906.
52. Arthur P. Davis to L.C. Hill, April 26, 1906, SRPA.
53. *Republican,* May 1 and 5, 1906.
54. *Ibid.,* May 5 and 8, 1906.
55. *Ibid.,* May 5, 1906.
56. *Ibid.,* May 5 and 8, 1906.
57. *Ibid.,* May 13, 23, 24 and 26, June 21, 1906; *Gazette,* May 4 and June 1, 1906.
58. *Republican,* May 23, 1906.
59. *Ibid.,* May 29, 1906.
60. *Ibid.*
61. *Ibid.*
62. *Ibid.,* June 1, 1906.
63. *Arizona Weekly Republican* (Phoenix), June 7, 1906.
64. *Republican,* June 3, 1906.
65. *Ibid.,* June 7 and 9, 1906; *Gazette,* June 6 and 9, 1906.
66. *Gazette,* June 8 and 9, 1906; *Republican,* June 9 and 10, 1906.
67. *Gazette,* June 13, 1906; *Final History to 1916,* Vol. I, p. 135; *Fifth Annual Report of Reclamation Service, 1905-06.* (Washington: Government Printing Office, 1907) p. 87.
68. *Final History to 1916,* Vol. I., pp. 132-133.
69. *Ibid.,* p. 135; *Gazette,* June 14, 1906.
70. *Republican,* May 19, June 16, July 5 and 22, 1906.
71. *Ibid.,* June 15, 1906; *Gazette,* July 25, 1906.
72. *Republican,* June 21 and 28, 1906; *Gazette,* June 23, 1906; *Final History to 1916,* Vol. I, p. 189.
73. *Gazette,* June 27, 1906.
74. *Republican,* June 30, 1906.
75. *Ibid.,* June 2, 1906.
76. *Ibid.; Final History to 1916,* Vol. I, pp. 192-194; *Fifth Annual Report of the U.S. Reclamation Service,* p. 90, plates VII-XI.
77. *Republican,* July 7, 1906; *Gazette,* July 7, 1906.
78. *Republican,* July 10, 1906.
79. *Ibid.,* July 14 and 15, 1906; *Gazette,* July 27, 1906.
80. *Republican,* July 22 and 29, 1906.
81. *Ibid.,* July 19, 1906.
82. *Gazette,* July 20, 1906; *Final History to 1916,* Vol. I, p. 126.
83. *Gazette,* July 27, 1906.
84. *Final History to 1916,* Vol. I, p. 185; *Republican,* July 26, 1906.
85. *Republican,* July 26, 1906.
86. *Gazette,* July 28, 1906; *Republican,* August 1, 1906.
87. *Republican,* August 1, 1906.
88. *Enterprise,* July 31, 1906; *Republican,* August 1, 1906.
89. *Republican,* August 1, 1906.
90. *Ibid.*
91. *Ibid.,* August 2, 3 and 19, 1906.
92. *Ibid.,* August 2, 1906.
93. *Ibid.,* August 7, 1906.
94. *Ibid.,* August 10 and 12, 1906.
95. *Ibid.,* August 10, 1906.
96. *Ibid.,* August 3, 12, 16 and 25, 1906.
97. *Ibid.,* August 19 and 21, 1906.
98. *Ibid.,* August 23, 1906.
99. *Ibid.*
100. *Gazette,* August 27, 1906; *Republican,* August 30, 1906.

September 1906 - February 1907

Early in September, workers completed the construction of a building 80-feet long and 30-feet wide in which to store cement at Granite Reef. Engineer Louis C. Hill of the Reclamation Service, in charge of the construction of Roosevelt and Granite Reef dams as well as a project at Yuma, Arizona, said September 4 that cement already had arrived from Roosevelt and was stored in the building. He said tents and other camp fixtures were going up. [1]

Hill said unless another flood delayed work at Roosevelt, the laying of the foundation for the dam could begin in 12 or 15 days. Indeed, about September 8, dam contractor John O'Rourke's men began blasting the bedrock in an area where the foundation cornerstone was to be laid and the first part of the dam was to rise. This work took place in the only section of the excavation cleared to bedrock. It began at the center of the stream at a point where the upper face of the dam would be and reached 100 feet to the south side of the river. The clearing extended 40 feet downstream from the line of the upper face. The purpose of the blasting was to create a staircase effect across the foundation, which would measure 165 feet from the upper to the lower face. The lowest point of the bedrock was along the line upon which the upper face of the dam would rise. The bedrock rose about 10 to 15 feet from that point to the lower face of the dam. The upper face of the dam was to curve a little on the upstream side. [2]

The trench to be cut into the bedrock across the foundation site was to be six-feet deep and 10-feet wide. The dam foundation to be built in the trench was to prevent seepage and was to anchor the dam to the bedrock to prevent it from sliding or slipping. The trench was to be channeled across the bedrock in practically a straight line. However, because of the formation of the bedrock, the trench at the south end of the dam would be about 50 feet from the upper face of the dam, and at the north end, about 15 feet. The trench was not to stop when it reached the sides of the river. Instead, it was to continue up the sides of the canyon walls to provide the slot into which the dam was to be secured to the mountain at both ends. [3]

The *Arizona Gazette* reported September 13 that W. Scott Smith, private secretary to Secretary of the Interior Ethan A. Hitchcock,

spent the day investigating the charges of corruption at the Tonto dam. . .he stated that it was true that his business here was in connection with those charges, but what they were or what he thought about them he declined to say.

Rumors of corruption at the dam have been in circulation here for many months, but as they seemed to be without strong foundation, the Gazette *has refrained from commenting upon them. The matter has now become public, however, and the charges will either be disproved or found to be true and the public will become aware of the situation.*

Mr. Smith goes from here to New Hampshire where he will meet Secretary Hitchcock to whom his report will be submitted. [4]

Apparently there was nothing to substantiate allegations of corruption because the *Gazette* failed to print any news about Smith's report.

Laying cornerstone for Roosevelt Dam in foundation excavation, September 20, 1906.

Frank T. Alkire, president of the Arizona Canal Water Users' Association, sent a letter to members informing them the price of water for members was $1.50 per acre and for non-members $3. He said all labor costs had been paid, but money was owed for materials and supplies, and these had to be paid. The Maricopa and Salt River Valley Canal companies put the price of water at $1.80 per acre. [5]

The afternoon of September 20, although only about a quarter of the excavation for the foundation had been completed, O'Rourke, his partner, George Steinmetz, Hill, and other Reclamation Service engineers gathered for the laying of Roosevelt Dam's cornerstone. Workmen and Roosevelt residents, whose duties allowed, joined in witnessing the event. While it was considered an important moment, one witness said it was "a pure business affair" because of the importance of getting as much work done as possible "while conditions were right"—meaning at a time when the river was down. At 5:05 p.m., a big derrick swung the huge cornerstone rock, weighing six tons, into place, setting it down at the upstream end of the excavation in the center of the channel, 32 feet below the normal bed of the river. This rock was the first for the upper face. Like all the rocks that were to go into the dam, it was thoroughly washed by a workman with a high-pressure hose to remove every particle of dirt, assuring the cement would firmly adhere. On the second day of construction about 40 cubic yards of masonry were put into place. [6]

The *Gazette* said September 21 that the Reclamation Service had taken the first step toward removing its main office from Roosevelt to Phoenix by assigning the purchasing agent to the city. [7]

On September 22, 15 members of the Salt River Valley Water Users' Association sent a letter to Hitchcock asking if some way other than the *Hurley v. Abbott* lawsuit could be found to adjudicate the water right of landowners. The letter, among whose signers were Vernon L. Clark, E. J. Bennitt, and Lloyd B. Christy, said the suit would result "in an almost endless litigation and that the entire community will be set every man against his neighbor." The writers said the business community would suffer most until the lawsuit was ended. Since the writers opposed the suit, they said an injustice was being done them because the Water Users' Association was taking their money and using it to prosecute the suit. They believed the interests of non-members of the association could be readily disposed of by contracts,

and as we understand the system of distributing the water after the completion of the irrigation system would be by giving each acre a pro rata share of the water distributed, we fail to see the necessity of a lawsuit to establish priorities that would afterward have to be ignored.

Hitchcock referred the letter to the U. S. Geological Survey. [8]

Dwight B. Heard presided at a meeting of some of the stockholders of the troubled and debt-ridden Appropriators' Canal Co. September 22. In order to avoid factional disputes, Heard proposed the lands under the canal be divided into five districts and each supply a representative to the board of directors to be elected at the annual meeting

October 1. The shareholders present gave the idea unanimous approval. [9]

Heard also proposed each candidate for the board be asked to pledge himself to a set of policies agreed to by the stockholders. The policies, read by Heard, included making the Appropriators' Canal "a part of the public north side water distribution system" as soon as possible, by selling to the government at a price that would enable the company's debts to be paid. Meantime, expenses for operating the company were to be reduced to the lowest possible figure so the debt could be paid with revenue from the sale of water. The policies were given unanimous endorsement. [10]

At a meeting of Cartwright district farmers September 26, H. A. Hughes attacked the idea of electing the Appropriators' directors from districts. He said the best men should be selected regardless of where they came from. Lincoln Fowler, the Appropriators' president, also opposed the district idea, and the Cartwright area farmers agreed to resist the proposal at the annual meeting. However, three of the remaining four districts elected representatives they wanted seated on the board. [11]

The *Arizona Republican* reported September 29 that the Arizona Water Co., in the opinion of the U. S. Department of Justice, did not own the land through which the canals passed and could not give a valid deed for the rights-of-way. Until the company could do this, the sale to the government could not be completed. Joseph L. B. Alexander, U. S. attorney for Arizona, said he expected it would be necessary for the company to obtain quitclaim deeds from the present owners of the land. [12]

At Granite Reef, about 30 men were busy building a camp under the direction of government engineer James W. Martin. Bunk houses, tents, and other structures were going up, but the the mess house had been completed. The kitchen was 30-feet square and diverging from it like the letter V were two dining rooms, each 16-feet wide and 18-feet long. One dining room was for the white workers and the other was for Mexicans. The camp's living quarters also were segregated. Each of the dining rooms contained a table in the shape of a hollow square, with one side opening to the kitchen for the waiters. Seats for the diners were on the outside of the tables. About 200 men could be fed at one time. The building's floors were cement. The walls were corrugated iron for a height of about six feet, at which point screen work two-feet high extended around the building providing ventilation. [13]

The only other thing completed was running the power line across the river. From a high cliff on the north side, a cable three-eighths of an inch in diameter dipped for a span of about 1,600 feet to the south side. From the cable, separated by triangle-shaped insulators, were suspended three electric wires over which the power was to be transmitted. A powerhouse was to be built to distribute the electricity. Two telephone lines also were carried across the river by the cable. Other works planned included a small gauge electric railroad running to two quarries, a cable tower on each side of the river for a cableway directly over the dam, and a footbridge over the river. The engineers also planned to build a cofferdam up the river to divert water during the construction of the diversion dam. [14]

Tempe Canal shareholders met September 29. After hearing Heard speak about the Granite Reef Diversion Dam, they adopted a resolution proposing the Tempe Canal Co. be allowed an interest in the dam by paying a pro rata share of the construction costs. The resolution was sent to engineer Hill. [15]

At the October 1 meeting of the Appropriators' Canal Co., Lincoln Fowler was elected without dissent to preside, but the moment he took the chair a motion was made to adjourn until Saturday, October 6. Heard, one of the leaders opposing Fowler, called for the adjournment so that a committee of credentials could decide who was eligible to vote. Heard said he understood Fowler held a large number of proxies from persons who it might be shown had no right to representation at the meeting. The motion to adjourn carried by voice vote, but Fowler ruled the vote had to be by shares. A roll call began. The company books were closely guarded for fear anti-Fowler people would try to capture them. But no attempt was made. The vote to adjourn was defeated 8,000 to 1,200 but the mood of the meeting was such it was apparent no business would be conducted, and adjournment was taken until Saturday. [16]

The Committee of Sixteen met October 4 to work on its final report to the Board of Governors and Council of the Water Users' Association. Although they did not complete the report, they arranged to meet with the Council and governors October 15. [17]

On October 5, a reply to the September 22 letter sent to Hitchcock by the anti-*Hurley* faction was completed by the Geological Survey and sent to the interior secretary. The reply noted that section 7 of article 5 of the Water Users' Association's articles of incorporation provided that the association would deliver to each shareholder the water he previously appropriated for irrigation. This must "have contemplated some adjustment of the rights to water which has been acquired independently of the government project," the reply said. The government position was this had to be done before delivery of water from the reservoir could start, which, from present conditions, might "be effected during the season of 1907." The anti-*Hurley* group was anxious to attempt to settle the question of priorities through contracts, but because nothing along this line had been accomplished, it was necessary to continue the lawsuit, the reply said. [18]

Hill reported the cement diversion dam for the power canal at Roosevelt was completed for 180 feet, and the rest of it, 220 feet, was four feet above water and should be finished in November. He said O'Rourke's force was laying from 50 to 70 yards of rock per day. In the center of the channel where the masonry was the highest, the upper face was about 12-feet high. Part of the bedrock had been cleared across the entire channel and rock had been laid. Hill said the plan now was to construct the upper face as high as possible above the trench that was to be cut in the bedrock. Once done, the foundation could be widened and a larger force employed to hasten the work. He also said a 7,000 gallon water tank had been erected at Granite Reef for camp purposes. From there,

the water was piped to the various parts of camp and the corrals. [19]

When the annual meeting of the Appropriators' Canal Co. was resumed October 6, Lincoln Fowler appointed two committees, one on resolutions and the other on credentials, to check the stock record and to report back the names of the stockholders and the number of shares each was entitled to vote. Fowler then read the annual report, including a financial statement, which showed the corporation to be in debt $35,000, which was more than authorized by its charter. Fowler said in the report the company was negotiating with the Interior Department for the sale and transfer of the canal to the government. Fowler said:

> . . .*we believe that an early proposition may be received from the government. It is recommended that these negotiations be continued and that when a proposition is secured that the whole matter be brought before the stockholders of our company for consideration and determination.* [20]

The **Republican** questioned Hill and Benjamin A. Fowler, president of the Salt River Valley Water Users' Association, about negotiations for purchase of the Appropriators' Canal Co. Both men said if there were negotiations, they were unaware of them. [21]

In the afternoon, the credentials committee proposed that "the question of proxies and unpaid stock being voted at this meeting be left to a vote of the stockholders present." A motion was made to limit voting to "those who have paid up for their stock in full and to whom their stock had been issued," which would have eliminated proxies. Several hours were taken up considering the fairness of the motion. Finally, there was a demand for a vote, and the question immediately arose as to whether proxies would be permitted. Lincoln Fowler ruled they would even though the credentials committee had said the vote should be limited to "the stockholders present." The voting went on for two hours, against a constant hubbub. When it was over, the three men charged with keeping the totals could not agree, and the meeting was adjourned until 10 a.m. Monday, October 8. Several of the men went to the courthouse to use an adding machine to get a correct total. Their figures showed the motion to limit voting to paid up stock had lost by 433 votes of 31,527 cast. Meanwhile, the anti-Fowler faction agreed to convene Monday morning before the resumed meeting to select a list of five candidates for the board of directors. [22]

Hill met with members of the Tempe Canal Co. October 6 to discuss the company's request to participate in the financing and ownership of the Granite Reef Diversion Dam. He said the contract between the Water Users' Association and the secretary of the interior appeared to limit the use of any of the facilities constructed by the government to members of the association. But Hill said he believed that, if the association and the government agreed, the Tempe company could use the diversion dam. However, completion of the dam was a long way off, and there was no use worrying about that now, he said. [23]

Monday morning before the Appropriators' Canal Co. stockholders assembled, the anti-Fowler faction gathered and agreed to form a ticket called "Square Deal for the Farmers" for the board of directors. Named to the ticket were Charles Goldman, Hosea Greenhaw Jr., James Ivy, A. W. Fredrick, and W. W. Cook. Goldman was the second heaviest creditor of the company. [24]

After the stockholders' meeting opened, Fowler called for the election of directors, but that was delayed in order to hear the report of the resolutions committee. The resolutions called for economical management of the company, fair distribution of water (Fowler had been in a continuing fight over this), and negotiations for government ownership of the canal. When nominations for directors started, the pro-Fowler forces nominated Fowler, Greenhaw, Goldman, Patrick T. Hurley, and Henry H. Renau. Others nominated, besides the anti-Fowler slate, were Henry Welborn, J. Stanley Howard, and John P. Orme. Before the vote started, a motion was carried that no candidate should be elected unless he had received a majority of the votes cast. The number cast was 31,187, which meant not less than 15,994 votes were necessary for election. [25]

The voting began at 1 p.m. and continued until 4:30 p.m. The results were not known until 9 p.m. Goldman, Greenhaw, Frederick, and Cook were elected, but Hurley fell 114 votes short of a majority, and after him came Ivy with 14,911 votes. A recess was taken until 10 a.m. October 11 to elect the fifth director. [26]

Hill said October 8 that the government would have to build a canal two-miles long on the south side of the Salt River at Granite Reef in order to connect with the head of the Consolidated Canal for the distribution of water. Hill said the government proposed enlarging the Arizona Canal on the north side to carry 80,000 inches of water instead of the current maximum of about 30,000. He said this work would begin as soon as the necessary machinery arrived. The first work on the dam itself would be the construction of the sluice gates and head gates at the ends of the dam. When this was done, the dam proper would be built out toward the main bed of the river. The excavation would be done a little at a time so if floods came all of the work would not be undone. Hill said the plan was still to construct a temporary dam to divert water into the two canals once the head gates were completed. [27]

The directors of the Arizona Canal Water Users' Association voted October 10 to sell winter water to grain growers for $1.50 per acre for the six months starting October 15, 1906, and ending April 15, 1907. The directors also decided to further repair the rock dam, which, when finished, was expected to be 30- to 40-feet wide at the base and 12-feet wide on top. [28]

Ivy was elected the fifth director of the Appropriators' after all other candidates withdrew. The four directors elected previously had said they wanted the fifth member to be someone with whom they could work smoothly. They raised the price of stock in the company from $1.50 to $2 per share and set the price of winter water at $1.50 per acre. The next day the board named Emil Ganz, president of the National Bank of Arizona, the heaviest creditor of the company, temporary secretary. [29]

The remainder of the Reclamation Service office staff and engineers, except for the men in actual charge of the construction of Roosevelt Dam, moved from Roosevelt to the government quarters in the Phoenix post office. [30]

Contractor O'Rourke arrived in Phoenix October 15 and said the face of the dam was about 25-feet high toward the south end. The cutting of the channel in the bedrock was about half completed, and one section of about 30-feet near the center of the riverbed already had been filled in, and construction was in progress over it. O'Rourke said the derricks were dividing time between placing the permanent rock in the foundation and removing the debris. He said his greatest problem was employing competent skilled labor. It was not wages, but the remoteness and lack of social opportunities for families that made hiring and keeping workers difficult. He said 40 to 50 quarrymen were at work, but more were needed. In all, 130 men were working, O'Rourke said. [31]

The Committee of Sixteen also met October 15 and turned over to the Council of the Water Users' Association a slightly amended version of the agreement reached in November 1905. The Council adopted the report and sent it to the governors with the recommendation it be presented to the shareholders for approval. The governors appointed a committee of three to consider the report. [32]

Directors of the Appropriators' Canal Co. met and elected Ivy president. Goldman was elected vice president; Greenhaw, treasurer; and Ganz, secretary. [33]

Engineer Chester Smith, in charge of the construction of Roosevelt Dam, said about a thousand yards of masonry had been laid and that the trench in the bedrock was almost completed across the river. He said a section about 90-feet long had been filled with rock and cement, and construction was proceeding above it. One slight annoyance was 110 degree water seeping from a seam in the bedrock about 10 feet below the face of the dam. To seal off the water, an iron pipe 15-feet high and about an inch in diameter was placed over the seepage so the water could rise inside. The masonry was built up around the pipe, and cement was run into the pipe to displace the water. The pipe was then covered. [34]

Work on the rock dam at the head of the Arizona Canal extension was completed the night of October 20, and the rails on which the rock had been carried were removed and stacked. Directors of the Arizona Canal Water Users' Association met October 22 and agreed to pay off the company's remaining indebtedness, which was $12,000 when they took control. [35]

Engineer Jay D. Stannard reported a survey of all the farmers in the area of the reservoir district showed about 97,500 acres irrigated in 1906. [36]

Secretary Hitchcock on October 27 replied to the anti-*Hurley* letter of September 22. Hitchcock sent with his answer a copy of the Geological Survey letter of October 5. Hitchcock reiterated, "It is absolutely necessary that these (water) rights be adjusted with as little delay as may be," but he said the Interior Department would "welcome any plan which would bring about such an adjustment, preferring that this be accomplished without resort to the courts, if that be possible." He noted the lawsuit had been pending for more than two years without progress toward a settlement. He continued:

Nor do you suggest any plan to reach that settlement. The department would gladly use whatever of influence it may have to secure a settlement of these claims by an agreement of the partners interested, thus obviating the necessity of prosecution of the proceedings already begun, but there can be no ground for offering suggestions in the matter unless, and until, some apparently feasible plan for amicable adjustment of the claim shall be presented. [37]

In the last days of October, excavation for the head gate walls for the canals at Granite Reef Diversion Dam began. One cement mixer was at the site and a second was on its way from Roosevelt. Two bunk houses, 18-feet wide and 100-feet long, were completed. At Roosevelt, the upper face of the dam extended nearly across the river, with an average height of 10 feet and a width of 40 feet. In the center, it was 18-feet high. Four derricks were in use. The diversion dam at the head of the power canal was completed October 29, but the apron was not finished until mid-November. It was almost identical in construction to the Granite Reef dam, but smaller in scale. J. E. Sturgeon sold his interests at Roosevelt and at Livingston, including his butcher business, to Johnson & Belcher of Roosevelt. [38]

On November 3, the Tempe and Mesa canal companies filed separate motions asking for separate trials in *Hurley v. Abbott.* The two companies also filed motions for a change in venue in which they charged they could not receive a fair trial because Judge Edward Kent was biased and prejudiced against their interests. Kent scheduled the motions for hearing November 10. [39]

Frederick H. Newell, chief engineer of the Reclamation Service, arrived in Phoenix and on November 8 appeared before the governors and told them that the large expenditure of money for the Salt River project had aroused considerable antagonism and hostility among people in other states. Because of this, Newell advised the people of the Valley to settle their differences over the *Hurley* suit and complete the adjudication over the priority of water rights. He said Roosevelt Dam would in a year be ready to store water, and the government would be faced with the question of water distribution. He said distribution could not be settled until priorities were settled. Yet, this was not done and progress was slow. Newell said there was a similar lack of progress in the Yakima, Washington, country. The government gave the people three months to resolve the problems, and they did, he said. [40]

Following Newell's remarks, the governors adopted the amended report of the Committee of Sixteen and ordered the printing of 2,000 copies of a memorandum of agreement in pamphlet form. The governors decided to present the agreement to the landowners in the hope the concurrence of three-quarters of them could be obtained so that the report could be submitted to the court. Although the governors took this action, new complications apparently arose in the agreement, and a subcommittee of three governors gave it new consideration. [41]

Newell visited Roosevelt November 9. By then, a portion of the upper wall of the dam was completed across the channel so that the visitor could get a view of its curved shape. About 44,000 yards of masonry were then in place. [42]

Judge Kent on November 10 denied the motions of the Tempe and Mesa canal companies for separate trials and a change of venue in the *Hurley* case. Before Kent ruled, attorney Thomas Armstrong Jr. appeared on behalf of the Bartlett-Heard Land & Cattle Co. and others to protest against the use of their names on the motions. Many of these persons had signed affidavits not realizing they were challenging the integrity of the court. In denying the motions, Kent said the number of defendants made it impractical to transfer the case, but he would remove himself as judge if a sufficient number of affidavits were submitted attesting the signers did not think they could get a fair and impartial trial before him. [43]

The *Republican* printed an editorial in defense of Kent, saying,

We do not believe that there is anywhere in this community an impression that Judge Kent is unfair, or that he is lacking in any judicial characteristic as to make him a dangerous judge, either in the pending case or any other which may come before him... When he came here, irrigation matters were in a chaotic state. He set out

Two views of foundation work at Roosevelt Dam, November 30, 1906.

The Salt River flowing over the upper cofferdam at Roosevelt, December 1906.

to undo the tangle, and while it is impossible to remove dissatisfaction so long as there is not enough water for all, he has accomplished much. One result has been that there is less litigation and a more equitable distribution of water. [44]

Construction at Granite Reef included railroad roadbed grading from the dam site to the quarries and the footbridge, which was completed in late November. In addition, preparations were underway for erection of the cableway. The two towers for the cable were each to be 100-feet high. Poles to carry the electric lines also were being set. [45]

The last week of November, rains fell over the watersheds, and a small rise in the Salt River occurred at Roosevelt, but it caused no damage and did not interfere with the work. Reclamation Service engineers proposed abandoning the term miners' inch and substituting second foot as a unit for measuring the flow of water. They also estimated the quantity of water needed to properly irrigate lands in the Valley at three to five acre-feet, depending upon crops and other conditions. [46]

Despite rainy weather, engineer A. H. Demrick and a crew of six men began surveying the route for the electric transmission line from Roosevelt to the Valley. While the original plan was to follow the course of the telephone line, the engineers decided to take a different route, which more nearly paralleled the road. They were motivated in part by the greater difficulty of getting the necessary equipment and supplies to the route taken by the telephone line. [47]

Rains returned to Arizona the first few days in December. On Sunday afternoon, December 2, contractor O'Rourke ordered his men to begin removing machinery and equipment from the excavation and to place them as high as possible along the river banks. The river rose throughout the evening and began washing the boulders and rocks piled against the upper cofferdam into the excavation. The water flow reached 60,000 cubic feet per second, and both the upper and lower cofferdams were damaged. By then, the upper face of the foundation was eight feet below the bed of the river, and it was about 20-feet wide on top. On the

downstream side, the foundation sloped downward in step fashion for a distance of 40 to 60 feet in different places, so that the width of the structure varied from 60 to 80 feet. [48]

The afternoon of December 3, the Salt River below the confluence with the Verde River submerged the rock dam at the head of the Arizona Canal extension. Contractor R. H. Collins said it appeared the loose stone on top of the dam had been washed away, but there was no rough water in the crest of the wave going over. He said this indicated the dam had not broken. However, he was certain part of the canal had washed away. The river also took out the footbridge at Granite Reef. [49]

At a meeting of the executive committee of the Arizona Canal Water Users' Association, the directors decided whatever repairs were necessary would be made. [50]

Collins reported December 4 there were breaks in the Arizona Canal below its old head. He said these were where the breaks usually occurred. The water in the Salt had risen at least 12 feet below the junction with the Verde. Upstream, the river closed the Roosevelt road. [51]

The next few days, it became evident the river had caused considerable damage to the Arizona Canal extension. Early reports were the extension had been filled with sand, but in reality, it had been obliterated. In addition, the flood had cut a new channel between the dam and the extension so, if the latter were rebuilt, the dam would also have to be extended. The estimated cost of this work plus repairing breaks in the canal totaled $8,125. A second plan, which involved abandonment of most of the extension and construction of a new rock dam across the river, was estimated to cost $6,255. The new rock dam was to be located between the old Arizona Dam and the existing rock dam. The two plans were developed by Collins and Dan McDermott, the canal superintendent, and were presented December 8 at a meeting of the stockholders of the Arizona Canal Water Users' Association. [52]

The shareholders discussed levying assessments of 50 cents, 75 cents, and $1 per share on the 12,539 shares of stock. Benjamin A. Fowler, speaking for the executive committee, said in addition to the costs of repairs, another $2,500 would be needed to pay for zanjero services and $745 in other fixed charges. If the decision was made to build the new rock dam, Fowler said he believed a cable and gasoline engine could be obtained from the government for the expense of removing them from where they were and placing them where needed. He said the government might later help with repairs but only at actual cost. He said the property would not be turned over to the government until May at the earliest and possibly not until October. When the government did take charge, it would neither assume nor pay any of the association's debts, Fowler said. He said it was necessary for the association to be prepared to turn over the canal at any time. [53]

A motion was made to levy a $1 assessment upon the stock. It was approved 65 to 3. However, Walter Bennett, association attorney, advised the vote had to be by stock. With that, members began rounding up a sufficient number of shareholders to assure a majority vote in favor. By 5 p.m.,

6,835 shares had voted yes and 300 shares no. [54]

The Salt River at Roosevelt lowered enough so it could be seen that a channel about 125-feet wide had been cut through the upper cofferdam and for 150 feet or more through the lower cofferdam. O'Rourke's men began making repairs to the cofferdams December 10. The sheet piling across the break in the upper dam was completed a week later so that the water again was diverted through the sluicing tunnel. [55]

Stages made the trip along the Roosevelt road, and a government engineering party began setting posts every mile to give travelers information about the distances. [56]

Collins had 60 men and 25 teams at work repairing the breaks in the Arizona Canal, and on December 18 it was announced Reclamation Service engineers at Granite Reef had been instructed to make a survey aimed at widening the extension from the canal head to a rock butte 900 feet upstream. The rock butte was the point at which the Arizona Canal Water Users' Association planned on building the new rock dam across the river. The Reclamation Service reported the survey was in connection with a tentative plan to divert the entire flow of the river at low stage through the Arizona Canal so the water would not interfere with putting in the foundation of the diversion dam. [57]

A hospital was under construction at Granite Reef, and wires had been run to the kitchen, bunk houses, and tents so they would have electric lights when power became available. A force of men was put on the north side of the river to begin construction of the cable tower, but the work was delayed because of the slow arrival of heavy timbers. A small rowboat was made, and a blacksmith shop was opened at the quarry. [58]

Jack Fraser bought from Adam Ator the buildings and equipment at Tortilla Flat, along the Roosevelt road, to make it into a stage station to replace the one at Mormon Flat. The other stage stations were at Government Well and Fish Creek. The Reclamation Service made a small dam across Tortilla Creek to provide a water supply and built a

Damage at upper coffer dam at Roosevelt Dam site, January 29, 1907.

wind mill and cement tank to pipe water to roadside troughs. [59]

The work of pumping water from the excavation at Roosevelt Dam began the morning of December 26, but two days later a flood larger than that of December 2 and 3 came down the river. The river rose throughout the day and night, sweeping away most of both cofferdams. A new gauge placed below the dam site showed the depth of the river at 8 a.m. December 28 at 2.75 feet. By 5 a.m. December 29, it rose to 12.6 feet and six hours later was a little more than 11-feet deep. The Roosevelt road between Roosevelt and Pine Creek was under 2 to 10 feet of water, while at Fish Creek, it was 5-feet deep. At the Arizona Canal head, the depth reached 15 feet, and it was estimated that 75,000 cubic feet of water per second came down the river. [60]

The deed transferring the Crosscut Canal of the Water Power Canal Co. to the federal government was filed December 29 in the Maricopa County recorder's office. [61]

Dr. Ralph Palmer took a half-dozen beds and bedding equipment to Granite Reef to outfit the camp hospital on January 1, 1907. Tim Hinchion, who served as steward at the Roosevelt hospital, was put in charge of the Granite Reef hospital. [62]

When the water lowered some, it was found the Arizona Canal had escaped serious damage except for the usual breaks. The river continued to run with a good flow but repairs began on the canal. The Arizona Canal Water Users' Association stockholders held their annual meeting January 8 and reelected the five directors and added two more, H. B. Lehman and J. W. Foss. [63]

Making milepost markers for the Roosevelt Road, December 6, 1906.

William H. Code, irrigation engineer for the Indian Service, visited Phoenix on January 11 and informed the *Republican* that proposals to bring electric power to the Gila River Indian Reservation were being considered by the Interior Department. Code said there were two plans. The first was to develop hydro-power at a point between the Arizona Canal head and Roosevelt, and the second was to run a branch transmission line from Roosevelt Dam to the reservation. The power was to be used to pump water from the ground for irrigation of reservation lands. [64]

The high water in the river cut a new channel that left the head of the Appropriators' Canal many feet away from the main flow of water. The head either would have to be lowered or extended. In addition, rocks and sand filled the head for a short distance and had to be removed. The cost of doing these things was estimated at $2,000. On January 16, the board of directors called a meeting for January 22 to consider an assessment of 50 cents per share. [65]

Benjamin Fowler returned January 18 from a two-day trip to the head of the Arizona Canal and the Granite Reef camp site. Fowler reported repair work on the canal was satisfactory and nearly all the preliminary work for the diversion dam had been completed. By this time the camp included four bunk houses, an office building, a mercantile store that used coupons and was operated by the government, and a large building with concrete floor and screened sides containing chairs and tables. In this latter building, cigars, soda water, and ice cream were sold as a department of the mercantile store. A little village of 20 houses built apart for Mexican laborers was known as "Mexico." There were 200 men in camp; common laborers were paid $2 per day; other laborers $2 to $3; drillers, $2.75; carpenters, $3.50 to $5; helpers, $2.50, and sub-foremen, $3.50. The government deducted 75 cents per day for meals. The cable tower on the south side was ready to be raised, and excavation for the north side tower was done. The 2-1/2 inch cable between the towers would span 1,600 feet and would

Traveling the Roosevelt road by buggy. First trip by auto was February 8, 1906.

sag 80 feet. A cage with a capacity of 35 men was to be attached to the cable to transport workers across the river. The narrow gauge railroad was completed, lacking only electricity to operate. The railroad ran to two quarries, the most distant 3,200 feet. On the south side, the excavation for the dam, sluice gates, and canal head gates was down to bedrock. [66]

The *Republican* reported January 22 that several holders of receivers' certificates from the Arizona Water Co. had received notification to forward them to the New York Trust Co. presumably to exchange for cash. The newspaper thought this meant the government had paid the company the purchase price of the canals, a supposition confirmed by Hill when he returned from Washington a few days later. However, R. E. Miner, secretary of the water company, said the transfer of the canals to the government was not expected until mid-May. He said the government still had to approve the abstracts of title to the Arizona, Maricopa, and Grand canals. [67]

Shareholders in the Appropriators' Canal Co. voted 9,085 to 3,247 against an assessment of 50 cents per share at their meeting January 22. By a voice vote, a levy of 15 cents per share was adopted, but there were objections the vote was illegal, and doubts were expressed that the directors would be able to collect the assessment. Before the votes were taken, the directors reported they had paid off about $14,000 of the old debt and several thousand dollars had been spent on repairs. [68]

On January 26, the *Republican* said engineer Hill had been furnished an automobile, a Stevens-Duryea, by the government, and a few days later he, Mrs. Hill, Fowler, Reclamation Service engineer Orville H. Ensign, and F. H. Ensign traveled in the vehicle to Granite Reef. The Ensigns were brothers. [69]

Demrick came in from Roosevelt and said O'Rourke's men for the past few days had been driving piling into the riverbed for the new cofferdams. Demerick said the dams were to be reinforced with concrete. [70]

Hill attended a meeting of the Arizona Canal Water Users' Association on January 29 and announced that because of practical ownership of the canal by the government, the Reclamation Service would widen the 900 feet of channel between the old head and the proposed new head. He said the ditch might not be widened as much as some persons had suggested, but it was part of the plan for the diversion dam construction to divert as much water as possible through the canals. This would make the handling of the remainder of the water by cofferdams much easier, Hill said. [71]

While the Reclamation Service intended to widen the canal, the responsibility for construction of the rock dam and the installation of the cable across the river remained with the association. Alkire wrote a letter to stockholders informing them of this, adding that they would be responsible for maintenance and operation expenses until October 1. He asked the shareholders to remit the assessment of $1 per share levied December 8. He said about two-fifths of the shares had paid. [72]

U.S. Reclamation Service headquarters building at Roosevelt, February 1907.

Hill also disclosed the contract for the powerline between Roosevelt and the Valley would soon be let. When the line reached Mesa, it would divide, one branch going south to the Gila River Indian Reservation, and the other running to Phoenix for use by the Pacific Gas & Electric Co. within the corporate limits of the city. [73]

Another bit of information learned from the Reclamation Service was that a survey for a new canal, the Eastern, which would be built east of the Highland, had been completed. In some places, the Eastern would be a half-mile distant from the Highland, and in others, less. A starting date for construction of the Eastern was not given. [74]

Shortly before noon, January 31, a mulatto named William Baldwin, 25, a laborer at the Roosevelt Dam, ran breathlessly into Roosevelt and reported two Mexicans had murdered Mrs. Harvey Morris and her daughter, Aminta, 5, on a ranch three miles east of town. Baldwin had a minor

gash on his throat and other slight injuries. He said he had suffered these wounds attempting to defend Mrs. Morris and her child, whose throats had been slashed. A posse of men was formed and went to the ranch. The bodies were found about 600 feet from the ranch house. The posse was unable to find any footprints in the vicinity except those of Baldwin, and suspicion soon fell on him as the murderer. The posse searched through the day for clues but was unable to find any, and Baldwin was held at the Roosevelt jail. He denied the crime. The following day, officers reported there may have been an attempted criminal assault of Mrs. Morris before she was slain. Feelings against Baldwin ran high, and some of the men decided to lynch him. They learned that Sheriff Thompson of Gila County planned to take Baldwin to Globe late the afternoon of February 1. Thompson, accompanied by deputies, left with Baldwin at 5 p.m. Two miles outside of Roosevelt, they spotted a group of armed horsemen approaching. Thompson and the deputies drew Winchester rifles and told the horsemen that if there was any attempt to take Baldwin, they would shoot. The horsemen rode off, and the sheriff reached Globe with Baldwin at 12:30 a.m. February 2. That night, members of the Morris family and friends arrived in town. They were joined by hundreds of others who had viewed the bodies, which had been brought to Globe. About a thousand people surrounded the Gila County jail, but Thompson had already taken Baldwin to the railroad where he obtained a handcar. The sheriff ordered Baldwin taken to Rice's station, then returned to Globe. Federal Judge Frederick S. Nave, who armed himself with a Winchester, and other citizens spoke to the crowd from the jail steps. Nave told them there would be no lynching, even if it cost him his life. Then he said Baldwin was not in the jail. The mob called for the keys, and a deputy sheriff turned them over. After a search of the jail was made,

Main street at Roosevelt, February 1907.

Thompson told them Baldwin was 50 miles away. With that, the crowd dispersed. It was then about 1 a.m., February 3. Thompson later took Baldwin to Bowie. From there, they went to Tucson where Baldwin was held in jail. He later was convicted of the murders and was sentenced to hang. [75]

The Salt River rose again February 1, disrupting work on the cofferdams. However, the rise was not as high as in January, and there was hope the work that had been done would stand. [76]

The three members appointed to study the memorandum of agreement developed by the Committee of Sixteen submitted a recommendation February 4 that the governors adopt a resolution approving the memorandum and urge landowners and water users to sign it. The governors delayed action until the next meeting. [77]

It was proposed at a meeting of the Arizona Canal Water Users' Association directors February 5 that the farmers under the lower north side canals join with the association in the construction of the new rock dam and save the expense of putting in their own brush dams. An immediate objection was that if the rock dam was ruined, the lower canals would have to rebuild their dams. Hill, who attended the meeting, said if the lower canals joined, he would guarantee the government would keep the dam in repair and replace it if it went out. He explained that if this was not done, he would have to build a cofferdam to both divert water into the Arizona Canal and to let water by the diversion dam construction to reach the lower canals. By construction of a proper rock dam and diversion of all the water through the Arizona Canal during the river's low stage, it might be possible to avoid building a cofferdam, or at least not a large one. The farmers would have to pay for the cofferdam in the long run, but if they pooled their money for the rock dam, that cost could probably be avoided, Hill said. Representatives of the other canals were invited to meet February 7. [78]

The Arizona Canal directors, at Hill's request, also agreed to keep water out of the canal for a month so the government could put men to work to deepen the ditch by five feet for some distance west of Granite Reef. This would be done to increase the canal's capacity. The directors also approved Alkire's sending a letter to stockholders informing them if they failed to pay the $1 assessment within 10 days, they would not receive water and their shares would be forfeited. [79]

At the February 7 meeting, Salt River Valley Canal representatives said they were reluctant to join in building the rock dam. They explained they were obligated to deliver water up to May 15, and the rock dam might not be completed in time to meet that commitment. They said they had $1,500, enough to build a brush dam at the Joint Head with the Maricopa Canal or to contribute to the rock dam. They said they could not do both. One argument in favor of the rock dam, aside from Hill's offer to keep it in repair, was that the brush dam could easily be taken out several times before May 15. The Arizona Canal directors said it made no difference what the other canals did, but the main argument was the potential savings from not building a cofferdam.

Fish Creek station along Roosevelt road.

Finally, the meeting chairman, Charles J. Hall, was instructed to name a representative from each of the other four canals and meet with them about the proposal. Hall later named John P. Orme, Benjamin Fowler, Nelson Bradley, and Walter Bennett. [80]

Hill, accompanied by his wife and daughter, Margaret, Orville Ensign, and W. H. Sanders, made the first trip to Roosevelt by automobile on February 8. They returned to Phoenix four days later. Hill said the auto climbed Fish Creek Hill in 16 minutes, a trip that usually took a man in an unloaded buggy 45 minutes or an hour with a load. The entire trip was made in six hours at about 10 miles an hour, which included making several stops to avoid freighters' teams. They ate dinner at the Fish Creek station, which was under the charge of Mr. and Mrs. F. M. Edward. Mrs. Edward's meals were sometimes compared to those of the Harvey Houses along the Sante Fe Railroad. As to conditions at Roosevelt, Hill said snow melting in the mountains kept more water in the Salt River than the sluicing tunnel could handle. He said construction of the upper cofferdam was progressing slowly. Once the river was low enough, he said, it would take three weeks to a month to clean out the excavation and resume work on the foundation. He said it was useless to speculate about when that would happen. [81]

At Granite Reef, Hill said, an inch and a quarter cable had been placed across the river to be used in moving material, but the situation would be improved even more when a big cable with large cages was in place. He said it would take about a minute to cross the river with the large cable. [82]

Hall and his four committee members visited Granite Reef and the Arizona Canal head February 14. They crossed to the government camp, riding in a carriage attached to the cable. [83]

Rain fell across the Valley on February 16, which brought a degree of relief to Arizona Canal farmers who worried it would be weeks before water would again be in their canal. An estimate also was made that a rock dam large enough to supply water for all the north side canals would cost about $12,000. Contractor Collins finished placing a small cable across the river at the head of the canal extension and expected to have a larger cable in place by February 19. A few days later, he expected to begin dropping huge rocks from the cable to start the foundation of the dam. [84]

The money due minority stockholders of the north side canals arrived at the Reclamation Service office February 18. The aggregate was more than $78,000, but after the debts of the companies were paid, the 100 shares of each company were to receive the following sums per share: Grand $204.88; Maricopa $199.50 and Salt River Valley $102.03. It also was believed the government would take control of the three canals May 15 because the three companies had sold water for delivery only to that date. [85]

Former Indian scout Al Sieber was killed the morning of February 19 when a large rock being removed by Apache Indians in the construction of the Tonto Creek road fell on him, mangling both legs and otherwise crushing him. He lost consciousness almost immediately and died in a brief time. He had worked for the government most of the time since the Roosevelt construction began. His main work had been directing Indians in road construction. [86]

Hill met with Hall's committee February 20. Because the farmers said they had no funds and had no way of making a fair collection of the money, Hill offered to pay the wages of the workmen and to collect the money after May 15 by increasing the levy for water. He said about 11,000 acres were under cultivation by each canal and that figure could be used as a basis for estimating the cost. Hill also said that should there be insufficient water through the Arizona Canal for all the north side ditches, he would keep in repair the brush dam at the Joint Head. His remarks were considered, but the Hall committee could reach no agreement. [87]

The first construction fatality at the Granite Reef Diversion Dam occurred the evening of February 25. Harry Cross, about 34, a former sailor from Detroit employed as a cablerigger, fell about 80 feet to his death. Cross was aboard one of the cable carriages when a flange on one side of one of the grooved wheels broke, causing the cable to wedge between the wheel and the carriage frame. Cross climbed out of the skip and got on top. But he was unable to repair it and apparently was preparing to ride the hoisting rope to the ground when a block on which he had placed his feet tipped over as he pulled a rope with one hand and grasped the carriage with the other. His feet came out from under him, and his hold on the carriage was jerked free. His other hand slipped down the rope until it reached the block, when he lost his hold and plunged earthward. He landed on his forehead and died at once. [88]

Arthur P. Davis, acting chief engineer of the Reclamation Service, wrote confidentially to Fowler on February 27 inquiring about progress in the *Hurley* suit. Davis said:

The matter is of extreme importance to the Reclamation Service as the progress in this case must guide its future policy.

The Government must be protected against any claims to the use of water stored in the Roosevelt reservoir. If no other protection is available it may become necessary to keep open the gates of the Roosevelt dam and not to store any water in the reservoir until this question has been definitely settled. [89]

In the last days of February, the electricity was turned on to the camp at Granite Reef, the power coming from Phoenix. Besides the bunk houses, dining halls, and street lights, the electricity was used to power the cable drawing carriages across the river and to operate the railroad to the quarry. [90]

---

1. *Arizona Gazette* (Phoenix), September 4, 1906.
2. *Ibid.,* September 4, 19, 1906; *Arizona Republican* (Phoenix), September 21, October 16, 1906.
3. *Republican,* October 16, 1906.
4. *Gazette,* September 13, 1906.
5. *Republican,* September 14, 21, 1906.
6. *Ibid.,* September 20, 23, 1906.
7. *Gazette,* September 22, 1906.
8. H. I. Latham, et al, to Ethan A. Hitchcock, September 22, 1906, *Republican,* November 6, 1906; Salt River Project Archives (hereafter SRPA).
9. *Republican,* September 23, 1906.
10. *Ibid.,* September 23, 27, 1906.
11. *Ibid.,* September 27, October 2, 1906.
12. *Ibid.,* September 29, 1906.
13. *Ibid.,* September 29, December 3, 1906, January 19, 1907; *Gazette,* November 5, December 24, 1906; *Salt River Project, Final History to 1916,* unpublished manuscript, Volume I, p. 187, SRPA.
14. *Republican,* September 29, 1906, January 19, 1907; *Gazette,* September 25, 1906; *Final History to 1916,* Vol. I, p. 189.
15. *Republican,* September 30, 1906.
16. *Ibid.,* October 2, 1906; *Gazette,* October 2, 1906.
17. *Republican,* October 5, 1906.
18. Acting Director, U. S. Geological Survey to E. A. Hitchcock, October 5, 1906, SRPA; *Republican,* November 6, 1906.
19. *Republican,* October 5, 1906; *Final History to 1916,* Vol. I, p. 187.
20. *Republican,* October 7, 1906.
21. *Ibid.*
22. *Ibid.*
23. *Ibid.,* October 8, 1906.
24. *Gazette,* October 8, 1906; *Republican,* October 18, 1906.
25. *Gazette,* October 8, 1906; *Republican,* October 9, 1906.
26. *Republican,* October 9, 1906; *Gazette,* October 9, 1906.
27. *Gazette,* October 9, 1906.
28. *Republican,* October 11, 12, 1906.
29. *Ibid.,* October 12, 13, 1906.
30. *Ibid.,* October 13, 1906.
31. *Ibid.,* October 16, 1906.
32. *Ibid.*
33. *Ibid.,* October 18, 1906.
34. *Ibid.,* October 21, 1906.
35. *Ibid.,* October 23, 1906.
36. *Ibid.,* October 25, 1906.
37. Hitchcock to Latham, et al, SRPA; *Republican,* November 6, 1906.
38. *Republican,* October 28, 30, 1906; *Gazette,* October 24, 30, November 5, 1906.
39. *Republican,* November 4, 11, 1906.
40. *Ibid.,* November 9, 1906.
41. *Ibid.*
42. *Ibid.,* November 10, 1906.
43. *Ibid.,* November 11, 1906.
44. *Ibid.*
45. *Ibid.,* November 11, 27, December 3, 1906; *Final History to 1916,* Vol. I, p. 187.

46. *Republican,* November 22, 27, 1906.
47. *Ibid.,* November 27, 1906.
48. *Ibid.,* December 4, 1906; *Final History to 1916,* Vol. I., p. 126; *Sixth Annual Report of the Reclamation Service, 1906-1907,* (Washington: Government Printing Office, 1908), p. 64.
49. *Republican,* December 4, 8, 1906.
50. *Ibid.*
51. *Ibid.,* December 5, 1906.
52. *Ibid.,* December 6, 9, 1906.
53. *Ibid.,* December 9, 1906.
54. *Ibid.*
55. *Ibid.,* December 7, 17, 1906; *Sixth Annual Report of the Reclamation Service,* p. 64.
56. *Republican,* December 17, 1906.
57. *Ibid.,* December 17, 19, 1906, January 30, 1907.
58. *Ibid.,* December 24, 25, 1906.
59. *Ibid.,* December 25, 1906, January 5, 15, 1905.
60. *Ibid.,* December 27, 29, 30, 1906, January 10, 1907; *Gazette,* December 29, 1906; *Sixth Annual Report of the Reclamation Service,* p. 64.
61. *Gazette,* December 29, 1906.
62. *Republican,* January 2, 1907.
63. *Ibid.,* January 3, 9, 1907.
64. *Ibid.,* January 12, 1907.
65. *Ibid.,* January 19, 1907; *Gazette,* January 15, 1907.
66. *Republican,* January 19, 1907; *Final History to 1916,* Vol. I, pp. 187, 197.
67. *Republican,* January 22, 29, 1907; *Gazette,* January 28, 1907.
68. *Republican,* January 23, 1907.
69. *Ibid.,* January 26, 29, 1907.
70. *Ibid.,* January 26, 1907.
71. *Ibid.,* January 30, 1907.
72. Frank T. Alkire to Stockholders, Arizona Canal Water Users' Association, *Republican,* January 30, 1907.
73. *Republican,* January 30, 1907.
74. *Ibid.*
75. *Ibid.,* February 1, 2, 3, 4, 1907, April 28, 1907.
76. *Ibid.,* February 2, 1907.
77. *Ibid.,* February 5, 1907; Charles Peterson, et al, report to President and Board of Governors, Salt River Valley Water Users' Association, February 4, 1907, SRPA.
78. *Republican,* February 6, 1907.
79. *Ibid.*
80. *Ibid.,* February 8, 10, 1907.
81. *Ibid.,* February 13, 1907.
82. *Ibid.*
83. *Ibid.,* February 15, 1907.
84. *Ibid.,* February 17, 19, 1907.
85. *Ibid.,* February 19, 1907; *Gazette,* February 18, 1907.
86. *Republican,* February 20, 1907.
87. *Ibid.,* February 21, 1907.
88. *Ibid.,* February 26, 1907; *Gazette,* February 28, 1907.
89. A. P. Davis to B. A. Fowler, February 27, 1907, SRPA.
90. *Republican,* March 1, 1907.

March - August 1907

The Board of Governors of the Salt River Valley Water Users' Association adopted a resolution March 4, 1907, endorsing the memorandum of agreement of the Committee of Sixteen and urging the Valley's water users to sign it as "the most equitable and expeditious basis for the settlement of the *Hurley v. Abbott* suit." This was the second time the governors had given their approval to the work of the Committee of Sixteen, but, as in the first, other water users found problems with it. [1]

Some of the water users under the Arizona Canal asked that water be let into the canal, but the board of directors of the Arizona Canal Water Users' Association met March 6 and decided against it. They said raising the head gates of the canal would interfere with construction work in progress. Engineer James W. Martin, in charge of the canal work and the Granite Reef Diversion Dam construction for the Reclamation Service, said he hoped to have the work of deepening the canal, including blasting and sand removal, completed in three weeks. The opinion was offered that not a great many crops would suffer. [2]

Meantime, contractor R. H. Collins' men began dumping rock into the Salt River for the foundation of the new dam to be built at the head of the Arizona Canal extension. The rock used was from deepening of the canal. This saved the government the expense of moving the rock and saved the Arizona Canal Water Users' Association the cost of quarrying rock. Collins met March 12 with the executive board of the Arizona Canal Water Users' Association, who authorized him to put on a night shift in order to hasten the building of the dam. [3]

There still was no decision about whether the water users under the Grand, Maricopa and Salt River Valley canals would join in paying the expenses of building the rock dam. The committee appointed to consider the proposal met several hours on March 12 with Louis C. Hill, Reclamation Service engineer in charge of all of the Salt River project work, but differences persisted, and the five committeemen adjourned subject to the chairman's call. Eventually, the canals participated in the construction, which cost $3,600 instead of the $1,500 originally estimated. [4]

By the middle of March, about 250 men were employed by the government at Granite Reef, and Martin said more workers were being hired each day. The north side cable tower was almost completed, and a locomotive for the electric railroad was in Mesa awaiting transportation. The new rock dam was in evidence for half the distance across the river channel. [5]

On March 20, Hill wrote from Laguna Dam, Arizona, to Benjamin A. Fowler, president of the Salt River Valley Water Users' Association, asking him to arrange a meeting concerning the desire of the Bureau of Indian Affairs,

to sign up 10,000 acres of (Gila River Indian Reservation) land under the reservoir, for which power is to be supplied them at the reservation line, they to pay all expense of transmission lines as well as ditches within the reservation, to share equally in the general maintenance and operation cost, and to pay their share in the first cost of the project, $100,000 toward the building of this transmission line to become immediately available.

The governors had earlier been informed by the Reclamation Service of the probable surplus of power, and they had suggested the Indians take electricity from Roosevelt Dam instead of from a contemplated project of their own. The meeting was to include the governors; Hill; Joseph B. Alexander, Indian agent for the Gila River Reservation; William H. Code, irrigation engineer for the Indian Service; and possibly W. H. Sanders, a Reclamation Service engineer. [6]

The stockholders of the Appropriators' Canal Co. met March 23 and adopted a resolution proposed by Dwight B. Heard stating they favored selling the canal to the government at whatever worth it might have "as a part of the general north side water distributing system" with the value to be determined by government representatives. The resolution also called for the election of three stockholders to enter into negotiations with the local Reclamation Service officials. Heard, John P. Orme, and Patrick T. Hurley were selected as the committee. [7]

The meeting passed a second resolution requesting the board of directors to ask persons holding water contracts to agree to pay 50 cents more per acre for water service, 25 cents of it by April 1 and the rest when called for by the board, for a trust fund "for the sole purpose of the maintenance of the Appropriators' canal." It also was provided the request would not become effective unless two-thirds of those with water contracts agreed. [8]

That same day, the Salt River rose four feet, and it was feared the Arizona Canal extension would fill with sand and delay its opening. However, the following day, March 24, it was reported little or no damage occurred. [9]

The *Arizona Republican* reported March 26 the name of the Reclamation Service had been changed to the U.S. Bureau of Reclamation, and it had been separated from the U.S. Geological Survey. Frederick H. Newell was named the first director of the bureau, and Arthur P. Davis was appointed chief engineer. [10]

At an April 1 meeting of the governors, Fowler read the February 27 letter from Davis dwelling upon the urgency of adjudicating water rights. Hill, who was present, said the project was so far along the settlement must come if the work was to continue uninterrupted. He said it did not matter to the government whether the settlement was by lawsuit or by agreement. He said in all the later projects undertaken by the Reclamation Service not a dollar was spent until the old rights were adjusted. Hill said if the government had not had confidence in the people, work both at Roosevelt and Granite Reef would have ceased. [11]

The governors also heard the Interior Department plan for conveying electric power to the Gila River Indian Reservation. They were told the Indians would be in the same position as the farmers in the Valley who proposed to use power to pump water. The Indians would pay the same proportionate cost of the Roosevelt Dam construction and later their share of the maintenance and operation expense. The Indians already had $100,000 appropriated by Congress to contribute. The transmission line would be built to the northern edge of the reservation. The Indians would be responsible for extending the power line onto the reservation and to their pumping plants. The governors agreed to invite Code to more fully explain the proposition. [12]

Alexander J. Chandler returned April 6 from an automobile trip with Hill and their wives to Roosevelt and reported the water was still high but was low enough so a large force of O'Rourke's men could work upon the upper cofferdam. Another group of men, government employees, were at work on the permanent powerhouse, which was being built on the south side of the river. The building was to be 40-feet wide, 120-feet long, and rise 40 feet. The walls were to be stone three-feet thick and concrete lined. The roof was to be made with reinforced concrete with five feet of gravel above it "to stop the career of any heavy stone that might possibly roll off the canyon wall in the years to come." Windows were to be installed not less than 16 feet above the ground. The upper end of the building was to rest upon the lower face of the dam. An upper door on the canyon wall side was to exit toward the temporary powerhouse. The machinery in the temporary plant was to be moved into the permanent powerhouse, which, when completed, was intended to have six generating units, five of them furnishing 1,000 kilowatts (equal to about 1,340 horsepower each), and the sixth, 2,000 kilowatts. It was intended three of the units would be supplied with water through a penstock passing through the dam from the reservoir with a head ranging from 100 to 225 feet and developing about 3,000 horsepower, and three from the power canal with a 225 foot head and providing about 4,000 horsepower. A pump was to be installed in the powerhouse in case water somehow got inside. [13]

The Reclamation Service also planned to construct a transformer house 600 feet downriver from the powerhouse. This was to be a red sandstone building quarried from the site. It was to measure 30-feet wide and 80-feet long. Eighteen transformers were to go into the building, three for each generator in the powerhouse. The transformers were to be placed in individual concrete cells to reduce the danger from explosion or fire. The machinery in the transformer house was to be operated by push button switches at the powerhouse. The transformers were to be oil-cooled. [14]

Water was turned into the Arizona Canal at 2 p.m. Sunday, April 7. Three hundred fifty feet of the rock dam had been completed, leaving 100 feet to reach the opposite shore of the river. [15]

The next day, Hill put the cage on the cable crossing the river at Granite Reef to a different use than carrying men and supplies. He drove his automobile inside, and it was lifted over the stream to the other side. [16]

With Herman McFall as the chauffeur, an automobile carrying five men made the trip from Roosevelt to Mesa in 3

Constructing the permanent powerhouse below Roosevelt Dam, spring 1907.

hours and 54 minutes on April 13. The time included a 30-minute stop for lunch at Fish Creek Station. The climb up Fish Creek Hill was made in eight minutes. F. A. Carr and J. G. Wheelock of Phoenix drove motorcycles over the Roosevelt road to Globe. Motor vehicle trips to Roosevelt became the thing to do. [17]

U.S. District Judge Edward Kent visited Granite Reef and the Arizona Canal head and returned with high praise for engineer Hill. Kent said all the cement foundations for the intake of the canal that would carry water from the diversion dam on the south side of the river had been laid, and construction of the dam proper was just beginning. He said the importance of the diversion dam to the Valley could not be overemphasized. [18]

The Appropriators' Canal Co. published an advertisement dated April 15 notifying its stockholders that more than two-thirds of the shareholders had signed for the additional 50 cents per acre agreed to at the stockholders' meeting March 23. Secretary Emil Ganz asked for quick payment to repair breaks in the canal. [19]

The governors met April 16 with Hill, Code, Alexander, Sanders, and Orville Ensign, chief electric engineer for the Reclamation Service. Fowler read Hill's March 20 letter, then asked him to elaborate. Hill restated what had been explained to the governors earlier, adding the Reclamation Service would direct the construction of the Gila River Indian Reservation pumping plants, which were to be paid for with funds already appropriated and available for irrigation of the Indians' lands; the Reclamation Service would direct the construction of canals to draw supplementary water from the Gila River for the lands to be irrigated primarily with pumped water; the Indians would "pay the same charge for construction and maintenance for power delivered to the reservation line as that assessed generally against the lands of the Salt River project," and $100,000 of the $300,000 available for the irrigation of the Indian land would "be advanced to the reclamation fund in order to aid the immediate construction of the transmission line from Roosevelt Dam to the boundary line of the reservation." [20]

Code spoke after Hill and said a suitable place on the Salt River below the reservoir site had been found for the development of power for the Indian reservation at a cost of approximately $300,000. After he had been informed the Salt River project would have surplus power, he discussed the governors' proposal with Hill that the Indian contract for some of the electricity. Code said he thought using the surplus power would be an advantage to the Indians as well as to the Salt River project, if an arrangement could be made that followed the previously outlined plan. Arizona Governor Joseph H. Kibbey, the Water Users' Association counsel, said he foresaw no insurmountable difficulties in making an arrangement. [21]

Following some additional discussion, the governors adopted a two-part resolution. First, it was "the sense of the board that the association deal with the government in the matter of supplying power to the Indians, if they can agree upon terms to conform with the reclamation act." Second, Kibbey and Fowler were named to form a committee of two to confer with the government and to draft the appropriate contract, which was to be submitted to the governors for approval. [22]

Engineer Jay D. Stannard of the Reclamation Service visited the Mesa area to examine the Highland Canal, whose owners had proposed to Hill it be purchased by the government. Stannard had gone to determine if the canal would fit into the irrigation system and, if so, to estimate its monetary worth. Stannard evidently found the Highland had no value to the government because it was not bought. [23]

Judge Kent on April 20 denied all demurrers to the lawsuit of *Hurley v. Abbott* and gave defendants who had not done so 20 days in which to answer. Kent said he hoped to hear testimony until hot weather arrived when the trial would be suspended until sometime in September. Kent suggested the litigants be arranged in groups, with those living within a certain section of land coming in at the same time to provide their proof. Those living within each section would be given a few days advance notice. [24]

Hill and Sanders returned April 23 from a trip to Roosevelt and the Gila River Indian Reservation. Hill said O'Rourke was pushing the building of the cofferdam, but little else was happening in the river except it was falling, and it was likely work would resume soon. In the afternoon, Hill met with Fowler and Kibbey to go over the draft of the contract prepared by Kibbey for supplying electric power to the edge of the Gila Reservation. Two days later, the contract was completed and was sent to Washington for approval. [25]

The *Republican* printed a long article about the contract, saying the plan for the Salt River project contemplated the construction of power plants on the canals in addition to the powerhouse at Roosevelt Dam, and the contract with the Indians would help accomplish this. The newspaper said "all those who are posted are aware the reclamation service has no more money." Hence, there could be no assurance the estimated $500,000 needed to build the additional power plants would be forthcoming. A few days earlier, the paper had published a story from Washington, D.C., pointing out that the Reclamation Service's financial problems stemmed from the doubling and more of the costs of labor and materials in three years. The story said,

The notable increased cost of construction has compelled a revision of the original estimates on all of the large projects, and if there is not a material improvement in conditions it may be necessary to postpone further construction work on some of these projects for an indefinite period. [26]

It is doubtful the Roosevelt Dam project would have been suspended, but without additional money, parts of it might have been delayed—such as the construction of the transmission line from Roosevelt to the Valley. Keeping in mind the project on the Salt River was intended as the showpiece in the early work of the national irrigationists and that the Reclamation Service needed money, the $300,000 approved by Congress for water development on the Gila River Indian Reservation must have appeared a ripe plum. The vehicle for picking it, whether originally intended or not, was Code's proposal for using electricity to operate pumps to provide the reservation with water. The *Republican* said of the "Roughly speaking" $500,000 needed for the canal power plants, "the Indians can advance one-fifth now, and two-fifths more later on." The source of the newspaper story was not identified, but it undoubtedly was Hill. For example, Hill wanted to excavate a new crosscut canal off the Arizona Canal so a powerhouse to develop 5,000 to 7,000 horsepower could be built. Hill also wanted a power plant erected on a south side canal to produce another 1,000 horsepower. He already had calculated that once a transmission line was built, $40,000 a year could be earned through the sale of electricity to the Pacific Gas & Electric Co., which retailed power in Phoenix. [27]

The Salt River at Roosevelt flowed at 1,026 cubic feet per second on April 26, all of which was diverted through the sluicing tunnel. It was the first time since December 2, 1906, that the volume of water in the river had been small enough to send through the tunnel. Construction on the cofferdam was nearing completion, and it was hoped the work of cleaning the excavation would soon start. [28]

At the end of April, a man could walk across the rock dam at the head of the Arizona Canal extension without getting wet. About 16,000 inches of water were running in the canal, and the farmers were taking 24 hours of water per quarter section. About 40 feet of the Granite Reef Diversion Dam were completed on the south side. [29]

Reclamation engineer W. A. Parish came in from Roosevelt on May 2 and said the powerhouse was taking shape, and four miles of the high line road up Tonto Creek had been completed. At Granite Reef, the two- and one-half inch steel cable arrived in a wagon pulled by 18 horses. The cable weighed eleven and one-half tons. Carpenters were preparing the woodwork at the top of the towers on each side of the river preparatory to stretching the cable. [30]

Secretary of the Interior James A. Garfield sent the following telegram to the Salt River Valley Water Users' Association on May 3:

Form of proposed contract relative to furnishing power for pumping for Pima Indians to irrigate some ten thousand acres of land satisfactory. [31]

The governors met May 6 to consider the contract. Before approving it, Hill told them the agreement would benefit both the Water Users' Association and the Indians. He said, "without more money, it would be impossible to construct the Power Crosscut Canal on the north side of the river for a great many years." The contract provided that 1,000 horsepower of electricity be delivered to the Gila Reservation line "out of the excess power over and above that which may be needed for use by the members" of the Water Users' Association. This was understood to mean that, if the association members required all of the electric power, none would be available for the Indians. Other provisions were that no water would be delivered to the reservation; that no more than 10,000 acres could be enrolled for membership in the association, but membership was dependent upon the Indians' ownership of their land "in fee simple;" that should the 10,000 acres be enrolled, they would be subject to their proportionate share of the costs of constructing the Salt River project and to the maintenance and operation. The Gila River Indians objected to using pumped water for irrigating their lands, and the majority report of a congressional investigation in 1912 concluded the contract was part of a larger scheme participated in by Code, Hill, and Newell to cheat the Indians out of 180,000 acres of their reservation. [32]

Before the governors adjourned their May 6 meeting, a motion was made renominating Kibbey to serve as the association attorney. Some of the governors did not want to act on the reemployment of Kibbey just then, and the selection of the attorney was put off until the next meeting. [33]

The executive board of the Arizona Canal Water Users' Association met May 7 to make arrangements for the transfer of the canal to the Reclamation Service on May 15. Hill attended the meeting and said because the water was appurtenant to the land, one man could not lend his flow of water to another or sell it to him. He said the government would only provide water for the lands lately receiving it, for it was only to such lands that a supply could be reasonably assured at present. He said there would not be an additional water charge because most of the water users had paid for water to October. Lastly, he said a measuring gate would be installed at each main lateral off the canal. [34]

The morning of May 11, the **Republican** printed a short letter from Hill announcing the Reclamation Service would take over all the north side canals, except the Appropriators' Canal, on May 15. The letter said the water service charge between May 15 and October 1 would be 60 cents per acre, payable no later than June 1, and no water would be delivered "if (the) service charge remains unpaid." In addition, Hill said water users could not get "double service." He explained,

By double service is meant double quantity on any acre by purchasing from two canals, but is not intended to mean the obtaining of a one half service from each canal.
The only other source of surface water on the north side after May 15, of course, was the Appropriators' Canal. [35]

The *Arizona Gazette* said May 11 the Water Users' Association had agreed to the 60 cents per acre charge. The

Gazette said while this presumably represented a little higher price than buying water by the inch, "the government takes the canal in poor condition and will have to spend a considerable sum of money getting it in proper running order." The price of water the previous summer had been 75 cents per inch to the water right owner and $1.50 to the non-water right owner. [36]

Hill returned May 14 from a trip to Roosevelt. He said while the new cofferdam had been completed some time ago, it leaked, and it would take another four or five days before all the cracks were filled. With that, the work of cleaning out the excavation would begin. Once done, work would resume on the big dam simultaneously with continuing the excavation. [37]

A large number of water users met May 15 to try to develop amendments that would make the memorandum of agreement more acceptable. Fowler was selected chairman of the group and Elliot Evans, secretary. [38]

The night of May 15, the center of the rock dam at the head of the Arizona Canal extension washed out for a distance of about 60 feet. The break in the dam came as a surprise because there was no special rise in the river. The Reclamation Service engineers determined the dam had been undercut at the deepest part of the river, and the rock had merely been spread out downstream. Round-the-clock repair work began at once, and the **Republican** praised Hill for having ordered the quarrying of a large quantity of rock beforehand for just such an emergency. The engineers said they believed the break would be repaired by Sunday, May 20, a timetable they met. In the meantime, workers repaired the brush dam at the Joint Head so the Salt River Valley and Maricopa canals received water. [39]

The water users chaired by Fowler met again May 18 and agreed upon three amendments to the memorandum of agreement. The first provided that once three-fourths of the water users had approved the memorandum, each who had signed would withdraw any disclaimer to the lawsuit of **Hurley v. Abbott.** The second provided the water to which the user was entitled not have to be delivered from a particular canal, and the third provided for the appointment of a committee of five to correct any errors in the designation of lands classified as cultivated. The committee was to complete its work within 30 days, after which no claim for correction could be made. [40]

The following day, a statement concerning the Committee of Sixteen's work prepared by Heard and the amendments proposed for the committee's consideration were published in the **Republican.** Heard's report was intended to inform the actual water user about the meaning of the memorandum. He said it was decided "that the most reasonable method of arriving at an agreement was to base the rights of the lands to water on the actual use of water which they had received during the past 14 years." The statement pointed out the distribution of water proposed in the memorandum would not apply except in times of shortages. The tables presented in the statement were based upon the average flow of irrigation water distributed by the canals for a 10-year period less 500 inches to the Indians on the Salt River Reservation north of the Salt River. Together, the canals' daily flow totaled 24,884 inches, or the equal of 622 acre-feet per day. The amount of land classified as cultivated in the original report of the Committee of Sixteen was 125,730 acres; but in the final report it was 132,539 acres. [41]

When the governors met the morning of May 20, they elected Kibbey by a vote of six to four with one governor absent to a six-month term as attorney of the Water Users' Association. The motion for a reduced term from the customary one year was made by Ralph Murphy, an opponent of *Hurley v. Abbott*. He was supported by G. M. Halm, E. J. Bennitt, C. A. Saylor, Charles Peterson, and W. W. Dobson. Opposed to the motion were Fowler, John P. Orme, Evans, and Nelson Bradley. Gaston P. Dismukes was absent. Kibbey let it be known he would not accept a reduced term, and Heard and Fowler set about trying to undo the vote. They got the governors to meet informally in the afternoon. While Kibbey's opponents did not apologize for their vote, they were persuaded that if the governor severed his relationship with the association at that time, it could prove damaging. For one thing, *Hurley v. Abbott* was scheduled for trial May 31, and Kibbey was to represent the association. The governors adopted a sense-of-the-meeting resolution that when they met in June, they would elect Kibbey for a full year. [42]

Charles Van der Veer, secretary of the Board of Trade, was elected by the governors to be the association's new secretary. Former secretary Frank H. Parker had informed the board he no longer would be able to serve. [43]

The Committee of Sixteen met May 21 and adopted two of the three resolutions presented May 18. The third resolution, providing for the five-member board of review, was modified but not adopted. The modifications were that when the board completed its work, it would report back to the Committee of Sixteen for review, and it would act in accordance with rules that would be devised by the committee. [44]

Another meeting of the committee was held May 23. While the committee adopted rules to guide the board of review, the committee members were not satisfied with them. [45]

The trial of *Hurley v. Abbott* opened May 31. Judge Kent denied a motion for a change of venue made on behalf of the Mesa Canal on grounds he was biased. Kent said two of the district's other judges were landowners in the Valley and had disqualified themselves from hearing the case, and the remaining two judges said they were too busy in their own districts to sit in the case before September. As to the persons who filed affidavits of bias against him, Kent said it was useless to say anything to them, but he could say he had not made up his mind about anything, and he could try the case impartially. Witnesses for the plantiff were called. There were objections to the proof and motions made to dismiss the suit. All were denied. A plan then was agreed upon about how to proceed. Called to testify when court resumed June 3 were landowners who occupied the ground south of the Salt River Valley Canal and north of the Salt River in township 1

north, range 3 east, beginning with the eastern section. [46]

In Washington on June 3, Garfield signed the contract that provided for the Salt River project to deliver 1,000 horsepower of electricity to the border of the Gila River Indian Reservation. [47]

The *Republican,* on June 5, published an article in which it warned that farmers under the north side canals who did not belong to the Water Users' Association should be aware that even though they were getting their water, as they did under a private corporation, the situation had changed. The newspaper said farmers with non-member land would be likely to have to pay more for the delivery of water than members. Further, the government intended to reduce the number of canals, which meant the ditch through which the non-member got water might eventually be abandoned. The government would see to it member lands received water through a new ditch, but it would not worry about farmers who did not belong. The *Republican* cited the Grand Canal as an example of a ditch that might be abandoned in favor of a larger ditch. The newspaper said,

The moral of all this is that a man who proposes to farm in this country has got to belong to the association if he makes a success of it. This is not a threat, but merely the stating of a fact. The books of the association were closed long ago, but a waiting list has been made available for the foolish virgins who had no oil in their lamps,

Two views of Roosevelt Dam construction, June 3, 1907. Top picture looking upstream.

a sort of second chance, as it were. Anyone who owns land signed to the association and now on the delinquent list should at once prepare to get right with the powers that be. Those who have lands that were never signed to the association should get on the waiting list at the earliest possible moment. [48]

Excavation of the foundation for the Roosevelt Dam resumed June 5. [49]

The Committee of Sixteen spent a large part of June 7 trying to agree on the principles by which the board of review would be guided, then adjourned until Wednesday, June 12. [50]

Testimony in the trial of **Hurley v. Abbott** was scheduled to resume at 9:30 a.m. June 10. At the proper time, Kent took the bench, but instead of a witness being called, United States District Attorney Joseph L. B. Alexander rose and read a motion. Alexander said the United States had become the owner of the property of the defendant north side canal companies; the United States was required to distribute at its dam on the Salt River water to lands on both the north and south sides of the river; the United States had no interest or claim to the water of the Salt and Verde rivers except to fairly distribute it; because of the differing claims of landowners to the prior right to the water, "the United States has become embarrassed and unable to determine who, among the respective claimants of said prior rights of said water, are entitled to the same and have a prior right thereto as between such claimants." In order to bring about a complete determination of the water rights, Alexander asked that the United States be substituted for the defendant canal companies; that it be allowed to interplead in the case; that it be given time to prepare its interpleading; and that the trial be suspended until then. [51]

Kent, after asking the attorneys present if there were any objections (there were none), said he viewed the government's action with "great satisfaction." Kent explained he believed in determining Hurley's rights it would be necessary to determine the water priority of all the defendants in the Valley. However, he said there were a number of defendants, acting under the advice of their attorneys, who "filed what they term disclaimers" because they agreed Hurley's right to water was ahead of theirs. Having filed disclaimers, these defendants did not plan to come into court to present proof as to the date of their own water claims. If they did not, no water would be distributed to them, Kent said. "That is a situation the court viewed with regret," he said, "because I should dislike to have to make a decree that would deprive a large number of people of water, when it is a matter of common knowledge that they were entitled to water at some stage." The judge said he presumed the United States' entry into the case,

in the nature of a stakeholder, asking to come in to have the rights of these various parties adjudicated as to the water that the government shall distribute, sets at rest, I presume, any question that may have been in the mind of counsel and individuals as to the power of the court to adjudicate in the action in its present form all the rights of the various defendants. [52]

Although Kent said "the court was in the position legally to proceed to determine the various rights of the various defendants," he privately was not entirely certain of his position. Sometime before, possibly at the time of his visit to Granite Reef in April, he told Hill and Charles W. Witbeck, Reclamation Service legal counsel, he wanted the government to interplead. Kent explained since the government had bought the north side canals and would soon control the distribution of water on both sides of the river, he believed it could come into the case as a disinterested party, as a stakeholder, and have the water rights of the various parties adjudicated. Thereafter, Alexander was called into consultation by Hill and Kent. Having been assured by "Hill that it was highly desirable and earnestly requested by the Department of the Interior. . .and on the advice and suggestion of Judge Kent," Alexander entered the motion to interplead. The procedure also had been urged by Kibbey and concurred in by Fowler, who told the *Gazette:*

It is not anything new, except for the general public, who were not informed of it. Six months ago Governor Kibbey and myself were talking of just such a move as was made this morning. I will say that I believe it to be for the best interests of all. [53]

Nor was it entirely clear the government could claim the position of stakeholder without any interest in the distribution of water of the Salt and Verde rivers. The government was the trustee for Indian lands using water from the river, but Alexander contended this did not matter because there was "no question among the claimants to this water in Salt River Valley as to the right of these Indians and the lands held by them to the right to use the waters of Salt River upon such lands." [54]

In court, after Kent had expressed his approval of Alexander's motion to interplead, Alexander said he had taken the action without consulting United States Attorney General Charles J. Bonaparte. After consulting with him, Alexander said,

I may bring an independent action, and not interplead at all, the only question being which is the best; or I may, upon advice from him, withdraw all interposition in the case. [55]

Kent, after denying an objection by Attorney Walter Bennett, who had arrived later, announced he would allow the United States to be substituted as a defendant and gave Alexander until September 1 to file pleadings. Kent suspended the trial until Monday, September 23. [56]

Hill wrote to Newell on June 11 concerning the events leading to Alexander's motion to interplead. Hill urged support for the interpleading, and said it was "not intended that the United States intervene, unless it should be deemed best to do so on behalf of the Indians, who have good priority rights which should be respected." [57]

The same day, Code wrote to Garfield from Los Angeles and urged that "The Indians' rights should be settled in common with those of the whites. . .[and] the U.S. District Attorney should be instructed to represent the Indians, and see their interests are properly safeguarded." Code identified the Indians' lands as the Salt River and Fort McDowell reservations and the Lehi settlement under the Utah Canal. He said the water rights of the Indians' Maricopa Settlement, southwest of Phoenix, were adjudicated earlier.

156

Code also said the water rights of the Phoenix Indian School should be determined. [58]

The Committee of Sixteen met June 12 but adjourned until October because of the development two days earlier in the *Hurley* suit. The government's entry into the case apparently ended the career of the Committee of Sixteen. [59]

Davis arrived in Phoenix June 14 and immediately departed for Roosevelt with Hill, making the drive in eight and one half hours, including two hours spent at Granite Reef. One reason Davis may have come to Arizona was to consult with Hill concerning a contract Hill was negotiating for the sale of Roosevelt Dam electricity to the Pacific Gas & Electric Co. [60]

From Roosevelt came news the work of cleaning out the excavation was progressing smoothly, and it was anticipated work on the foundation of the big dam would resume soon. This, plus the latest development in the water suit and the work at Granite Reef, led the *Republican* to observe,

The valley's greatest prosperity is yet to come in the settlement of ten thousand families in small farm homes in the few years that are immediately to follow. What has thus far occurred has been in great measure speculative. That is the people with money realized the future and realized that valley lands were ridiculously cheap. They bought, sold and bought again, etc. But even with that, and the consequent increase of fifty per cent in the price of lands, acreage is still held at bargain prices when the productivity of the soil and water are considered, together with the possibilities of nearby markets. Lands will yet double in price, before the opportunity for even speculative profit taking shall give way to the permanent prosperity of the intensive tilling of the soil. [61]

The work of laying masonry at Roosevelt Dam began again on Saturday, June 15. This was reported by Davis upon his return from Roosevelt. Meantime, quantities of rock were piled into the river bottom to be ready for immediate use on the foundation. Hill said the trip back took five hours for an average of 16 miles an hour—12 to 15 miles an hour in the mountains and about 22 miles an hour on the desert. O'Rourke had 160 men at work. [62]

Hill, Davis, Fowler, and Orville Ensign toured the Valley on June 17, which included looking over the route proposed for the new crosscut canal south from the Arizona Canal. The crosscut was to run along the eastern side of John W. Murphy's Ingleside development and through the sandstone buttes, one of which was known as hole-in-the-rock. The final route where the penstock would be constructed for the development of hydropower had not been selected, but the *Republican* commented that with the 5,000 horsepower produced there added to what would come from Roosevelt, it was estimated there would be 12,000 to 14,000 horsepower,

available for commercial purposes. This is not an official announcement, nor a promise, but undoubtedly the government will be most anxious to sell surplus power to all comers after the pumping needs have been satisfied. The irrigation or pumping demands are first to be considered but after that there will be still a large amount of power available and nearly half of it will be right here in the valley only a few miles from where it will be used. [63]

Reclamation Service engineer Howard Reed, in charge of water distribution on the north side, announced June 20 that beginning Sunday, June 30, the canals would be paired and

water would run in them alternately for seven days at a time, always beginning on Sunday morning. The Arizona and the Maricopa would get water first, then the Appropriators' and Salt River Valley. This was a change from a six-day alternating schedule for the Arizona and the Appropriators', and four days for the Maricopa and Salt River Valley canals. Disapproval of the system came from farmers who said watering once each 14 days, instead of every eight days, would make growing table vegetables and small fruits impossible. Reed responded that persons growing such crops would receive two wettings, the first at the start and the other at the end of the run. Reed said it was intended to give each farmer the water he needed. [64]

The Reclamation Service also announced a new footbridge had been built across the river at Granite Reef, eliminating the need to transport workers in the cable basket. [65]

The Appropriators' Canal Co. was attached by the Phoenix Flour Mill for a debt of $500 and interest. This was said to be one of a number of overdue debts and notes of the Appropriators'. Some of the debtors expected the Appropriators' to be sold to the government and to receive payment out of the proceeds of the sale. [66]

The contract between the Reclamation Service and Pacific Gas & Electric Co. for the latter to buy power at a cost of one and one-half cents per kilowatt hour was signed June 22 by Hill and two utility representatives, F. H. Ensign, manager, and W. L. Percy, secretary. The contract, which at that time was not announced to the public, provided the electricity be supplied to Pacific Gas & Electric from "a power plant at the Roosevelt reservoir site or other source of hydraulic power on the Salt River" over "a transmission line or lines" the government planned on building to the Salt River Valley. The Reclamation Service agreed to provide a maximum load of 1,500 kilowatts and reserved for itself the right to sell "blocks of 100 to 500 kilowatts and over to anyone to be used for manufacturing industries, waterworks, or pumping plants" in the city of Phoenix. However, the Reclamation Service agreed that during the life of the contract, which was to extend for 10 years from the date the government began providing electricity, it would not enter "into a general retailing of power to customers in the city of Phoenix, Arizona," nor would it furnish "power to anyone in said city to be again sold or retailed." [67]

At Roosevelt, a June 28 fire in a hoisting house on the south side of the river caused one of the big cables being used by O'Rourke to drop to the river. This was the cable installed for work on the downstream portion of the dam. Hill said the fire would delay the excavation somewhat until the cable could be reinstalled. Each cable was really three cables, below the big one being suspended a second, or button line, which regulated the third, or fall line. The fall line was the one to which rock or other materials was attached. No one was injured in the incident, but damage was estimated at $10,000. [68]

The Reclamation Service announced July 8 that, beginning July 14, it would resume the former water delivery schedule. It was explained the new schedule was not intended to be permanent if it was not satisfactory to the farmers. Also it was said that should there be a flood in the river, water would be turned into all the canals. [69]

Hill and Reed toured the Valley on July 10 trying to figure out ways to conserve water, such as reducing the number of laterals. Also, they said the stealing of water would not be tolerated. This subject was raised because several locks had been broken on headgates west of Phoenix. The farmers suspected were confronted, and they readily admitted it, contending they had a moral if not a legal right to the water. The Reclamation officials said in stealing water, it was not being taken from the government, nor from a water company against whom the farmers may have held a grudge, but from neighbors and friends. Future thefts would be prosecuted, the officials said. [70]

Killer William Baldwin was hanged at 8:45 a.m. July 12 in Solomonville for the murders of Mrs. Harvey Morris and her daughter, Aminta, 5, the previous January 31 at a ranch outside Roosevelt. According to a news account,

For the first time in Arizona, two young girls witnessed an execution. They were a daughter and niece of the murdered woman, Eunice Morris, and Maggie Nelson. They came one hundred and fifty miles and begged for the privilege. Harvey Morris, the husband, missed the train and failed to arrive in time, after traveling on horseback all night. [71]

Moses Murphy, 37, was killed Sunday morning, July 14, when one of the iron skips used to lower rock and cement to the Roosevelt Dam dropped and landed on him. Murphy, a cement expert and foreman for the government, had gone alone to the dam to inspect some work, and there apparently were no witnesses. The skip was operated with electric power, but something overhead broke, allowing it to fall. Murphy's wife and four children lived at Roosevelt. [72]

Alexander received a letter July 20 from the United States attorney general directing him to protect "the rights of the Indians living on reservations" by intervening in the case of *Hurley v. Abbott,* or if Alexander believed it to be a more effective course, to bring an independent suit on behalf of the government. [73]

The *Republican* reported July 22 the upstream face of Roosevelt Dam on the south side was 13 feet above the bed of the river and on the north side four and one-half feet. In a few days, it was expected the north side would be brought to eight feet. That was as high as the engineers could carry the dam until the foundation was made wider. The newspaper said the effect of having the dam at that height was that if flood water poured over it would fill the excavation, but no damage would result. [74]

Construction of the transmission line from Roosevelt began July 22. The trail had been made for about six miles, and holes had been dug for about two miles. At Granite Reef, it was expected that 200 feet of the main dam would be completed by the end of July, and iron frames for the sluice gates on the south side were being set. The same work was expected to be completed on the north side in a few days. [75]

F. H. Ensign returned from Los Angeles on July 22 where he had gone to arrange for the purchase of machinery to equip a new substation in Phoenix for the Pacific Gas & Electric Co. to receive power from Roosevelt Dam. This evidently was the first public disclosure that the Reclamation Service had contracted with the company for the sale of power for commercial purposes. The *Republican* said, "the revenue. . .will be applied to the payment of the cost of the water storage project," which it estimated would be between $25 and $30 per acre (or double original estimates of about $15 per acre). Terms of the contract were not disclosed, but Ensign said Pacific Gas & Electric's substation would cost $60,000 to $70,000. [76]

On July 23, a small flood came down the Salt River and went over the north wall of the upper face of Roosevelt Dam. The water filled the excavation and covered the machinery, delaying work for about a week. [77]

The *Gazette* commented upon the blessings of government control of the north side canals, saying when flood waters from Cave Creek broke the Arizona Canal toward the end of July,

contrary to past custom there was no necessity for a call of this or that water users' committee and no general stockholders meeting was held to devise ways and means of repairing the damage. The reclamation officials simply gave the necessary orders and almost immediately a force of men and teams was put to work repairing the rents. There was no worry, no inconvenience, on the part of the ranchers; it was all done without their help and when they were again ready for water it was found in the big ditch as though nothing had happened. [78]

Hill on August 2 sent a telegram from Yuma to Kibbey asking him to come to Yuma to meet Garfield, who was due there the morning of August 4 and in Tempe the following morning. Hill said Garfield's party would immediately leave from Tempe for Granite Reef and from there for Roosevelt. Kibbey replied he would depart Phoenix the night of August 3. Hill also wired his secretary, S. B. Taggart, saying the party expected to reach Phoenix the evening of August 7. [79]

Garfield and the men accompanying him ate breakfast aboard a special train that arrived at the Mesa depot at 6 a.m. August 5. The train, arranged for by Epes Randolph, president of the Southern Pacific in Arizona, consisted of Randolph's private car, a private car for Garfield, and a parlor car. The party, which included Newell, Fowler, Kibbey, and Judge Richard E. Sloan of Prescott, traveled in three automobiles to the pumping plant operated by Chandler, then returned to Main Street in Mesa where members of the Chamber of Commerce presented grapes, peaches, figs, and cantaloupes to the travelers before they went to Granite Reef. They took lunch at Granite Reef about 11 o'clock and started for Roosevelt at noon. On the way, the three automobiles were joined by two others that had been stationed along the road by Hill's orders, to be ready for use in case of a breakdown or accident. The party arived at Roosevelt at 6 p.m. [80]

August 6 was spent visiting the works at Roosevelt, including the diversion dam at the head of the power canal. The party arrived in Phoenix early the afternoon of August 7. Comments made by Garfield and Newell to the press were positive about the work being done, and they expressed support for Hill, who had been attacked by newspapers in California. Garfield would not comment about the accuracy of a report that Kibbey had submitted his resignation as governor and a man would be appointed in his place who supported joint statehood for Arizona and New Mexico. [81]

Garfield and Newell were to meet with the governors that afternoon. Before they arrived, Kibbey told the governors he had discussed with Newell the problem that ranchers and farmers on school lands were unable to give the government proper security in order to gain reservoir rights. Kibbey said Newell had agreed title to the school lands should remain in the United States until Arizona became a state, and in the meantime, the lands would be permitted to receive water and would become subject to the reclamation laws. When Newell arrived, he said the problem of the school lands probably would be brought to Garfield's attention, but,

It is the policy of the secretary and the administration to encourage the territories to hold onto their land. He does not wish you to emulate the example of Ohio and other eastern states and let go school lands worth thousands of dollars to you. [82]

In other remarks, Newell recommended the governors push the *Hurley* lawsuit because "the adjustment of the water rights in the valley is of fully as much importance as the completion of the dam." Newell also spoke of the difficulty of the past year being,

One that tried men's souls and squeezed their pockets. Prices of labor have advanced 60 per cent and material has increased in cost fully one-half. Many contractors have failed, so the progress made during this time is a matter of congratulations, considering the conditions. [83]

The *Arizona Democrat,* on August 8, published an interview with Hill about the contract between the government and Pacific Gas & Electric Co. The article gave details of the contract, explaining that Pacific Gas & Electric had acquired the assets of the Phoenix Light & Fuel Co., which had a 25-year contract with the Arizona Water Co. to develop electricity at Evergreen, two miles west of Granite Reef, by carrying water through a crosscut canal to the power plant and then dumping it into the river for use by south side irrigators. Hill said the United States took over the contract when it bought the Arizona Water Co., and it had to be taken into consideration. He said,

The government was tied up with this old contract for 25 years, and we had to make mutual concessions in order to cut it down to 10 years and to get the government in complete control of the Arizona canal. We could not afford to build the Granite Reef dam and leave a private company with the right to divert all the water that belonged to the south side out of our canal and back into the river. [84]

At the end of 10 years, the government could do anything it wanted with the electricity. In the interim, Hill said it did not intend to enter the retail business, but it had reserved the right to furnish power to streetcar lines in Phoenix and elsewhere, to manufacturing plants inside the city, and to those who wanted to retail it outside of Phoenix. Previous to the contract, the worth of electricity had been estimated at $50 per horsepower a year, but the price of 36 cents per kilowatt day to Pacific Gas & Electric meant a value of about $85 per horsepower per year, Hill said. If 10,000 horsepower could be sold each year, it would bring in something like $800,000 a year to the reclamation fund, he said, adding,

High water the last week of August 1907 wrecked the footbridge in foreground.

We do not want to say that this money will be received in time to pay for the reservoir, for it is going to take time to develop all of this power. In fact, it may be 10 years before it is all developed, as the government does not expect to put in the power falls [along the canals] until it is seen that the power can be disposed of. It will tie up too much money and is going to cost a million or so to develop the power. [85]

The *Republican,* August 9, carried a report that 270 feet of the main dam at Granite Reef had been completed, 50 feet on the south side and the remainder on the north. The government had 225 men at work. Some of the work was delayed because all of the machinery for the large cable had not arrived. [86]

The directors of the Appropriators' Canal Co. met August 10 and levied an assessment of 10 cents per share "for urgent needs of the company." The assessment was to be paid by September 15. [87]

Motorcyclist Carr rode his Curtiss machine to Roosevelt in four hours and 25 minutes on August 11, the arrival time being attested to by J. C. Evans, Roosevelt justice of the peace. [88]

Hill, following a trip to Roosevelt, reported August 13 an average height of 10 feet had been reached on the upper face of the dam and progress from then on should be rapid. He said there would be no leakage of water because the dam would act as its own coffer. All water going over the dam into the excavation would be pumped out in a short time. Hill said O'Rourke had cleared out half of the excavation, and masonry was being laid. The powerhouse was going up at a rapid rate, and four miles of the transmission line had been completed. He said it would be built at the rate of about six miles per month. In the mountains, the line would be carried on steel towers set on concrete anchors, but in the Valley it would be on steel poles. [89]

The Reclamation Service announced August 16 the charge for water from October to June would be $1 per acre or $160 per quarter section. The *Republican* said this compared with $120 for the purchase of sixty-six and two-

Flood waters filled the excavation at the site of Roosevelt Dam, August 31, 1907.

thirds inches at $1.80 per inch, but it was not often the buyer got the water for which he contracted. "Under the new plan each will receive whatever he pays for," the newspaper said. The Reclamation Service also said that surplus water, when there was any, would be sold at 50 cents per acre, but this would not establish a water right. [90]

Heavy seasonal rains on the watershed put high water in the Salt and Verde rivers the last week of August, washing away at least 200 feet of the rock dam at the head of the Arizona Canal. The Joint Head of the Maricopa and Salt River Valley canals was weakened and eventually went out. The telephone to Roosevelt was knocked out. The excavation had filled with water, and work had halted. Five derricks in the riverbed were wrecked. The footbridge over the river just above Rooosevelt Dam was almost totally destroyed. [91]

On August 31, Alexander filed an "Answer and Cross Complaint" in **Hurley v. Abbott.** The court was asked to decree the right of the United States to use sufficient water to irrigate the lands on the Phoenix Indian School, the Salt River Indian Reservation, the Fort McDowell Indian Reservation, and the Lehi Settlement of the Salt River Reservation. The government requested the plaintiff, defendants and all parties to the suit establish in court their claims to water "and that the court. . .fix, determine and establish the nature, the extent and the order in time" of the claims. The government asked for 75 inches of water for the Indian School; 500 inches for 4,256.42 acres under the Arizona Canal on the Salt River Reservation, 300 inches for 1,073.2 acres under the Utah Canal on the same reservation; and 425 inches for 1,311.26 acres on the Fort McDowell Reservation. [92]

1. *Arizona Republican* (Phoenix), March 5, 1907.
2. *Ibid.,* March 7, 1907.
3. *Ibid.,* March 10, 12, 13, 1907.
4. *Ibid.,* March 13, 1907; *Arizona Gazette.* (Phoenix), May 15. 1907.
5. *Republican,* March 18, 19, 1907.
6. Louis C. Hill to B. A. Fowler, March 20, 1907, Salt River Project - U. S. Reclamation Service letter file, Salt River Project Archives (hereafter SRPA); W. H. Code to E. A. Hitchcock, January 23, 1907, SRPA.
7. *Republican,* March 24, 1907.
8. *Ibid.*
9. *Gazette,* March 23, 24, 1907.
10. *Republican,* March 26, April 2, 1907.
11. *Ibid.,* April 2, 1907.
12. *Ibid.*
13. *Ibid.,* April 7, 11, 1907, January 3, 1908, December 30, 1910;

Sixth Annual Report of the Reclamation Service, 1906-07, (Washington: Government Printing Office, 1908) p. 65; Minutes of the Salt River Valley Water Users' Association, Board of Governors, May 6, 1907.
14. *Republican,* January 3, 1908.
15. *Gazette,* April 8, 1907.
16. *Republican,* April 11, 1907.
17. *Ibid.,* April 14, 16, 1907.
18. *Gazette,* April 20, 1907.
19. *Republican,* April 20, 1907.
20. *Ibid.,* April 17, 1907.
21. *Ibid.;* Code to Hitchcock, January 23, 1907.
22. *Republican,* April 17, 1907.
23. *Gazette,* April 17, 1907.
24. *Republican,* April 21, 1907.
25. *Ibid.,* April 24, 26, 1907.
26. *Ibid.,* April 9, 26, 1907.

27. *Ibid.,* April 26, 1907; *Report in the Matter of the Investigation of the Salt and Gila Rivers—Reservations and Reclamation Service* (Washington: Government Printing Office, 1913), p. 488; Minutes of the Board of Governors, SRVWUA, May 6, 1907, SRPA; Louis C. Hill to A. P. Davis, February 7, 1907, SRPA, Hill wrote, "The Phoenix Light & Fuel Co. will probably start in with cash returns amounting to about $40,000 a year..." but Pacific Gas & Electric Co. by then had taken over the assets of the Phoenix Light & Fuel Co. and Hill's reference to that company is in error.

28. *Republican,* April 27, 1907.

29. *Ibid.,* April 28, 29, 1907.

30. *Ibid.,* May 3, 1907; *Gazette,* May 3, 1907.

31. James A. Garfield to Salt River Valley Water Users' Association, May 3, 1907, SRPA.

32. *Investigation of the Salt and Gila Rivers,* pp. 8-11; 126, 151-155, 162-166, 326; Minutes of SRVWUA, Board of Governors, May 6, 1907.

33. *Republican,* May 7, 1907.

34. *Ibid.,* May 8, 1907.

35. *Ibid.,* May 11, 1907.

36. *Gazette,* May 11, 1907.

37. *Ibid.,* May 15, 1907.

38. *Republican,* May 19, 1907.

39. *Ibid.,* May 17, 24, 1907.

40. *Ibid.,* May 19, 1907.

41. *Ibid.*

42. *Ibid.,* May 21, June 1, 1907; *Gazette,* May 20, 21, 1907.

43. *Republican,* May 21, 1907.

44. *Ibid.,* May 22, 1907.

45. *Ibid.,* May 24, June 8, 1907.

46. *Ibid.,* June 1, 1907.

47. *Investigation of the Salt and Gila Rivers,* p. 164.

48. *Republican,* June 5, 1907.

49. *Sixth Annual Report of the Reclamation Service,* p. 65.

50. *Republican,* June 8, 1907.

51. Joseph L. B. Alexander, *Patrick T. Hurley v. Charles F. Abbott et al.* Case No. 5464, Third Judicial District, Territory of Arizona, June 10, 1907, SRPA; *Gazette,* June 10, 1907; *Republican,* June 11, 1907.

52. *Hurley v. Abbott,* proceedings of June 10, 1907; *Gazette,* June 10, 1907; *Republican,* June 11, 1907.

53. Louis C. Hill to F. H. Newell, June 11, 1907; J. L. B. Alexander to Charles J. Bonaparte, U. S. Attorney General, June 17, 1907, SRPA; *Gazette,* June 10, 1907.

54. Alexander to Bonaparte, June 17, 1907; *Hurley v. Abbott,* proceedings of August 31, 1907, SRPA.

55. *Hurley v. Abbott,* proceedings of June 10, 1907; *Gazette,* June 10, 1907; *Republican,* June 11, 1907.

56. *Ibid.*

57. L. C. Hill to F. H. Newell, June 11, 1907, SRPA.

58. W. H. Code to J. R. Garfield, June 11, 1907, SRPA.

59. *Republican,* June 13, 1907.

60. *Ibid.,* June 15, 16, 1907; *Investigation of the Salt and Gila Rivers,* pp. 379-381.

61. *Republican,* June 15, 1907.

62. *Ibid.,* June 17, 1907.

63. *Ibid.,* June 18, 1907.

64. *Ibid.,* June 21, 24, 1907.

65. *Ibid.,* June 21, 1907.

66. *Gazette,* June 21, 1907.

67. *Investigation of the Salt and Gila Rivers,* pp. 379-381; *Arizona Democrat* (Phoenix), August 8, 1907.

68. *Republican,* July 2, 3, 1907; *Gazette,* July 3, 1907.

69. *Republican,* July 9, 1907.

70. *Ibid.,* July 11, 1907.

71. *Ibid.,* July 13, 1907.

72. *Ibid.,* July 16, 1907; *Gazette,* July 15, 1907.

73. C. J. Bonaparte to J. L. B. Alexander, July 15, 1907, SRPA; *Republican,* July 21, 1907.

74. *Republican,* July 22, 24, 1907.

75. *Ibid.*

76. *Ibid.,* July 23, 1907; *Gazette,* July 23, 1907.

77. *Sixth Annual Report of the Reclamation Service,* p. 65.

78. *Gazette,* August 1, 1907.

79. *Ibid.,* August 3, 1907; *Republican,* August 3, 1907.

80. *Democrat,* August 5, 1907; *Gazette,* August 5, 1907; *Republican,* August 6, 1907.

81. *Democrat,* August 8, 1907.

82. *Democrat,* August 7, 1907; *Gazette,* August 8, 1907; Board of Governors, SRVWUA, Minutes, Book 2, SRPA.

83. *Gazette,* August 8, 1907.

84. *Democrat,* August 8, 1907.

85. *Ibid.*

86. *Republican,* August 9, 1907.

87. *Ibid.,* August 20, 1907.

88. *Ibid.,* August 13, 1907.

89. *Ibid.,* August 14, 1907.

90. *Ibid.,* August 18, 1907.

91. *Ibid.,* August 30, 31, September 21, 1907.

92. *Hurley v. Abbott, Answer and Cross Complaint,* August 31, 1907, SRPA; *Gazette,* August 31, 1907; *Republican,* September 1, 1907.

September 1907 - February 1908

Governor Joseph H. Kibbey, attorney for the Salt River Valley Water Users' Association, in early September 1907 addressed the National Irrigation Congress in Sacramento, California, on the subject of water users' associations. In the course of his speech, he mentioned at least 80 percent of the landowners who might benefit from the Roosevelt reservoir had joined the Water Users' Association. He said,

The question naturally presents itself, what is the situation of the 20 percent who remain out. The answer is obvious: their rights will be ascertained by judicial inquiry, fairly, legally, but strictly measured, and thereafter respected, subject to all the variableness, uncertainty, inadequacy and unreliabiity that has heretofore characterized, and of course will hereafter attend them. Whatever of uncertainty, unreliability and inadequacy that have heretofore characterized the rights of their neighbors who have joined the association will be corrected, made reliable and adequate by recourse by them to the added supply made available by the government works. [1]

The telephone line to Roosevelt, knocked out when lines were blown together between Tortilla Flat and Mormon Flat, was restored September 5. However, repeated small floods came down the river, and contractor John O'Rourke's men were unable to resume either the excavation work or the laying of masonry on the Roosevelt Dam. [2]

The *Arizona Republican* published an article September 12 explaining the error of farmers who failed to join the Water Users' Association. Non-members were charged more for water. The newspaper said this was justified because members paid assessments to the Water Users' Association and also would pay the costs of the project. As for non-members, the *Republican* said,

Unless they are charged more for water delivery than the members are, they would have all the benefits of the members who made storage and an ample supply possible with none of the costs, worry, trouble or expense. [3]

On September 13, a train carrying 50 Italian laborers from New York arrived in Mesa. They were on their way to Roosevelt to work for O'Rourke. They went to the dam site in Shattuck & Desmond's wagons. [4]

That same day in Roosevelt, Leonicia Duarte, 7, was kicked in the abdomen by a horse and died a few hours later. She was buried next to an infant sister, who had died four days earlier. They were the children of the Rafael Duartes. [5]

The laying of masonry on Roosevelt Dam resumed Monday, September 16, but the footbridge across the river just above the dam had not been repaired, and children from Camp O'Rourke, in order to reach school in Roosevelt, either had to cross the river in one of the cable carriages or by foot over the cofferdam. Because of that few of the children were enrolled. Lumber for repair on the bridge had been hauled in, but the effort to speed work on the dam was so great laborers were unavailable to fix the bridge. The bridge was finally restored October 4. [6]

The Reclamation Service reported from Granite Reef on September 19 that the last layer of heavy rock would be placed atop the rock dam at the Arizona Canal extension that day, and by the next day, crevices in the dam would be filled and the canal would carry a full head of water. It also was revealed that Louis C. Hill, supervising engineer for projects in Arizona and Southern California, had been given the additional duties of supervising construction in New Mexico, Kansas, and Oklahoma. [7]

With the hot weather gone and construction progressing on the Roosevelt and Granite Reef dams and the transmission line, Phoenix businessmen and landowners were preparing to advertise the Valley as an attractive place for home seekers. The *Republican* printed a long article September 21 describing the fertility of the ground and detailing the rising value of the land. It pointed out that orange groves now priced at $150 per acre a year earlier could have been bought for $75 to $100 per acre. General crop lands, selling from $40 to $60 per acre 12 months earlier, were now worth $40 to $100 per acre depending upon location and other conditions. The newspaper said lands in the Valley could be expected to at least double in value in two years or go even higher. The paper said the farmers "are now revelling in prosperity" and the Roosevelt reservoir "will merely make that prosperity continuous and certain." While the estimated cost of the reservoir project had about doubled because of the development of electric power, the newpaper said,

There will be a never ending revenue that will pay for the reservoir construction in part, and perhaps entirely, or failing to do so within ten years, it will later return a dividend, so that in a quarter of a century from now the Salt River Valley will have a reservoir worth millions that did not cost it a cent, and cost Uncle Sam nothing but the interest on his money while it was loaned to the people. [8]

A correspondent from Roosevelt reported that on the morning of September 21, three large stones were blasted out in the No. 1 quarry and one of them, weighing an estimated 20 tons, struck a derrick and broke half of it to splinters. The workmen immediately began construction of a new derrick. Meanwhile, one of four derricks at work on the dam toppled when a large stone it was raising struck a leg and smashed it. Three of the derricks were used for laying stones and the other was used for excavation at the downstream end of the dam site. The contractors were laying stone to bring the back of the dam to the height of the face. [9]

Judge Edward Kent on the morning of September 23 resumed the case of *Hurley v. Abbott.* United States District Attorney Joseph L. B. Alexander, who had filed an answer and cross complaint on behalf of the federal government August 31, said he wanted some sort of response before going to the expense of printing the pleading he had filed. Alexander said the response might come in the form of objections from attorneys to whom copies had been sent. Several attorneys wanted delays to examine the government's cross complaint. Kent said that, while opposing attorneys were deciding what sort of response they would make, there was no reason why testimony in the case should not continue. Kent said testimony would be taken up the following morning, but instead, he issued an order the next day admitting the government's answer and cross complaint and directing all parties to show why they should not be required to establish the priority of their water claims. [10]

Attorney Walter Bennett moved on various grounds on October 2 to strike the United States' answer and cross complaint from the lawsuit. A number of water users under the Tempe Canal also filed objections to the government's entry into the suit. However, Kent, on October 4, overruled the objections and ordered that all answers previously filed in the case stand as answers to the cross complaint. He gave those who wanted to submit a different answer or to enter a pleading 20 days in which to do it. Kent also restated he welcomed the government's entrance into the case because it precluded the possibility anyone legally entitled would be deprived of water. [11]

Dwight B. Heard, as a member of a committee from the Appropriators' Canal Co., which was appointed to confer with the Reclamation Service concerning the latter's interest in acquiring the canal, met October 6 with Hill. Heard, in connection with the annual meeting of the canal company scheduled for two days later, asked Hill for a letter explaining where matters stood. Hill wrote the letter, which was presented at the Appropriator's meeting. Hill said:

I have had a survey made of both the Grand and Appropriators' canals to determine what portion of the Appropriators' canal would be of service in the future system of irrigation in the Salt River Valley. From time to time I have taken this matter up with your committee and with Washington. From correspondence I feel certain that negotiations continued along the line indicated in your resolution will be favorably passed upon in Washington so the property may be turned over to and operated by the United States in the near future. I would advise pending these negotiations that your water contracts be made co-existent with ours. [12]

The present indebtedness of the company was $37,000. It was estimated that $18,000 would be needed to operate in the next year, so the shareholders voted to deliver water at $1.25 per acre for the season. They also agreed not to deliver water to land not already receiving it and to deny water to any stockholder who was delinquent in payments. The stockholders elected as directors Charles Goldman, John P. Orme, A. M. Fredericks, Hosea Greenhaw Jr., and H. M. Welborn. A few days later the directors elected Orme president. [13]

Hill and Kent returned October 8 from a visit to Roosevelt and reported the upper face of the dam was 10 to 13 feet above the level of the riverbed. From there, it sloped downstream for about 110 feet, or two-thirds of the intended width of the foundation. For the remaining one-third of the intended width, no rock had been laid, and a large part of the foundation itself was two to five feet below datum, or the bed of the river. About 23,000 yards of masonry had been laid, leaving about 17,000 yards to complete the foundation. [14]

A reporter for the *Republican* visited Granite Reef on October 13 and found 450 feet of the dam foundation had been completed, 350 feet of it on the north side, all on a solid rock bed. A cofferdam had been built to divert the water from a 175-foot section where the work was then in progress, that section being a part of 450 feet in the sandy riverbed where bedrock had not been reached and "through which the water runs like a sponge." The workmen were constructing an apron 19 feet below the sand of the riverbed. Work on the dam had been delayed because of the failure of the sellers of the big cable to supply the carriers, but the Reclamation Service had arranged for some temporary buckets, and these were to go into service within a few days. Because the cable had not been in operation, the cement for the dam, head gates and sluiceway on the north side had to be hauled by teams. In addition, a rock quarry had to be opened on the north side. This meant the rock quarry and railroad on the south side had been virtually useless. But now that the temporary buckets were almost installed, it meant these could be used, reducing both time and expense. [15]

The headworks, diversion gates, sluiceway, and all auxiliary works had been completed on the south side and were within a short time of being completed on the north side. Construction went on seven days a week with 70 men working the night shift and 175 the day shift. [16]

The Reclamation Service was busy restoring the dredge it had acquired when it bought the north side canals. Once done, its first job would be to widen the head of the Arizona Canal. It would then be floated to a point near Scottsdale and work its way back upstream. It was estimated the dredge could clear away 1,500 yards of material every 24 hours. [17]

A meeting of the Phoenix and Maricopa County Board of Trade was scheduled October 14 to consider advertising the Valley to attract settlers and to raise money for that purpose. The *Republican,* commenting on the meeting, said,

The purpose is in no sense a philanthropic one. What the Valley wants to do is to help itself and if it can help others at the same time the incentive is still greater. It is one time when both parties can make a profit on a transaction. The few who contend that it is too soon to advertise should bear in mind that it is not flash in the pan advertising that pays but steady and persistent work whether the magnitude be large or small and the larger the plan of action, if persistently followed, the greater the results proportionate with the investment.

The newspaper said no country had as much to offer as the Salt River Valley to "farmers who have a few dollars, enough to buy themselves homes and enter upon the tilling of the soil under circumstances more favorable than can be found anywhere else." The paper said the purpose of the advertising was to present the Valley "as a place for home building" in keeping with the intent of the reclamation law, and not speculation. It said the results of the advertising could not be expected for a year, which would be about the time water should be in storage behind Roosevelt Dam. [18]

All the speakers at the meetings were in agreement about the need to advertise the Valley, and almost all had the same observation—people may have heard frequently about Roosevelt Dam and occasionally about Phoenix, but they did not connect the two. In addition, some of the people confused the Laguna Dam with Roosevelt Dam, and they knew little about the lands to be served under them. There also was agreement that better railroad connections at Maricopa would encourage more people to make a side trip to the Valley. Travelers disliked waiting overnight at

Maricopa or being delayed several hours in getting the train to the Valley. C. M. Scott, superintendent of the Maricopa & Phoenix railroad, arrived at the meeting just as it adjourned. Learning about the criticism, he said the railroad was willing to cooperate, and he had made efforts in that direction, such as running special trains at a loss, or going to Maricopa in his motor car and bringing travelers to the Valley. [19]

Reclamation Service officials announced October 14 that widening of the Grand Canal would begin by the end of the week or early the following week. The widening was expected to take one to one and one-half years. On the western part of the canal, starting near the Phoenix Indian School, the bottom of the canal was to be widened to 34 feet, gradually narrowing as the amount of land to be watered lessened. The Reclamation Service could not say what would be done along the eastern portion of the canal because it ran so close to the Appropriators', and could not be enlarged without making some sort of arrangement, such as buying or otherwise acquiring the Appropriators'. [20]

Sales of winter water ended the evening of October 16, and the Reclamation Service reported the next day that $41,894 had been paid by farmers under the Arizona, Maricopa and Salt River Valley canals. Most of the water was sold at $1 per acre to association members. Officials said no more than a half-dozen non-members paid for water, which meant that more than 41,000 acres were to be cultivated. [21]

Late the night of October 17, Pinal Creek, which runs by Globe in Gila County, discharged about 3,000 cubic feet of water per second into the Salt River above Livingston. Early the next day, the flood covered the Roosevelt Dam, filled the excavation, and submerged three derricks. That afternoon, a flood of about 3,000 cfs came down Tonto Creek, so that about 6,000 cfs ran at the dam. At Granite Reef, the men used the big cable to remove machinery and equipment from the low points along the river. [22]

The night of October 19, Hill returned from a visit to the Arizona Canal head and said about 70 feet of the crest of the rock dam had been washed over, and there was damage to the canal. However, there was still water in the canal, while the Appropirators', Maricopa, and Salt River Valley canals ran bank full. [23].

The river fell and on October 20, laborers were put to work repairing the lower cofferdam at Roosevelt. Repairs also were made to the Arizona rock dam. [24]

Kent, the morning of October 21, set the case of *Hurley v. Abbott* for further trial on November 25. He said proof would be taken under the Salt River Valley canal in township 1 north, range 2 east, westward through the cultivated land. [25]

Additional rains brought expectations the Salt River would rise again, and on October 24 the river was again flooding at Roosevelt but was not as high as before. The flow reached 4,532 cubic feet per second at Roosevelt and was slowly rising, with the greater part of the water coming from Tonto Creek. At the Arizona head, the flow was 2,007 cfs. [26]

The river below the mouth of the Verde River rose to 9,000 cfs on October 25, and for the next few days

maintained a good run. By October 29 at Roosevelt, the river had fallen sufficiently to divert the full flow through the sluicing tunnel. The back flow through the lower cofferdam had to be stopped, but O'Rourke hoped to resume laying masonry by the end of the first week in November. A larger problem was the scarcity of labor. Because the laborers could not know how long the floods would last, and their expenses of not less than $1 per day continued, they would seek employment elsewhere. Work resumed on the Arizona rock dam, which survived the latest flood without much more damage. [27]

Reclamation engineer A. H. Demrick arrived in the Valley to prepare for the survey of the transmission power line from Mesa to the Gila River Indian Reservation border. [28]

At Roosevelt, Mrs. Morris Williams closed out her interest in the boarding house she had operated in the large tent formerly used for the camp hospital. Mrs. B. B. Warnock, who had been living on the O'Rourke side of the river, succeeded her. Mrs. Warnock was said to be an experienced restaurant woman. Charles Mow, "a Chinaman, who had been in the restaurant business in Roosevelt for several months, died suddenly from hemorrage of the lungs." [29]

Another rise in the Salt River on November 3 put more water over the upper face of the dam at Roosevelt and into the excavation. The hydraulic pumps were put to work removing the water, and by the morning of November 5 the masonry work began again. The *Republican's* correspondent reported November 15 an average of 500 cubic yards of masonry were laid each day, and the roof was ready to be installed upon the powerhouse. [30]

Attorney Alexander on November 13, in response to a letter from George W. Hance of Camp Verde about *Hurley v. Abbott,* wrote he would ask Kent to appoint a commissioner to take depositions from Verde Valley residents when the time arrived to take testimony from them in the case. Hance had written there were about 140 residents of the Verde Valley interested in the litigation, and it would save money if their testimony could be taken there. [31]

The big dredge was put to work the morning of November 20, its goal to expand the capacity of the Arizona Canal from 40,000 to 80,000 inches of water. The dredge was floated down the canal about a mile before starting to work back toward the head gates. [32]

Testimony in *Hurley v. Abbott* resumed November 25 as scheduled. Evidence about lands under the Appropriators' Canal began November 27. [33]

F. W. Griffin and Earl Brown drove motorcycles to Roosevelt on November 27. On their return, Griffin wrote an account, saying,

The work on the dam was in active progress and from the high road several hundred feet about the scene of operations, the brilliantly lighted canyon was a beautiful sight. . . Taking advantage of the present conditions, the contractor is pushing the work night and day. Rock is taken from the quarries during the night and placed in convenient locations where the workmen on the day shift can make the best use of it. The night workmen were a sociable lot and kindly offered to allow Mr. Brown and the writer to take a view of operations from the cable across the canyon. This cable is four hundred and fifty feet high. It was too good an opportunity to be missed and on one of the empty skips on which rock is let down from the quarry, the ascent was made. . .A sensation is felt while swinging and swaying that distance in the air with nothing between one and eternity but a few pieces of iron forming a small platform about ten feet square. . .The big arc lights in the pit look like small candles way down below. [34]

About 10 a.m. December 4, a large quantity of water going down the Approrpiators' Canal caused a break near the Phoenix Indian School. News of the break was carried a short distance to the Reclamation Service force engaged in enlarging the Grand Canal. Under the direction of K. W. Sibley, about 30 men went to the point of the break in the Appropriators' Canal. Using lumber and sacks filled with dirt they stopped the break in about an hour. [35]

That afternoon, the *Arizona Gazette* reprinted an article from the *Prescott Journal-Miner* saying the Verde Valley water users had passed a resolution thanking Alexander for agreeing to the appointment of a commissioner to take their testimony in *Hurley v. Abbott.* Hance, a pioneer of the Verde Valley, said the people "are naturally indignant over the insinuation of the suit. . .They deplore the action of the water users of the Salt River Valley in instituting the suit, but have full confidence that the courts will give ample opportunity to every settler to show his rights to the use of the water." Hance said farmers had 8,000 acres of land under cultivation, and they were watered from 67 ditches. [36]

Hill said the footing and foundation for the first 100-foot section of the Granite Reef Diversion Dam, beyond the point where it left bedrock, had been completed. Despite the cofferdam to divert the river water, enough percolated through the dam and the ground below to keep several large pumps busy. [37]

The Reclamation Service sent letters to Salt River Valley farmers asking them to supply statements concerning their successes through "the most difficult irrigation period of the entire year." The service asked the farmers to detail "the amount of your crops, the methods employed in cultivating the same, the costs of production and profits received therefrom." The letter said the information was not prompted by curiousity,

but by a sincere wish to know what can be and is done in the Salt River Valley, which was the first to receive attention under the national irrigation act and which has been, and still is, considered the banner project of the many now under construction. . . .

The information was to be forwarded to the director of the Reclamation Service for use in demonstrating to the Eastern section of the nation the advantages of irrigated country. [38]

Demrick reported the crew installing the foundation for the transmission line towers was at Mormon Flat and would soon move to Government Well. [39]

Excavation on the north side of the Roosevelt Dam site was finished the night of December 7, while at Granite Reef the dam from the north side was completed for 580 feet, and the foundation for another 140 feet had been brought up to water level. That left 280 feet of foundation to build, and a cofferdam was being constructed around the next 75-foot section of that distance. [40]

Hill returned December 24 from a visit to Roosevelt and reported the contractor was almost "out of the woods" insofar as the work being stopped by flood waters. Hill drew a diagram of the work for a *Republican* reporter, who described it this way:

Though it is slightly curved, in a general way the foundation of the dam is a parallelogram. The upper face of the dam for about one-quarter of the distance from the north bank of the river, is about nine feet above datum or normal water level. From the point last described to the south bank of the river the face is from twenty to twenty-two feet above the datum. The down-stream or lower face of the dam is about four feet above datum at the north bank

Electric car hauling tubs of rock to site of Granite Reef Diversion Dam.

and for a quarter of the distance across the river. From that point to the south bank the lower face is five or six feet above datum. Dividing the dam into three sections, the dividing lines running parallel with the river, it might be said that the north section is nine feet above datum on the upper side and four feet above on the lower side, retreating from these two walls to a point in the center of the section where the foundation is still considerably below datum; a hole or sump as it were. The other two sections are twenty-two feet above datum on the upper side and six feet above on the lower side. Next to the south bank the working surface of the dam would present a series of steps like the face of the pyramids, from the lower face of the dam to a point a few feet back of the upper face. Toward the north section there is less work done, the south end of the dam being kept ahead all the time. [41]

Hill said the work had reached a point at which the upper coffer dam had about outlived its usefulness and one day soon would be blown up with powder. He said the upper face of the north end of the dam would not be constructed any higher before the winter floods, so that when the water came, the north end would serve as a sluiceway. The running of the water would cause no harm, he said, and once the floods were passed, the laying of rock would resume. About 10,000 yards of rock were being laid each month with about eight feet being gained per month in the height of the dam. [42]

The work of installing the big gates in the sluicing tunnel was to start in a few weeks. While this was being done, the entrance to the tunnel was to be sealed. But before that, it was hoped the entire foundation of the dam would be up to datum, but the tunnel would be closed in any case before the winter floods. [43]

Hill also reported the electric railroad at Granite Reef would soon be taken to Roosevelt where it would connect the cement mill and the clay banks. [44]

Thomas McGraw, who worked in the cement mill, died Christmas day when his left arm was caught in some machinery and torn from his body. McGraw was attempting to enter the bin area of the mill through a low door when he suddenly lost his footing, and he thrust his arm forward to balance himself, his arm catching in the machinery. He died almost immediately. Little was known about him except that at one time he had been a sailor and was said to be about 60. [45]

Material was delivered to construct a telephone line between Roosevelt and Mesa and then to Sacaton on the Gila River Indian Reservation. The telephone line was to operate in connection with the transmission line to the reservation's edge. Four railroad cars of copper wire arrived at Mesa for the transmission line. It was estimated that 1 million pounds of copper would be used in the line. Where the line crossed cultivated areas, it was to be at least 35-feet high, and where it crossed railroad lines, 40 feet. [46]

The upper face of Roosevelt Dam was 28 feet above datum except for where the water was expected to pass over on the north side when the river was in flood stage. [47]

By January 5, 1908, visitors just returned from Granite Reef reported that from the north bank of the river the dam was finished to water level for about 700 feet and from the south bank 38 feet. There remained 262 feet of foundation to lay. The Arizona rock dam was in good shape and the canal carrying all the water it could hold. [48]

Upstream face of Roosevelt Dam, January 5, 1908.

Work on the Roosevelt Dam the week of January 5 was confined to filling the excavation and it was completed to within two feet of datum. The highest point on the south side was 30 feet above datum. [49]

The *Republican* on January 15 reprinted an article from the *Los Angeles Times* about the gates that were to be installed in the sluicing tunnel at Roosevelt Dam. The story said the gates had been manufactured in Los Angeles by the Llewellyn Iron works at a cost of $200,000 "and are the main mechanical features of the stupendous project." The article continued,

At almost the last minute, the government had the misfortune to smash one of the costly parts of the equipment, an immense bronze casting, and this is being replaced at great cost at the Los Angeles foundry. Fortunately for the local manufacturers, the accident occurred after the casting had been delivered to the government and the loss will fall on the United States.

The gates, of which there are six, are to be used in a great sluicing tunnel at the side of the dam—a water passage that is 10 x 13 feet in size for most of its length, widening out into a roomy chamber at the point where the gates are to be installed.

There are two sets of three gates each, and each gate has an opening measuring 4-1/2 x 10 feet. One set will be known as the service gates and will be in constant use, except when repairs may be needed; then the other set provided for cases of emergency, will come into play.

Each of the six gates weighs ten tons. There are more than 400 tons of material in all. Seventy tons of bronze is used in the working faces of the gates, this provision being required because of the large proportion of salt carried by the water, which would cause corrosion of the iron if that material alone were to be used. . .

The gates are of what is known to engineers as the Stoney type. They will operate under the heaviest pressure of any of the same type in use in the world. There will be a depth of 230 feet of water above the gates—a tremendous pressure. The gates will be operated by hydraulic cylinders and will be easy of manipulation.

It will probably take sixty days to install the gates, when the Llewellyn works will receive the last payment on its contract. The work will be in the charge of Walter Taylor, vice president of the local concern, and will be under the supervision of the United States engineers at the head of the big project. . . .

It was a good deal of a task to get the 400 tons of material for the gates from Los Angeles to the dam. Roosevelt is seventy miles from Mesa, a railroad station on the Southern Pacific, fifteen miles beyond Phoenix. From Mesa all of the material was hauled by government wagon trains to the same site. . . . Many wagons broke down under the load of the heavy castings, but this was a matter of no local concern. [50]

Hill, on January 25, said,

Both the Roosevelt and Granite Reef dams are so high above water level now that no flood can delay their construction, unless it is an extraordinary flood, such as that of 1905, and that but for a day or two, while it is pouring over.

He said the north end of Roosevelt Dam was now practically all above datum, the lower end being four feet above water level and the upper face nine feet. At Granite Reef, he said the foundation had been completed across the portion of the river where bedrock could not be reached and had been anchored to the south side bedrock. He said it would be a short time until the entire foundation was up to water level. [51]

Demrick reported three carloads of the steel needed to fashion the 624 towers between Roosevelt and the Highland Canal were on their way. He said the towers should arrive at the rate of 60 or 70 per week until all were in. He expected the cement work for the tower foundations to be completed by the end of January. Demrick said four miles of service telephone line to parallel the transmission line had beem completed between Mormon Flat and Government Well. [52]

Speculation on the exact route of the Eastern Canal, east of Mesa, continued to run high, and the **Republican** reported all the lands that could possibly come under it had been filed upon by homesteaders. The generally accepted route was that the canal, beginning north of the Roosevelt road, would be a half-mile to the east of and parallel to the Highland Canal, but that south of the road, the distance between the canals would be a quarter-mile. At some point farther south, it was said the Eastern Canal would cross the Highland to the west. Delay in the canal's construction was blamed on the financial panic of 1907. [53]

The **Gazette** published an account January 27 of a trip to

Flood waters washing over the Roosevelt Dam construction site, February 4, 1908.

Roosevelt written by one of its reporters, who said the first thing he noticed when boarding the stage in Mesa was the driver had a revolver in a holster on the side of the boot. The weapon was there because of a recent order from the government to thwart any robbery attempts. Including the starting team of four horses, the animals were changed five times so that 20 different horses were used. Freight was carried on the stage at the rate of 2 cents per pound. The cost was 1 cent shipped by wagon. [54]

Workmen began planking shut the entrance to the sluicing tunnel at the start of February, but rains on the watershed sent a flood down the Salt River on February 4. This was the first flood in three months, and for the people at Roosevelt it provided a dramatic change from earlier ones. The erection of the dam had created a small lake because the river flow had exceeded the capacity of the sluicing tunnel. Now, with the sudden rise, the water ran over the dam and showed the people of the town the dam had reached a height where it would not be long before the water backing up would endanger the community. And, indeed, Reclamation Service engineers already had begun surveying for a new Roosevelt. [55]

The peak flow of 79,000 cubic feet of water per second was measured at 11:30 a.m. and it remained at that level for several hours. The water deposited a considerable amount of sediment in the sluicing tunnel and carried away two of the derricks used in the dam building. The footbridge to Camp O'Rourke was torn to pieces, but before it broke it served as a dam for trees and limbs that came down the river. The water reached to within a few inches of the powerhouse floor and soaked more than 200 sacks of cement, which were to be used in the building. The water flooded the Roosevelt road, delaying the stages in both directions for a few days. [56]

At the Arizona rock dam, the water rose from 20,000 cubic feet per second to 60,000 cubic feet per second in the 30 minutes between 8 and 8:30 a.m. The flood completely washed away 100 feet of the dam and damaged it for a few hundred feet more. It took out the suspension bridge upstream of the dam. Work on the Granite Reef Diversion Dam halted, but the damage was not great, and the water fell rapidly the following day. [57]

The **Republican** took the occasion to recall the coming submersion of Roosevelt would not be the first time a community in Arizona had ended in that fashion. The newspaper said,

It was the occasion of the construction of the Walnut Grove dam a great many years ago. A village almost as large as the town of Roosevelt grew up in the basin during the construction period partly of the men employed and partly of miners and cattlemen operating in that vicinity that made it headquarters as long as the town remained. But when the big dam was finished, the town was mostly moved away and the rest of it submerged, remaining so until the dam, which was defectively constructed, gave way one awful night a few years later, swept destruction before it down the Hassayampa river and bringing death to between one and two score of people who lived below the dam. [58]

The laying of masonry at Roosevelt resumed February 8, and carpenters began again to build bulkheads to close the sluicing tunnel. On February 11, the government's head carpenter, George Greenwald, 33, was killed when a raft loaded with lumber was carried through the floodway at the north quarter of the dam. Greenwald and two other carpenters were guiding the raft toward the tunnel when it got too far out into the river. Two of the men jumped into the water and swam to shore, but Greenwald stayed with the raft, apparently trying to save the lumber. As the raft started over the dam, a rope was thrown to Greenwald from a bridge suspended between the dam and the land. Observers said he did not seem to understand the situation and made no effort to save himself. The raft tipped as it hit the stones at the downstream end of the dam, and Greenwald was pitched into the water. Greenwald had come to Phoenix from California about a year before construction began on the Roosevelt Dam and had married Selma Johnson. They had one child. [59]

Construction of the transformer house began February 12. The Reclamation Service also announced that a second crew would be formed to work on the transmission line, one crew working in the mountain section and the other in the desert. The river rose again February 16, but it was for a short time, and the main thing it did was put water into the sluicing tunnel over the bulkhead. The highest point on the dam was thirty-seven and one-half feet above datum by February 22 and 13 feet on the downstream face. [60]

The first tower on the transmission line was raised February 24, and by the end of the week more than a half-mile of them were up. Twelve men were employed in assembling the towers and about half that number in raising them. Also during the week, the penstock from the power canal to the powerhouse was completed. [61]

Hill attended the annual meeting of the Mesa Canal Co. on February 27 and revealed the government intended to buy the Consolidated Canal Company. Hill said that, while no deal had been completed, arrangements for the purchase were being made. He also described the course of the future Eastern Canal, saying it would intersect with the Highland Canal, about four miles east of Mesa. [62]

1. *Arizona Republican* (Phoenix), September 5, 1907.
2. *Arizona Gazette* (Phoenix), September 5, 1907.
3. *Republican,* September 12, 1907.
4. *Ibid.,* September 14, 1907.
5. *Ibid.,* September 21, 1907.
6. *Ibid.,* September 21, 23, October 13, 1907.
7. *Ibid.,* September 20, 1907.
8. *Ibid.,* September 21, 1907.
9. *Ibid.,* September 29, 1907.
10. *Ibid.,* September 24, 25, 1907.
11. *Ibid.,* October 3, 5, 1907.
12. *Ibid.,* October 8, 1907.
13. *Ibid.*
14. *Ibid.,* October 9, 1907.
15. *Ibid.,* October 14, 1907.
16. *Ibid.*
17. *Ibid.*
18. *Ibid.*
19. *Ibid.,* October 15, 1907.
20. *Ibid., Gazette,* December 4, 1907.
21. *Republican,* October 18, 1907.
22. *Ibid.,* October 19, 1907.
23. *Ibid.,* October 20, 1907.
24. *Ibid.,* October 22, 24, 1907.
25. *Ibid.,* October 22, 1907.
26. *Ibid.,* October 25, 1907.
27. *Ibid.,* November 5, 1907.
28. *Ibid.,* October 30, 1907.
29. *Ibid.,* November 5, 1907.
30. *Ibid.,* November 10, 18, 1907.
31. *Gazette,* December 4, 1907.
32. *Ibid.,* November 20, 1907; *Republican,* December 4, 1907.
33. *Republican,* November 27, 28, 1907.
34. *Ibid.,* November 29, 1907.
35. *Gazette,* December 4, 1907.
36. *Ibid.*
37. *Republican,* December 4, 1907.
38. *Ibid.,* December 6, 1907.
39. *Ibid.,* December 8, 1907.
40. *Ibid.,* December 9, 10, 1907.
41. *Ibid.,* December 25, 1907.
42. *Ibid.*
43. *Ibid.*
44. *Ibid.*
45. *Ibid.,* January 3, 1908.
46. *Ibid.*
47. *Ibid.*
48. *Ibid.,* January 6, 1908.
49. *Ibid.,* January 17, 1908.
50. *Ibid.,* January 15, 1908.
51. *Ibid.; Gazette,* January 25, 1908; *Republican,* January 26, 1908.
52. *Republican,* January 24, February 2, 1908.
53. *Ibid.*
54. *Gazette,* January 27, 1908; *Republican,* January 18, 1908.
55. *Republican,* February 5, 12, March 7, 12, 1908.
56. *Ibid.,* February 12, March 5, 1908.
57. *Gazette,* February 4, 1908; *Republican,* February 5, 6, 1908.
58. *Republican,* February 7, 1908.
59. *Ibid.,* February 14, 19, 1908.
60. *Ibid.,* February 19, 26, 1908.
61. *Ibid.,* March 5, 1908.
62. *Ibid.,* February 29, 1908.

March - August 1908

The actual work of installing the sluicing tunnel gates began March 2. The bulkhead at the entrance to the tunnel had been raised and strengthened to keep water and sand out should a second flood come. Another bulkhead was constructed for the tunnel exit to keep water from backing in. [1]

Supervising engineer Louis C. Hill of the Reclamation Service reported March 3 that 9,000 cubic yards of rock were laid at the Roosevelt Dam in February. He said the upstream face of the dam was at 40 feet above datum and the downstream face 25 feet, except for approximately the north one-third where 2,500 cubic feet of water per second was pouring over. This section remained at 9 feet above datum on the upstream face and 4 feet on the downstream end. Hill said this section would remain as it was until the water could again be sent through the sluicing tunnel. He said the volume of water the sluicing tunnel could handle would increase from the present 1,200 cubic feet per second by about three times when the water depth was 50 feet and to about 10,000 cubic feet per second when the reservoir was full. [2]

At Granite Reef, Hill said the foundation for the diversion dam was completely across the stream and about 500 feet of the main dam had been finished. On the south end, virtually everything in the way of work that could be done had been completed. On the north side, everything would be finished by the middle of the following week except for cutting into the Arizona Canal. [3]

The *Arizona Republican* said March 4 the Reclamation Service reportedly was willing to buy the Appropriators' Canal for $13,000. This amount was not agreeable to the canal company's creditors, who were owed $28,000. It was suggested an assessment be levied on the stock of the company to raise the $15,000 difference so the government could acquire the canal. The shareholders met March 7 and levied an assessment of 50 cents per share. [4]

Another flood came down the river at Roosevelt on March 4, but the water did not go over the entire dam because the portion to the south was nine feet higher than when the flood came in February. The effect of the flood was to delay work the afternoon of March 4 and the morning of the following day. On March 7, the flow reached 20,000 cubic feet per second, all of it going over the lower end of the dam. [5]

The last of the testimony in *Hurley v. Abbott,* except for "some loose ends," was heard March 13, 1908. [6]

On March 15, the *Republican* carried an item about the sale of two orchards—the first of 40 acres for $200 per acre and the second of 20 acres, including 10 acres in oranges, for $600 per acre. The paper said the highest quotation was only about 50 percent of prices for similar land in California. [7]

It was about this time too that what may have been the first cement lining of an irrigation ditch in the Valley was completed. The *Republican* said it had been thought when the government took over the north side irrigating system

the ditches would be lined with cement, and George H. Halm was among the first landowners to inquire about it. When it was determined that could not be done under the National Reclamation Act, the Reclamation Service nevertheless agreed to supply cement at its cost. The government engineers also leveled the ditch and provided specifications for the lining, which was completed under a contract Halm and William J. Murphy made with M. L. Vieux. The lining involved more than a quarter-mile of irrigating ditch between the lands of Halm and Murphy. [8]

In a March 17 article from its Washington correspondent, the *Republican* quoted Reclamation Service statistician C. J. Blanchard about the good feeling he had found upon a visit to the Valley:

If I were asked what one thing attracted my attention most, I would say it was the atmosphere of cheerful optimism which seems to prevail everywhere. The crops of 1907 were the best for many years, owing to the more satisfactory distribution of water among the irrigators, for which, I understand, the reclamation service is entitled to some credit as it had charge of the apportioning of water in the several canals. The whole valley is awakening and the number of new settlers is surprising. I was particularly interested to note, among the new comers, several practical orange growers from California, who are already starting new groves. They expressed themselves as much pleased with the outlook for this industry.

There was a time in the valley, and not so very long ago, when the condition was one of discouragement, almost despair. The water supply was not dependable. No man felt sure of a crop. Today all is changed. Every man has become a booster. All are sure that with the close of the diversion dam at Granite Reef and the completion of the great Roosevelt dam, the future is sure. [9]

The Board of Governors of the Salt River Valley Water Users' Association, preparing for the annual election in April, ruled that no person would be permitted to vote unless in possession of a deed to the property signed with the association. This exluded from voting persons buying land on time, farming under a lease, or cultivating school lands. Nonetheless, the number of persons eligible to vote rose from 1,455 in 1907 to 1,573 in 1908. The increase was cited as an indication the number of large holdings of more than 160 acres was being reduced. It also meant in some instances husbands, wives, and adult children became sole owners of their individual 160 acres. [10]

In late March, the first setting of the service gates in the sluicing tunnel at Roosevelt Dam was finished. The first of the gates was about 150 feet from the mouth of the tunnel and just forward of the upstream face of the dam. Two pillars were constructed for each gate. The *Republican* reported,

The gate and its setting can well be compared to a window with its frame work. The casing of this windowlike construction is of bronze and the castings are all put together with bronze bolts and the gates rest on bronze wheels about six inches in diameter which run on grooves in the bronze casing. It will be seen that all parts on which there is great wear are made of bronze which is the most enduring of metals. The gates are of solid cast iron a foot thick, six feet wide and measure ten feet long. The pressure of the water against these gates will depend of course upon the amount of water

Laying masonry on south side of Roosevelt Dam, circa March 1908.

in the reservoir but the maximum pressure will be about 600,000 pounds. It will require considerable power to raise the gates which are heavy in themselves and with the pressure of the water against them the resistance is much increased. They will be operated by water power. Every piece of casting in the gates has been perfectly made and matched at the factory so it is not necessary to make the smallest alteration in the fittings.

At the entrance to the sluicing tunnel, an arched grate made of steel bars and concrete was erected to stop debris from entering the tunnel. The grate was about 90-feet high. [11]

On April 1, the *Republican* published a "Homeseekers' Edition" describing the attractions of the Salt River Valley. An article about the benefits of water storage said the south two-thirds of Roosevelt Dam was nearing 45 feet in height, sloping back to about 15 feet lower on the downstream face.

The story said,

The dam is built of solid blocks of stone throughout and is not of two walls filled in loosely as is wrongly supposed by some persons.

Of the estimated 300,000 cubic yards of masonry that were to go into the dam, 60,000 yards had been laid, the newspaper story said. While the dam would gradually narrow to 16 feet at the top, it would broaden to about 700 feet at the level of the bridges over the spillways connecting with the roadway over the top of the dam. The article said orders had gone out for the removal of the buildings at Roosevelt to the new town. The cost of the dam and other works was put at about $6 million, and it was anticipated the largest part of this sum, advanced by the federal government, would be repaid with the profits earned from the sale of hydroelectric power. The electricity, in addition to extracting water from underground at central pumping stations, would be used to lift water from one canal to another of a higher level to supply lands inaccessible by gravity; to operate "trolley lines, both freight and passenger," to connect all parts of the Valley to make "business and social intercourse quick and convenient"; to light farmhouses and do domestic and other farm chores; and to operate machinery in mines and factories—all of this in addition to the 1,000 horsepower to be supplied the Gila River Indian Reservation. The Granite Reef Diversion Dam, which would have 40,000 yards of masonry, was 75 percent completed. It was expected it would back up a body of water a quarter-mile wide and a mile long. In the water distribution system of the future, the Maricopa and Salt River Valley canals would disappear. The organization of the Salt River Valley Water Users' Association had in five years replaced discord with harmony, contention with satisfaction. Land values had jumped, mostly in the past six months, but there was opportunity for homeseekers. The newspaper said "there are only a little over 100,000 acres of land now in cultivation in the valley," while the water in storage in the reservoir would "mean the irrigation of additional acres up to the total of 200,000." In this connection, the *Republican* said the Mesa Improvement Co., controlled by Alexander J. Chandler, intended to divide 15,000 acres of the Chandler ranch and offer them "in small holdings in compliance with the government's scheme to make the valley maintain the maximum of population." Additionally, the newspaper said Augustus C. Bartlett and Dwight B. Heard, proprietors of the 7,000 acre Bartlett-Heard Land & Cattle Co. south of the river, were "seriously considering sub-dividing about 4,500 acres of this property, under the San Francisco Canal, into twenty and forty acre farms." [12]

At a meeting April 6, the governors were informed about a notice from the Reclamation Service describing a method by which farmers could earn cash credits by hiring themselves and their animals to construct ditches and other works. For his work, the farmer would receive a check which would be presented to the secretary of the association, who would then issue a voucher acceptable at face value for payment in buying the next season's water, or for payment of reservoir assessments once it was determined which lands would be included. [13]

President Benjamin A. Fowler of the Water Users' Association was unopposed for another two-year term in the annual election April 7. Indeed, the election went off so quietly the *Republican* said,

The election looked at from one viewpoint is about the strongest possible endorsement of the present administration. It was an admission that the relations between the government and the association are harmonious almost to the point of dullness and that the people have so much confidence in the association they are hardly alive to its existence. [14]

That same day, the Phoenix, Tempe, and Mesa Boards of Trade joined with the Maricopa Commercial Club in sending a letter to the Maricopa County Board of Supervisors asking it to investigate the construction of a wagon bridge over the Salt River. [15]

The evening of April 8, the shaft of the water wheel operating the generator in the power plant at Roosevelt Dam broke, cutting off all electricity to the cement plant, the hoists, and other equipment. The shaft, made of steel, was 6 inches in diameter and 21-feet long. Apparently it broke because it had crystallized. Instructions for manufacture of a new shaft were sent immediately to the Llewellyn Iron Works in Los Angeles, which worked round-the-clock to make it. Meantime, an unsuccessful effort was made to put into operation a second generator. It took the Llewellyn Iron Works about five days to produce the new shaft, which arrived by train in Mesa the morning of April 16, and was immediately loaded on a wagon and started for Roosevelt. It arrived the afternoon of April 17 and the work of installing it was started at once. By April 20, the generator was back in operation and work resumed on the dam the next day. [16]

One thing the power failure did not delay was construction of the penstock through the dam. Hill, who reported the dam at the highest point on the upper face was about 50 feet above datum and on the lower face about 45 feet, said the diameter of the penstock pipe was 10 feet. It was made of steel plates three-quarters of an inch thick, each plate measuring 6 x 15 feet. The plates were riveted together. The length of the penstock was 140 feet. The base of the pipe entered the powerhouse about 40 feet above the riverbed, while the intake on the face of the dam began about 72 feet above datum. The penstock was to connect with three pipes connecting with the water wheels of three generators in the powerhouse. Hill said it was necessary to release as much stored water as possible through the penstock to generate electricity, but if more water was needed for irrigation, it would come through the sluicing tunnel. [17]

By the second week in April, 15 miles of transmission line

towers had been erected from the Highland Canal eastward toward Goldfield. Between the two points there were 191 towers 30-feet high set on anchor plates about two feet in diameter and buried from four to five feet in the ground. From Roosevelt to Goldfield there were 422 towers mounted on concrete bases or anchored to solid rock. These towers ranged in height from 15 to 90 feet. The distance from Roosevelt to the Highland Canal was 48 miles. When the workers, mainly Indians who excavated and built the concrete bases, reached Weekes station about 18 miles from Mesa, they had divided into two camps, the first one erecting towers toward Roosevelt and the second group working toward the Highland Canal. From there to Phoenix, which was 17 miles, 276 steel poles were set in concrete. Most of the poles were 50-feet high. The switching station to carry the line south to the Gila River Indian Reservation was a mile east of Mesa. This line ran for 15 miles and had 266 poles, most of them 45-feet high except at crossings where they were 50 feet. At Desert Wells, two machines for use in stringing the wire were constructed. The copper wire came in two-mile lengths on reels. The copper line was attached to a two-mile long steel messenger wire, which was drawn up over rollers on the towers. The wire was then drawn to tension by horses. The messenger wire was detached and carried by mules back to the starting point until each two-mile stretch of six wires was completed. The route of the line from the Mesa switching station to Phoenix was along the north city limit of Mesa, then along the railroad tracks through Tempe where the line turned north to cross the Salt River after passing between the Buttes, then west along the railroad tracks to Phoenix. [18]

The Reclamation Service announced April 10 the sale of summer water would begin May 1 at a price of 60 cents per acre, but any landowner who owed money to the Water Users' Association for failure to pay the annual assessment could not get water. [19]

Sometime during the week of April 12, a director of the Maricopa County Commercial Club mentioned to Francis

View of a portion of the penstock through Roosevelt Dam, circa spring 1908.

Transformer building construction (foreground) below Roosevelt Dam site, March 31, 1908.

A. Jones, club manager, that there was a contract, negotiation, or other matter pending between the Reclamation Service and the Pacific Gas & Electric Co. that might be detrimental to the interests of Phoenix and the valley. Jones was asked to investigate and on April 15 went to the Reclamation Service offices. Jones asked to see the contract between Pacific Gas & Electric and the Reclamation Service. Jones said he "made direct inquiry as to the status of the situation and got an evasive reply, except that it was stated by Mr. Standard (sic), who was then in charge of the office, that there were negotiations pending." Jay D. Stannard, in the absence of Hill who was in Mexico, was in charge of the Reclamation Service offices. Stannard said he did not think there was a contract, but there was an agreement dated June 22, 1907, which would grant Pacific Gas & Electric an exclusive contract to buy power from Roosevelt Dam for resale to customers within the city of Phoenix. Jones notified the Commercial Club directors, who called for a meeting April 17 with directors of the Maricopa and Phoenix Board of Trade. The presidents of the two organizations along with the directors who attended quickly agreed that an irreparable wrong was being committed against the people and called for Phoenix Mayor L. W. Coggins to join them. In a body they went to the Reclamation Service office where J. W. Foss, president of the Board of Trade and a member of the Council of the Water Users' Association, asked to see the agreement and to be allowed to make a copy. Stannard refused to provide a copy of the agreement without permission from Hill but said it would be two or three months before a contract was signed. Stannard produced a copy of the agreement, which Foss read aloud. The group returned to the offices of the Commercial Club with each one convinced,

that the public had been most beautifully and thoroughly betrayed, and instead of relief from excessive light rates, the valley was thoroughly bottled up so far as competition of a municipal lighting plant is concerned.

Phoenix residents were paying 20 cents per kilowatt hour for electric lighting to Pacific Gas & Electric, while the agreement with the Reclamation Service provided that the company would pay one and one-half cents per kilowatt hour for the 1,500 kilowatts it had the right to buy for a period of 10 years beginning with the availability of the power. The main objections to the agreement were that there was nothing in it limiting the price at which Pacific Gas & Electric could retail the electricity to customers, including to the city, and that it created a monopoly for Pacific Gas & Electric for the sale of power from Roosevelt Dam within Phoenix. The businessmen were upset because they had visions of cheap power to induce the opening of factories in Phoenix, but the effect of the agreement was that Pacific Gas & Electric would be the only source of power unless a factory bought 100 kilowatts or more from the Reclamation Service. After discussing the agreement, Coggins, the directors of the Commercial Club, and the Board of Trade sent the following telegram to Secretary of the Interior James A. Garfield:

We, representing the city government of Phoenix, its commercial interests and its taxpayers, as well as the farmers of this valley, only learned today of the existence of an agreement between the reclamation service and the local electric lighting company whereby in June of last year an exclusive agreement for electricity for lighting purposes was granted such company at a nominal rate. We protest against the execution of any contract under this agreement as contrary to public policy, and would ask that no further action be taken until the public of Phoenix and the Salt River valley can be heard. This telegram is authorized at a joint meeting of the undersigned.

Signing the wire with Foss and Coggins was C. H. Akers, president of the Commercial Club. [20]

The directors also decided to seek legal advice, and the information they had gathered was given to County Attorney George Purdy Bullard and City Attorney T. J. Prescott. The two attorneys reported at a meeting Monday night, April 20, which was attended by Governor Joseph H. Kibbey, attorney for the Water Users' Association. Bullard said the United States government was not obligated to honor the 1901 contract between the Arizona Water Co. and Pacific Gas & Electric as successor to the Phoenix Light and Fuel Co. Bullard said the contract was a restraint of trade and in violation of the Sherman antitrust law and would be nullified if taken into court. Similarly, the agreement between the Reclamation Service, as successor to the Arizona Water Co., and Pacific Gas & Electric represented a restraint of competition and would be voided. Prescott said the city could enact an ordinance fixing the price of gas, electric light, and electric power if a satisfactory agreement was not reached with Pacific Gas & Electric. [21]

Kibbey urged that nothing be done until Hill could be consulted because if the matter became public it might be considered a censoring of the government. The directors also read a letter from Robert Craig, superintendent of the city water department. Craig said the city was paying 5 cents per kilowatt hour to light 102 street lights and three and one-fourth cents per kilowatt hour for power for pumping water. At the current price of oil, he wrote, the city could pump water for two and one-half cents per kilowatt hour; by the addition of a 150-horsepower engine and other equipment,

174

the city could generate electricity for lights for city streets for 2 cents per kilowatt hour. Oil sold for $1.68 per barrel. [22]

Also in attendance were several Commercial Club directors from Mesa and Tempe. While they were not members of the Water Users' Association, they were concerned about any contract Hill might have made with Chandler, who sold electricity to the two south side cities from his powerhouse on a crosscut canal. A proposal that a mass meeting of the farmers be called, including running a special train from Mesa and Tempe, was deferred after a few of the directors objected. [23]

Another meeting was called for the following morning, April 21, and Stannard was asked to attend. At this meeting, Stannard said he had made further investigation and had learned the agreement with Pacific Gas & Electric was actually a contract that had been signed July 10, 1907. Foss said he knew nothing of the contract. Kibbey said he may have heard talk or rumors of it but he had no official knowledge of it. Joseph L. B. Alexander, United States district attorney, the day before had said he knew nothing about the matter. [24]

The news that the agreement was really a contract meant that the telegram sent April 17 was pointless. Bullard advised that a committee be appointed to confer with the city council with the aim of the council's appointing a committee, and both committees going directly to Pacific Gas & Electric to determine if an amicable agreement on prices could be made. If the company resisted, then the council could pass an ordinance regulating the prices charged by all public utilities. Kibbey objected, saying Hill should be heard before anything was done, but Bullard said no harm could be done Hill by taking it before the city council. Kibbey withdrew his objection and a committee of six was named. [25]

This meeting "at times was stormy as the result of opposition that was made to the public being informed of what was taking place," and that afternoon the *Arizona Democrat* and the *Arizona Gazette* published the first accounts about what had been going on. The *Democrat's* position was summed up by the statement that the committee named at Bullard's suggestion would point out to the city council,

the need of immediately taking steps to prevent the Pacific company getting this valley in the grip of a monopoly that will for the coming ten years retard its development and deny the property owners the fruits of their labor.

The paper also printed some comments from F. H. Ensign, general manager of Pacific Gas & Electric, who said the firm's purchase of a maximum of 2,000 horsepower of the 20,000 horsepower to be produced by the government did not "look as if we had a monopoly." Ensign said the government had to respect the 25-year contract signed in 1901. He said Pacific Gas & Electric was even then paying the government $550 per month for power generated at the Arizona Falls, and the company would have to build an $80,000 powerhouse before it could take delivery of electricity from Roosevelt Dam. "There was nothing secret about making this contract," Ensign said. [26]

The *Gazette's* story was biased against Pacific Gas &

Electric, too, but the *Republican* said there was nothing new about the contract. The *Republican* pointed out it had given "the news and substance of it to the world in its issue of July 23, (1907)" and that the *Democrat* on August 8, 1907, had done the same thing. The *Republican* said the contract was "exclusive only in so far as it applied to houselighting," while "any private individual who may want power for running the city water plant or any manufacturing industry, in quantities of more than 100 kilowatts, may secure it." According to Ensign, "the advantage to the company lies in securing large patrons of power," a feature eliminated in its contract with the Reclamation Service. The *Republican* said:

The government transmission lines will furnish power all over the valley to farmers, and to industries requiring it. The only reservation of exclusiveness is in the little square representing the city of Phoenix. Out of this little section will come every industry that requires more than 100 kilowatts. The city can secure power direct also if it desires it to run its water plant. There is nothing left in the way of a monopoly, except the house lighting and any company that chooses to put in a half million dollar plant and become a competitor has the opportunity and privilege of doing so. [27]

Graciano Narez, 17, a laborer at the Granite Reef Diversion dam, was walking across a footbridge about 6:30 a.m. April 22 when he lost his footing and fell into the river. It was believed his head struck something, or he was frightened, and he was swept over the apron of the dam and was found dead about 50 feet below. The foreman, an anglo, jumped into the water to rescue him, but the current was too strong for him to hold Narez, and the foreman was himself in danger of drowning. Another Mexican leaped into the river and caught hold of the foreman, saving him. A man could easily have waded at the point where Narez was found, which suggested he probably was injured in the fall. [28]

Raising an electric transmission line tower in the desert, March 20, 1908.

The afternoon of April 22, the *Gazette* printed an editorial in which it urged the people to "proceed calmly" in considering the contract made by the government with Pacific Gas & Electric. The newspaper said it was sure "the matter was going to come out all right." It said,

> *This belief is based in a great measure on the confidence we have in Mr. Louis C. Hill, a confidence, we might add, which every citizen of the valley shares and this confidence leads us to the opinion, no matter what the facts appear to be, that Mr. Hill will be able to explain to the satisfaction of the people the terms of the contract and why it was made.*
>
> *However, this declaration did not alter the* Gazette's *stand that the provisions of the contract "are not entirely just to the people of this city, for the reason that it allows the company to charge a higher price for its lights than is reasonable under existing conditions."* [29]

In a news story, the *Gazette* said it would take a large manufacturer to use 100 kilowatts or more because the city itself did not use that much—it was using 65 kilowatts. The story said the Commercial Club and Board of Trade were continuing to work toward an annulment of the contract if lower light rates were not obtained, and a meeting with the city council was being arranged. The article noted that Pacific Gas & Electric would have to spend $80,000 for an additional plant,

> *and it is not intended that it shall be forced into making its charges so low that it cannot pay fair dividends to its stockholders.* [30]

The *Republican* on April 23 printed article 11 of the contract with Pacific Gas & Electric:

> *The party of the first part (the government) further agrees, while serving power to second party (Pacific Gas & Electric) under the terms of this contract to refrain from entering into a general retailing of power to customers in the city of Phoenix, Arizona, or from furnishing power to anyone in said city to be again sold or retailed. It is agreed, however, that the party of the first part shall have the right to sell or lease power in the city of Phoenix, Arizona, at any time in blocks of 100 to 500 kilowatts and over to anyone to be used for manufacturing industries, waterworks or pumping plants.* [31]

Meanwhile, the joint committee from the Commercial Club and the Board of Trade had decided on a course of action. The committee got Coggins to call a meeeting of the city council at 7:30 p.m. April 23. Ensign was to be asked to provide a written agreement lowering the light rates for houselights. If he failed to do that, the city council would be asked to pass an ordinance fixing the maximum rates that could be charged for power, light, and gas by public utilities. If both Ensign and the council failed to act, the plan was to take the issue to Washington, D.C., and to court if necessary. [32]

The upshot of the meeting with the council was the appointment of Coggins and C. W. McKee as chairmen of the joint committee to meet with Ensign to learn what concessions would be made by Pacific Gas & Electric. When the question of haste in moving on the matter was raised, it was pointed out the time to resolve the issue was before Pacific Gas & Electric began getting power from Roosevelt Dam, not after. Coggins and McKee met the afternoon of April 24 with Ensign, who asked for and received 10 days within which to learn from his superiors in the utility what

concessions could be made. Ensign assured them the company officials would be reasonable and would make agreements fair to all parties. [33]

The *Los Angeles Times* printed an article about the contract April 25. Without naming the officials it said it was quoting, the *Times* said representatives of the Reclamation Service and Pacific Gas & Electric contended the contract was in the best interests of the Valley because the old 25-year contract with Phoenix Light and Fuel Co., now owned by Pacific Gas & Electric, "formed a sort of barrier to plans that had been made for the benefit of the valley." The *Times* article said:

> *Under this contract, power was being supplied for the lighting of Phoenix from two power houses on the Arizona canal, the plants running when there was water in the canal, which was not often. The plants had been bonded for an immense amount, and were generally considered failures, owing to the indeterminate water supply. But the dry condition soon will be changed and the Arizona canal will have water constantly when the Roosevelt dam is done. So the lighting company drove a hard bargain with the reclamation service, and traded its obstructing rights for a new contract with especially favorable terms to the corporation.*
>
> *The officials of the Salt River Water Users' Association, which has the interests of the valley farmers in hand, states that they knew nothing of the terms of the contract, and admit that it is very much one-sided.* [34]

John Loser, a German stonemason, shortly before noon April 25 was crushed to death between a derrick and the rocks on the north side of the Roosevelt Dam. Fellow workmen saw the derrick bearing down on Loser too late. He "was crushed like a fly between the rocks and the derrick. His death was instantaneous, and he presented a horrible sight when his body was reached." His fellow workers erected a monument to him, which can still be seen at the Roosevelt Cemetery. [35]

The *Republican* said in an article April 27 that tourists to Roosevelt were increasing and were welcomed, but if they planned to be housed and fed at the government quarters, they had better check first with the Reclamation Service office in Phoenix to make certain they could be accommodated. The newspaper said most of the tourists going to Roosevelt expected to secure billeting with the government because the accommodations were better and the town was preparing for its removal. [36]

John P. Orme, president of the board of the Appropriators' Canal Co., disclosed April 28 the company would not be sold to the government until October and for that reason water contracts would be made for the period between May 15 and October 15. Meanwhile, the titles to the land and other papers necessary for the transfer were to be prepared. [37]

On May 4 the *Republican* reported J. W. Crenshaw, the commissioner of immigration for Maricopa County, was answering many letters inquiring about the Valley. Most of the questions asked about what parts of the Valley would be opened for acquiring land, the manner in which the government would dispose of the ground, and when water would be turned on it. Crenshaw advised the writers that no land was available from the government within the reservoir district, and that the best way to get land, priced at from $50 to $150 per acre, was to buy through real estate agents. He explained practically all the land for which there was water was already being irrigated. [38]

Kibbey was asked informally by the governors to present a statement about the power contract at their next meeting. Ensign, accompanied by company attorney H. L. Chambers, met with the joint committee of the Commercial Club and the Board of Trade and informed the members that Pacific Gas & Electric would not take up the question of electric prices until the government was prepared to deliver the power. [39]

At a meeting of the Board of Trade, on May 5, there was a call to construct a bridge across the Salt River "at some point between South Seventh Avenue and Tempe" and to raise $5,000 to spend on advertising in the last six months of the year. The board's advertising committee advised the advertising be directed at the farming and dairying classes of the West and Middle West, and added,

We would like to especially reach the intending tourists, also, but advertising of this nature is extremely expensive and the results are admittedly less important than the securing of actual settlers. [40]

Work on the Roosevelt Dam was going slower than usual because of the work involved in putting in the penstock, but, at its highest point on the south end, the dam was 65 feet above datum. In connection with the growing height of the dam, the **Republican** cautioned that the only lands that would be benefited by any water in storage in the fall would be those already under cultivation. This was mainly because the amount of water in storage would be small, and water continued to run over the much lower north end. However, available flood water was to be sold for 30 cents per acre, while water for the summer season under the Arizona, Grand, Maricopa, and Salt River Valley canals would cost 60 cents per acre and would be sold through May 25. [41]

Statistician Blanchard wrote to Fowler May 6 informing him that he was planning to have printed an illustrated folder describing the Salt River project. Blanchard said the Reclamation Service was "receiving about 1,000 inquiries a week from homeseekers," and the advertising matter it had did not adequately answer all the questions. He asked for signed testimonials from farmers explaining the advantages of farming in the Valley. [42]

Ensigns' disclosure that Pacific Gas & Electric would not immediately enter into an agreement about electric rates prompted Foss, Akers, Coggins, and three members of the city council to write a letter May 7 to Secretary Garfield asking for a modificaion or abrogation of the contract. They wrote the city of Phoenix had signed more than 2,000 acres (the actual figure was 1,760 acres) of its land toward the reclamation project. They said besides being obligated to pay more than $60,000 toward the work, taxpayers and citizens were interested "both from the standpoint of beneficiaries from power sold and to the end that its people be protected in securing reasonable rates for lighting and power for industrial purposes, which. . .the contract does not appear to provide." The letter continued, in part:

As the effect of this contract gives a private corporation a complete monopoly of lighting and a practical monopoly of the distribution of power in the city of Phoenix for 10 years, her citizens readily appreciated that the inducements, so long held forth by those prominent in the management of the water users' association, of cheap light and power was left entirely optional with a corporation. . .

It is said by those interested in defending the contract that certain rights were possessed by the Pacific Co. in power privileges in the Arizona Canal, acquired by the Government in the furtherance of its plans of distributing water from the Roosevelt project; that the Government was bound morally and legally to recognize these rights; and that this exclusive contract was in lieu of the old Arizona Canal contract.

It is a matter of common knowledge locally that the value of this old contract was uncertain, because of the fact that the manner of securing water for canals was not dependable until the Government, through its storage plans, corrected the uncertainty.

The letter signers had no objection to Pacific Gas & Electric "being granted all that they had under former conditions," but they wanted the "exclusive" feature of the contract eliminated to permit competition or to allow Phoenix to buy power for its street lights and other municipal purposes, and to permit the federal government to acquire power for the Indian School and for the territorial government buildings. [43]

McKee on May 8 addressed his own letter to Garfield, explaining that action upon the Pacific Gas & Electric contract was not taken earlier because the contract "was made without any publicity and entirely without the knowledge of the citizens of Phoenix or the members of the Water Users' Association." McKee enclosed with his letter the one written the day before by Foss, et al. Garfield referred the letters to Frederick H. Newell, director of the Reclamation Service. [44]

Tourist interest in Roosevelt Dam led the Phoenix Auto Co. to lease a 15-passenger Manhattan touring car owned by the Castle Hot Springs Hotel Co. for runs over the Roosevelt road. The car left Mesa on its inaugural trip at 10 a.m. May 10 and arrived in Roosevelt at 6 p.m. On the way back, the travelers visited Granite Reef where 72 feet of concrete work remained before the diversion dam would be completed. One of the travelers, E. A. Marshall, described some of what he saw:

We arrived at Roosevelt at 6 p.m. and were most courteously received and entertained by the government officials of the reclamation service. That night we strolled through the town which is soon to be submerged and coming down by the lower road saw the great dam by moonlight. My first glimpse of this structure from the top of the hill as the car turned the curve was rather disappointing. The mountains and all around were so very, very big and way down 400 feet below the dam looked so very, very small. That night however, as I stood on the bank of the river and looked up at the dam's present height of seventy-five feet and across its present width of one hundred and twenty-five feet and realized that the foundation was thirty-five feet below and that the dam when completed would be in the stupendous class. . .

The next morning we were escorted by an accomplished assistant and went on the top of the dam and saw the huge granite rocks weighing tons and tons skillfully and permanently placed in their cement bed never to be moved again—nowhere in the world is there to be witnessed such a triumph of man over nature and so many intricate engineering feats as one can see at Roosevelt. . . [45]

C. E. Tait, the Reclamation Service's inspector of canals, arrived in Mesa on May 11 to begin a survey of all the canals

177

in the Valley regarding the costs of maintaining, cleaning, and building them in each of the districts. Chandler escorted Tait on May 12 on a tour of the canals in the Mesa area. [46]

In Roosevelt, the evening of Tuesday, May 12, about a dozen businessmen met with Chester W. Smith, Reclamation Service engineer in charge, to discuss the permanent location of the new Roosevelt. The businessmen said dam contractor John O'Rourke had invited them to build on his side of the river, agreeing to assist them in arranging for a water supply and in any other way he could. They thought the location would be advantageous to ranchers, stockmen, and prospectors. Smith responded the government already had surveyed a site above the water line about a mile from the present Roosevelt. Smith said the final location was up to Hill, and the businessmen agreed to wait and talk it over with him when he next came to Roosevelt. [47]

Hill returned to Phoenix on May 17 from a long trip which included a visit to Washington. He said he had not intended going there, but in the past few months the work had proceeded so fast at Roosevelt there was a danger of running out of money or of delaying the work at Granite Reef and on the canals. Hill said he was successful in getting enough money to continue. He also had been directed to make a report to Washington about a dispute with Mexico over the use of Colorado River water. Hill was not quoted in the newspapers as having made any comments concerning the Pacific Gas & Electric contract, but he no doubt discussed the matter of the contract with Newell while in Washington. [48]

Newell on May 21 directed separate letters to McKee and to the Water Users' Assocation. Newell told McKee it would take approximately 20 days "before action can be taken upon your communication." In that period Newell expected to learn the attitude of the Water Users' Association about the contract. He enclosed with the letter to the association copies of McKee's letter and the one written May 7 by Foss, et al. Newell said to the association,

This office will be glad to have from your Association an expression of its views relative to the allegations contained in these letters in order that as complete information as it is possible to obtain may be at hand in taking action upon the matters discussed in the communications. [49]

A committee of Roosevelt businessmen visited the land proposed by O'Rourke for the new Roosevelt on May 21. The next day they met with Smith and told him the site was unsuitable for a town, and they were ready to occupy the ground proposed by the Reclamation Service. Smith said the water for the town would have to be piped in from Cottonwood Canyon, which would be expensive, but the cost was to be shared by all moving there, and water would be available to meet all needs. Hill and the businessmen talked May 26. Their main concerns were whether they could obtain deeds for land in the new town and when they should begin moving. Hill said he could not provide deeds, but he could think of no reason why anyone need worry about that so long as he conducted himself lawfully. He advised moving as soon as possible because he expected the sluicing tunnel to open in seven or eight days. When that

happened, O'Rourke would begin closing the gap on the north side of Roosevelt Dam. At the latest, it was expected the move should be completed by October or November, before the winter rains. [50]

The Reclamation Service was preparing for the closing of the low place in the dam and the formation of the lake behind it by ordering a ferryboat wide and long enough to transport a wagon and team. In addition, a gasoline launch was ordered for use between Port Roosevelt and Port O'Rourke on the Roosevelt reservoir. The launch would continue in use until the road across the top of the dam was completed. [51]

The work of building the Granite Reef Diversion Dam was completed Wednesday, May 27, but the connecting of the Arizona Canal on the north side and the building of two miles of canal on the south side remained to be done. To begin the latter work, Hector Gillis, one of the superintendents at Granite Reef, arrived in Mesa to secure 100 horses to pull the scrapers and dirt conveyors. [52]

The directors of the Maricopa County Commercial Club met May 29 to consider the letter sent by Newell. The directors agreed if relief from the contract was not obtained from the Reclamation Service or the United States Department of the Interior, it probably would be necessary to go to court. [53]

At their regular monthly meeting June 1, the governors adopted a resolution giving unanimous approval to the contract between the Reclamation Service and Pacific Gas & Electric. In the absence of Fowler and George Christy, vice president, the governors selected from their number H. L. McClung to preside. McClung was a stockholder in Pacific Gas & Electric and was cashier of the Phoenix National Bank. In reporting the meeting, the **Republican** said,

It is understood that since the attack on the contract was initiated, the most of the board of trade directors and the mayor have grown lukewarm in the matter and are even disposed to drop it. [54]

Before adoption of the resolution, the governors heard from Kibbey and Hill. Kibbey reviewed the history of the Phoenix ordinances dealing with the right to sell electricity inside the city, noting that the Phoenix Light and Fuel Co. was developing about 1,000 horsepower of electricity from two power plants through its contract with the Arizona Water Co. before passage of the reclamation act and formation of the Water Users' Association. Kibbey said he had no doubt as to the validity of the ordinances and contract,

and if I had any say I am disposed to believe that it would not now be good faith, if it was desirable, for the Water Users' association, to attempt to impeach them and there was never a time when it would have been good policy or to our advantage to do so. . .

(As) It is stated, . . . in the letter of the board of trade,. . .that "it is a matter of common knowledge, locally, that the value of the old contract was uncertain because of the fact that the manner of securing water for the canals was not dependable until the government through its storage plans corrected the uncertainty,"is hardly accurate—at least it is incomplete. There was complete certainty that at some time the water flowing in Salt river would be diverted continuously and permanently for the irrigation of lands

on both sides of the river. This could not be done without rendering capable of use that flow for the development of power. If the electric company's contract was a valid one, then that company became necessarily the beneficiary.

Kibbey said the contract was an obstruction to the government's plan to build the Granite Reef Diversion Dam. He said the government had five options: to recognize the contract; to ignore it and face litigation, which would have been expensive and caused delays; to purchase the rights to Pacific Gas & Electric under the contract; to condemn the right of the company to use the water, which also would have meant going to court; to negotiate a new contract, which was the course adopted. Hill said he had driven a good bargain with Pacific Gas & Electric. He said if the company had been buying power the past year from the Arizona Water Co., it would have paid $5,000 under the old contract compared to the $40,000 it would have paid and would be paying the government for the reservoir project for at least 10 years. [55]

The governors then approved the following resolution:

Having considered the letter of the director of the Reclamation Service relating to the contract between the government and the Pacific Gas & Electric Co., and documents and statements concerning it, it was resolved unanimously by the board that the contract is plainly to the best interests of the members of the association and to the water users of the valley, and that it meets the entire approval of the board, and that the secretary so advise the director of the reclamation service. [56]

The governors also appointed Kibbey and two of their number, Charles Peterson and Orme, to arrange for a celebration to mark the completion of the Granite Reef Diversion Dam. Hill said the camp was being dismantled but everything would be done to accommodate visitors. A few days later, Hill set June 13 as the day for the festivities to coincide with the turning of water into the Arizona Canal. [57]

At 2:30 p.m. June 2, the gates in the sluicing tunnel at Roosevelt Dam were opened allowing the river to run through, but it was not until June 8 that O'Rourke's men were able to begin laying masonry on the north end of the dam. [58]

Kent announced June 6 he would take additional testimony in **Hurley v. Abbott** on June 12. Several farmers had informed the court they had accumulated additional evidence important to their water priority claims. [59]

Hill met in his office June 11 with members of the joint committee of the Board of Trade and Commercial Club to discuss the contract with Pacific Gas & Electric. He told them he doubted they would succeed in breaking the contract if they went to court, and if they did succeed, the only thing they would accomplish would be the reinstatement of the original contract to which Pacific Gas & Electric and the United States government were the successors. He said the utility would have cheaper power and other prerogatives that would hamper the Reclamation Service's operations. After the meeting the committee issued a statement pledging to continue the fight against the contract, but it could expect no help from the Interior Department because Newell on June 12 wrote to Charles Van der Veer, secretary of the Water Users' Association, acknowledging receipt of the governors' resolution dealing with the contract and Kibbey's comments and saying,

I am pleased to note that the Association finds this contract satisfactory and agrees with the Service that it is eminently for the best interests of the project. [60]

On June 12, Heard and three other members of the Phoenix and Southside Bridge Co. visited Maricopa and Pima Indian settlements on the Gila River Reservation to

General view of Granite Reef Diversion Dam on the Salt River, May 2, 1908.

enlist the Indians' aid in building a wagon bridge over the Salt River at the foot of Central Avenue. The committee traveled in Heard's Pierce Great Arrow, which was "decorated with fluttering American flags," driving first to a Maricopa village southwest of Phoenix. There the visitors dined on barbecue prepared by the women. Afterward, they assembled in the schoolhouse where Heard explained the bridge project and how the Indians would be employed. The Maricopas consented to help and the *Republican* reported,

This was accomplished through a signed agreement, many of the Indians being able to write while others affixed their mark. The first name signed was Buffalo Bill. William McKinley signed towards the last.

The committee was equally successful in its meeting with the Pimas at Gila Crossing and another agreement was signed. Heard said the assistance from the Indians made the bridge a certainty, provided the county contributed to the construction. Heard said:

Otherwise plans will be considered for a toll bridge. However that is not thought probable as with the cooperation of the south side land owners, the Indians and the Phoenix businessmen, the county at comparatively small expense will be able to offer the long needed free bridge to the people. [61]

Between 1,200 and 1,500 people were on hand when Hill, about 1:30 p.m. June 13, asked for their attention so he could begin the ceremonies dedicating the Granite Reef Diversion Dam. Although it was an intensely hot day and the people were assembled on a shadeless area of sand just above the Arizona Canal, the people listened closely to what was said and loudly cheered the speakers. Many of the people had camped overnight and others had driven in by wagon and auto during the morning and early afternoon. Others came by horseback, bicycle, and motorcycle. Water had been backing up against the dam for four days and a lake had formed above the dam and water poured over it. Later, in order to allow visitors from the south side to walk across the dam without getting wet, the sluice gates were opened sufficiently to draw down the lake. The gates were then shut, the pond rose, and some latecomers waded through the water coming over the dam to reach the ceremonial site. The cutting off of the water to form a pond caused the deaths of thousands of fish downstream; to entertain themselves, some of the boys at the dedication pulled hundreds of fish from a pool immediately below the dam. A temporary booth was erected for the entertainment of the official party, which arrived in two automobiles. One brought Hill, Kent, Van der Veer, and Stannard. In the other car were Kibbey, Orme and Mr. and Mrs. Heard and their son, Bartlett. Mrs. Heard set out lunch with the assistance of Mrs. James W. Martin, whose husband had overseen the construction of the Granite Reef dam. [62]

Kibbey was introduced by Hill, and the governor told the crowd that,

What we do here today and whatever may be said, are merely to formally fix a date from which henceforth we reckon our progress—it is the planting of a milestone, to note for the future the point in the program of time at which this great work was completed and its use inaugurated.

Kibbey briefly reviewed the history of the national reclamation law, saying it "came as a surprise to us of this valley. It had been beyond our hopes." He said the diversion dam was second in importance to the Roosevelt Dam and listed the features of the Salt River project, adding he hoped in the near future it would include "the impounding of the waters of the Verde." Kibbey praised the men of the Geological Survey for the confidence they showed in the people of the Valley by proceeding with the Roosevelt Dam. He said Hill had won the respect, admiration, and gratitude of the people. Kibbey ended by congratulating the people for the completion of the dam,

to your use, to your benefit and to the use and benefit of those who may succeed you. [63]

Kent also paid tribute to Hill, but the judge also spoke of the great advantage it would be if all landowners in the Valley joined the Water Users' Association. Kent said,

. . .let any number of men stay out and refuse their aid and assistance in making this great scheme of irrigation one great comprehensive whole, and new and difficult questions as between those outsiders and the government, and between these outsiders and those who are in, are sure to arise as to who may be entitled to water against the other, and as to the means of delivery, and the times and the amount. [64]

After remarks were made by Orme and Peterson, the *Republican* reported,

Kibbey walked to the center of the head gates and placed his hand on the lever while all eyes turned toward him and the row of flags with which the gates were adorned and as he pulled the lever, the flags rose, slowly, the water shot through the open gateways [into the Arizona canal] as in a millrace, under pressure of full catchment basin, and a mighty cheer rent the circumambient atmosphere and fluttered the forty-foot flag that hung on a sixty-foot mast that crowned the summit of the huge 100-foot cable tower in the rear of the crowd, a wavering response was noted from the dozens of little flags that ornamented the big cable its entire length across the river, and, the celebration was over. [65]

Virtually unnoticed on the day of celebration was the start of work on the South Canal that would provide the link between the diversion dam and the Consolidated Canal. However, no water was to be given to the Highland Canal, but the Reclamation Service would make a connection if a new Highland (the Eastern) were dug. Hill told the Highland homeowners the government did not have money to build the new canal and probably would not have it for a year or two. He suggested landowners form an organization within the Water Users' Association, and on June 15 the *Republican* printed an announcement from a committee of seven men, among them Ethelbert W. Wilbur and Harry L. Chandler, the brother of Alexander Chandler, calling for a meeting in Mesa on June 20 to discuss the matter. [66]

During the week of June 14, the Reclamation Service put men to work in Roosevelt taking down buildings and machinery and moving what it wanted to salvage above the anticipated high water line of the reservoir. Some of the businessmen began the construction of new buildings in the new Roosevelt, while others made arrangements to move present buildings. The merchants had to begin building by August 1 or lose the ground allotted to them. Among the businesses planning to make the move were T. T. Emery and Emery Strait, who bought the ice cream and cold drink

Two views of Roosevelt Dam construction looking downstream, June 30, 1908.

establishment of W. A. Thompson; M. C. Webb and Sons, general merchandise, who bought the stock of rival Joe T. Akers, who had started at Roosevelt with a capital of $500 and had goods worth $5,000 and money in the bank; John Belsar, butcher; and F. A. Durate, general merchandise. Belsar and Webb and Sons began construction of a cement dam across Cottonwood Canyon from behind which water would be brought through pipe to the town. [67]

At the meeting of the Highland Canal owners June 20, Wilbur was appointed chairman, and a motion was approved the group assume the cost of building a new canal east of the Highland, providing the Reclamation Service superintend the undertaking. A committee of five including Wilbur and Harry Chandler was appointed to meet with Reclamation Service officials to find out what the government would supply and what the Highland owners would need themselves in money, material, and equipment. [68]

The Maricopa and Phoenix Board of Trade met June 24 and listened to Heard, its finance chairman, describe a plan to raise funds to attract a thousand or 2,000 new farm families to the Valley. Heard's plan, which was adopted, was to assess every businessman, every farmer and rancher, and every non-resident landowner on the premise that all would prosper by cutting up the land into small holdings and attracting new settlers. The Board of Trade already had made contracts to advertise in farm and dairy publications. Hill also spoke at the meeting, saying indications were that water storage could begin in the winter and by summer there should be enough water in storage to furnish at least two irrigations for the 116,000 acres in cultivation. By the summer of 1910, he said it should be possible to store water for all the lands signed and accepted into the association. All the masonry work on the dam should be completed by then, and the contractor should be finished with all his work by January 1911, Hill said. Thus, the conditions in the Valley were far different than ever before and the only thing lacking was advertising to bring in the small farmer. [69]

Elmer Cox, who was working on the construction of the

transmission line for the Reclamation Service, drowned the evening of June 27 about five miles below Roosevelt Dam. Cox and several fellow employees went to the river to swim after work that day. They entered the water together. Later, on the way back to camp, it was noticed that Cox was missing. The men returned to the river to hunt for Cox. Some distance below where they had been swimming, they found his body in a pool of water three-feet deep. [70]

Hill returned from Roosevelt the evening of June 28 and reported the gap on the north side of the dam at the lowest point was 22 feet above datum. The high point remained at 75 feet on the dam's south side. He said the first building completed at the new Roosevelt was a carpenter shop put up by Dick Behr. Hill also said that on the way in he had passed a big load of pipe intended for the waterworks. He said the water from Cottonwood Canyon would be enough for drinking. Additional water would have to come from the power canal. [71]

Gifford Pinchot, forester for the United States Department of Agriculture, wrote to Fowler on June 19 informing him two members of the Forest Service would depart from Phoenix on September 1 to investigate "the effects of sheep and goat grazing upon watersheds within National Forests which are important to irrigation." The examination was to be undertaken in cooperation with the Reclamation Service, and the Water Users' Association was invited to have its representatives accompany the Forest Service men, Albert F. Potter and D. D. Bronson. [72]

Demrick said on July 6 that construction of the power line had been completed between the Highland Canal and Government Well, a distance of about 20 miles. Construction of the towers had been completed to a point about four miles below Roosevelt. In Roosevelt, United States postmaster George Burtis said he wanted the new post office at O'Rourke's camp because more people were there. [73]

Secretary Emil Ganz of the Appropriators' Canal Co. turned over the company records to Van der Veer. It was explained that the Water Users' Association had nothing to do with the Appropriators' Canal, but it was convenient to have all water distribution records in one location. [74] [7]

The governors met July 6 with a delegation from the Highland Canal. The delegation proposed that the new Highland Canal be built under the cooperative plan proposed by the Reclamation Service. The new canal was to be about 16 miles long and cost an estimated $36,000 to $40,000. Most of the land to be served already was signed into the association, and the request of the Highland owners revived a question that had been fought over at the time the articles of incorporation were adopted: Who would pay for the local improvement, in this case the new Highland Canal, the entire Water Users' Association or the landowners who would farm under the new canal? By the same token, who was to pay for the north side canal system, the north side farmers and ranchers alone or the entire association? The *Republican* raised the point that by the time the government got ready to collect, "every section will have had special benefits of some sort that were not conceived when the association was organized. . ." The Granite Reef Diversion Dam was an example of an improvement that was not planned on at the beginning but was of benefit to all. Water conservation on the north side benefited the south side. Many of the association leaders anticipated that when the time came all the expenses would be shared pro rata. [75]

The north side of the Roosevelt Dam reached 27 feet above the low water mark by the second week of July, while the river itself was at its lowest point in two years. A few days later, however, heavy rains fell, and on July 16 both the Salt River and Tonto Creek rose, but not dangerously. The water topped the old cofferdam at the front of Roosevelt Dam, but the sluicing tunnel lacked 18 inches of running full at the top. The night of July 17, a Friday, a severe wind and thunderstorm visited Roosevelt, ripping loose some tents and soaking everything. The river rose a little, but between 2 and 3 p.m. July 18 the river rose six feet in an hour. It continued to rise, and while not so rapidly, it was fast enough to cause O'Rourke to remove all of the derricks from the north end of the dam. By Sunday morning, the river had backed up a couple of miles. The water came to within 12 inches of the top of the lowest part of the dam before it stopped rising. [76]

In new Roosevelt, all of the water pipes were in and the exodus of houses and tents from the old to the new community continued. The cost of the cement dam and the water pipes was more than $3,000. A telephone line between Globe and Payson was completed. [77]

Reclamation Service engineer S. K. Baker and a surveying party of eight men arrived at the head of the Consolidated Canal July 20 preparatory to starting the survey for the new Highland Canal. [78]

Attorney Chalmers told the *Republican* in an interview July 28 that the Pacific Gas & Electric Co. contemplated a new rate schedule after it began getting power from the government. He said the company was now examining rates in comparable Eastern and Western cities. Chalmers said the company desired good relations with the community. [79]

A definite location for the Roosevelt post office remained unsettled, Burtis now desiring to locate it at Roosevelt-on-the-Hill. In response, residents circulated a petition calling for the post office to be located in the new town. [80]

Another severe windstorm hit the Roosevelt area, ripping off about half the metal roof of the cement warehouse and the wooden roof of one of the oil reservoirs. The river ran higher than it did earlier in the month, but it did not top the dam because several feet had been added to the north end. [81]

At the dam, the low point on the north end at the end of July was 30 feet above datum and on the south end 80 feet. The last of the transmission line towers had been set, and the transformers that were to be installed in the transformer house were carried by wagon from Mesa to Roosevelt. [82]

The governors on August 3 adopted the cooperative plan of construction for building the new Highland Canal; the plan also was adopted for similar work in all other districts. Under the plan adopted for the Highland, the landowners were to form an organization, the Highland Canal Construction Co., to settle the questions of who would hire the labor, buy equipment and supplies, and run the camp. The Water Users' Association would advertise for bids, giving the maximum prices that would be paid for excavation, hauling, and other work. The Highland Canal Construction Co. would bid for the work and would accept certificates in payment, which would later be accepted in payment for Roosevelt Dam and other works. [83]

Burtis received permission to locate the post office "on-the-hill" at Roosevelt, but this met with opposition from Reclamation Service officials as well as townspeople. They collected more than 300 signatures on their petition, including the names of the government men, to have the post office in new Roosevelt. "I want to do the best I can for the people and will go where the greatest number will be benefited," Burtis said. O'Rourke said he would like the post office at his camp, but "we will not feel badly if we are left out." [84]

Heavy rains fell over the watershed in mid-August and the river began rising rapidly at Roosevelt. By the end of August 17, the water ran five-feet deep over the lower end of the dam. On August 18, the river at its confluence with Tonto Creek was five miles wide and the lake was more than 10 miles in length. While the water halted work on the north end of the dam, construction continued on the south end. [85]

Appropriately, the ferryboat for use at Roosevelt arrived in Mesa. It was loaded aboard two large freight wagons for shipment over the Roosevelt road. [86]

Meantime, the modes of transportation from one side of the river to the other were reduced to two: the overhead cables of O'Rourke & Co. and a small boat added by the Mesa-Roosevelt Stage Co. The water stopped flowing over the lower end of the dam by August 27, but it rushed through the sluicing tunnel with the level of the lake gradually falling. [87]

---

1. *Arizona Republican* (Phoenix), March 5, 1908.
2. *Ibid.,* March 4, 1908.
3. *Ibid.*
4. *Ibid.,* March 4, 8, 1908.

5. *Ibid.,* March 7, 12, 1908.
6. *Ibid.,* March 14, 1908.
6. *Ibid.,* March 14, 1908.
7. *Ibid.,* March 15, 1908.
8. *Ibid.*
9. *Ibid.,* March 17, 1908.
10. *Ibid.,* March 18, 27, 1908.
11. *Ibid.,* March 20, 28, 1908.
12. *Ibid.,* April 1, 1908.
13. *Ibid.,* April 7, 1908.
14. *Ibid.,* April 8, 1908.
15. *Ibid.,* April 9, 1908.
16. *Ibid.,* April 13, 14, 17, 29, 24, 1908; *Arizona Gazette* (Phoenix).

17. *Republican,* April 14, 17, 24, 1908.
18. *Ibid.,* April 17, July 9, 1908; *Salt River Project Final History to 1916,* unpublished manuscript. Vol. III, pp. 511-520, Salt River Project Archives (hereafter SRPA).

19. *Republican,* April 11, 1908.
20. *Arizona Democrat* (Phoenix), April 21, 1908; *Gazette,* April 21, 1908; *Republican,* April 22, 2908; *Report in the Matter of the Investigation of the Salt and Gila Rivers—Reservations and Reclamation Service* (Washington: Government Printing Office, 1913), pp. 444-446.

21. *Democrat,* April 21, 1908; *Gazette,* April 21, 1908; *Republican,* April 22, 1908.

22. *Democrat,* April 21, 1908; *Republican,* April 22, 1908.
23. *Democrat,* April 21, 1908; *Republican,* April 1, 1908.
24. *Democrat,* April 21, 1908; *Republican,* April 22, 1908; *Gazette,* April 21, 1908. The *Gazette* said it was S. B. Taggart, Hill's private secretary, who revealed that the agreement was actually a contract, but the *Republican* identified the person as Stannard, as did Francis A. Jones in testimony before a congressional committee in 1912.

25. *Ibid.*
26. *Democrat,* April 21, 1908.
27. *Gazette,* April 21, 1908; *Republican,* April 22, 1908.
28. *Republican,* April 23, 25, 1908.
29. *Gazette,* April 22, 1908.
30. *Ibid; Republican,* April 23, 1908.
31. *Republican,* April 23, 1908.
32. *Democrat,* April 23, 1908; *Gazette,* April 23, 1908.
33. *Democrat,* April 24, 1908; *Gazette,* April 24, 1908; *Republican,* April 25, 1908.

34. *Los Angeles Times,* April 25, 1908, reprinted *Gazette,* April 29, 1908.

35. *Gazette,* April 21, 1908.
36. *Republican,* April 27, 1908.
37. *Democrat,* April 28, 1905; *Gazette,* May 5, 1908.
38. *Republican,* May 4, 1908.
39. *Republican,* May 5, June 2, 1908.
40. *Ibid.,* May 6, 1908.
41. *Ibid.,* May 3, 8, 10, 1908.
42. C. J. Blanchard to B. A. Fowler, May 6, 1908, SRPA.

43. *Republican,* May 30, 1908; *Report in the Matter of the Investigation of the Salt and Gila Rivers,* pp. 648-649.
44. C. W. McKee to James A. Garfield, May 8, 1908, SRPA; *Republican,* May 30, 1908.
45. *Republican,* May 9, 12, 13, 1908.
46. *Ibid.,* May 13, 1908.
47. *Gazette,* May 18, 1908.
48. *Republican,* May 18, 19, 1908.
49. *Ibid.,* May 30, 1908; F. H. Newell to Salt River Valley Water Users' Association, May 21, 1908, SRPA.
50. *Gazette,* May 23, June 4, 1908.
51. *Republican,* June 1, 1908.
52. *Ibid.,* May 27, 28, 1908.
53. *Ibid.,* May 30, 1908.
54. *Report in the Matter of the Investigation of the Salt and Gila Rivers,* pp. 445-446; *Republican,* June 2, 1908.
55. *Republican,* June 23, 1908.
56. *Ibid.,* Charles Van der Veer to F. H. Newell, June 5, 1908, SRPA.
57. *Republican,* June 2, 5, 1908.
58. *Gazette,* June 4, 1908; *Republican,* June 3, 9, 1908.
59. *Gazette,* June 6, 1908; *Republican,* June 7, 1908.
60. *Republican,* June 12, 1908; F. H. Newell to Charles Van der Veer, June 12, 1908, SRPA.
61. *Republican,* June 13, 1908.
62. *Gazette,* June 13, 1908; *Republican,* June 14, 1908.
63. *Ibid.*
64. *Ibid.*
65. *Republican,* June 14, 1908.
66. *Gazette,* June 15, 1908; *Republican,* June 16, 1908.
67. *Gazette,* June 16, 1908; *Republican,* June 21, 24, 28, 1908.
68. *Gazette,* June 20, 1908; *Republican,* June 22, 1908.
69. *Republican,* June 24, 1908.
70. *Ibid.,* June 30, 1908; the victim was identified as Elmer Carson in the *Gazette,* July 2, 1908, and as Elmer Carlson in the *Republican,* July 5, 1908.
71. *Republican,* June 30, 1908.
72. Gifford Pinchot to B. A. Fowler, June 29, 1908, SRPA.
73. *Republican,* July 6, 1908; *Gazette,* July 8, 1908.
74. *Republican,* July 7, 1908.
75. *Ibid.; Gazette,* July 6, 1908.
76. *Republican,* July 12, 22, 1908.
77. *Gazette,* July 18, August 8, 1908.
78. *Ibid.,* July 21, 1908; *Republican,* July 21, 1908.
79. *Republican,* July 29, 1908.
80. *Gazette,* July 29, August 8, 1908.
81. *Republican,* August 3, 1908.
82. *Ibid.*
83. *Ibid.,* August 4, 1908.
84. *Ibid.,* August 10, 12, 1908; *Gazette,* August 8, 1908.
85. *Republican,* August 19, 21, September 4, 1908.
86. *Gazette,* August 18, 1908; *Republican,* August 30, 1908.
87. *Republican,* August 30, 1908.

September 1908 - February 1909

At a meeting September 1, Albert F. Potter of the forestry service outlined plans for a three week trip to investigate whether grazing sheep and cattle had damaged the watersheds in the national forests covering the Salt and Verde rivers. Potter said the intent of the investigation was not to halt grazing; rather, it was to protect the water supply. If it was shown grazing had damaged the watershed, steps had to be taken to stop it, such as dividing the range between the different classes of livestock and limiting their numbers. Potter met with representatives of the Reclamation Service, Salt River Valley Water Users' Association, Arizona Wool Growers' Association, and Arizona Cattle Growers' Association. [1]

Supervising engineer Louis C. Hill of the Reclamation Service said in an interview with a reporter for the *Arizona Republican,* on September 2, that if there was no interference, the Roosevelt Dam would be 100-feet high across the entire river channel by January 1, 1909. Hill said water could be stored to within 25 feet of the top of the dam, which meant a reservoir of 42,000 acre-feet of water. By February 1, 1909, if all continued well, the dam would be 125-feet high, which would increase the reservoir capacity to 110,000 acre-feet of water. With that amount of stored water, there would be enough "for at least two emergency irrigations when the dry times come next season" in addition to the general irrigations, the newspaper reported. The *Republican* added in an editorial,

What this means to the Salt river valley can hardly be hinted at. The fulfillment of all prophecies as to area cultivated, as to the wonderful development to follow in the building of cities and towns and country homes, cannot come for years for this is but the beginning of an expansion that will continue until a time beyond which we of the present day are not concerned. But for those who have lived and struggled for a quarter of a century in this chosen land, a paradise lacking only water; those who have improved their lands with an abiding confidence in both God and government; those who have toiled, and prayed and cursed, have bought water and stolen water that others had bought; those who were patient enough to bear the burden that they might wear the crown; this glad news is a fulfillment of prophecy, a reward for past industry and faithfulness in overcoming what often seemed to be insurmountable obstacles. [2]

Four men were injured in an explosion of methane gas at 11:15 a.m. Sunday, September 6, in the power plant at Roosevelt Dam. The injured were Almon H. Demrick, chief electrician, who was badly burned on the face, arms, and chest; R. H. Spencer, electrician, burned on the face and arms and cut in the scalp over the left forehead; William Harvey, power plant operator, burned on the face, chest, and arms; and Thomas A. Crow, workman, burned on the face, neck, and arms, and right shoulder hurt by being thrown against a wall. Three other men escaped injury, and those who were hurt were expected to recover. The *Republican* printed this account of the incident:

Just after the big turbine wheel which drives the dynamo developing all the electrical energy used at this place for construction work, etc., was stopped at 11 o'clock yesterday [Sunday], for general adjustment and inspection, a very unusual and peculiar accident occurred. The machine plates on the big steel jacket were being removed. When the lower manhole was opened Chief Electrical Engineer Demrick with six men in attendance was examining the wheel, when a lighted candle caused a violent explosion by the ignition of methane gases developed from the vegetable matter contained in the water. A terrific long-drawn flare emanated from the manhole, burning the faces, breasts, and arms of the men who were thrown violently from the aperture into which they were looking. Their clothing was torn to shreds. [3]

Four government carpenters, who struck for higher wages and rebelled at working on Labor day, September 7, and attempted to induce others to join them, were fired. Word seeking replacements for them was sent to Phoenix. [4]

The Reclamation Service announced September 8 the price of winter water for the period between September 15 and May 15, 1909, would be $1 per acre and would be on sale between September 15 and 30. The price of flood water was set at 50 cents per acre. The sale of flood water later drew protests from some farmers who said it was delivered while water was in short supply or when there were less than 50,000 miners' inches in the river. The Appropriators' Canal Co. set its winter water price at $1.25 per acre and 75 cents for flood water. [5]

The lake that had formed behind Roosevelt Dam because of the August rains had completely disappered by September 10 and a vast expanse of mud flats was left in its place. The ferryboat and gasoline launch ordered by the government arrived, but the launch lacked a propeller and steering wheel, items which either were omitted or were lost in transit. A rowboat also was delivered but without oars. [6]

The relocation of the Roosevelt post office was still not decided. About half the population already had moved to the new town and the other half waited for the stage company to move. Stage company officials said they could not move until they knew where the post office was going. [7]

Engineer S. K. Baker of the Reclamation Service completed the survey of the new Highland Canal on September 11. The survey party was able to bring additional land under the canal by changing the course of a former survey in an easterly direction. The survey provided for a canal 16-feet wide across the bottom at its beginning at the Consolidated Canal head, gradually narrowing to six feet at its end. [8]

The Reclamation Service's proposed contract for purchase of the Consolidated Canal Co. from Alexander J. Chandler was discussed by Hill with the governors of the Water Users' Association at a meeting September 14. The *Arizona Gazette* commented that, "It was not necessary that this contract be approved by the Board of Governors, but it was done, merely to show that the Water Users' Association did not disapprove of the deal." The *Republican* said the intent of the Reclamation Service was "to do for the south side water users just what has been done for the north side water users, and is therefore the taking of one more of the big steps toward the completion of the Salt River project." The

Reclamation Service itself later reported that if it was "to serve the lands on the south side, it was necessary either to construct a canal practically parallel to the Consolidated or use the latter canal. . ." The Consolidated Canal passed through particularly difficult terrain, climbing along a side hill for about five miles to reach the mesa from which Mesa derived its name. To put the canal in shape so that it would stand was going to require "several years of extensive repair work and a good many dollars," but the alternative was for the Reclamation Service to build a parallel canal that would pass through the same ground and probably would be "subject to the same difficulties." In addition, south side farmers would receive no benefit from the Granite Reef Diversion Dam for the year or two it would take to build the parallel canal. The Reclamation Service determined the cost of duplicating the Consolidated Canal Co. system was very high. It was after that that Hill entered into negotiations with Chandler. Hill said the principle adhered to in purchasing any canal system was this: "If we could purchase the system at a reasonable price, it was but fair to do that rather than to build a parallel canal and ruin that investment." The usual basis for setting a price for the canals was the cost of excavating the various materials, but the Consolidated Canal Co. property was bought at its original cost of construction less the cost of its headworks, diversion gates, division boxes, sluice gates, and all but two or three laterals that were useable. Also deducted was the cost of putting the lower part of the Consolidated Canal into good repair, including the removal of silt, trees, and other debris. After making all these deductions, Hill said, "the cost of it all was so considerably less than the cost we would be put to build a parallel canal that we were very glad to accept his price for the property." Except that the price was not Chandler's. The Reclamation Service proposed $187,000 and Chandler accepted. There were no negotiations. The purchase of the Consolidated Canal was attacked in the majority report of a House subcommittee that investigated the Reclamation Service and the Salt River project in 1912. The subcommittee concluded the land served by the Consolidated Canal had been fraudulently obtained by Chandler. The subcommittee charged once the canal had been used to obtain the land,

The canal was allowed to run down. When the Reclamation Service came there were from 4 to 5 feet of sand and numerous trees and other obstructions in the ditch. One bank had been washed away for a distance of nearly a mile and a half near the intake, and it was hardly possible to travel along the banks. . .Reclamation reports show it cost $100,000 to put the canal in repair. When repaired, it served to reclaim the very lands of which the Government had been defrauded. Also Hill permitted Chandler to reserve a power site at which power is developed to operate pumps which supply additional water for Chandler's use. Hill also gave Chandler a contract similar to that given to other large land speculators, by which the Government of the United States, in effect, guarantees to deliver water to such persons as Chandler may induce to settle upon 160 acre tracts or less. [9]

As part of the proposed contract, Chandler retained the power plant he had built on the crosscut canal from which water was diverted from the Main Canal (the old Mesa Canal) through the West branch, or Tempe Crosscut Canal,

to the Tempe Canal. The powerhouse was constructed at a point where the water dropped 42 feet to the Tempe Canal and developed 300 kilowatts of electricity with a flow of 125 cubic feet of water per second. The electricity was sold to Tempe and Mesa in addition to being supplied to the Chandler Ranch for its pumps. Chandler was to pay the government an average of one-half cent per kilowatt hour for the electricity, and Hill estimated the revenue to the government would reach $10,000 per year. The Reclamation Service had the option of providing Chandler with a maximum load of 300 kilowatts in lieu of the water. [10]

The other Consolidated Canal Co. property included the Main Canal, which ran from the south bank of the river about eight miles to what was known as the division gates; the Eastern branch, which ran from the division gates south for a distance of 18 miles; the West branch, running west from the division gates for about two miles to the power division gates, where the canal split to allow water to run either through or around the powerhouse and then in a northerly direction to the Tempe Canal; and the contract between the Consolidated Canal Co. and the Mesa Canal Co. entered into January 10, 1891. Under this contract, the Consolidated Canal Co. delivered water to the Mesa Canal Co. at the rate of $8.75 per share per year for the total of $3,500 per year. Hill said most of the lands under the Mesa Canal were signed into the association. Since under the new conditions the water could be delivered at much less expense per share, he believed the Mesa Canal Co. owners would be pleased to turn their canal over to the government as soon as they could. [11]

The contract provided the government would pay the $187,000 in three installments: $50,000 on January 1, 1909, or as soon thereafter as title was conveyed to the government; $50,000 on January 1, 1910, and $87,000 on January 1, 1911. The *Republican* erroneously reported that for the agreement between the government and Chandler to become effective, it required only the approval of the secretary of the interior. In fact, the dealings between Hill and Chandler continued so the actual agreement was not signed by them until November 19, 1908, and Secretary of the Interior James R. Garfield did not approve the contract until January 11, 1909. [12]

Chandler on December 23, 1912, signed a contract with the government modifying the terms of the agreement as they pertained to the electrical delivery. Under the new contract, Chandler could take delivery of up to 600 kilowatts of electricity for a period of 10 years at the rate of 1 cent per kilowatt hour with a minimum charge of $2.50 per kilowatt per month. The new contract also provided for the delivery of the power to Chandler's substation near Mesa and to other substations near the towns of Chandler and Tempe if requested. [13]

Other actions taken by the governors, besides approving the contract for the government's buying the Consolidated Canal Co. property, were the appointments of committees to consider the construction of a "water temple," which was a building to house Water Users' Association and Reclamation Service offices, and to inquire into the construction of laterals along the lower portion of the Grand Canal under the cooperative plan approved for building the new Highland Canal. Together the association and the service were paying $1,800 per year in rent, and the lease was due to expire in May 1909. It was contended the rent bill for eight or ten years would equal the cost of a building made to suit the rquirements of the association. [14]

Hill, Governor Joseph H. Kibbey, attorney for the Water Users' Association, and Benjamin A. Fowler, association president, met September 16 in Mesa to discuss the proposal for building the new Highland Canal with the landowners. Kibbey said the estimated cost of the Salt River project was $6 million, and the government was without funds to dig the ditch itself and would be that way for two or three years. However, the certificates (or scrip) the government would issue the landowners for the money they put up or work performed would be limited in use to pay for the entire reservoir project and would not be acceptable in payment for water service or for annual operation and maintenance expenses. Kibbey said the landowners had the choice of doing the work through individual contracts or through one large contract, but all work must be acceptable to the Reclamation Service. Hill estimated 115,000 yards of gravel would have to be excavated in the hilly section of the canal alignment and 100,000 yards off the desert on the mesa. He thought the work would be comparatively easy and could be accomplished with ordinary scrapers and teams with the cost 10 cents per yard overall and less than 30 cents per yard at the upper end. He said the Reclamation Service would do all the cement work. Harry L. Chandler said he had calculated the cost would equal $5 per acre. Chandler, Tom W. Smith, and others urged the landowners to sign their land to build the canal. [15]

Professor F. H. Bigelow arrived in Phoenix on September 16 to confer with Hill about building a plant at or near Roosevelt to measure water evaporation. [16]

A new steam dredge built by the Reclamation Service for use in continuing the enlargement of the Arizona Canal was launched September 20. However, machinery remained to be installed. [17]

From Roosevelt came word that construction of a new schoolhouse in new Roosevelt had been completed in time for the opening of the fall term. Meantime, a new school district had been formed to accommodate children on the O'Rourke side of the river. The high line road to Globe formed the main street through the new Roosevelt. Two side streets provided the frontage for other buildings and tents. A few stores and tents as well as the post office remained in the old town. [18]

Toward the end of September, the lowest part of the dam was 54 feet above datum, and contractor John O'Rourke used about as much cement as the cement mill could produce. Of the four men injured in the explosion September 6, only Demrick remained in the hospital. He was able to get around but his hands and portions of his face and chest were still bandaged. [19]

C. W. McKee, chairman of the joint committee of the Maricopa County Commercial Club and the Maricopa and Phoenix Board of Trade, wrote to President Theodore Roosevelt on September 26 appealing to him to do something about the Reclamation Service contract with Pacific Gas & Electric Co. McKee said, in part:

The recipient of this valuable contract, the Pacific Gas & Electric Co., are greatly overcapitalized. Their president states that their property is worth but $200,000, thus getting a reduction of taxes from the assessed valuation of $140,000, yet it is bonded and capitalized for six hundred thousand or more dollars.

Our citizens have grounds for fearing that instead of the promised benefits of cheap electric power from the Roosevelt reclamation project they will be forced to pay rates that will yield a private monopoly interest on an excessive capitalization.

Because of banking interests represented in the control of the Water Users' Association and also interested in the Pacific Gas & Electric Co. it may be difficult to get an expression from the former of the members of the Water Users' Association. . . .

This contract, being a creature of the local reclamation managers, is naturally defended by them and because of the fear expressed on many sides that any criticism of the contract might have the effect of the Government discontinuing the work on the Roosevelt project and for reasons above stated the directors of the Water Users' Association approved the contract one year after it was made.

Having exhausted our resources direct with the department in interest, we appeal to you to take such action as will free our people from this ten year exclusive contract. [20]

The work of making holes for the transmission line towers at the Buttes in Tempe began. The workers discovered the ground was solid rock, and the excavation of the holes, two-feet across and five-feet deep, required considerable blasting and drilling. The last tower before crossing the river was up by September 30. It stood high enough on the side of a butte so the wire that would eventually stretch from it would cross a span of 800 feet to another tower to rise from a caisson built in the riverbed. Another 800-foot span would then link to a tower on the north side of the river. Also under construction was the Mesa substation on the southwest corner of the Bullock Ranch. The men excavating the South Canal experienced considerable difficulty because of the large number of boulders and the rocky formation. [21]

Shareholders of the Appropriators' Canal Co. met October 5 in a spirit of harmony and reelected the board of directors, which in turn reelected John P. Orme president. The company's indebtedness had been reduced to $6,800, and it was predicted by the following spring it would be down to $2,500. [22]

Judge Edward Kent on October 7 heard evidence concerning the water rights of the Fort McDowell Indian Reservation in the case of *Hurley v. Abbott.* Also present was George W. Hance, who was there to represent himself and the interests of others who lived along the upper Verde River. [23]

The following day, the *Republican's* correspondent at Roosevelt reported the dam at its lowest level was 60 feet above datum and the work was progressing at the rate of 600 cubic yards of cement per day. O'Rourke employed about 400 men, working them in day and night shifts. The river was very low and resembled "a good-sized creek cut through a mud flat, with four- to six-foot banks on each side." Tonto

Creek was so low it could be jumped across and several boats were stranded high on the mud. [24]

Demrick got out of the hospital and returned to work, but one hand was still tied up and over the other he wore a cotton flannel glove to protect it. [25]

Carpenters fashioned the forms for the concrete and stone work that would encase the penstock at the face of the dam. The masonry was being laid when all work on the dam was called to a halt on October 22 because the cement had not been burned long enough. This was detected by D. O. White, a government chemist, and more than 9,000 barrels of cement, which were too green, were discarded. The opening of the penstock was closed with timbers to prevent an inflow of water. [26]

On the same day in Phoenix, the Reclamation Service resolved the question of who was to haul 33,000 barrels of oil to Roosevelt for use in the cement mill. Shattuck-Nimmo Warehouse Co., the present contractor, was scheduled to deliver the last of 50,000 barrels of oil by the end of October. The price for the oil delivered at Roosevelt was $3.48 per barrel but Shattuck-Nimmo's bid for the new consignment was $5.05 per barrel, including $3.30 per barrel to haul the oil from Mesa to Roosevelt. The low bid for the oil and its delivery to Roosevelt was made by the Pioneer Consolidated Transfer Co. of Phoenix at $4.40 per barrel, but the company operators later abandoned the bid because they could not deliver at the stated price. Shattuck-Nimmo, to carry through its original contract, had spent at least $35,000 on wagons, tanks, horses, shops, and stations along the way. In good weather the trip required eight days, with each man delivering two tanks containing from 13 to 19 barrels each. There was talk of the government taking over the delivery of the oil, but the expenses were such that Shattuck-Nimmo and the Reclamation Service reached a compromise price of $3.15 per barrel to haul the oil from Mesa. This was in addition to the price of oil delivered to Mesa, which was about $1.75 per barrel. [27]

Santiago Gomez was buried alive by cement in a bin at the cement mill late in the night of October 26 or early in the morning of October 27. Gomez and two co-workers were occupied filling buckets of cement, which were transferred to the dam by a continuous cable. After they cleared the cement from the front of the bin, Gomez entered to start the cement, which had collected in a high wall or break off, in a flow toward the front of the bin. When he failed to come out of the bin after about 15 minutes, his comrades entered and found him buried in the cement. The cement was about a foot over his head. Gomez was buried at Roosevelt October 28. [28]

The gates in the sluicing tunnel at Roosevelt Dam were closed the night of November 5 to determine if they were working properly preparatory to closing them to allow water to be stored to a height 25 feet below the top of the dam. In connection with that, workmen put up forms for the continued extension of the shaft through which the gates were operated. The shaft rose as the dam rose and would do so to the top of the dam. Carpenters also prepared the forms to bring upward at the head of the sluicing tunnel the grillwork, which had been started earlier. [29]

In Roosevelt, the last restaurant had been closed and moved to the new town. There nevertheless remained at the old town about nine houses and tents, a store, a place to buy soft drinks, the stage office, and the post office. [30]

The Highland Canal landowners received a letter November 6 from the Water Users' Association advising them they would have to submit a petition to the association asking it to request the Reclamation Service for permission to build the new canal under the cooperative plan. The Highland owners were under the impression all they had to do to begin construction was raise enough money to guarantee interest on the money that would be invested by the Highland Canal Construction Co. in building the canal. Circulation of a petition was started immediately and was soon in the hands of the Water Users' Association. [31]

The governors agreed to a proposal by Hill that new bridges, to be built over the Grant Canal in connection with its widening and deepening, be made of concrete. The governors said they approved concrete bridges when it was assured there would not be a need for further changes in the canal; when there was a chance of this, bridges of less expense and permanance were preferred. Hill already had arranged with the Santa Fe Railroad for construction of a steel bridge where the tracks crossed the canal alongside Grand Avenue. [32]

Dr. B. B. Moeur of Tempe received a telephone call on Saturday afternoon, November 7, asking him to hurry to Roosevelt to care for Mrs. John Chapman, who had taken ill. Moeur telephoned the Ainsworth garage in Phoenix asking for its fastest car. With Joe Volz at the wheel, they left Tempe at 5 p.m. and arrived in Roosevelt at 11 p.m. They started back from Roosevelt at 3 a.m. with Mrs. Chapman, the wife of a government engineer at the dam, and arrived in Tempe at 8 a.m. The *Republican,* in reporting this incident, failed to specify Mrs. Chapman's illness except to say "she is suffering from complications" but was not critically ill, and that the trip had been made in the fastest time thus far. [33]

For travelers who did not expect such a rapid trip, the Roosevelt Stage Co. offered a one-way trip from Mesa to Roosevelt for $6 with five changes of horses and arrival in 10 hours. [34]

O'Rourke's men resumed laying rock and concrete at the dam on November 10, using the cement produced at the cement mill the previous two weeks. However, the supply did not last long and within a week the concrete work at the dam was again at a standstill. [35]

A postal official arrived in Roosevelt November 12 to decide where the post office should be located. A decision was becoming critical because the lowest elevation of the dam was about 85 feet and the high point was 97 feet above datum. That put the lowest part of the dam 10 feet higher than the elevation of the post office, which meant that if the gates were closed and the water was allowed to rise within 25 feet of the top of the lowest part of the dam, there would be a 15-foot margin of safety. The stage company office stood at the same elevation as the post office, but the company's barn and corral were from 12 to 20 feet lower. Once the gates were closed and a lake was formed, virtually anything in the way of a flood would have saved the post office and stage company the trouble of moving. The plan was to close the gates after the reservoir reached the desired level. Then they were to be opened sufficiently to maintain the height. However, the need to adjust the machinery operating the gates delayed their immediate closing. [36]

The new Roosevelt had about 400 residents and 10 businesses. The latter included three general stores, two restaurants, a jewelry and gun store, a butcher shop, a bakery, and two barber shops. [37]

The *Republican* reported November 19 that Hill had just signed a contract with the Southwestern Sugar and Land Co. to draw water from the Arizona Canal to fill one or two reservoirs with a total capacity of 260 acre-feet of water. The newspaper said the company had bought an unencumbered title to 8,135 acres of land from the Detroit Trust Co., all of it under the Arizona Canal and all of it signed into the Water Users' Association. The property was valued at $1.6 million. The sugar company planned to build one or two reservoirs, and the Reclamation Service was to have the right to use them during the nine months of the year when the factory was not operating. Most of the water used in the factory was to be turned into a lateral for use by farmers under the Arizona Canal. Some of the water, however, would have quantities of lime. That water was to be drawn off separately until its potential effect on the land could be determined. The factory was to replace this water with pumped water. [38]

P. H. Greer of the Greer-Robbins Co. of Los Angeles claimed the record round trip in an automobile from Phoenix to Roosevelt after passing over the route in 8 hours and 37 minutes on November 19. Greer, accompanied by R. L. Greer and Dale Carleton of Los Angeles, drove a four cylinder, 20 horsepower Mitchell runabout. The time to Roosevelt was 4 hours and 16 minutes; the return was 4 hours and 21 minutes. P. H. Greer, who never before had been over the road, said he passed 25 teams traveling in both directions, and this caused some delay because he had to wait in sidings for them to pass. Greer commented:

...a race over this road, which in my estimation is one of the finest motor courses in the country, would fill the adventurous spirit with joy. The chances of dropping over a precipice would make it most interesting. I have just come from a 600-mile trip through California and with the single exception of the Yosemite, think this the most beautiful motor trip in America. [39]

On November 22, the last of the copper wire for the transmission line between Roosevelt and Mesa was put in place, and City of Tempe officials received a letter from Hill saying the government expected to be ready to deliver electricity to the Valley sometime in the spring. [40]

Hill on November 27 ordered there be no more car racing over the Roosevelt road. He reminded the road was built for hauling freight and construction of the dam, not for racing. Hill said there were constantly 20 to 60 teams on the road, and the lives of the teamsters and the animals should not be endangered by speeding automobiles. [41]

An application by J. M. O'Rourke & Co. for an extension of time to complete Roosevelt Dam was granted December 1 by the secretary of the interior. The extension was for five months, advancing the completion date to March 10, 1909. [42]

The cement mill at Roosevelt was shut down for two days. On Monday morning, December 7, workmen started a small fire under an iron 20-barrel fuel oil tank in the mill to thaw congealed oil. A drain in the tank had been left open, and the fire ignited the oil, causing two explosions in the globe valves connecting the oil pipes. With the blasts, fire erupted, burning through many of the timbers in the building, including the wooden clay and rock bins. The iron roof held together because it was riveted, but the intense heat caused the iron rafters and braces to twist and bend and the roof sagged and appeared ready to collapse. A hoist outside the mill was destroyed and damage was estimated at $9,000. It was estimated it would take about two weeks to repair the building. This did not mean an immediate stopping of all the work on the dam because some cement was on hand. However, it meant a delay when the cement supply ran out except that a stoppage already had been planned because the engineers intended to extend the power canal penstock into the powerhouse to connect with two additional water wheels. To accomplish this, it was necessary to shut off the power, which would have cut the electricity to the cement plant as well as to the derricks, hoists, and other equipment. [43]

The governors approved the plans of the Highland Canal Construction Co. and authorized publication of a call for bids. The Highland landowners, meantime, changed the name of the projected canal from the Highland to the Eastern, and it was under the latter name that the following advertisement was published December 10 in the *Republican:*

Proposals will be received at the office of the Salt River Valley Water Users' association, at Phoenix, Ariz., until 2 o'clock p.m., December 23rd, 1908, for excavation work on the EASTERN CANAL (commonly known as the new Highland canal).

Estimates will be received for one or more divisions, or subdivisions thereof consisting of approximately 2,000 cubic yards, as shown on the profile.

Profile may be examined and forms of proposal obtained at the office of the Water Users' association, Phoenix; the U.S. Reclamation Service, Phoenix, or the Mesa City Bank, Mesa, Arizona.

The canal was to be nineteen and one-half miles long, and about 225,000 yards of various formations were to be excavated. The estimated cost was $3,000 per mile. The canal would pass within four miles of Mesa on the east and serve as the reservoir district's east boundary south of the river.

The excavation was divided into eight divisions with the formation varying from solid rock to soft earth. Contractors could bid on the entire work or on one of the divisions. [44]

Rain fell over the watershed in the early part of December raising the levels of the Salt River and Tonto Creek. The sluicing tunnel carried all the water, but the increased volume interfered with additional cement work involving the forms holding the tunnel gates. Work on the dam continued, and the highest point approached 90 feet above datum and the lowest about 75 feet. [45]

Jesse Earl Parker, a shift foreman for the Reclamation Service at Roosevelt Dam, was fatally hurt at 11:30 a.m. December 12 while aiding in the repair of the cement mill. Parker was standing by a large timber resting on a hydraulic jack holding up the roof. The foundation for the jack gave way, causing another large timber to fly out and hit Parker, who fell 12 feet to a concrete floor. His head hit the concrete and he died at 9 o'clock that night. Parker was survived by a wife and child. [46]

Light rain began falling December 13 and continued for the next two days and nights, picking up in intensity as time passed. On Monday, December 14, postmaster Burtis received orders to relocate the Roosevelt post office to near the Reclamation Service office at Roosevelt-on-the-Hill. Just before sundown December 15, it was noticed Tonto Creek and the Salt River had started to rise. But in the words of S. S. Thompson, the **Republican's** Roosevelt correspondent, "nothing was expected to develop into a dangerous situation therefrom, and all went to sleep in peace." By 7 a.m. Wednesday, "the bottom of the reservoir was covered up to about the height it was a short while back, when a lake was formed here." Thompson said, "Parties who still lived on the bottom did not feel any apprehension," and all went to work at the cement mill, including Thompson. He said no one expected any further rise in the reservoir because the gates in the sluicing tunnel were wide open. After it began raining again, he congratulated himself for working under shelter that day. Thompson's description of the submerging of Roosevelt and the surrounding area continued:

At eight o'clock a fellow workman called our attention to the fact that a small cabin was afloat on the edge of the lake. It dawned on our dilatory mind that that was an odd thing, as we were under the impression that that particular cabin was all right when we went to work. Even as we stood watching it, one nearby commenced to show water between it and the shore. Something doing sure, and not much time to hesitate, either. We dropped our tools and commenced to stampede towards home. On the way we passed several cabins, the owners of which were transferring their contents toward higher levels. . . Our house was situated on the highest point of what has since become an island and soon afterward part of the bottom of the lake. We still thought that we would escape, as we were a few feet higher than the lowest part of the dam, and that when the water began to flow over, that it would not rise any higher, such being the decision of one of the engineers also.

The post office was 10 or 15 feet lower than our location and on the same piece of land, and it was thought that the water would just about reach it. Mr. Burtis thought that this was a little nearer than would be comfortable, so he proceeded to move at once. . . Every thing was got out safely, but there had to be some tall hustling on the part of the postmaster to do it. . .

As to ourselves, we waited for the water to stop until 10:30, but it didn't know how, it seems, as it came creeping, creeping up like the rising tide. We had one tent a little lower by some six feet than our main habitation, and it was stored full of goods and, just to be absolutely safe, we decided to move them. . .

Up to this time we had labored under the impression that our other tents were absolutely safe, but word came that the water passing the [power canal] intake was equal to the amount passing the dam, and that the Tonto had to be reckoned with also, in excess of this. We proceeded at once, and with the aid of eight additional men to transport the rest of our household goods to the side of the mountain opposite, and got the contents and upper parts of two of the tents across to the mainland—we had just before this been transformed into an island—by making a temporary bridge. . . It was not very long till the island began to be awash, and shortly afterward disappeared from view. . .

It rained most of the night and every once in a while the tent would whip loose from one corner of the building directly over our bed and relieve itself of all surplus water onto the bed covers. In the meantime the lake was up to within four feet of our floor, and every time we woke up we would heave out a rock with which we had provided ourselves before retiring to see if the water had reached us yet. Providentially, the rise of the lake stopped at about three feet below our level. . . All night the crash of adobe walls could be heard as the water reached them. All night, also, could be heard at intervals the last cry of some unfortunate cat which had found some wall as a temporary place of safety, and succeeding the crash of the wall would come the cry of the feline that had placed too much faith on its stability and whose faith was rewarded with a watery grave. . . In the morning we found. . .over a dozen houses were caught by the water and some of them with all their belongings. The post office building floated up stream about a hundred yards, and the waters having since receded some several feet, have left it standing in the mud. Many people who have visited Roosevelt and stopped at the Hotel de Akers can form somewhat of an idea of the recent rise when informed that the water rose above the counters in the store that was situated on the first floor of that hostelry. The church building was flooded almost up to the eaves of that building. . .

The government launch has been kept busy, and Mr. Depew, who has been finding time hanging heavily on his hands on account of lack of water to run his boat, has had to work overtime in trying to fill all demands that have been sprung upon him. A boom has been stretched across the river above the dam to impound lumber, houses and driftwood, of which large bodies cover the lake, from going over the dam. All derricks were taken off the dam in time to keep them from being washed away. Some lively work had to be done at the powerhouse to keep the water going over the dam from getting in among the electrical machinery. . . The water going over the dam sends up a spray higher than the dam itself as it strikes the bottom on the lower side. All that could be seen of the dam while the water was going over full force was a course of three large stones that constituted the highest part of the dam. . . Reports from up the Tonto state that it was the highest rise in years, in fact, since 1891. . . The waters of the lake are backed up, both rivers out of sight, and this flood ought to put a quietus on the croakers that have been laboring under the illusion that we never get enough rain in Arizona. . .to fill the reservoir site at the Roosevelt Dam. [47]

The *Gazette* reported the afternoon of December 16 that water more than six-feet deep was passing over Roosevelt Dam and more than seven-feet deep over Granite Reef Diversion Dam with the volume of water at the diversion dam flowing at the rate of 60,000 cubic feet per second. The *Republican* said the stream over Roosevelt Dam was 125-feet wide and eight feet in the deepest place. About 8 p.m., the water running over Roosevelt Dam was about 13-feet deep and was within two feet of the highest point on the structure. In the Valley, the gage on the Verde River at the 16-foot level was covered, and the Arizona Canal was broken in numerous places including 14 breaks made by Cave Creek northwest of Phoenix. A crew of men under the direction of Demrick was sinking a caisson in the Salt River at Tempe to support the transmission line, but a rise of about 12 feet in the river interrupted that work. The caisson, measuring 5 feet 6 inches in diameter, was being sunk to bedrock 35 feet below. [48]

Looking downstream from above powerhouse roof (foreground), circa December 1908.

The river crested at Granite Reef about 11 p.m. December 16, reaching a depth of 7 feet 2 inches. The crest at Roosevelt passed at 1:30 a.m. December 17 and was about 18 inches over the highest place on the dam. [49]

Hill was at Laguna Dam, Arizona, at this time, and on December 17 he sent the following letter to Fowler:

As you know, I have received a number of applications for power from the Globe district, and feel reasonably certain that I can dispose of such power as we feel that we can spare in that district at very good prices.

I would like to have from the Water Users' Association an expression of the opinion as to the policy they wish to pursue in cases of this kind. I would like to have this expression in the form of a resolution, if it is convenient. [50]

Fowler replied December 21, saying he did not,

think it would be wise to bring this matter before the Board of Governors of the Water Users' Association before your return. It is important that you be present at this meeting to answer questions and give information upon which the Board could base intelligent decision.

Personally, I have no doubt at all that the policy of the Board will be to dispose of such power as can be wisely sold without detriment to the interests of the valley, but this is a large and important question which could not be decided off hand or without your personal assistance and advice. [51]

The rivers receded and by December 21 the flow over Granite Reef Diversion Dam was 18 inches. The same day six inches ran over the low point of Roosevelt Dam. Water coming over the dam had flooded the chamber containing the machinery for operating the sluicing tunnel gates and workmen were assigned to clean it. Once the chamber was cleared, the gates were partially closed to keep the lake at a regular level. The gasoline launch on the lake was kept busy carrying people and mail across the lake. The edges of the lake were covered with driftwood and timber, but gathering it, as some did, for firewood was difficult because of the mud. [52]

F. H. Ensign announced December 23 Pacific Gas & Electric Co. would spend $75,000 to build a new plant "in order that my company may make changes and reductions in our lighting rates at such time as we commence using power furnished under the government contract." Ensign said the plant would transform the current generated at Roosevelt to make it suitable for supplying the city. [53]

Two bids were submitted for construction of the Eastern Canal, but the governors rejected both at a meeting December 24 and decided to ask for new bids. The bids were rejected because they were incomplete and were submitted conditionally. Some surprise was expressed at the lack of interest in bidding on the job, but it unquestionably was because the contractor was to be paid in certificates from the Water Users' Association. While the certificates were transferable, they would not be redeemable except in making payments for the Salt River project when they came due, and the contractor, in effect, was being asked to finance the construction without any provision for paying him interest on his money. A group of the landowners met December 29 to discuss the situation, and it appeared to them that the canal would not be built under such conditions. They met with the governors on December 31 and talked about the Highland Canal Construction Co. doing the work. If the landowners decided to build themselves, they would take the certificates and the only cash they would have to raise would be that which was necessary to cover the amount a bank or capitalist would discount for advancing funds. [54]

On January 1, 1909, the power at Roosevelt Dam was turned off to extend the power canal penstock. The dam at its high point on the south end was about 108 feet, at the center about 90 feet, and at the lowest about 75 feet. Carpenters began dismantling the Roosevelt church so it could be relocated at new Roosevelt. The building was to serve as a public hall and as a school for Indian children. The building was to go up on a lot that originally had been saved for the post office. The Reclamation Service also announced it planned to build a warehouse on S. Second Avenue just below Jackson Street in Phoenix. [55]

The *Republican* announced the first day of the new year the Reclamation Service had taken complete charge of the Appropriators' Canal. The newspaper said the canal company had paid off all its debtors and had given the government a quitclaim deed the day before. In reality, the agreement for the sale of the canal and the quitclaim deed were not signed and filed until January 19. The government paid $1 for the canal, but it also agreed to provide water at its own expense to irrigators who had contracted with the Appropriators' Canal Co. for water through May 15. Once the canal came under control of the Reclamation Service, the task of completing the enlargement of the Grand Canal was started. In some places the Grand and Appropriators' canals were united, in others the Appropriators' replaced the Grand and the unused portions of both were filled in. [56]

The December floods in the Salt River washed away the head and the upper part of the Utah Canal, which led the canal management to seek the aid of the Reclamation Service. The canal directors met with Hill, making a tentative agreement for the government to buy the canal in the future based on the cost of excavating the parts of the ditch that would fit into the south side canal system. Payment for the canal would be in certificates, redeemable as cash in payment for the reservoir. Meantime, the Reclamation Service agreed to furnish water to the Utah Canal through the Consolidated Canal, which meant the construction of a connecting canal about a mile in length. The directors of the Utah Canal approved the agreement at a meeting in Mesa on January 4. [57]

That same day in Phoenix, the governors met with Hill to consider a policy for disposing of surplus electric power and approved the following resolution:

Resolved, that it is the sense of this board that all power developed and generated by works connected with the Salt River project, over and above the demands therefore for the purpose of this association, be leased by the government upon the best possible terms, having due regard always for the best advantage that may accrue to this association and to the people of this valley by the disposition of such surplus power.

The governors also appointed Fowler, Kibbey, and George M. Halm, a member of the board, to serve as a committee to deal with contracts and other such matters when they arose. [58]

Hill estimated the potential for electric power at no less than 25,700 horsepower produced at nine sites with the initial power coming from three locations: Roosevelt Dam, 7,200 horsepower; Arizona Falls, 700 horsepower with the installation of new machinery to replace equipment then used by Pacific Gas & Electric; and South Canal, 1,500 horsepower. The other locations were: midway between Roosevelt and Fish Creek, 3,500 horsepower; near Bagley Flat and a little west of the mouth of Cottonwood Wash, 2,500 horsepower; a short distance above the mouth of the Verde River, 4,500 horsepower; the Chandler plant, 1,000 horsepower; opposite the Joint Head in a proposed drop from the restructured Grand Canal to the Maricopa Canal, 300 horsepower. Of the 9,400 horsepower to be available from the initial three sources, 5,500 were reserved for use by Pacific Gas & Electric, the Gila River Indian Reservation, and irrigation pumping plants within the reservoir district. However, until all of the pumping plants were built, it was estimated that 5,000 horsepower would be available for sale—at $50 per horsepower, a minimum of $250,000 per year, but probably at a higher price. When all nine power sites were in operation, perhaps as much as 20,000 horsepower would be available for sale, or a minimum of $1 million per year if sold at $50 per horsepower (which was considered a low price). In reporting this, the *Republican* presented a bright picture for the farmers with their not having "to put up a cent" to pay for the irrigation works. And, once "title to the project has passed to the association the annual dividends to the farmers will make the county taxes look like popcorn money at Christmas time." [59]

Hill told the governors a corporation at Globe wanted to contract for 2,500 horsepower and another wanted an indefinite amount. A company in the Kelvin-Ray district indicated a desire for power. Hill said there doubtless would be others in the near future. [60]

Attorney George Stone of Globe told a *Gazette* reporter Globe interests were very anxious to get electricity from Roosevelt Dam and if enough power could be obtained, a transmission line would be built from Globe to Roosevelt. Stoneman said the Globe area was booming. He estimated that four-fifths of the mining property in the district had changed hands in the past five years. [61]

New bids for construction of the Eastern Canal were opened in the Water Users' Association office on January 6. W. S. Dorman of Mesa offered a bid on one section of the work, while the Highland Canal Construction Co. and a San Francisco contractor, R. A. Moncure, proposed building the entire canal. If the Highland Canal Construction Co. received the contract, it was expected it would sublet the work and perhaps even pay a bonus since the company's objective was to have the canal built as quickly and cheaply as possible. The bonus would be in lieu of interest the company might have to pay some other contractor on the certificates the Water Users' Association would issue. [62]

Shattuck-Nimmo Warehouse Co. received a new 11-passenger Concord stage from M. P. Henderson & Sons of Stockton, Calif., the manufacturer, for use on the run between Mesa and Roosevelt. Shattuck-Nimmo planned to retire an 8-passenger stage used on the line since April 1905. [63]

After the sluicing tunnel gates were closed at Roosevelt Dam, Reclamation Service engineers discovered the large amount of water that had come over the dam had scooped

Two views of electric transmission line towers, February 1909.

out to bedrock all the loose dirt, gravel, and rock immediately below the dam. A considerable pile of this debris accumulated at the exit of the sluicing tunnel. This was cleared away and a concrete extension of the tunnel was built to prevent a recurrence of the problem. Work also proceeded on the addition to the power canal penstock into the powerhouse, while the penstock through the dam was covered with asphaltum paint. [64]

Engineer Jay D. Stannard proposed the Water Users' Association join with other associations in opposing a bill before Congress that would prevent the Reclamation Service from spending any money after July 1 without permission of Congress. Stannard said the work of the U.S. Geological Survey had been weakened by such a provision, and he expressed concern the Reclamation Service would be unable to get appropriations to complete the work at Roosevelt. He said protests to the legislation from the Reclamation Service would do little good. The protests had to come from the people, he said. [65]

Reclamation Service engineers reported to the Water Users' Association on January 16 that the bid of the Highland Canal Construction Co. was the lowest for building the Eastern Canal. [66]

Early the week of January 17, water again flowed over the lowest point of Roosevelt Dam. The plan was to let the water run over the dam for a few days to carry off the driftwood. Then the gates would be opened and the lake drained. When the lake was empty, the gates would be shut again. By the time water began going over the dam again, it was thought the extension work on the sluicing tunnel and other repairs would be completed. [67]

The gates were opened about January 22 and electric power at the dam turned on. The cement mill went back into operation the next day and the first dance in the new Roosevelt was held at the public hall that night. Several feet of water drained out of the lake over the weekend, but rains began falling over the watershed. On January 25, work on the dam was again in full swing, but the in-flow of water into the lake from Tonto Creek and Salt River soon began to exceed the volume let out by the sluicing tunnel. By January 28, water poured over the low part of the dam at a depth of eight feet. However, the flow began dropping, and, in a few days, the lake was again below the level of the dam. [68]

Statistician Blanchard wrote to Fowler on January 22 expressing concern about the rising price of land in the Valley:

. . .the real estate boom in the valley has assumed such proportions, and the land values have increased to such an extent,

that many would-be settlers are being turned away. . . With land prices soaring as they are in the valley I have hesitated about directing anyone to that section of the country. . . Present land owners cannot claim that they are in any sense responsible for this big increase in values, and if they put their prices too high it is quite probable that large areas will remain unsettled until the time comes for the Water Users' Association to put it on the market. This, of course, would result in bringing down values, and would be followed by a great outcry on the part of the landowners. [69]

In the Valley, construction of the transmission line was within two miles of the Salt River Crossing at Tempe by January 25. Poles also had been set, except for the last seven, to the Pacific Gas & Electric plant in Phoenix. Six miles of the line to the Gila River Indian Reservation from the substation east of Mesa were completed. [70]

Representative Frank DeSouza of Maricopa County on January 29 introduced in the House of the Legislative Assembly a memorial to Congress asking for an investigation of the contract between the Reclamation Service and Pacific Gas & Electric. The memorial was unanimously approved in the House and went immediately to the Council, where it also was approved by a vote of 10 to 2. After citing the section of the contract the memorial said "creates a monopoly and a trust in favor of said Pacific Gas & Electric Co. in said city of Phoenix, relieving it from competition and allowing it to charge consumers in the city of Phoenix charges for electric power controlled and governed only by its desire and conscience," it petitioned Congress,

To call upon the Secretary of the Interior to produce said contract and all correspondence and papers relating thereto, and to investigate said contract, and if upon investigation it appears that said contract is unjust, illegal, and creative of a monopoly, that proper proceedings be brought to obtain the abrogation and annulment of the same. . . [71]

A subcommittee of the House Committee on Expenditures in the Interior Department heard testimony concerning the contract when it met in Phoenix from April 23 through May 2, 1912. The majority report said, in part,

The real important fact. . .which Hill and his associates persist in overlooking is that the act of Congress authorizing the generation of power provides that the municipalities shall be given the preference in the sale of such power and that Hill had no more right to sell the power to a private corporation without first giving the city of Phoenix a chance to purchase it than he would have had to sell the Roosevelt Dam to that same company. . . Your committee believes that some action should be taken by the proper officials of the Government, either through the courts or otherwise, looking to the setting aside of this illegal and vicious contract, and that the Department of Justice should institute such criminal proceedings as the facts warrant. [72]

The advice of the majority was not followed.

Fowler responded to Blanchard's letter on January 30, saying,

With the general proposition that possibly there may in time be danger of "land prices soaring" in this valley I agree. But when you consider the profits being made by many land owners, $200 per acre for good farm lands, well situated in fertile soil sections of the valley, with good school accommodations, and near to railroad and town, does not seem too high. [73]

Harry Williams, 11, was electrocuted January 31 after climbing a Reclamation Service transmission tower near the

Pacific Creamery in Tempe. He reached out with his foot and touched a line of the Tempe Light & Power Co., which passed close to the government line at that point. Williams had gone to the site with a friend, Victor Corbell. They had removed their shoes in order to climb the government's towers. Corbell was on the ground when the accident happened. Ray Nichols of the creamery said he noticed Williams on the tower but glanced away. When he next looked, he saw the boy's head had fallen back. Nichols said Williams was limp for perhaps a minute before falling 35 or 40 feet to the ground. [74]

Although work on Roosevelt Dam had resumed, the main business of contractor O'Rourke's men was to add to the portion of the dam behind the front wall. Five derricks were used on the dam early in February and rock was placed in position as fast as it could be supplied from the quarries. The lake was maintained about five feet below the dam's low point. It backed up along the Salt River for about four miles and along Tonto creek about three and one-half miles. DePew reported he carried 600 teams and 1,400 persons across the water during January. [75]

In a letter February 4, Blanchard agreed with Fowler that because of the advantageous location of the Salt River Valley, the land might not be overpriced, but Blanchard thought the newcomer "is entitled to a little of the unearned increment arising from the expenditure of the Government of seven millions of dollars in your valley." Blanchard said in too many places the price of land had been set so high "settlers do not come in" and he hoped this was not going to happen in the Valley. But there was another matter on Blanchard's mind, and he wrote:

The time is not very far distance. . .when the Government is going to demand a payment for water rights on the Salt River project. What will be the attitude of the speculators and owners

One of the skips used in construction of Roosevelt Dam, February 29, 1909.

194

who are controlling excess areas [of land]? Is the situation going to be the same in the Salt River Valley as it is in other sections? Are we going to have the complaint that the people have not been able to dispose of their property and a request for more time before the Government receives its money? It strikes me that it would do no harm to have this matter discussed in the press of the valley, and to have the attention of the people called to the fact that the day of reckoning is not far off. I am bringing this matter up to you at this time for the reason that I shall be very much disappointed if, in the final analysis, we are confronted with the same conditions in your valley that we have had to meet in other sections not so favorably situated. [76]

The morning of Sunday, February 7, fire destroyed the wooden building that was the Mesa-Roosevelt Stage Co. station at Government Well, the first station east of Mesa. One of the guests was Demrick, government engineer in charge of the transmission line. He lost a portion of his clothing. He and other guests were awakened, dressed, and reportedly helped fight the fire. [77]

The **Republican** reported February 14 the Reclamation Service was constructing four concrete bridges over the Grand Canal and it planned to build 10 or more 5- or 6-room houses around the Valley for use by zanjeros and others. Houses were to be built on both the north and south sides of the river at the Granite Reef Diversion Dam and at the Mesa switching station. Engineer W. A. Farish was in charge of the bridge building. [78]

Three government workers drowned the evening of February 17 at Granite Reef. At the end of the work day, eight men each got into two boats to row across the lake from the north to the south side. The boats had just got under way when an oar of one of them broke and the two craft came together with a jolt. Frightened, some of the men in one boat stood up. Antonio Durana called for them to sit, but one dived into the water, causing the boat to rock and take on water. This further frightened the others, and three more jumped into the water, causing the boat to overturn. A strong current carried the boat and men toward the open sluice gate. R. C. Ochoa saved himself by catching hold of an iron casing, but the other seven were drawn through the gate. Durana, Romaldo Leon, and Eriberto Trasvina drowned, while the others saved themselves. [79]

The committee appointed by the Phoenix City Council to investigate electric power and light rates reported February 18 that Pacific Gas & Electric was overcapitalized and that electric rates were at least 123 percent too high. The committee said the average rate was seventeen and one-half cents per kilowatt hour, and it should be not more than 7 cents. The committee said "that the present rates are an imposition on the public, the poorer people are deprived of convenience of lights and suffer the discomfort due to the excessive cost of fans in summer." The committee urged passage of an ordinance fixing rates and requiring full reports from all public utilities. [80]

Southwestern Sugar Co., in conformance with the national irrigation law, began disposing of its land holdings in excess of 160 acres with an advertisement February 22 in the **Republican**. Through H. I. Latham Co., Southwestern Sugar offered 4,333 acres of land for sale in tracts of 40 acres and up for prices ranging from $125 to $175 per acre. Most of the ground was offered for $150 per acre, and Latham said, the next day, he had sold three of the ranches before noon. Portions of the Jack Rabbitt Ranch went on sale February 23 with the explanation that "the owner's sole reason for reducing his holdings" was the reclamation law's limit on the size of farms. This ground was offered in tracts of 20 acres and up for $125 per acre. The terms were one-fifth cash and one-fifth cash for each of the next five years at 8 percent interest. The water for the land offered by the sugar company and the ranch came through the Arizona Canal. [81]

To a renewed attack in the **Arizona Democrat** upon the government contract with Pacific Gas & Electric, the **Republican** said editorially:

Partisan politics and corporation-phobia lead their victims to great lengths, yet we should think there would be some point at which they would stop short of the lunatic asylum. All are aware how great damage to this valley might have resulted from the assaults which have been made upon the reclamation service in connection with the Pacific Gas and Electric Co. contract, if the government had not known that the assailants did not represent the best and most progressive sentiment of the community. [82]

At the end of February, the high point on Roosevelt Dam was 115 feet above datum, the middle of the dam was 100 feet, and the low point was 83 feet. The water stood at a height of 50 feet against the dam. The **Republican's** correspondent wrote,

Anyone who has not viewed the dam since operations were commenced after New Years would be very much surprised at the strides being taken and the changed appearance of that structure. It is sure beginning to loom up. [83]

---

1. *Arizona Republican* (Phoenix), September 2, 1908.
2. *Ibid.*, September 4, 1908.
3. *Ibid.*, September 8, 10, 1908; *Arizona Gazette* (Phoenix), September 7, 1908.
4. *Republican*, September 13, 1908.
5. *Ibid.*, September 8, 20, October 4, 1908.
6. *Ibid.*, September 13, 1908.
7. *Ibid.*
8. *Ibid.*, *Gazette*, September 11, 1908.
9. *Gazette*, September 14, 1908; *Republican*, September 14, 1908; *Salt River Project, Final History to 1916*, unpublished manuscript, Vol. II, pp. 334-335, Salt River Project Archives (hereafter SRPA); *Report of the matter of the Investigation of the Salt and Gila Rivers--Reservations and Reclamation Service* (Washington:

Government Printing Office, 1913), pp. 13, 587-588.
10. *Final History to 1916*, Vol. II, pp. 337-344; *Republican*, September 15, 1908; *Gazette*, September 14, 1908; *Investigation of the Salt and Gila Rivers*, p. 307.
11. *Final History to 1916*, Vol. II, pp. 337-344; *Republican*, September 15, 1908.
12. *Final History to 1916*, Vol. II, pp. 337-344.
13. *Ibid.*, pp. 352-359.
14. *Gazette*, September 14, 1908; *Republican*, September 15, 17, 1908.
15. *Gazette*, September 17, 1908; *Republican*, September 17, 19, 1908.
16. *Republican*, September 17, 1908.
17. *Ibid.*, September 23, 1908; *Eighth Annual Report of the*

Reclamation Service, 1908-1909, (Washington: Government Printing Office, 1910), p. 45.

18. *Republican,* September 20, 22, 1908.
19. *Ibid.,* September 22, 1908.
20. *Investigation of the Salt and Gila Rivers,* p. 650.
21. *Republican,* September 25, October 1, 1908; *Gazette,* September 24, October 7, 1908.
22. *Republican,* October 6, 1908.
23. *Ibid.,* October 7, 1908.
24. *Ibid.,* October 11, 1908.
25. *Ibid.,* October 11, 18, 1908.
26. *Ibid.,* October 18, 25, 1908.
27. *Ibid.,* August 31, 1908; *Gazette,* August 21, 26, October 22, 24, 1908.
28. *Gazette,* October 17, 1908; *Republican,* November 2, 1908.
29. *Republican,* November 9, 22, 1908.
30. *Ibid.,* November 9, 1908.
31. *Gazette,* November 7, 1908; *Republican,* November 19, December 10, 1908.
32. *Republican,* November 7, 1908.
33. *Ibid.,* November 9, 1908.
34. *Ibid.*
35. *Ibid.,* November 15, 22, 1908.
36. *Ibid.*
37. *Gazette,* November 26, 1908.
38. *Republican,* November 19, 1908.
39. *Ibid.,* November 20, 1908.
40. *Ibid.,* November 22, 1908; *Gazette,* November 26, 1908.
41. *Ibid.,* December 2, 1908.
42. *Ibid.,* December 2, 1908.
43. *Ibid.,* December 8, 13, 1908.
44. *Ibid.,* December 9, 10, 1908; *Gazette,* December 12, 1908.
45. *Republican,* December 13, 1908; *Gazette,* December 17, 1908.
46. *Republican,* December 15, 16, 1908.
47. *Ibid.,* December 14, 1908; *Gazette,* December 21, 1908.
48. *Gazette,* December 16, 17, 1908; *Republican,* December 17, 1908.
49. *Gazette,* December 17, 1908; *Republican,* December 18, 1908.

50. Louis C. Hill to B. A. Fowler, December 17, 1908, SRPA.
51. B. A. Fowler to Louis C. Hill, December 21, 1908, SRPA.
52. *Republican,* December 21, 27, 1908; January 4, 1909.
53. *Ibid.,* December 24, 1908.
54. *Ibid.,* December 25, 30, 1908, January 1, 1909.
55. *Ibid.,* January 4, February 1, 7, 1909; *Gazette,* December 17, 1908, January 1, 1909.
56. *Republican,* January 1, 1909; *Final History to 1916,* Vol. II, pp. 304-309.
57. *Republican,* January 5, 1909.
58. *Ibid.,* January 5, 1909; Charles Van der Veer to Louis C. Hill, January 4, 1909, SRPA.
59. *Republican,* January 5, 6, 1909.
60. *Ibid.,* January 5, 1909.
61. *Gazette,* January 8, 1909.
62. *Republican,* January 7, 1909.
63. *Ibid.,* January 12, 1909.
64. *Ibid.,* January 18, 1909.
65. *Gazette,* January 15, 1909.
66. *Republican,* January 17, 1909.
67. *Ibid.,* January 18, 24, 1909.
68. *Ibid.,* February 1, 7, 1909.
69. C. J. Blanchard to B. A. Fowler, January 22, 1909, SRPA.
70. *Republican,* January 23, 25, 1909.
71. *Ibid.,* January 30, 1909; *Gazette,* January 29, 1909; *Investigation of the Salt and Gila Rivers,* p. 649-650.
72. *Investigation of the Salt and Gila Rivers,* p. 19.
73. B. A. Fowler to C. J. Blanchard, January 30, 1909, SRPA.
74. *Republican,* February 1, 1909.
75. *Ibid.,* February 7, 14, 1909.
76. C. J. Blanchard to B. A. Fowler, February 4, 1909, SRPA.
77. *Republican,* February 9, 1909.
78. *Ibid.,* February 14, 1909.
79. *Ibid.,* February 19, 1909.
80. *Gazette,* February 19, 1909.
81. *Republican,* February 22, 23, 1909.
82. *Ibid.,* February 24, 1909.
83. *Ibid.,* February 28, 1909.

March - August 1909

A section of land [640 acres] under the Utah extension ditch, or the Eureka Canal, sold for $80,000. The buyer was W. J. Clemans. The land, sold by A. J. Peters and George Taylor, four years earlier had been bought for $16,000, or $25 per acre. Clemans and his wife paid $125 per acre. The *Arizona Republican* wrote March 4, "This is a splendid illustration of the remarkable advance in real estate values in the Salt river valley in recent years." [1]

On March 5, the Highland Canal Construction Co. signed a contract with Tom W. Smith and others to build the Eastern Canal. Smith and his partners were landowners under the canal. They received a bonus of $13,000 raised by the landowners to serve as interest on the money they would put up to build the canal under the Reclamation Service's cooperative plan. The first dirt in the construction of the canal was removed March 13. The construction was under the direction of Reclamation Service engineer S. K. Baker. The certificates that Smith and partners were to get from the government were printed in Washington, D.C., in denominations of $5, $10, $50 and $100 and resembled paper money. [2]

Secretary of the Interior Richard A. Ballinger, in one of the first acts of the administration of President William Howard Taft, issued some regulations affecting reclamation projects, including one that required a homesteader,

shall claim at least one-half of the total irrigable area of his land for agricultural purposes, and no right to the use of water for such lands shall permanently attach until such reclamation has been shown. [3]

S. S. Thompson, the *Republican's* correspondent at Roosevelt, wrote on March 11 the highest elevation of Roosevelt Dam was 117 feet, the highest average for two-thirds of the dam 108 feet, and the lowest third 88 feet. Because of snowfall and melt, runoff into the rivers had raised the elevation of the lake in a week from 55 to 62 feet although the sluicing tunnel gates were wide open. As to the dam at that point, it,

is built from one side of the canyon to the other in the shape of a semi-circle with the apex upstream. The length of the dam at datum is about 240 feet, while the top of it is now about 500 feet long. The thickness of the dam at datum is 170 feet and this narrows down as the dam is elevated until now the top of the dam is about 80 feet thick. The upstream side of the dam is perpendicular, while the narrowing down of the dam is done from the lower or down-stream side, and the dam on the lowest side appears to be a long flight of steps, each two or three feet high. The dam when finished is to be 270 feet high.

Two large steel cables extend across the canyon, running parallel and directly above the dam. They are at an elevation of about 500 feet and are capable of sustaining a weight of fifteen tons guaranteed. These are used to carry rock from quarries Nos. 1 and 2 and cement from the mixer. These are delivered to the top of the dam, where five large derricks are situated at intervals of between 80 and 100 feet apart. These derricks have a reach of about 40-foot radius and pick up the material and set it in place. All rock for use in the dam has to be first inspected by competent men in the employ of the government before it can be placed in the dam. . .

. . .as the larger stones require less mortar per cubic yard than the small stones, so this lowers the cost. In laying these large stones considerable care must be taken. First, the stone is let down into the mortar, and if it does not move easily in the mortar, this shows it is resting on stone, and the derrick lifts it and more mortar is put under it. Between the large stones small spalls are used to reinforce the concrete. . . The down-stream face is made of selected stone, but it is not cut more than to form the arch of the dam. The stone on this face is set back six inches to the foot and will be so continued to the top. . . [4]

Ballinger on March 13 sent a letter to Benjamin A. Fowler, president of the Water Users' Association, expressing concern because landowners in some localities were ignoring the requirement that the lands be divided into small holdings for occupation by actual settlers and were instead "increasing them for speculative purposes." The effect was to raise land values so that homeseekers were discouraged, and this, in turn, "imperiled. . .the repayment of the Government's investment in not more than ten annual installments," said Ballinger. He said some landowners had demanded extensions of time and easier terms for payment and others were contemplating doing so "ostensibly. . .to longer hold their lands for advanced prices." Ballinger asked for a report on the breaking up of large holdings in the Salt River Valley, including the value of land with and without water, and whether the officers or principal members of the Water Users' Association were buying or selling land. [5]

The *Republican* reported March 13 the automobile record for climbing Fish Creek Hill had been lowered from 13 minutes to 10 minutes by an Oldsmobile driven by Hughie Hughes, but this was lowered to six and one-half minutes on March 17 by a Winton driven by Herman McFall. On that trip, McFall drove from Roosevelt to Tempe in 3 hours 30 minutes, lowering the record by 50 minutes. McFall was accompanied by Dr. H. H. Stone, owner of the Winton, who said freighters met on the road had no objection to automobiles if the drivers exercised care and did not frighten teams. Some teamsters, however, told stories of discourteous motorists causing near accidents. Stone, a member of the Board of Governors of the Water Users' Association, said the Winton reached the speed of 50 miles an hour while crossing parts of the desert. [6]

Reclamation Service engineers expected to complete the construction of the transmission line from Roosevelt to Phoenix in about three weeks and to then move the workers south of Mesa to complete the line to the Gila River Indian Reservation. [7]

The gates in the Roosevelt Dam sluicing tunnel were closed March 16 to shut off the flow of water into Salt River so sheep could make a downstream crossing of the river into the Valley for shearing. Closing of the gates did not affect the distribution of water because the Verde River supplied enough for irrigation. The gates reopened at 7 p.m. March 18. [8]

Fowler and Louis C. Hill, supervising engineer of the Reclamation Service, met March 23 with a delegation representing about 6,000 acres of land south of the Salt

River. The land was signed into the Water Users' Association, but so far there was no canal to furnish water. The simplest way to bring water to their land was to extend the Wormser branch of the Tempe Canal westward, which the landowners proposed doing under the cooperative plan. But because the Tempe Canal was independent of the government, that could not arbitrarily be done. Hill said if the people under the Tempe Canal failed to come into the association, some other means of bringing water to the delegation's lands would have to be found, but he could not tell them just then what course would be taken. [9]

Judge Edward Kent announced in United States District Court on March 27 he would take additional testimony April 5 in the case of *Hurley v. Abbott*. Kent said testimony concerning the cultivation of land had been compared with records on file with the Water Users' Association and the Reclamation Service. In some instances, water was now being delivered to land about which there was no testimony; in other cases, water was not being delivered to lands that had a right to it. It was to clear up these discrepancies that Kent said he had set April 5 to hear witnesses. [10]

The *Republican* reported March 29 that President Theodore Roosevelt before leaving office had set aside the Roosevelt reservoir as a breeding ground for native birds. No hunting would be allowed on the lake or within its borders. [11]

The evening of March 31, homesteaders east and south of the line of the Eastern Canal met to discuss drilling for wells and asking the Reclamation Service to furnish power for pumping. The homesteaders had heard the government would not deal with them individually but would supply power through a company at a price of 2 cents per horsepower per hour. If the government was unable to supply power, the homesteaders proposed using gasoline engines. However, the Reclamation Service was soon to complete the transmission line to the Gila River Indian Reservation, and it was anticipated power could be obtained from it. In addition, the Reclamation Service was then engaged in drilling batteries of wells south of Mesa to provide pumped water to bring additional lands within the reservoir district into cultivation. [12]

At the end of March, the highest point of the dam above datum was 126 feet with the two-thirds of the dam towards the south averaging 116 feet above water level and the remaining one-third about 96-feet high. The lake against the front of the dam was 70-feet high. [13]

Judge Richard E. Sloan of Prescott was expected to succeed Joseph H. Kibbey, attorney for the Water Users' Association, as governor of the Arizona Territory, and was sworn in as the last territorial governor on May 1, 1909. Plans for the Center Street bridge arrived and went on display in the office of the Maricopa and Phoenix Board of Trade. The bridge plans, prepared by the National Bridge Co. of Indianapolis, Indiana, called for 29 concrete steel arches to support a span more than 2,100 feet in length and 20-feet wide. At the south end of the bridge there was to be a causeway 900-feet long. The bridge was to be higher than the causeway so unusually high flood water would cross the causeway and not the bridge. It was believed the causeway could be repaired at comparatively little expense. Of the 29 piers, 28 would be 6 feet 6 inches wide by 28 feet 6 inches long. The piers would extend 10 feet below the surface of the river bottom and would be set into 25 steel pointed piles, 30 feet in length, and driven into the bed of the river. The central pier was to be twice as large as the others with an underpinning of 50 steel-shod piles. The roadway was to consist of three-quarter inch steel rods laid nine inches apart and covered by gravel from the river. [14]

Contractor John M. O'Rourke said April 3 he believed the Roosevelt Dam would be completed within 12 months, but construction at the end would appear to progress much slower. He said this was because the dam was lengthening out, but this also would make room for additional derricks. [15]

The governors of the Water Users' Association on April 5 authorized Fowler to buy from the Young Men's Christian Association for $8,000 the northwest corner of block 93 of the original townsite of Phoenix. The northwest corner of block 93 forms the southeast corner of the intersection of Second Avenue and Van Buren. The intent of the governors was to construct an office building, the so-called water temple, at a then-projected cost of $22,000 to $24,000 to house the offices of the Water Users' Association and the Reclamation Service. Fowler, who was president of the Young Men's Christian Association as well as president of the Water Users' Association, without leaving his seat, immediately approved the transaction, which, the *Republican* explained, had been under consideration for some time. The association was to pay $2,000 down, another $2,000 on December 1, and the remaining $4,000 in the fall of 1910. The association had $2,000 on hand, and it expected to get the rest of the money through the Reclamation Service's purchase from the association of the Lee Ranch at the Tonto Basin. The association had bought the ranch to settle a dispute over the price of the land between the government and the Lees. [16]

At the same meeting of the governors, Fowler read the March 13 letter from Ballinger and discussed the requirement that landowners dispose of land in excess of 160 acres. Fowler, in a letter April 6 to C. J. Blanchard, Reclamation Service statistician, said that the governors decided "that it was unnecessary and unwise to have this matter discussed in the press of the Valley at the present time." Fowler also said, in compliance with Ballinger's request, statistics concerning excess lands were being gathered, but he assured Blanchard, "There never has been serious thought of requesting the Government for more time to pay assessments that may be levied. . .for reimbursing the Government expenditures." Fowler said good orange land was selling for $100 to $150 per acre, and good farm land with alfalfa or a crop of beets would bring $150 per acre. He added, "some of our land is selling for $1,000 an acre, orange land and residential sections, but that is the great exception, and it is worth the money." Fowler also pointed out the number of persons eligible to vote in the association's election, being held that day, was 16 percent higher than the previous year. In actual numbers, 1,829 landowners could have voted in 1909 compared to 1,573 in 1908 and 1,455 in 1907. [17]

The election produced few surprises, with John P. Orme defeating Lin B. Orme for governor in the 2nd district by 777 votes. Stone won by 300 votes over Charley Barkley in the 1st district and Joseph Cope defeated F. C. Norris by almost 1,000 votes in the 5th district. The other seven governors were unopposed. [18]

A meeting was held April 6 at the Board of Trade to petition the Maricopa County Board of Supervisors to call a special election at which the taxpayers would be asked to approve $50,000 for construction of a $100,000 bridge across the Salt River at the foot of Center Street. The other $50,000 was to be raised through subscriptions, and Dwight B. Heard announced the Bartlett-Heard Land and Cattle Co. would contribute $20,000 cash provided the owners of 11,500 acres on the south side of the river would raise $15,000, and the merchants and citizens of Phoenix $5,000. In addition the U.S. Indian Service was to give $5,000 and was to guarantee $5,000 worth of labor by Indians. [19]

Fowler reported to the meeting efforts to work with Tempe and Mesa interests toward a two-bridge project, one at the Tempe Crossing and the other south of Phoenix, had failed. The Tempe and Mesa people maintained the Tempe bridge should be built first because it was the better location. Once done, they would support the construction of the Center Street bridge. Meantime, they circulated a petition of their own asking the Board of Supervisors to schedule a special election to build the Tempe bridge. The supervisors set an election June 10 on three propositions: building a bridge at the foot of Center Street, building at the Tempe Crossing, and building across the Agua Fria River. [20]

The Phoenix City Council on April 8 formally received the report of the committee assigned to investigate electric and gas rates. The council was told a number of businessmen would soon apply for a franchise to begin a company competitive with Pacific Gas & Electric Co. One stipulation of the franchise the businessmen would present would be a readiness to turn the company over to the city when that appeared advisable. Attorney L. H. Chalmers, president of Pacific Gas & Electric, and F. H. Ensign, the company manager, attended the meeting. Chalmers said as soon as the company began taking power from the government, which was expected no later than September 1, Pacific Gas & Electric's rates would be lowered. Chalmers said:

It is a mistaken idea that we get our power cheaper than the companies that use water power. We don't make the profit; the government makes it. One and a half cents a kilowatt sounds cheap, but it is just what it would cost us to produce the power with coal at $9.60 a ton and oil at $1.50 a barrel. We were fools to make that ten years' contract and we know it now. If the government sells all its power at the same price that we pay for it the cost of the dam will be paid for in ten years and every acre of land in this valley under the reclamation project will pay a dividend of $15.

Ensign said bids for the construction of the company's new powerhouse would be taken April 10. He said the electric rates would be reduced, but not because the company would get hydropower. Rather, Ensign said it was because of the growth of Phoenix and the increase in the number of patrons. [21]

The gates in the Roosevelt Dam sluicing tunnel were closed for about 36 hours beginning the afternoon of April 12 to accommodate sheep men who wanted to cross the river April 13 and 14. While the gates were closed, the water in the reservoir rose five and one-half feet to a depth of eighty-four and one-half feet. [22]

Blanchard wrote to Fowler April 14, saying he trusted that Fowler's "predictions that no requests for deferment of payments will come from the Salt River Valley will be fulfilled." Fowler's predictions proved wrong. Farmers in the Salt River Valley and their political leaders began agitating in the summer and fall of 1911 for an extension in the time over which the federal government would be repaid the costs of building Roosevelt Dam and the associated irrigation works.[23] The Salt River Project made its final payment to the federal government in 1955.

By mid-April, Roosevelt Dam at its highest point was 132 feet above the riverbed, but this, as usual, covered only a very small area. A much broader area of the dam, the south one-third, was 128-feet high; the middle third 112-feet high; and the north third about 120 feet high. Construction began on a large concrete settling basin at the end of the power canal at the point where the water entered the penstock. The intent was to capture sand in the settling basin to reduce the wear small stones caused on the water wheels that turned the generators. Workmen at the dam also noticed large numbers of fish just below the dam. It was assumed the fish were trying to reach the headwaters of the river but were unable to pass through the sluicing tunnel because of the force of the water coming through. [24]

On April 16, the *Republican* published an advertisement titled, **"THE TRUTH ABOUT THE BRIDGE,"** signed by the Tempe Bridge Committee. The advertisement, besides citing the reasons why the first bridge across the Salt River should be built at Tempe, included a map showing the lands of the Bartlett-Heard Land and Cattle Co. The map showed the Center Street bridge entered directly onto Bartlett-Heard lands, and the accompanying text maintained "that no taxpayer would vote for a bridge at Mr. Heard's ranch." The advertisement contained additional statements relating to Heard, including:

We have been criticised by some of the persons interested in the bridge at Heard's ranch because we mention Mr. Heard in this discussion. They say that we are making a personal fight of the matter. The fact of the matter is that no one blames Mr. Heard for trying to get the taxpayers to let him have their money to build a bridge at his ranch and mostly for his own personal benefit. . . The fact alone that Mr. Heard and his associates find it necessary to raise a bonus in order to try and get the vote of the county shows that they recognize the weakness of their proposition and are trying to influence the taxpayers to vote for the bridge at Heard's ranch when they know that if the question were left to a vote of the taxpayers on the merits of the case they would not have one chance in a hundred. . . We are making no fight against Mr. Heard as an individual, but we do object to the plans of Mr. Heard as the representative of the Bartlett-Heard Land & Cattle company, when these same plans have for their object the building of a bridge at a point where most of the taxpayers do not want it and the building of which would be an injury to our town under present circumstances.

The advertisement noted a road Heard proposed building from Center Street south of the river to connect with a corner of Mesa would pass a mile south of Tempe. The Tempe Bridge Committee said the construction of this road (today's Broadway Road) would have to be graded and graveled and would cost the county more than the $50,000 bonus offered by Heard and his associates. The committee said the present road from Tempe to Phoenix was three miles shorter and from Tempe to Mesa two miles shorter. In addition, the bridge site at Tempe was superior because it was only 1,400-feet wide and the bridge would stand on a rock foundation. The committee said the site of the Center Street bridge had "no bank to the river and because the engineers recognize the fact that it will be dangerous to build a low bridge of the type that the advocates of this lower site propose, they propose to build a two-thirds bridge and the rest of the channel to be dammed with a causeway, or, in plain English, a dirt fill, over which it is proposed to let the water run when it is high enough to be dangerous to the bridge." The committee contended the bridge would cost $175,000, not $100,000, and it would be so low it would act as a dam by collecting brush and trees coming down the river, and this would raise the level of the river upstream so the water "would either destroy the land south of the bridge or sweep through the streets of Phoenix as it did in 1891." The committee argued it would be better to build a Center Street bridge after the Heard Ranch was subdivided into small tracts and the taxable value of the land doubled. At that time, "a $200,000 bridge could be built at Center Street, and the people who would be benefited would be paying for their share." To the Tempe Bridge Committee, the question of where the first bridge would be erected was of paramount importance. The committee said that if the Center Street bridge was built, and this was followed by construction of Heard's proposed road to Mesa, and there was no bridge at Tempe,

We would be on one side of the new territorial road across the territory; that unless they had special business in our town none of the large numbers of people who are coming to this valley in the next few years would pass through our town. This means that the citizens of Tempe are being asked to build a bridge and tax themselves for the maintenance of the same bridge, when this bridge will injure one of the oldest communities in Arizona, when it will practically kill our town. This is a life and death matter with the residents of Tempe, and we do not believe that the taxpayers of this county are going to compel us to do anything of this kind, particularly in the interests of a real estate scheme, pure and simple. Gentlemen, put yourselves in our place. [25]

The Center Street bridge interests gave their answer to the Tempe Bridge Committee when they met April 17 to organize a propaganda campaign on behalf of the south-of-Phoenix bridge. Fowler said there was no reason for recrimination over the location of a bridge. He said the interests of any part of the county were the interests of all, and he said there was no reason for anger over a difference of opinion. Attorney Charles F. Ainsworth responded directly to the Tempe people, saying they had made no move to build a bridge when one of the railroad companies was constructing a span over the river and it was suggested a wagon road be attached. He said Tempe also took no

interest when it was suggested the piers of the old Maricopa & Phoenix railway could be bought cheaply for use in building a wagon way. Ainsworth said the Heard lands were less than 7,000 acres of the 35,000 acres that would be served by the Center Street bridge. He said the flood in Phoenix in 1891 came from broken canal banks and not from a halt and rise of water at Center Street. In going before the Legislature, Ainsworth said, Tempe interests said they wanted a bridge so Tempe people could trade in Phoenix, an argument defying the usual business attitude of a community. He said it appeared Tempe did not want a bridge so long as Phoenix did not get one. L. M. Hoghe, a member of the County Board of Supervisors, said he was in favor of as many bridges as the people wanted, and he had interests along the road to Tempe as well as south of the river from Phoenix. But he said he favored the Center Street bridge because he did not think it was right that during times of high water people south of the river should have to travel 13 miles to Tempe, stable their horses, take a train to Phoenix, and return in the same way. [26]

Frederick H. Newell, director of the Reclamation Service, arrived in Phoenix April 17 to tour the work in the Valley and to visit Roosevelt. After making the trip and returning, Newell reminded there was a day of reckoning coming when the government would stop spending money and the people would have to repay the costs. He said he hoped the people would readily and willingly do their part, and to accomplish this, he encouraged immigration of small farmers and not more speculators. Newell said the small farmer would come only if it could be shown to him it would be in his financial interest. He said newcomers were entitled to a share of the unearned increment, or speculative profit, the reservoir would bring, but this could not happen if land prices were set too high. [27]

The last week of April, two of the three service gates at Roosevelt Dam again were shut to permit the passage of 20,000 sheep across the lower Salt River and to allow the water to rise to the 100-foot level with the aim of having the stored water available for summer irrigation. The third service gate in the sluicing tunnel was to be shut the night of April 30 to allow Almon H. Demrick and A. L. Harris, Reclamation Service engineers, to make an inspection of the gates and tunnel the following morning. The highest point on the dam had reached 141 feet above datum while the average of the lowest one-fourth on the north side was 108 feet. The lowest point of the dam was 99 feet but this was only for a few square yards. [28]

Demrick drowned in the sluicing tunnel about 9 a.m. May 1 and Harris narrowly escaped death. As was customary, in order for Demrick and Harris to enter the tunnel a small temporary dam of between one and two feet was built across the mouth of the sluicing tunnel. This backed up the water so the men could row a boat upstream into the tunnel to the gate structure. This method of entering the tunnel was devised because during the construction of the tunnel the floor had been blasted and there were holes and pits, some of which had been enlarged to four- and six-feet deep by the constant washing of the water. Demrick and Harris were to meet the gatekeeper at 7 a.m., but he failed to appear in 30 minutes so the two engineers decided to enter the tunnel. The gatekeeper was supposed to lower the service gate of the middle of the three compartments through which the water flowed, then raise the emergency gate of the middle compartment. Demrick and Harris had been in the tunnel about an hour when the gatekeeper began raising the emergency gate, not realizing the service gate had not been lowered. This allowed the water to surge through, catching Demrick. Harris said he was on a ladder in one of the two side compartments when he heard Demrick call to him. Harris said he started down the ladder, but when he was about eight feet from the bottom it began to topple in the swirling water, and he jumped into the water. As he jumped, he said he caught sight of Demrick on the crest of a wave, throwing his hands wildly. Harris said the next thing he remembered was trying to swim out of a big pool in the river below the dam. He was aided by a workman who had been near the mouth of the sluicing tunnel and had seen Demrick shoot by an instant before Harris. In aiding Harris, the man had lost sight of Demrick, whose body was found about an hour later. Harris was unhurt [29] and the following day completed the inspection of the gates. Harris reported:

All the roller trains were either entirely gone or broken in two and partly gone. Some of the deflector plates belonging to the walls and piers above each of the gates had been carried away or loosened. The bronze gate seats were all damaged by the blows of iron or other loose parts, the worst of these being where a strip patched on to the river side gate seat had been knocked loose by a heavy blow. Various bolts in the other castings were loose, apparently by turning caused by vibration. The large nuts securing the piston rods to gate leaves were turned, the worst one being about four inches out of position. The cast iron struts behind and above the gate had become loosened in several cases and slipped out of place. One or two of the guide strips in front of the gates had been torn off.

The concrete in the floor, roof and piers was badly eroded by the water jets. A large piece about 10 feet in diameter had fallen from the tunnel roof about 20 feet downstream from the gates and the concrete floor originally extending about 20 feet below the gates had been undercut several feet back toward the piers.

The threat was the piers would wash out or collapse if the strata composing the tunnel floor continued to erode. The engineers considered keeping the gates shut until permanent repairs and additions could be made, but because it was the time of year when the farmers were especially in need of water, they decided to try to keep the middle gates open with temporary repairs. [30]

The Phoenix Citizens' Bridge Committee on May 1 published an advertisement in the *Arizona Gazette* explaining why a Salt River bridge should be built at the foot of Center Street and not at Tempe. The committee began by saying that Phoenix's population was 20,000 and its taxable property valued at nearly $6 million, while Tempe's population did not exceed 2,000 and the valuation of its property was $300,000, which meant Phoenix had a population 10 times greater and an assessed valuation 20 times larger. The committee argued the Center Street bridge would serve two-thirds of the people in the county and would provide access to 37,000 acres of land, including 13,000 under cultivation south of Phoenix, compared to only 3,500 acres adjacent to Tempe that would be better served by a Tempe bridge. "The greatest good to the greatest

number, is an axiom that is as old as civilization," the committee said. "It was born of good government and human progress, and taking this as a basis for our claims for the Center Street location, it leaves little to be said in behalf of Tempe." The committee said the Center Street bridge would open many thousands of acres to new settlement, which would mean hundreds of thousands of dollars on the tax rolls, while a Tempe bridge would not open new land for development nor offer any new markets for trade. [31]

On May 3, the *Republican* printed a long article under the title, "Hour for Exultation," explaining the meaning of having 100 feet of stored water in the Roosevelt reservoir. "It means a supply of 108,880 acre-feet, or sufficient to give every acre in the valley under cultivation two thorough irrigations," the newspaper said. It continued:

The work is not all done, but no fatal interference is longer possible in any quarter, save the precipitation of final planetary chaos, or the destruction of the government. The people of the valley may now, with the confidence of certainty, lift up their voices and invite the homeseekers of the world to come to God's most favored land, wrought into Edenic fitness as an abiding place, through the agency of the world's most beneficient government.

The *Republican* quoted Hill as saying the reservoir, when full, would insure the Valley sufficient stored water to irrigate 200,000 acres for two- and one-half years, even if the annual rainfall and river flow in that period did no more than equal the year of the lowest recorded rainfall and runoff. "For years and years the people of this valley have sung a song the burden of which is, wait until we have the assurance of a permanent water supply, a supply, not merely in prospect, but an assurance verified by availability," the paper said. "That assurance has, to use a colloquial expression, 'done arrived.' " [32]

Heard and Augustus C. Bartlett appeared before the governors on May 3 and submitted a proposition to give the San Francisco Canal to the government and to sign the 4,500 acres under the canal into the Water Users' Association, including payment of all back assessments totaling 32 cents per acre, providing the governors would agree to extend for five years the time in which they would have to dispose of their lands in excess of 160 acres. They said the proposition was agreeable to the Interior Department if it was okay with the Water Users' Association. Heard and Bartlett said they intended to subdivide the ranch into 40-acre parcels and sell them off on long-time payments. They did not believe the parcels could be sold within the present time the government would allow for the disposal of excess lands. In addition, they believed Valley land prices would fall if they offered excess land for sale in addition to what then was being offered by others. They believed they had 80 percent of all the water they would ever need without joining the association through their early water rights and pumping plant, but they preferred to make the reservoir district harmonious and to insure an abundant water supply by donating the ditch and paying the assessments. Of course, extending the time for them to dispose of excess land would set a precedent; indeed, it was because of the anticipated objection of other large landowners that the matter had not been presented to the governors two years earlier. The governors took no action, but as soon as the proposition became public knowledge, James C. Goodwin of Tempe used it to attack the Center Street bridge proposal. [33]

Goodwin said the intention of Heard and Bartlett to delay disposing of their land showed "it is their policy to allow other lands to be sold and they will hold theirs until they can get the cream of the market," which meant $50 to $100 per acre more than it was presently worth. Goodwin charged the Board of Trade was allowing itself to be used to further the interests of Bartlett, Heard, "and other private speculators," and that the majority of the men "howling the loudest for the bridge at Center Street are either agents of corporations, speculators, or paid henchmen." [34]

Water users under the Mesa and Utah canals on May 6 were reported circulating a petition protesting the Reclamation Service's shutting off and on the flow of water in the Salt River because it made it impossible to regulate the distribution of water from their canals. That same day, temporary repairs to the middle gates in the sluicing tunnel at Roosevelt Dam were completed and the gates were opened. [35]

At a dinner in the Adams Hotel the night of May 6 in support of the Center Street bridge, Bartlett said he thought the Bartlett-Heard Land and Cattle Co. would make some money out of the sale of land if the bridge were built, but he could not say how much nor did the subdividing of the land depend upon construction of the span. Bartlett said the land was bought for the purpose of developing one of the finest ranches in the nation, and it was Hill who suggested the area be subdivided. Bartlett said he thought the bridge should be built "where it will be of the greatest benefit to the greatest number, without reference to the corporation whose interests lie on the south side of the river." Chalmers said Phoenix people could not afford to put aside the bridge because it would benefit some persons more than others, and Vernon Clark credited W. S. Pickrell with coming up with the idea to build a concrete bridge at that point. Fowler announced the appointment of a 10-member committee to seek greater newspaper support for the bridge. There also was an 11-member Center Street Bridge Committee, which opponents characterized as "Mr. Heard's Bridge Committee." Among its members were Fowler, Chalmers, Clark, Heard, Ainsworth, Eugene B. O'Neill, and Aaron Goldberg. [36]

The morning of May 8, the **Republican** printed a letter from the Center Street Bridge Publicity Committee in which it was said the Reclamation Service was considering construction, south of the river, of a high line canal to irrigate 11,240 acres of homestead lands above the existing gravity ditch—the Wormser branch of the Tempe Canal. The proposed plan was to use pumps to drain Tempe lands adjacent to the east and to raise this excess water into a high line canal to serve the homestead lands between the Wormser Canal and the Salt River Mountains. The letter said the water could be delivered to the canal through a pipeline less than a half-mile long. Much of the homestead land was signed into the Water Users' Association. [37]

Reclamation Service engineers ordered the gates in the

Roosevelt Dam sluicing tunnel closed the morning of May 8 so another inspection could be made of the gates and tunnel. The engineers reported that,

It was found that about two-thirds of the lower end of the river pier was entirely gone from [the] floor to two feet below [the] roof and back to the firm column casting. The floor had undermined and washed out back to the point of piers. The concrete had washed out from inside of the spreader castings of service gates top and bottom until in one case a passage had been made entirely under the sill of gate.

The engineers decided they had no alternative but to close the gates until repairs were made (news of this did not reach the Valley until May 10). This meant drastically reducing the amount of water to the Valley. The power canal penstock discharged 4,000 inches (equal to 100 cubic feet per second, or 198 acre-feet per 24 hours) almost continuously. The Verde River contributed to the flow through the Valley but the engineers did not consider it enough. To increase the water supply, they ordered contractor O'Rourke "to remove a portion of a fresh course of masonry from the lowest part of the dam and. . .to remove a notch about 40 feet wide for the water, which had about five feet to rise before going over [the dam] at an elevation of 106.4 [feet]." [38] Because of the emergency, Ballinger permitted the order of necessary materials for the tunnel repair on proposals rather than bids. The plan was to line the bottom of the tunnel with concrete—which was begun at once—and to line the entire surface of the tunnel with steel plates to a point 25 feet below the gates. In addition, the entire pier area was lined with cast steel floor and deflector plates installed between the service (front) and emergency (downstream) gates. Special bronze gate faces and anchor bolts were used. The Reclamation Service reported the tunnel floor,

was made of 3/4" steel plate and the roof and sides of 5/8" steel. The plates lapped and the lap joints fastened together with 1-1/8" screws rivet-headed. Anchor bolts of special design which allowed the heads of nuts to come nearly flush with the surface of plates were set in concrete and rock for holding fast the plates. [39]

Another result of the problems with the sluicing tunnel was a decision to construct a second outlet tunnel on the north side of Roosevelt Dam with its center at 115 feet above the river bed. When it was completed, the Reclamation Service described it as follows:

This outlet consists of three lines of 5-foot [diameter] cast-iron pipe through the dam discharging into a tunnel 260 feet long excavated in rock. The tunnel is 9 feet in diameter at its minimum section and it is lined with concrete throughout. The discharge to the pipes is controlled by means of 58-inch balanced valves.

The water was taken through the reservoir through the valves, which were located on the face of the dam. The three lines of cast-iron pipe measured in length 69 feet 6 inches, 80 feet 4 inches and 93 feet, and were imbedded in masonry and concrete all the way to their downstream end. At that point, the tunnel began with a breast of 14-feet width and 9 feet in height. [40]

Additional attacks on Heard by the Tempe Bridge Committee prompted Bartlett to write to the editor of the **Republican** on May 10. Bartlett said that, if members of the Tempe Bridge Committee,

actually believe that we are conscienceless south side land speculators having no thought for the public weal, but are in this community for the sole purpose of seeing how many dollars we can ruthlessly squeeze out of the present residents of the valley and the future home-making immigrants, I wish they would manfully state their views over their own signature.

Bartlett said his company sought no special privilege or advantage, and he and Heard preferred the government extend the time for disposing of excess land to every landowner in the district. He said it was true the Center Street bridge would add to the value of their land, but in the long run, it would be many times more valuable to Phoenix. Further, if the governors had shown an interest in their proposition when it was first discussed informally two years earlier, some "portion of the land would have been sold before the bridge was even 'in the air.' " [41]

The *Republican,* in reporting the closing of the sluicing tunnel gates on May 11, said the Reclamation Service officials in Phoenix did not learn what happened May 8 because the telephone line went out of commission. On Sunday, May 9, a telegram was received from Roosevelt and two Reclamation Service engineers left for Roosevelt. Telephone service was restored May 10 and a full explanation of the sluicing tunnel problems was given. The engineers predicted water would run over the 40-foot notch in Roosevelt Dam in three days, slowly at first, but after a few hours in a volume sufficient to represent the river's normal flow. The newspaper also reported, "The sluicing tunnel was never intended to serve as the regular outlet of the reservoir after the dam is finished." The paper said once the work was completed, the gates might be closed and not opened again, except in an emergency. It said the normal outlet from the reservoir would be through the powerhouse penstock placed through the dam 75 feet above datum. The penstock could not be used then because the powerhouse machinery had not been installed. The newspaper said all the water needed to irrigate the Valley would come from the main penstock and the power canal penstock. [42]

Water began to trickle over the lowered portion of Roosevelt Dam May 14, and it was estimated it would take three months to get the materials and to complete the sluicing tunnel work. The high point on the dam had reached 148 feet and the average 127 feet. A flow one-foot deep over the dam was expected to discharge about 4,500 inches, two feet about 13,500 inches, and three feet about 24,000 inches. Meantime, the Reclamation Service announced water between May 15 and September 15 would cost 60 cents per acre. [43]

The *Republican* printed a letter May 16 from a dozen south-of-the-river farmers and ranchers who disliked being characterized by the Tempe Bridge Committee "as peons of Mr. Heard without any substantial interests." The writers, among them Wolf Sachs, M. R. Horovitz, and Joseph Lambeye, said during periods of high water Tempe residents had a train connection with Phoenix, but for them it meant traveling upwards of 40 miles. They said the Center Street bridge would mean better mail service because at present the mail was left on the north bank of the river at the foot of Center Street. Neighbors delivered the mail to one another, but when water was high, getting mail meant a trip via

Tempe. The writers also pointed out that not including the Bartlett-Heard Ranch, there were then in cultivation on the south side 5,000 acres of non-Indian and 3,000 acres of Indian lands. [44]

The morning of May 17, the water coming over Roosevelt Dam was 18-inches deep and 40-feet wide, providing a volume of about 280 second feet, or 11,200 inches. By Wednesday morning, May 19, the water depth had increased to twenty-six and one-half inches, or about 400 second feet. Another 90 second feet was discharged through the penstock tunnel for a total in excess of 19,000 inches. That, combined with 7,500 inches from the Verde River, meant farmers badly needing water were getting some or hoped to get it soon. [45]

Fowler received from Sen. Thomas H. Carter, chairman of the Senate Committee on Irrigation and Reclamation, notification the committee expected to arrive in Phoenix the morning of October 21 and would visit Roosevelt and Granite Reef Diversion dams before leaving the night of October 24. The committee posed 19 questions concerning the operation of the reclamation law and local conditions. [46]

The depth of the water flowing through the notch in Roosevelt Dam continued to rise daily, reaching a depth of 4.2 feet May 27. This sent 1,069 second feet spilling down the dam's rock steps to the river below and prompted the *Republican* to comment,

There must come a time when the water stops rising and begins to fall, but old Mr. River is doing beautifully so far, and if the valley were inclined to pagan methods, it would be almost time to begin erecting an altar for its worship. It has kept up surprisingly well, but in so doing illustrating one of the beauties of river regulation, one of the first fruits of the dam. Under similar conditions in other years, it would merely have been a good river, all running to the sea, while now a nice surplus is being restrained daily over and above the urgent needs.

The next day, the depth of water increased another tenth of a foot, where it was to remain for a few days. Water backed up the Salt River for a distance of eight miles and up Tonto Creek for seven miles. The width of each of these bodies of water was at least a half-mile. [47]

Meanwhile, construction continued on the dam, reaching a peak of 152 feet above datum on the south end by the end of May. The elevation on both sides of the gap where the water passed stood at about 118 or 120 feet. By June 1, the contractor expected to have placed 241,121 cubic yards of material, while the dam, when completed, was supposed to contain 326,000 cubic yards. [48]

Some Phoenix businessmen began circulating a petition agreeing to join in an application to the city for a franchise to construct an electric light and gas plant, pledging that electricity for lighting would not exceed 10 cents per kilowatt hour, and that gas would not be in excess of $1.50 per thousand cubic feet. [49]

Another letter from Goodwin was printed in the *Republican* on May 30. Goodwin said false statements concerning the Tempe Irrigating Canal Co. were printed in a pamphlet issued by the Center Street Bridge Committee headed by Fowler. The pamphlet asked if it was not possible that objections of the Tempe Canal people,

to the Center Street Bridge is based in part upon a hope that by defeating that project they may succeed in keeping the Bartlett-Heard Land and Cattle company out of the association and their subdividing their property and thus avoid being all alone in their independence?

Goodwin pointed out that Heard and Bartlett only offered to bring that part of their lands which was under the San Francisco Canal into the Water Users' Association and not the portion of the ranch under the Wormser extension of the Tempe Canal. Goodwin said the lands watered by the Wormser extension were in excess of 3,000 acres. He also said his discussing this should not be construed as a personal attack on Fowler or Heard. [50]

Pacific Gas & Electric Co. mailed notices to its electric customers on May 31 outlining new lower rates that would go into effect starting August 1. The new rate schedule was based on 15 cents per kilowatt hour for the first 100 kilowatt hours while the old rate began at 20 cents per kilowatt. The schedule, which was the same for business and commercial customers, called for 14 cents per kilowatt hour for the second 100 kilowatt hours. The remainder of the schedule was as follows: 12 cents per kilowatt hour for the next 200 kilowatt hours; 10 cents for the next 200 kilowatt hours; 8 cents for the next 200 kilowatt hours; 6 cents for the next 200 kilowatt hours. All electricity in excess of 1,000 kilowatt hours was put at 5 cents per kilowatt hour. The minimum charge was $1.50 per month. Business and commercial users, who paid bills before the 10th of the month, could get 10 percent discounts. [51]

Lands west of the Agua Fria River were opened for homesteads on June 3. There were 73 filings for approximately 25,000 acres of ground. That same day, the articles of incorporation of the Arizona Orange-Land Water Association were filed with the territorial auditor. The association, owned by Phoenix businessmen, planned to irrigate the lands with underground water brought to the surface by pumps operated with electricity bought through Pacific Gas & Electric, which planned to extend its line to Glendale, to the sugar beet factory, and to the association's lands. Also planning to use electricity to pump water were homesteaders east and south of the reservoir district. Hill sent a letter to the Queen Valley Development Co. saying the Reclamation Service would not install a new substation along the line to the Gila River Indian Reservation to serve a small district. Hill added there was no objection to selling the company "power at a reasonable rate" provided it furnished its own step-down transformer and came to the government substation east of Mesa to get the electricity. He advised against any contract, however, until the company had proven the adequacy of the pumped water supply with a steam or gasoline engine. Hill also said, "there is no use in attempting to go into this business of pumping water. . . unless you intend to raise high grade crops." [52]

Without ceremony, Reclamation Service engineer Howard Reed, Water Commissioner Frank P. Trott, and L. N. Jesunofsky of the Weather Service opened the gates of the Granite Reef Diversion Dam on June 4 to let water into the South Canal for the first time. Jesunofsky also planned to install instruments at the diversion dam to measure water evaporation. [53]

The governors on June 7 discussed the proposition of the Bartlett-Heard Land and Cattle Co. to donate the San Francisco Canal and bring lands under it into the Water Users' Association, but they said without taking formal action there was one part of the proposal they could not accept. That part was that if at the end five years any land under the San Francisco Canal remained unsold, the company's water rights in the canal would be restored to the extent of the unsold land. Several members of the board spoke against this clause, indicating that if the company would drop it, they would support the rest of the proposition. [54]

The governors also authorized the preparation of detailed plans for the water temple to be built on the lot bought from the Young Men's Christian Association. The reinforced concrete building, as presented by an architect, resembled the territorial capitol building in architecture and shape. It was rectangular with a dome over the center and had a projected cost of $35,000. [55]

Last, the governors instructed Kibbey to attend the Phoenix City Council meeting that night with the goal of assuring that nothing was done to harm the Water Users' Association's interest in the expected application of a number of businessmen to have the people vote on a franchise permitting them to start a gas and electric company to compete with Pacific Gas & Electric. The governors acted after being read a letter from Hill in which he said that if a competing company entered and captured a quarter of the business, it would cost the government—or association—an estimated $100,000. But the businessmen delayed their request because a compromise on Pacific Gas & Electric's new rates was effected between the company and the businessmen. Pacific Gas & Electric, in exchange for a six-month delay of the franchise request beginning August 1, in order to learn the effect of the company's operation with power from Roosevelt Dam, agreed to reduce the minimum charge from $1.50 to $1 per month; to permit a 10 percent reduction for residential users if they paid their bills by the 10th of the month; and to charge merchants 10 cents per kilowatt hour. [56]

An election eve torchlight parade through the streets of Phoenix in support of the Center Street bridge was conducted the night of Wednesday, June 9, by the Center Street Bridge Committee. The parade, which stretched for four blocks, came together at City Hall plaza. The citizens heard speeches by Fowler, Chalmers, Ainsworth, Kibbey, Heard, and Roy S. Goodrich. The speakers expressed no animosity toward Tempe and several of them pledged to work for a territorial bridge at that point, once construction of the Center Street bridge was assured.

The election drew more than 1,400 voters to the polls, but only the proposal to build the Center Street bridge drew "Yes" votes from more than half the voters, a requirement of the law for the bridge to be built. The vote in favor of the Center Street bridge had a majority of about 100. The proposition for building a bridge at Tempe lacked about 20 votes of having a majority, and the proposition to construct a bridge across the Agua Fria River lacked more than 300 votes for a majority. The people at Tempe immediately began campaigning for construction of a bridge either by the territory or by another vote of county taxpayers. [57]

In the middle of June, the main talk at Roosevelt concerned a possible halt in construction for one- and one-half to two- and one-half months beginning in mid-July. A provision of the contract between the government and O'Rourke provided that after the dam had been completed to the 150-foot level, it was up to the government engineers in charge as to whether masonry work on the dam would be permitted in the months of June, July, August, and September. In building the dam, the Reclamation Service engineers were worried that the intense heat might adversely affect the setting of the concrete. The dam at the highest point was about 163 or 165 feet above the riverbed. The *Republican's* correspondent reported it was expected the cement mill and sand crushers would be shut down and the hauling of oil to the dam would stop. On the other hand, the cement work in the sluicing tunnel and the quarry work would continue. In addition, O'Rourke was to construct the tunnel on the north side of the dam. The power canal settling basin was expected to be completed in early July. Hill said it was unlikely the work in the sluicing tunnel would be finished before September because of the time it would take to get the steel plates to be used in lining the portion below the gates. The cement floor in the tunnel was being laid at the rate of 16 to 18 feet per day. [58]

A petition asking for the resignation of Fowler as president of the Water Users' Association circulated in Phoenix on June 17. The petition objected to the $2,000 per year salaries paid to both Fowler and Kibbey and to the general conduct of the association. The governors had prepared a new budget, starting September 1, showing a levy of 10 cents per share on the owners of 212,500 shares outstanding. The levy was scheduled to be set July 5. Of the $21,250 that would be collected with a 10 cent levy, $8,000 was intended for the Young Men's Christian Association to pay for the water temple lot. [59]

At a special meeting of the Phoenix City Council on June 19, two separate requests for gas and electric light franchises were presented. Both proposed a maximum rate of 10 cents per kilowatt hour for electricity and a minimum charge of $1 per month. One offered to sell the property to the city at the end of 10 years at cost plus 7 percent interest per annum while the other proposed selling to the city after 10 years at cost. [60]

The first drowning in Roosevelt Lake apparently occurred the evening of June 20. The victim was a boy about 10, the stepson of Manuel Guzman of Roosevelt. The boy and two friends started for the lake to swim but the companions turned back. That was the last seen of the victim until his body was found the following day. He was buried June 22 in the Roosevelt cemetery. [61]

L. A. "Bud" Norton, who carried freight between Mesa and Roosevelt with his own string of horses and equipment, added to his operation with the purchase of the Roosevelt to Payson and Roosevelt to Globe stage lines from the Shattuck-Nimmo Warehouse Co. on June 21. [62]

The *Republican* on June 24 printed an article attempting to put the water temple question in perspective. It began by quoting Hill on the need for the building primarily because of the economy and the advertising it would give the Valley. The newspaper said:

It is true that the association at this time does not require a vast amount of room and has but few employees but it is true that the reclamation service has many employees. . . It is true also that the office force of the reclamation service will begin to diminish before a great while, but just as fast as it does the force in the association will necessarily increase. As the government eliminates itself from the project the association will have to take hold. There may be fewer draftsmen but there will be more administrative officials and plenty of work so that it is not thought there will ever be fewer employees in the combined office service here in the valley than now. [63]

At the start of July, a report circulated in Roosevelt that Reclamation Service officials in Washington had been persuaded to permit work on the dam to continue. Another report was that work on the dam would stop August 1 and would resume October 1, but on July 12 it was learned that work would be reduced but not halted. Water continued to run over the low point in the dam at a depth of about three feet, but farmers continually complained that not enough water was available. [64]

The governors met July 5, then adjourned to July 20. In considering the annual assessment, they intended to discuss making it large enough by an additional 5 cents per acre to begin to pay the cost of building the water temple. [65]

A postal inspector visited Mesa the first week of July to determine whether the mail service between there and Roosevelt should be discontinued. Mesa postmaster W. M. Newell received a letter July 8 recommending the Mesa-Roosevelt mail service be stopped. This prompted an immediate petition in protest among Mesa people and others. [66]

Fowler, prompted by opposition to the water temple, announced a special meeting of water users would be held at 2 p.m. July 14 to explain the need for the building. Kibbey and Hill were expected to attend. They believed it would be better to construct the office building at once while shareholders were not burdened with the expense of repaying the government the costs of the Roosevelt Dam. [67]

Hill, who was soon to leave for Washington, D.C., returned July 9 from a visit to Roosevelt. He reported the dam at its high point was 175 feet above datum. Continued funding for the Salt River project was among the things Hill was to take up in Washington. [68]

At the meeting July 14 presided over by Fowler, Kibbey said both the Reclamation Service and the Water Users' Association needed better quarters. Kibbey said one thing the building would have was a vault in which to store papers, some of which were not replaceable, and others of which would cost an estimated $50,000 if destroyed. He said the association was paying $1,800 per year in rent, which was equal to 6 percent annually on $30,000. This did not include the rent paid by the Reclamation Service, which the farmers would ultimately pay. Hill supported Kibbey's statements concerning the inadequacy of the quarters and the value of the papers, while Fowler read three letters in support of the water temple. These were from Newell, Dr. H. H. Stone, a member of the Board of Governors, and J. C. Waite, a Reclamation Service employee working in Chicago to find and to aid people in moving to federal reclamation projects. Waite called attention to the "advertising value. . .such a building would be." He wrote:

In my work in Chicago. . .there is one matter that comes up daily for discussion, and that is the character and permanence of the organization that is to continue the operation and control of the irrigation works after the government ceases to exercise jurisdiction. This is considered very important by prospective settlers and investors and anything which will stimulate their confidence is obviously of direct benefit to the project. The erection of a building such as that contemplated by the association will, I believe, very greatly increase the regard in which the Salt River project is held to a person seeking a home on irrigated land. [69]

J. P. Ivy led off the opposition to the construction of the water temple. In addition to opposing it, he said the Water Users' Association was an unneeded organization. However, he praised the government engineers. His remarks drew frequent applause, indicating he had supporters among the 75 or so water users at the meeting. Joining in the criticism were H. A. Bustrin and Lin B. Orme. Orme offered a resolution that said:

Resolved, That the water users of the association in mass meeting assembled, are opposed to the construction of a water temple or other official building and request the board of governors to drop the matter.

A voice vote left unsettled whether the resolution was adopted, so a call for a standing vote followed, in which the resolution lost 24 to 20. At that point, a motion to adjourn carried without opposition. [70]

After the meeting, Fowler said he knew of threats he and the entire board would be replaced at the next election if they made an assessment for the office building. Fowler said:

As long as I am president of this association I am going to act according to my best judgment. The threat has been made, I am told, that if the board of governors vote that assessment there will be an entire new staff of officers in here next year. Such threats as that cannot change me a particle. I was elected to perform the duties of this office as I saw fit, and I am not going to change my convictions just because some farmer out under the Agua Fria or away up under the Arizona Canal, who isn't anywhere near the center of things, takes it into his head that this or that is right or wrong.

Fowler said as much as he appreciated being president of the association, he appreciated the prosperity of the association more. He said he would vote for the assessment even if he knew it meant certain failure of reelection, and he hoped and believed the governors would do the same. [71]

On July 17, an order was issued by an assistant postmaster general in Washington discontinuing the mail route between Mesa and Roosevelt. [72]

Roy McCormick, in charge of the Reclamation Service's well-drilling operations south of Mesa, said the underground water supply was the best he had ever seen, and it appeared to be sufficient to meet all ordinary irrigation needs. Three wells were drilled for each battery. The underflow in the section south of Mesa was encountered at the 300-foot level and rose to within 20 to 25 feet of the surface. Flows of about 2 cubic feet of water per second were developed. [73]

The Water Users' Association issued a statement July 19 explaining the need for construction of a building. It pointed out the location for the building was selected by Fowler, H. J. McClung, and John Orme. It labeled as "tommyrot" talk about "mahogany desks, plush covered chairs, Turkish rugs, etc." and said these things were said in order to prejudice farmers against the association and Reclamation Service. The statement said the association and Reclamation Service now had 30 employees, but the number would grow as the association took over the responsibilities and as the volume of business increased. [74]

Farmers in the Alhambra area, geographically in district 4 of the Water Users' Association, met July 19 and passed a resolution to protest the levying of any assessment, contending there was enough money on hand to meet current expenses. They also protested "against the undertaking to construct a water temple at this time and we are very strongly opposed to the action taken in purchasing ground to erect a temple upon." Among the 19 signers were Ivy and Lin Orme. Farmers in the Murphy and Wilson districts adopted similar resolutions. [75]

Five members of the Board of Governors, including Fowler, met July 20 to set the assessment, but they could not take action because six members were required for a quorum. Governors present were Orme, Cope, E. J. Bennitt, and Charles Peterson. Cope personally favored the office building but was opposed officially because his constituents were against it. The attitudes of two of the governors, C. A. Saylor and W. W. Dobson, were not known because they were away from the Valley. The remaining governors were known to be for the water temple, but they apparently decided not to levy an assessment because of threats of legal action. The governors were advised they had authority to indebt the association up to $50,000, but legal action was threatened if they did this. The five members at the meeting set a new meeting for the next afternoon. It was anticipated, however, that no action would be taken, and the governors would embark upon a program of education among dissident farmers. [76]

The *Republican* on July 21 printed an account of the organizing of the Paradise Valley Homesteader's Association, which was formed to drill a test well. Most of the land represented in the organization was one and one-half to 3 miles north of the Arizona Canal and 5 to 6 miles north of Scottsdale. If the land could be cultivated with well water, it could be obtained under the homestead law. Much of the land had been cleared by settlers under the old Rio Verde Land and Power Co. [77]

Four governors were present when the board reconvened on July 21—Fowler, Orme, Bennitt, and Peterson. Because a quorum was not present, they again could not meet formally, but they could have adopted an assessment, which would have been legal if approved at the next regular monthly meeting. However, they did not. Instead, they held a frank discussion about the water temple with some of the protesters. One opponent said the farmers would be better able to afford the office building after they had ample water for a few years, whereas the extra assessment would cause hardship. Kibbey said that was the first reasonable argument he had heard against the assessment. The objectors also said they would be willing to abide by the result of a vote of the entire association at the election in April 1910. [78]

The Reclamation Service on July 23 warned that the power in the transmission line from Roosevelt was likely to be turned on at anytime. Parents were warned to keep children away from the poles. [79]

Summer rains produced a rise in the Salt and Verde rivers, and on July 26 the water going through the notch at Roosevelt Dam was 3.6-feet deep. The next day the flow was 4-feet high. [80]

Postmaster Newell of Mesa received a telegram at 4 p.m. July 28 informing him that the order issued July 17 discontinuing the mail route to Roosevelt had been rescinded. [81]

About two-dozen Alhambra district water users met July 29 to discuss how the questions posed by the Senate Irrigation Committee, coming to the Valley in October, should be answered. They decided this should be done through school district meetings at which delegates would be elected to a convention of farmers. In an 8 to 5 vote, a series of resolutions condemning the Water Users' Association were approved. The resolutions said the association was "ill advised and premature" under section 6 of the reclamation law; that there was "no good and sufficient reason for its existence;" "that it is a useless and expensive burden to the farmers;" and that its membership was obtained "by

representation to the farmers that unless they joined" the Roosevelt Dam would not be built. The resolutions, while praising the Reclamation Service overall, condemned it for charging higher rates for water to non-association members, contending that this was "illegal and without authority of law and is for the sole purpose of forcing water users to join said association and help bear the burden of high-salaried officials and their expenses for a long period of years during which time they are rendering no assistance either towards construction of irrigation works or the service of water therefrom." The resolutions attacked the Reclamation Service for failing to provide stored water from the reservoir that summer. Several speakers were bitter because the Reclamation Service denied water to some farmers in order to deliver it to those raising cantaloupes and sugar beets. Some of the farmers urged caution, and one of them, Stanley Howard, said there was no assurance the delegates to district meetings would represent the farmers any better than the governors. He thought the best way was to cooperate with the governors. Because some things were wrong did not make them all wrong, he said. [82]

Sometime in the last week of July, a workman named Maul Estado was crushed to death when caught in a rock slide at the sand quarry at Roosevelt. He was said to have been survived by a wife and three children. He was buried at Roosevelt. [83]

The first test of the transmission line between Roosevelt, Mesa, and Phoenix was made Sunday, August 1. The current was allowed to flow for a few minutes, and nothing out of the ordinary occurred. While the Reclamation Service

The Salt River flows through a notch in Roosevelt Dam, July 31, 1909.

said the Mesa and Phoenix plants should be ready to expect electricity at any time, neither was ready to receive it. Manager Ensign of Pacific Gas & Electric said he hoped everything would be ready by September 1. [84]

G. R. Brewster, who presided at the meeting of Alhambra water users July 2, issued a call for water users to meet the night of August 5 in the schoolhouses of their respective districts to select delegates for a convention to reply to the Senate committee's questions. The same day, August 2, the governors adopted a resolution calling for a meeting of water users in each of the association's districts between September 15 and October 1 for the purpose of each selecting one delegate to meet with the governors to consider the questions, and to develop answers to the questions representing the majority opinion of the water users. The governors directed that a copy of the questions be sent to each member of the association accompanied by a blank for answer. The governors noted the letter from Carter accompanying the questions said it would not be possible for the committee "to examine or accord a hearing to all members of respective water users' association, but, at the same time, it is very desirable that the judgments of all, as expressed through the majority, should be ascertained." [85]

In response to the complaints of farmers that the Reclamation Service had not completed the widening of the Arizona Canal, which meant water had been wasted down the Salt River, the *Republican* on August 3 published a story detailing what had been done but including the fact that no one could say when the work of enlarging the canal would be finished. The story recalled the dredger excavated 10,400 cubic yards of the hardest kind of material from October 1907 until the boat gave out late in 1908. Early in 1909, the machinery was put on a new hull, and in May another excavator, this one running on rails beside the canal, was put in operation. Through the month of June, the two machines had removed 115,000 cubic yards of rock, boulders, and some dirt. In addition, teams and scrapers had removed another 30,000 cubic yards of rock and dirt. In July, when the dredger and excavator moved into dirt, 47,000 yards of soil were removed. The dredger had a crew of 10, and the excavator a crew of 12. In the past two years the number of men engaged in enlarging the canal had ranged from 25 to 250. The *Republican* said, "it can hardly be said in fairness that [the canal] has been neglected or entirely overlooked." [86]

During the first week of August, piping for the Roosevelt Dam's north side tunnel began to arrive at Roosevelt. O'Rourke's men had excavated 50 feet of the new tunnel. [87]

In response to Brewster's call for district meetings, six were held and two of those attracted too few farmers to take action. A third postponed the meeting. Farmers in the Scottsdale, Isaac, and Murphy districts elected three delegates each to the proposed convention to be held later. The sense of the Scottsdale district meeting was that the water temple should not be built, the Water Users' Association should be kept alive, but the salaries of the officers should be trimmed, and the Reclamation Service should be supported, but water should be delivered more often than once in 12 days so that small truck crops could be grown. Murphy district farmers wanted the salaries of the association's officers reduced, and they noted the association was quick to ask the farmers to respond to the Senate committee's questions only after a move to do this had been started in the Alhambra district. [88]

The water going through the low spot in Roosevelt Dam reached a depth of 4.8 feet the morning of August 9, which was said to make a beautiful waterfall. The water was described as greenish white as it started over, but lashed into a white foam the whole distance as it struck the rock in the dam. The foam hid the rocks entirely, so that the torrent was said to look bigger and deeper than it was. The water created a small whirlpool at the bottom and appeared to run off like an ordinary stream. [89]

Fowler was elected president of the National Irrigation Association at its annual meeting, which began August 10 in Spokane, Washington. His election led the *Republican* to remark editorially August 14 that, "It is probable that as a result of Mr. Fowler's election, his connection with the Salt River Valley Water Users' Association will be severed, since it is understood that the irrigation congress will maintain permanent headquarters in Chicago." [90]

Secretary Charles A. Van der Veer of the Water Users' Association received a letter August 14 from Senator Carter, who said the Senate Irrigation Committee would be delayed "owing to the protracted session of Congress," and it would arrive in the Valley sometime in November. [91]

The water going through the notch in Roosevelt Dam had climbed steadily, reaching 7.6 feet in depth August 16. This meant the elevation at the top of the water was 113 feet. A few days later, the dam at the highest point was 182 feet, while the average height was 150 feet. [92]

About 7 a.m. Sunday, August 29, what apparently was the first automobile fatality on the Roosevelt road occurred a few miles east of Government Well between Weekes Station and Goldfield. The victim was the car's driver, Al Miller of Tempe, who was the oldest son of Tempe pioneer Winchester Miller. Something was wrong with the steering wheel, and the car drove into an embankment and overturned. Two passengers, Dr. B. B. Moeur and Halbert Miller, were thrown clear and suffered bruises. The *Republican* said Al Miller was unable to get out from under the car and was caught beneath it. The top was down at the time, leaving bare the top support, an iron rod in the shape of an arm attached to the front seat. As the machine fell, Mr. Miller was caught on his back, and this iron arm was forced completely through his right lung, pinning him to the ground. Moeur and Halbert Miller lifted the heavy car off Miller, who was conscious and tried to assist. In about three to five minutes, however, he lost consciousness and died. Moeur had been called to Fish Creek to aid a sick child. His automobile was not working and he employed the Millers to take him. The car had wheel trouble all along the road, and Moeur and Halbert Miller suggested Al Miller stop and repair it. Al said he thought it would be okay, but it failed to take a turn and went into the embankment. Moeur estimated the car was traveling at least 40 miles an hour. [93]

1. *Arizona Republican* (Phoenix), March 4, 1909.
2. *Ibid.,* March 6, 15, 16, 1909.
3. *Ibid.,* March 8, 1909.
4. *Ibid.,* February 2, 1908, March 7, 14, 1909.
5. R. A. Ballinger to B. A. Fowler, March 13, 1909, Salt River Project Archives (hereafter SRPA).
6. *Republican,* March 13, 14, 1909; *Arizona Gazette* (Phoenix), March 18, 1909.
7. *Republican,* March 16, 1909.
8. *Ibid.,* March 18, 21, 1909.
9. *Ibid.,* March 26, 1909.
10. *Ibid.,* March 28, 1909.
11. *Ibid.,* March 29, April 1, 1909.
12. *Ibid.,* March 25, 30, April 2, 1909; Richard E. Sloan, *Land and Water Rights, Salt River Project* (unpublished manuscript, May 10, 1922), p. 16, SRPA.
13. *Republican,* April 4, 1909.
14. *Ibid.,* April 1, 7, 1909.
15. *Ibid.,* April 4, 1909.
16. *Ibid.,* April 6, 1909.
17. *Ibid.,* March 28, 1909; B. A. Fowler to C. J. Blanchard, April 6, 1909, SRPA.
18. *Republican,* April 7, 1909.
19. *Ibid.,* April 7, 1909.
20. *Ibid.,* April 7, 8, June 11, 1909.
21. *Ibid.,* April 9, 1909.
22. *Ibid.,* April 18, 1909.
23. *Ibid.,* August 27, October 11, 1911; *Gazette,* August 9, September 12, 1911; C. J. Blanchard to B. A. Fowler, April 14, 1909.
24. *Republican,* April 11, 18, 1909.
25. *Ibid.,* April 16, 1909.
26. *Ibid.,* April 18, 1909.
27. *Ibid.,* April 17, 22, 1909.
28. *Ibid.,* May 2, 3, 1909.
29. *Ibid.,* March 3, 1909; *Salt River Project, Final History to 1916* (unpublished manuscript), Vol. I., p. 99, SRPA.
30. *Final History to 1916,* Vol. I, pp. 99-100.
31. *Gazette,* May 1, 1909.
32. *Republican,* May 3, 1909.
33. *Ibid.,* May 4, 5, 11, 1909; A. C. Bartlett to the editor of the *Republican,* May 10, 1909, printed *Republican,* May 11, 1909.
34. James C. Goodman to the Editor of the *Republican,* May 4, 1909, printed *Republican,* May 5, 1909.
35. *Republican,* May 6, 9, 1909.
36. *Ibid.,* May 7, 1909.
37. *Ibid.,* May 8, 1909.
38. *Ibid.,* May 11, 1909; *Final History to 1916,* Vol. I, pp. 100-101.
39. *Final History to 1916,* Vol. I, p. 101.
40. *Ibid.,* p. 145; *Ninth Annual Report of the Reclamation Service, 1909-1910* (Washington: Government Printing Office, 1911), p. 63, SRPA.
41. *Republican,* May 11, 1909.

42. *Ibid.*
43. *Ibid.,* May 9, 12, 13, 14, 16, 1909.
44. *Ibid.,* May 16, 1909.
45. *Ibid.,* May 18, 19, 1909.
46. *Ibid.,* May 19, 20, 1909.
47. *Ibid.,* May 28, 29, 30, 1909.
48. *Ibid.,* May 30, 1909.
49. *Ibid.,* May 28, 1909.
50. *Ibid.,* May 30, 1909.
51. *Ibid.,* June 1, 1909.
52. *Ibid.,* May 31, June 3, 4, 1909; *Gazette,* June 4, 1909.
53. *Republican,* June 3, 4, 1909.
54. *Gazette,* June 7, 1909; *Republican,* June 8, 1909.
55. *Republican,* June 8, 1909.
56. *Ibid.,* June 8, 10, 1909.
57. *Ibid.,* June 10, 11, 12, 1909.
58. *Ibid.,* June 13, 16, 17, 1909; *Gazette,* June 14, 1909; *Report in the Matter of the Investigation of the Salt & Gila Rivers - Reservations and Reclamation Service* (Washington: Government Printing Office, 1913), p. 508.
59. *Gazette,* June 17, 18, 1909; *Republican,* June 18, 24, 1909.
60. *Republican,* June 20, 1909.
61. *Ibid.,* June 27, 1909.
62. *Ibid.,* June 19, 27, 1909.
63. *Ibid.,* June 24, 1909.
64. *Ibid.,* July 4, 9, 13, 1909.
65. *Ibid.,* July 17, 1909.
66. *Ibid.,* July 9, 1909.
67. *Ibid.,* July 10, 1909; *Gazette,* June 22, 1909.
68. *Republican,* July 12, 1909.
69. *Ibid.,* July 15, 1909; *Gazette,* July 14, 1909.
70. *Gazette,* July 14, 15, 1909; *Republican,* July 14, 1909.
71. *Republican,* July 15, 1909; *Gazette,* July 15, 1909.
72. *Republican,* July 29, 1909.
73. *Ibid.,* July 19, 1909.
74. *Ibid.,* July 20, 1909.
75. *Ibid.,* July 21, 22, 1909.
76. *Ibid.,* July 21, 1909; *Gazette,* July 21, 1909.
77. *Republican,* July 21, 1909.
78. *Ibid.,* July 22, 1909; *Gazette,* July 22, 1909.
79. *Republican,* July 25, 1909.
80. *Ibid.,* July 27, 28, 1909.
81. *Ibid.,* July 29, 1909.
82. *Ibid.,* July 30, 1909.
83. *Ibid.,* August 8, 1909.
84. *Gazette,* August 6, 1909.
85. *Republican,* August 2, 3, 1909.
86. *Ibid.,* August 3, 1909.
87. *Ibid.,* August 8, 1909.
88. *Gazette,* August 7, 1909.
89. *Republican,* June 1, August 10, 1909.
90. *Ibid.,* August 13, 14, 1909.
91. *Ibid.,* August 15, 1909.
92. *Ibid.,* August 18, 23, 1909.
93. *Ibid.,* August 30, 31, 1909.

September 1909 - February 1910

Engineer W. A. Farish of the Reclamation Service issued a warning September 1 that fast driving automobiles along the mountainous sections of the Roosevelt road would not be permitted, and persons who disregarded the edict would be banned from the road. Farish's order, in response to the death August 30 of Al Miller in the wreck of an automobile, was not for the purpose of protecting the motorist against himself, the *Arizona Republican* reported. "He may break his bones or smash up his own car if he wants to, for the government is not concerned in that," the newspaper said. Rather, the government wanted to protect teamsters and their teams of mules and horses. The speed on the mountainous sections was not to exceed 15 miles per hour. [1]

On September 2, engineer Jay D. Stannard of the Reclamation Service returned from a tour of the six batteries of wells six to eight miles south of Mesa. Stannard said if the wells worked out others would be installed. He said one well produced a constant flow of 125 miners' inches. [2]

The water going through the notch in Roosevelt Dam had decreased to a depth of 5 feet on September 4, but rain began falling on the watershed and the water began climbing on Monday, September 6. The following day, the depth was 9.8 feet, and on September 8 it was 13.5 feet. Water also flowed over the Granite Reef Diversion Dam at a depth of 1.2 feet for the 1,000-foot length of the structure. The water at Roosevelt Dam reached its maximum depth of 13.9 feet on September 9. The canals, laterals, and small ditches in the Valley ran full and the river was unfordable. [3]

On September 11, the Reclamation Service announced the price of water between September 15, 1909, and May 14, 1910, would be $1 per acre, while flood water was priced at 50 cents per acre. [4]

In mid-September, the highest point of the Roosevelt Dam was 190 feet above datum, and the distance from the front to the rear of the dam at that spot was 30 feet. The night of September 17, dam contractor John O'Rourke's men finished drilling through the mountain for the tunnel on the north side of the dam. [5]

On September 18, the Salt River Valley Water Users' Association revealed Secretary of the Interior Richard A. Ballinger had disapproved of the cooperative plan for construction of irrigation works, and President William Howard Taft had sustained that decision. Benjamin A. Fowler, president of the association, sent a telegram to Frederick H. Newell, director of the U.S. Reclamation Service, asking for a clarification of Ballinger's ruling. Fowler's wire said:

Recent department ruling directing cessation of co-operation plan of canal construction threatens to stop work on Eastern canal and entail crop loss of more than $100,000. Can you secure early adoption of plan to continue work? This is urgent and we respectfully request early consideration to avert serious injury to farmers under said canal.

Attorney Morris Bien, counsel for the Reclamation Service, replied to Fowler with the following telegram on September 18:

Attorney general's and secretary's ruling prevent new co-operation contracts, also prevent issue of receipt of certificates on pending contracts so far as reclamation service is concerned. Compensation will be made for work hereafter reported under pending contract. Outstanding certificates or claims for certificates not issued will be settled under plans now being considered.

Fowler and Joseph H. Kibbey, the association's attorney, interpreted Bien's reply to mean no new work could be started under the cooperative system; no more certificates were to be issued under any circumstances; plans were being made to compensate in some way for the certificates already issued; work already contracted for could continue and a way would be found to pay for it. [6]

Electricity generated at Roosevelt Dam was tested by Pacific Gas & Electric Co. in machinery at its new Phoenix substation on September 28. The Reclamation Service sent an inspector to check the transmission line and found vandals had shot apart two insulators. Pacific Gas & Electric hoped to begin taking the power on a permanent basis starting September 30, but this did not happen until October 1, and Phoenix took it without special notice. This prompted the *Republican* to comment:

In any community more excitable than this—and what other community is not more excitable?—such an important event as the beginning of service by the electric power line from Roosevelt to Phoenix would have been the occasion of a day's celebration. Here, however, it was merely a part of the day's work.

Nevertheless, the installation of this electric service is an epoch-making event. Over a line sixty miles in length, a line having no superior in the world, electric power is conveyed from the great Roosevelt dam to the Salt River valley. Within a year various pumping plants in the valley will be adding thousands of inches to the supply of water for irrigation.

The completion of the power line is next to the final step in the government's vast storage project for the valley. The completion of the dam is but a year away. [7]

Charles A. Chambers, a homesteader under the Eastern Canal, five miles east of Mesa, was electrocuted Sunday, October 3, when he climbed one of the government transmission line poles and came in contact with a wire. Chambers, 36, had turned his horses out on the desert the night before and about noon the next day left the house to look for them. They were not in sight and, as he had done before, he climbed a tower to extend his view. The *Republican* reported,

Before he had never climbed as high as the wires. This time he evidently put his head among them, for when the body was found the head was nearly burned off and a great gash in the throat showed the point of contact... The clothing was entirely burned off of him. The front of the abdomen, where it had been in contact with the tower, was burned away and the entrails had fallen out. The corpse was a black and shapeless figure...

The tower was in sight of his house. His wife had gone to the door to see if he was coming to dinner and she was horrified at the sight of him, a blazing mass, at the top of the tower. As she looked she saw him fall to the ground. All the time she could hear the angry hissing of the wire until it burned in two, letting her husband fall.

Chambers, besides his wife, was survived by six children, the oldest 13. He carried life insurance policies totaling $3,000. [8]

On October 4, the Board of Governors of the Water Users' Association named a committee of three, Governors John P. Orme and Joseph Cope and the counsel, Kibbey, to meet with farmers in the districts to help frame answers to the 19 questions concerning the reclamation law and irrigation posed by the Senate Irrigation Committee. This action was taken because of the small response the association had received to the mailing of the questions to all the members along with a blank on which to write answers. The committee was instructed to meet either in private or in public with the farmers and to present the answers for ratification or amendment at the November meeting of the governors. The committee later decided to ask each governor to appoint five members from his district to meet together to prepare answers to the questions. [9]

The governors gave the Highland Canal Construction Co. an extension until November 1 to complete the Eastern Canal. The problem in the work was there was more rock to excavate than had been anticipated. Contractor Tom Smith was also concerned about having enough money to complete the work, though there were then 100 men and 120 mules on the job. In addition, the Reclamation Service was building a cement bridge over the canal were it crossed the Roosevelt road and was cementing the lateral heads where they emerged from the main canal. [10]

At Roosevelt, Reclamation Service engineers reported the steel plates had been laid on both the sides and the bottom of the dam's sluicing tunnel, and the roof would be completed in about two weeks. After that, fine cement was to be pumped behind the plates and let rest for 10 days, so the cement would harden. Thereafter, the gates would be raised and the water let through until the lake was lowered sufficiently to allow the gap on the north side of the dam to be filled. The gates would be closed again as soon as it was believed the dam was high enough to keep the water from flowing over. [11]

Secretary Ballinger arrived in Phoenix the morning of October 19 to tour the Valley and visit Granite Reef Diversion and Roosevelt dams. An *Arizona Gazette* writer questioned him about the government's contract with Pacific Gas & Electric Co. Ballinger said he had given his office orders to investigate the contract, but he understood that when the government took over the irrigation system "it was found necessary to assume an existing contract with the local electric company. That makes a vast difference. But when power is to be sold at public auction, municipalities have first call." Ballinger said because the government was not a retailer of power, under proper limitations, it was the policy of the Interior Department to give exclusive contracts to private corporations. However, government policy and law were to give a preference to municipalities. He could not say offhand how Pacific Gas & Electric's contract for exclusive sale of power in Phoenix might affect the city's right to purchase power then or in the future. [12]

In a meeting with some of the governors of the Water Users' Association, Ballinger asked if the people would be able to meet the payments to the government. Kibbey and others said they would. Kibbey also said there was no reason

for an extension of time for payments, but one member of the board disagreed. Ballinger said in some instances water users thought they should have up to 40 years to repay the construction costs of irrigation works. He said extending the time would take an act of Congress, but he intimated it was possible for him to defer the start of payments (by delaying the date on which the project was declared open). Ballinger said he thought it would be reasonable too, to make it possible for farmers, in case of fire, flood, or some other disaster, to delay payments for a year. He then gave two reasons why he thought delaying the start of repayments was not good: first, by adhering to the law, it would attract a better class of settlers because they would not undertake farming until they assured themselves they could meet the payments; second, delaying the payments would defeat the part of the national law establishing a revolving fund to finance irrigation works. Some of the men present said the established farmers would probably find it easier to make payments than those starting with new land. [13]

Concerning the abandonment of the cooperative plan for paying for construction of irrigation works, Ballinger said that was one reason why he told the Senate irrigation committee the Interior Department wanted authority to issue bonds and repay them with revenue from the projects. Money from the bonds would be used to complete the construction of present projects. He said the idea had the support of the president. [14]

After visiting Roosevelt Dam on October 20, Ballinger again spoke with reporters, telling them no new features or works would be undertaken at any of the projects because there was no money. He said the power produced at Roosevelt Dam would produce a source of revenue to the water users for all time to come. Ballinger said his own preference was for municipal ownership of lighting plants, but he understood that had not been a matter of consideration in the contract with Pacific Gas & Electric Co. He also thought once the possibilities of the Valley were understood, people of substance from around the country would be attracted. He added,

and that is just what you want. No other kind of settler will have any business here or under any other reclamation project. There will naturally be a burden which a man without money cannot undertake unless he is an exceptionally resourceful man. Such a man might succeed, but such men are comparatively few. But the man with some money and judgment will find here an admirable opportunity to increase his substance. [15]

The *Republican* reported October 22 that during Ballinger's visit to Roosevelt Dam, a laborer, not identified by the newspaper, fell to his death. Ballinger witnessed the accident, the man landing within 50 feet of the secretary and his companions. L. J. Fremeau, who drove the car that took Ballinger to the dam, also saw the man fall. Fremeau said he was walking toward the powerhouse when the accident occurred. Several workmen were at the very top of the dam slowly working a huge stone into place with the aid of a derrick. The man who fell stepped out to swing the stone into position. His foot came down in green cement and he slipped. He tried to save himself by jumping to the rock step immediately below, and "for a moment he balanced, swinging his arms. Then he toppled, striking the steps far below on his back and rebounding to the stones lower down. The third time he struck on his head and was undoubtedly killed at that point." He rolled or fell the remaining distance to the bottom. The distance the man fell was something more than 180 feet. [16]

On October 26, a committee of seven farmers met to refine answers to the 19 questions posed by the Senate Irrigation Committee. The replies had been adopted at a general meeting of farmers, the delegates to that meeting having been selected at school district meetings. It still was not known just when the Senate committee would arrive. [17]

Dwight B. Heard issued a call for occupants of land south of the river above the high line of the Wormser extension of the Tempe Canal to meet at his office October 30 to devise ways and means of securing water for the spring planting season. [18]

The Water Users' Association committee to supply answers to the Senate Irrigation Committee questions met October 27 with the governors to give a report, which was accepted by them in anticipation of their meeting November 1 with five representatives from each district in the association. The November 1 plan was to merge the ideas of the association's committee with those of the district representatives and then to call a mass meeting of all farmers. [19]

At the October 27 meeting, Kibbey spoke for the committee composed of himself, Orme, and Cope. Kibbey thought it was ill-advised, unfortunate, and untimely to agitate the question of extending the time for government repayment of the Salt River project construction costs. He said it was true the cost of the project was two times or more than was first contemplated, but that was because the only things expected when it started were construction of Roosevelt Dam and a plant to provide electrical energy for the sole purpose of building the dam. Kibbey said it was at the request of the landowners that 20 feet were added to the height of Roosevelt Dam, a powerhouse was added, Granite Reef Diversion Dam was built, the north side and some of the south side canals were bought, and the canals were being extended, enlarged and improved. He said:

I think it cannot be fairly said that the cost of this project has been either unwarrantably or unfairly increased. It was all done at our own request, and the burden of the cost of the acquisition, enlargement and improvement of the canals and the construction of the Granite Reef dam which were originally our own burden was assumed at our request by the government. . . .

The elements of our burden have not been increased at all. All the things being furnished us by the government had to be supplied, and I cannot assume that we would not have to pay for them. Of course, we would not object to the extension of time for these payments over a longer period or a diminution of the amount.

It has long been contemplated by the reclamation service, and certainly very earnestly wished for by us, that other plants for the generation of electrical energy should be installed so that from them a revenue might be derived to materially reduce the cost to us of our irrigation works. . . .

The one difficulty is the lack of money in the reclamation fund. . . With the expenditure of an additional million dollars on our project we can install power plants which will enable us to furnish power at the most conservative estimate netting to us an

annual revenue of from $300,000 to $600,000 per year. That means a reduction of our assessments for payment for the project of from $1.50 to $3 per acre per year, and after the payment to the government of the cost of the project, an assured revenue far in excess of the cost of operation, repairs and maintenance of the whole system. . . .

I think it must be assumed that we can pay [for the project]. If we can't, we need hope for no further expenditures by the government in a project that can't pay for itself in ten years without any interest charge. I do not care to even discuss the matter upon the hearing that we wish to avoid our obligations. Such a suggestion as that would instantly show that we were entitled to no consideration at all. . . .

Mr. Hill says that the further expenditure of $600,000 will at once, at the most conservative estimate, give a net revenue of $300,000 per annum. We hope to get this money of the government, but certainly we need not expect the government to advance it in the face of our efforts to be relieved from our present obligations to it. The government will hardly borrow money and pay interest on it and advance it to us when we are asking it to forbear what we already owe. . . .

A tentative proposition is already under consideration. It is this: That if the money cannot be obtained from the reclamation fund, then that we have the secretary [of the interior] declare officially that the proposed electric power plants are a part of the project, and that the project will not be declared completed until their instalment. That in the meantime the water users assess themselves for sufficient money to install these works within two or three years.

That will work out somewhat in this way. If the project is declared completed without the electric power plants, and the secretary may probably do that within the next year, then the ten year term begins, with payments approximately of $4 or $4.50 per acre per year. If, however, the secretary will withhold his announcement of the completion of the project until we can furnish the money to install the power plants, upon condition that we assess ourselves for that purpose, we will have this situation: That for the first, second and even third year we need assess ourselves for only $1.50, or at most $2, an acre. That will raise ample funds to install power plants sufficient to net us a revenue of $300,000 to $500,000 per year which will reduce our ten year assessment by $1.50 to $2 per acre per year, making them only $2 to $2.50 per year. To do this, however, we must have the cooperation of the secretary of the interior and possibly of congress—and that, I think, we may not hope to have if we oppose their known policies with reference to these payments.

Kibbey said he also had heard that the Senate Irrigation Committee would be presented with "small grievances arising out of the details of administration by the reclamation service in the valley, or of the Water Users' Association itself." While those grievances were important to the individuals, he said the Senate committee was not constituted to deal with them and he advised against presenting them, for the only result would be to irritate the committee. Concerning complaints against the association, Kibbey said the remedy was to "appeal to the shareholders at the next election." [20]

Hill told the *Gazette* the Eastern Canal would not be ready to receive water until December 1, and then it would be entitled only to the flood water of the river until such time as Judge Edward Kent made a decision in the case of *Hurley v. Abbott*. Hill said he thought the decision would be made by Christmas, and whatever it was, it would be strictly followed. [21]

South side settlers, who met with Heard to try to devise a way to get water for lands above the Wormser extension, passed resolutions asking the Reclamation Service to furnish them with a plan for a pumping plant and its estimated cost. The settlers wanted the government engineers to tell them whether it would be better to sink deep wells on high levels or to elevate water from lower points where the wells would not be so deep. [22]

Kent announced the final day for giving evidence in **Hurley v. Abbott** would be November 6. He said he wanted to give his decision before the end of the year. [23]

Word came from Roosevelt on October 31 the construction work on the sluicing tunnel at Roosevelt Dam was about completed and it was expected water would flow through it November 8. It was expected to take until that date for the concrete to set. When the tunnel was back in use, the contractor was to begin immediately closing the gap in the dam. [24]

On November 1, the governors, the representatives from each of the districts appointed by them, and a delegation from the farmers' group met to complete the Water Users' Association's answers to the Senate Irrigation Committee's 19 questions. According to an account of the meeting published in the **Republican,** the first question, "Is the existing reclamation law satisfactory, and if not, in what respect should it be amended?" produced the biggest difference of opinion during the day with H. A. Bustrin and James P. Ivy of the farmers' group offering in answer, "Yes, it is," which was rejected 24 to 5 in the day's only recorded vote. The **Gazette** said the first question caused more discussion than any of the others except No. 8, while the **Republican** said No. 8 was "easily disposed of." At the meeting's end, it was decided a mass meeting was unnecessary, and Fowler was directed to appoint a committee of five to present the association's answers to the senators and to draw up a resolution commending the reclamation act and the Reclamation Service. Fowler on November 6 named himself, Heard, Orme, Charles Peterson, and Joseph H. Trotter. [25]

At 11:30 a.m. November 8, the center gates of the service and emergency gates in the Roosevelt Dam sluicing tunnel were raised three feet and water began flowing through. In a short time, the lake behind the dam lowered eight inches, but it was not until November 13 that the water was down enough for O'Rourke's men to begin closing the notch in the dam. The **Republican** said the motive power for operating the gates was to be changed from hydraulic to motor power. [26]

Hill sent a telegram from Yuma November 14 asking that the Senate Irrigation Committee and party be met in Mesa the next morning by enough automobiles to carry the visitors to Granite Reef and then to Roosevelt. There were 12 persons in the senatorial party, including Senators Thomas H. Carter of Montana, F. E. Warren of Wyoming, and W. L. Jones of Washington. As planned, the party arrived in Mesa November 15 and departed for Roosevelt. It was announced the committee would assemble at 7:30 p.m. November 16 at the Board of Trade and would leave Phoenix the same night. [27]

Following dinner at the Heard home on November 16, the senators went to the Board of Trade where about 150 businessmen and farmers had gathered. Fowler opened the meeting, asking speakers to limit themselves to five minutes. Kibbey read a resolution in praise of Hill, the Reclamation Service, and the work they had done. The resolution contained this passage:

> *. . .while not unmindful that in minor details in the progress of the work there may have appeared to have been some mistakes and not in any way minimizing the annoyance that may have arisen therefrom, we are fully aware that such mistakes, if they were indeed mistakes, were inevitable in the course of a work of such magnitude and extent as the Salt River project. That if there were mistakes or miscalculations, they have been so infrequent and in comparison with the magnitude of the work so unimportant and of so little comparative disadvantage and wholly of so temporary a character that they rather emphasize the splendid ability, wisdom and foresight of those who designed and have superintended the construction of the works of the project.*

Kibbey then read aloud the 19 questions and answers. Following this, the senators asked questions. When that was done, Fowler informed the committee another set of answers had been developed, and these were presented by Ivy. Some of the answers given by Ivy differed very little or not at all, but in others the approach taken by the Water Users' Association and the group represented by Ivy were at great variance. Here are the answers of both groups to questions upon which they differed:

No. 1—Is the existing reclamation law satisfactory, and if not, in what respect should it be amended?

Association—Yes. We are informed through our land office that less than 100 homesteads (16,000 acres) are now being held under the Salt River project, or rather under the reservoir district, and that practically all of this land is signed up with the Water Users' association. Under existing laws, title to such homestead land will not be issued until payments for the reservoir rights are all made—the payments being made through our government land office. We believe that when final five-year proof is made and accepted, patents should be issued to all homestead lands under this project, and all collections made for reservoir rights by the local Water Users' association, the land being held by the association as security for the payments assessed by the government against said lands, as is the case of holdings in private ownership.

Ivy's group—In so far as the general terms of the reclamation laws are concerned, we do not find anything to suggest in the way of amendments or additions, except to urge that the time of payment to the government of the sum expended in the building of reclamation works be extended in such a manner as will bring the annual payments of the land holders under such reclamation works within the estimates first made by the reclamation officials, that is in the case of the Roosevelt dam, $1.50 per acre per annum.

No. 2—Are the local laws governing the appropriation and use of water for irrigation satisfactory in their application to lands being reclaimed by the government or through private enterprise, and if not, what amendments are required?

Association—Yes.

Ivy—The laws governing the appropriation and use of water are sufficient, but we have no laws governing the administration or distribution of water.

No. 4—Is your water supply adequate both for irrigation and domestic uses?

Association—Not under present conditions, but it will be when the reclamation project is fully completed.

Ivy—The water supply may be adequate for domestic use, but it certainly has been insufficient for irrigation purposes. By the Reclamation Service attempting to irrigate more land than the available water will cover beneficially, farming has generally been unprofitable the past year. The supply of water for irrigation purposes has been so irregular and uncertain in time and insufficient in quantity that we are in no wise certain of getting a paying crop under present conditions.

No. 6—Is your canal and distribution system satisfactory, and if not, what are the defects, what caused them, and what remedy is proposed?

Association—The distributing system under the canals acquired by the government is steadily improving, and under those canals on the south side of the river which have for years been controlled and operated by the people who own the lands under them, the distributing system is in a very satisfactory condition. On the north side, the enlargement of the Arizona canal should be pushed to early completion.

Ivy—No—Our canal and distributing or lateral system are not satisfactory. The defects are: An incomplete canal and lateral system. Remedy: The early completion of the canal and lateral systems as planned by the Reclamation Service, and we earnestly petition your honorable committee to use every honorable means to secure such an appropriation as will enable the Reclamation Service to complete the canal and lateral system as planned.

No. 7—Can the cost of maintaining and operating the canal and distributing system be reduced, and if so, in what way and to what extent?

Association—On the north side of the river, under government operation, we believe the cost of maintaining the canals and distributing the water can be reduced by lessening the number of canals and decreasing the number of small private ditches.

Ivy—Yes, in several ways. First, by a reduction of clerical and office forces; second, by a reduction of ditch cleaning forces; third, by a reduction in the forces of overseers, bosses and sub-bosses; fourth, by compelling workmen to work eight full hours instead of counting "a day" from time of leaving camp to returning thereto.

No. 8—Can the water users by employing reasonable industry and economy promptly make all payments required by the existing law?

Association—Yes.

Ivy—We believe the land owners can make all payments, based upon original estimates. But if there is an excess of cost in construction of the Salt River project, Roosevelt dam, over original estimates, we think there ought to be more time given equal to the excess.

No. 19—How, in your opinion, can congress best promote the general welfare of the water users and carry out the purposes of the reclamation act?

Association—We approve the plan suggested by President Taft for a liberal appropriation to the cause of national irrigation, to be repaid from money received from the sale of public lands in the states comprised in the national irrigation act.

Ivy—By seeing that the every phase of the original Newlands-Hansbrough law be carried out, both in letter and in spirit.

Carter said he objected to the Taft plan of issuing bonds for reclamation purposes because the money received through the proceeds from reclaimed lands would have to go into the treasury to repay the bonds instead of into the reclamation fund for widening that work. Carter said bonds would mean an end to the reclamation fund, and he preferred issuing warrants against the fund. He also warned that farmers of the Mississippi Valley objected to the competition being generated from the West through government expense. He said other interests also opposed the reclamation act and continued to regard it as unconstitutional, and if it were to come to a vote in the Congress, it might be repealed. [28]

H. E. Bierce of Globe, a mining engineer, told a *Gazette* reporter November 18 the Globe-Miami area could use at least 10,000 horsepower of electricity from Roosevelt Dam. Bierce said more than $1 million worth of electricity each year was being consumed in that area. He said he thought the Salt River project could realize a million dollars per annum from the sale of power within five years, which would more than pay the yearly cost of the dam and leave a profit of $200,000 each year. The cost of Roosevelt Dam and other irrigation works connected with the Salt River project was then about $8 million. [29]

By November 29, the lowest part of the dam had been brought to 150 feet above datum, which meant 400,000 acre-feet of water could be stored. This was the elevation that was supposed to have been reached within two years after the signing of the contract. Instead, because of the many delays, it took four years, seven months, and 21 days before the entire dam was at 150 feet or more. [30]

A power substation near Sacaton on the Gila River Indian Reservation was completed in November, but it was not until June 1910 that power generated at Roosevelt Dam was delivered to operate irrigating pumps on the reservation. [31]

Construction of the Eastern Canal was completed by the start of December, but contractor Tom Smith refused to turn the canal over to the Reclamation Service because he had not been paid. The Reclamation Service refused to put water in the canal until it took possession. Smith was to have been paid with government certificates under the cooperative plan of construction, but this could not be done because the cooperative scheme had been declared illegal. Interior Department officials in Washington, D.C., were trying to decide what to do to pay Smith, who was owed $92,000. [32]

The governors at their meeting December 6 authorized Fowler and Kibbey to take the steps necessary to have the members of the Water Users' Association vote at a special election about whether to build a water temple. This was done after every governor said he personally favored the construction of the office building. Hill said if a building was not erected, he would seek other quarters for the Reclamation Service, which probably would cost more. [33]

There followed a long discussion about the power possibilities of the project and the best way to use them. One fear was any proceeds from the sale of electricity would be taken by the government and put into the reclamation fund, but Hill said if the association shareholders invested their own money in the construction of power plants, they should be able to retain the proceeds themselves. Hill supposed Ballinger would delay the opening of the project if the association undertook building the plants. The association could raise about $400,000 by assessing each acre $1 per year for two years, a sum which it was thought would pay for the crosscut power plant and at least one other. Some governors thought the burden would be too heavy if at the same time the interior secretary opened the project, and the farmers had to repay construction costs. Hill thought the $400,000 would be returned in power sales in two years, and from then on the revenue would be net profit less maintenance costs.

Additionally, he said the plant at the Arizona Falls on the Arizona Canal could be improved so that by itself it could produce all the electricity required under the contract with Pacific Gas & Electric Co. [34]

Another area of talk involved how to furnish power to individual farmers for domestic purposes. Hill suggested community electrical companies that might involve four contiguous sections of land or more. The small company would supply a small transformer, wires, poles, and other machinery and retail power obtained from the government to pay off the costs of the equipment. Hill suggested trying this along the power line running to the Gila River Indian Reservation. This led the governors to discuss disposing of electrical power outside the reservoir district. Hill said the Avondale Co. and the Marinette Co., both engaged in reclaiming acreage west of the Agua Fria River, talked about buying government power. One proposal was the companies construct the lines to connect with the government lines and be given credits for their use of power until their construction costs were paid off. Then the lines would be turned over to the government and the companies would thereafter buy their power. [35]

The evening of December 8, the *Gazette* published an article showing that Pacific Gas & Electric's net profit in 1908 was twenty-one and one-half percent. The story said the company capitalized its rights and franchises for $515,000 but paid taxes on only $185,200 in Phoenix. The newspaper revealed the secretary and treasurer of the Edison Electric Co. in California were the vice president and secretary, respectively, of Pacific Gas & Electric. The *Gazette* said Edison Electric served Los Angeles and nearby towns including Pasadena, which had its own plant and was in competition with Edison. Because of the competition, Edison sold power for 5 cents per kilowatt in Pasadena, while Pacific Gas & Electric charged 15 cents per kilowatt hour in Phoenix. The *Gazette* urged building a municipal plant in Phoenix, and the city council on the night of December 10 ordered the city attorney to determine the measures necessary to have Congress allow the city to bond itself for $300,000 to construct a municipal lighting plant. The council had received a petition from 500 citizens asking this be done. The original proposal before the council was to bond the city for $200,000, but Fowler told the council that Hill had told him within the past few hours the city could not build a plant for that sum. Fowler said the council was acting hastily, an opinion joined in by Joseph Thalheimer. Fowler also said there would be opposition in Congress to the bonds, and the bonds would go unsold if approved because people would not buy because Phoenix already had a company serving light and power. [36]

Because of the slow use of water in the Valley, the gates in the sluicing tunnel at Roosevelt Dam were closed. The only water running in the Salt River came from that used to generate power, and this came to approximately 2,500 inches. The elevation of the reservoir was 96 feet. [37]

In Phoenix, December 21, Hill met with the board of directors of the Mesa Canal Co., who wanted the government to take control of the canal system. The

directors left the meeting with the understanding stored water from the reservoir would not be delivered to any corporation before the Salt River project was opened. The Mesa Canal Co. was a corporation with 400 shares outstanding, the holdings ranging from one-half to 15 shares. In the delivery of water, the Reclamation Service intended to deal only with individuals and not corporations. Almost all the land served by the Mesa Canal Co. was signed into the Water Users' Association, and it had been the plan of the stockholders to turn their interests in the canal over to the association when Roosevelt Dam was completed. Because of the Reclamation Service's position, Mesa Canal Co. directors called a meeting January 3, 1910, to test the sentiment of the stockholders toward selling to the government. Members of the Utah Canal Co. were invited to attend. [38]

Reclamation Service officials reported in the last week of December the highest point on Roosevelt Dam was 228 feet, or a dozen feet from the crest of the final structure. The lowest point was between 150 to 156 feet above datum, while elevation of the water was 97 feet. The valves in the north side tunnel were in place, and it was expected the outlet could be used for the discharge of water, if necessary, by the end of the month. The capacity of the tunnel was put at 1,500 cubic feet of water per second. [39]

Rains on the Salt River watershed increased runoff into the Roosevelt reservoir with the water on December 25 and 26 running two-feet deep over the power canal intake dam. A New Year's flood came down the Verde River, causing water to go over the Granite Reef Diversion Dam at a depth of 4 feet. By January 3, the lake at Roosevelt was a little more than 101-feet deep. [40]

On January 5, 1910, by a vote of 15 to 2, the Council of the Water Users' Association approved the governors' resolution calling for the purchase of ground and the construction of an office building, including furnishings, for no more than $40,000 for joint use of the association and the Reclamation Service. The Council also recommended the question be voted upon at the association's April 1910 election, and not at a special election. The Council gave approval to a resolution recommending the governors begin an educational campaign among shareholders concerning the value of assessing each acre $1.50 to $2 per year for two years to raise funds for building power plants. This was premised upon the secretary of the interior agreeing to delay the opening of the project and the apportionment of water to the lands. [41]

At a meeting of the governors the same day, they agreed to put the office building question on the April election ballot. They also authorized Kibbey and Fowler to go to Washington, if necessary, to present the self-assessment proposal for power plants to Ballinger. [42]

Hill met with Mesa Canal Co. shareholders January 8. On the question of how much the government would be willing to pay for the canal, Hill said he could not give an answer. He said that was a matter for negotiation between the canal company directors and the Reclamation Service officials, but the price would be calculated upon the cost of duplicating the facilities the government could use in the distributing system. This meant the government would not buy the water carrying right the Mesa Canal held in the Consolidated Canal. The government would not distribute water based upon the number of shares held in the Mesa Canal Co., nor would stored water be furnished unless the stockholders were members of the Water Users' Association. The Mesa Canal Co. shareholders were entitled to natural flow rights of the river and this they would get. A question was raised as to whether the company, if taken over by the government, could appeal the decision in *Hurley v. Abbott* if the shareholders were dissatisfied with Kent's ruling. Hill saw that as no problem, saying the decision would be made before the negotiations were completed. He said he knew of no reason why the company could not appeal simply because it had sold one of its possessions. Alexander J. Chandler moved that the question of price to be paid for the canal be placed in the hands of the board of directors to take up with the Reclamation Service. The motion was approved. [43]

The Phoenix City Council on the night of January 11 scheduled an advisory vote of taxpayers February 24 to decide whether the city should ask Congress to authorize it to sell $300,000 worth of bonds for construction of a municipal lighting plant. While the council's vote for the election was unanimous, the proposal met with opposition from a number of speakers who thought it was more important for the city to own its own sewer system and to have paved roads. [44]

The *Republican* reported January 12 the water in the Roosevelt reservoir was at the 108-foot level and this meant 140,000 acre-feet of water was in storage. The low point of the dam was 160 feet above the riverbed, and construction was proceeding at about 10 feet per month. The newspaper said it was impossible to give the exact date of the completion of masonry work, but it was not too early for the Valley to begin speculation on what form of celebration would occur at Roosevelt to mark the event. [45]

Reclamation Service officials reported January 12 the Interior Department had found a legal provision by which the government could pay for the construction of the Eastern Canal under the cooperative plan. Officials said the cash would come out of the reclamation fund and $92,000 would be allotted for the Eastern Canal. [46]

In response to a letter from Hill, the governors met January 17 to consider whether the government should purchase the Mesa and Utah canals. The governors gave their approval after a brief discussion. [47]

Plans to extend the Eastern Canal a mile farther south were announced by Reclamation Service engineers on January 26. The engineers also expected water would be distributed to lands lying under the canal early in February. [48]

On January 30, the *Republican* disclosed the decision in the case of *Hurley v. Abbott* had been delivered to the printer, but the terms of Kent's findings had not been given. [49]

W. E. Barry and J. T. Bone sent a letter to fellow members of the Council asking the office of counsel to the Water Users' Association be abolished and the salary of the association president be reduced. The letter did not specify the amount of reduction desired in the president's salary. Bone and Barry also called for a change in the association articles of incorporation to require that members of the Board of Governors live within the district they represented. Governors identified as living outside their districts, though possessing holdings in them, were Orme, Cope, George M. Halm, H. H. Stone, Elliott Evans, and H. J. McClung. [50]

The governors on February 7 voted to supply all landowners in the Water Users' Association with a copy of the decision in *Hurley v. Abbott* and to have an additional supply on hand for future landowners, for nonmembers who would be interested, and for realty agents. The governors agreed to sell them for 50 cents per copy, which was said to be little more than the cost of printing. [51]

Some rules concerning the distribution of water from Roosevelt Lake to members of the Water Users' Association were announced by the Reclamation Service on February 15. The first statement was no single landowner would receive stored water for more than 160 acres of land. Some landowners had been under the impression this provision of the reclamation law would not be enforced until after the project was declared open by the secretary of the interior. If an owner of land in excess of 160 acres sold the excess to a buyer not already holding a right to water for 160 acres, the buyer would be automatically entitled to water for up to 160 acres. The Reclamation Service said the rule requiring the landowner to live on or near his land would not be enforced until the project was opened. The distribution of the natural flow water of the river would be guided by the decree in *Hurley v. Abbott.* Lands signed into the association receiving flood water when it was available would continue to get it, provided they were included in the reservoir district when it opened. [52]

On February 21, the Council announced it would meet March 3 to consider amending the articles of incorporation, as requested by Bone and Barry. The Council also said it would consider the salaries of the president and counsel. [53]

On February 24, Phoenix property taxpayers voted 346 to 206 to ask Congress to authorize the city to sell $300,000 in bonds for building a municipal light plant. [54]

Judge Kent announced February 26 that his decision in *Hurley v. Abbott* would be handed down at 9 a.m. Tuesday, March 1. The decision had been expected February 26, but it was delayed because maps to be attached to it had not arrived from Denver. [55]

At the end of February, Roosevelt Dam measured 645 feet in total length. The height of the dam beginning at the south end was 228 feet above datum for the first 60 feet, 238 1/2 feet for 30 feet, 228 feet for the next 100 feet, 212 feet for 60 feet, 200 feet for 100 feet, 192 feet for 85 feet, 180 feet for 60 feet, and 190 feet for 150 feet. [56]

1. *Arizona Republican* (Phoenix), September 2, 1909.
2. *Ibid.,* September 3, 1909.
3. *Ibid.,* September 9, 10, 1909.

4. *Ibid.*, September 12, 1909.
5. *Ibid.*, September 19, 1909.
6. *Ibid.*
7. *Ibid.*, September 29, 30, October 2, 1909.
8. *Ibid.*, October 4, 1909; *Arizona Gazette* (Phoenix), October 4, 1909; the *Gazette* reported his first name was Arthur.
9. *Republican,* October 5, November 17, 1909.
10. *Ibid.*, October 8, 9, 1910.
11. *Gazette,* October 13, 1909.
12. *Ibid.*, October 19, 1909.
13. *Ibid.; Republican,* October 20, 1909.
14. *Republican,* October 20, 1909.
15. *Ibid.*, October 21, 1909.
16. *Ibid.*, October 22, 1909.
17. *Ibid.*, October 27, 1909.
18. *Ibid.*
19. *Ibid.*, October 28, 1909.
20. *Ibid.*
21. *Gazette,* October 28, 1909.
22. *Republican,* October 31, 1909.
23. *Ibid.*, November 1, 1909.
24. *Ibid.; Gazette,* November 2, 1909.
25. *Gazette,* November 1, 1909; *Republican,* November 2, 7, 1909.
26. *Gazette,* November 12, 1909; *Republican,* November 17, 1909; *Salt River Project,Final History to 1916* (unpublished manuscript), Vol. I, p. 130, Salt River Project Archives.
27. *Republican,* November 15, 16, 1909.
28. *Ibid.*, November 17, 1909; *Gazette,* November 17, 1909.
29. *Gazette,* November 18, 1909; *Republican,* November 1, 1909.
30. *Final History to 1916,* p. 130; *Republican,* December 7, 1909.

31. *Ninth Annual Report of the Reclamation Service, 1909-1910* (Washington: Government Printing Office, 1911) pp. 64, 65, 68.
32. *Gazette,* December 10, 13, 1909; *Republican,* December 10, 1909.
33. *Republican,* December 7, 1909.
34. *Ibid.*
35. *Ibid.*
36. *Ibid.*, December 10, 1909; *Gazette,* December 8, 1909.
37. *Republican,* December 19, 1909.
38. *Gazette,* December 23, 1909; *Republican,* December 23, 1909, January 4, 1910.
39. *Republican,* December 23, 28, 1909.
40. *Ibid.*, January 4, 1910.
41. *Ibid.*, January 6, 1910.
42. *Ibid.*
43. *Ibid.*, January 9, 10, 1910.
44. *Ibid.*, January 11, 1910.
45. *Ibid.*, January 12, 1910.
46. *Gazette,* January 13, 1910.
47. *Republican,* January 18, 1910.
48. *Ibid.*, January 26, 27, 1910.
49. *Ibid.*, January 30, 1910.
50. *Ibid.*, February 4, 23, 1910.
51. *Ibid.*, February 8, 1910.
52. *Ibid.*, February 16, 1910.
53. *Ibid.*, February 22, 1910.
54. *Ibid.*, February 25, 1910.
55. *Ibid.*, February 27, 1910.
56. *Ibid.*, March 9, 1910.

March - August 1910

JudgeEdward Kent, sitting as the district judge in the 3rd Judicial District of the Territory of Arizona on March 1, 1910, filed his decision and decree in the case of *Patrick T. Hurley v. Charles F. Abbott and Four Thousand Eight Hundred Others,* ordering that it go into effect April 1. However, it did not become effective until noon April 25 because of a delay in gathering data and in installing gauging equipment by the Reclamation Service. In booklet form, the decree was 80-pages long including 22 pages of text and the remainder in 10 tables and two maps. The tables showed the dates the land within the reservoir district of the Salt River Valley Water Users' Association came under cultivation, and, hence, the date of appropriation from which priority of right to water was established, beginning in 1869 and continuing through 1909. Kent divided the land into three classes, designating them class "A," class "B," and class "C." Class A lands were those with a continuous history of cultivation from the various dates to 1909. Continuous did not necessarily mean in every successive year, but with a constantness to evidence a desire to cultivate. Class B lands were those with some continuous history of cultivation but which had not been cultivated for at least five years before the taking of testimony in the case began. Class C lands were those within the reservoir district without a history of cultivation. Class A lands totaled 151,083 acres with 91,813 acres on the north side of the river and 59,270 acres on the south side. Class B lands totaled 28,887 acres of which 14,792 were on the north side and 14,095 acres on the south side. Class A and Class B lands aggregated 179,970 acres. [1]

Kent fixed at 48 miners' inches the constant flow of water to which each 160 acres, or quarter section, was entitled, subject to an increase or decrease "after due trial of such amount as such standard." Forty-eight inches meant one miners' inch for every three- and one-third acres, or 5.4 acre-feet per acre per year. When the water was not measured at the land, there was to be added to the flow, to account for evaporation and seepage, one percent for each mile of canal the water moved from the point of diversion at the river to its release from the ditch. [2]

The court said the right of a landowner to divert water from a natural non-navigable stream and to apply it for beneficial use upon the land always had been recognized in the territory. This appropriation was "not a right to the water itself, but a right to the use of the water. Its application to a beneficial use upon the land is as necessary in order to complete the right as is the diversion thereof from the stream." Further, the court said when the water was "no longer applied to the land for which it was diverted, the right of appropriation of such water for such land ceases. . . The right to appropriate is a right that belongs to the landowner, but the water appropriated is appropriated for the land, and when so appropriated its use belongs to the land and not to the appropriator." [3]

Kent defined the "normal flow of the river" as,

the flow of water in the river at its varying stages available for appropriation. The maximum normal flow is the total amount to be diverted from the river for the cultivation of all the parcels of land to which water has been appropriated.

He said maximum normal flow plus the water estimated to be lost in carrying it through the canals was approximately 58,000 miners' inches (which would equal 1,047,915 acre-feet in a year if the flow were constant). "Flood water" was defined as that "over and above the maximum normal flow," while "surplus water" was "the flow of the river, both normal and flood, not needed or used." "Stored water" was that impounded behind Roosevelt Dam. [4]

For the Salt River Indian Reservation, Kent decreed 700 miners' inches of water with a right of appropriation ahead of all others. The Fort McDowell Indian Reservation received 390 miners' inches. The Hayden Flour Mill at Tempe was awarded 1,100 miners' inches. Kent appointed Frank P. Trott as water commissioner to carry out the provisions of the decree. Kent declined at that time to determine the rights to the use of Verde River water by Verde Valley water users as against Salt River project water users. The court also retained for itself,

jurisdiction of the case and of the issues embraced therein. From time to time, as conditions may require an enlargement or modification of the decision and decree, application for such modification or enlargement may be made to the Court, and if granted, the same shall be entered at the foot of the decree herein. [5]

The *Arizona Republican* printed the text of the Kent

Judge Edward H. Kent

Decree, as it came to be called, in its March 2 edition. The newspaper also published an analysis by Joseph H. Kibbey, who recalled,

One of the questions that most perplexed the organizers of the Salt River Valley Water Users' association (for it was one, the solution of which had to be provided for as a condition precedent to the construction of the Roosevelt dam), was that of the individual rights of the water claimants. Vested rights could not be disturbed by the operation of the reclamation act, but until these rights could be determined, or their determination provided for, the government could not proceed at all. As a condition to the undertaking by the reclamation service of the construction of the Salt River project, the organizers of the Water Users' association agreed to institute the necessary proceedings to procure an adjudication of these rights.

Kibbey said a vast amount of patience was displayed by Kent in the trial of the case, which involved the claims of more than 4,800 defendants. [6]

On the afternoon of March 1, the *Arizona Gazette* reported John P. Orme, a member of the Board of Governors of the Water Users' Association and a member of the Maricopa County Board of Supervisors, was "said to have backing of a goodly number of prominent ranchers" for the presidency of the Water Users' Association. The newspaper said it was "more than a personal issue" (an allusion to differences between him and Benjamin A. Fowler, president of the association since its inception). The *Gazette* said,

that it involves the future policy of the Water Users' association on all matters of vital interest to the valley. For Mr. Orme it is claimed that he stands and has always stood for the small farmer against the speculator, and for the policy of referendum; that is, to refer important matters involving the expenditure of money, or giving of rights to a vote of the people. Mr. Orme contended that the question of building a water temple should be referred to the water users and finally that policy was adopted. [7]

Twenty-one members of the Council of the Water Users' Association convened the morning of March 3. A resolution was introduced to reduce the salaries of the president and legal counsel from $2,000 to $1,000 per annum. The resolution was referred to a committee of three. While the committee was out, the Council took up the question of requiring governors and Council members to live within the districts they represented. During the discussion, a suggestion was made to do away with the Council itself. Some of the members said they would like to hear from Kibbey on that, and a telephone call was made asking him to appear. Meantime, the committee on salaries returned, and it was agreed to consider the salaries of the president and attorney separately. A resolution to reduce the president's salary to $1,000 was unanimously approved. The Council was considering the attorney's salary when Kibbey arrived. He offered to withdraw while that was being done, but the members said they preferred to first hear his opinion on the suggestion the Council be disbanded. Kibbey explained the origin of the Council, saying it would be impractical to attempt to represent 4,000 to 5,000 shareholders by other than an elective body such as the Council. With that, the Council dropped the discussion. Kibbey withdrew, and the members returned to the question of the legal adviser's

salary. After discussion, the Council voted 13 to 8 to reduce the salary to $1,000. Following a recess for lunch, a committee on bylaws reported favorably on a resolution to require governors and Council members to live within the district represented. The resolution met with considerable resistance, and Patrick T. Hurley and others asked Kibbey be summoned for an opinion. Kibbey said he saw no valid reason for changing the law. If the shareholders wanted to insist upon their representatives living within their districts, they could already do that by electing such men. A motion to table the resolution was approved 10 to 9. At that point, Kibbey asked if he was wanted for anything further. Informed he was not, he told the Council that when the governors met Monday, March 7, he would tender his resignation. Kibbey thanked them for past courtesies and said he had no doubt they could find other attorneys who would serve at the salary they were willing to pay. [8]

The following day, John W. Foss, one of the Council members who voted against reducing the attorney's salary, said he thought it would be very difficult for the Water Users' Association to find an attorney for $1,000 who could pick up the threads of the work being done by Kibbey, including preparation of a brief asking the shareholders be allowed to assess themselves to construct power plants. On the street, there was hope the Council members elected at the April 5 election would reverse the action. [9]

Visitors returning from Roosevelt Dam reported the structure at one small point at the south end near the spillway had been completed to the maximum 240 feet above the riverbed. The rest of the dam was not far behind in height, and the reservoir was at a depth of about 117 feet. [10]

On March 5, the *Republican* printed a long editorial sarcastically attacking the action cutting in two the salary of the legal counsel to the Water Users' Association (the paper said it would deal with the president's salary at another time). The editorial said the reduction in salary,

may be attributed in large part to the general demand for a reduction in the cost of living. . . The salary of the association's counsel having been $2,000 a year, every shareholder of the corporation was groaning under the burden of paying his share of this salary.

The newspaper pointed out that rounding the association's acreage to 200,000 acres, the cost per year for Kibbey's salary was 1 cent per acre, or 80 cents per year if the average farm was 80 acres. The *Republican* said the "bold stroke" of cutting the salary reduced the attorney's pay to a level about equal with the farmer's hired hand. The paper wondered if the lawyer, however, should be allowed the liberality of not reporting for duty until 8 o'clock in the morning, quitting at 5 in the afternoon, and "working in the shade." [11]

Motions for a new trial in *Hurley v. Abbott* were filed March 5 on behalf of the Tempe Irrigating Canal Co., the Mesa Canal Co., the Utah Irrigation Canal Co., and the Utah Canal Enlargement and Extension Co. The Mesa and Tempe companies argued on somewhat the same grounds that under the Kent decree newer lands that came under cultivation would be denied water. The companies said that since 1890, the year the canal companies entered into an agreement concerning the division of water, all lands under the canals shared in the water. In the case of the Tempe company, it was estimated that 13,000 of the 24,000 acres served by the canal would not receive the water they got under the present distribution. Because this and the other matters raised were pretty well thrashed out during the course of the trial, the general opinion was that Kent would deny the motions. The thinking was Kent would not want to undertake another five-year trial. [12]

Kibbey's letter of resignation was read to the governors when they met the morning of March 7. He noted his term of employment had about two months to run, but said he should resign immediately so the new legal adviser could be involved in matters of importance to the association from the start. After hearing the letter, the nine governors present instructed the association secretary to prepare a resolution expressing confidence in Kibbey and rejecting his resignation. [13]

Dr. Ethelbert W. Wilbur asked the governors to consider two rulings of the Reclamation Service and the Water Users' Association that appeared in need of adjustment. The first was a Reclamation Service order that reservoir water be distributed only to members of the association and the second was an association rule that a person could not vote in association elections unless he was an "owner of record" of the land he irrigated. While the rules were considered fair, they presented a hardship in the disposing of excess land. Unless a person bought land for cash, he could not receive title and be identified as the "owner of record" eligible to be a member of the association and receive stored water nor vote in elections. Few cash sales were possible. The problem was referred to the legal counsel. [14]

The *Gazette* on March 8 printed a short story attempting to pinpoint the support for Orme and for Fowler in the April 5 election for president of the Water Users' Association. The newspaper quoted Supervisor L. M. Hoghe as saying Orme's campaign was fully launched, and the boom for him was growing. The third sentence from the end of the item said:

There has been a report current that Mr. Orme might have a clear field but that has not been authenticated. [15]

Three more motions appealing the decision in *Hurley v. Abbott* were filed in U. S. District Court, two of them on behalf of individuals and the third for the Bartlett-Heard Land and Cattle Co. All of the motions filed were on behalf of residents and companies operating south of the Salt River. [16]

Supervising Engineer Louis C. Hill of the Reclamation Service returned to Phoenix March 10 after a two-week trip that took him to Washington, D.C. Hill said he had received from Secretary of the Interior Richard A. Ballinger a commitment of $575,000 from the Reclamation Fund to complete construction of Roosevelt Dam. In addition, Hill said Ballinger would look favorably upon the proposal to delay the formal opening of the Salt River project two years while the Water Users' Association shareholders assessed themselves $2 per acre per annum for the construction of power plants, including one to be built on a new crosscut

canal from the Arizona Canal. Fowler and Kibbey were credited with developing this plan, which would require approval of the shareholders at a special election. In an editorial, the *Republican* said of the scheme to build power plants:

It must be borne in mind, of course, that this plan has not yet been formally laid before the secretary of the interior. It must be remembered that in order to have the plan accepted by the government there will necessarily be negotiation with the authorities at Washington—and above all, intelligent and acceptable representation of the Water Users' association at Washington. [17]

Phoenix Mayor Lloyd Christy called on Hill to investigate the possibility of securing power from Roosevelt Dam to operate the city's domestic water pumps. Hill said the government was ready at any time to enter into a contract with the city. [18]

Water ceased passing over the Granite Reef Diversion Dam on March 10, and the next night the Reclamation Service raised the gates in the Roosevelt Dam sluicing tunnel. The lake was at a depth of one hundred twenty and one-fourth feet, which meant 200,275 acre-feet of water in storage. Construction of a new brush and rock dam at the Joint Head was completed March 11, and the next day 3,000 miners' inches of water flowed into the canal. [19]

Dwight B. Heard, in an attempt to clarify the situation about the presidency of the Water Users' Association, met with Orme and Roy S. Goodrich. The difficulty, as Heard and some others saw it, was that both Orme and Fowler stood for the same policies, and if an opposition candidate appeared, the vote might be so divided that neither Orme nor Fowler would win. Under those conditions, it was hoped one or the other would withdraw. The result of the meeting was

John P. Orme

Heard and Orme agreed to name 12 men to meet and discuss the matter. Named were Heard, Goodrich, Foss, Hurley, H. B. Wilkinson, James H. McClintock, Aaron Goldberg, Selim Michelson, Charles Goldman, H. P. DeMund, E. J. Bennitt, and Walter Talbot. McClintock was not a member of the Water Users' Association and did not want to be a member of the group, but he was told his interest and his knowledge of the situation was as great as the others. The men met the morning of March 12 in Heard's office. Fowler and Orme were interviewed separately, and both were said to have agreed to abide by a vote of the dozen men as to who should run for president. A vote was said to have been taken with Fowler getting the votes of seven—Heard, Goldberg, Goodrich, Bennitt, Talbot, Wilkinson, and McClintock. There reportedly were two votes for Orme and three abstentions. McClintock was thought to be a partisan of Orme's. Asked later why he did not support Orme, McClintock said while he considered Orme one of the best men in the Valley, Fowler could better represent the association in pending negotiations in Washington with the Interior Department. [20]

Orme said later in the day he intended to be a candidate, and he would issue a statement concerning his candidacy. Fowler said he had no statement to make. [21]

The afternoon of March 14 the *Gazette* reported the committee had passed a resolution or motion that it was the sense of the group to keep the meeting secret, but one man, apparently McClintock, said he did not believe in transacting public business in private, and he was not bound by the action of a committee to which he had been appointed without his knowledge, and on which he agreed to serve only after considerable solicitation. Other committee members also were said to have objected to the meeting and would have nothing more to do with it. The vote that was taken reportedly was to have Fowler run for president and Orme for vice president. Editorially, the *Gazette* called the meeting "a very bad precedent" and said it regretted,

that whenever any public question is before the people there is a tendency toward committee, instead of leaving the matter to the people to decide. However well intentioned these committees may be or however respectably constituted, the rule of a committee or caucus is opposed to the idea of popular self-government. [22]

Orme on March 16 made a statement of candidacy:

Under the conditions existing in the association, at the present time and after consultation with my friends, there seems nothing for me to do but to be a candidate for the office of president.

I am thoroughly conversant with the affairs of the association and with the running of water in the valley, having been superintendent of one of the canals for twelve years. I am thoroughly in accord with the policies of the government with respect to reclamation and especially with respect to the irrigation system of this valley and, further, I believe that I can do more to harmonize the people on both sides of the river, though in the matter of irrigation, there should not be two sides, than any other man. My work as harmonizer was shown in the affairs of the Appropriators' canal whose members were broken up into factions until at a meeting of the directors the secretary was directed to cast the unanimous vote for me for president and thereafter the affairs of the company proceeded smoothly and successfully.

As to the meeting of the committee of twelve last Saturday for the purpose of selecting a candidate, there was no vote taken on

that question and I have been told by Roy S. Goodrich and other members of the committee that I am in no wise bound by any action taken by that committee.

Orme also said he thought he was as close to the Reclamation Service officials as any man and had confidence in the service and Hill. Orme said he was the only member of the governors to have served continuously since the first board. [23]

The Board of Supervisors on March 16 received a bid of $99,000 to build the Center Street bridge, and the Reclamation Service announced a force of men was employed 16 miles east of Mesa putting bird guards on the transmission line poles to save the lives of hawks and other large birds. The guards were to be put on as far as Government Well because from there east through the mountainous region the birds were less likely to settle on the transmission poles. There was no problem with the birds landing in the towers, but many of them, when they spread their wings to fly away, touched two wires, electrocuting themselves and causing the circuit to short out. In a few instances, the wires burned through. The engineers said on every inspection trip at least a half-dozen of the large birds were found dead. The guards being placed on the towers were made of tin and sharp pointed lengths of wire. These were placed over the insulators and midway between. [24]

The *Republican* on March 18 extolled Fowler in an editorial, but said either he or Orme would be a safe choice for election as the Water Users' Association president. [25]

At Roosevelt, a stone mason, W. Dillon, employed by dam contractor John O'Rourke, fell from the highest point of the dam into the lake and drowned. For some reason, another workman called to Dillon, "Look out!" This caused Dillon to suddenly turn, lose his footing, and plunge into the water. Dillon's wife and children were in England. [26]

Fowler said on March 22 he would not be a candidate for reelection as president of the Water Users' Association. He said he had reached the decision several days earlier. The *Republican* said Fowler's decision was based upon the existence of "a considerable element of opposition." The newspaper said he was anxious to avoid "acrimonious discussion," and having never announced he was a candidate, he had nothing from which to withdraw. [27]

The directors of the Mesa Canal Co. called a meeting for April 2 at which shareholders would hear Hill explain what the government was willing to pay for the canal. [28]

A committee favorable to electing Orme as president met the morning of March 23 at Melczer's Hall. Committees to campaign for Orme in the various districts were organized. Hill was summoned and addressed the crowd about the proposed power plants. He advised the Water Users' Association's counsel be instructed to draw up a tentative contract for submission to the secretary of the interior, and that an election be held in the spring among the shareholders. Hill estimated the new crosscut canal and the power plants would cost $800,000 but their completion and sales from the other plants would bring a net revenue of $200,000 annually. He also said 25,000 to 30,000 acres would be brought into cultivation using pumped water, but no one landowner would have a better right to the underground water than any other. On a motion by Orme, the committee endorsed the construction of the works outlined by Hill and approved a separate resolution in support of Hill and the Reclamation Service. [29]

While the Orme committee met, attorneys in U.S. District Court argued their objections to the Kent ruling in *Hurley v. Abbott,* and testimony was heard in support of requests to modify the decree as it pertained to the classification of some of the land. Kent indicated the motions for a new trial would be denied, but modifications in the decree would be made. [30]

In an editorial March 24, the *Republican* reviewed, to a degree, Fowler's presidency, saying,

Fowler naturally felt that if his ten years' record of splendid achievement in behalf of the valley did not speak for itself it was not up to him to make an aggressive campaign for the retention of the presidency of the association. . . It is timely and worthwhile to say that the services of Benjamin A. Fowler to this valley have been of value beyond the possibility of realization by any citizen who has not kept books on his work. . . This community will never forget what B. A. Fowler has done for it. [31]

Secretary Charles A. Van der Veer of the Water Users' Association sent a letter to shareholders explaining the need for an office building and urging them to vote April 5. Orme said on March 25 he strongly favored the building. There would be a meeting hall in it where farmers' organizations could gather at no charge, he said. [32]

Kent on March 26 denied the motions for a new trial in *Hurley v. Abbott* and issued a supplementary decree reclassifying some of the lands. Kent said it was true under his decision the Mesa Canal water users might receive less water than before, but under the decree, they had been apportioned exactly the same amount as lands with similar rights. He said he did not see how the Mesa water users could object to being on an equal basis. Notices of appeal to the Supreme Court of the territory were made, but it was not expected any of the attorneys intended to actually make an appeal. [33]

On March 26, Orme issued a statement outlining his views concerning the power plants and the desire of south side homesteaders to build a pumping plant on ground higher than the Wormser extension of the Tempe Canal. Orme said he favored the power plant improvement, which would cost not more than $850,000, and would mean a shareholder assessment of $2 to $2.25 per acre a year for two years. He favored building the pumping plant for homesteaders with money they were ready to advance, and to either pay them back with power receipts from the Salt River project or to credit the money they gave toward their payments to the government. [34]

The Water Users' Association reported the number of landowners eligible to vote in the April 5 election had increased to 2,130 compared to 1,829 in 1910. The greatest gain was 129 landowners in the Phoenix area, where the land had been subdivided into tracts of 2, 3, 5 and 10 acres. [35]

Word leaked out the Reclamation Service was going to offer $43,000 for the Mesa Canal Co., or $107.50 per share for the 400 shares, which for years had been quoted on the local market at $800 per share. In addition, the cost per acre for maintenance and operation was expected to rise from 50 cents to $1.60 cents. [36]

Hill informed the Mesa Canal Co. stockholders on April 2 the $43,000 the government was offering would not be paid in cash. Rather, the money, which was equal to about $3 for each acre under the canal, would be credited to the land in paying the government for the project construction. Some stockholders expressed concern that if the canal ownership were transferred to the government, it would preclude a planned lawsuit aimed at readjudicating the prorating of the water to the canal. Nevertheless, after Hill and officials of the Water Users' Association left the meeting, the directors of the company were instructed to confer with the company attorney and prepare a contract for submission to the Reclamation Service. [37]

Fowler and Kibbey at a meeting of the Board of Governors April 4 reported they had delayed developing an agreement with the interior secretary for the power plants because only recently had Hill returned with news the proposition would get Ballinger's approval. More importantly, because developing and marketing electricity would be a new venture for the association, it would require a change in the articles of incorporation and approval from the shareholders. It was recalled that when the articles were originally drawn, there was a section covering this, but it had been stricken because it was thought the association would never desire to engage in such business. Another reason for striking the article was the owner of the local gas and electric company, an enthusiastic supporter of the Water Users' Association, thought it would be inimical to the interests of his company. Since eliminating the article cost the association nothing, it was stricken. It was pointed out any proposed contract for the power plants would first have to meet approval of the governors, then the secretary of the interior, and finally the shareholders. Moreover, Kibbey said he did not think it was propitious for him to begin the work before a change in the association administration. However, the governors disagreed and they approved a motion directing Fowler to appoint a committee of three to meet with Hill and draw up an agreement for presentation to the interior secretary. Fowler appointed Orme, H. H. Stone, and Kibbey. [38]

Another meeting April 4 involved the shareholders of the Tempe Canal, who assembled to hear a report on the decision in *Hurley v. Abbott* and to discuss the drainage of 10,000 to 12,000 acres of land served by the canal. The canal's attorneys advised against an appeal of Kent's decree, a proposal which met no opposition. Concerning the need to drain the land, a committee headed by C. M. Mullen proposed one or more drainage ditches be built running north and south so the water could run into the river. Several stockholders disagreed. They believed it would be best to pump out the water and to use electric power furnished by the government. To better accomplish this, it was suggested the Tempe Canal enter the Water Users' Association. Heard spoke in favor of this, saying he thought an agreeable deal could be developed, and he urged the shareholders meet with Hill and talk about it. A motion was made to invite Hill to a meeting. The idea engendered considerable debate, but it was finally approved unanimously. [39]

At the election of the Water Users' Association on April 5 the proposal to build an office building was carried by a vote of 21,588 to 12,780. In the election for president, Orme received 33,068 votes and Fowler got 782. In district 7, banker George M. Halm was ousted as governor by E. O. Brown, who won 2,775 to 2,499. The other governors elected were Stone, George L. Wilky, H. J. McClung, E. E. Jack, Joseph Cope, E. J. Bennitt, C. A. Saylor, Ethelbert W. Wilbur, and Wilson W. Dobson. [40]

Stockholders in the Utah Canal met April 6 at the Mesa Opera House to hear a report on discussions with Hill about turning the canal over to the Reclamation Service. The meeting chairman, Dobson, said it was his understanding the government was willing to pay $30,000 for the capital stock of the canal, which would mean the purchase of the main ditch and laterals. The main objection to selling to the government involved the $1.60 per acre maintenance and operation levy the Reclamation Service would impose. Alexander J. Chandler moved the stockholders vote on whether they would accept an offer from the Reclamation Service, but the motion did not come to a vote. Instead, a committee was appointed to confer with Hill. Another committee was appointed to consider whether the company should incorporate. Incorporation was considered because the Reclamation Service, in buying canal companies, would deal only with the company and not with the individual stockholders. [41]

The Reclamation Service reported the first 30 feet of the south end of Roosevelt Dam was finished to the top of the roadway, or 240 feet above datum, the final level. The next 100 feet were finished to within 18 inches of the top. The next 60 feet were at an elevation 193 feet above the riverbed, and the rest varied from 193 to two hundred thirty-eight and one-half feet. The reservoir was 125.22-feet deep, but the gates were open because the amount of water coming down the Verde was small. [42]

Ballinger on April 11 authorized the Reclamation Service to execute a contract for purchase of the Mesa Canal at the proposed price of $43,000 with the money to be credited to the individual landowner for his part of the project construction cost. The purchase price was based on the estimated cost of duplicating the canal. [43]

Hill's meeting with Tempe Canal shareholders took place April 11 and was attended by several hundred persons, including some from Phoenix and Mesa. Hill said he thought it would be possible to drain waterlogged lands with a series of ditches, but he did not view this as the best method because of the flatness of the land. He thought draining should be accomplished with pumps with the water being used to irrigate the highlands along the Salt River Mountains to the southwest. Hill indicated that should a contract be signed admitting the Tempe lands to the Water Users' Association, sufficient power and money were available to begin the drainage project at once. Many questions were asked, including whether "the ruling that no individual is to be served with reservoir water for more than

160 acres" could be changed. This was not a ruling but part of the reclamation law, Hill said. During the discussion, it was brought out that a man owning more than 160 acres could deed portions of his property to his wife and children, even if the children were minors, in order to get water. In draining the land, the stockholders wanted to know if the government would guarantee to keep the water level 8 to 10 feet below the surface. Hill said he thought that was possible, but he could guarantee that no more than he could guarantee the Roosevelt Dam would not go out or the Granite Reef Diversion Dam would remain where it was. Except for authorizing the company president to appoint a committee of seven to confer with Hill about the possibility of selling to the government, the shareholders took no other action. [44]

By April 14, a proposed agreement for the purchase of the Mesa Canal was completed and a copy was sent to every shareholder. A meeting of the stockholders to approve the agreement was scheduled Saturday, April 16, but fear was expressed that, as in the past, not enough of them would attend. With 400 shares of stock outstanding, approval was required by at least owners of 267 shares. [45]

Eleven men met the evening of April 15 to discuss an idea put forward by H. P. DeMund to have the Salt River Valley Water Users' Association buy the Salt River project outright from the federal government, paying for it in full just as soon as it was completed. This was to be accomplished by having the Water Users' Association issue bonds for 30, 40 or 50 years or longer, if possible, at the lowest rate obtainable, with the association and its land pledged as security. It was argued the land, with a minimum value of $100 per acre on 250,000 acres, was worth $25 million and would easily be accepted as security on the $8 million to $10 million in bonds that would have to be sold to repay the federal government for the Roosevelt project. This would give the government money in the reclamation fund to spend on other projects. Proponents of the bond plan said the purpose was to extend the time of paying for the project from 10 to 50 years or more. They believed the farmers in 20 or 30 years would be better able to afford to make the payments, and the burden of the debt would be partly borne by the next generation, which would reap the greater fruits of the reservoir construction. They figured the revenue generated from the sale of electricity would pay all the interest and would leave enough to create a sinking fund to eventually pay off the bonds. The bond plan was not seen as an immediate thing, but it would allow for the proposed delay in the opening of the project and the construction of the additional power plants. Another advantage was that with the Water Users' Association in charge and the government out, the limitation on the distribution of water to one owner for not more than 160 acres could be ignored. However, some feeling was expressed that small landowners would object to elimination of the 160-acre limit. Some persons friendly to Pacific Gas & Electric Co. objected to the Water Users' Association's building additional power plants, while others thought it wrong to burden the next generation with debt because it would have its own. Another objection was in repaying the government, the farmers were not paying interest, but they would have to pay interest for the bonds. Fear also was expressed that if there was a default in payment, the reservoir and canals would pass into private ownerhsip. However, it was pointed out the plan was to mortgage the land and not the water storage dam and water distribution facilities. [46]

The *Republican* said the scheme was such a "grotesque absurdity. . .it is entertaining to think about," but suspected it was a product of "Halley's Comet. . .getting in its work on the mental processes of our good citizens." The newspaper contrasted the rosy future with the situation as it was versus what it would be if the scheme, which went nowhere, succeeded. The paper said:

At the end of the ten-year period, the land owners will own the storage and irrigation and power plant free of all debt. Thereafter the rancher will pay absolutely nothing for his irrigation water. The revenue from power will pay not only the expenses of upkeep for the entire irrigation system, but will yield a profit to the shareholders of the association. In other words, the rancher will pay nothing for his water, and will get dividends on his stock in the association. . .

What is the fantastic scheme which is proposed to take the place of this ideal arrangement? It is, in short, a proposition that the association shall exchange a short-time debt which bears no interest for a long-time debt bearing interest. . .sold at par at 6 per cent, the interest charge on eight million dollars would be the mere trifle of $480,000 a year,. . .if any disaster overtakes the project within the ten-year period, the expense of repair will be made good by the government. . . [47]

Three meetings were held on the south side of the river April 16, one in Mesa and two in Tempe. In Mesa, 230 shares of stock were represented at a meeting of the owners of the Mesa Canal. That was not enough to adopt a resolution approving the sale of the canal to the government, but it was sufficient to get a motion approved, 221 1/60 to 12 1/4, amending the bylaws to say, "No sale shall be made involving 50 per cent or more of the property assets of this company except upon the vote of two-thirds or more of the stockholders. . ." Because it was believed virtually impossible to get two-thirds of the stockholders together at a meeting an amendment to the bylaws was suggested to allow for the sale through the signatures of a two-thirds majority of the stockholders. But the company attorney said he did not believe the government would accept a transfer of the canal in that manner, and corporations did not do business in that fashion. Wilbur suggested an ice cream social be held to improve attendance at the next meeting, and a committee was appointed to gather proxies. [48]

At Tempe, Roy Goodrich presided at a meeting of landowners south and west of the Tempe Canal. They were encouraged at the prospect of getting water by the use of pumps to drain waterlogged Tempe Canal land along lines suggested by Hill. Following up on Hill's suggestion, the landowners raised $300 to send Goodrich to Washington to present their situation to the Interior Department. The second meeting involved the Tempe Canal's committee of seven, which had been devoting its time to getting the sentiment of shareholders concerning the proposed sale of the canal to the government. Heard, Vernon Clark, and H. C. Yaeger, who had come from Phoenix, told the committee

it was going about the business in the wrong way. They suggested the committee meet with Hill, get a proposition from him, then call a stockholders' meeting. The committee agreed to the suggestion. Owners of land under the Tempe Canal system, who were signed into the Water Users' Association, wanted the company sold, while the other landowners generally did not. [49]

Tuesday morning, April 19, the last load of oil for use in the cement mill at Roosevelt Dam departed Mesa. The *Republican* reported it was "pretty generally understood" the company doing the hauling, the Shattuck-Nimmo Warehouse Co., "will leave the local field with a loss." The newspaper said it was estimated the company lost upwards of $30,000 in taking over the original contract to deliver 50,000 barrels of oil at $3.48 per barrel. Shattuck-Nimmo sold its stations at Fish Creek and Tortilla Flat, but it still owned those at Government Well and Desert Wells. Whether the company would continue its Mesa-Roosevelt Stage Co. depended upon whether it got a renewal of its contract to carry the mail to Roosevelt. [50]

Hill and the committee of seven from the Tempe Canal spent three hours together April 21 with the committee requesting he submit a written proposition. He said he would be unable to do that until he corresponded with the secretary of the interior. He said he thought an arrangement could be made whereby landowners who did not want to join the Water Users' Association could remain out but would sell their interest in the canal. He said the government had to own the entire canal or not at all. Hill also said that if the government took up drainage of the land, it would use additional means besides pumps if that became necessary. [51]

Construction of a $100,000 factory to produce alfalfa meal and mixed feeds for cattle, chickens, horses, ostriches, and other stock was promised by the Arizona Alfalfa Milling Co. if competitive freight rates were granted by the railroads. The company intended to buy electric power from the Reclamation Service and was looking for a factory site near the railroad tracks in Phoenix. [52]

Mesa Canal Co. shareholders met April 23 at the Opera House in Mesa. When it was found 319 of the 400 shares were represented, one of the company directors telephoned the Reclamation Service and was assured the government would consider that number of shares a fair representation in any decisions that were reached. The shareholders later voted 309 to 9 to sell to the government. [53]

With the sale of the Mesa Canal Co. assured, Hill met April 25 with representatives of the Utah Irrigating Ditch Co., the Utah Extension and Enlargement Co. and the Eureka Canal Co., the latter two extensions of the original Utah Canal. After the meeting, it was rumored the government would not offer more than $20,000 for the three companies, and approximately one-third of the canal system would be abandoned. [54]

To get more definite data for negotiations with the Tempe Canal Co., Hill sent two parties of Reclamation Service engineers into the field to make surveys and to more definitely locate the water level. [55]

The *Gazette* on April 26 said when the new Council and

Board of Governors of the Water Users' Association took office Monday, May 3, the salary of $2,000 per annum for the legal counsel would be restored. Kibbey was asked if he would accept the position if the salary was restored, and he said he did "not care to make any statement upon the point" because the salary had not been offered him. In reply to the question of whether he would accept if offered, Kibbey said, "I do not think the time has come to tell the public what I would do under those circumstances." [56]

Stockholders in the Utah Canal met April 27 and heard they were now getting water in accordance with the Kent decree, and unless they turned the canal over to the government within two weeks, the crops would burn because they would not get reservoir water. It was suggested that if a majority voted to sell, Hill could be persuaded to deliver stored water until all the owners agreed. A committee was appointed to try to get all shareowners to the next meeting. [57]

At 4 p.m. April 28 at Roosevelt, the last clinker was burned at the cement mill. It was estimated it would take six weeks to grind the clinker into the finished product, but in the meantime, the quarrying of rock and digging of clay and the transporting of both to the mill was over. The mill's furnaces were expected to be dismantled in June or July. The closing of most of the cement mill and the near completion of the dam caused an exodus of workmen and an extra stagecoach was put on Sundays to handle the departures from Roosevelt. [58]

In Phoenix on April 28 the Reclamation Service approved new water distribution regulations. The rules said water available at Granite Reef Diversion Dam and the Joint Head would be distributed to class A land in the amount and order fixed by the Kent decree. Class A and B lands were to get stored water in such quantities as the government had available to furnish; but no one, neither individual nor corporation, would get water for more than 160 acres. The charge was 60 cents per acre for water for the period June 1 to October 1. In addition, water users were told it was up to them to construct and maintain their ditches. [59]

At April's end, Roosevelt Dam was 95 percent completed with but 12,000 cubic yards of masonry to be laid. The lowest point on the dam was 193 feet above datum. For 230 linear feet, the elevation was 238 feet and the remainder of the structure was 205- to 215-feet high. The bridges were to be built, one at each side of the river over the spillways, and the road across the top was to be finished off with low protecting walls of cement. The cost of the Salt River project was then $8,640,000. There was a movement to have former President Theodore Roosevelt open the project on his birthday, October 27. [60]

The new Council and Board of Governors met May 2. The Council elected Daniel P. Jones of Lehi as its new chairman, then took up the question of the salary for the legal adviser. A bylaws committee recommendation that the salary be retained at $1,000 per annum was defeated in a 16 to 10 vote. The Council then approved a motion, 13 to 11, instructing the committee to report a bylaw making the salary $2,000. When the bylaw was reported, it was adopted 17 to 9. A bylaw to establish the secretary's salary at between $1,500 and $1,800 per year was approved 24 to 2. The Council approved unanimously a letter, drafted by Orme, Stone, and Kibbey, concerning the proposed power plants and also agreed upon a campaign to educate shareholders as to the value of the electrical facilities to the reservoir district. [61]

When the governors met, Van der Veer reported on the activities of the Water Users' Association for the previous year. He said that 3,851 acres additional had been subscribed to the district, bringing the total within its borders to more than 216,000. A resolution commending Fowler for his years of service was adopted, following which Kibbey addressed the board concerning Fowler. Among Kibbey's remarks were these:

After the history of the Salt River Valley Water Users' association shall have been written, if it ever shall be written at all, it will embody the history of the life and work of B. A. Fowler for the past ten years. During all of that time he has devoted his time, his energy and his splendid ability to the promotion of the ends and purpose that we have sought to accomplish by means of this association. He spared neither his time nor his money. Long before the organization of the association he had enlisted himself energetically and effectually in the cause of a safe water supply for the lands of this valley. . .

I think I can say, and I say it without abating one bit of, or detracting at all from, the credit due the many others who worked so long and steadfastly in that cause, that to B. A. Fowler we owe more than to any other one man our present fortunate situation.

There is much of the history of these efforts that will never be written, it will probably never be known, but through all discouragements, at times so overwhelming that failure seemed inevitable, Mr. Fowler held a steady hand and drove staight ahead.

I want, gentlemen, to pay this slight word of tribute to Mr. Fowler and his work, on the eve of his severance of his official connection with the Salt River Valley Water Users' Association. [62]

The governors approved the power plant letter to Ballinger, then reelected Van der Veer as association secretary and F. D. Lane as treasurer. A secret ballot was taken on continuing Kibbey as legal adviser and he was retained 8 to 2. The governors instructed Orme to appoint a committee to negotiate a price for the Young Men's Christian Association lot for the office building, then they set Van der Veer's salary at $1,800. The governors sent a letter to Kibbey informing him of his selection as legal adviser, but he replied that while,

I appreciate the compliment implied by the action of the board, yet I am compelled to decline the employment at the compensation fixed. [63]

Utah Canal shareholders met May 4 at the Mesa Opera House. It was made known to them that if they could not agree upon selling the entire canal system to the government, the Reclamation Service was prepared to buy the Eureka Canal, which covered the heart of the irrigated area. In that case, the water that usually flowed in the Utah Canal to the Eureka would be sent through the Mesa Canal and would be delivered by a new crosscut that would be dug by the government. Eureka Canal Co. owners owned shares in both the Utah Irrigating Ditch Co. and the Utah Extension and Enlargement Co., but no outsiders owned shares in the

Electric railway alongside the power canal with Roosevelt Lake in backgound, April 1910.

Eureka, and the Eureka landowners were determined to sell. [64]

Hill issued a new warning about auto speeding on the Roosevelt road. He said that within the past few days at least three cars had made the trip in what might be considered record time, but the government did not build the road for that purpose, and speeders would be ordered off. [65]

President F. F. Towle of the Globe Chamber of Commerce said he had been assured by Hill that if a local power company were formed, ample power was available from Roosevelt Dam at a good price to serve the community. Towle, who said he had no interest in forming a company, quoted Hill as saying the price would be comparable to that given Pacific Gas & Electric Co. in Phoenix. [66]

Although the Eastern Canal had been built, the Water Users' Association had not changed the boundaries of the reservoir district to take in the land between the Eastern and the Highland canals, the latter serving as the existing eastern border. At the suggestion of Hill, the landowners between the two canals circulated a petition asking the association to extend the boundary east to the Eastern Canal. [67]

President Charles Peterson signed a petition on May 7 conveying the Mesa Canal to the government. The contract provided $107.50 credit for "each shareholder of stock" in the company upon the construction charges in connection with building the Salt River project. This provision in the agreement did not satisfy the stockholders, so the contract was modified May 27 to provide that no credit would be given "except upon the evidence of a certificate of stock" in

the company. This stipulation was approved by a shareholders' vote of two hundred twenty-five and three-eighths to six and one-fourth at a meeting April 4, 1911. Part of the contract provided for the company to convey the rights in 16 small ditches to the government, and the company secured deeds to the ditches from each of the owners. The Reclamation Service considered the deeds defective, and in late 1914 got affidavits from water users under these laterals attesting the conveyance of the ditches. The deed to the canal was not executed by the government until November 26, 1915. [68]

Homesteaders living immediately east and south of the Eastern Canal formed an organization May 8 to devise a way to get water, pumped or otherwise, but the Reclamation Service showed no interest in helping them reclaim the land. J. D. Attaway was named chairman of the group. [69]

The governors met May 10 to consider a successor to Kibbey. Richard E. Sloan, governor of Arizona Territory, was suggested and a committee made up of Cope, Stone, and Wilbur called upon him and offered him the position at $2,000 per year. Sloan accepted upon approval of the secretary of the interior. The governors also directed the committee negotiating for the Young Men's Christian Association lot to pay up to $9,000, which was $1,000 more than the original price. The governors were told the price increase was to account for interest, taxes, and other incidental expenses. [70]

At a meeting of the Utah Canal Co. stockholders May 11, 97 of the 128 shares were represented, and 90 voted to sell to the government and 7 opposed the proposition. One provision of a proposed sales agreement was all of the shareholders had to agree to sell. But it was hoped that because the overwhelming sentiment was for selling, the interior secretary would not insist upon every share agreeing to the sale. The price the government reportedly was willing to pay for the Utah Canal was $6,760, while the Utah and its extensions and laterals together would bring about $15,000. [71]

Plans for another pumping plant several miles west of Tempe to add to the flow of the San Francisco Canal were disclosed by the Bartlett-Heard Land and Cattle Co. The company hoped to develop 500 miners' inches of water and obtain power to operate the pumps from the Reclamation Service. [72]

Sloan advised the governors by letter May 13,

I find that, after consultation with the secretary of the interior, it is inadvisable for me to accept, inasmuch as contingencies may arise which might make the full discharge of my duty to your association incompatible with the full discharge of my duty as an officer of the government. . . [73]

The **Republican** reported May 19 owners of 13 of the 128 shares of the Utah Canal refused to agree to sell the ditch to the government. The 13 shares represented about 800 acres of the approximately 11,500 acres under the canal, its extension, and laterals. The newspaper said it was unknown how long the Reclamation Service would continue to provide stored water to the canal under the circumstances. The answer to that came the next day when the Reclamation Service stopped stored water from flowing into the canal, leaving only the water awarded to the lands under the Kent decree. That spring was an especially dry one, which meant the rivers were running low, and it was thought that the cutoff of the reservoir water would soon force the holdouts to change their minds. [74]

Hill on May 23 delivered a letter from Ballinger to the Water Users' Association in which he said he was prepared to delay the opening of the project for two years to allow the association to accomplish the following tasks: construction of a new crosscut canal from the Arizona Canal to the Grand Canal; enlargement and extension of the Grand Canal to connect with the new crosscut canal; building of a power plant on the South Canal to generate 3,000 horsepower of electricity; building of a power plant on the crosscut canal to generate 6,000 horsepower; and building of a power plant at the Arizona Falls to generate 700 horsepower. When the work was done, all of it was to become a part of the project "and be the property of the United States as the other parts of the project are." [75]

Kent announced on May 24 that **Hurley v. Abbott** would be reopened May 28 to hear additional proof regarding class B lands. [76]

The governors at a meeting May 26 endorsed Hill's action in repeatedly urging the Interior Department to reject applications by the United States Department of Agriculture to grant permission to farmers to run canals through government land on the watersheds of the Salt and Verde rivers in order to divert water from those rivers. Hill took the position that all the runoff from the watersheds had

been appropriated for the lands under the Salt River project. The governors also discussed a contract with the Interior Department for building the power plants, but no action was taken on the contract because it was not in its final form. [77]

Another meeting of the governors was held May 31. They again went over the proposed power plant contract, each of them expressing personal support, but they delayed a formal vote because they wanted the opinions of Hill and Arthur P. Davis, chief engineer of the Reclamation Service, who was visiting. Hill and Davis had gone to Roosevelt but they were expected back in time for a meeting June 2. [78]

Roosevelt Dam at the end of May was 96 percent completed with 330,000 yards of masonry laid. The top of the dam between the spillways measured 650 feet; including the spillways the dam's length was 1,080 feet. Virtually all of the dam was up to the level of the spillways or higher except for a few feet on the north side. Some 250 feet of the dam were between 219- and 228-feet high, and the remaining 400 feet were two hundred thirty-eight and one-half to 240 feet above the river bed. [79]

On June 2, the governors approved the form of the contract with the Interior Department for the power plants and authorized Orme to take it to Washington for approval. The governors were aided in the preparation of the contract by Charles Witbeck, attorney for the Reclamation Service, because new counsel for the association had not been hired. The governors also had a private attorney, Thomas Armstrong Jr. of Phoenix, go over the contract. [80]

The Council of the Water Users' Association met June 6 and decided it would be unwise just then to extend the boundaries of the reservoir district east to the Eastern Canal. Council members pointed out that the lands were class C, and there was no water available for them; hence, they had nothing to lose by waiting until the secretary of the interior made a final determination about which lands were to be served by the reservoir. [81]

The governors adopted a budget of $31,366 for the year, starting September 1, 1910, and ending August 31, 1911, setting an assessment of 15 cents per acre on the 217,200 acres enrolled in the association. The budget included $20,000 for purchasing a building site and for starting the erection of the building, and $3,800 for costs in **Hurley v. Abbott**. [82]

The afternoon of June 7, the **Gazette** published a lengthy article explaining the Roosevelt Dam had in the present drought conditions proved itself. Citing figures furnished by the Reclamation Service, the **Gazette** said there were 155,000 acre-feet of water in storage, enough to last for 100 days, or until September 14. It said there were 40,644 miners' inches flowing in the river, 28,951 of it coming from the reservoir. Without the additional water coming from the reservoir, and in accordance with the Kent decree, lands whose cultivation began after 1879 would have been without water. This would have meant ruin for all the crops and orchards on association lands north of the Maricopa Canal on the north side of the river, for all of the lands under the Consolidated Canal, and most of the lands under the Mesa Canal south of the river. The Mesa Canal, under the Kent decree, was entitled to receive 732 miners' inches, but because there was stored water, 6,800 inches were available. [83]

Reclamation Service engineers were in the field south of the river working out a system of plats showing the lands susceptible of irrigation between the Highland and Eastern canals. The *Republican* reported the engineers had drawn the line for another canal east of the Eastern, and the landowners east of the Eastern and south of the base line were of the opinion they had received assurance they would receive reservoir water if there was any. These same landowners also had been encouraged by Ballinger's letter concerning the additional power plants. If not reservoir water, they believed they could get electric power from the government at a price cheap enough so they could put pumped water on the land. [84]

Director Frederick H. Newell of the Reclamation Service sent the following telegram to the Reclamation Service office on June 10:

Secretary on June 9th authorized execution Salt River contract to construct canals and power plants, as presented by John Orme. [85]

The works were to be constructed at a cost not exceeding $900,000. [86]

Tempe landowner H. C. Yaeger announced on June 9 the Reclamation Service began delivering stored water to his land through a new lateral it had dug in six days. Yaeger, who for a long time had been a supporter of the reservoir, said the water was not delivered through the Tempe Canal. Rather, it came through a lateral off the Consolidated Canal. He said he had gone to Hill and asked if he could get water for his ranch, which had 460 acres in cultivation including 200 acres in sugar beets, if he paid all the back assessments of the Water Users' Association. Yaeger said Hill told him he could. [87]

Hill met June 11 with members of the Tempe Canal committee of seven, who presented him a list of 23 questions. Two of the key questions were whether the government would take over the management of the canal if the entire interest in it was not surrendered, and whether the Tempe Canal could have its water diverted at the Granite Reef Diversion Dam if it paid its proportionate share of the cost. [88]

The Reclamation Service reported on June 15 it had approved a contract for the Eureka Canal Co. to become the property of the government, and a force of men was to be put to work to bring water to the ditch from the Mesa Canal. The actual contract, which was not signed until August 1, provided that the government was to credit each of the 130 shares $71.30 for the cost of the Salt River project, or a total of $9,269. Ballinger approved the contract October 22, 1910, but not until April 20, 1916, did the government receive a quitclaim deed for the canal and certain laterals. [89]

The governors approved the power plant contract at a meeting June 16. The contract contained one added provision calling for construction of a crosscut canal to connect the Grand Canal with the west end of the Salt River Valley Canal, two miles west of Alhambra. The Reclamation Service reportedly intended to completely eliminate the Salt River Valley and Maricopa canals. [90]

On June 18, the Council met and approved the power plant contract. Two days later, the governors set July 21 as the date for an election to get the approval of shareholders. It was explained that if the shareholders approved, the govenors would levy an assessment of $2.25 per acre per year for two years for the power plants and other work. That meant for the next year the assessment would total $2.40 per acre because of the earlier assessment of 15 cents per acre. The assessments could be met in two payments, the first in September and the second in March. [91]

In connection with its operation of the Consolidated, Mesa, and Eastern canals on the south side, the Reclamation Service announced the water would be distributed solely on the basis of acreage and not on the number of shares in any previous system. Four zanjeros had been appointed, including one to oversee water deliveries south of the base line. The service said Mesa Canal's custom of using a bulletin board to post water delivery times would be continued. Payments for water were being accepted through July 2 at the Chandler building in Mesa. [92]

Hill commented concerning the Tempe Canal that if the government was unsuccessful in obtaining it, there was but one thing to do—build a canal paralleling it and extend it westward to the territory on the south across the river from Phoenix. Doing that would take some time and money, while with the Tempe Canal it could be accomplished with an extension. Hill also said he had prepared answers to the questions submitted by the Tempe Canal committee, but he would first have to send them to Washington. [93]

Meantime, Yaeger and his son, L. D. Yeager, asked the United States District Court to modify the Kent decree to give legal affirmation to the delivery of water to their land through laterals from the Consolidated Canal rather than through the Tempe Canal. The court did this on June 21, giving further credence to the theory the water was attached to the land and the landowner could get his water through any means of delivery open to him. Tempe Canal attorney Charles Woolf contended unsuccessfully the Yaegers were stockholders in the Tempe Canal and had a contract with it for the delivery of the water. Attorney Witbeck argued for the Reclamation Service the government had no interest in the contract between the Yaegers and the Tempe Canal. Rather, if the Yaegers were members of the Water Users' Association and they wanted to get delivery of their water through a government canal and it was available to them, they had a perfect right to do so. Kent's decision in favor of the Yaegers was considered important because other landowners under the Tempe Canal, who were association members, were ready to petition the court to have water brought to their acreage via laterals from the Consolidated Canal. The judge gave authority to Trott, the water commissioner, in the absence of the court, to make similar changes. Efforts to stop him failed. [94]

A conference to fix a date for dedicating Roosevelt Dam was held June 25 in the Water Users' Association office. The result of the conference was a decision the dedication should not be held earlier than February 22, 1911, and many of the participants thought a month later would be better. There was sentiment for holding the celebration in the fall, but it was pointed out that while the dam would be practically finished, the cleaning up and removal of unwanted buildings, machinery, and other materials would still be in progress. In addition, unless there happened to be heavy rains, the reservoir would be a mud puddle. The conference members agreed it would be better if winter runoff produced a full reservoir and water rushing over the spillways. Among the conferees were Hill, Fowler, Orme, Cope, Foss, Heard, Bennitt, William J. Murphy, and McClintock. McClintock represented the Rough Riders' Association, which planned to entertain Roosevelt if he accepted an invitation to the dedication. [95]

Hill wrote to Newell on June 28, saying negotiations with the Tempe Canal had progressed to a point where the stockholders wanted a letter embodying the terms under which the government would be willing to purchase the canal and furnish water to the landowners under it. Hill wrote:

The water rights of the lands under the Tempe canal are better than those under any canal system in the Salt River Valley, excepting only the Salt River Valley Canal, and it is more desirable to add, if possible, these lands to the Salt River project, as the amount of water they would demand from the reservoir would be comparatively small, and their contribution would be equal to those of any other lands embraced in the project. The Tempe Canal and its branches also so fit into the general system that will supply water in the future to the lands under the Salt River project as to make it very desirable indeed, from an economical standpoint, to acquire this property, if it is possible. . .

A careful canvass has been made and it has been ascertained that out of a total of 24,000 acres, probably the owners of 17,000 acres under the Tempe Canal system will sign in the project. The owners of all of the rest of the lands, it is anticipated, will sell their interests in the canal and its branches to the United States, provided their water is delivered to them for a fair remuneration. An arrangement of this kind would clearly be to their advantage, as they would always be sure of the diversion of their water by the Granite Reef dam instead of being obliged to depend on a temporary structure like the Tempe dam.

The question, therefore, which is submitted for consideration is the expediency of acquiring a canal system covering some 24,000 acres, under an agreement to supply at a fixed price to 30 percent of these lands, river water which they have appropriated, for the purpose of getting the remainder into the project.

I believe such an arrangement to be extremely desirable. . .

Hill proposed a charge of $1.80 per acre per year to non-members of the Water Users' Association for the diversion of water at Granite Reef and for its carriage and delivery. He also submitted a proposed letter to be written by Ballinger containing a price of $156,843 to be paid for the Tempe holdings as follows: for the Tempe pumping plant and equipment, $40,000; Tempe Canal, $77,000; Kirkland-McKinney ditch, $6,300; Western (Wormser) Canal, $9,600; first section of the South Extension Canal, $15,800, and second section of the South Extension Canal, $8,143. The letter stated no more than 30 percent of all lands then served by the Tempe Canal would be eligible to remain out of the Water Users' Association and receive normal flow water delivered by the government for $1.80 per acre. Last, the government would agree to construct and maintain suitable drainage works for the lands signed into the Water Users' Association. [96]

The Reclamation Service also let it be known its surveyors were in the field laying out lines for ditches to bring water to landowners under the Tempe Canal who were signed into the Water Users' Assocation. The engineers said it was up to the landowners to bring pressure upon stockholders who did not want to sell to the government to make the paralleling of ditches unnecessary. [97]

On June 29, the Reclamation Service announced the cement plant at Roosevelt would be sold at auction in the service's Phoenix office on July 25. The sale was to include the machinery and the cement mill building. [98]

Arthur G. Keene took over the Mesa-Roosevelt Stage Co. the morning of July 1. Keene had won the mail contract between Mesa and Roosevelt for a four-year period. [99]

At a meeting of the governors on July 5, owners of class C lands as well as homesteaders and others questioned whether they should be assessed the $2.25 per acre for power plants, providing the shareholders approved of the plan, because they had no assurance of ever getting reservoir rights. They feared some of the land on the fringe of the reservoir district would be trimmed when the final designation of lands was made. The governors believed the money would be returned to lands that did not ultimately come into the district. [100]

Orme was directed to write a letter to Theodore Roosevelt inviting him to attend the dedication of Roosevelt Dam on February 22, 1911, if convenient for him or for him to name a later date. It was hoped, however, the dedication would not be much later so the Valley could be seen in its spring attire. [101]

Ballinger on July 6 approved a letter drafted by Newell outlining the basis of a contract to be drafted between the government and the Tempe Irrigation Canal Co. and the Tempe Pumping Co. Newell's letter summarized the proposals contained in Hill's letter of June 28. Newell on July 7 sent a copy of the letter approved by Ballinger to Hill. [102]

Continued drought caused farmers to plead for more water from the reservoir; and the Reclamation Service increased the flow from Roosevelt Lake by 305 acre-feet per day so the daily flow was 1,749 acre-feet. The morning of July 9, the depth of the lake was 98.80 feet, and the water in storage was about 105,000 acre-feet. Howard S. Reed, assistant engineer of the Reclamation Service in charge of operation and maintenance, said at the present rate of release, the water would last until September 6. [103]

Van der Veer on July 14 sent a letter to each shareholder in the Water Users' Association explaining the power plant proposition they were to vote on July 21. He pointed out a two-thirds approval was required for an expenditure of more than $50,000 in a year. He also reminded them that without a favorable vote, the project might be officially opened in the fall and the first of 10 annual payments of $4.50 per acre would become due beginning January 1, 1911. Approval of the power plants meant a two-year delay in the opening. Incorporated in Van der Veer's letter was a letter from Hill to the Water Users' Association explaining the horsepower to be developed by the power plants and the amount contemplated as available for sale. Hill said judging from the applications on file for electricity, there should be no trouble in disposing of all the horsepower produced. He estimated not less than 5,500 horsepower available for sale of a probable minimum 9,000 horsepower and a maximum 18,000 horsepower. [104]

In another letter sent July 14 to the Tempe Irrigation Canal Co., Hill conveyed the terms of the basis for a contract as provided by Newell, and added that because the matter had been reviewed by the Interior Department, he "would not feel justified in recommending any material modifications of the above terms." Hill also sent responses to the 23 questions submitted by the company. [105]

Van der Veer on July 18 said that because of a lack of apparent opposition to the power plant proposal, the vote July 21 might be light. It was the desire of the governors and the Council that a heavy vote be cast. Van der Veer said he knew of one man who said he was going to vote against the proposition on grounds the government would build the power plants with part of $20 million voted by Congress for the reclamation fund. Van der Veer said the man was mistaken because Congress provided the funds could only be used to complete existing projects and could not be used to start new work. [106]

Shareholders in the Water Users' Association approved building the powerhouses by a vote of 33,669 to 2,162 at the election July 21. The reaction of the **Republican** was to charge in an editorial that the water users who had opposed the Kibbey and Fowler management of the association had been outmaneuvered by the Interior Department into assessing themselves for construction of the power plants. The newspaper said,

It was the plan of Judge Kibbey and President Fowler to postpone all negotiations for an assessment contract until it was seen whether congress would make the proposed appropriation [of $20,000,000]. It was their plea, if this appropriation should be made, to insist upon getting one million of it for the Salt River valley, and to "stand pat" on that proposition. Their suggestions of postponement were angrily received, however, and they were accused of "knocking" a most meritorious scheme.

In negotiations for an allotment of a part of the appropriation for the benefit of this valley there would have been so many advantages on the side of the association that it is more than reasonable to suppose that the association would have won, had the policy of Judge Kibbey and Mr. Fowler been followed and had negotiations been entrusted to them. . .

The new management of the association ought to have kept constantly in mind the fact that, whereas heretofore the interests of the government and the association had been the same, the two parties to the reservoir contract were approaching the point of diverging interests, and it behooved the association to see that its side in all negotiations was shrewdly and firmly conducted.

It would have been worth a great deal to the valley if this million dollars which now must be raised by assessments upon the ranchers could have been left in their pockets during the next two years—a great deal more, let us say, than the petty savings that is made in officers' salaries, under the new regime. [107]

A group of Mesa men bought the kilns and grinding machinery of the Roosevelt Dam cement mill for $10,500. It was said the buyers intended to reconstruct the mill either at a point near Phoenix or at Winkelman. [108]

Tempe Canal company owners met July 25 in Cosmopolitan Hall and heard the answers that Hill had made to their questions. When this was done, Clark proposed a resolution to sell the canal to the government and to appoint a committee of three to negotiate a formal agreement with the Reclamation Service. The resolution provoked a series of speeches, Walter Wilbur saying there was no hope of the body of canal owners ever entering the reservoir system together. Thomas Armstrong said that while he presumed he had been paying about 40 cents per acre for water, he thought it was in the best interest of the community because it would enhance the value of his land and because he feared so many others under the canal would find alternate ways to get their water that the maintenance fee for those remaining would rise above $1.80 per acre. W. J. Kingsbury, who had an interest in 2,100 acres of Tempe land, said he feared the day was coming when a share in the Tempe Canal, which had fallen from $8,000 to $1,200 with the government offer, would be worth nothing. Kingsbury said:

I know there is no possibility of ever getting the Tempe system in as a whole. I know there are a half dozen stockholders in this organization who will not sign up or sell their shares in the canal under any circumstances. They came here in an ox cart and they are still in one; you can't get them to come out and take an airship.

C. T. Hirst, representing Heard, favored the resolution, but John Birchett said $1.80 per acre for water was too much. A call for a vote was made, and while the vote was being tabulated, a motion to adjourn was approved. The vote was 36 to 22 in favor of the resolution, but persons who understood the situation said the canal would not be sold then. This was correct. Deeds for the Tempe Irrigating Canal Co. and the Tempe Pumping Co. were not transferred to the United States until October 1924. [109]

The governors also met July 25, to approve purchase of the Young Men's Christian Association building lot for $9,000 with the price to be paid in two installments of $4,500. The first payment was made the following day. [110]

Hill visited the Gila River Indian Reservation on July 26 to inspect Reclamation Service work. Upon his return to Phoenix, he said that when the pumping stations being installed at wells already constructed on the reservation and south of Mesa were completed, 15,000 acres of agricultural land would be added to the area of the Salt River Valley without the use of a drop of water from Roosevelt Dam. He put the price of constructing each well and pump at $10,000. [111]

Hill also said that since the meeting of the Tempe Canal owners, a number of large blocks of Tempe land had been signed into the Water Users' Association. He added:

I have had a corps of surveyors at work south of the base line for some little time running lines, and I expect to have a map made up at once showing the lines of the proposed new canals. We will be prepared in a very short time now to come under the Tempe canal with new canals wherever necessary to supply water to those who sign up. [112]

A rainstorm sent 16,000 miners' inches of water over the power canal intake dam east of Roosevelt near Livingston on July 27. Part of the water coming down the river was diverted into the power canal. Also entering the canal were a great number of fish that clogged the screen at the head of the power canal penstock. As a result water was cut off, which, in turn, stopped the generation of electricity to Phoenix. But the city got electricity once again after the Pacific Gas & Electric Co. fired up its steam plant. Government men were put to work shoveling fish out of the canal. [113]

The governors met July 29 and selected the firm of Trost & Trost of El Paso, Texas, represented in Phoenix by R. W. Lescher, to prepare plans for the water temple. Lescher submitted a building plan with a subdued Spanish style of architecture, which was the type adopted for the Young Men's Christian Association building on the same block. This was a change from the sketch provided earlier by architect Thornton Fitzhugh, whose concept resembled the state capitol building. [114]

The city of Mesa and the Reclamation Service agreed to a two-year contract similar to one proposed for Phoenix in May 1910, providing for the government to supply water "for the irrigation of shade trees, fruit trees, shrubs, flowers, lawns and small gardens." The maximum quantity of water per acre was not to exceed four acre-feet in a year. [115]

At the end of June, the dam proper of the Roosevelt Dam was completed, except for the roadway on top and the bridges over the spillways. [116]

Summer storms put a small rise in the Verde River on August 1, and 30,000 miners' inches flowed over the Granite Reef Diversion Dam. The Tempe Canal ran full. [117]

On August 2, Orme and Van der Veer sent the following letter to former President Roosevelt in care of The Outlook in New York City:

On behalf of the Salt River Valley Water Users' Association we desire to extend to you an invitation to visit Phoenix and take part in the dedication of the Roosevelt dam. This structure with its accompanying distribution system is fast nearing completion, and has been in partial use this summer, so that the water stored in the reservoir has saved the farmers what would otherwise have been almost a total failure of crops. The engineers advise us that the dam and its approaches will be wholly completed by next February. It has been suggested that if the date is convenient to you it would be

desirable to have the dedication of this—the largest of the projects so far undertaken by the reclamation service and one which will be the model for the whole world—on Washington's birthday, February 22, 1911. We are extending this invitation so far in advance in order that we may have the first call upon your attendance at that date, and trust that you have no other engagements to interfere with this tentative program. The exercise would necessarily consist of a trip from Phoenix to the reservoir for its formal dedication, and also a hurried survey of the valley, which is receiving such great benefits, and will continue to receive them in greater proportion from this immense structure, which bears your name. [118]

The little floods coming down the Verde led the Reclamation Service to close the gates at Roosevelt Dam, allowing a gain of 863 acre-feet in water storage. But by noon August 3 they were reopened. [119]

A meeting of the Council was called August 15 to discuss the advisability of closing the gates at Roosevelt Dam so that some water would be available for fall planting. The meeting was attended by a large number of farmers, who were unanimous the water should be used until it was gone—then there would be nothing to argue about. Engineer Jay D. Stannard of the Reclamation Service said because of the flows in the Verde River, only 3,000 acre-feet of water had been withdrawn from the reservoir in the first 15 days of August. He said that compared with 44,000 acre-feet in July. If the Verde kept up its flow, the reservoir would not be seriously depleted. [120]

The *Republican* reported August 19 a letter had arrived from Stuart Hill, a secretary to Roosevelt, saying Roosevelt would not be able to be in Arizona "at the time you mention, though he hopes to visit the state (sic) the following month." Orme wrote back, suggesting to Roosevelt the date be sometime between March 1 and May 15. [121]

On August 21, there was a report the capstones were being laid on the top of Roosevelt Dam, that the work was about 98 percent completed. Some work remained on one of the spillways as well as the bridges. [122]

Ballinger on August 30 signed the contract delaying the opening of the Roosevelt project and authorizing the Water Users' Association to build power plants and make other improvements. [123]

1. *Patrick T. Hurley v. Charles F. Abbott, Decision and Decree,* No. 4564, Judge Edward Kent, District Court of the Third Judicial District, Territory of Arizona, March 1, 1910, pp. 13-15; *Arizona Republican* (Phoenix), March 2, April 21, 1910.
2. *Hurley v. Abbott,* pp. 11-12.
3. *Ibid.,* pp. 8-9.
4. *Ibid.,* p. 10.
5. *Ibid.,* pp. 17-22.
6. *Republican,* March 2, 1910.
7. *Arizona Gazette* (Phoenix), March 1, 1910.
8. *Republican,* March 4, 1910.
9. *Gazette,* Mach 4, 1910.
10. *Republican,* March 3, 5, 1910.
11. *Ibid.,* March 5, 1910.
12. *Ibid.,* March 6, 1910; *Gazette,* March 5, 1910.
13. *Gazette,* March 7, 1910; *Republican,* March 8, 1910.
14. *Republican,* March 8, 1910.
15. *Gazette,* March 8, 1910.

16. *Republican,* March 9, 1910.
17. *Ibid.,* March 11, 1910.
18. *Gazette,* March 11, 1910.
19. *Republican,* March 14, 1910.
20. *Ibid.,* March 13, 1910.
21. *Ibid.*
22. *Gazette,* March 14, 1910.
23. *Ibid.,* March 16, 1910; *Republican,* March 17, 1910.
24. *Republican,* March 17, 1910.
25. *Ibid.,* March 18, 1910.
26. *Ibid.,* March 22, 1910; *Gazette,* March 21, 1910.
27. *Republican,* March 23, 1910.
28. *Ibid.*
29. *Ibid.,* March 24, 1910; *Gazette,* March 24, 1910.
30. *Gazette,* March 23, 1910; *Republican,* March 24, 1910.
31. *Republican,* March 24, 1910.
32. *Ibid.,* March 26, 1910; *Gazette,* March 25, 1910.
33. *Republican,* March 27, 1910; *Gazette,* March 26, 1910.

34. *Republican,* March 27, 1910.
35. *Ibid.,* March 28, 1910.
36. *Ibid.*
37. *Ibid.,* April 3, 1910.
38. *Ibid.,* April 5, 1910.
39. *Ibid.*
40. *Ibid.,* April 6, 13, 1910.
41. *Ibid.,* April 7, 8, 1910.
42. *Ibid.,* April 8, 1910.
43. *Ibid.,* April 12, 1910.
44. *Ibid; Gazette,* April 12, 1910.
45. *Republican,* April 15, 16, 1910.
46. *Ibid.,* April 16, 1910; *Gazette,* April 16, 18, 1910.
47. *Republican,* April 17, 1910.
48. *Ibid.*
49. *Ibid.*
50. *Ibid.,* April 19, 20, 1910.
51. *Ibid.,* April 22, 1910.
52. *Gazette,* April 23, 1910.
53. *Republican,* April 25, 1910.
54. *Ibid.,* April 26, 27, 1910; *Salt River Project,Final History to 1916* (unpublished manuscript), Vol. II, p. 383.
55. *Republican,* April 26, 1910.
56. *Gazette,* April 26, 1910.
57. *Republican,* April 28, 1910.
58. *Ibid.,* April 29, May 3, 1910.
59. *Ibid.,* May 1, 1910.
60. *Gazette,* April 29, 30, May 6, 1910.
61. *Republican,* May 3, 1910.
62. *Ibid.*
63. *Ibid.,* May 3, 6, 1910.
64. *Ibid.,* May 5, 1910; *Final History to 1916,* Vol. II, pp. 383-384.
65. *Republican,* May 5, 1910.
66. *Gazette,* May 6, 1910.
67. *Republican,* May 6, 1910.
68. *Ibid.,* May 8, 1910; *Final History to 1916,* Vol. II, pp. 360-364.
69. *Republican,* May 10, 1910.
70. *Ibid.,* May 11, 1910.
71. *Ibid.,* May 12, 1910; *Gazette,* May 12, 1910.
72. *Republican,* May 12, 1910.
73. *Ibid.,* May 15, 1910.
74. *Ibid.,* May 19, 21, 1910; *Gazette,* May 19, 1910.
75. *Republican,* May 24, 1910.
76. *Ibid.,* May 25, 1910.
77. *Ibid.,* May 27, 1910.
78. *Ibid.,* June 1, 1910.
79. *Ibid.,* June 10, 1910.
80. *Ibid.,* June 3, 1910.

81. *Ibid.,* June 7, 1910.
82. *Ibid.*
83. *Gazette,* June 7, 1910.
84. *Republican,* May 25, June 9, 1910.
85. *Ibid.,* June 11, 1910.
86. *Ibid.,* June 12, 1910.
87. *Ibid.,* June 13, 22, 1910.
88. *Ibid.,* June 13, 1910; Tempe Canal Committee to L.C. Hill, June 11, 1910, Salt River Project Archives (hereafter SRPA).
89. *Republican,* June 16, 1910; *Final History to 1916,* pp. 385-395.
90. *Republican,* June 17, 20, July 15, 1910.
91. *Ibid.,* June 17, 21, 1910.
92. *Ibid.,* June 23, 1910.
93. *Ibid.,* June 21, 1910; *Gazette,* June 21, 1910.
94. *Republican,* June 22, July 2, 7, 9, 1910.
95. *Ibid.,* June 26, 1910.
96. L.C. Hill to F. H. Newell, June 28, 1910, SRPA.
97. *Republican,* June 30, 1910.
98. *Ibid.*
99. *Ibid.,* June 13, July 2, 1910.
100. *Ibid.,* July 6, 1912.
101. *Ibid.*
102. F.H. Newell to R.A. Ballinger, July 6, 1907; F.H. Newell to L.C. Hill, July 7, 1907, SRPA.
103. *Gazette,* July 9, 1910.
104. *Republican,* July 15, 1910.
105. *Ibid.,* July 16, 1910.
106. *Ibid.,* July 19, 1910.
107. *Ibid.,* July 23, 1910.
108. *Ibid.,* July 26, 1910.
109. *Ibid.,* July 26, 1810; *Gazette,* July 26, 1910; P.W. Dent, acting commissioner, U.S.R.S., to chief engineer, Denver, Colo., June 25, 1925, SRPA.
110. *Republican,* July 27, 1910.
111. *Gazette,* July 27, 1910.
112. *Republican,* July 28, 1910.
113. *Ibid.,* July 28, 1910.
114. *Ibid.,* July 30, 1910.
115. *Ibid.,* July 31, 1910.
116. *Ibid.,* August 9, 1910.
117. *Ibid.,* August 2, 1910.
118. *Ibid.,* August 19, 1910.
119. *Ibid.,* August 5, 1910.
120. *Ibid.,* August 16, 1910.
121. *Ibid.,* August 19, September 16, 1910.
122. *Ibid.,* August 21, 1910.
123. *Gazette,* September 12, 1910.

September 1910 - February 1911

The Roosevelt reservoir continued to supply water to the Salt River Valley farmers though the amount of water in storage tended to decrease. Occasional rains in the Verde River watershed helped keep the canals full and on September 1 and 2, so much water came down the Salt River Valley Canal—the Town Ditch—that it overflowed its banks between Seventh and Second Streets. However, no damage of consequence was reported. [1]

The *Arizona Republican* reported September 7 that it was expected that the bridges at Roosevelt Dam would be completed by November 1, but getting the work done depended upon the employment of stonemasons. Supervising engineer Louis C. Hill of the Reclamation Service visited the dam a few days later and on return said he thought the work would be completed by the end of October. He said there had been some delay because of the scarcity of the type of stone being used in the parapet, but he said the north side bridge was finished. The newspaper said the side railings, four-feet high, were tall enough so "It is estimated that no animal no matter how greatly frightened will be able to jump over. . ." [2]

Deputy Sheriff W. A. Burton warned against drinking water coming into the canals from Roosevelt Lake. Burton said the water probably was polluted. He explained that cattle came to the lake's edge to drink and some of them got caught in the mud along the shore and remained there until they starved or were killed. In riding along the perimeter of the reservoir, he said he found 65 head of cattle in various stages of decomposition. [3]

Completion of a new lateral from the Consolidated Canal in the Kyrene section south of Tempe was reported September 14 by the Reclamation Service. There also was a report the service was planning to water certain lands under the Utah Canal by extending laterals west from the Consolidated Canal. [4]

President John P. Orme of the Salt River Valley Water Users' Association received a letter in mid-September from a secretary to former President Theodore Roosevelt acknowledging receipt of the letter suggesting Roosevelt Dam be dedicated anytime between March 1 and May 15. A few days later, Orme received a note from Roosevelt:

In a very few days I will send you the date for the dedication. It is necessary to work out the schedule of my journey.
I will let you know as soon as possible. [5]

At the annual meeting of the Tempe Irrigation Canal Co. on September 24, L. E. Pafford, secretary, submitted a report showing that 22,510 acres had been irrigated in the fiscal year ending September 15, 1910, at a total expense of $8,965.89, which included legal expenses of more than $3,100, or a fraction less than 40 cents per acre. The account in the *Republican* called it "one of the most remarkable records ever established in any canal." [6]

Dwight B. Heard told the meeting of the Tempe Canal owners that the time had come to decide once and for all whether the lands were to be signed into the reservoir district and what was to be done about draining the ground. Heard also said the landowners needed to decide whether the water was going to be distributed by priority of appropriation or by pro rata as was then being done. He said he hoped the will of the majority would prevail. While his comments concerning the distribution of water provoked some sharp verbal tilts, nothing was settled. The question of drainage produced a sentiment from the shareholders that the company undertake the matter, not the Reclamation Service. A motion was made and passed calling upon the company president, C. G. Jones, to appoint a committee of five shareholders to investigate the drainage situation. [7]

Benjamin A. Fowler was reelected president of the National Irrigation Congress on September 30 in Pueblo, Colorado. [8]

Archie Roosevelt, son of the former president, arrived in Phoenix the morning of October 2. Young Roosevelt spent several hours seeing the sights before continuing to Mesa and to the private Evans School, which was located about two miles south. Archie's cousin, Nicholas Roosevelt, had attended the Evans School the year before. [9]

At a meeting October 3, the governors of the Water Users' Association voted to pay off the $4,500 still owed the Young Mens' Christian Association for the water temple building lot. The governors were told the association had money sitting idle so it might as well be used to pay the debt. [10]

The city of Mesa, in connection with a proposed contract between itself and the United States Department of the Interior for the delivery of water for municipal purposes, first wanted to extract itself from membership in the Water Users' Association. Mesa's dilemma started coming toward some sort of resolution when the city received a bill for $960 from the Water Users' Association for assessments. When the association was seeking shareholders in 1903, Mesa was signed in for its incorporated area of 640 acres. It regularly paid the assessments levied by the association, but the city council thought the burden had become excessive with the association assessments for the power plants in addition to the $1.60 per acre each year to the Reclamation Service for the cost of water. Additionally, the city employed a zanjero and paid to keep the ditches clean. Because the national reclamation law provided that no individual or corporation could receive water for more than 160 acres, Congress in 1906 amended the law so that a corporation could receive water for more than 160 acres provided it was a municipality. The city council did not want to sign a contract with the Reclamation Service to receive up to four acre-feet of water per acre at a cost of $1.25 per acre-foot unless it could pull out of the Water Users' Association, thereby eliminating the debt. The council on October 5 ordered the city attorney to prepare a petition asking the governors to allow the city to leave the association. [11]

On October 6, the *Republican* printed an editorial saying:

The electric current from Roosevelt Dam went off at 1:30 p.m. October 15 because of a 25-foot break in the bank of the power canal about ten miles above the dam. The break apparently resulted from a gopher hole. Repair of the break was finished by 2 a.m. October 16, but the power was not restored for a few hours in order to allow the water in the power canal to soak into the repaired bank. [13]

Withdrawal of the city of Mesa from the Water Users' Association was approved by the governors at a meeting October 17. This cleared the way for Mesa to enter the contract to buy water from the Reclamation Service. Governor Richard E. Sloan, acting as legal adviser, said corporations could not become members of the association. Therefore, all corporations were absolved from any agreement with the association. This applied to both the cities of Phoenix and Glendale, the lands of which were signed into the association, but not to Tempe, which did not sign. [14]

A report on the 1910 crop year in the Salt River Valley, prepared by the Reclamation Service, became available in mid-November. It said water was furnished through 490 miles of canals for 131,364 acres, the largest area ever watered in the Valley. Although it was a season of unusual drought, the report said the croplands received more than five acre-feet of water each. Alfalfa was the most important crop with about 65,000 acres harvested. More than 5,000 acres were in cantaloupes and other melons. [15]

About the only construction work going on in the Valley by the Reclamation Service involved the continued enlargement of the Arizona Canal and the improvement of lateral ditches. A dredger and excavator were about one and one-third miles east of the Arizona Falls and were working west in that direction. The dredger was making about 250 feet per day. When the dredger reached the falls, it was to be taken back to the head of the canal and there begin another westward trek to make the canal even wider. The excavator, meanwhile, was to continue west widening the canal to its end. [16]

Judge Edward Kent announced November 25 that he would hear additional evidence December 3 concerning the use of water upon class C lands in his ruling in *Hurley v. Abbott*. Kent said that would be the last opportunity to make changes in the decree. [17]

All bids for construction of the Water Users' Association's office building were rejected at a meeting of the governors on December 5. The low bidder failed to qualify properly so the governors directed the project be readvertised and set December 20 as the date for opening bids. [18]

The *Arizona Gazette* said in an article December 6 that one of the wells the Reclamation Service was developing southeast of Mesa was in operation and a second one would soon be ready for operation. Construction of the pumping plants was completed in the fall of 1909, but a shortage of funds delayed the installation of equipment and this was not completed until June 1913. The *Gazette* said the,

Wells are doing great work for this section and they will be the means of saving much water for the canals, as already the water in the Consolidated Canal that supplies that section has been cut down to the extent of the flow from the wells. [19]

John Miller, an Indian employed by the Reclamation Service as a teamster, was killed December 12 on the Lehi Road north of Mesa. Miller's wagon was the last of a small train. As the wagons descended from the mesa, his team suddenly broke into a run and became unmanageable. Just before the wagon reached the bottom of the hill, Miller was thrown from the wagon. His clothes caught in a rope and he was dragged several hundred yards. His head was crushed

Enlarging the Arizona Canal with Camelback Mountain in the background, circa winter 1910-11.

and his jugular vein was severed. [20]

Kent entered a third supplemental decree in *Hurley v. Abbott* on December 13. [21]

Five bids were opened December 20 by the governors' building committee for construction of the water temple. The low bid of $31,998 was submitted by Olson & Co., which agreed to erect the building in 120 days and turn the completed work over to the Water Users' Association by June 1. The building was to front on Van Buren Street. The building was to be made of concrete and brick. The governors awarded the contract December 22 and ground was broken the morning of December 29. [22]

Water users under the Wormser branch of the Tempe Canal met the morning of December 22 to hear a proposition from the Reclamation Service. Supervising engineer Hill told the landowners that the Reclamation Service, in order to serve acreage west of the Tempe district, would either have to gain control of the existing canal or construct a parallel canal. Hill proposed buying the Wormser Canal, but to continue serving the water users their regular water as they then received it. However, the government wanted to enlarge the canal to four times its existing capacity. Hill said the government was willing to pay about $10,000 for the canal and to make a contract to perpetually carry and distribute the water, making a nominal charge. He said the charge would be less than the cost of maintaining the ditch. The landowners appointed a committee of three to consider the proposal. Heard was one of the committee. The same afternoon, Hill met with owners of the Kyrene ditch and made the same sort of proposition. [23]

The Wormser ditch owners met with Hill December 29 and made a counter offer: that the owners be allowed to retain the ditch, but grant the government permission to enlarge the canal and run water through it to its patrons. If the government had accepted, it would have meant a partnership situation, something which the Reclamation Service repeatedly refused. As a consequence, the Reclamation Service was unable to make deals with either the owners of the Wormser or Kyrene ditches and parallel canals were constructed. [24]

At Roosevelt, the work of fully equipping the power plant below the dam was in progress. This had been delayed primarily because there had not been enough money. Hill said the plan then was for six units, five of them furnishing 1,000 kilowatts, or about 1,340 horsepower each. The sixth unit was to be twice the size of any of the other units, making a total of 7,000 kilowatts, or about 9,000 horsepower. Three of the 1,000-kilowatt generators were already working and the generators for the other 1,000-kilowatt units were at the powerhouse. Water wheels for the two units had been advertised and bids were being awaited. Advertisements were soon to be made for the generator and wheel for the final unit. [25]

Hill said Pacific Gas & Electric Co. sometimes used as high as 1,500 kilowatts and the company was paying about $5,000 per month for the electricity it bought. He said there was a ready market for the additional power and he had many applications, but he had nothing to sell. However, he said the Arizona Alfalfa Milling Co. was prepared to use 150 kilowatts and at 2 p.m. December 31 the company became the second business to receive electricity generated at Roosevelt Dam. The Lount Ice Works also was ready to receive power, but because there was not a large demand for ice in the winter, it had not started taking it. [26]

The cement mill at Roosevelt had been dismantled and on December 30 the last wagon carrying some of the parts began transporting them over the Roosevelt road to the Salt River Valley. The Arizona Portland Cement Co., which owned the equipment, intended to build a plant north of the Salt River opposite Tempe. [27]

As 1910 closed, the dam was completed except for about 160 feet of parapet wall. Both of the road bridges over the spillways were completed in December 1910. [28]

With the start of the new year, the Mesa-Roosevelt Stage Co. reduced its service from daily to every other day. The company expected to maintain this schedule until the camp of dam contractor John O'Rourke shut down. Meantime, with little work remaining at Roosevelt, the stage schedule was cut back. [29]

The week of January 8, 1911, rain and snow fell over the watersheds of the Verde and Salt rivers. The Verde River ran rather well, sending a flow of water four-feet deep over the Granite Reef Diversion Dam by the morning of January 12 when the river started to drop. The reservoir behind Roosevelt Dam rose from 66.35 feet January 11 to 80.70 feet the following day, representing an increase of 27,784 acre-feet of water. The reservoir was still rising, but Reclamation Service officials did not expect it to rise above its former high mark of 126 feet when 233,640 acre-feet of water were in storage. A flood of water also came down Cave Creek, washing out about 70 feet of the south bank of the Arizona Canal northwest of Phoenix. [30]

Contractor John O'Rourke and his partner, George N. Steinmetz, visited Hill in Phoenix January 16. The *Republican* reported there was no special concern, only the closing details of the job. O'Rourke said all his work would be finished by the end of January or early in February but it would be until at least March 1 before the contractors were packed up and gone. He said 600 tons of machinery and material had to be brought over the Roosevelt road to Mesa and stored until a decision was made about where to send it. Financially, O'Rourke said he did not care to comment about how his company fared in the construction of the dam and other works, except that while no money had been lost, not as much had been made as hoped. He said there was great satisfaction in completing an undertaking for which many had predicted disaster. O'Rourke described his relationship with Hill and the Reclamation Service as cordial with Hill always ready to assist in smoothing conditions when irritations and differences arose. The contractor said that so long as the water was not spread too thin by trying to cultivate too much land, the prosperity of the Valley would be perpetual and to an extent that could not scarcely be conceived of then. [31]

Water was turned out of the Arizona Canal January 18 to

give the Reclamation Service ten days in which to deepen the canal through rock formation for a distance of about 2,000 feet. More than 300 men were camped near the site, working both day and night shifts, blasting rock and removing it. [32]

On January 23, Orme received a letter from Frank Harper, private secretary to Roosevelt, announcing the date of the Roosevelt Dam dedication. The letter said:

Mr. Roosevelt desires me to acknowledge receipt of your letter to say that he hopes to reach Phoneix on the morning of Saturday, March 18th, at 9 o'clock. He would then like to motor from Phoenix in order to reach Roosevelt Dam in the early afternoon. He will then stay at Roosevelt for the night in a cottage to be reserved for him. Mr. Clarence John Blanchard, U.S. Reclamation Service, Washington, D.C., has been into the office several times regarding these arrangements, and it would be well for you in making your arrangements to get in touch with Mr. Blanchard so that there may be no hitch in the matter. On Sunday, March 19th, Mr. Roosevelt will motor from Roosevelt to Mesa and will stay at Mesa for Sunday night. On Monday morning he will leave Mesa for Phoenix and will stay in that town until 7:30 that evening, when he will have to leave for Los Angeles. He will be accompanied by Mrs. Roosevelt and Miss Roosevelt, and probably by about three friends. If there is anything further you would like to know I hope you will not fail to write, and when your program is sufficiently advanced I hope you will send me a copy in order to see that everything is in order. [33]

In response to the letter, a meeting of the governors was called for Saturday, January 28. The **Republican** said that while the Roosevelts and party would be guests of the Water Users' Association, it was expected the Board of Trade would cooperate in the event. The newspaper also said Roosevelt was expected to arrive via the Santa Fe Railroad in a private car. [34]

Arthur P. Davis, chief engineer of the Reclamation Service, and a party of other U.S. Reclamation Service engineers, arrived in Tempe the morning of January 25 and immediately left for Roosevelt by car. They returned to Mesa the following day and arrived in Phoenix the evening of January 26. The visitors reported the coping was being installed on the dam. Davis said the coping was particularly attractive, being built with rock of varying colors and appearing quite ornamental, massive and secure. Still remaining to be built but not part of the contractor's work, were a gate house and tool houses at either end of the dam. Davis also spoke about the increase in the number of little springs that had appeared in the river banks or canyon walls below the dam. Before the dam, there were a few of these and the larger number resulted from the great pressure of water stored above. The water emerged from miniature fissures or crevices and when the reservoir was full, their number might grow even larger. But as the years passed they would gradually fill because of the silt carried into them. Another thing that could be expected was that one day the dam would crack or have a number of cracks, and if it did not, it would forever remain in a class by itself. Davis said all large dams cracked, but that was nothing to cause alarm. He said it would come as a result of the expansion and contraction, expanding with the summer heat and contracting in the winter. Davis said the cracks would not be dangerous and a tourist need not flee to the surrounding hills if he should spot them. [35]

Orme named himself and governors Ethelbert W. Wilbur, H. H. Stone, E. J. Bennitt and E. E. Jack as a committee for the dedication of Roosevelt Dam. They were to be assisted by Governor Richard Sloan, association lawyer, and Charles Van der Veer, secretary. [36]

On January 30, the reservoir behind Roosevelt Dam was 108.80 feet deep and contained 144,032 acre-feet of water. This compared with an elevation of 61.75 and 22,094 acre-feet January 1. Despite the improvement in storage, there were complaints from some farmers about using water to operate the generators through the power canal so that Pacific Gas & Electric Co. would have electricity to sell. These farmers thought 250 second feet, the capacity of the power canal, were being used for this purpose. They maintained Pacific Gas & Electric should start up its auxiliary steam plant and produce power that way, at least until the water in storage was large enough for all agricultural purposes. [37]

The water in storage climbed to 145,760 acre-feet by the morning of January 31. [38]

The Council of the Water Users' Association met February 1 and agreed to amend the bylaws so that the assessments payable September 1 and March 1 would be due November 1 and May 1 each year. One reason for the change was that March was in between markets and might be burdensome to small farmers. The Council also agreed to spend an additional $500 to enlarge the basement of the water temple to better accommodate farmers and their families. [39]

The dedication arrangements committee met February 2 and established a tentative schedule for Roosevelt's visit and the dedication. The Roosevelt party would be met at the Santa Fe depot at 9 a.m. and would at once be placed in automobiles. The number of autos would depend upon the number of persons in the official party but, in any event, the first car would be occupied by Roosevelt, Orme and Hill, the latter two to inform the visitor about the magnitude and meaning of the dam and other works. The trip to Roosevelt would be made via Granite Reef Diversion Dam, and they would arrive at the dedication site at 4 p.m. The dedication would begin at once and would be conducted on top of the dam. Orme would begin the program, then turn it over to Sloan who would preside. The list of speakers was not final. At the conclusion of the program, Roosevelt would be asked to press a button to release a flow of water from the reservoir for a few minutes, thus officially putting Roosevelt Dam into service. If the water in the reservoir was high enough, the water would exit through the tunnel on the north side of the dam. Water coming through the tunnel would create a waterfall, which would be visible to the crowd. If the lake was too low to use the north side tunnel, the button would be attached to the gates in the sluicing tunnel. The water from the sluicing tunnel would not be visible from the top of the dam. [40]

As nightfall came, Roosevelt's daughter, Ethel, would be asked to press a button to illuminate the dam in lights. The lights included those installed atop a series of pilasters constructed into the downstream wall of the dam to give it greater strength. The pilasters rose to the top of the coping. These lights were intended for permanent use. On the upper face of the dam along a ledge just outside the coping would be placed an electric wire across the length of the dam. The line would have numerous sockets for bulbs. The visitors would view the illumination from a spot on the hillside beside the dam. [41]

The speaker's stand was to be at the south end of the dam on the spot reserved for the later erection of a tool house. The area was 18-feet square, just off the road where the bridge above the spillway joined the dam. It was estimated that 1,600 persons could assemble along the roadway within hearing of the speakers and a great many more people could crowd farther back. [42]

The Reverend Bertrand R. Cocks, superintendent of the St. Luke's home, east of Phoenix, said he had received a letter from the Right Reverend Julius W. Atwood, bishop of Arizona, saying Atwood had visited Roosevelt in New York and the former president had promised to dedicate the home during his visit in Phoenix on March 20. [43]

By the morning of February 5, the elevation of the water in the Roosevelt reservoir was 119.90 feet for a total of 198,332 acre-feet. Engineer Howard Reed, in charge of water distribution for the Reclamation Service, announced the government was ready to deliver water to all class A and B lands. [44]

Later on February 5, the last stone on the coping of Roosevelt Dam was placed, completing the construction of the dam. The gate house was under construction by government forces, who also were to build the tool houses and lighting system. [45]

Reclamation engineers measuring the water in the reservoir the morning of February 7 found the elevation was 127.20 feet, more than ever before, and the acre-feet in storage totaled 240,970. [46]

Hill said statements that 250 second feet of water were being discharged from the reservoir for the production of electricity were incorrect. He said the amount coming through the power canal varied from 60 to 70 second feet but in any case except in time of flood, the water used to make electricity also was needed in the Valley for irrigation. This water would be needed whether or not there was a powerhouse. He said the loss of water for a few days during floods was all it cost the irrigation interests for all the electricity sold in a year. Hill said the water in storage was sufficient to provide six irrigations, exclusive of pumped water, and in about a week the Reclamation Service expected to begin irrigating about 1,000 acres with pumped water from the Olsen wells six miles southwest of Mesa. [47]

On February 17, a letter arrived from Harper saying that Roosevelt had approved the main features of the program for his visit, but the colonel wanted time set aside so he could meet with members of the Rough Riders regiment who happened to be in the area. The committee on arrangements proposed a horseback ride from Roosevelt on Sunday morning, March 19, to the cliff dwellings six miles distant, but that was scrapped in favor of a buffet luncheon at the Ford Hotel in Phoenix at 1 p.m. March 20. [48]

Harper's letter said the party would be limited to Roosevelt and his wife, their daughter, Ethel, a friend of Ethel's, Cornelia Landon, and Harper. They were to travel in what was known as the Santa Fe Railroad's private "Business Car No. 3." [49]

The committee on arrangements issued formal invitations to the dedication February 17. The language of the engraved invitations was as follows:

The Board of Governors
of the
Salt River Valley Water Users' Association
Phoenix, Arizona
Requests the Honor of Your Presence
at the Exercises Commemorating
the Completion of the
ROOSEVELT DAM
A Part of the Salt River Project,
Saturday, Sunday and Monday,
March Eighteenth, Nineteenth and Twentieth
Nineteen Hundred Eleven
JOHN P. ORME,
President
CHAS. A. VAN DER VEER
Secretary
R.S.V.P. [50]

On a card within the invitation the program outlined was as follows:

Saturday
Phoenix to Roosevelt
Dedicatory Address at the Dam by
Hon. Theodore Roosevelt
Sunday
Roosevelt to Mesa City.
Monday
In the Salt River Valley. [51]

Pacific Gas & Electric Co. announced new electric rates, lowering the initial charge from 15 cents to 12 cents per kilowatt hour. [52]

Sunday, February 19, Hill conducted a dedication of the road over the Roosevelt Dam. He drove his car across the bridges above the spillways to contractor O'Rourke's house on the north side of the river. Among those accompanying Hill on the drive back over the dam were Mr. and Mrs. Steinmetz, Mrs. Hill and the Hills' daughter, Margaret. [53]

Hill reported February 25 that the gate house at the dam had been completed. [54]

The morning of February 28, the elevation of the water in Roosevelt Lake was 131.30 feet and the water in storage totaled 300,605 acre-feet. [55]

---

1. *Arizona Republican,* September 2, 1910.
2. *Ibid.,* September 7, 12, 1910.
3. *Ibid.,* September 9, 1910.
4. *Ibid.,* September 11, 15, 1910.
5. *Ibid.,* September 16, 1910; *Arizona Gazette* (Phoenix), September 21, 1910.
6. *Republican,* September 21, 1910.
7. *Ibid.,* September 25, 1910.
8. *Ibid.,* October 1, 1910.
9. *Ibid.,* October 3, 1910.
10. *Ibid.,* October 4, 1910.
11. *Ibid.,* October 6, 8, 1910; *Gazette,* October 18, 1910.

12. *Republican,* October 6, 1910.
13. *Ibid.,* October 16, 18, 1910.
14. *Ibid.,* October 18, 1910; *Gazette,* October 18, 1910.
15. *Republican,* November 15, 1910.
16. *Ibid.,* November 22, 28, 1910.
17. *Ibid.,* November 26, December 4, 1910.
18. *Ibid.,* December 6, 1910.
19. *Gazette,* December 6, 1910; *Salt River Project, Final History to 1916* (unpublished manuscript), Vol. III, p. 531.
20. *Republican,* December 13, 1910.
21. *Final History to 1916,* Vol. III, p. 486.
22. *Republican,* December 21, 1910; *Gazette,* December 22, 29, 1910.
23. *Republican,* December 23, 1910.
24. *Ibid.,* December 30, 1910; conversation with Ted Walker, right-of-way section, Salt River Project, July 29, 1981; map of the Salt River Project, U.S. Reclamation Service, May 1915.
25. *Republican,* December 30, 1910.
26. *Ibid.,* April 7, December 30, 1910; January 1, 1911.
27. *Ibid.,* December 31, 1910.
28. *Final History to 1916,* Vol. III, p. 136.
29. *Republican,* January 3, 1911.
30. *Ibid.,* January 13, 1911.
31. *Ibid.,* January 17, 1911.
32. *Ibid.,* January 22, 1911.

33. Frank Harper to John P. Orme, January 16, 1911, reprinted *Republican,* January 24, 1911.
34. *Republican,* January 24, 1911.
35. *Ibid.,* January 24, 28, 1911.
36. *Gazette,* January 30, 1911.
37. *Ibid.,* January 31, 1911; *Republican,* January 31, 1911.
38. *Republican,* February 1, 1911.
39. *Ibid.,* February 2, 12, 1911.
40. *Gazette,* February 2, 1911; *Republican,* February 4, 1911.
41. *Republican,* February 4, 1911.
42. *Ibid.,* February 26, 1911.
43. *Gazette,* February 2, 1911.
44. *Republican,* February 6, 1911.
45. *Ibid.,* February 8, 1911; *Final History to 1916,* Vol. I, p. 137; *Republican,* February 8, 1911, also said the last stone was laid on Monday, February 6, 1911.
46. *Republican,* February 8, 1911.
47. *Ibid.*
48. *Ibid.,* February 18, March 20, 1911.
49. *Ibid.,* February 18, 1911.
50. *Ibid.*
51. *Ibid.*
52. *Gazette,* February 17, 1911.
53. *Ibid.,* February 25, 1911; *Republican,* February 26, 1911.
54. *Republican,* February 26, 1911.
55. *Ibid.,* March 1, 1911.

March 1-18, 1911

M. C. Webb of Roosevelt and his son, A. C. Webb, secretary of the Overland Telephone Co., owners of the Roosevelt Mercantile Co., bought the mercantile business and ice plant of J. M. O'Rourke & Co., contractor for construction of Roosevelt Dam. The Webbs also leased "The Lodge," which had been used as headquarters by O'Rourke, for use as a hotel, but no liquor was to be dispensed. The Webbs also took over the O'Rourke bunkhouses containing 300 cots and the dining facilities. Anticipating a large attendance at the Roosevelt Dam dedication March 18, the Webbs laid in a good supply of gasoline and lubricating oils. [1]

Supervising engineer Louis C. Hill of the Reclamation Service issued an order that no horse-drawn vehicles would be allowed on the Roosevelt road on March 18 so there would be no delay in the line of automobiles that would make the trip from Phoenix to the dam. In addition, no motor vehicle was to be permitted to travel either west or east on the road unless it would pass Government Well before noon. If a vehicle failed to pass that point, Hill said it would be detained on the road until after the dedication party passed. Persons going to the dam for the dedication were advised to go the day before or to start early on the morning of March 18 so they could keep far ahead of the automobiles that would bring former President Theodore Roosevelt and the official dedication party. [2]

On March 6, Secretary of the Interior Richard E. Ballinger approved an agreement between Hill and Dwight B. Heard, vice president of the Bartlett-Heard Land and Cattle Co., for sale of the San Francisco Canal to the government for $12,840. The purchase committed the Reclamation Service to sinking wells for a,

pumping plant of sufficient capacity to furnish a supply of water which when added to the amount to which the lands under the San Francisco Canal are now entitled from the natural flow of Salt River, will afford an adequate supply of water for the irrigation of about 4,300 acres of land lying under and irrigable from the San Francisco Canal: It is understood that if sufficient water should not be developed at said plant the United States may furnish water from any other sources to complete said supply for the proper irrigation of said lands. [3]

The agreement provided that all the lands under the San Francisco Canal were to be signed into the Salt River Valley Water Users' Association. Heard's company was given until the opening of the Salt River project to sell its land under the canal. If all the land was not sold by the time the project was opened by the secretary of the interior, the unsold portion would not be entitled to reservoir water. The deed giving the government possession of the San Francisco Canal was not executed until December 31, 1912, and the Reclamation Service did not take over the operation of the canal until January 1, 1913. [4]

Roosevelt Lake behind Roosevelt Dam gained 88,194 acre-feet of water in the 24 hours between the morning of March 6 and 7. This raised the elevation of the lake to 150.50

feet and the water in storage to 409,722 acre-feet. [5]

Hill received a letter March 11 from Arthur P. Davis, chief engineer for the Reclamation Service, saying Davis would be unable to attend the dedication of Roosevelt Dam because he would be on his way to St. Petersburg, Russia, to undertake an assignment of several months for the Russian government in Turkestan. [6]

Hill also announced the growing volume of water in storage made it possible to distribute water to some class C as well as class B lands. The water was to be sold with the understanding that under no circumstances was the delivery of water to "become the basis of a permanent water right." [7]

The morning of March 13, the gauge at Roosevelt Dam showed there were 500,234 acre-feet of water in the reservoir. In an editorial, the *Arizona Republican* reminded readers the quantity was twice that impounded the previous winter, when in a year of severe drought it carried "this valley prosperously through a rainless summer." The newspaper continued:

Hence we already know that there will be an abundance of water for irrigation throughout this year. The ranchers will have far more water this year than ever before in the history of the incomparable Salt River Valley.

This means a record year of prosperity for rancher, for business man, for laboring man, for everybody. [8]

Because of high water in the Verde River, it was announced March 13 that Roosevelt and his party would not visit Granite Reef Diversion Dam on the way to Roosevelt. Water in the Salt River below the dam made the river impassable, and it was expected that would still be the condition by Saturday. Plans were made to route the travelers over the Center Street (Central Avenue) bridge, which was near completion except for parapets and other minor work. Members of the official party were directed to assemble at 8 a.m. Saturday, March 18, at the office of the Water Users' Association so they could be ready for a quick start when Roosevelt's train arrived. The name of Governor Richard E. Sloan was added to those of Hill and John P. Orme, president of the Water Users' Association, to ride with Roosevelt in the first car. A driver for the car was still to be named. [9]

On March 14, the Water Users' Association opened bids for the turbines and electrical equipment to be used in the proposed power plant on the South Canal. Only one bid was made, it coming from S. Morgan Smith Co. of York, Pennsylvania, which furnished turbines for Roosevelt Dam's powerhouse. Five companies offered bids to supply the electrical machinery for the South Canal plant. [10]

The *Arizona Gazette* reported on March 15 that Roosevelt and his private secretary, Frank Harper, had left El Paso, Texas, that morning aboard a private railroad car and that night they would join Mrs. Roosevelt, daughter Ethel, and Sloan at Albuquerque, New Mexico. The party was to reach the Grand Canyon in Arizona on March 16 where it would be joined by Archie Roosevelt, son of the former president, Judge Edward Kent, and Bishop Julius W. Atwood. [11]

With Leon Jacobs, assistant clerk of the Maricopa County Board of Supervisors, at the wheel, an Apperson automobile became the first to be driven across the Central Avenue bridge the morning of March 16. Passengers were Supervisors Orme and L. M. Hoghe, and L. M. Acuff, county road superintendent. [12]

Later that day, the *Gazette* reported the river was down at Granite Reef Diversion Dam and that likely would be the route taken by the dedication party. The following day, March 17, Hill said Granite Reef definitely would be the route. However, motorists who wanted to take the Central Avenue bridge were informed they could, but to exercise caution because the parapets were not up. They also were advised that a large derrick was on the bridge, leaving a seven-foot clearance. Motorists were advised not to try to cross the bridge at night. [13]

In anticipation of the Saturday arrival of Roosevelt, Phoenix citizens busied themselves cleaning up their properties and giving the city a patriotic look. Special emphasis was given Washington Street between Fourth Street and Fourth Avenue. Flags would wave in front of every building. Al Williams, proprietor of the Ford Hotel at Second Avenue and Washington where Roosevelt would lunch with the Rough Riders, covered a considerable portion of the front of the building with flags and bunting. Electric light bulbs were strung on both sides of Washington from Fourth Street to Fourth Avenue and lights were strung along some of the side streets. A speaker's stand and press box were put up at City Hall Plaza on Washington Street between First and Second streets where Roosevelt would speak on Monday, March 20. [14]

Engineer William A. Farish of the Reclamation Service left Phoenix on March 17 to establish patrols along the Roosevelt road to make certain the rules-of-the-road laid down by Hill were enforced. Motorists were advised that if any stops were made along the road even for four or five minutes, it would be necessary to send back a flagman a far enough distance to alert any on-coming motorist. [15]

A. M. Smith, government electrician in charge of arranging the light display at Roosevelt Dam, wrote to his wife, Agnes, 20, in Phoenix to join him at Roosevelt for the dedication. She was the only passenger aboard the stagecoach the morning of March 17 when it left Mesa with Bud Norton at the reins. Coming down Fish Creek Hill not far from Fish Creek Station the stage came upon an automobile stopped in the road. The *Gazette* said, "...just as the stage team passed, the chauffeur crawled from beneath the car. This startled the horses, and they started at a mad gallop...Norton tried to keep his team close to the mountain, and might have succeeded in controlling it had the stage not dropped off a culvert and hurled its occupants with terrific force head foremost into the rocky hillside." The *Republican* reported the stage went over a steep embankment at a sharp curve, the coach rolling several times. When it came to a stop, Mrs. Smith and Norton were pinned beneath. Mrs. Smith suffered a fractured skull and was unconscious, while eight of Norton's ribs were fractured. The horses broke free from the stage when it left the road and they continued to Fish Creek Station. A party was immediately organized to go back up the road to learn what had happened to the stage. The searchers found Mrs. Smith and Norton and carried them to Fish Creek Station.

Roosevelt Dam

Doctors were summoned from Mesa and Roosevelt. After doctors performed surgery on Mrs. Smith, she was taken by car to the hospital in Roosevelt. Norton remained at Fish Creek Station. Mrs. Smith died at 2 o'clock the afternoon of March 18. Besides her husband, she was survived by a year-old son and her parents, Mr. and Mrs. James K. Anderson of Phoenix. [16]

Sloan returned to Phoenix from the Grand Canyon on the train that arrived Friday night, March 17, and said that if nothing unforeseen happened, the Roosevelts should arrive in Phoenix at 9 o'clock the following morning. [17]

Readers of the *Arizona Republican* on the morning of Saturday, March 18, found a photograph of a bespectacled Theodore Roosevelt looking out at them from the newspaper's front page. The caption beneath the picture did not identify Roosevelt by name. Instead, it said:

The World's First Citizen [18]

The private railroad car occupied by the Roosevelts was attached to the end of the Santa Fe train. Accounts of the arrival time in Phoenix that morning vary as do some of the other minor details of Roosevelt's visit and the dedication of Roosevelt Dam. The Roosevelts were said to be still at breakfast when the train rolled to a stop at 9:20 a.m. Even before it halted, James H. McClintock bounded up the steps into the car and was followed by Heard, Sloan, Orme, and Charles Van der Veer, secretary of the Water Users' Association. Ten minutes elapsed before Kent appeared on the back platform of the car, followed moments later by Roosevelt, who squinted through his glasses at the crowd and waved his black fedora. From the "enormous crowd" came shouts of "There he is!" and other greetings. Scattered among the hundreds of persons were men wearing Rough Riders yellow badges in the lapels of their coats. The automobiles that were to carry the visitors and members of the official party to the dam were lined up beside the railroad car, and Roosevelt was directed to the Kissel Kar in which he was to ride. At the wheel was former Rough Rider Wesley A. Hill of Tempe, wearing a linen coat. Roosevelt, discerning that was "the regulation uniform" for the road, donned a similar coat over his khaki trousers tucked into leather leggings, black coat and vest, turned down collar and tie. Roosevelt sat in the front seat, beside the driver, while Sloan, Orme, and Louis Hill sat in the rear seat. In the second auto went Mrs. Roosevelt, Archie Roosevelt, Mrs. Sloan, and Heard. Ethel Roosevelt, her friend, Cornelia Landon, Ora Orme, and Van der Veer went in the third car. The rest of the official party was distributed in 21 other cars according to a previously arranged plan. [19]

Almost before the riders were fully settled, Wesley Hill stepped on the gas pedal and the 60-horsepower engine in the Kissel Kar propelled the vehicle across the railroad tracks to Central Avenue where the driver turned north. People lined the streets through the business district to get a glimpse of Roosevelt and to shout greetings. Once past Washington, the car picked up speed. [20]

A couple of minutes later, a lookout on top of the highest building at the Phoenix Indian School alerted school superintendent C. W. Goodman, faculty, students, and about a thousand other visitors, that the cars were on their way up Central Avenue and would shortly enter the grounds. The pupils were lined up by the girls' building, the boys "in natty uniforms" holding polished rifles, and everyone else, "from the teachers down to the tiniest child, was in holiday attire." As Roosevelt's car entered the circular roadway inside the school grounds, the school band played ***Hail to the Chief,*** and the cadets presented arms. A cheer went up for Roosevelt, and Goodman and his staff greeted him. Roosevelt rose and delivered a brief address, saying there were in his regiment in the war with Spain a number of "full blooded members" of the Indian race and that "they made just as good soldiers as were in that regiment." He said there was "more than being good soldiers," and he urged the students to take advantage of the opportunities at the school and the teachers to instruct them well. When he finished speaking, he sat down and the crowd applauded. An Indian stepped forward to crank up the car. As the motor started, Roosevelt reached out of the car and shook hands with the Indian and thanked him. Roosevelt waved his hat as Wesley Hill steered the auto out the school's west road onto Central Avenue, where the car went north a short distance to the Grand Canal. There, the car was driven onto the road along the canal to where the canal intersected Indian School Road, west of today's 16th Street. From there, the caravan followed Indian School Road to the crosscut canal at today's 48th Street. The cars turned north on the canal bank and traveled a short distance to the south bank of the Arizona Canal, where the road was followed to the Granite Reef Diversion Dam. Whenever possible, the drivers sped as fast as possible, stirring up considerable dust, but every few miles the lead car slowed enough to allow the others to close and to make certain the party was intact. Behind the last guest auto came car No. 13, which was occupied by mechanics to make repairs if needed along the road. [21]

At Granite Reef, a short rest was taken. Roosevelt got out of the auto and viewed the diversion dam from different angles. Louis Hill explained the purpose of the dam and Roosevelt asked some questions. Back on the road, the car drivers were instructed to maintain intervals of about 1,000 feet, or far enough to keep out of the dust of the vehicle ahead, but once past Government Well the distance was lessened to about 300 feet, which was the space kept the rest of the way to the dam. [22]

The automobile carrying Roosevelt arrived at Mormon Flat at 1:15 p.m., which news was carried to the office of the *Arizona Democrat* in Phoenix by carrier pigeon. The note said Roosevelt and party had been greeted by men and women in front of every farmhouse, or along the road, in the flat country, and by miners and prospectors in the canyon country. [23]

The *Gazette* reported the trip to Roosevelt Dam "was made without episode," but the *Republican* said Roosevelt stopped at Fish Creek Station long enough to visit stagecoach driver Norton, who had expressed a desire to see the former president (the *Republican* also said Roosevelt visited Norton on the way back to Phoenix). Some of the autos had difficulty on the long grades, but the *Gazette* said

175 cars made the trip from the Salt River Valley and about 50 more from Globe. The *Democrat* said its auto passed 14 disabled vehicles along the Roosevelt Road. [24]

At 4:15 p.m., the car carrying Roosevelt rounded the point along the road from which he got his first view of the Roosevelt Dam and the reservoir, which contained 526,857 acre-feet of water and was at elevation 163.15 feet on the dam. The appearance of Roosevelt's car was the signal for the discharge of 11 guns at the dam, followed by cheers from the hundreds of persons (upwards of a thousand people). The reverberation of the guns fluttered the United States flag and the blue Reclamation Service flag floating above the parapets of the dam. At the top of the hill overlooking the dam, the car halted, signaling another gun salute and more shouts and yells from the crowd, which included a contingent of Apache Indians. Roosevelt, a yellow badge attached to the left lapel of his coat, Sloan, McClintock, Kent, Joseph H. Kibbey, and the others came down the roadway to the southern bridge of the dam. They walked across to the speaker's platform with pauses to greet people and shake hands. While this went on, Mrs. Roosevelt, who was heavily veiled, Miss Roosevelt, and the other ladies were seated. When the speakers were on the platform, Orme called the assemblage to order and introduced Bishop Atwood, who gave the invocation, which he concluded by reciting the Lord's Prayer accompanied by the crowd. [25]

Orme introduced Sloan, the chairman of the dedication, who said the dam was "a vindication of the wisdom and foresight and a justification of the effort and labor of all those who were instrumental in bringing about the adoption of the national irrigation policy." [26]

Sloan said he was sure the people of the Salt River Valley appreciated the way the irrigation law had been administered, and he believed they were "determined to show their appreciation. . .by fulfilling their obligations to the government in the utmost good faith and in strict compliance with the terms of their contract." [27]

Louis Hill was the first speaker introduced by Sloan. Hill described the main features of the Salt River Project, and revealed that,

The latest extension will be the addition of five feet to the height of the spillways, thus adding 100,000 acre-feet at a cost of 3 cents an acre-foot, to the capacity of the reservoir. . . [28]

Hill said that, even though the reservoir was less than half-full, all of the land served by the Water Users' Association was "safe from drought for two years, even if no flood comes," all of which water would have been lost for use without Roosevelt Dam. [29]

Statistician Charles J. Blanchard of the Reclamation Service spoke on behalf of Frederick H. Newell, director of the service, who was unable to attend. Blanchard said it required,

no particular acumen to predict a time when in the Salt River Valley there will be developed the most nearly ideal conditions of living and the best type of citizenship this world has ever known. [30]

Benjamin A. Fowler, as president of the National Irrigation Congress, briefly reviewed the work of the congress in behalf of a national irrigation policy in order to make clear "the obligation which the Salt River Valley is under to the organization [congress]." Fowler said the dam,

will stand as an everlasting sentiment to serve, conserve and safeguard the interests of all the people alike. To its builders it is a splendid monument. To a great and growing community in an arid region, it is a guarantee for all time of prosperity and happiness, comfort and peace. [31]

Roosevelt was the last speaker and he spoke extemporaneously. He recalled that about a week after he became president, Newell and Gifford Pinchot called upon

Former President Theodore Roosevelt at the dam's dedication, March 18, 1911

him to urge that he take up the policy of national irrigation. Knowing "the utter impossibility of expecting the larger schemes to be developed by private enterprise unless we were content to have the larger schemes become private monopolies," Roosevelt said he threw his weight behind the National Reclamation Act. He said there were two achievements of his administration of which he was very proud, "this reclamation work in the West and the Panama Canal." Among his other remarks were these:

. . .first of all, I want to thank you for having named the dam after me. I do not know if it is of any consequence to a man whether he has a monument. I know it is of mighty little consequence whether he has a statue after he is dead. If there could be any monument which would appeal to any man, surely it is this. You could not have done anything which would have pleased and touched me more than to name this great dam, this great reservoir site, after me, and I thank you from my heart for having done so.

I want to recollect the men who built the dam, who made that road to the Roosevelt Dam from Phoenix. I hope my people will realize, which I am bound to say, I did not, or never realized until this morning, what an extraordinary, beautiful and picturesque strip of country this is. I think that the drive from the beautiful city of Phoenix, especially the last few miles down the extraordinary gorge, then to see this lake and dam, I think is one of the most spectacular, best worth seeing in the world, and I hope our people will realize that. I want to see them come in by the tens of thousands here just as they go to the Yosemite, to the Grand Canyon and Yellowstone Park. . .

As soon as it was done [the National Reclamation Act signed into law], I called in Mr. Newell and I said, "Now I want this work divided fairly. There will be great pressure by different senators and congressmen who will honestly think that their state has the first claim, that they have the meritorious project, and as Arizona and New Mexico have not any senators or congressmen and as I raised three-fourths of my regiment in New Mexico and Arizona, I will take their place, and now I want to see that they get a fair deal." Mr. Davis and Mr. Newell answered at once that they were perfectly easy in Arizona. Mr. Newell said that there were two projects that they regarded as two of the most important, if not the most important, projects of the Reclamation Service. Mr. Newell and Mr. Davis took the keenest personal interest in everything connected with starting this work just as if they had been citizens of Arizona who were directly to be benefited by the proposed work and they couldn't have been more devoted to it or towards it or have served it or have more conscientiously worked to see this policy adopted in a form that would make it of the widest and most far reaching benefit to the people of the Salt River Valley. [32]

Following the benediction by Atwood, at 5:48 p.m., Roosevelt pressed a button to allow the release of water from the reservoir, and, according to the *Republican,*

A mighty roar of water rushed through the canyon and the dedication of the greatest storage dam and reservoir on earth was an accomplished fact. [33]

1. *Arizona Gazette* (Phoenix), January 9, 1911; *Arizona Republican* (Phoenix), March 3, 1911.
2. *Republican,* March 3, 1911.
3. *Salt River Project, Final History to 1916* (unpublished manuscript), Vol. II, pp. 397-403, Salt River Project Archives.
4. *Ibid.,* pp. 396-403.
5. *Republican,* March 8, 1911.
6. *Ibid.,* March 12, 1911.
7. *Ibid.*
8. *Ibid.,* March 14, 1911.
9. *Ibid.,* March 14, 17, 1911.
10. *Ibid.,* March 15, 1911.
11. *Gazette,* March 15, 1911.
12. *Republican,* March 17, 1911.
13. *Gazette,* March 16, 17, 1911.
14. *Ibid.,* March 15, 1917; *Republican,* March 17, 1912.
15. *Republican,* March 18, 1911.
16. *Ibid.,* March 19, 1911; *Gazette,* March 20, 1911; *Arizona Democrat* (Phoenix), March 20, 1911.
17. *Republican,* March 18, 1911.
18. *Ibid.*
19. *Ibid.,* March 19, 1911; *Gazette,* March 20, 1911; *Democrat,* March 20, 1911.
20. *Republican,* March 19, 1911; *Gazette,* March 18, 1911.
21. *Ibid.*
22. *Ibid.,* March 18, 1911; *Gazette,* March 18, 1911.
23. *Democrat,* March 18, 1911.
24. *Ibid.,* March 18, 1911; *Gazette,* March 20, 1911; *Republican,* March 19, 20, 1911.
25. *Gazette,* March 18, 1911; *Republican,* March 19, 1911.
26. *Democrat,* March 20, 1911; *Republican,* March 19, 1911.
27. *Ibid.*
28. *Republican,* March 19, 1911.
29. *Ibid.*
30. *Ibid.*
31. *Democrat,* March 20, 1911.
32. *Ibid.; Republican,* March 19, 1911; *Gazette,* March 20, 1911.
33. *Republican,* March 19, 1911.

INDEX

A

Adams Hotel, 43, 48, 77, 202
Adams, John C., 32, 77, 88
Agua Fria River, 199, 204, 216
Ainsworth, C.F., 119, 123-124, 136, 200, 202, 204
Akers, C.H., 174, 177
Akers, Joe T., 181, 190
Alexander, Joseph L.B., 63, 77, 106, 140, 151, 156, 158, 163, 165-166, 175
Alkire, Frank T., 48, 82, 90, 127, 132, 140, 146, 148
Apaches, 53, 93, 116, 124, 149, 244
Appraisal Commission, 108, 117-121, 129
Appropriators Canal, 92, 95, 103-104, 106-107, 115-118, 120-121, 127, 130, 133-134, 140-142, 146, 151-152, 154, 157, 159, 164, 181-182, 185, 187, 192
Arizona Agricultural Assoc., 30
Arizona Alfalfa Milling Co., 225, 237
Arizona Canal, 15, 21-26, 31, 45-48, 52, 56, 62, 91-92, 96, 102, 104, 106-108, 113-118, 120-124, 129, 131-132, 135-136, 142, 144-146, 148, 151-153, 157-158, 160, 163, 165-167, 177-180, 187, 189-190, 195, 206, 208, 216, 228, 236-237
Arizona Canal Protective Association, 96, 115-116, 119-124, 127
Arizona Canal Water Users' Assoc., 127, 131-133, 140, 142, 144-146, 151
Arizona Dam, 25, 61, 65, 69, 78-79, 88-89, 91, 95-96, 101-108, 113-115, 118, 127, 135
Arizona Falls, 21-22, 103, 127, 175, 192, 216, 228, 236
Arizona Improvement Co., 23, 25
Arizona Water Co., 22, 47, 62, 78, 89, 91-92, 103-109, 113-124, 127, 130, 134-135, 140, 146, 159, 174, 178
Armstrong, Thomas Jr., 92-93, 96, 107, 143, 228, 231
Avondale Co., 216

B

Baker, Albert C., 21, 84
Baker, C.D., 26
Baker, Sheldon, 93, 182, 185, 197
Ballinger, Richard A., 197-198, 211-212, 215-216, 221, 223-224, 226-227, 229-230, 232, 241
Barnett, Warren, 90, 106
Bartlett, Augustus C., 29, 58-59, 131, 172, 201-203
Bartlett-Heard Land & Cattle Co., 29, 38, 58, 69, 143, 172, 199, 202-204, 221, 228
Bennett, Walter, 87, 90, 123, 144, 148, 156, 164
Bennitt, E.J., 134, 140, 155, 206, 222, 230, 238
Bien, Morris, 101-102, 130, 135-136, 211
Blanchard, C.J., 171, 177, 193-194, 198-199, 238, 244
Board of Trade, 30-32, 37, 45, 53, 66-67, 75-77, 87, 90, 116, 164, 174-177, 179, 181, 198
Bowen & Grover stage line, 90
Bradley, Nelson, 148, 155
bridges, 199-204, 222, 242
Broadway Canal, 117
Brodie, Alexander O., 52, 63-64, 69, 77, 96
Broomell, J.H., 27, 57
Buckeye Canal, 32
Bullard, George P., 174-175
Bustin, H.A., 206, 214
Buttes dam site, 27

C

C.R. Eager & Co., 94-95, 105, 113-114
Camp O'Rourke, 116, 123, 136, 163, 165, 168, 178, 181, 187
Carter, Senator Thomas H., 203, 214-215
Casa Grande Valley Water Users' Assoc., 59, 64

Cave Creek, 136, 158, 190, 237
cement mill, 51, 68, 75-81, 83-86, 87-96, 102-104, 129
Center Street Bridge, 199-200, 202-204, 222, 242
Chalmers, Louis H., 119, 177, 182, 199, 202
Chandler, Dr. Alexander J., 25, 29, 31, 33, 48, 67, 82, 90, 102, 109, 152, 158, 172, 175, 178, 185, 186
Chandler, Harry L., 180-181, 187
Christy, William, 31-33, 43, 45, 48, 55-56, 104, 148, 178
Clark, Vernon, 30, 57, 75, 77, 90, 140, 202, 225
Cleary, William, 47, 92, 103-104, 106-107
Code, William, 106, 146, 151-154, 156-157
Coggins, L.W., 174, 176-177
Collins, R.H., 132, 136, 144-145, 148
Commercial Club, 173-179, 187
Committee of Sixteen, 108, 117, 136, 141-143, 148, 151, 154-157
Committee on Irrigation, 79, 207
Consolidated Canal, 25, 31-33, 35, 38, 102, 142, 169, 180, 182, 185-186, 217, 228-229, 235-236
Cope, Joseph, 199, 206, 212-213, 224, 227, 230
Crosscut Canal, 65, 92, 104, 119, 145

D

Davis, Arthur P., 27-28, 32, 34-36, 38-39, 44, 49, 51-52, 62, 69-70, 75-89, 101-102, 108, 117-118, 130, 132, 135-136, 149, 151, 157, 228, 238, 241
deaths, 92-94, 101, 108-109, 116, 118, 121, 124, 127-129, 131-132, 135, 147, 149, 158, 163, 165, 167, 169, 175-176, 181, 188, 190, 194-195, 200, 205, 207-208, 211-213, 222, 236, 242-243
Democratic Party, 33, 45, 75, 104
Demrick, A.H., 144, 146, 165-166, 168, 181, 185, 187-188, 190, 195, 200
Department of Justice, 75, 91, 140
Desert Land Act, 22
Dorris Theatre (Opera House), 55, 88, 93, 130
Dobson, W.W., 155, 206, 224
Duryea, Edward T., 77, 83, 96

E

E.F. Kellner & Co., 78, 121
Eastern Canal (also see Highland), 147, 168, 180, 189, 191-193, 197-198, 212-213, 215, 227-229
Ely, Sims, 30, 81-82
Ensign, F.H., 131, 146, 157-158, 175-177, 191, 199
Ensign, Orville H., 94, 146, 148, 152, 157
Etter, Cleon M., 127, 129
Eureka Canal, 197, 225-227, 229
Evans, Elliot, 154, 217
Evergreen Power Plant, 131, 134, 136, 159

F

Farish, Thomas E., 24-25
Farish, William A., 80, 123, 153, 195, 211, 242
Fish Creek Hill, 76, 80, 82-83, 88, 90, 93, 148, 152, 197
Fish Creek Station, 13, 75, 90, 106, 145, 242
floods, 59, 91, 96, 101-102, 117-118, 129, 131, 136, 144-145, 160, 168, 190, 237
Ford Hotel, 239, 242
Fort McDowell Indian Reservation, 27, 156, 160, 187, 219
Foss, Dr. John W., 123, 129, 145, 174, 177-178, 220, 222, 230
Fowler, Benjamin, 15, 19, 30, 32-34, 37-39, 43-48, 52-55, 58-70, 75-84, 87-93, 101-102, 104-108, 114, 116-117, 119-120, 122, 127, 132, 141, 144, 146, 148, 151, 173, 187, 191, 199, 211, 220-221, 223, 226, 230-231, 235, 244-245
Fowler, Lincoln, 23, 25, 29, 37-38, 92, 107-108, 115-116, 119-124, 129-131, 134, 136, 140-142, 149, 151, 153-155, 157, 177, 181, 192,

204-206, 208, 214-216
Fredrick, A.W., 142, 164

G

Ganz, Emil, 142, 152, 181
Garfield, James R., 158-159, 177, 186
Gila River, 23, 27, 29-30, 152
Gila River Indian Reservation, 25, 27, 31, 35, 43, 47, 54, 145-147, 151-154, 165, 167, 172-173, 179, 192, 194, 197-198, 204, 215-216, 231
Gila Valley Globe & Northern Railway, 75, 80
Goldberg, Aaron, 29, 202, 222
Goldfield, 75, 80, 90, 105-106, 109, 173
Goldman, Charles, 35, 115, 142, 164, 222, 243
Goodrich, Roy S., 204, 221-222, 225
Grand Canal, 19-23, 26, 45-48, 62, 65, 67, 69, 81, 90, 92-93, 96, 103-104, 107, 113, 115-122, 129, 133, 135, 146, 149, 151, 155, 164, 177, 192, 195, 228-229, 243
Granite Reef Dam, 121, 129, 131-132, 134-136, 139-146, 148-152, 157, 159, 163-166, 171-172, 177-180, 182, 186, 204, 211, 213, 224, 229-230, 232, 237-239, 241-243
Greenhaw, Hosea, 142, 164
Griffin Ditch Co., 20-21

H

Hall, Charles J., 115, 118, 121-123, 127, 148-149
Halm, George H., 171, 192, 217, 224
Hancock, William A., 24, 26
Hansbrough-Newlands Act., 37, 39, 43
Harris, A.L., 134, 200
Harrison Act, 77
Hassayampa River, 14, 21-22, 25, 168
Hayden, Carl, 15, 56-59, 69, 88
Hayden, Charles Trumbull, 21
Hayden's Ferry, 20-21
Hayden Flour Mill, 219
Heard, Dwight B., 14, 29, 32, 35, 37-39, 43-45, 47-48, 50, 53-54, 56, 61, 65-70, 91-92, 104-105, 116-118, 129-131, 140-141, 151, 154, 164, 172, 179-181, 199-202, 213-214, 221-222, 225, 230, 235, 241-242
Highland Canal, 23, 26, 31-32, 43, 45, 48, 117, 147, 153, 168-169, 173, 180-182, 185, 187-189, 191-193, 197, 212, 227, 229
Highline Road, 88-91, 96
Hill, Louis C., 15, 75, 78, 81, 82, 87-91, 93, 96-97, 104-106, 113, 115-116, 118-119, 121, 123-124, 131-132, 135-136, 139-142, 146, 148-149, 151-154, 157-158, 163-164, 167-169, 171-176, 178, 180-181, 185-189, 191-192, 197, 201-202, 204-205, 213-217, 221-225, 228-231, 235, 237-239
Hinton, Richard J., 24-25
Hirst, C.T., 102, 104, 129, 231
Hitchcock, Ethan A., 32-36, 39, 43-44, 51-52, 57-59, 61-69, 75, 77-80, 82, 84, 89, 92, 96, 106, 108, 113, 120, 122-124, 127, 135, 139, 141-142
Hoghe, L.M., 200, 221, 242
Holdren & Sons Stage, 106, 110, 117
Holmes, Jim, 115-116, 124
Holt, Judge George, 113, 127, 133
Hudson Reservoir & Canal Co., 26-27, 29-31, 33, 36, 43-44, 61, 81-82, 133
Hughes, Ward, 45, 48
Hunt, George W.P., 13-14
Hurley, Patrick T., 92, 115, 142, 151, 220, 222
Hurley v. Abbott and others, 95-96, 101-105, 108-110, 117, 130, 133-136, 140-143, 149, 151, 153-160, 163, 165-166, 171, 179, 187, 198, 213-214, 217, 219-221, 223, 228, 236-237

I

Indian Service, 99
Indians (see also individual tribes), 29, 43, 76, 90, 94, 101, 124, 127,

131, 154, 156, 179, 180, 199
Italians, 133-134, 163
Ivy, James, 142, 206, 214

J

Jack, E.E., 129, 224, 238
jail, Roosevelt, 124, 147
Jamison, Julius M., 123, 135
Joint Head, 107, 121, 226
Jones, C.G., 69, 235
Jones, Daniel Webster, 20, 226

K

Kent, Judge Edward, 39, 65, 93, 107, 113, 115, 117, 122, 127, 131, 133, 143, 152-153, 155-156, 163-164, 180, 187, 198, 213-214, 217, 219-220, 223, 229, 236-237, 242
Kent Decree, 226-227, 229
Kibbey, Joseph H., 14-15, 23, 26, 35, 46-49, 51-57, 62, 69, 77-78, 81-84, 87-88, 91, 93, 95-97, 102-103, 105, 108, 113-117, 119, 121-122, 129-130, 135-136, 153-156, 158-159, 163, 174-175, 177-180, 187, 192, 198, 204-205, 207, 211-216, 220, 223, 226, 231, 244
Kibbey Decree, 103-105, 133
Kimball, William, 115, 117
Kingsbury, W.J., 102, 231
Kirkland-McKinney Ditch, 230
Kyrene Ditch, 237

L

Landowners' Cooperative Water Co., 32
liquor, 108, 115-116, 131, 241
Llewellyn Iron Works, 93, 167, 173
Lount Ice Works, 237

M

Mann, Henry, 29, 44, 80
Maricopa & Phoenix Railroad, 61, 101, 105, 118, 200
Maricopa Canal, 20-23, 45-46, 48, 57, 62, 67, 69, 81, 90, 92-93, 96, 107, 113, 115-118, 120-121, 129, 133, 135, 140, 148-149, 151, 154, 157, 160, 172, 177, 229-230, 235
Maricopa County Board of Supervisors, 114, 134, 173, 222
Maricopa County Board of Water Storage Commissioners, 33-39, 43, 45, 75, 104
Maricopa County Enabling Act, 37-38, 43
Maricopas, 39, 69, 179
Martin, James W., 140, 151, 180
Maxwell, George H., 14-15, 27, 30, 32-34, 36, 38, 44-49, 51-54, 56-59, 62-68, 70, 75-77, 84, 93
McClintock, James H., 24-25, 27, 222, 230, 244, 247
McClung, H.J., 131, 178, 206, 217, 224
McCowan, S.M., 30-33, 46
McCormick, Roy, 206
McDermott, Dan, 113, 115, 124, 127, 132, 144
McDowell reservoir, 32, 34
McKee, C.W., 176-178, 187
McKinley, William, 35
Mesa Canal, 20-21, 23, 25-26, 32, 45, 48, 52, 56, 69, 109, 117, 143, 155, 169, 186, 202, 216, 217, 220, 222, 224-226, 228
Mesa Opera House, 224-226
Mesa-Roosevelt Stage Co., 117, 124, 182, 188, 195, 225, 230, 237
Mexicans, 109, 116, 134, 140, 146-147, 175
Moeur, Dr. B.B., 188, 208
Moffat, Rev. Thomas C., 116, 120
Monterey Ditch Co., 20-21
Mullen, C.M., 223
Murphy, Nathan O., 29-30, 81
Murphy, Ralph, 123, 135-136
Murphy, William J., 15, 25, 29, 31, 33-34, 37, 39, 48, 82, 96, 102, 115, 123-124, 171, 230

N

Nash, Frank, 96, 117
National Central Committee of Irrigation, 19, 37
National Irrigation Act (movement), 44, 53, 55, 59, 64, 66, 70, 93
National Irrigation Assoc., 15, 30, 37, 44, 51, 64, 75, 93, 208
National Irrigation Congress, 25, 27, 30, 32, 33, 48-49, 75-76, 163, 208, 235
National Reclamation Act., 15, 46, 54-55, 59, 64, 70, 101, 171, 178, 250
Negroes, 134-36, 147
New York Trust Co., 113, 127, 146
Newlands, Frank, 34-37
Newell, Frederick H., 27, 29-30, 39, 43-45, 51-52, 57-58, 64, 68-70, 75, 77, 79-80, 82, 84, 87, 90-91, 105, 108, 121, 129, 130, 143, 151, 154, 156, 158-159, 177-179, 200, 206, 211, 229-230, 244
Nicholson Building, 56
Norton, John R., 24, 33, 68-69, 79

O

Olberg, Charles R., 68, 78, 92
O'Neill, Eugene B., 46-47, 202
Orme, John P., 13, 62, 68, 76, 91-92, 102, 115, 129, 134, 142, 148, 151, 164, 176, 179-180, 187, 199, 206, 212-214, 217, 220-223, 226, 230, 232, 235, 237-238, 241-242
Orme, Lin R., 48, 199, 206
O'Rourke & Co., 97, 101, 103, 110, 114-115, 118, 120-124, 127, 131, 133-136, 139-141, 145, 153, 157, 165, 182, 189, 241
O'Rourke, John M., 103, 109, 142, 144, 178, 182, 187, 198, 202, 205, 237, 239

P

Pacific & Eastern Railroad, 127
Pacific Gas and Electric, 131, 134, 147, 153, 157-159, 174-179, 182, 187, 191-192, 194-195, 199, 204, 208, 211-212, 216, 224, 227, 232, 237, 238
Palmer, Dr. Ralph F., 92, 96, 109, 115, 116, 124, 127, 131-132, 145
Papagos, 66
Parker, Frank H., 32, 43, 45, 48, 53, 66, 94, 104-105, 116, 120, 122, 124, 127, 155
Peters, A.J., 57, 197
Peterson, Charles, 135, 155, 179, 180, 206, 214, 227
Phelps, Joe, 115, 134
Phoenix and Eastern Railroad, 101, 118
Phoenix & Southside Bridge Co., 179
Phoenix Indian School, 46, 84, 157, 160, 243
Phoenix Light and Fuel Co., 103, 107, 119-120, 124, 131, 134, 159, 174, 176, 178
Pimas, 27, 39, 46, 64-66, 69-70, 179-180
Pinchot, Gifford, 44, 181, 244
Porter, Judge DeForest, 21-22
Potter, Albert, 181, 185
power canals, 52, 76-78, 81, 83-84, 88-89, 93, 97, 105, 119
Priest, J.T., 35, 43

R

races, 113, 197, 211
railroads, 55, 79, 83, 87, 93, 101, 103, 132, 146, 151, 227
Randolph, Charles, 31, 33, 57, 68, 77-78, 81, 120, 122-124, 127
Randolph, Epes, 158
Reed, Howard, 157-158, 204, 230, 239
Reppy, Charles C., 59, 64, 66, 76
Republican Party, 31, 33, 47, 78, 81, 85, 93
Rio Verde Canal, 25-26, 29
roads, 68-69, 75-79, 87, 90, 94, 101, 106
  bonds, 77-78, 82-84, 88
  Roosevelt road, 13-14, 87-89, 93-97, 101, 104, 114, 146, 189, 211, 227
Roosevelt Dam,
  cornerstone, 140
  dedication, 13, 235, 244-245

Roosevelt, town of (Newtown), 14, 78-79, 81-83, 85, 88-90, 96, 105, 109-110, 115, 121, 127, 134-135, 147, 182, 188-190, 193
Roosevelt, Theodore, 13, 35-36, 38-39, 44, 49, 51, 63-64, 66, 68, 70, 77, 80, 96, 187, 226, 230, 235, 237, 241-245

S

Salt River Indian Reservation, 33, 37, 70, 103, 106, 120, 123, 131, 150-154, 160, 219
Salt River Valley Canal Co., 20-21, 23, 26, 45, 48, 62, 67, 81, 90, 92-93, 96, 107, 113, 115-118, 120-121, 129, 133, 135, 140, 148-149, 151, 154, 157, 160, 172, 177, 229-230, 235
Salt River Valley Water Storage & Reservoir Co., 31-32, 43
San Carlos Dam, 51-52, 57, 59, 63-66, 76-77, 93
San Carlos Indian Reservation, 30, 77, 127
San Carlos reservoir, 30, 35-37, 39, 43-44, 46
San Francisco Canal, 21, 23, 32, 38, 45, 48, 56, 103-104, 109, 117, 172, 201, 204, 228, 241
Sanders, W.H., 135, 148, 151, 153
Santa Fe Railroad, 38, 82, 188, 239
sawmill, see August 1903—March 1904, 79, 96
Saylor, C.A., 155, 206, 224
Scott, Winfield, 29, 123, 129
Select Committee on Irrigation & Reclamation of Arid Lands, 24-25
Shattuck & Desmond, 114, 117, 124, 131, 134, 163
Shattuck-Nimmo Warehouse Co., 188, 192, 205, 225
Sieber, Al, 109
Sierra Anchas, 22, 24, 51, 90, 95
Sloan, Richard E., 198, 227, 236, 238, 241-242, 244
Smith, Chester W., 95, 115, 142, 178
Smith Marcus A., 37-39, 93
Smith, Tom W., 187, 197, 212, 215
Smith, W. Scott, 122, 124, 139
South Canal, 135, 180, 187, 192, 204, 228, 230, 241
Southern Pacific Railroad, 38, 132, 158
Southwestern Sugar & Land Co., 189, 195
stagelines, 106, 109-110, 114, 117, 168, 242
Stanford, M.A., 56, 65
Stannard, Jay D., 153, 174-175, 180, 193, 211, 232
Steele, Hiram R., 105-106, 113-117, 121-124, 130
Steele, Porter, 131, 135
Steinmetz, George N., 103
Steinmetz, John, 116, 129-130, 134, 136, 140, 237, 239
Stewart, I.V., 135
Stone, George, 78, 199
Stone, Dr. H.H., 206, 217, 223-224, 226-227, 238
Storrs, Henry A., 68, 78
Sturgeon, J.E., 79, 96, 127, 143
sugar beet factory, 116, 123, 136, 204
Swilling Irrigating and Canal Co., 20

T

Taft, William H., 197, 211
Talbot, Walter, 77, 90
Tempe Bridge Committee, 200, 202-203
Tempe Canal, 20-21, 23, 25-26, 29, 32, 45, 48, 53, 56-57, 59, 61, 66-70, 103-104, 109, 117, 141, 143, 164, 186, 198, 203, 204, 213, 220, 223-225, 229-231, 235
Tonto Creek, 14, 22, 24, 26, 39, 108, 133, 182, 187-188, 194, 202
Trott, Frank, 34, 38-39, 61, 133, 204, 219, 229

U

Utah Canal, 20-21, 23, 25-26, 32, 45, 48, 56-57, 61, 69, 109, 117, 156, 192, 197, 202, 216, 220, 224, 226-228, 235

V

Valley Bank, 45, 56
Van der Veer, Charles, 155, 179-180, 208, 223, 226, 230-232, 238-239, 242
Verde River, 22-28, 32, 47, 49, 61

W

Walcott, Charles D., 27, 32, 39, 44, 52, 57-59, 61, 62, 64, 66-70, 77, 95, 106
Wallace, W.H., 48, 56
Walnut Grove Dam, 21-25, 168
Walnut Grove Water Storage Co., 23
Water Power Canal Co., 107, 145
Water Storage Conference Committee, 29-35, 37, 43, 45-50, 51-56, 61, 69
water temple, 186, 206, 232, 235
Webb & Sons, 181, 241
weddings, 101
Weedin, Thomas, 51, 63, 64, 70
Western (Wormser) Canal, 230, 237
Western Union, 117

Wilbur, Ethelbert W., 26-27, 38-39, 48, 52-54, 56, 61, 80, 88, 104-105, 109, 129-130, 180-181, 221, 224, 227, 238
Wilson, John F., 30, 33, 44, 46-47
Wisner, George Y., 118, 121, 130
Witbeck, Charles W., 156, 228-229
Wolf, Sachs, 95, 101, 131
Woolf, John W., 27, 29, 38, 43, 48, 53-54, 56, 59, 61-62, 67, 69
Wormser, et.al. v. the Salt River Valley Canal Co., et.al., 103
Wormser, Michael, 23, 26, 38, 46

Y

Yeager, H.C., 225, 229

Z

zanjeros, 113, 120, 144, 195, 229

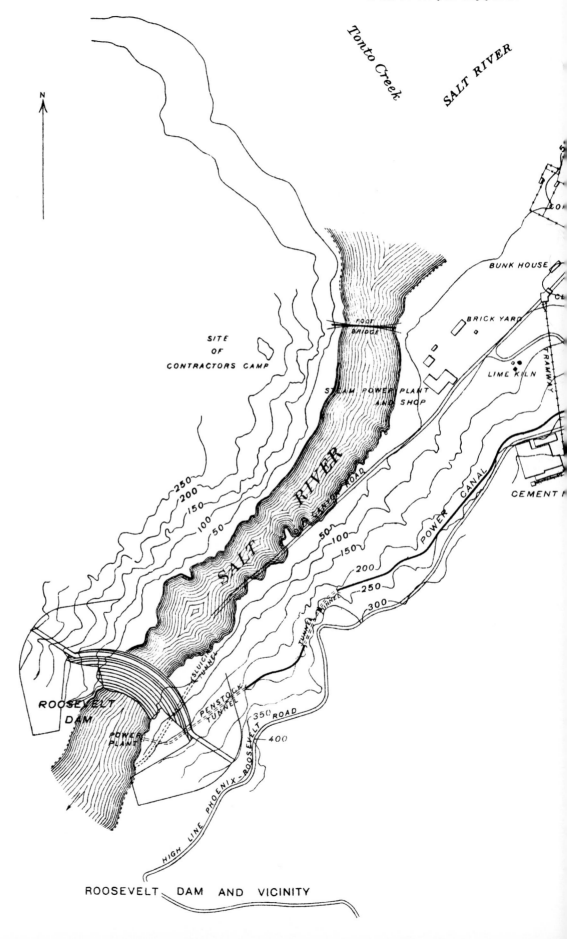

River bottoms of shifting sand changing channels

Tonto Creek

SALT RIVER

BUNK HOUSE

SITE
OF
CONTRACTORS CAMP

FOOT
BRIDGE

BRICK YARD

STEAM POWER PLANT
AND SHOP

LIME KILN

TRAMWAY

CEMENT

SALT

RIVER

SERVICE ROAD

250
200
150
100
50

50
100
150

POWER CANAL

200

250

300

SLUICE TUNNEL

TUNNEL TUNNEL

PENSTOCK TUNNEL

ROOSEVELT
DAM

POWER
PLANT

350 ROAD

400

HIGH LINE PHOENIX-ROOSEVELT ROAD

ROOSEVELT   DAM   AND   VICINITY

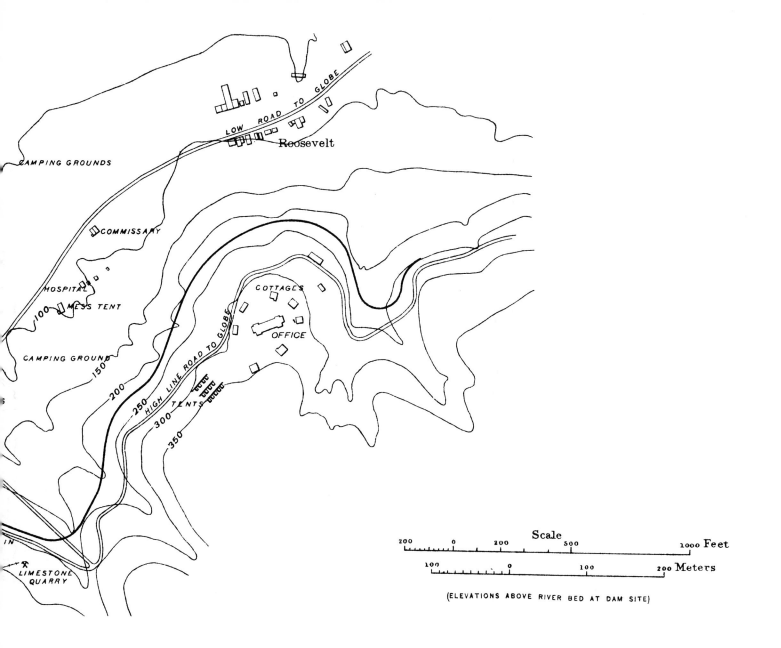

CAMPING GROUNDS

LOW ROAD TO GLOBE

Roosevelt

COMMISSARY

HOSPITAL

MESS TENT

100

CAMPING GROUND

150

200

250

HIGH LINE ROAD TO GLOBE

TENTS

300

350

COTTAGES

OFFICE

IN

LIMESTONE QUARRY

Scale

200   0   200   500   1000 Feet

100   0   100   200 Meters

(ELEVATIONS ABOVE RIVER BED AT DAM SITE)